THE
CONSERVATIVE
MIND

THE CONSERVATIVE MIND

From Burke to Eliot

Seventh Revised Edition

RUSSELL KIRK

Regnery Publishing, Inc.
Washington, D.C.

The Library of Congress has catalogued the 1986 Edition as follows:

Kirk, Russell.
      The conservative mind.

      Rev. ed. of: The conservative mind from Burke to Santayana 1953.
      Bibliography, p.
      Includes index.
      1. Conservativism—History. I. Kirk, Russell, Conservative mind, from Burke to Santayana. II. Title.
B809.K57 1986   890.5'2   86-42909
ISBN 0-89526-171-5

Published in the United States by
Regnery Publishing, Inc.
An Eagle Publishing Company
One Massachusetts Avenue, NW
Washington, DC 20001
www.regnery.com

Distributed to the trade by
National Book Network
4720-A Boston Way
Lanham, MD 20706

Printed on acid-free paper
Manufactured in the United States of America

10 9 8 7 6 5 4

Books are available in quantity for promotional or premium use. Write to Director of Special Sales, Regnery Publishing, Inc., One Massachusetts Avenue, NW, Washington, DC 20001, for information on discounts and terms or call (202) 216-0600.

Contents

The Making of *The Conservative Mind*
by
Henry Regnery

B Y THE 1950s, with the work of Albert J. Nock, T.S. Eliot, Richard Weaver, and Eliseo Vivas, among many others, the criticism of liberalism had grown into a substantial literature, but what was lacking was a point of view, or perhaps better, an attitude that would bring the conservative movement together and give it coherence and identity.

It was the great achievement, one might even say the historic achievement, of Russell Kirk's *The Conservative Mind*, which was published in 1953, to provide the needed unifying concept. He not only offered convincing evidence that conservatism was an honorable and intellectually respectable position, but that it was an integral part of the American tradition. It would be too much to say that the postwar conservative movement began with the publication of Kirk's book, but it did give conservatism its name and, more important, the coherence that had been lacking.

When the book that made his reputation was published, Russell Kirk was an instructor in history at Michigan State College. He had written one earlier book, *John Randolph of Roanoke,* and numerous essays, many of them for English magazines. Canon Bernard Iddings Bell had spoken to me of Kirk, but I came to know him and became his publisher through a mutual friend, Sidney Gair, who had been a textbook traveler for one of the large Eastern publishers, and after his retirement had become associated with our firm.

Gair was a delightful man—a good conversationalist, widely and well read, and courtly in manner. Confirmed conservative that he was, he was a great admirer of Paul Elmer More and Irving Babbitt. What it all comes down to, he used to say, is that a conservative knows that two plus two always, invariably, equals four, a fact of life that a liberal, on the other hand, is not quite willing to accept. It was through him that I met Russell Kirk and published *The Conservative Mind*, for which I will always remember Sidney Gair with gratitude.

Returning in the early part of 1952 from a trip to some of the colleges in Michigan, Gair told me that a friend of his, a young instructor at Michigan State, had written a manuscript he thought I would be interested in. I remember his description of the young man very clearly: "...the son of a locomotive engineer, but a formidable intelligence—a biological accident. He doesn't say much, about as communicative as a turtle, but when he gets behind a typewriter the results are *most* impressive."

Some time later, Gair asked me to read a letter Kirk had written to him from St. Andrews in Scotland, in which he described a ninety-mile walk he had just made "from Edinburgh to Alnwich, in Northumberland, over the desolate Lammermuirs and along the Northumbrian coast." After describing various adventures, he expressed the hope that he and I might meet during the summer, and from this beginning a correspondence soon developed.

In reply to my expression of interest in his manuscript, Kirk told me that it was on offer to Knopf, but if they declined it, he would send it to me. "There has never been a book like it," he remarked in this letter, "so far as breadth of subject is concerned, whatever its vices may be. The subtitle is 'An Account of Conservative Ideas from Burke to Santayana.'" This letter was followed by a postcard from Trier, Germany, showing a photograph of the Roman Porta Negra, which was my publishing insignia.

Then, on July 31, 1952, Kirk wrote from St. Andrews that Knopf would be willing to publish his manuscript only if he would reduce it to about one-half of its original length, and that he was sending it to me. His manuscript, he said,

is my contribution to our endeavor to conserve the spiritual and intellectual and political tradition of our civilization; and if we are to rescue the modern mind, we must do it very soon. What Matthew Arnold called "an epoch of concentration" is impending, in any case. If we are to make that approaching era a time of enlightened conservatism, rather than an era of stagnant repression, we need to move with decision. The struggle will be decided in the minds of the rising generation—and within that generation, substantially by the minority who have the gift of reason. I do not think we need much fear the decaying "liberalism" of the retiring generation; as Disraeli said, "Prevailing opinions are generally the opinions of the generation that is passing." But we need to state some certitudes for the benefit of the groping new masters of society. More than anyone else in America you have been doing just this in the books you publish.

On August 21st, I acknowledged this letter and the receipt of the manuscript, which after his description I was most anxious to read. My judgment of manuscripts has often been faulty, but with this one I knew that I had an important, perhaps great book, and although I had some doubts about its commercial possibilities— which proved to be unfounded—I was determined to publish it. In reply to my letter to this effect, Kirk, after urging me "not to forsake our Lake States for the East," had this to say about the battle we both felt we were engaged in:

It may well be that we shall be trampled into the mire, despite all we can do. But Cato conquered. And we shall, in any event, be playing the part which Providence designed for us. Even the failure of Charles I, after all, was in the long view of history a considerable success. By opposing what seems inevitable, often we find that its force is not irresistible; and at the worst, we have the satisfaction of the heroic attitude of the Sassenach confronting Roderick Dhu's crew

Come one, come all; this rock shall fly
From its firm base as soon as I!

The manuscript was in beautiful shape, and could have been sent out for typesetting as it had come in, except for the original title, which none of us thought would do—"The Conservative Rout." Sidney Gair suggested "The Long Retreat," which was worse (he thought "rout," as I mentioned to Kirk in a letter, "sounded 'too hasty'"). Russell replied, not too helpfully, that "there is a rather fife-and-drum sound to 'rout,'" but we kept trying until someone suggested "The Conservative Mind," which Kirk readily accepted.

Great care was given to the design of the book, which I wanted to be appropriate to the dignity of its language and the importance of what it has to say. The jacket confidently and, as it turned out, correctly predicted that this was a book which "will become a landmark in contemporary thinking," and on the back of the jacket, to make it evident that *The Conservative Mind* was not a solitary effort on our part, we listed four recently published books: *The Republic and the Person,* by Gordon Chalmers; *The Return to Reason,* essays in rejection of naturalism by thirteen American philosophers and Charles Malik of Lebanon; *The Forlorn Demon: Didactic and Critical Essays,* by Allen Tate; and Wyndham Lewis' *Revenge for Love.*

In March or April 1953, we sent out review copies; and with some fear and trepidation, since this book represented a major commitment on our part, we awaited the response, which was not long in coming, and far exceeded our most optimistic expectations.

Kirk approached the difficult task of presenting conservatism as a tradition relevant to our time with two enormous advantages: great skill in organizing a vast body of knowledge with which he was thoroughly familiar, and a superb literary style. "To review conservative ideas, examining their validity for this perplexed age," he explains, "is the purpose of this book." It is not, he says further, "a history of conservative parties…[but] a prolonged essay in definition. What is the essence of British and American conservatism? What system of ideas, common to England and the United States, has sustained men of conservative instincts in their resistance against radical theories and social transformation ever since the French Revolution?"

Any informed conservative, he continues, "is reluctant to con-

dense profound and intricate intellectual systems to a few pretentious phrases.…Conservatism is not a fixed and immutable body of
dogma, and conservatives inherit from Burke a talent for re-expressing their convictions to fit the times. As a working premise, nevertheless, one can observe here that the essence of social conservatism
is preservation of the ancient moral traditions of humanity."

Kirk was a young man when he wrote *The Conservative Mind;* he
was in his late twenties when, still a graduate student at St. Andrews
University in Scotland, he began researching the book and in his
early thirties when it was finished. One senses in it the freshness of
discovery, the immense pleasure of a young man, searching for his
way in a confused and confusing age, who had discovered a view of
life that satisfied him, gave him direction, and seemed to answer
his most pressing questions.

For all its maturity and sound scholarship, Kirk is able to maintain the quality of discovery throughout the entire book that is evident in the first chapter; he may have been, as a young man, "about
as communicative as a turtle," as his good friend Sidney Gair
described him, but he wrote with the passion of a man who has discovered a great truth and wishes to communicate his discovery to
others. It is this quality of the freshness of discovery as much as its
scholarship, perhaps, which carried the day for *The Conservative
Mind* and made it one of the most influential books of the postwar
period.

The first indication that the response to Kirk's book might be
favorable was an advance notice from the somewhat unpredictable
Kirkus Book Review Service on March 15th, which was all we could
have asked for, and certainly more than I had expected: "A fine study
of conservative thought in politics, religion, philosophy and literature from 1790 to 1952." This was followed by a recommendation in
the *Library Journal* on May 1st that "since the book is sure to provoke
heated controversy…libraries should have copies available."

On May 17th, the day before publication, the *New York Times* Sunday Book Review Section raised our hopes and spirits immeasurably with an excellent, half-page review in a prominent position, by
Gordon Chalmers.

The book was beginning to show signs of life, and in a letter to Kirk I reported that we were selling about one hundred copies a week. But what really put it into the center of discussion was a long, intelligent review in the July 4th issue of *Time* (dated July 6th). The whole book review section was devoted to one book, *The Conservative Mind;* with George Washington on the cover and the Kirk book taking up the entire book review section—it was also mentioned in the news pages—the theme of the issue could be taken to be the continuity of the American conservative tradition.

The review, which I am told was written by Max Ways, was not only favorable, it was the kind of review that stimulates the interest and curiosity of the reader, which is not true of every review, favorable or not. All this, and the circumstances of the review having appeared in this issue and featured as it was, made the publication of *The Conservative Mind* a significant event. Sales increased immediately—to four hundred a week, I wrote Kirk—and the first printing was sold out before the end of July. A second printing of five thousand was delivered in August and a third before the end of the year. Russell Kirk, from having been a rather obscure instructor at what he was later to call "Behemoth U," had become a national figure.

The impact of *The Conservative Mind* when it first appeared in 1953 is hard to imagine now. After the long domination of liberalism, with its adulation of the "common man," its faith in mechanistic political solutions to all human problems, its rejection of the tragic and heroic aspects of life, and the not exactly inspiring prose in which its ideas are usually expressed, after all this, I repeat, such sentiments as "the unbought grace of life," the "eternal chain of right and duty which links great and obscure, living and dead," a view of politics as "the art of apprehending and applying the Justice which is above nature," came like rain after a long drought.

August Hekscher began his review in the *New York Herald-Tribune* (August 2, 1953): "To be a conservative in the United States has for so long been considered identical with being backward, and even faintly alien, that Mr. Kirk's proud justification of the term is to be welcomed." Harrison Smith, in a syndicated review which appeared in many papers including the *Washington Post,* welcomed the book

with the words, "Thoughtful Americans concerned with the rapid-
ity with which totalitarian theories and revolutions are spreading
over a large part of the world should read Russell Kirk's landmark
in contemporary thinking."

Peter Viereck reviewed the book in the *Saturday Review;* there
was a most favorable and effective review in *Fortune;* and *Partisan
Review* discussed the book at length in two separate issues. A long
essay about *The Conservative Mind* appeared in the *Kenyon Review* by
John Crowe Ransom (later reprinted in a collection of his essays),
and another, in part a reply to Ransom, by Brainard Cheney in the
Sewanee Review. It was reviewed in the *London Times Literary Supplement,* and both Golo Mann and Wilhelm Roepke wrote extended
essays about the book in German publications. The post–World
War II conservative movement had attained intellectual respectability and an identity, and was on its way.

For the review in *Time* we are indebted to Whittaker Chambers.
I had first met him in 1952, when he was given an honorary degree
by Mount Mary College in Milwaukee. Hearing that he was in Milwaukee, I called to ask if I might see him. I did this, I must say, with
some hesitation, since I was reluctant to intrude on his privacy, and
was therefore all the more pleased when he told me that he would
be delighted to see me, and to come along at once.

The admiration I had felt for him ever since reading *Witness*
quickly developed into warm friendship. I visited Chambers a number of times at his Maryland farm, visits of which I have the most
pleasant memory, and corresponded with him to the end of his life.
To have known Whittaker Chambers, and to have been able to
regard him as a friend, was a great privilege. Feeling as I did about
the manuscript, I spoke to Chambers about *The Conservative Mind*
soon after I had read it, and sent him a set of proofs as soon as they
became available.

His response was the following letter, dated June 26, 1953:

I wrote Roy Alexander, the editor of *Time*, recently, to say that I thought
that Russell Kirk's book was one of the most important that was likely to
appear in some time, and to suggest that *Time* might well devote its entire

Books section to a review of it....I also told *Time* why I thought the *Conservative Mind* important, what it was and did.

Yesterday, Roy telephoned to say that *Time* agreed and that his whole forthcoming Books section will be devoted to Kirk's book. It will be the July 4 issue with G. Washington on the cover. So I am able at last to do something, in a small way, for you who have done so much for us—and to do something for Kirk's book, which you and I both would agree is the big thing. Incidentally, this shows that by simply picking up a pen, things can be done if we have the will to overcome inertia.

I can make no claim that I ever did anything for Whittaker Chambers beyond offering him my friendship; I felt more than repaid by the return of his. He was one of the great men of our time, and by assuming the terrible burden of being, as he put it, "an involuntary witness to God's grace and to the fortifying power of faith," all of us are immeasurably in his debt.

The sense of exaltation we all felt when the advance copies of the *Time* review came in is still very clear in my memory. Sidney Gair, who had recommended the book to me in the first place, was in a state bordering ecstasy. "Just look," he said, striking the magazine with his hand for emphasis, "pictures of Paul Elmer More and Irving Babbitt in *Time* magazine, and all because you decided to go into the publishing business."

Not all the reviews, needless to say, were favorable, and neither *Harper's* nor the *Atlantic* could find space to review the book at all. The die-hard liberals of the academy, in particular, were unwilling to concede anything to Kirk. Peter Gay of Columbia University, for example, ended his review in the *Political Science Quarterly* (December 1953) with the observation: "In trying to refute Lionel Trilling's position (that American conservatives have no philosophy and express themselves only 'in action or irritable mental gestures'), Kirk has only confirmed it."

Stuart Garry Brown reviewed the book in *Ethics* (October 1953), a quarterly published by the University of Chicago, and was not at all impressed. He reviewed Scott Buchanan's *Essays in Politics* at the same time, which, he said, "is much the better book." Norman

Thomas, in the *United Nations World* (August 1953), concluded a long and wordy review, which gives the impression that his reading of the book was rather spotty, with the remark, "What he has given us is an eloquent bit of special pleading which is, in part, a false, and, in sum total, a dangerously inadequate, philosophy for our time."

In contrast to the opinions of Peter Gay and Stuart Garry Brown, Clinton Rossiter, in the *American Political Science Review* (September 1953), states flatly that Kirk's "scholarship is manifestly of the highest order," and concludes his review: "Certainly the so-called 'new conservatism' of the postwar period takes on new substance and meaning with the publication of this book." L.P. Curtis reviewed *The Conservative Mind* together with Richard Pares' *King George II and the Politicians* in the *Yale Review* (Autumn 1953), and expressed the opinion, "This eloquent and confident book should hearten present conservatives and open the eyes of many of them to the splendor of their moral heritage. It should give pause to those scientistic planners and sentimentalists who dismiss the forebodings of Shakespeare's Ulysses as old hat...in spite of shortcomings Kirk fulfills one of the higher aims of the historian: he teaches us a way of life, and one, moreover, that is tried in experience and sprung from our condition."

The acceptance of "conservatism" as the description of the growing movement in opposition to the rule of liberalism was not automatic nor without strenuous opposition. Both Frank S. Meyer, who eventually became one of the acknowledged leaders of the conservative movement, and F.A. Hayek, who did as much as any other single person to give direction and a sound footing to the movement in opposition to the planned economy, wrote vigorously against conservatism as a description of their position.

Although recognized as one of the founding fathers of the conservative movement, Hayek had never been willing to describe himself as a conservative; he preferred to be known as an "Old Whig," a label that requires several pages of explanation which probably convinced everyone who read it, except Professor Hayek himself, that he really was, at heart, a conservative. All of which provides a fine example of "the proliferating variety and mystery of traditional life," which, Kirk tells us, conservatives particularly cherish.

Hayek's rejection of conservatism was first given in the form of a paper at a meeting of the Mont Pelerin Society, an international organization of liberal—in the traditional sense—economists and others who share their concern for the free society.

The first meeting of the society took place in Switzerland in April 1947; ever since its annual meetings, which usually are held in September, have provided opportunity for the consideration on the highest level of contemporary problems and issues. Hayek was the founder of the society, and was still its president when he gave his paper, "Why I am not a Conservative" at the 1957 meeting. He included this paper, as a postscript, in his monumental book, *The Constitution of Liberty,* which was first published in 1968.

While neither *The Conservative Mind* nor Russell Kirk was specifically mentioned in the paper, it was obviously inspired by the success of Kirk's book and the influential position the ideas it set forth had attained, which is attested by the fact that Kirk was invited to defend his position immediately afterward, which he did extemporaneously, without notes of any kind, and with great brilliance and effect.

This encounter in an elegant Swiss hotel before a distinguished international audience between one of the most respected economists of his time, who had been honored by professorships at the universities of Vienna, London, and Chicago, and the young writer from Mecosta, Michigan, was a dramatic and memorable occasion; as a rather biased witness, I would not be prepared to say that the young man from Mecosta came out second best.

As related earlier, Russell Kirk was an instructor of history at Michigan State College (later University, of course) when *The Conservative Mind* was published. Michigan State is one of those vast educational conglomerates which have developed in consequence of the widely held belief that if a college education is useful and helpful to some, justice and the principles of democracy demand that it be made available to all. Courses are offered, as Kirk remarked, in everything from medieval philosophy to elementary and advanced fly casting, and its chief function, in his opinion, is to deprive the young people who pass through its gates of whatever prejudices and moral principles they bring with them, to send them out into the world having given them nothing in return in the way of values or understanding to help them come to terms with the realities of life.

Not long after the publication of *The Conservative Mind* Kirk resigned his position at Michigan State, using the occasion to get off a blast at then-president, John Hannah—"a bachelor of poultry husbandry and honorary doctor of laws at his own institution" as he was later to describe him—and at the whole concept as well of such an institution as Michigan State.

When he told me of his intention to do this, I had urged him to reconsider, pointing out the advantages of a relatively secure academic post with its monthly check as opposed to the uncertainties of living as a writer and lecturer, to say nothing of the retribution to be expected from the academic establishment. To this admonition he replied, in a letter, in his characteristic fashion:

Poverty never bothered me; I can live on four hundred dollars cash per annum, if I must; time to think, and freedom of action, are much more important to me at present than any possible economic advantage. I have always had to make my own way, opposed rather than aided by the times and the men who run matters for us; and I don't mind continuing to do so.

Make his own way he did; Russell Kirk, one can truthfully say, became one of the most influential men of our time: we listened to him because he spoke with authority, not with the outward authority of the tax collector or public official, but with the inner authority of a man who had thought deeply about what he said, meant it, and was willing to put himself on the line for it.

He chose to live in that small town in northern Michigan, Mecosta, where he had spent many happy summers as a boy with various relatives, in a region of small lakes, sand hills, and the stumps of the great pines that once covered the land. The house of his great-grandfather, where Kirk had lived as a bachelor, burned to the ground, ghosts and all, about the time his new house, a large, solid, brick house surmounted by a cupola rescued from a demolished public building, was being finished, providing ample room for his family, his charming, down-to-earth, energetic wife and their four daughters, and for the numerous visitors. Most appropriately, as the home of its most prominent citizen, it dominates the village.

A former woodworking shop some quarter of a mile away was converted into a study and there, surrounded by the books accumulated during years of disciplined study, he did his work. A student or protégé was usually in residence, and groups of students came during holidays for study and discussion. The rather remote, obscure village of Mecosta became an important intellectual center, and doubtless had more positive influence in the world of ideas than the huge "universities" that Kirk had abandoned in its favor.

One of the most remarkable aspects of Kirk's career was its determined consistency. In a disorderly age, he tirelessly and eloquently made clear the necessity and sources of order. Against the false prophets who proclaimed that all values were relative, derived from will and desire, he showed their immutability. And to those who believed that man is capable of all things, he taught humility and that the beginning of wisdom was respect for creation and the order of being.

While Russell Kirk is no longer among us, we can still take solace and strength from his words and his works, his landmark writings, chief among them, *The Conservative Mind*.

Chicago, Illinois
June 1995

Foreword to the
Seventh Revised Edition

Written some thirty-five years ago—chiefly at haunted St. Andrews and in the old country houses of Fife—this prolonged essay in the history of ideas has obtained an influence unusual for such books in our time. A few brief comments by the author may be pardoned here.

First published by Henry Regnery in 1953, *The Conservative Mind* has run through six revised editions in the English language—including Faber and Faber's London edition, arranged by T.S. Eliot—and also translations published at Zurich and Madrid. This seventh revised edition, to which these paragraphs are prefaced, presumably is the final version of the book.

Its author, thirty years old when he began to scribble away at this second book of his, expected his study of conservative thought to move public opinion. But the book's success exceeded his hopes. Heartily commended in the major book-review media during the spring and summer of 1953, *The Conservative Mind* became known to a much broader public than ordinarily takes up serious studies in history and political theory. It was discussed, too, in critical quarterlies and learned journals, and re-reviewed. Directly or in someone's paraphrase, presently its chapters reached those people who, Dicey says, are the real (if unknowable) shapers of public opinion: a multitude of thinking men and women, obscure enough, who influence their neighbors and their communities. The book was read by professional people in particular. It appeared soon on the desks of political administrators, legislators, leaders of parties; it began to work as a catalyst in the renewal or the recrudescence of a conservative polity—or so, later, the author would be told by the mighty, even presidents of the United States. The public's response, in short, to this rather difficult study in the history of ideas was comparable, almost, to the cordial reception by the French public of Chateaubriand's *Genius of Christianity,* a century and a half earlier.

Being no leader of the crowd, the author was surprised to find that he had contributed through the power of the word to a large political movement in America—to a movement which, within a few years, would supplant in power America's latter-day liberalism. Indeed, his original title for the book had been *The Conservatives' Rout,* he apprehending that the conservatives of America and Britain, during the course of two centuries, had been beaten back from ditch to palisade. But the book's publisher persuaded him to alter the title to *The Conservative Mind.* That decision itself seemed to have converted a rout into a rally. As if this profession of intelligence had erased John Stuart Mill's libel upon conservatives as "the stupid party," soon American conservatives proceeded to take thought and to act. More books of a conservative persuasion were written by scholars and men of letters; conservative weeklies and quarterlies were founded; university students formed conservative discussion clubs.

Friends to this new book declared that the author had conjured up the forgotten genius of conservatism. Certain liberal and radical critics, on the other hand, suggested that the author had sown dragons' teeth. But the author was not sounding a call to arms, really; rather, he aspired to renew that "armed vision" to which, in Coleridge's phrase, the razor's edge becomes a saw. For only by means of a reawakened moral imagination, the young author argued, might order and justice and freedom be sustained through our time of troubles.

Fluttering the liberal dovecotes of 1953, the book took by surprise many of the accustomed arbiters of American literary criticism and political opinion; months or even years elapsed before those guardians could agree upon a common front against such views, as startling as they were antique. So many feathers flew in this battle of ideas over *The Conservative Mind* that its author was tempted to cry, in Coriolan's fashion, "Alone I did it!" Eventually he was repelled from the literary ramparts of Corioles—of New York City, that is—and took to the life of a literary guerrilla, finding its adventures congenial.

Why all this stramash about a solitary volume? Because the book served as "the voice of a dispossessed and forlorn orthodoxy" (to borrow Santayana's phrases), "prophesying evil." Somehow the liberal classes, Santayana remarks, were unable to silence such a voice: "and what renders that voice the more disquieting is that it can no longer be understood." The dangerous thing about this particular book was its relative lucidity: conceivably some readers might understand it; and at that prospect, there shivered the people whom Gordon Chalmers, in those years, called the "disintegrated liberals."

The Conservative Mind describes a cast of intellect or a type of character, an inclination to cherish the permanent things in human existence. On many prudential questions, and on some general principles, conservatives may disagree from time to time among themselves; so this book offers a certain diversity of opinions. Yet the folk called "conservative" join in resistance to the destruction of old patterns of life, damage to the footings of the civil social order, and reduction of human striving to material production and consumption.

The book distinctly does not supply its readers with a "conservative ideology": for the conservative abhors all forms of ideology. An abstract rigorous set of political dogmata: that is ideology, a "political religion," promising the Terrestrial Paradise to the faithful; and ordinarily that paradise is to be taken by storm. Such *a priori* designs for perfecting human nature and society are anathema to the conservative, who knows them for the tools and the weapons of coffeehouse fanatics.

For the conservative, custom, convention, constitution, and prescription are the sources of a tolerable civil social order. Men not being angels, a terrestrial paradise cannot be contrived by metaphysical enthusiasts; yet an earthly hell can be arranged readily enough by ideologues of one stamp or another. Precisely that has come to pass in a great part of the world, during the twentieth century.

To general principles in politics—as distinguished from fanatic ideological dogmata—the conservative subscribes. These are principles arrived at by convention and compromise, for the most part, and tested by long experience. Yet these general principles must be applied variously and with prudence, humankind's circumstances differing much from land to land or age to age. The conservative refuses to accept utopian politics as a substitute for religion. (In Eric Voegelin's phrase, the ideologue immanentizes the religious symbols of transcendence.) *The Conservative Mind* in part treats of such general principles; but it does not point the way to Zion.

This book, then, is an historical analysis of a mode of regarding the civil social order; it is no manual for partisan action. To define the terms "conservative" and "conservatism" by reference to the opinions and actions of certain important writers and public men; to apprehend the conservatives' principles of moral and social order—such are the limited ends of *The Conservative Mind*.

This book was written from conviction, though not from ideological motive. "Aphorisms burst like bombs from Kirk's pen," one early and unconservative reviewer declared. Perhaps so; the author was youthfully sanguine, even sanguinary, although he stood defiant upon the stricken field of the conservatives' rout, where "the flame that lit the battle's wreck/ Shone round him o'er the dead." These metaphorical bombs of his were intended to ward off literal bombs—to withstand the anarchy of the antagonist world.

The conservative fyrd, as matters would turn out, was not so fatally stricken as radicals had hoped and conservatives (with some liberals) had dreaded. Early in the 1950s, public opinion in America and Britain had begun to shift toward conservative measures and candidates, what with the menace of Soviet power and with popular disappointment at the fruits of political humanitarianism. This book, and others, provided an explanation and a justification of the conservative impulse. Public-opinion polls and other indices, over the succeeding years, would show that an ever increasing proportion of the American public—and, less markedly, of the

British public—were ready to call themselves conservatives. By 1980, both American liberalism and British socialism lay in the sere and yellow leaf.

Yet such electoral successes may be delusory. It is possible to win at the polls even while being overwhelmed by social circumstances; and material prosperity may mask, for a time, moral dissolution.

For the present general state of this world is an advanced decay. During the years that have slipped by since the first edition of this book was published, whole cultures have sunk to their final ruin. The most remote quarters of the world, previously little affected by modern technology and ideological fury, have been the worst devastated since the 1950s by the Four Horsemen of the Apocalypse: Tibet, Indochina, El Salvador, Afghanistan, Ruanda, Timor, Cyprus, nearly every old refuge of custom, convention, tradition. "Emergent" Africa, during this book's brief span of influence, has become submerged Africa, drowned in violence and economic folly. Millions of human beings have been slaughtered or starved in Asia. Representative government and the rule of law now seem tolerably secure in a few countries merely. Within such nations as still retain the framework of a tolerable civil social order, there has occurred Ortega's famous revolt of the masses: since the 1950s especially, the destruction of standards of all sorts, the widespread reduction of civilized life to the gross satisfaction of petty material appetites.

The egalitarian dystopias of Jacquetta Hawkes, Robert Graves, Aldous Huxley, and George Orwell have taken on flesh. The world's evanescent liberal era, in fulfillment of Santayana's predictions, is giving up the ghost. The outer order of the state falls into the clutch of merciless ideologues or squalid oligarchs: the inner order of the soul is broken by the "reductionism" of fashionable recent notions and by the triumph of destructive appetites.

But this Foreword is no place for disquisition upon the character of our woes. For an account of what ails mankind today, we can listen to the nobly prophetic voices of our generation: to the Russian Alexander Solzhenitsyn, to the Englishman Malcolm Muggeridge, to the Swiss Max Picard, to the Frenchman Gustave Thibon, to yet others endowed with the moral imagination and the tragic sense of life. There comes to mind, for eminent instance, the book entitled *The Tares and the Good Grain,* by the Swedish philosopher Tage Lindbom—once a Marxist, today a subject of the Kingdom of God.

Lindbom tells us movingly that, deserting the Kingdom of God, mankind has descended into its own Kingdom of Man: and that the Kingdom of Man will suffer destruction. Enslaved by our readily gratified lusts, reduced to fatuity by our own ingenious toys, we ignore the *mene, mene, tekel, upharsin* upon our wall.

"It is only since World War II that we have entered the time of the great harvest of the Kingdom of Man," Lindbom writes. "We have now to deal with a secularized generation for which material existence is everything and spiritual life is nothing. It is a generation for which all that is symbolic becomes ever more incomprehensible....It is a generation which is in the process of eliminating from its consciousness the notion of the family....

"The chaos from which we have for so long been preserved arises as a menace before us. And this menace cannot be turned aside by secular guidance except in certain manner: by a dictatorship, a technocratic dictatorship. In reality this dictatorship has already begun to make its entrance step by step.

"The exterior chaos and this exterior menace of dictatorship are nevertheless not the essential. They are but the projection of something incomparably more serious and more dangerous—interior chaos, the confusion that reigns in the hearts of men. It is now an affair of a generation which, in its ensemble, is incapable of discerning truth from lies, the true from the false, the good from the bad. The time of harvest is come for the Kingdom of Man."

Lindbom's voice echoes that of Edmund Burke, two centuries gone. Those who, impossibly demanding, revolt against law and nature do work their own ruin, Burke cried: "and the rebellious are outlawed, cast forth, and exiled, from this world of reason, and order, and peace, and virtue, and fruitful penitence, into the antagonist world of madness, discord, vice, confusion, and unavailing sorrow."

How much of the world of law and nature still may be preserved? In the United States, at least, there stirs increasingly a vague impulse of guardianship, of defense against the enemies of order and justice and freedom. The noun "conservative" signifies guardian or defender, the conservator. May that impulse be directed by imagination and right reason? When the Kingdom of Man is harvested and found to be a yield of tares, fit only for burning—why, will nothing of our civilization be spared? Nothing at all of our vainglory?

It remains conceivable even now that much worth conserving in our culture may be protected and renewed—granted some conservative will and talent among the rising generation. No universal fall into the antagonist world is decreed ineluctably by a deified History. Burke, in 1795, denied with vehemence that great states inescapably are subject to cycles of growth and decay:

"At the very moment when some of them seemed plunged in unfathomable abysses of disgrace and disaster, they have suddenly emerged. They have begun a new course, and opened a new reckoning; and even in the depths of their calamity, and on the very ruins of their country, have laid the foundations of a towering and durable greatness. All this has happened without any apparent previous change in the general circumstances which had brought on their distress. The death of a man at a critical juncture, his disgust, his retreat, his disgrace, have brought innumerable calamities on a whole nation. A common soldier, a child, a girl at the door of an inn, have changed the face of fortune, and almost of Nature."

In those last two sentences, Burke refers to the reverses of Pericles, of Coriolanus, of the elder Pitt, of the Constable of Bourbon. His common soldier is Arnold of Winkelried, who flung himself upon the Austrian spears at Sempach; his child is Hannibal, taking at the age of twelve his oath to make undying war upon Rome; his girl at the door of an inn is Joan of Arc. Chance, providence, or more individual strong wills, Burke declares, abruptly may alter the whole apparent direction of a nation or a civilization.

Men and women with a disposition to preserve and an ability to reform need to bear often in mind this argument of Burke: it may hearten them on dark days. To remind such men and women of their inheritance of thought and feeling, *The Conservative Mind* was written.

This seventh revised edition of the book reaches a new generation of readers. "I attest the rising generation!" Burke exclaimed, in his final speech to the House of Commons. And indeed that rising generation of Englishmen came to act in conformity to the counsels of the dead Burke. It may come to pass that the chastened rising generation of these twilight years of the twentieth century, perceiving the soreness of our straits, will labor energetically to keep what is worth keeping here below.

This book presents to you a body of conventional wisdom. Sophisters, economists, and calculators of our era often employ derogatorily this phrase "conventional wisdom"—as if both convention (that is, general agreement) and wisdom (that is, good judgment based on experience) were contemptible. This book holds otherwise—agreeing with Robert Frost's observation that

Most of the change we think we see in life

Is due to truths being in and out of favor.

For rightly understood, the conventional wisdom is made up of Frost's "truths we keep coming back and back to."

Both the impulse to improve and the impulse to conserve are necessary to the healthy functioning of any society. Whether we join our energies to the party of progress or to the party of permanence must depend upon the circumstances of the time. Of rapid change, healthy or unhealthy, we seem sure to experience more than enough in the concluding years of this century. Whether the conservative impulse within modern society can suffice to prevent the disintegration of the moral order and the civil order by the vertiginous speed of alteration—why, that may hang upon how well today's conservatives apprehend their patrimony.

—R. K.
Piety Hill, Mecosta, Michigan
July, 1986

IN EVERY STATE, not wholly barbarous, a philosophy, good or bad, there must be. However slightingly it may be the fashion to talk of speculation and theory, as opposed (sillily and nonsensically opposed) to practice, it would not be difficult to prove, that such as is the existing spirit of speculation, during any given period, such will be the spirit and tone of the religion, legislation, and morals, nay, even of the fine arts, the manners, and the fashions. Nor is this the less true, because the great majority of men live like bats, but in twilight, and know and feel the philosophy of their age only by its reflections and refractions.

—Coleridge, *Essays on His Own Times*

THE
CONSERVATIVE
MIND

I

The Idea of Conservatism

"THE STUPID PARTY": this is John Stuart Mill's description of conservatives. Like certain other summary dicta which nineteenth-century liberals thought to be forever triumphant, his judgment needs review in our age of disintegrating liberal and radical notions. Certainly many dull and unreflecting people have lent their inertia to the cause of conservatism: "It is commonly sufficient for practical purposes if conservatives, without saying anything, just sit and think, or even if they merely sit," F.J.C. Hearnshaw observed.[1] Edmund Burke, the greatest of modern conservative thinkers, was not ashamed to acknowledge the allegiance of humble men whose sureties are prejudice and prescription; for, with affection, he likened them to cattle under the English oaks, deaf to the insects of radical innovation. But the conservative principle has been defended, these past two centuries, by men of learning and genius. To review conservative ideas, examining their validity for this perplexed age, is the purpose of this book, which does not pretend to be a history of conservative parties. This study is a prolonged essay in definition. What is the essence of British and American conservatism? What sentiments, common to England and the United States, have sustained men of conservative impulse in their resistance against radical theories and social transformation ever since the beginning of the French Revolution?

Walk beside the Liffey in Dublin, a little way east of the dome of the Four Courts, and you come to an old doorway in a blank wall. This is the roofless wreck of an eighteenth-century house, and until recently the house still was here, inhabited although condemned: Number 12, Arran Quay, formerly a brick building of three stories, which began as a gentleman's residence, sank to the condition of a shop, presently was used as a governmental office of the meaner sort, and was demolished in 1950—a history suggestive of changes on a mightier scale in Irish society since 1729. For in that year, Edmund Burke was born here. Modern Dublin's memories do not extend much beyond the era of O'Connell, and the annihilation of Burke's birthplace seems to have stirred up no protest. Sill more recently many of the other old houses along the Quays have been demolished; indeed most of the eighteenth-century town falls into dereliction. The physical past shrivels. Behind Burke's house (or the sad scrap of it that remains), toward the old church of St. Michan in which, they say, he was baptised, stretch tottering brick slums where barefoot children scramble over broken walls. If you turn toward O'Connell Street, an easy stroll takes you to the noble façade of Trinity College and the statues of Burke and Goldsmith; northward, near Parnell Square, you may hear living Irish orators proclaiming through amplifiers that they know how to lead the little streets against the great. And you may reflect, with Burke, ''What shadows we are, and what shadows we pursue!''

Since Burke's day, there have been alterations aplenty in Dublin. Yet to the visitor, Ireland sometimes seems a refuge of tradition amidst the flux of our age, and Dublin a conservative old city; and so they are. A world that damns tradition, exalts equality, and welcomes change; a world that has clutched at Rousseau, swallowed him whole, and demanded prophets yet more radical; a world smudged by industrialism, standardized by the masses, consolidated by government; a world crippled by war, trembling between the colossi of East and West, and peering over a smashed barricade into the gulf of dissolution: this, our era, is the society Burke foretold, with all the burning energy of his rhetoric, in 1790. By and large, radical thinkers have won the day. For a century and a half, conservatives have yielded ground in a manner which, except for occasionally successful rear-guard actions, must be described as a rout.

As yet the causes of their shattering defeat are not wholly clear. Two general explanations are possible, however: first, that throughout the modern world *things* are in the saddle, and conservative ideas, however sound, cannot resist the unreasoning forces of industrialism, centralization, secularism, and the levelling impulse; second, that conservative thinkers have lacked perspicacity sufficient to meet the conundrums of modern times. And either explanation has some foundation.

This book is a criticism of conservative *thought;* and space does not allow any very thorough discussion of the material forces and political currents which have been at once the forcing-bed and the harvest of conservative ideas. For similar reasons, one can deal only laconically with the radical adversaries of conservatism. But there are good political histories of the years since 1790, and the doctrines of liberalism and radicalism are sufficiently established in the popular mind; while conservatism has had few historians. Although the study of French and German conservative ideas (linked with British and American thought by the debt to Burke of Maistre, Bonald, Guizot, Gentz, Metternich, and a dozen other men of high talents) is full of interest, that subject is too intricate for treatment here; only Tocqueville, out of all the Continental men of ideas, has been properly recognized in this volume, and he chiefly because of his enduring influence upon Americans and Englishmen.

The Conservative Mind, then, is confined to British and American thinkers who have stood by tradition and old establishments. Only Britain and America, among the great nations, have escaped revolution since 1790, which seems attestation that their conservatism is a sturdy growth and that investigation of it may be rewarding. To confine the field more narrowly still, this book is an analysis of thinkers in the line of Burke. Convinced that Burke's is the true school of conservative principle, I have left out of consideration most anti-democratic Liberals like Lowe, most antigovernmental individualists like Spencer, most anti-parliamentary writers like Carlyle. Every conservative thinker discussed in the following chapters—even the Federalists who were Burke's contemporaries—felt the influence of the great Whig, although sometimes the ideas of Burke penetrated to them only through a species of intellectual filter.

Conscious conservatism, in the modern sense, did not manifest itself until 1790, with the publication of *Reflections on the Revolution in France.* In that year the prophetic powers of Burke fixed in the public consciousness, for the first time, the opposing poles of conservation and innovation. The Carmagnole announced the opening of our era, and the smoky energy of coal and steam in the north of England was the signal for another revolution. If one attempts to trace conservative ideas back to an earlier time in Britain, soon he is enmeshed in Whiggery, Toryism, and intellectual antiquarianism; for the modern issues, though earlier taking substance, were not yet distinct. Nor does the American struggle between conservatives and radicals become intense until Citizen Genêt and Tom Paine transport across the Atlantic enthusiasm for French liberty: the American Revolution, substantially, had been a conservative reaction, in the English political tradition, against royal innovation. If one really must find a preceptor for conservatism who is older than Burke, he cannot rest satisfied with Bolingbroke, whose skepticism in religion disqualifies him, or with the Machiavellian Hobbes, or that old-fangled absolutist Filmer. Falkland, indeed, and Clarendon and Halifax and Strafford, deserve study; still more, in Richard Hooker one discovers profound conservative observations which Burke inherited with his Anglicanism and which Hooker drew in part from the Schoolmen and their authorities; but already one is back in the sixteenth century, and then in the thirteenth, and this book is concerned with modern problems. In any practical sense, Burke is the founder of our conservatism.

Canning and Coleridge and Scott and Southey and Wordsworth owed their political principles to the imagination of Burke; Hamilton and John Adams read Burke in America, and Randolph promulgated Burke's ideas in the Southern states. Burke's French disciples adopted the word "conservative," which Croker, Canning, and Peel clapped to the great party that no longer was Tory or Whig, once the followers of Pitt and Portland had joined forces. Tocqueville applied the wisdom of Burke to his own liberal ends; Macaulay copied the reforming talents of his model. And these men passed on the tradition of Burke to succeeding generations. With such a roster of pupils, Burke's claim to speak for the real conservative genius should be difficult to deny. Yet scholars of some eminence have endeavored to establish Hegel as a kind of coadjutor to Burke. "Sir," said Samuel Johnson concerning Hume, "the fellow is a Tory by chance." Hegel's conservatism is similarly accidental, as Tocqueville remarks: "Hegel exacted submission to the ancient established powers of his own time; which he held to be legitimate, not only from existence, but from their origin. His scholars wished to establish powers of another kind....From this Pandora's box have escaped all sorts of moral disease from which the people are still suffering. But I have remarked that a general reaction is taking place against this sensual and socialist philosophy."[2] Schlegel, Görres, and Stolberg— and Taine's school, in France—were admirers of both Hegel and Burke, which perhaps explains the confounding of their superficial resemblance with their fundamental inimicality. Hegel's metaphysics would have been as abhorrent to Burke as his style; Hegel himself does not seem to have read Burke; and people who think that these two men represent different facets of the same system are in danger of confusing authoritarianism (in the political sense) with conservatism. Marx could draw upon Hegel's magazine; he could find nothing to suit him in Burke.

But such distinctions are more appropriate in a concluding chapter than in a preface. Just now, a preliminary definition of the conservative idea is required.

Any informed conservative is reluctant to condense profound and intricate intellectual systems to a few pretentious phrases; he prefers to leave that technique to the enthusiasm of radicals. Conservatism is not a fixed and immutable body of dogmata; conservatives inherit from Burke a talent for re-expressing their convictions to fit the time. As a working premise, nevertheless, one can observe here that the essence of social conservatism is preservation of the ancient moral traditions of humanity. Conservatives respect the wisdom of their ancestors (this phrase was Strafford's, and Hooker's, before Burke illuminated it); they are dubious of wholesale alteration. They think society is a spiritual reality, possessing an eternal life but a delicate constitution: it cannot be scrapped and recast as if it were a machine. "What is conservatism?" Abraham Lincoln inquired once. "Is it not adherence to the old and tried, against the new and untried?" It is that, but it is more. F.J.C. Hearnshaw, in his *Conservatism in England,* lists a dozen principles of conservatives, but possibly these may be comprehended in a briefer catalogue. I think that there are six canons of conservative thought—

(1) Belief in a transcendent order, or body of natural law, which rules society as well as conscience. Political problems, at bottom, are religious and moral problems. A narrow rationality, what Coleridge called the Understanding, cannot of itself satisfy human needs. "Every Tory is a realist," says Keith Feiling: "he knows that there are great forces in heaven and earth that man's philosophy cannot plumb or fathom."[3] True politics is the art of apprehending and applying the Justice which ought to prevail in a community of souls.

(2) Affection for the proliferating variety and mystery of human existence, as opposed to the narrowing uniformity, egalitarianism, and utilitarian aims of most radical systems; conservatives resist what Robert Graves calls "Logicalism" in society. This prejudice has been called "the conservatism of enjoyment"—a sense that life is worth living, according to Walter Bagehot "the proper source of an animated Conservatism."

(3) Conviction that civilized society requires orders and classes, as against the notion of a "classless society." With reason, conservatives often have been called "the party of order." If natural distinctions are effaced among men, oligarchs fill the vacuum. Ul-

timate equality in the judgment of God, and equality before courts
of law, are recognized by conservatives; but equality of condition,
they think, means equality in servitude and boredom.

(4) Persuasion that freedom and property are closely linked: separate property from private possession, and Leviathan becomes
master of all. Economic levelling, they maintain, is not economic
progress.

(5) Faith in prescription and distrust of "sophisters, calculators, and economists" who would reconstruct society upon abstract designs. Custom, convention, and old prescription are checks
both upon man's anarchic impulse and upon the innovator's lust
for power.

(6) Recognition that change may not be salutary reform: hasty
innovation may be a devouring conflagration, rather than a torch
of progress. Society must alter, for prudent change is the means
of social preservation; but a statesman must take Providence into
his calculations, and a statesman's chief virtue, according to Plato and Burke, is prudence.

Various deviations from this body of opinion have occurred,
and there are numerous appendages to it; but in general conservatives have adhered to these convictions or sentiments with some
consistency, for two centuries. To catalogue the principles of their
opponents is more difficult. At least five major schools of radical
thought have competed for public favor since Burke entered politics: the rationalism of the *philosophes*, the romantic emancipation
of Rousseau and his allies, the utilitarianism of the Benthamites,
the positivism of Comte's school, and the collectivistic materialism of Marx and other socialists. This list leaves out of account
those scientific doctrines, Darwinism chief among them, which
have done so much to undermine the first principles of a conservative order. To express these several radicalisms in terms of a
common denominator probably is presumptuous, foreign to the
philosophical tenets of conservatism. All the same, in a hastily
generalizing fashion one may say that radicalism since 1790 has
tended to attack the prescriptive arrangement of society on the
following grounds—

(1) The perfectibility of man and the illimitable progress of society: meliorism. Radicals believe that education, positive legislation, and alteration of environment can produce men like gods; they deny that humanity has a natural proclivity toward violence and sin.

(2) Contempt for tradition. Reason, impulse, and materialistic determinism are severally preferred as guides to social welfare, trustier than the wisdom of our ancestors. Formal religion is rejected and various ideologies are presented as substitutes.

(3) Political levelling. Order and privilege are condemned; total democracy, as direct as practicable, is the professed radical ideal. Allied with this spirit, generally, is a dislike of old parliamentary arrangements and an eagerness for centralization and consolidation.

(4) Economic levelling. The ancient rights of property, especially property in land, are suspect to almost all radicals; and collectivistic reformers hack at the institution of private property root and branch.

As a fifth point, one might try to define a common radical view of the state's function; but here the chasm of opinion between the chief schools of innovation is too deep for any satisfactory generalization. One can only remark that radicals unite in detesting Burke's description of the state as ordained of God, and his concept of society as joined in perpetuity by a moral bond among the dead, the living, and those yet to be born—the community of souls.

So much for preliminary delineation. The radical, when all is said, is a neoterist, in love with change; the conservative, a man who says with Joubert, *Ce sont les crampons qui unissent une génération à une autre*—these ancient institutions of politics and religion. *Conservez ce qu'ont vu vos pères.* If one seeks by way of definition more than this, the sooner he turns to particular thinkers, the safer ground he is on. In the following chapters, the conservative is described as statesman, as critic, as metaphysician, as man of letters. Men of imagination, rather than party leaders, determine the ultimate course of things, as Napoleon knew; and I have chosen my conservatives accordingly. There are some conservative thinkers—Lord Salisbury and Justice Story, for instance—about whom I would have liked to write more; some interesting disciples of Burke, among them Arnold, Morley, and Bryce, I have omitted because they were not regular conservatives. But the main stream of conservative ideas is followed from 1790 to 1986.

In a revolutionary epoch, sometimes men taste every novelty, sicken of them all, and return to ancient principles so long disused that they seem refreshingly hearty when they are rediscovered. History often appears to resemble a roulette wheel; there is truth in the old Greek idea of cycles, and round again may come the number which signifies a conservative order. One of those flaming clouds which we deny to the Deity but arrogate to our own employment may erase our present elaborate constructions so abruptly as the tocsin in the Faubourg St. Germain terminated an age equally tired of itself. Yet this roulette-wheel simile would be repugnant to Burke (or to John Adams), who knew history to be the unfolding of a Design. The true conservative thinks of this process, which looks like chance or fate, as, rather, the providential operation of a moral law of polarity. And Burke, could he see our century, never would concede that a consumption-society, so near to suicide, is the end for which Providence has prepared man. If a conservative order is indeed to return, we ought to know the tradition which is attached to it, so that we may rebuild society; if it is not to be restored, still we ought to understand conservative ideas so that we may rake from the ashes what scorched fragments of civilization escape the conflagration of unchecked will and appetite.

II

Burke and the Politics of Prescription

When the age of Miracles lay faded into the distance as an incredible tradition, and even the age of Conventionalities was now old; and Man's Existence had for long generations rested on mere formulas which were grown hollow by course of time; and it seemed as if no Reality any longer existed, but only Phantasms of realities, and God's Universe were the work of the Tailor and the Upholsterer mainly, and men were buckram masks that went about becking and grimacing there,—on a sudden, the Earth yawns asunder, and amid Tartarean smoke, and glare of fierce brightness, rises Sansculottism, many-headed, fire-breathing, and asks: 'What think ye of me?'

SO CARLYLE WROTE of the eruption of 1789; his *French Revolution,* said Lord Acton, "delivered the English mind from the thraldom of Burke." Acton, by the way, would have hanged Robespierre and Burke on the same gallows, a judgment so sentimentally representative of Liberal opinion in this matter during the nineteenth century as its execution would have been abhorrent to Liberal practice.[1] From Carlyle's day onward, a great part of the serious public believed that the truth about the Revolution must lie somewhere between Edmund Burke and—why, Condorcet, if one needs to choose a name.

Throughout its hundred years of ascendancy, Liberal criticism maintained that Burke had blundered disastrously concerning the significance of the Deluge; Buckle went so far as to explain, in mournful pages, that Burke had gone mad in 1790.[2] Despite this, the intellectual defences of the Revolution never recovered from the fire of Burke; James Mackintosh, in Burke's own generation, surrendered without conditions to his great adversary, the Romantics deserted the egalitarian cause in answer to Burke's appeal, and Carlyle could not find it possible to share the ecstatic vision of Paine. Burke's *Reflections* captured the imagination of the most powerful part of the rising generation, for his style "forked and playful as the lightning, crested like the serpent" (Hazlitt's description) had outshone the flame of Rousseau in the eyes of most young Englishmen of parts: his work had not only survived Paine's assault, but had eclipsed it. He had set the course for British conservatism, he had become a model for Continental statesmen, and he had insinuated himself even into the rebellious soul of America. Buckram masks could not escape the Deluge, which Burke himself proclaimed the revolution "most astonishing that has hitherto happened in the world." But Burke was not of buckram; nor did he belong to the age of Conventionalities. He believed in the age of Miracles—the old age of Miracles, not the new age of human endeavors at miracle-manufacturing. He kindled a fire to stifle the blaze in France.

So late as the summer of 1789, Thomas Paine himself (whom Burke had previously befriended) wrote from Paris to Burke in the hope that the great orator might be persuaded to introduce into England "a more enlarged system of liberty" and become the spokesman of public discontent and popular sovereignty. Mirabeau, too, quoting to the National Assembly long passages from Burke's speeches (sometimes with acknowledgement and sometimes without) praised the leader of the Whigs with fervor. These recollections may be startling now, but they were hardly odd then, when the youthful Dupont might in all candor expect a commendation of the Revolution from the opponent of George III. Burke the conservative was also Burke the liberal—the foe of arbitrary power, in Britain, in America, in India. But with consistency he set his face against the Revolution in particular and against revolution in general.

Burke the lover of tradition was a commoner and a new man. The concluding third of the eighteenth century was an era dominated by new men: throughout western Europe, and in England most of all, that intellectual and spiritual equality, which the revolutionaries soon would demand with passion, already had been attained, substantially, some years before the Bastille fell. An actual ascendancy of "enterprising talents" made possible the success of that revolutionary cataclysm which was professed to be a necessary prelude to the rewarding of obscure merit. In Burke's generation, the most eminent names of Englishmen are new men's, come from the middle classes or up even steeper stairs: Smith, Johnson, Reynolds, Wilkes, Goldsmith, Sheridan, Crabbe, Hume, and so many others. A roster of the *philosophes* reads much the same. That natural aristocracy to which Burke would have entrusted national destinies was about him as he spoke in St. Stephen's Hall.

This new man, this son of a Dublin lawyer, had become the philosopher and organizer of aristocratic liberalism. Writing of Burke and John Randolph of Roanoke, and asking why the former was not a Tory and the latter not a Federalist, J.G. Baldwin says, "They were Whigs, in the ancient sense, because of their strong love of personal freedom—alone as deep and unconquerable as their pride; and because of their strong *caste* feelings; in other words, devotion to their own rights and to those of their order."[3]

To define Whiggism is not easy. The Whigs were opponents of arbitrary monarchical power, advocates of the internal reform of administration, men generally dubious of England's ventures abroad. When Burke entered the House of Commons, the party was seven reigns old: about as old as the present Conservative party is today. It was linked, although only vaguely, with the commerical interest as well as with the great landed proprietors. Much in the Whig program could attract the imagination of a young man like Burke: freedom under law, the balancing of orders in the commonwealth, a considerable degree of religious toleration, the intellectual legacy of 1688. The Tories, too, would have welcomed such a recruit, and Burke did not lack acquaintance among them; but they stood for the influence of a stubborn king, a scheme of colonial and domestic management sometimes stupidly rigorous in application, and a short way with dissenters abhorrent to one who had witnessed the disabilities of Irish Catholics. Not an atom of radicalism lived in either faction, nor yet of truly conscious conservatism. Burke chose the Rockingham Whigs, who needed him.

"Even in those affairs of state which took up most of the Whigs' time, they troubled little with the dry details of economic theory or administrative practice," Lord David Cecil observes. "Politics to them meant first of all personalities, and secondly general principles. And general principles were to them an occasion for expression rather than thought. They did not dream of questioning the fundamental canons of Whig orthodoxy. All believed in ordered liberty, low taxation and the enclosure of land; all disbelieved in despotism and democracy. Their only concern was to restate these indisputable truths in a fresh and effective fashion."[4]

The deficiencies of the Whig system need little comment; and the indefatigable recruit whom Lord Rockingham secured set to work at once, mortaring the perilous crannies in their rambling Whig country house. Deeply interested in political economy, capable of mastering a welter of details hopelessly repellent to most politicians, Burke alone could draw up and push through the Commons their plan of economical reform; yet he was at the same time the very man to express more lucidly and beautifully those general ideas they loved. He was willing to work, which virtue few Whig leaders shared; he was the greatest orator of an age of talk; he was a writer affectionately admired even by that pungent critic Dr. Johnson. Upon Burke descended almost the whole intellectual burden of his party, and a disproportionate share of its administrative duties, even after Fox had come to stand by Burke's side. Here was a genius who, as Johnson said, could do anything and everything—could have been bishop, governor, poet, philosopher, barrister, professor, soldier, all with a high degree of success. Even in Burke's aristocratic era, however, it was surprising that such

a man could be one of the managers of a great party. He was brilliant; and men of genius frequently fail in the political world. It
is difficult to imagine Burke enjoying similar power had he taken
to the hustings after 1832. Lacking the suppleness of Disraeli and
the self-righteous astuteness of Gladstone, the man who was rejected by the electors of Bristol disdained the arts of democratic
management.

Four enormous subjects separate the career of Burke into distinct periods: the restraining of royal authority; the American controversy and Revolution; the Indian debates and the trial of
Hastings; the French Revolution and consequent war. Only in
the first of these struggles did Burke effect a practical triumph.
He and his colleagues were unable to arrange conciliation with
America; Hastings went free; and even England's course in the
war against Jacobin France was conducted by Pitt and Dundas
in a fashion very different from that Burke advocated. In yet another principal effort of his parliamentary career, the economical
reform—dim enough to us now, but then a measure of the first
magnitude—Burke was more fortunate, and conferred an enduring
benefit upon British administration. For our present purpose, what
matters is the devleopment of Burke's conservative ideas as he dealt
with these pressing questions; and a steady continuous development it was, from the time of his protest against corruption by
the court faction to the *Regicide Peace*. "There is no shallower criticism than that which accuses Burke in his later years of apostasy
from so-called liberal opinions," says Augustine Birrell. "Burke
was all his life a passionate maintainer of the established order
of things, and a ferocious hater of abstractions and metaphysical
politics. The same ideas that explode like bombs through his dia-
tribes against the French Revolution are to be found shining with
a mild effulgence in the comparative calm of his earlier writings
….Burke, as he regarded humanity swarming like bees into and
out of their hives of industry, is ever asking himself, How are these
men to be saved from anarchy?"[5]

Conservatism, steadily; but conservation of what? Burke stood
resolutely for preservation of the British constitution, with its tradi-

tional division of powers, a system buttressed in Burke's mind by the arguments of Hooker and Locke and Montesquieu, as the system most friendly to liberty and order to be discerned in all Europe. And he stood for preservation of the still larger constitution of civilization. Anacharsis Cloots might claim to be the orator of the human race; Burke was the conservator of the species. A universal constitution of civilized peoples is implied in Burke's writings and speeches, and these are its chief articles: reverence for the divine origin of social disposition; reliance upon tradition and prejudice for public and private guidance; conviction that men are equal in the sight of God, but equal only so; devotion to personal freedom and private property; opposition to doctrinaire alteration. In the *Reflections,* these beliefs severally find their most burningly earnest expression:

As the ends of such a partnership cannot be obtained in many generations, it becomes a partnership not only between those who are living, but between those who are living, those who are dead, and those who are to be born. Each contract of each particular state is but a clause in the great primaeval contract of eternal society, linking the lower with the higher nature, connecting the visible and invisible world, according to a fixed compact sanctioned by the inviolable oath which holds all physical and all moral natures, each in their appointed place....

Prejudice is of ready application in the emergency; it previously engages the mind in a steady course of wisdom and virtue, and does not leave the man hesitating in the moment of decision, skeptical, puzzled, and unresolved. Prejudice renders a man's virtue his habit; and not a series of unconnected acts....

You would have had a protected, satisfied, laborious, and obedient people, taught to seek and to recognize the happiness which is to be found by virtue in all conditions; in which consists the true moral equality of mankind, and not in the monstrous fiction, which by inspiring false ideas into men destined to travel in the obscure walk of laborious life, serves only to aggravate and embitter that real inequality, which it never can remove; and which the order of civil life establishes as much for the benefit of those whom it must leave in an humble state, as those whom it is able to exalt to a condition more splendid, but not more happy...

In this partnership all men have equal rights; but not to equal things....

By this wise prejudice we are taught to look with horror on those children of their country, who are promptly rash to hack that aged parent in pieces, and put him into the kettle of magicians, in hopes that by their poisonous weeds, and wild incantations, they may regenerate the paternal constitution, and renovate their father's life.

But this is to anticipate. A moral order, good old prescription, cautious reform—these are elements not merely English, but of general application; for Burke, they were as valid in Madras as in Bristol; and his French and German disciples, throughout the nineteenth century, found them applicable to Continental institutions. The intellectual system of Burke, then, is not simply a guarding of British political institutions. If it were only this, half his significance for us would be merely antiquarian. Yet a brief glance at the particular Constitution which Burke praised may repay attention—a glance at that eighteenth-century society upon which it rested, and which, in turn, depended upon that political constitution. Recently much nostalgic eulogy has been lavished upon the eighteenth century; but there are sound reasons why modern men may admire that age.

The constitution of England existed for the protection of Englishmen in all walks of life, Burke said: to ensure their liberties, their equality in the eyes of justice, their opportunity to live with decency. What were its origins? The tradition of English rights, the statutes conceded by the kings, the arrangement established between sovereign and parliament after 1688. In the government of the nation, the people participated through their representatives—not *delegates*, but representatives, elected from the ancient corporate bodies of the nation, rather than from an amorphous mass of subjects. What constituted the people? In Burke's opinion, the public consisted of some four hundred thousand free men, possessed of leisure or property or membership in a responsible body which enabled them to apprehend the elements of politics. (Burke granted that the extent of the suffrage was a question to be determined by prudence and expedience, varying with the character of the age.) The country gentlemen, the farmers, the professional classes, the merchants, the manufacturers, the university graduates, in some constituencies the shopkeepers and prosperous artisans, the forty-shilling freeholders: men of these orders had the franchise. It was a proper balancing and checking of the several classes competent to exercise political influence—the crown, the peerage, the squirearchy, the middle classes, the old towns and the universities of the realm. Within one or another of these categories, the real interest of every person in England was comprehended. In good government, the object of voting is not to enable every man to express his ego, but to represent his interest, whether or not he casts his vote personally and directly.

Now everyone knows the catalogue of charges against the electoral system of eighteenth-century Britain. No one understood better than Burke (who was editor of the *Annual Register*) the state of the nation; no one better apprehended the arguments for reform. But reform, said Burke, needs a delicate touch. With the rotten and pocket boroughs, the imperfectly—represented new industrial towns, the corruption common about the hustings and touching Parliament itself, the preponderance of the great Whig magnates—with all these he was acquainted. Reform, achieved by patching and reinforcing the fabric of British society, he was willing to promote; but not the alleged reform of a brand-new suit of clothes, breaking the continuity of political development. With the Duke of Richmond's demand for universal suffrage and annual parliaments, he had no sympathy; he was always a liberal, never a democrat. Of the elements that qualify men for the franchise, two at least—land and leisure—may have been as widely diffused then as now; education has spread since his day, but not commonly education of the sort Burke meant; and while personal incomes have gravitated toward equality, the proportion of people with the income Burke thought proper for a voter bulks no greater in the whole population, probably. Burke would have dreaded the modern democratic state.

Often Burke's age is called aristocratic. But in the stricter sense, it was not: the basis of power was far broader than nobility and gentry. Burke himself drew much of his support from the middle classes, and could say, "I am no friend to aristocracy...I would rather by far see it [government] resolved into any other form, than lost in that austere and insolent domination."[6] The scholarship of Tocqueville describes succinctly this liberal England: "At first blush it would appear that the old constitution is still in force in England; but, on a closer view, this illusion is dispelled. Forget old names, pass over old forms, and you will find the feudal system substantially abolished there as early as the seventeenth century: all classes freely intermingled, an eclipsed nobility, an aristocracy open to all, wealth installed as the supreme power, all men equal before the law, equal taxes, a free press, public debates—phenomena which were all unknown to medieval society. It was the skillful infusion of this young blood into the old feudal body which preserved its life, and imbued it with fresh vitality, without divesting it of its ancient shape."[7] Spiritual continuity, the immense importance of keeping change within the framework of custom, the recognition that society is an immortal being: these deep truths were impressed upon Burke's mind through his observation of free English institutions. Certain writers who ought to know better are fond of saying that Burke considered society an "organism"—a term redolent of positivism and biological evolution. In actuality, Burke was careful not to bind himself by that rash analogy. He spoke of society as a *spiritual* unity, an eternal partnership, a corporation which is always perishing and yet always renewing, very like that other perpetual corporation and unity, the church. Upon the preservation of this view of society, Burke thought, the success of English institutions depended—defending a view implicit in English thought so early as Hooker, but never before so clearly enunciated.

Liberty, Burke knew, had risen through an elaborate and delicate process, and its perpetuation depended upon retaining those habits of thought and action which guided the savage in his slow and weary ascent to the state of civil social man. All his life, Burke's chief concern had been for justice and liberty, which must stand or fall together—liberty under law, a definite liberty, the limits of which were determined by prescription. He had defended the liberties of Englishmen against their king, and the liberties of Americans against king and parliament, and the liberties of Hindus against Europeans. He had defended those liberties not because they were innovations, discovered in the Age of Reason, but because they were ancient prerogatives, guaranteed by immemorial usage. Burke was liberal because he was conservative. And this cast of mind Tom Paine was wholly unable to appreciate.

With the eighteenth-century political life touched upon here, Burke was substantially content. Being no meliorist, he preferred this epoch of comparative peace and tranquillity, whatever its failings, to the uncertain prospect of a society remoulded by visionaries. With all the titanic power of his intellect, he struggled to protect the chief lineaments of that age. Yet it is one of the few charges that can be preferred successfully against Burke's prescience (to digress for a moment) that he seems to have ignored economic influences spelling death for the eighteenth-century milieu quite so surely as the *Social Contract* repudiated the eighteenth-century mind. He was thoroughly acquainted with the science of political economy: according to Mackintosh, Adam Smith himself told Burke, "after they had conversed on subjects of political economy, that he was the only man, who, without communication, thought on these topics exactly as he did."[8] But what is one to say about Burke's silence upon the decay of British rural society? Innovation (as Burke, and Jefferson, knew) comes from the cities, where man uprooted seeks to piece together a new world; conservatism always has had its most loyal adherents in the country, where man is slow to break with the old ways that link him with his God in the infinity above and with his father in the grave at his feet. Even while Burke was defending the stolidity of cattle under the English oaks, wholesale enclosures, the source of much of the Whig magnates' power, were decimating the body of yeo-

men, cotters, rural dwellers of every humble description; as the
free peasantry shrank in numbers, the political influence of landowners was certain to dwindle. "To what ultimate extent it may
be wise, or practicable, to push inclosures of common and waste
lands," wrote Burke, "may be a question of doubt, in some points
of view; but no person thinks them already carried to excess."
His misgivings went no farther.

    This is an exception, however. Burke did not often leave im-
portant material influences out of consideration; he was eminently,
almost omnisciently, practical. "I must see the things; I must see
the men." He elevated political "expedience" from its usual
Machiavellian plane to the dignity of a virtue, Prudence. "I heaved
the lead every inch of the way I made," Burke once said of his
political practice.

    Heaving the lead is not a practice for which Irish orators are
renowned; Burke's flights of eloquent fancy everyone knows; and
surely Burke did not seem at Hastings' trial, to frightened Tory
spectators, a man sworn to cautious plumbing of the depths. Yet
Burke spoke accurately of his general policy as a statesman, for
he based his every important decision upon a close examination
of particulars. He detested "abstraction"—by which he meant
not *principle*, but rather vainglorious generalization without respect
for human frailty and the particular circumstances of an age and
a nation. Thus it was that while he believed in the rights of Englishmen and in certain natural laws of universal application, he
despised the "Rights of Man" which Paine and the French doctrinaires were soon to proclaim inviolable. Edmund Burke believed
in a kind of constitution of civilized peoples; with Samuel Johnson,
he adhered to the doctrine of a universal human nature. But the
exercise and extent of these rights can be determined only by
prescription and local circumstances; in this Burke read Montesquieu much more faithfully than did the French reformers. A
man has always a right to self-defense; but he does not have, in
all times and all places, a right to carry a drawn sword.

    Nearly sixty years old when the French cauldron commenced
to bubble, grown gray in opposition to the government, denied

office except for two fleeting periods during his whole parliamentary career, Burke must have seemed to Paine and Mirabeau and
Cloots the most natural leader imaginable for making a sweep of
the old regime in Britain. For decades he had been denouncing
men in authority with a vehemence which no one in France, not
even Voltaire, dared imitate: Burke had called the king of England a scheming tyrant and the conqueror of India an unprincipled despoiler. But what Paine and Mirabeau and Cloots forgot
was that Edmund Burke fought George III and Warren Hastings
because they were innovators. He foresaw in the Age of Reason
a scheme of innovation which was designed to turn society inside
out, and he exposed this new menace to permanence with a passion of loathing that exceeded all his invectives against Tories and
nabobs. For the great practical spokesman of the Whigs knew more
of the wants of mankind than did all the galaxy of French
economists and men of letters. "Burke has endured as the permanent manual of political wisdom without which statesmen are
as sailors on an uncharted sea." It was not Churchill who said
this, nor Taft, but the late Harold Laski. To Burke's analysis
of revolutionary theories, philosophical conservatism owes its
being.

2

Reflections on the Revolution in France was published in 1790, after
Burke had broken with Fox's Whigs; *A Letter to a Member of the
National Assembly* and *An Appeal from the New to the Old Whigs* appeared in the following year; *A Letter to a Noble Lord* and the earlier letters of *Thoughts on a Regicide Peace*, in 1796; the conclusion
of the latter series, in 1797. Together, these works of a giant near
his end are the charter of conservatism. Disdainful as he was of
closet-philosophies and systems abstractly fabricated, Burke made
little effort to form his ideas into a regular compendium of political
doctrine; but the universal principles he applies to the transitory
French scene of terror transcend their immediate topic. That very
wealth of historical and biographical detail in which Burke's opin-

ions are embedded often makes his thoughts twice as readable as the treatises of his opponents. His pamphlets first checked in Britain an enthusiasm for French innovation; presently made possible Pitt's rallying of British patriotism against France; and then inspired a reaction against levelling principles which kept the English constitution almost unaltered during four decades. His influence is still strong in the world.

Until very recent years, the bulk of serious criticism of Burke's ideas was written by Liberals, men unable to share Burke's suspicion of "progress" and "democracy," optimists (writing before the First World War and the Russian Revolution) who looked forward to a charming vista of material and cultural achievement throughout society. Certainly Burke must have misunderstood the general tendency of the revolutionary movement in France, these critics agreed; for the Revolution was a necessary step toward universal equality, freedom, and prosperity, however unpleasant its immediate manifestations. But the course of events seems to have vindicated Burke's prophecies, after all, and our present time of troubles has seen the literal disintegration of those illimitable hopes of the Age of Revolution: the gods of the copybook headings with fire and slaughter return. He habitually thought in terms of long-run tendencies and consequences. All the vaticinations of Burke have come to pass: the dissolution of nations into mere aggregations of individuals, the reapportionment of property by political machinery, the era of merciless war, the appearance of men on horseback to forge tyranny out of anarchy, the ghastly sickness of morality and social decencies. Burke found the source of these terrors in the radical visions of the revolutionary thinkers.

Until 1914, it was common among commentators on Burke to observe that he exaggerated, besides, the immediate danger to England from Sansculottism. These critics had not witnessed the triumph of Marxism in Russia, of all European states apparently the least suited for communistic experiments. Possibly Burke may have overestimated the strength of radicalism in England; but how far the triumph of conservatism resulted directly from Burke's own admonitions and from Pitt's precautions, one can hardly tell now

—except that Burke's and Pitt's policies were vastly important. Burke blocked the current of fervor for abstract doctrines of equality which by 1790 had made such progress in Britain that the Duke of Bedford should pose as an English Philip Égalité; that peers, notably Richmond, Derby, Norfolk, Selkirk, and Effingham, were members of the radical Constitutional Society; that Fox and Sheridan should mistake the direction of the revolutionary wind; that the young men later to become Burke's disciples—Coleridge, Southey, Wordsworth—were enraptured with levelling fancies; that even scholars like Soame Jenyns, "the cosmic Tory," should approve the "principle of sortition" and other adaptations from classical democracy. The state of the English agricultural laborer, oppressed by the enclosures; the terrible life of the mining communities and of the new industrial classes in the North; the ferocious London mob that could paralyze the capital with no better leader than the opéra-bouffe Lord George Gordon; the Leith riots; the awful glowering of Ireland in those years; the sentimental radicalism of the rationalistic parsons, more than half of whom seem originally to have been in sympathy with the upheaval in France—Burke was accustomed to draw parallels. Material circumstance in France had hardly been more propitious to a conflagration; revolutionary propaganda had supplied the tinder. Burke was determined to snuff the spark on his side of the Channel. If he had not pinched the wick, or at least if he had joined Fox in applauding liberty, equality, and fraternity, perhaps no man could have extinguished the flame. Burke's critics wrote less than a century after the event, and one century is a short time in which to estimate the consequences of having turned the world upside down. One commentator on Burke, himself an eminent partisan of democracy, was wiser than most. "Burke was himself, and was right," when he warned England against the Revolution in France. These are the words of Woodrow Wilson.[9]

Framing a system to refute the assumptions of egalitarianism was a task uncongenial to Burke's nature. Even when he set himself doggedly to it, as in the *Reflections*, he could express principles in the abstract only for a few consecutive paragraphs. Yet he perceived the necessity for opposing ideas with ideas, in spite of his distaste for generality divorced from contingency, and by 1793 his tremendous countermine had effectively thwarted the British devotees of revolutionary reform. "I am come to a time of life, in which it is not permitted that we should trifle with our existence," he wrote to Lord Fitzwilliam, in that fearsome year. "I am fallen into a state of the world, that will not suffer me to play at little sports, or to enfeeble the part I am bound to take, by smaller collateral considerations. I cannot proceed, as if things went on in the beaten circle of events, such as I have known them for half a century. The moral state of mankind fills me with dismay and horrors. The abyss of Hell itself seems to yawn before me. I must act, think, and feel according to the exigencies of this tremendous reason."[10] Never was statesman more reluctant to turn political philosopher; but never, perhaps, was the metamorphosis more consequential.

"Nothing can be conceived more hard than the heart of a thoroughbred metaphysician," he had written. "It comes nearer to the cold malignity of a wicked spirit than to the frailty and passion of a man. It is like that of the principle of evil himself, incorporeal, pure, unmixed, dephlegmated, defecated evil." In 1798, nevertheless, the reluctantly awed Hazlitt told Southey that "Burke was a metaphysician, Mackintosh a mere logician."[11] By the clutch of circumstance, Burke had been compelled to enter the realm of abstraction, although he went not one step farther into that windy domain than exigency demanded. Like Johnson, he was convinced that first principles, in the moral sphere, come to us through revelation and intuition.

Edmund Burke's conservative argument was a reply to three separate radical schools: the rationalism of the *philosophes*; the romantic sentimentalism of Rousseau and his disciples; and the nascent utilitarianism of Bentham. One hardly can catalogue here the infinite projects and theories of Voltaire, Holbach, Helvétius, Diderot, Turgot, Condorcet, Sièyes, Rousseau, Morelly, Mably, Paine, Godwin, Price, Priestley, and all the rest of the eloquent innovators of the Age of Reason, let alone distinguish accurately among them. Burke was quite aware of the hostility between the rationalism of Voltaire's associates and the romantic idealism of Rousseau's adherents; he assaulted both camps, although generally training his heavy guns upon Rousseau, "the insane Socrates." In the course of his assault upon these differing systems, Burke disavowed a great part of the principles of Locke, the official philosopher of Whiggism. The theories of Locke were inherited by such diverse legatees as Rousseau in Geneva, Price in the Old Jewry, Fox in St. Stephen's, Bentham in his library, and Jefferson at Monticello; but from among the general ideas of that philosopher, conservatism after Burke retained almost nothing but Locke's contention that government originates out of the necessity for protecting property.

In spite of differences among these schools, Burke knew himself to be contending against a spirit of innovation possessed of a recognizable general character. One may venture to condense the tenets of radicalism at the end of the eighteenth century into the following catalogue:

(1) If there is divine authority in the universe, it differs sharply in its nature from the Christian idea of God: for some radicals, it is the remote and impassive Being of the deists; for others, the misty and new-modelled God of Rousseau.

(2) Abstract reason or (alternatively) idyllic imagination may be employed not merely to study, but to direct, the course of social destiny.

(3) Man naturally is benevolent, generous, healthy-souled, but in this age is corrupted by institutions.

(4) The traditions of mankind, for the most part, are tangled and delusory myth, from which we learn little.

(5) Mankind, capable of infinite improvement, is struggling upward toward Elysium, and should fix its gaze always upon the future.

(6) The aim of the reformer, moral and political, is emancipation—liberation from old creeds, old oaths, old establishments; the man of the future is to rejoice in pure liberty, unlimited democracy, self-governing, self-satisfying. Political power is the

most efficacious instrument of reform—or, from another point of view, the demolition of existing political power.

To these professions of radicalism, the utilitarian and collectivistic school afterward submitted amendments; but we are concerned just now with the innovating theories which Burke confronted. He conceded his enemies not one premise. He began and ended his campaign for the conservation of society upon the grand design of piety; in his reverent eyes, the whole of earthly reality was an expression of moral order.* This it is which lifts Burke so far above "political science" that some scholars have confessed themselves unable to follow his chain of ideas; and still Burke remains so attentive to practicality that he leaves some metaphysicians at a loss. In examining Burke's conservative system, therefore, it is well to commence on the lofty plane of religious belief. For Burke, the formulas upon which man's existence rested never had grown hollow.

3

"The Tory has always insisted that, if men would cultivate the individual virtues, social problems would take care of themselves." So, contemptuously, Granville Hicks once wrote of Robert Louis Stevenson. There is a good deal in this observation, although it is more nearly true of Johnson than of Burke. It is not the whole of Burke's opinion upon the ills of society, for no one knew better than he the power for good or evil that lies in establishments; but it is true that Burke saw politics as an exercise in morals. And a great part of conservative doctrine on this point comes from Burke. To know the state, first we must know the ethical man, Burke thought.

"Rousseau is a moralist, or he is nothing." After delivering this judgment, Burke rises to an assault upon the Genevese so

---

*John Adams, censorious always, suspected both Burke and Johnson of being "political Christians"; but Adams knew neither of them, and the verdict of their biographers does not bear Adams out.

merciless that one is tempted to add the quip, "and he is not a moralist." Yet Burke did not underestimate the *Social Contract.* Rousseau's was a false morality, but pretentious; against it must be set a nobler. A new-fangled morality was a monstrous imposture; Burke turned in this matter, as in most, to prescription and precedent, old materials ready to the true reformer's hand, to supply this opposing morality which might heal the wounds inflicted by revolutionary moral doctrines. The praise of humility was often on Burke's lips; and in his system of morals, at least, he showed himself a humble man. Disdaining a vain display of invention, he burnished up the arguments of Aristotle and Cicero, of the Fathers of the Church, of Hooker and Milton, and put new warmth into their phrases, so that their ideas flamed above the Jacobin torches. Rejecting the notion of a world subject only to sudden impulse and physical appetite, he expounded the idea of a world governed by strong and subtle purpose. Into this old morality he poured the catalyst of his Irish imagination, which transformed the flicker of classical thought and neo-classical formal religion into a sheet of fire.

Revelation, reason, and an assurance beyond the senses tell us that the Author of our being exists, and that He is omniscient; and man and the state are creations of God's beneficence. This Christian orthodoxy is the kernel of Burke's philosophy. God's purpose among men is revealed through the unrolling of history. How are we to know God's mind and will? Through the prejudices and traditions which millennia of human experience with divine means and judgments have implanted in the mind of the species. And what is our purpose in this world? Not to indulge our appetites, but to render obedience to divine ordinance.

This view of the nature of things may appear delusory to the utilitarian and the positivist; it will seem transcendently true to the religious man; but whether sound or erroneous, there is nothing incomprehensible about this confesstion of faith, or even obscure. Burke's position is stated above in the simplest terms; he makes his own case in language at once more lucid and more noble. For a thousand years, hardly a learned man in Europe dissented from this belief. Yet the scholars of "political realism" in the twentieth century, full of the notion that society can be managed on scientific principles, have gone so far as to call this "obscurantism"— this defense of a moral tradition Socratic and Pauline in its origins. Professor R. M. MacIver exclaims with a vehemence resembling horror, "It was no service to our understanding when Burke enveloped once more in mystic obscurity the office of government and in the sphere of politics appealed once more against reason to tradition and religion."[12]

But is not this objection simply begging the question? The Age of Reason, Burke protested with all his splendor of rhetoric, was in reality an Age of Ignorance. If (as most men, since the beginning of human history, have believed) the foundation of human welfare is divine providence, then the limitation of politics and ethics to a puny "reason" is an act of folly, the refuge of a ridiculous presumption. Precisely this blindness to the effulgence of the burning bush, this deafness to the thunder above Sinai, is what Burke proclaims to be the principal error of the French "enlightenment." Even Rousseau cries out against such overweening confidence in a human rationality which, although insolently disavowing supernatural direction, asserts its own infallibility. Almost no disputes concerning first principles ever are settled, and Burke himself would have agreed that if the arguments of Aristotle, Seneca, and Aquinas concerning purpose in the universe cannot convince the skeptic, he never will be converted but by grace. Burke was indignant, however, at the fashion in which the philosophers of the Enlightenment casually dismissed the faith of ages and the proofs of genius with a complacent formula or a sniggering witticism. For Burke's lofty spirit, there could be no satisfactory suspension of judgment in these things. Either order in the cosmos is real, or all is chaos. If we are adrift in chaos, then the fragile egalitarian doctrines and emancipating programs of the revolutionary reformers have no significance; for in a vortex of chaos, only force and appetite signify.

I allow that, if no supreme ruler exists, wise to form, and potent to enforce, the moral law, there is no sanction to any contract, virtual or even actual, against the will of prevalent power. On that hypothesis, let any set of men be strong enough to set their duties at defiance, and they cease to be duties any longer. We have but one appeal against irrestible power—

> *Si genus humanum et mortalia temnitis arma,*
> *At sperate Deos memores fandi atque nefandi.*

Taking it for granted that I do not write to the disciples of the Parisian philosophy, I may assume, that the awful Author of our being is the author of our place in the order of existence; and that having disposed and marshalled us by a divine tactic, not according to our will, but according to His, He has, in and by that disposition, virtually subjected us to act the part which belongs to the part assigned to us. We have obligations to mankind at large, which are not in consequence of any special voluntary pact. They arise from the relation of man to man, and the relation of man to God, which relations are not a matter of choice....When we marry, the choice is voluntary, but the duties are not a matter of choice....The instincts which give rise to this mysterious process of nature are not of our making. But out of physical causes, unknown to us, perhaps unknowable, arise moral duties, which, as we are able perfectly to comprehend, we are bound indispensably to perform.[13]

This is great preaching. No one ever expressed more persuasively the impotence of human reason before divine mystery, or the necessity for cheerful obedience to the moral order if "the great mysterious incorporation of the human race" is to endure. We never will penetrate, in this brief life, says Burke, to precise knowledge of providential aims; the philosopher who wastes his time in endeavoring to rationalize the transcendent can accomplish no more than the stimulation of a shallow, sour skepticism among men whose only surety lies in obedience to prescriptive truths. If there is no superhuman sanction for morality, then "reason," "enlightenment," and "pity" are so many figments of dreams, for in a world without justice and purpose, men may as well forget the notions of knowledge and charity. "To illuminate the struggles of the past, to dignify and intensify the responsibilities of the present, and to guarantee the future against the decadence and defeat with which, in a world of turbulent human wills, it is constantly menaced, it seemed to him the sheet anchor of a true political faith that the whole great drama of national life should be reverently recognized as ordered by a Power to which past, present, and future are organically knit stages in one Divine plan,'' says J. H. MacCunn of Burke's faith.[14] "There is an order that keeps things fast in their place," said Burke himself, penetrating to the very root of conservative instinct; "it is made to us and we are made to it."

Burke does not approve religion because it is a bulwark of order; instead, he says that mundane order is derived from, and remains a part of, divine order. Religion is not merely a convenient myth to keep popular appetites within bounds; he had no sympathy with Polybius' suggestion that the ancients invented religion to save men from anarchy, or with Plato's willingness to create religious mythology out of whole cloth so that man will reverence the established order in the illusion that it was ordained from the very beginning of things. Politics and morals, Burke saw, are deduced from belief or skepticism; men never really succeed in convincing themselves of the reality of things supernatural merely to sustain things natural. Implicit in Burke's writings are the proofs of Aristotle and the Schoolmen and the English divines for the reality of providential purpose and intelligent direction in the cosmos. The universal instinct for perpetuation of the species; the compulsions of conscience; the intimations of immortality; the profound consciousness in men that they partake of some great continuity and essence—these evidences sparkle through his works from first to last, but Burke does not attempt fanciful new proofs, leaving theology to the schools. A man always desperately busy, lacking time to chop logic, he shared Dr. Johnson's exasperation at haggling over intuitive truths—the conviction of instinctive knowledge which provoked Johnson to growl, "Why, sir, we *know* the will is free, and there's an end of it!" Only the restless, shallow, self-intoxicated atheist, who refuses to admit the existence of anything greater than himself, really can have the impudence to deny these sources of religious insight. And the spectacle of Burke's ranging intellect thus humbly convinced, his erudition supporting the verdict of the Christian fathers, his prudent, practical, reforming spirit submitting to the discipline of religious tradition, is perhaps as good a proof as any direct evidence available to man that our world is only a little part of a great spiritual hierarchy. It is the faith of a man steeped in Christian and classical wisdom. An Hellenic piety, almost Platonic in its tone, suffuses Burke's declaration that the state is divinely ordained: "He who gave us our nature to be perfected by our virtue, willed also the necessary means of its perfection.—He willed therefore the state.—He willed its connexion with the source and original archetype of all perfection."[15]

The sentimental advocacy of indiscriminately generous human sympathies, or the prevalence of universal pity, cannot suffice to save a society which has denied its divine ordination.* Every state is the creation of Providence, whether or not its religion is Christianity. Christianity is the highest of religions; but every sincere creed is a recognition of divine purpose in the universe, and all mundane order is dependent upon reverence for the religious creed which a people have inherited from their fathers. This conviction redoubled Burke's detestation of Hastings: the Governor-General had ridden rough-shod over native religious tradition and ceremonial in India.

Burke could not conceive of a durable social order without the spirit of piety. Statesmen, quite as much as bishops, fulfill a consecrated task: "This consecration is made, that all who administer in the government of men, in which they stand in the person of God himself, should have high and worthy notions of their function and destination; that their hope should be full of

---

*"I have observed that the philosophers in order to insinuate their polluted atheism into young minds systematically flatter all their passions natural and unnatural. They explode or render odious or contemptible that class of virtues which restrain the appetite. These are at least nine out of ten of the virtues. In place of all this, they substitute a virtue which they call humanity or benevolence. By this means their morality has no idea in it of restraint, or indeed of a distinct settled principle of any kind. When their disciples are thus left free and guided only by present feeling they are no longer to be depended upon for good or evil. The men who today snatch the worst criminals from justice will murder the most innocent persons tomorrow."—Burke to the Chevalier de Rivarol, 1791 (Wentworth Woodhouse Papers, Book I, 623).

immortality; that they should not look to the paltry pelf of the moment, nor to the temporary and transient praise of the vulgar,
but to a solid, permanent existence, in the permanent part of their
nature, and to a permanent frame and glory, in the example they
leave as a rich inheritance to the world.''[16] A popular government,
even more than monarchy or aristocracy, requires such consecration, because the people then enjoy a share of power, and must
be made to understand the responsibilities of power. "All persons
possessing any portion of power ought to be strongly and awfully
impressed with an idea that they act in trust: and that they are
to account for their conduct in that trust to the one great Master,
Author, and Founder of society.''

   To describe as "obscurantism" and "mysticism" this vivid and
sagacious piety of Burke's is a gross abuse of philosophical terms,
illustrating the semantic Dark Age into which the twentieth century has been slipping. Burke's was a lofty faith, but it was also
the faith of a practical man, joined to ideas of public honor and
responsibility. A man who believes that a just God rules the world;
that the course of history has been determined, though commonly
in ways inscrutable, by His Providence; that individual station
in life is assigned by "a divine tactic"; that original sin and aspiration toward the good both are part of God's design; that the
reformer first should endeavor to discern the lineaments of a
providential order, and then endeavor to conform political arrangements to the dictates of a natural justice—skeptics may believe
a man who declares these convictions to be mistaken, but skeptics are muddled if they call him a "mystic." These are the religious principles of a man profoundly familiar with the world of
experience. And Burke proceeds to make his creed still more a
part of private and political life. If our world indeed is ordered
in accordance with a divine idea, we ought to be cautious in our
tinkering with the structure of society; for though it may be God's
will that we serve as his instruments of alteration, we need first
to satisfy our consciences on that point. Again, Burke states that
a universal equality among men exists; but it is the equality of
Christianity, moral equality, or, more precisely, equality in the

ultimate judgment of God; equality of any other sort we are foolish, even impious, to covet. Leonard Woolf, the shrewdest of humanitarians, recognizes this bond between Christianity and social conservatism: "Christianity envisages a framework for human society in which earthly miseries have a recognized, permanent, and honourable place. They are trials sent by Heaven to test and train us; as such, it is impious to repine against them."[17] Burke would have accepted this impeachment.

Contemptuous of the notion of human perfectibility, Burke modelled his psychology on this Christian picture of sin and tribulation. Poverty, brutality, and misfortune are indeed portions of the eternal order of things; sin is a terribly real and demonstrable fact, the consequence of our depravity, not of erring institutions; religion is the consolation for these ills, which never can be removed by legislation or revolution. Religious faith makes existence tolerable; ambition without pious restraint must end in failure, often involving in its ruin that beautiful reverence which solaces common men for the obscurity and poverty of their lot.

To inculcate this veneration among men, to consecrate public office, Burke believed that the church must be interwoven with the fabric of the nation. His Church is an idealized Anglican establishment, but more than Anglican. There is something classical in it; something Catholic, too, so that bigots (including the old duke of Newcastle) whispered that Burke must have been educated in the Papist seminary at St. Omer. "Religion is so far, in my opinion, from being out of the province of a Christian magistrate," Burke wrote, "that it is, and it ought to be, not only his care, but the principal thing in his care; and its object the supreme good, the ultimate end and object of man himself."[18] But it was not wholly the medieval church-idea. As Alfred Cobban justly remarks of Burke, "His ideal is neither Protestant Erastianism nor Catholic Theocracy; it is much more like the kingdom of God on earth."[19]

Though state and church ought never to be separate entities, true religion is not merely an expression of national spirit; it rises far superior to earthly law, being, indeed, the source of all law.

With Cicero and Philo, Burke enunciates the doctrine of the *jus naturale*, the law of the universe, the creation of the divine mind, of which the laws of man are only the imperfect manifestation. "All human laws are, properly speaking, only declaratory; they may alter the mode and application, but have no power over the substance of original justice."[20] Men have no right to alter the laws as their fancy suggests; the superior law is not in the power of any political community to amend.

Ours is a moral order, then, and our laws are derived from immortal moral laws; the higher happiness is moral happiness, says Burke, and the cause of suffering is moral evil. Pride, ambition, avarice, revenge, lust, sedition, hypocrisy, ungoverned zeal, disorderly appetites—these vices are the actual causes of the storms that trouble life. "Religion, morals, laws, prerogatives, privileges, liberties, rights of men, are the *pretexts*" for revolution by sentimental humanitarians and mischievous agitators who think that established institutions must be the source of our afflictions. But the human heart, in reality, is the fountain of evil. "You would not cure the evil by resolving, that there should be no more monarchs, nor ministers of state, nor of the gospel; no interpreters of laws; no general officers; no public councils....Wise men will apply their remedies to vices, not to names."[21]

This moral order cannot be transformed by the process of counting noses, any more than it can be improved by violating ancient establishments. "When we know, that the opinions of even the greatest multitudes are the standard of rectitude, I shall think myself obliged to make those opinions the masters of my conscience. But if it may be doubted whether Omnipotence itself is competent to alter the essential constitution of right and wrong, sure am I, that such *things*, as they and I, are possessed of no such power."[22] Now and again, Burke praises two great virtues, the keys to private contentment and public peace: they are prudence and humility, the first pre-eminently an attainment of classical philosophy, the second pre-eminently a triumph of Christian discipline. Without them, man must be miserable; and man destitute of piety hardly can perceive either of these rare and blessed qualities.

For solitary man in search of spiritual peace, for society in search of permanent order, Providence has furnished means by which mankind may apprehend this moral universe. Tradition and prescription are the guiding lights of the civil social man; and therefore Burke elevates to the dignity of social principles those conventions and customs which, before the eighteenth century, most men accepted with an unreflecting confidence.

4

"The reason first why we do admire those things which are greatest, and second those things which are ancientest, is because the one are the least distant from the infinite substance, the other from the infinite continuance, of God."[23] Burke could repeat from memory this sentence of Hooker's; and it expresses the soul of their prescriptive philosophy.

Burke faced the necessity of re-stating, in the Age of Reason, the premises of men who have faith in an enduring order of life. What is the foundation of authority in morals and politics? By what standard may men judge the prudence of any particular act, and the justice of it? To rely upon divine inspiration certainly will not suffice for the ordinary courses of life: one cannot expect the supernatural universe to manage the routine concepts of the natural universe. Burke answered that Providence had taught humanity, through thousands of years' experience and meditation, a collective wisdom: tradition, tempered by expedience. A man should be governed in his necessary decisions by a decent respect for the customs of mankind; and he should apply that custom or principle to his particular circumstances by a cautious expediency. Burke, though a contemner of abstractions, was far from rejecting general principles and maxims. His doctrine of divine purpose puts a great gulf between his "expedience" and the expediency of Machiavelli—and, for the matter, it separates him from the geographical and historical determinism of Montesquieu and of his own pupil Taine. The individual is foolish, but the species is wise; prejudices and prescriptions and presumptions are the instruments which the wisdom of the species employs to safeguard man against his own passions and appetites. At times, Burke approaches very nearly to a theory of a collective human intellect, a knowledge partially instinctive, partially conscious, which each individual inherits as his birthright and his protection. Awake to all the mystery of human character, interested in those complex psychological impulses which associationist theories cannot account for, Burke implicitly rejected Locke's *tabula rasa* concept as inadequate to explain the individuation of character and imaginative powers which distinguish man from the animals. Human beings, said Burke, participate in the accumulated experience of their innumerable ancestors; very little is totally forgotten. Only a small part of this knowledge, however, is formalized in literature and deliberate instruction; the greater part remains embedded in instinct, common custom, prejudice, and ancient usage. Ignore this enormous bulk of racial knowledge, or tinker impudently with it, and man is left awfully afloat in a sea of emotions and ambitions, with only the scanty stock of formal learning and the puny resources of individual reason to sustain him. Often men may not realize the meaning of their immemorial prejudices and customs—indeed, even the most intelligent of men cannot hope to understand all the secrets of traditional morals and social arrangements; but we may be sure that Providence, acting through the medium of human trial and error, has developed every hoary habit for some important purpose. The greatest of prudence is required when man must accommodate this inherited mass of opinion to the exigencies of new times. For prejudice is not bigotry or superstition, although prejudice sometimes may degenerate into these. Prejudice is prejudgment, the answer with which intuition and ancestral consensus of opinion supply a man when he lacks either time or knowledge to arrive at a decision predicated upon pure reason.

In the twentieth century, speculative psychologists have begun to investigate the concepts of collective mind in men and animals, with increasing seriousness; these prescient opinions of Burke's, together with his allied emphasis upon the importance of custom in the life of society, and the predominance of habitual or instinctive motives over reason in the ordinary affairs of mankind, already have displayed a wide influence, which may be traced, variously, in the ideas of Coleridge, Maine, Bagehot, Graham Wallas, A. N. Whitehead, and a dozen other important thinkers. No really educated man today is likely to maintain that human nature is so simple as Condillac, for instance, believed it was. Burke, rather than being an old-fashioned apologist for dying superstitions, struck through the mask of the Age of Reason to the dark complexities of human existence, so that he remains a living influence upon thought when most of his radical opponents are no more than names in a history of intellectual tendencies.

The Romantics followed Burke in this; yet by most writers, during the nineteenth century, Burke was praised as a sort of utilitarian, under the assumption that his psychology was founded upon the simple calculus of Locke. There is no shallower view of Burke's premises. Burke knew that just under the skin of modern man stirs the savage, the brute, the demon. Millennia of bitter experience have taught man how to hold his wilder nature in a precarious restraint; that dread knowledge is expressed in myth, ritual, usage, instinct, prejudice. The Church, too, always has sensed this truth (as Paul Elmer More remarks with a brooding admiration in his essay on Lafcadio Hearn) and has looked with suspicion upon the advance of scientific rationalism because it may unveil to modern man the hideous secrets of his brutal origin.

Yet Burke has been mistaken for a precursor of empiricists and pragmatists, chiefly because he expressed his determination to deal with circumstances, not with abstractions. Buckle is enthusiastic about this fancied side of Burke's character, and says that Burke resisted the temptation to rely on his own generalizations, and "made his opinions subservient to the march of events; that he recognized as the object of government, not the preservation of particular institutions, but the happiness of the people at large ....Burke was never weary of attacking the common argument, that, because a country has long flourished under some particular custom, therefore the custom must be good."[24]

Buckle is perverse here, translating Burke's exceptions into Burke's rules. The test of the greatest happiness of the greatest number, and the examination of every custom in the light of immediate utility, were characteristic of the recluse Bentham, not of the statesman Edmund Burke. Above all else, Burke's philosophy has Principle and Prescription stamped upon the face of it; Burke attacks abstraction and abuse, not principle and prescription. "I do not put abstract ideas wholly out of any question, because I well know that under that name I should dismiss principles; and that without principles, all reasonings in politics, as in everything else, would be only a confused jumble of particular facts and details, without the means of drawing out any sort of theoretical or practical conclusion."[25]

Principle is right reason expressed in permanent form; abstraction is its corruption. Expedience is wise application of general knowledge to particular circumstances; opportunism is its degradation. One arrives at principle through comprehension of nature and history, looked upon as manifestations of divine purpose; one acquires prudence by patient observation and cautious investigation, and it becomes the director, the regulator, the standard" of all the virtues. Expedience implements principle, but never supplants principle. For principle is our expression of cognizance of providential purpose.

History (and Burke's historical knowledge was respected by Gibbon and Hume) is the gradual revelation of a supreme design—often shadowy to our blinking eyes, but subtle, resistless, and beneficent. God makes history through the agency of man. Burke has no tinge of Hegel's Categorical-Imperative determinism, for Burke, faithful to the Christian doctrine of free will, says history is directed not by an arbitrary, unreasoning urge, but by human character and conduct. Providence works in natural ways. It may be impious to resist this grand design, if its direction is clearly to be seen; but a full comprehension of God's ends seldom is within our powers. The statesman and the philosopher must know more than history: they must know nature. Burke's "nature" is human nature, the springs of conduct common to civilized peoples, not the Romantics' quasi-pantheistic nature. The phrase "state of nature" was irritating to Burke's accurate intellect; "natural rights," as asserted by Rousseau and Paine, he denied; but the usage of "nature" which Cicero employed was Burke's also. Knowing history and nature, a man may humbly aspire to apprehend providential dispensations.

Yet the study of history and human character never can encompass the greater part of human wisdom. The experience of the species is treasured up chiefly in tradition, prejudice, and prescription—generally for most men, and sometimes for all men, surer guides to conduct and conscience than books and speculation. Habit and custom may be the wisdom of unlettered men, but they come from the sound ancient heart of humanity. Even the wisest of mankind cannot live by reason alone; pure arrogant reason, denying the claims of prejudice (which commonly are also the claims of conscience), leads to a wasteland of withered hopes and crying loneliness, empty of God and man: the wilderness in which Satan tempted Christ was not more dreadful than the arid expanse of intellectual vanity deprived of tradition and intuition, where modern man is tempted by his own pride.

We are afraid to put men to live and trade each on his own private stock of reason; because we suspect that this stock in each man is small, and that the individuals would do better to avail themselves of the general bank and capital of nations and ages. Many of our men of speculation, instead of exploding general prejudices, employ their sagacity to discover the latent wisdom which prevails in them. If they find what they seek, and they seldom fail, they think it more wise to continue the prejudice, with the reason involved, than to cast away the coat of prejudice, and to leave nothing but the naked reason; because prejudice, with its reason, has a motive to give action to that reason, and an affection which will give it permanence.[26]

This veneration of habit and custom, incidentally, is one of the chief distinctions between Burke and the Romantics. Romanticism (except for those writers directly influenced, sometimes at the expense of their consistency, by Burke), as Irving Babbitt writes, is "clearly hostile to habit because it seems to lead to a stereotyped world, a world without vividness and surprise." Burke dreaded a consuming individualism; habit and prejudice induce that conformity without which society cannot endure. Encouraging moral extravagance for the sake of novelty is as dangerous an experiment as man can undertake.

"Prejudice"—the half-intuitive knowledge that enables men to meet the problems of life without logic-chopping; "prescription"—the customary right which grows out of the conventions and compacts of many successive generations; "presumption"— inference in accordance with the common experience of mankind: employing these instruments, men manage to live together in some degree of prosperity and amicability. The English constitution is prescriptive, and "its sole authority is that it has existed time out of mind. Your king, your lords, your juries, grand and little, all are prescriptive." Prescription, presumption, and prejudice suffice to direct the individual conscience and conscript fathers. Without them, society can be saved from destruction only by force and a master. "Somewhere there must be a control upon will and appetite; and the less of it there is within, the more of it there must be without." If these checks are abolished, only one instrument remains for preventing man from relapsing into that primitive state from which he has crept up so painfully through the millennia, and which existence Burke (though in most matters at war with Hobbes) also knew to be "poor, nasty, brutish, and short." That surviving instrument is rationality. And Reason, dear to the illuminati of the eighteenth century, seemed to Burke a tool weak at best, frequently treacherous. The mass of mankind, Burke implies, reason hardly at all, in the higher sense, nor ever can: deprived of folk-wisdom and folk-law, which are prejudice and prescription, they can do no more than cheer the demagogue, enrich the charlatan, and submit to the despot. The common man is not ignorant; but his knowledge is a kind of collective wisdom, the sum of the slow accretions of a thousand generations. This lost, he is thrown back upon his own private stock of reason, with the consequences which attend shipwreck. Even the shrewdest of men are puffed up with vanity if they try to set the product of their reason against the consensus of the centuries. It is possible, Burke concedes, that in one respect or another times may have changed, past experience in that particular is invalid, and the innovator is right; but the presumption ordinarily is to the contrary; and in any case, it may be wiser to continue an old practice, even though it seem the child of error, than to break radically with custom and run the risk of poisoning the body social, out of a doctrinaire affection for mathematical precision or bluebook uniformity. "You see, sir, that in this enlightened age I am bold enough to confess, that we are generally men of untaught feelings; that instead of casting away all our old prejudices, we cherish them to a very considerable degree, and, to take more shame to ourselves, we cherish them because they are prejudices; and the longer they have lasted, and the more generally they have prevailed, the more we cherish them."

Burke's affection for prejudice and prescription was not new in English thought. Chesterfield had written, "A prejudice is by no means (though generally thought so) an error; on the contrary, it may be a most unquestioned truth, though it be still a prejudice in those who, without any examination, take it upon trust and entertain it by habit....The bulk of mankind have neither leisure nor knowledge sufficient to reason right; why should they be taught to reason at all? Will not honest instinct prompt, and wholesome prejudices guide them, much better than half reasoning?"[27] This is precisely what Burke meant. And Hume (as Carl Becker reminds us in *The Heavenly City of the Eighteenth-Century Philosophers*) displayed a strong deference to prejudice and its social advantages when, alarmed at his own speculations into the origin of morals, he asked, "But are such ideas very *useful?*"—and locked his notes away in his desk. Yet Burke's onslaught upon new-fangled Reason ran counter to the great fashionable intellectual tendency of his time, the movement characterized by the Encyclopaedia. Courage was required to make declarations in defense of prejudice; in a lesser man, such an attitude would have met with the contempt of the literary public. Burke they could not scorn, however; for reason was as conspicuous in him as in any man in England.

It is some indication of the strength of Burke's Christian humility that he, with his acute and far-ranging mind, could be the partisan of the instincts of the species against the vanity of the man of genius.

Men's appetites are voracious and sanguinary, Burke knew; they are restrained by this collective and immemorial wisdom we call prejudice, tradition, customary morality; reason alone never can chain them to duty. Whenever the crust of prejudice and prescription is perforated at any point, flames shoot up from beneath, and terrible danger impends that the crack may widen, even to the annihilating of civilization. If men are discharged of reverence for ancient usage, they will treat this world, almost certainly, as if it were their private property, to be consumed for their sensual gratification; and thus they will destroy in their lust for enjoyment the property of future generations, of their own contemporaries, and indeed their very own capital:

One of the first and most leading principles on which the commonwealth and its laws are consecrated, is lest the temporary possessors and life-renters in it, unmindful of what they have received from their ancestors, or of what is due to their posterity, should act as if they were the entire masters; that they should not think it among their rights to cut off the entail, or commit waste on the inheritance, by destroying at their pleasure the whole original fabric of their society; hazarding to leave to those who come after them a ruin instead of a habitation—and teaching these successors as little to respect their contrivances, as they had themselves respected the institutions of their forefathers. By this unprincipled facility of changing the state as often, and as much, and in as many ways, as there are floating fancies or fashions, the whole chain and continuity of the commonwealth would be broken. No one generation could link with another. Men would become little better than the flies of a summer.[28]

The modern spectacle of vanished forests and eroded lands, wasted petroleum and ruthless mining, national debts recklessly increased until they are repudiated, and continual revision of positive law, is evidence of what an age without veneration does to itself and its successors. Burke saw into the future, where Condorcet and Mably saw merely the rosy interior of their own fantasies and mistook it for the prophetic afflatus.

Prejudice and prescription, despite their great age—or, rather, because of it—are delicate growths, slow to rise, easy to injure, hardly possible to resuscitate. The abstract metaphysician and fanatic reformer, intending to cleanse society, may find he has scrubbed it clean away: "An ignorant man, who is not fool enough to meddle with his clock, is however sufficiently confident to think he can safely take to pieces, and put together at his pleasure, a moral machine of another guise, importance, and complexity, composed of far other wheels, and springs, and balances, and counteracting and co-operating powers....Their delusive good intention is no sort of excuse for their presumption."[29]

Does the observance of prejudice and prescription, then, condemn mankind to a perpetual treading in the footsteps of their ancestors? Burke has no expectation that men can be kept from social change; neither is rigidity of form desirable. Change is inevitable, he says, and is designed providentially for the larger conservation of society; properly guided, change is a process of renewal. But let change come as the consequence of a need generally felt, not inspired by fine-spun abstractions. Our part is to patch and polish the old order of things, trying to discern the difference between a profound, slow, natural alteration and some infatuation of the hour. By and large, change is a process independent of conscious human endeavor, if it is beneficial change. Human reason and speculation can assist in the adjustment of the old order to new things if they are employed in a spirit of reverence, awake to their own fallibility. Even ancient prejudices and prescriptions must sometimes shrink before the advance of positive knowledge; but the Jacobin mind is unable to distinguish between minor inconvenience and actual decrepitude. The perceptive reformer combines an ability to reform with a disposition to preserve; the man who loves change is wholly disqualified, from his lust, to be the agent of change.

The case of tradition against abstract reason never was put so well before. Yet Burke could little arrest the proclivity of his age to let every man form his own opinions after his own lights, according to transitory circumstances and imperfect knowledge. The increase of literacy, the cheapness of books and newspapers, and the natural attraction of individualistic doctrines for the mass of men—these influences were too much for Burke's persuasive powers. Graham Wallas understands Burke's conviction that men cannot act wisely from their private reasoning: "But the deliberate following of prescription which Burke advocated was something different, because it was the result of choice, from the uncalculated loyalty of the past. Those who have eaten from the tree of knowledge cannot forget."[30] Irving Babbitt believes that the battle for prejudice and prescription has been lost; "a wisdom above reflection" no longer dominates the lives of the industrial millions. "It is no longer possible to wave aside the modernists as the mere noisy insects of an hour, or to oppose to an unsound activity of intellect mere solidity and imperviousness to thought—the great cattle chewing their cud in the shadow of the British oak."[31] These criticisms are rather sweeping; after all, prescription in favor of local rights and private property and habits of life, prejudice in favor of old decencies, the family, and religious dogmas, still are forces of great power among the most urbanized and industrialized of nations. And it is easier to expose the weakness of Burke's defences than to provide some alternative system for resisting a corrosive intellectual atomism. Immensely expensive systems of state schooling have not succeeded in repairing the damage to private character and public life that was done when personal judgment began to supplant traditional opinion.

In one respect, however, Burke triumphed over the indiscriminate innovating impulse. He taught English statesmen how to meet change with courage and dexterity, softening its consequences, preserving the best of the old by reconciling the innovators to its survival. Not a single formidable rebellion has occurred in England since Burke retired from politics—nothing worse than riots and eccentric conspiracies; and had Burke's recommendations for Ireland been put into execution, it is possible that the record of society might have been as admirable there. In the present decade, government in England is exchanged between parties bitterly inimical, without disturbance, because Englishmen know that if change must come, it comes less injuriously when the peace is kept.

We must all obey the great law of change. It is the most powerful law of nature, and the means perhaps of its conservation. All we can do, and that human wisdom can do, is to provide that the change shall proceed by insensible degrees. This has all the benefits which may be in change, without any of the inconveniences of mutation. This mode will, on the one hand, prevent the *unfixing old interests at once:* a thing which is apt to breed a black and sullen discontent in those who are at once dispossessed of all their influence and consideration. This gradual course, on the other hand, will prevent men, long under depression, from being intoxicated with a large draught of new power, which they always abuse with a licentious insolence.[32]

Conservatism never is more admirable than when it accepts changes that it disapproves, with good grace, for the sake of a general conciliation; and the impetuous Burke, of all men, did most to establish that principle.

5

Radicalism at the end of the eighteenth century expressed its case in terms of "natural rights." Ever since Paine's *Rights of Man* was published, the notion of inalienable natural rights has been embraced by the mass of men in a vague and belligerent form, ordinarily confounding "rights" with desires. This confusion in definition plagues society today, notably in the "Universal Declaration of Human Rights" drawn up by the United Nations Organization: thirty articles, and a somewhat greater number of "rights" defined therein, including the right to free education, the right to "enjoy the arts," the right of copyright, the right to an international order, the right to "the full development of personality," the right to equal pay, the right to marry, and a great many more which actually are not rights at all, but merely aspirations. The conservative adage that all radical "natural rights" are simply, in substance, a declaration of the Right to be Idle is suggested in Article 24: "Everyone has the right to rest and leisure, including reasonable limitation of working hours and periodic holidays with pay." This lengthy catalogue of "rights" ignores the two essential conditions which are attached to all true rights; first, the capacity of individuals to claim and exercise the alleged right; second, the correspondent duty that is married to every right. If a man has a *right* to marry, some woman must have the duty of marrying him; if a man has a *right* to rest, some other person must have the duty of supporting him. If rights are confused thus with desires, the mass of men must feel always that some vast, intangible conspiracy thwarts their attainment of what they are told is their inalienable birthright. Burke (and after him, Coleridge), perceiving this danger of fixing upon society a permanent grudge and frustration, tried to define true natural right and true natural law.

At a time when the world was infatuated with constitution-manufacture, when Abbé Sièyes was drawing up organic documents wholesale, when every coffee-house had its philosopher qualified to revise the statutes of the nation on a rational plan, when America had just got up fourteen new constitutions and was thinking of more, Burke declared that men do not make laws: they merely ratify or distort the laws of God. He said that men have no rights to what they please: their natural rights are only what may be directly deduced from their human nature. The Whig reformer, the advocate of enlightened expediency, told England that there is indeed an immutable law, and there are indeed inalienable rights, but they are of origins and character profoundly different from that *philosophes* and levellers take them for.

Unlike Bolingbroke and Hume, whose outward politics in some respects resembled his own, Burke was a pious man. "The most important questions about the human race Burke answered from the Church of England's catechism."[33] He believed in a Christian universe, to which a just God has given moral order to permit of man's salvation. God has given man law, and with that law, rights: this is Burke's premise in all moral and juridical questions. But that law, and the rights which derive from it, have been misunderstood by the modern mind.

The rights of *men*, that is to say, the natural rights of mankind, are indeed sacred things; and if any public measure is proved mischievously to affect them, the objection ought to be fatal to that measure, even if no charter at all could be set up against it. If these natural rights are futher affirmed and declared by express covenants, if they are clearly defined and secured against chicane, against power, and authority, by written instruments and positive engagements, they are in a still better condition: they partake not only of the sanctity of the object so secured, but of the solemn public faith itself, which secures an object of such importance....The things secured by these instruments may, without any deceitful ambiguity, be very fitly called the *chartered rights of men*.[34]

So Burke spoke on Fox's East-India Bill, between two revolutions, concerning those assertions of natural right which were about to convulse the world. There lingers in this speech a certain reluctance to come to grips with the general question, perhaps; Burke shows, however, that he is dubious of abstract and undefined rights, devoted to prerogatives that are guaranteed by prescription and charter. Soon he was compelled to make his distinctions more emphatic.

Much as purpose may be discerned, however dimly, in history, says Burke, so there exist eternal enactments of divine authority which we can endeavor to apprehend through the study of history and the observation of human character. Man's rights exist only when man obeys God's law, for right is the child of law. All this is radically different from the "natural rights" of Locke, whose phraseology Burke sometimes adopts; and Burke's concept of natural right, obviously, is descended from sources quite separate from Rousseau's. Rousseau deduces natural right from a mythical primeval condition of freedom and a psychology drawn chiefly from Locke; Burke's natural right is the Ciceronian *jus naturale,* reinforced by Christian dogma and English common-law doctrine. Now Hume, from a third point of view, maintains that natural right is a matter of convention; and Bentham, from yet another, declares that natural right is an illusory tag. Burke, detesting both these rationalists, says that natural right is human custom conforming to divine intent.

Burke does not look upon natural right as a suitable weapon for political controversy: he has too much reverence for its origin. Whether in the role of reformer or of conservator, he rarely invokes natural right against his adversaries' measures or in defense of his own. He dislikes having to define it closely; natural right is an Idea comprehended only by the divine intellect; precisely where it commences and terminates, we are no fit judges. To think that divine law could not operate without the sanction of our human legislation would be presumptuous. But so far as we can delineate the features of natural justice, Burke suggests, it is the experience of mankind which supplies our knowledge of divine law; and the experience of the species is taught to us not only through history, but through myth and fable, custom and prejudice.

From the beginning to the end of his career, Burke denounced the idyllic fantasy of a free, happy, lawless, and propertyless state of nature which Rousseau popularized. Neither history nor tradition, Burke thundered, sustain this idea of a primeval condition in which man, unfettered by mundane convention, lived contentedly according to the easy impulses of natural right. Natural law can enter our cognition only so far as it is embodied in social prescription or charter. The rest remains a sealed book to us. We know God's law only through our own laws that attempt to copy His; for He has given us no facile covenant, no utopian constitution. Most certainly, as Cicero demonstrates, human law is not sufficient unto itself; our imperfect statutes are only a striving toward an eternal order of justice; but God seldom literally writes upon a wall. We grope toward His justice slowly and feebly, out of the ancient imperfections of our nature.

Although it is foolish to think that man might follow natural law without the defining force of social law, Burke implies, it would be no less conceited to attempt defining in statutory enactment the whole of natural law. At one time or another, the *philosophes* committed both errors. God, and God's nature (for Burke would have inverted Jefferson's phrase) can guide us, indeed, to a knowledge of justice, but we need to remember that God is the guide, not the follower. Vainglorious man in the role of guide, equipped with a map compiled from his own abstractions, would lead society to destruction. The work which first brought Burke to public notice was his *Vindication of Natural Society*, a burlesque both of rationalism and of the idyllic fantasy; and the *Regicide Peace*, resplendent with his dying genius, is impassioned in its distinction between the real and the pretended rights of men. Burke was always on his guard against concepts of natural law that were dangerously vague and concepts that were dangerously exact.

Like Dr. Johnson, Burke loathed the idea of nature unrefined: for "art is man's nature," he wrote. In Burke's opinion, human nature resides in man at his highest, not his simplest. "Never, no never, did Nature say one thing and Wisdom say another. Nor are sentiments of elevation in themselves turgid and unnatural. Nature is never more truly herself than in her grandest forms ....The Apollo of Belvedere (if the universal robber has yet left him at Belvedere) is as much in nature as any figure from the pencil of Rembrandt, or any clown in the rustic revels of Teniers."[35]

Not "natural" man, but civilized man, is the object of Burke's solicitude. And if society tries to apply the "natural rights" possessed by a hypothetical savage to the much more real and valuable privileges of an Englishman—why, terrible risk is the penalty. "These metaphysic rights entering into common life, like rays of light which pierce into a dense medium, are, by the laws of nature, refracted from their straight line. Indeed in the gross and complicated mass of human passions and concerns, the primitive rights of men undergo such a variety of refractions and reflections, that it becomes absurd to talk of them as if they continued in the simplicity of their original direction."[36] Man's nature is intricate, society is wondrously complex: primitive simplicity is ruinous, when applied to the political concerns of great states. "When I hear the simplicity of contrivance aimed at and boasted of in any new political constitutions, I am at no loss to decide that the artificers are grossly ignorant of their trade, or grossly negligent of their duty." In his *Tracts on the Popery Laws* (published posthumously), Burke again attacks social primitivism. The purpose of civil society is "a conservation and secure enjoyment of our natural rights"; and to abolish or suspend these true natural rights, in order to conform to some fanatic scheme for establishing fancied rights of man, or on the pretext of protecting them more securely, "is a procedure as preposterous and cruel in argument as it is oppressive and cruel in its effect."[37]

Egalitarian proposals to accomplish the restoration of a pretended "natural right" of equality, abolishing both artificial and natural aristocracy, display this cruel and fallacious character. "The state of civil society, which necessarily generates this aristocracy, is a state of nature; and much more truly so than a savage and incoherent mode of life. For man is by nature reasonable; and he is never perfectly in his natural state, but when he is placed where reason may be best cultivated, and most predominates....We are as much, at least, in a state of nature in formed manhood, as in immature and helpless infancy."[38] Here as elsewhere, Burke is readier to say what the laws of nature are *not* than to tell what they are; nor does he attempt hiding his reluctance to enter into exact definition. He writes of his enemies the egalitarian men of letters:

The pretended rights of these theorists are all extremes; and in proportion as they are metaphysically true, they are morally and politically false. The rights of men are in a sort of *middle*, incapable of definition, but not impossible to be discerned. The rights of men in government are their advantages; and these are often in balances between good and evil, and sometimes between evil and evil....Men have no right to what is not reasonable, and to what is not for their benefit.[39]

Natural right, he goes on to explain, is not identical with popular power; and if it fails to accord with justice, it ceases to be a right. For the *administration* of justice (though justice itself has an origin higher than human contrivance) is a beneficial artificiality, the product of social convention. In social compacts, the chief purpose is to facilitate this administration of justice. To obtain it, ''natural'' man gave up long ago (and by his implied assent, continues to surrender) the anarchic freedom which is inconsistent with justice. This social compact is very real to Burke—not an historical compact, not a mere stock-company agreement, not even simply a juridical concept, but rather a contract that is reaffirmed in every generation, in every year and day, by every man who puts his trust in another. For our common welfare, our ancestors agreed, and we agree today, and our descendants will agree, to yield up an unrewarding natural ''freedom'' in order to receive the benefits of trust enforced by mundane justice. Accordingly, no natural right exists which excuses man from obedience to the executors of justice. ''One of the first motives to civil society, and which becomes one of its fundamental rules, is, *that no man should be judge in his own cause.* By this each person has at once divested himself of the first fundamental right of uncovenanted man, that is, to judge for himself, and to assert his own cause. He abdicates all right to be his own governor. He inclusively, in a great measure, abandons the right of self-defense, the first law of nature. ...That he may secure some liberty, he makes a surrender in trust of the whole of it.''[40]

But a surrender in *trust*, one notes; although a man cannot enjoy civil and uncivil rights simultaneously, when he gives up anarchy, he receives in its place a guarantee of justice. Violation of that trust can justify resistance, but nothing else can. Not only the dictates of justice bind men to mutual dependence, but the dictates of general morality also. Neither the savage nor the civilized man can help elbowing his neighbors; and whenever he does, in some degree his ''natural'' freedom must be restrained, for it endangers the prerogatives of others. The French devotion to ''absolute liberty'' (still demanded without qualification by Lamartine, half a century after Burke wrote) was historical and social nonsense: "As to the right of men to act anywhere according to their pleasure, without any moral tie, no such right exists. Men are never in a state of total independence of each other. It is not the condition of our nature; nor is it conceivable how any man can pursue a considerable course of action without its having some effect upon others; or, of course, without producing some degree of responsibility for his conduct."[41]

And natural rights do not exist independent of circumstances; what may be a right on one occasion and for one man, may be unjust folly for another man at a different time. Prudence is the test of actual right. Society may deny men prerogatives because they are unfit to exercise them. "But whether this denial be wise or foolish, just or unjust, prudent or cowardly, depends entirely on the state of the man's means."[42]

All of these things, natural right is *not*. Of what, then, does it consist? Of very practical and indispensable benefits, Burke declares, the preservation of which is the chief aim of this mundane order. Burke's best description of true natural right occurs in the *Reflections:*

Far am I from denying in theory, full as far as is my heart from withholding in practice, (if I were of power to give or to withhold,) the *real* rights of men. In denying their false claims of right, I do not mean to injure those which are real, and are such as their pretended rights would thoroughly destroy. If civil society be made for the advantage of man, all the advantages for which it is made become his right. It is an institution of beneficence; and law itself is only beneficence acting by rule. Men have a right to live by that rule; they have a right to do justice, as between their fellows, whether their fellows are in public function or in ordinary occupation. They have a right to the fruits of their industry, and to the means of making their industry fruitful. They have a right to the acquisitions of their parents; to the nourishment and improvement of their offspring; to instruction in life, and to consolation in death. Whatever each man can separately do, without trespassing upon others, he has a right to do for himself; and he has a right to all which society, with all its combinations of skill and force, can do in his favour. In this partnership all men have equal rights; but not to equal things. He that has but five shillings in the partnership, has as good a right to it, as he that has five hundred pounds has to his larger proportion. But he has not a right to an equal dividend in the product of the joint stock; and as to the share of power, authority, and direction which each individual ought to have in the management of the state, that I deny to be amongst the direct original rights of man in civil society; for I have in my contemplation the civil social man, and no other. It is a thing to be settled by convention.[43]

In all Burke's works, the passage above is perhaps his most important contribution to political thought. Equal justice is indeed a natural right; but equal dividend is no right at all. The laws of nature,—that is, the nature humankind acquires in civilization—make no provision for sharing goods without regard for individual energies or merits, nor is political power naturally egalitarian. How far economic and political levelling should be carried is a question to be determined by recourse to prudence. Security from trespass is a natural right; power to trespass upon others is not. To assure the reign of justice and to protect the just share of each man in the social partnership, government is established. Government is a practical creation, to be administered according to practical considerations; for Burke distinguishes between the "state" or social being, which is ordained of God, and "government," or political administration, which is the product of convention. The foundation of government is "laid, not in imaginary rights of men, (which at best is a confusion of judicial with civil principles,) but in political convenience, and in human nature; either as that nature is universal, or as it is modified by local habits and social aptitudes." Government is intended to provide for our wants and enforce our duties. It is not a toy to manipulate according to our vanities and ambitions.[44]

Infatuation with natural right in the practical concerns of government must end in anarchy, in a fiery and intolerant individualism. Even parliaments cannot endure if the doctrinaires of natural rights are triumphant, for any form of representative government is in some degree an invasion of "absolute liberty." Here Burke assails Rousseau's inchoate vision of a general will, in which all men participate without the interposition of parliamentary institutions. "They who plead an absolute right cannot be satisfied with anything short of personal representation, because all *natural* rights must be the rights of individuals; as by nature there is no such thing as politic or corporate personality; all these ideas are mere fictions of law, they are creatures of voluntary institution; men as men are individuals, and nothing else." But personal participation in all the concerns of government, or sending a personal deputy, is a complete absurdity in great modern states. Such a fanatic determination to participate directly in the complexities of government is sure to undo the very "natural rights" for which such zeal is professed; since before long, any government so conducted tumbles into anarchy, in which any description of right is unrecognized, Burke pronounces. To such catastrophes the confusion of pretended rights with real rights always tends.

The true natural rights of men, then, are equal justice, security of labor and property, the amenities of civilized institutions, and the benefits of orderly society. For these purposes God ordained the state, and history demonstrates that they are the rights desired by the *true* natural man. These genuine rights, without which government is usurpation, Burke contrasts with the fancied and delusory "rights of men" so lusted after across the Channel—"rights" which really are the negation of justice, because if (impossible contingency) actually attained in the absolute sense demanded by their devotees, they would at once infringe one upon another and precipitate men into moral and civil chaos. "Absolute liberty," "absolute equality," and similar projects, far from being natural rights, are conspicuously unnatural conditions —using the term "nature" in the sense of Rousseau—for they can exist, even temporarily, only in highly civilized states. In confounding matters of social convenience and convention with the subtle and almost indefinable natural order of God, the philosophers of the Enlightenment and the followers of Rousseau threaten society with the dissolution of artificial institutions.

For these several reasons, Burke rejects with contempt the arbitrary and abstract "natural right" of the metaphysicians, whether of Locke's school or Rousseau's. Yet natural principle society must have, if men are to be saved from their passions. What other basis exists for realizing the natural moral order in society? "Reason," Voltaire might have answered; "Utility," Bentham was to say; "material satisfaction of the masses," the Marxists would reply six decades later. Burke looked upon reason as a feeble prop, quite insufficient for most men; utility was for him a test only of means, not of ends; and material satisfaction an aspiration grossly low. Another foundation for social principle is Burke's. "Obey the divine design"—so one may paraphrase his concept of obedience to a natural order. By a proper regard for prescription and prejudice, we discover the means of dutiful obedience. The collective wisdom of the species, the filtered experience of mankind, can save us from the anarchy of "the rights of man" and the presumption of "reason."

True conformity to the dictates of nature requires reverence for the past and solicitude for the future. "Nature" is not simply the sensation of the passing moment; it is eternal, though we evanescent men experience only a fragment of it. We have no right to imperil the happiness of posterity by impudently tinkering with the heritage of humanity. An enthusiast for abstract "natural right" obstructs the operation of true natural law:

A nation is not an idea only of local extent, and individual momentary aggregation; but it is an idea of continuity, which extends in time as well as in numbers and in space. And this is a choice not of one day, or one set of people, not a tumultuary and giddy choice; it is a deliberate election of ages and of generations; it is a constitution made by what is ten thousand times better than choice, it is made by the peculiar circumstances, occasions, tempers, dispositions, and moral, civil, and social habitudes of the people which disclose themselves only in a long space of time. Nor is prescription of government formed upon blind, unmeaning prejudices—for man is a most unwise and a most wise being. The individual is foolish; the multitude, for the moment, is foolish, when they act without deliberation; but the species is wise, and, when time is given to it, as a species it always acts right.[45]

Enunciating general principles only with reluctance if they were divorced from particular practical questions, Burke applied these views immediately to the great egalitarian movement of his time. Social and political equality, he declared, do not fall within the category of the *real* rights of man; on the contrary, hierarchy and aristocracy are the natural, the original, framework of human life; if we modify their influence, it is from prudence and convention, not in obedience to "natural right." These are the postulates for his praise of natural aristocracy and his condemnation of levelling.

6

Is equality of any sort consequent upon the nature with which God has endowed us? One sort only, says Burke: moral equality. Divine mercy judges us not by our worldly estate, but by our goodness, and this, after all, far transcends mundane political equality. Reproaching the French, Burke expresses this opinion in a passage characterized by that high pathos he frequently employs:

You would have had a protected, laborious, and obedient people, taught to seek and to recognize the happiness that is to be found by virtue in all conditions; in which consists the true moral equality of mankind, and not in that monstrous fiction, which, by inspiring false ideas and vain expectations into men destined to travel in the obscure walk of laborious life, serves only to aggravate and embitter that real inequality, which it never can remove; and which the order of civil life establishes as much for the benefit of those whom it must leave in a humble state, as those whom it is able to exalt to a condition more splendid, but not more happy.[46]

In nature, obviously, men are unequal: unequal in mind, in body, in energies, in every material circumstance. The less civilized a society, and the more generally will and appetite prevail unchecked, the less equal is the position of individuals. Equality is the product of art, not of nature; and if social levelling is carried so far as to obliterate order and class, reducing a man to "glory in belonging to the Chequer No. 71," art will have been employed to deface God's design for man's real nature. Burke loathed the barren monotony of any society stripped of diversity and individuality; and he predicted that such societies must presently sink into a fresh condition of inequality—that of one master, or a handful of masters, and a people of slaves.

Majority rule is no more a natural right than is equality. When we accept the principle of majorities in politics, we do so out of prudence and expediency, not because of an abstract moral injunction. Possessing the franchise, holding office, and entrusting powers to the people—these are questions to be settled upon practical considerations, varying with time, circumstance, and the temper of a nation. Democracy may be wholly bad, or admissible with certain reservations, or wholly desirable, according to the country, the age, and the particular conditions under which it is adopted. Burke cites Montesquieu in support of this position. If we appeal to the natural order of things, moreover, we will destroy majority rule, because this mode of decision is a highly elaborate artifice. "Out of civil society nature knows nothing of it; nor are men, even when arranged according to civil order, otherwise than by very long training, brought at all to submit to it....This mode of decision, where wills may be so nearly equal, where, according to circumstances, the smaller number may be the stronger force, and where apparent reason may be all upon one side, and on the other little else than impetuous appetite; all this must be the result of a very particular and special convention, confirmed afterwards by long habits of obedience, by a sort of discipline in society, and by a strong hand, vested with stationary, permanent power, to enforce this sort of constructive general will."[47]

As the most eloquent champion of parliamentary liberties, Burke believed in majority rule, properly understood. But expedience always puts the question, What constitutes a true majority? Dismissing the "natural right" of men to exercise political power as a fiction without historical or physical or moral foundation, Burke maintains that a proper majority can be drawn only from a body qualified by tradition, station, education, property, and moral nature to exercise the political function. In Britain, this body, "the people," included some four hundred thousand men, Burke said; and a competent majority should be a majority of these persons, not merely of the whole population taken indiscriminately. Sharing in political power is not an immutable right, but rather a privilege to be extended or contracted according to the intelligence and integrity of a population. "And I see as little of policy or utility, as there is of right, in laying down a principle that a majority of men told by the head are to be considered as the people, and that as such their will is to be law."[48] If natural right be called into question, indeed, men do possess a natural right to be *restrained* from meddling with political authority in a fashion for which they are unqualified and which can bring them nothing but harm. The nature which we inherit is not simply a nature of license; it is also a nature of discipline. Not every real natural right which man possesses is always palatable to him, but the limitations of our nature are designed for our protection. The stern old Tory plebian publican in Drinkwater's play *The Bird in Hand* echoes this ancient conservative principle (which Burke expresses better than anyone else) when he grunts that the purpose of the state is to govern those that are not fit to govern themselves.

"Government is a contrivance of human wisdom to provide for human *wants*," says Burke. "Men have a right that these wants should be provided for by this wisdom. Among these wants is to be reckoned the want, out of civil society, of a sufficient restraint upon their passions. Society requires not only that the passions of individuals should be subjected, but that even in the mass and body, as well as in the individual, the inclinations of men should frequently be thwarted, their will controlled, and their passions brought into subjection. This can be done only *by a power out of themselves;* and not, in the exercise of its function, subject to that will and to those passions which it is its office to bridle and subdue. In this sense the restraints on men, as well as their liberties, are to be reckoned among their rights."[49] The extent of this restraint will vary with the degree of civilization and of religious veneration in a society; it cannot be settled upon abstract rules.

Burke's denial of the theory of the omnicompetent majority (which is not competent, from its very excess of power, to restrain itself) and the one-man, one-vote idea of democracy is at its most vigorous in an earlier passage from the *Reflections:* "It is said, that twenty-four millions ought to prevail over two hundred thousand. True; if the constitution of a kingdom be a problem of arithmetic. This sort of discourse does well enough with the lamp-post for its second; to men who *may* reason calmly, it is ridiculous. The will of the many, and their *interest,* must very often differ; and great will be the difference when they make an evil choice."[50]

Though Burke's political principles have given so much ground before utilitarian and egalitarian ideas in our age, his penetrating criticism of the natural-rights concept of democratic political authority has vanquished the abstractions of his opponents. Intelligent supporters of democracy in the twentieth century find the basis for a wide diffusion of political power not in a natural law of equality, but in expediency. David Thomson expresses this prevailing opinion, which Burke and Disraeli imprinted upon political thought: "The case for universal suffrage and political equality does not rest on any superstition that all men, by acquiring the vote, become equally wise or equally intelligent. It rests, both historically and philosophically, on the belief that if any section of the community is deprived of the ability to vote, then its interests are liable to be neglected and a nexus of grievances is likely to be created which will fester in the body politic."[51]

Political equality is therefore in some sense unnatural, Burke concludes; and aristocracy, on the other hand, is in a certain sense natural. The Whig leader admired aristocracy only with numerous reservations: "I am no friend to aristocracy, in the sense at least in which that word is usually understood."[52] Unchecked, it is "an austere and insolent domination." "If it should come to the last extremity, and to a contest of blood, God forbid!—my part is taken; I would take my fate with the poor, and low, and feeble."[53] But nature has furnished society with the materials for an aristocracy which the wisely-conducted state will recognize and honor—always reserving, however, a counterpoise to aristocratic ambition. Just as it is a fact of nature that the mass of men are ill qualified for the exercise of political power, so it is written in the eternal constitution of things that a few men, from various causes, are mentally and physically and spiritually suited for social leadership. The state which rejects their services is doomed to stagnation or destruction. These aristocrats are in part "the wiser, the more expert, and the more opulent," and they are to conduct, enlighten, and protect "the weaker, the less knowing, and the less provided with the goods of fortune."[54] Birth, too, Burke respects; but he mentions more particularly the clergy, the magistracy, the teachers, the merchants: not the accident of birth, but nature, has made these men aristocrats. It is wise and just and in accord with the real law of nature that such persons should exercise a social influence much superior to that of the average citizen. "A true natural aristocracy is not a separate interest in the state, or separable from it. It is an essential integrant part of any large body rightly constituted. It is formed out of a class of legitimate presumption, which, taken as generalities, must be admitted for actual truths." The description of this aristocracy which is inextricably interwoven with the fabric of every civilized society is one of the more memorable passages in Burke; it has had its share in preserving British and American constitutional government:

To be bred in a place of estimation; to see nothing low and sordid from one's infancy; to be taught to respect one's self; to be habituated to the censorial inspection of the public eye; to look early to public opinion; to stand upon such elevated ground as to be enabled to take a large view of the wide-spread and infinitely diversified combinations of men and affairs in a large society; to have leisure to read, to reflect, to converse; to be enabled to draw the court and attention of the wise and learned wherever they are to be found; to be habituated in the pursuit of honour and duty; to be formed to the greatest degree of vigilance, foresight, and circumspection, in a state of things in which no fault is committed with impunity, and the slightest mistakes draw on the most ruinous consequences; to be led to a guarded and regulated conduct, from a sense that you are considered as an instructor of your fellow-citizens in their highest concerns, and that you act as a reconciler between God and man; to be employed as an administrator of law and justice, and to be thereby amongst the first benefactors to mankind; to be a professor of high science, or of liberal and ingenuous art; to be amongst rich traders, who from their success are presumed to have sharp and vigorous understandings, and to possess the virtues of diligence, order, constancy, and regularity, and to have cultivated an habitual regard to commutative justice—these are the circumstances of men, that form what I should call a *natural* aristocracy, without which there is no nation.[55]

More than any other order in history, perhaps, the British upper classes of the eighteenth and nineteenth centuries deserved this eulogium: as a body, honorable, intelligent, moral, and vigorous. The ascendancy of this class, says Burke, is truly natural. Domination of society by mediocrity is contrary to nature. One of the duties of a statesman is to employ the abilities of the natural aristocracy in the service of the commonwealth, rather than to submerge them in the mass of the population, where they could only menace the stability of society.

Leadership by men of ability, birth, and wealth is one of the most natural, and most beneficial, aspects of civilized life. "Nature" is the character of man at his highest, within a civilized order. Man's rights are linked with man's duties, and when they are distorted into extravagant claims for a species of freedom and equality and worldly aggrandizement which human character cannot sustain, they degenerate from rights to vices. Equality in the sight of God, equality before the law, security in what is one's own, participation in the common activities and consolations of society—these are the true natural rights. The presumptuous demands of Rousseau, Condorcet, Helvétius, and Paine for absolute liberties which no state in history ever could accord are the very reverse of natural justice; they are unnatural because impious, "the result of a selfish temper, and confined views." In the political sphere, these claims are absurd, for the exercise of any right must be circumscribed and modified to suit particular circumstances.

Real harmony with the natural law is attained through adapting society to the model which eternal nature, physical and spiritual, sets before us—not by demanding radical alteration upon fantastic claims of social primitivism. We are part of an eternal natural order which holds all things in their places. "Our political system is placed in a just correspondence and symmetry with the order of the world, and with the mode of existence decreed to a permanent body composed of transitory parts; wherein, by the disposition of a stupendous wisdom, moulding together the great mysterious incorporation of the human race, the whole, at one time, is never old, or middle-aged, or young, but, in a condition of unchangeable constancy, moves on through the varied tenor of perpetual decay, fall, renovation, and progression. Thus, by preserving the method of nature in the conduct of the state, in what we improve, we are never wholly new."[56] Political reform and impartial justice conducted upon these principles embody the humility and prudence which men must cultivate if they are to conform to a transcendent moral order. These definitions of nature and right, these views of permanence and change, lift Burke to a plane of reflection far above the simple postulates of French reforming speculation, and give his ideas an enduring elevation superior to the vicissitudes of politics.

7

Though Burke could not make the British constitution and prescriptive society immutable—even had he wished to oppose all change, which never was his object—still the restraining influence of his ideas upon the tendency of politics and speculation has been incalculably powerful. Burke himself, late in 1791, despaired of affecting the current of innovation; he saw Jacobinism sweeping everything before it, deluging even the Whig party, and he wrote to Earl Fitzwilliam, who as yet had not been completely persuaded of Burke's prescience: "You see, my dear Lord, that I do not go upon any difference concerning the best method of preventing the growth of a system which I believe we dislike in common. I cannot differ with you, because I do not think any method can prevent it. The Evil has happened; the thing is done in principle and in example; and we must wait the good pleasure of a higher hand than ours for the time of its perfect accomplishment."[57] He was too humble. That real Jacobinism never has come to Britain or America is in some considerable measure the work of Edmund Burke's conservative genius. He first succeeded in turning the resolute might of England against French revolutionary energies; and by the time of his death, in 1797, he had established a school of politics founded upon the concepts of veneration and prudence, which ever since has opposed its talents to the appetite for innovation. "We venerate what we cannot presently understand," he taught the rising generation. His reverence for the wisdom of our ancestors, through which works the design of Providence, is the first principle of all consistent conservative thought.

Burke knew that economics and politics are not independent sciences: they are no more than manifestations of a general order, and that order is moral. He applied his great practical intellect to a glowing delineation of this principle of order, and his work is suffused with the imagination of a poet and the keenness of a critic. Greatly though he disliked an easy familiarity with metaphysics, he saw that the struggle between order and innovation in modern times has its cause in a metaphysical and religious problem: as Basil Willey points out to us, Burke perceived that the root of evil in society "lay in the meddling instinct which presumes to interfere with the mysterious march of God in the world. Burke was of the company of those who are continually conscious of the weight of all this unintelligible world; he was more aware of the complex forces which hem us in and condition all we do, than of any power in us to act back and modify the very environment that limits us."[58] Men never will be gods, Burke was convinced; all their will and virtue is required if they are to attain mere genuine humanity; and (as Aristotle said) a being that can exist in isolation must be either a beast or a god. Radical innovations would cut us off from our past, destroying the immemorial bonds that join generation to generation; they would leave us isolated from memory and from aspiration; and in that condition, we would sink to the level of beasts, "We have not (as I conceive) lost the generosity and dignity of thinking of the fourteenth century; nor as yet have we subtilized ourselves into savages." But how are we to be saved from the fierce tide of demoniac energy, the flood of unprincipled aspiring talents and ferocious envy, which is called Jacobinism?

Our hope for safety against the consequences of intellectual fallacies lies in our steadfast adherence to right opinion. Taken as a whole, Burke's accomplishment is the definition of a principle of order; and a brief examination of that principle is a recapitulation of this chapter. His system is an anticipatory refutation of utilitarianism, positivism, and pragmatism, as well as an attack on Jacobinism. Burke's almost unparalleled talent for social prediction informed him that the Revolution in France was no simple political contest, no culmination of enlightenment, but the inception of a moral convulsion from which society would not recover until the disease, the disorder of revolt against Providence, had run its course. To check it, he adapted the reverential view of society, the idea of Aristotle, Cicero, the Schoolmen, and Hooker, to the conundrums of the modern world.

An order in society, good or evil, just or tyrannical, must always exist. We have been "marshalled by a divine tactic" to unite in a state which recognizes the true idea of justice. Men are saved from anarchy by veneration of the divine and fidelity to prescriptive wisdom. They are saved by prejudice and gradation. There is only one way really to appreciate Burke, and that is to read him through. But, reducing vast splendid profundities to little meagre paraphrases, one can outline what Burke means by obedience to a providential order. To attempt more, with an author like Burke —why, "the rest is vanity; the rest is crime."

(1) This temporal order is only part of a transcendent order; and the foundation of social tranquillity is reverence. Veneration lacking, life becomes no more than an interminable battle between

usurpation and rebellion. Though Burke did not carry the advocacy of ordination and subordination so far as Dr. Johnson did, he is emphatic that the first rule of society is obedience—obedience to God and the dispensations of Providence, which work through natural processes. "Out of physical causes, unknown to us, perhaps unknowable, arise moral duties, which, as we are able perfectly to comprehend, we are bound indispensably to perform." W. Somerset Maugham, in an interesting essay on Burke's style, observes that we moderns are unable to enter into the spirit of veneration.[59] He is right, or nearly right. But when veneration goes out of society, so much sinks with it, as Burke knew, that a cyclical process seems to be set in motion, insuring that mankind shall presently experience disaster, then fear, then awe, and at last resurrected veneration. Veneration may be the product of a patriarchal social outlook. When it is eradicated by sophistication, Providence has a way of returning us, rudely, to patriarchy.

(2) After the order of God, Burke states, comes an order of spiritual and intellectual values. All values are not the same, nor all impulses, nor all men. A natural gradation teaches men to hold some sentiments dear and others cheap. Levelling radicalism endeavors to put all emotions and sensations upon the same level of mediocrity, and so to erase the moral imagination which sets men apart from beasts. "On this scheme of things, a king is but a man, a queen is but a woman; a woman is but an animal, and an animal not of the highest order." When Burke wrote of how "learning will be cast into the mire, and trodden down under the hoofs of a swinish multitude," the phrase which excited more bitter criticism (even from John Adams) than anything else he said, Burke was simply paraphrasing Matthew, vii, 6, of course; and he meant what some eminent socialist critics are coming to dread, that the mass of men, shorn of proper intellectual leadership, "all the decent drapery of life torn rudely off," will be indifferent, or perhaps hostile, to anything that is not flesh.

(3) Physical and moral anarchy is prevented by general acquiescence in social distinctions of duty and privilege. If a natural aristocracy is not recognized among men, the sycophant and the

brute exercise its abandoned functions in the name of a faceless "people." If high character, strong intellect, good birth, and practical shrewdness are honored in society, then ''so long as these endure, so long the Duke of Bedford is safe, and we are all safe together,—the high from the blights of envy and the spoliations of rapacity, the low from the iron hand of oppression and the insolent spurn of contempt.'' This must be a true natural aristocracy, rather than an administrative corps of ambitious and clever reformers. Against the innovating idea of an ''elite'' recruited out of conformity to party fanaticism and enthusiastic adherence to a venomous intellectual credo, Burke wrote in the second letter of the *Regicide Peace:* ''To them, the will, the wish, the want, the liberty, the toil, the blood of individuals is nothing. Individuality is left out of their scheme of government. The state is all in all. Everything is referred to the production of force; afterwards, everything is trusted to the use of it. It is military in its principle, in its maxims, in its spirit, and in all its movements. The state has dominion and conquest for its sole objects; dominion over minds by proselytism, over bodies by arms.'' These were the Jacobins; the description applies as well to the Communist and the Nazi rule of an ''elite.'' Here one grasps in a moment all that Burke's principle of order is *not;* and here one perceives the gulf that separates Burke from Hegel. But Burke's constructive imagination means even more to the twentieth century than his denunciation of fanatic social planning, of plebiscitary democracy; and possibly the present generation will begin to struggle back toward his principle of true order, a society guided by veneration and prescription.

Society is immeasurably more than a political device. Knowing this, Burke endeavored to convince his generation of the immense complexity of existence, the ''mysterious incorporation of the human race.'' If society is treated as a simple contraption to be managed on mathematical lines—the Jacobins and the Benthamites and most other radicals so regarded it—then man will be degraded into something much less than a partner in the immortal contract that unites the dead, the living, and those yet unborn, the bond between God and man. Order in this world is contingent upon order above.

If one visits Beaconsfield today, he will not find Burke's country house of Gregories, for it burned long ago; but in the fine old church is a modest tablet recording that Edmund Burke is buried somewhere here. Precisely where, no one knows; for Burke, fearing the triumphant English Jacobins would desecrate his bones, left instructions for his body to be interred secretly. That day of profanation never came; British society moved instead in a conservative direction, of which impulse Burke himself was the prime mover. The memory of Burke and Disraeli seems to have enchanted Beaconsfield, and little has changed here: the good old houses of four centuries, the tidy half-timbered inn, the great oaks and the quiet lanes are as they were in Burke's day, though the villadom and new-housing-scheme expanses of London bite deep into Buckinghamshire, and light industry is invading the neighboring towns. At Stoke Poges, only a few miles distant, a tremendous and hideous housing estate of unredeemed monotony has shouldered right against Gray's country churchyard. But Beaconsfield Old Town is an island of ancient England in an industrial and proletarian sea of humanity.

Burke's ideas did more than establish islands in the sea of radical thought: they provided the defenses of conservatism, on a great scale, that still stand and are not liable to fall in our time. More than a century and a half after Burke's death, what Matthew Arnold called "an epoch of concentration" seems to be impending over the world once more. Revolutionary impulses and social enthusiasms, expansive since their explosion in Russia in 1917, are beginning to yield ground before the conservative spirit. England in Arnold's "epoch of concentration," the England of Scott, Coleridge, Southey, Wordsworth, Pitt, and Canning—in spite of its disillusion—was a society of high intellectual attainment, the revolutionary energy latent in it diverted to reconstructive ends. That the epoch of concentration displayed moral and intellectual qualities so vigorous, Arnold attributed to the influence of Burke. Our age, too, seems to be groping for certain of the ideas which

Burke's inspiration formed into a pattern of social preservation. Failing these or some other genuine principles, our own epoch of concentration is liable to descend into sardonic apathy and fatigued repression.

III

John Adams and Liberty Under Law

Jus cuique, the golden rule, is all the equality that can be supported
or defended by reason or common sense....My 'Defence of the
Constitutions' and 'Discourses on Davila' were the cause of that
immense unpopularity which fell like the tower of Siloam upon me.
Your steady defence of democratical principles, and your invariable favorable opinion of the French revolution, laid the foundation for your unbounded popularity. *Sic transit gloria mundi.*

J OHN ADAMS, son of a Braintree farmer, let his enemy persuade him to write a book. *A Defence of the Constitution of Government of the United States of America* was the book, and Thomas
Jefferson was the enemy—a friend at the moment, however, and
then for long years an adversary, and toward the end a friend once
more. Shocked at the fancies of Lafayette, Rochefoucauld, Condorcet, and Franklin, condemning their ignorance of history, this
severe and forthright little Massachusetts lawyer spent the greater part of his life declaring, with perfect indifference to popularity, that freedom can be achieved and retained only by sober men
who take humanity as it is, not as humanity should be. His learning and his courage made him great, and he became the founder
of true conservatism in America. Thirteen years after Adams had
lost the presidency of the United States, he wrote the passage
above, without acrimony, to the man who had beaten him. In
general, the Federalists were a gloomy set; and Adams underesti-

mated the influence his ideas and his example would exert upon future generations in America. Despite grave faults, the United States remain today a nation strong and prosperous, where property and liberty are tolerably secure. John Adams, who entertained no exaggerated opinion of the wisdom and virtue possessed by the mass of mankind, might have been reasonably satisfied with this accomplishment. More than anyone else, he taught the value of good and practical laws, transcending the passions of the hour. And more than anyone else, he kept the American government one of laws, not of men.

By and large, the American Revolution was not an innovating upheaval, but a conservative restoration of colonial prerogatives. Accustomed from their beginnings to self-government, the colonials felt that by inheritance they possessed the rights of Englishmen and by prescription certain rights peculiar to themselves. When a designing king and a distant parliament presumed to extend over America powers of taxation and administration never before exercised, the colonies rose to vindicate their prescriptive freedom; and after the hour for compromise had slipped away, it was with reluctance and trepidation they declared their independence. Thus men essentially conservative found themselves triumphant rebels, and were compelled to reconcile their traditional ideas with the necessities of an independence hardly anticipated. It was a profound problem: the Republicans Jefferson being chief among them, endeavored to solve it by the application of *a priori* concepts, and came to sympathize with French egalitarian theories. Their opponents, the Federalists, appealed to the lessons of history, the legacy of British liberties, and the guarantees of prescriptive constitutions.

These Federalists, the first conservative faction in an independent America, found themselves menaced by two radicalisms: one of French origins, the same enormous social and intellectual convulsion that Burke confronted; the other a growth in part native and in part English, the levelling agrarian republicanism of which Jefferson was the chief representative, zealous to abolish entail, primogeniture, church establishments, and all the vestiges of aristocracy, and to oppose centralization, strong government, public debt, and the military. The Federalists tended to be the party of the towns, the commercial and manufacturing interests, and the creditors; the Republicans, the party of the country, the agricultural interests, and the debtors. Shays' Rebellion, and later the Whiskey Rebellion, gave the Federalists a highly unpleasant notion of the power and aspirations of their opponents, inspiring in them an almost desperate resolution to oppose local radicalism by means of conservative consolidation.

Among the agrarian and democratic Republicans looms the angular figure of Jefferson, whose doctrines always were more radical than his practice and far less extreme than French notions of liberty. Jefferson tried his hand at everything, and often succeeded; and as his talents were immensely varied, so did his character display odd and sometimes inconsistent facets. This advocate of political purity and simplicity could recommend the infamous Gideon Granger, who "bought and sold corruption in the gross," for appointment to the Supreme Court of the United States; this exponent of strict construction of the Constitution could acquire Louisiana. Despite his love of variety and ingenuity, he could lay out the Northwest Territory on a checkerboard "sophisters' and calculators'" pattern that still makes the states which have been carved from that region dismally monotonous in their road-patterns and arbitrary in their internal boundaries. Yet for all this, and for all his acquaintance with the *philosophes* and his affection for France, Jefferson had Coke, Locke, and Kames for his real political mentors; and, like them, he had half a mind to be a conservative—and sometimes more than half a mind for it.

Nevertheless, if a true American Revolution can be said to have occurred, it came with the successes of Jefferson and the Republicans that culminated in 1800; it was an alteration internal and nearly bloodless. What was best in Federalism did not wholly die after 1800, however; it is not extinct even now. John Adams had a great share in its perpetuation.

Nowadays John Adams is not read; I was the first man to cut the pages in the ten big volumes of my set of his works, although they were published a hundred years before. Adams wrote with vigor, wit, and enviable accuracy, but people do not read him: his ideas have penetrated the American mind more by osmosis than by conscious assimilation. It is to Hamilton that most Americans turn when they look for a conservative among the founding fathers—not that they read Hamilton, either, for Hamilton was a gentleman of personalities and particularities, and (with the partial exception of *The Federalist*) he wrote very little which can be considered social thought. Yet Alexander Hamilton the financier, the party-manager, the empire-builder, fascinates those numerous Americans among whom the acquisitive instinct is confounded with the conservative tendency; and they, in turn, have convinced the public that "the first American businessman" was the first eminent American conservative. Hamilton was not that; but he was significant of the American future, and he and Fisher Ames and John Marshall share this chapter with Adams because they were the best exemplars of the anti-democratic, property-respecting, centralizing, rather short-sighted Federalism to which Adams often rose superior. Men like Hamilton and Ames and Pickering and Dwight seem to have believed in something very like old Toryism. Adams, broader of vision and keener in discerning the lineaments of the future, represented instead that coalescing of liberal ideas with prescriptive wisdom to which Burke's disciples gave the name conservatism. The brilliant family he founded—resembling in their stiff patriotism some ancient Roman house—for generations leavened the American social dough with John Adams' prudent integrity.

Always austere, sometimes pompous, and almost perversely contemptuous of public enthusiasms, Adams; on the face of things, it is surprising that he ever could attain a popularity sufficient to make him president of the United States. A great part of the common people, however, revered this man who would not flatter them; they recognized his complete honesty, his indefatigable diligence, his devotion to old simplicities and loyalties. They trusted him as the Athenians trusted Nicias, and with results more fortunate. Hamilton, intriguing against Adams before the elections of 1796 and 1800, found it easy enough to detach the party bosses from their allegiance to the tart Massachusetts statesman; but neither Hamilton nor his lieutenants ever could encompass the defection of the mass of Federalist voters. "No democracy ever did exist or can exist," said Adams, roundly; and his very audacity endeared him to the farmers and fishermen and tradesmen who sent him to Philadelphia in 1774, to Paris in 1777, to London in 1785, and to Washington in 1793 and 1797. But before examining the resolute opinions of this conservative who was a revolutionary leader, one needs to look at the more nearly orthodox Federalism of Hamilton and Ames.

2

"In the commencement of a revolution, which received its birth from the usurpations of tyranny, nothing was more natural than that the public mind should be influenced by an extreme spirit of jealousy." So Alexander Hamilton spoke to the Convention of New York, in 1788. "To resist these encroachments, and to nourish this spirit, was the great object of all our public and private institutions. The zeal for liberty became predominant and excessive. In forming our Confederation, this passion alone seemed to actuate us, and we appear to have had no other view than to secure ourselves from despotism....But there is another object, equally important, and which our enthusiasm rendered us little capable of regarding. I mean a principle of strength and stability in the organization of our government, and of vigor in its operations."

Both the virtue and the weakness of Hamilton as a conservative thinker may be detected in this brief passage. His political principles were simple: he distrusted popular and local impulses, and he believed that salvation from the consequence of levelling ideas lay in establishing invincible national authority. He would have liked a central government; perceiving this wholly unacceptable to America, he settled for a federal government, and became its most vigorous organizer and pamphleteer. To him, with Madison and Jay, the United States owe the adoption of their Constitution. Such was Hamilton's wisdom and such were his achievements, and they have kept his memory fresh even in this generation, celebrating the Constitution's bicentenary, which in many ways badly misunderstands Hamilton. But General Hamilton was not vouchsafed the gift of prophecy, the highest talent of Burke and (in a lesser degree) of Adams. It seems hardly to have occurred to Hamilton's mind that a consolidated nation might also be a levelling and innovating nation, though he had the example of Jacobin France right before him; and he does not appear to have reflected upon the possibility that force in government may be applied to other purposes than the maintenance of a conservative order. Even in political economy, he was a practicing financier rather than an economic thinker, and he ignored the probability that the industrialized nation he projected might conjure up not only conservative industrialists, but also radical factory-hands— the latter infinitely more numerous, and more inimical to Hamilton's old-fashioned idea of class and order than all the agrarians out of Jefferson's Virginia. Now Hamilton's scheme for stimulating American industry was neither narrow nor selfish, it ought to be said; he looked forward to benefits truly general. "Hamilton asked for protection, not to confer privilege on industry, or to swell its profits, but to bring the natural occupation of a free country, namely, agriculture, into the stream of cultural advance," writes C. R. Fay.[1] Still, his splendid practical abilities had for their substratum a set of traditional assumptions almost naïve; and he rarely speculated upon what compound might result from mixing his prejudices with the elixir of American industrial vigor.

Vernon Parrington, though now and then guilty of using the terms "Tory" and "liberal" in a sense hardly discriminating, is accurate when he remarks that Hamilton was at bottom a Tory without a king, and that his teachers were Hume and Hobbes. All his revolutionary ardor notwithstanding, Hamilton loved English society as an English colonial adores it. His vision of the coming America was of another, stronger, richer eighteenth-century England. To the difficulties in the way of his dream, he was almost oblivious. American hostility to his proposal for a more powerful chief magistracy, preferably hereditary, grieved and rather surprised him, and with pain he relinquished this plan. As England was a single state, its sovereignty indivisible and its parliament omnicompetent, so should America be: he shrugged impatiently away those considerations of territorial extent, historical origin, and local prerogative which Burke would have been the first to recognize and approve.

"It is a known fact to human nature, that its affections are commonly weak in proportion to the distance or diffusiveness of the object," wrote this "bastard brat of a Scotch pedlar" (Adams' epithet) from Nevis; he had none of those local attachments of ancestry and nativity that caused leaders like Josiah Quincy and John Randolph to love their state with a passion beside which nationalism was a feeble infatuation. "Upon the same principle that a man is more attached to his family than to the community at large, the people of each State would be apt to feel a stronger bias toward their local governments than towards the government of the Union; unless the force of that principle should be destroyed by a much better administration of the latter."[2] But Hamilton's very exoticism, which enabled his patriotism to ignore local distinctions, tended to conceal from him the obdurate resolution which was latent in the several state governments and local affections. Despite his remarks above, generally he mistook these profound impulses for mere transitory delusions; he thought they could be eradicated by the strong arm of national government—by the federal courts, the Congress, the tariff, the Bank, and his whole nationalizing program. In the long run, his instruments did indeed crush particularism to earth; but only by provoking a civil war which did more than all of Jefferson's speculations to dissipate the tranquil eighteenth-century aristocratic society that really was Hamilton's aspiration. Hamilton misunderstood both the tendency of the age (naturally toward consolidation, not localism, without much need of assistance from governmental policies deliberately pursued) and the dogged courage of his opponents. A political thinker of the first magnitude possesses greater prescience.

Similarly, that industrialization of America which Hamilton successfully promoted was burdened with consequences the haughty
and forceful new aristocrat did not perceive. Commerce and
manufactures, he believed, would produce a body of wealthy men
whose interests would coincide with those of the national commonwealth. Probably he conceived of these pillars of society as being
very like great English merchants—purchasing country estates,
forming presently a stable class possessed of leisure, talent, and
means, providing moral and political and intellectual leadership
for the nation. The actual American businessman, generally speaking, has turned out to be a different sort of person: it is difficult
to reproduce social classes from a model three thousand miles over
the water. Modern captains of industry might surprise Hamilton,
modern cities shock him, and the power of industrial labor frighten
him: for Hamilton never quite understood the transmuting properties of social change, which in its operation is more miraculous
than scientific. Like Dr. Faustus' manservant, Hamilton could
evoke elementals; but once materialized, that new industrialism
swept away from the control of eighteenth-century virtuosos like
the masterful Secretary of the Treasury. Indeed, Hamilton was
contemplating not so much the creation of a new industrialism,
as the reproduction of European economic systems which the spirit
of the age already was erasing:

To preserve the balance of trade in favor of a nation ought to be a leading aim of its policy. The avarice of individuals may frequently find
its account in pursuing channels of traffic prejudicial to that balance,
to which the government may be able to oppose effectual impediments.
There may, on the other hand, be a possibility of opening new sources,
which, though accompanied with great difficulties in the commencement,
would in the event amply reward the trouble and expense of bringing
them to perfection. The undertaking may often exceed the influence and
capitals of individuals, and may require no small assistance, as well from
the revenue as from the authority of the state.[3]

This is mercantilism. Hamilton had read Adam Smith with attention, but his heart was in the seventeenth century. The influence
of government, in his view, might properly be exerted to encourage

and enrich particular classes and occupations; the natural consequence of this would be an ultimate benefiting of the nation in
general. Had America left fallow what Hamilton took in hand,
her industrial growth would have been slower, but no less sure;
and the consequences might have been perceptibly less rough-
hewn. Hamilton, however, was fascinated by the idea of a planned
productivity: "We seem not to reflect that in human society there
is scarcely any plan, however salutary to the whole and to every
part, by the share each has in the common prosperity, but in one
way, or another, will operate more to the benefit of some parts
than of others. Unless we can overcome this narrow disposition
and learn to estimate measures by their general tendencies, we
shall never be a great or a happy people, if we remain a people
at all."[4] Burke—who, despite his reforming energy, would have
delayed indefinitely any alteration if it menaced the lawful property and prerogative of a single tidewaiter—was extremely suspicious of such doctrines in their English form. To excuse present
injustice by a plea of well-intentioned general tendency is treacherous ground for a conservative; and in this instance the argument
is suggestive of how much more familiar Hamilton was with particularities than with principles.

For the rest, Hamilton gives small hint as to how this mercan-
tilistic America is to be managed; he appears to have thought (since
he had a thoroughgoing contempt for the people) that somehow,
through political manipulation, through firm enforcement of the
laws and national consolidation, the rich and well-born could keep
their saddles and ride this imperial system like English squires.
These are the hopes of a man who thinks in terms of the short
run. Seven years before, the shrewd young John Quincy Adams
had written from Europe to his father, "From the moment when
the great mass of the nations in Europe were taught to inquire
why is this or that man possessed of such or such an enjoyment
at our expense, and of which we are deprived, the signal was given
of a civil war in the social arrangements of Europe, which cannot
finish but with the total ruin of their feudal constitutions."[5] Those
powers which Hamilton was so ready to bestow upon the state

eventually would be diverted to ends at the the antipodes from Hamilton's; and the urban population that Hamilton's policies stimulated would be the forcing-ground of a newer radicalism. The conservative side of Jefferson's complex nature frowned against this arbitrary meddling with populations and occupations, and presently Randolph, and after him Calhoun, denounced with impotent fury the coming of the new industrial era, more hideous in their eyes than the old colonial condition. In several respects, they were sounder conservatives than Hamilton: for he was eminently a city-man, and veneration withers upon the pavements. "It is hard to learn to love the new gas-station," writes Walter Lippmann, "that stands where the wild honeysuckle grew." But Hamilton never penetrated far beneath the surface of politics to the mysteries of veneration and presumption.

For all that, one ought not to confuse Hamilton with the Utilitarians; if he erred, it was after the fashion of the old Tories, rather than that of the philosophic radicals. He remained a Christian, in the formal eighteenth-century way, and wrote of the follies of the French Revolution, "The politician who loves liberty, sees them with regret as a gulf that may swallow up the liberty to which he is devoted. He knows that morality overthrown (and morality *must* fall with religion), the terrors of despotism can alone curb the impetuous passions of man, and confine him within the bounds of social duty."[6] Burke's vaticinations had stirred him here, as they affected John Adams, J. Q. Adams, Randolph, and so many other Americans; but the influence of Burke went no deeper. Hamilton was a straggler behind his age, rather than the prophet of a new day. By a very curious coincidence, this old-fangled grand gentleman died from the bullet of Aaron Burr, friend and disciple of Bentham.

3

"It is indeed a law of politics as well as of physics, that a body in action must overcome an equal body at rest."[7] This, said Ames, is an eternal handicap of conservatism; and he thought the game already played out and lost in the United States.

Fisher Ames, of Dedham in Massachusetts, whom Beveridge calls "that delightful reactionary," was many years dying. It was his invalid constitution, perhaps, that kept him from fulfilling the splendid promise of his early years in Congress, when he had beaten Samuel Adams at the polls—although his congenital moroseness of temper and his disdain for humanity were not qualities calculated to bring success in his rough times of national fermentation. The most eloquent of the Federalists, he exhibited a succinct mastery of literary style which might have led to great things; but he confined himself to occasional speeches and pamphlets and letters, and lived to see the prolonged triumph of the Jeffersonians, and expired sunk deep in despair, prophesying mediocrity in spirit, anarchy in society.

Long after the Federalist party had ceased to be, John Quincy Adams compressed into a few sentences their history and their epitaph:

The merit of effecting the establishment of the Constitution of the United States belongs to the party called Federalists—the party favorable to the concentration of power in the federal head. The purposes for which the exercise of this power was necessary were principally the protection of property, and thereby the Federal Party became identified with the aristocratic part of the community. The principles of Federalism and aristocracy were thus blended together in the political system of the Federalists, and gathered to them a great majority of the men of wealth and education throughout the Union. The anti-Federalists had always the advantage of *numbers*. Their principles, being those of democracy, were always favored by the majority of the people; and their cause, being more congenial to our Revolution, gave them the opportunity of making their adversaries obnoxious as Tories. The remnants of the Tories of the Revolution generally sided with the Federalists and produced an effect doubly disadvantageous to them; first, by infusing into their principles opinions adverse to the Revolution and to republican government; and, secondly, by exposing the whole Federal Party to the odium and obloquy of those opinions. This mixture of Tory doctrines with the principles of Federalism was the primary cause of their disasters and of all their subsequent errors, till their ostensible dissolution as a party.[8]

Of this aristocratic proclivity among the Federalists which the younger Adams remarks, Ames was the ablest spokesman; he was a stern moralist, and with few exceptions conventional moralists have doubted the virtue of the common man in politics. And the foreboding Ames was the most cogent representative, too, of that pessimistic inclination toward contracting their lines which prevailed among the Federalists after they began to lose ground to Republicanism. Hamilton, Marshall, and Cabot were consistent advocates of economic and territorial expansion, of an active nationalism; but Ames, speaking for the majority of the party, soon began to dread the innovating potentialities within the national government—a path which in time led them to the Hartford Convention. Ames' only counsel was to stand desperately firm against change: a conservatism as doomed to destruction as that of Eldon and Croker and Wellington, born with the sardonic grin of death upon its countenance, but which Ames expressed with an irony and penetration worthy of Voltaire. Looking back upon the rawness of the Jeffersonian democracy that Ames beheld, with its apparent threat to "proscribe the aristocracy of talents," one can make allowance for the exaggerated gloom of Ames. It has become customary among American historians and critics to deride the whole tendency of Ames' analysis of the American mind. Yet that very insensitivity to his thrusts partially vindicates his arraignment of democracy. "Our country is too big for union, too sordid for patriotism, too democratick for liberty. What is to become of it, He who made it best knows. Its vice will govern it, by practising upon its folly. This is ordained for democracies."[9]

A work never published during his lifetime, *The Dangers of American Liberty*, was Ames' most closely-reasoned and nervous criticism of American idealism; but the same general ideas he disseminated among his admirers year after year, languishing in his Dedham farmhouse. Government, he says, has for its object the protection of property and the tranquillity of society. Democracy fails in both these essentials; for democracy—pure democracy, toward which he perceived America slipping—is founded upon the quicksand of idyllic fancy. Even Federalism was based upon a fallacious premise: "the supposed existence of sufficient political virtue, and on the permanency and authority of the publick morals." On the contrary, however, passion, deluded sentiment, and a destructive yearning for simplicity (simplicity which means despotism) are characteristics of peoples who have exchanged the leadership of "the good, the rich, the well-born"* for the intoxication of self-expression and the negation of discipline. "The people, as a body, cannot deliberate;" therefore their appetites are flattered by demagogues, who satisfy the popular impulse toward action by the exhibition of violence and the spectacle of incessant change.

Politicians have supposed, the man really is what he should be; that his reason will do all it can, and his passions and prejudices no more than they ought; whereas his reason is a mere looker-on; it is moderation, when it should be zeal; it is often corrupted to vindicate, where it should condemn; and is a coward or a trimmer, that will take hush-money. Popular reason does not always know how to act right, nor does it always act right, when it knows. The agents that move politicks, are the popular passions; and those are ever, from the very nature of things, under the command of the disturbers of society....Few can reason, all can feel; and such an argument is gained, as soon as it is proposed.

The seventeenth-century pith in these sentences, the flavor of Thomas Fuller, is characteristic of the Federalist pamphleteers, who generally were men read in Harrington and Sidney and Hobbes and Locke. As time runs on, Ames grows more intense. Democracy cannot last; for presently military despotism succeeds to the intolerable and consuming tyranny of "what is called the people." When property is snatched from hand to hand, when tranquillity is hideously murdered, then society submits cravenly to the immorality of rule by the sword, preferable at least to ex-

---

*This phrase, so frequently encountered in the pages of Ames and Hamilton, was not originated by John Adams—who, indeed, uses it in a sense more cautionary than commendatory.

tinction. "Like the burning pestilence that destroys the human body, nothing can subsist by its dissolution but vermin."

Of all the terrors of democracy, the worst is its destruction of moral habits. "A democratick society will soon find its morals the incumbrance of its race, the surly companion of its licentious joys....In a word, there will not be morals without justice; and though justice might possibly support a democracy, yet a democracy cannot possibly support justice." Here speaks the old Calvinism which finds milder expression in John Adams.

Is there no check upon these excesses? Some people think that a free press "has risen, like another sun in the sky, to shed new light and joy on the political world." This is fatuity. For in actuality, the press supplies an endless stimulus to popular imagination and passion; the press lives upon heat and coarse drama and incessant restlessness. "It has inspired ignorance with presumption, so that those who cannot be governed by reason, are no longer to be awed by authority."

Nor can constitutions, however artfully designed, suffice to restrain men who have embraced the doctrines of complete equality and an inalienable popular right to power. "Constitutions," says Ames, "are but paper; society is the substratum of government." Like Samuel Johnson, the New England pessimist finds the key to political decency in private morality. "There are many, who, believing that a pen-full of ink can impart a deathless energy to a constitution, and having seen, with pride and joy, two or three skins of parchment added, like new walls about a fortress, to our own, will be filled with astonishment....Our present liberty was born into the world under the knife of this assassin, and now limps a cripple from his violence." Corruption is not intimidated by a mere flimsy charter. When the old respect for hierarchy and prescriptive title are swallowed up, only naked force counts, and a constitution may be torn into scraps in an instant. Such is the state of America; in consequence, "to mitigate a tyranny, is all that is left for our hopes."

Very little novelty exists in Ames' denunciations of equality and innovation; a dreadful beauty of invective, to which one can hardly do justice here, is their merit. Ames can even laugh, but it is the laughter of the damned: "Our disease is democracy. It is not the skin that festers—our very bones are carious, and their marrow blackens with gangrene. Which rogues shall be first, is of no moment—our republicanism must die, and I am sorry for it. But why should we care what sexton happens to be in office at our funeral? Nevertheless, though I indulge no hopes, I derive much entertainment from the squabbles in *Madam* Liberty's family. After so many liberties have been taken with her, I presume she is no longer a *miss* and a virgin, though she may still be a goddess."[10]

As Ames' voice faded, the approaching War of 1812 was casting its shadow over New England. This impending catastrophe, the unchecked ascendancy of Jeffersonian doctrines, the Napoleonic victories, and the internal decay of Federal principles combined to demonstrate, in the fanatic conservative's view, that the fountains of the great deep were broken up and American society was foredoomed to degeneration. Ames was wrong, so far as the immediate future was concerned; for already a counterbalance to American radicalism was making its weight felt. That saving influence was in part the product of an innate moderation in the planter society Jefferson represented, and in part of the sobering practicality of the Adamses, father and son, who converted a lost cause into an American tradition. But this Ames could not perceive; in 1807, he shrugged his shoulders, and turned to the wall, and said goodbye to a friend with that courageous charm which now and then flickered across his melancholy career:

My health is exceedingly tender. While I sit by the fire and keep my feet warm, I am not sick. I have heard of a college lad's question, which tolerably describes my case: 'Whether bare being, without life or existence, is better than not to be, or not?' I cannot solve so deep a problem; but as long as you are pleased to allow me a place in your esteem, I shall continue to hold better than 'not to be' to be,

Dear sir,
Your friend, &c.
Fisher Ames[11]

4

Between the centralizing and acquisitive principles of Hamilton and the beetling defiance of Ames stands John Adams, the real conservative. "He is a man of an imagination sublimated and eccentric; propitious neither to the regular display of sound judgment, nor to steady perseverance in a systematic plan of conduct," Hamilton wrote of Adams in 1800. "I began to perceive what has been since too manifest, that to this defect are added the unfortunate foibles of a vanity without bounds, and a jealousy capable of discoloring every object."[12] Coming from Hamilton, this judgment is rather amusing; but no article of it lacks a kernel of truth. In consequence of their long array of diaries and letters, the Adams presidents are known more thoroughly by historians than are any other Americans of mark. John Adams was guilty of some of the foibles of genius, and yet blessed with qualities which genius too often lacks: industry, chastity, absolute honesty, and piety. He was a very wise man, but often impolitic, for political expediency sometimes dictates that truth be left unuttered. Adams scorned to buy a little popularity with a little discretion, and through his boldness he shattered his own career, but his candor helped to save America from the worst consequences of two radical illusions: the perfectibility of man and the merit of the unitary state.

For a sample of the audacious vigor of this sublimated Puritan, take his anathema against Paine, in a letter to Benjamin Waterhouse, in 1805:

I am willing you should call this the Age of Frivolity, as you do: and should not object if you had named it the Age of Folly, Vice, Frenzy, Fury, Brutality, Daemons, Buonaparte, Tom Paine, or the Age of the burning Brand from the bottomless Pit: or anything else but the Age of Reason. I know not whether any man in the world has had more influence on its inhabitants or affairs than Tom Paine. There can be no severer satire on the age. For such a mongrel between pig and puppy, begot by a wild boar on a bitch wolf, never before in any age of the world was suffered by the poltroonery of mankind to run through a career of mischief. Call it then the Age of Paine. He deserves much more than the courtesan who was consecrated to represent the goddess in the temple at Paris, and whose name Tom has given to the age. The real intellectual faculty has nothing to do with the age, the strumpet, or Tom.[13]

These are the phrases of a man censorious, practical, ironic, and heroic, a man not afraid to risk hanging for the liberties of Massachusetts, not afraid to plead for Captain Preston after the Boston Massacre, not afraid to denounce the Gallophilic enthusiasm raised by Citizen Genêt. The uncompromising independence of Adams' nature induced him to publish, in 1787, his *Defence of the Constitutions*; and thus he became an avowed conservative three years before Burke denounced French delusions.

Like Burke, Adams had come to detest the fancies of the *philosophes* and of Rousseau's disciples during the course of a residence in France; like Burke, he had been taken for a liberal innovator, and again like that other practical statesman, he had been aghast at the visionary character of French political speculation. Adams himself had been a farm boy, a teacher, a lawyer, a legislator, an ambassador; he knew men and things; talk concerning a "state of nature" or "natural equality" or universal benevolence exasperated both his common sense and his New England morality. He saw French notions of liberty gaining currency in the states of the Confederation, and to counteract them he wrote that interminable, erudite treatise the *Defence*, which was published in hope of influencing the delegates to the Constitutional Convention.

The *Defence* is a refutation of Turgot's and Rousseau's theories of democratic absolutism. Three years later, at the very time Burke was launching his great assault on radicalism, Adams published a series of newspaper essays entitled *Discourses on Davila*—a refutation of Condorcet's notion of human and institutional perfectibility, and of certain French revolutionary assumptions. In 1814, old, withdrawn from the world, Adams engaged in a correspondence with Jefferson concerning aristocracy and democracy; and the following year he addressed to John Taylor of Caroline a series of letters on similar topics. Taken all in all, this body of political thought exceeds, both in bulk and in penetration, any other work on government by an American.

When Adams refers to Burke, usually his tongue is rough, rather as if the Federalist were anxious to be considered as representing a mean between the extremes of English reaction and French Jacobinism; but the radicals cut at him as savagely as they hacked at Burke, and indeed it is difficult to draw any clear line of demarcation between the ideas of the Whig and of the Federalist. Both declare the necessity of religious belief to sustain society, both exalt practical considerations above abstract theory, both contrast man's imperfect real nature with the fantastic claims of the *philosophes*, both stand for a balanced government which recognizes the natural distinctions of man from man, class from class, interest from interest. Burke hardly goes farther than John Adams in his horror at the French Revolution—no farther, certainly, than the younger Adams, in the *Letters of Publicola*. Only Burke's attachment to the idea of the English crown (a respect for hereditary magistracy which Adams was widely, though mistakenly, accused of sharing) and Burke's defense of church establishments are in conflict with Adams' principal ideas. John Adams, veering gradually toward Unitarianism, could not abide Catholic or Anglican or Presbyterian churches; but he did not yield to Burke in his devotion to religion: "Is there a possibility that the government of nations may fall into the hands of men who teach the most disconsolate of all creeds, that men are but fireflies, and that this *all* is without a father?" Rather than this, "Give us again the gods of the Greeks." So Adams writes in his *Discourse on Davila*. With a coincidence nearly so remarkable as the similarity between *Candide* and *Rasselas*, Burke declared about the same time that such atheistic premises reduce men to the level of "the flies of a summer."

These two great conservatives occupy common ground, but they press their separate assaults against radicalism with different weapons. Where Burke talked of prejudice, prescription, and natural rights, Adams attacked the doctrine of perfectibility and the idea of a unitary state. Without much regard for the chronological development of Adams' ideas, there follows a brief examination of his principles: first, his analysis of human nature; second, his analysis of the state.

Napoleon coined the word "ideology"; and Bonaparte's detestation of the spirit which that epithet defined was not more intense than Adams'. "Our English words, Idiocy or Idiotism, express not the meaning or force of it. It is presumed its proper definition is the science of Idiocy. And a very profound, abstruse, and mysterious science it is. You must descend deeper than the divers in the Dunciad to make any discoveries, and after all you will find no bottom. It is the bathos, the theory, the art, the skill of diving and sinking in government. It was taught in the school of folly; but alas! Franklin, Turgot, Rochefoucauld, and Condorcet, under Tom Paine, were the great masters of that academy!"[14] Among these speculators, Adams selects the Marquis de Condorcet as the especial target of his fire in *Discourses on Davila*. What are the motives of men? Adams turns psychologist, and in the Socratic sense of that term he displays great shrewdness.

Old John Adams has been curiously commended, on the score of his "utilitarianism" and "materialism," by some writers whose good opinion he might resent. The source of most such observations is his remark to John Taylor, "That the first want of man is his dinner, and the second his girl, were truths well known to every democrat and aristocrat, long before the great philosopher Malthus arose, to think he enlightened the world by the discovery."[15] Yet this is a mere contemptuous half-concession; man's nature, Adams believed, is something much deeper than his simple material wants. Men are weak and foolish, especially when deprived of proper leadership and good institutions; but they are not mere creatures of appetite; nor are they by instinct selfish. La Rochefoucauld erred when he thought self-love was the ruling passion of humanity—or, at least, he did not define that longing properly, which is more specifically "a desire to be observed, considered, esteemed, praised, beloved, and admired by his fellows."[16] The yearning for good repute, then, may be diverted from a possible course of vice to one of general benefit. But the weakness and ignorance of man leave him continually exposed to tempting love of gold, love of praise, and ambition, as well as impulses less grand than these "aristocratical passions." Only religious faith, stable institutions, and candid recognition of his own failings can withhold man from the spiritual destruction that lurks at the back of such appetites.

"It is weakness rather than wickedness which renders men unfit to be trusted with unlimited power. The passions are all unlimited; nature has left them so; if they could be bounded, they would be extinct; and there is no doubt they are of indispensable importance in the present system. They certainly increase, too, by exercise, like the body." Men must try to attain a balance of the affections and appetites, governed by reason and conscience. "If they surrender the guidance for any course of time to any one passion, they may depend upon finding it, in the end, a usurping, domineering, cruel tyrant. They were intended by nature to live together in society, and in this way to restrain one another, and in general they are a very good kind of creatures; but they know each other's imbecility so well that they ought never to lead one another into temptation. The passion that is long indulged and continually gratified becomes mad; it is a species of delirium; it should not be called guilt, but insanity."[17]

Despite Adams' observation that he learned from Plato two things only (that hiccoughs are a cure for sneezing and that husbandmen and artisans should not be exempted from military service), one remarks the tinge of Platonic method here—the comparison of emotion in individuals with emotion in society. Social order, like human sanity, is dependent upon the preservation of a delicate balance; and precisely as men who, abandoning that balance, destroy themselves, so any society which tosses away the weights at one end of the scale must end in a condition broken and desolate. The social scale is Justice; abandon balance, and justice goes with it, and the result is tyranny.

Condorcet, trusting in a natural benevolence of human character, would discard all the weights that maintain balance, and rely upon pure reason as society's guide. Adams, outraged at this fatuous confidence in a human intellect which he knew to be faltering and fallible, proceeds at exhaustive length to demonstrate by historical precedent the unreasonableness of man. Looking upon this controversy from the vantage-point of the twentieth century, it appears that in Condorcet, with accuracy, Adams chose his most irreconcilable antagonist: Condorcet, who believed that all institutions have for their aim the physical, intellectual, and moral benefit of the poorest classes; Condorcet, who proclaimed, "Not only equality of right, but equality of fact is the goal of the socialist art"—this unquenchable optimist, unshaken in his convictions even while the tumbrils carried his associates to the scaffold, was in moral philosophy the negation of all that Adams believed. Upon recognition of individual fallibility, respect for property, and acceptance of natural, inescapable differences among men rests the tranquillity of the human race; and all this, Condorcet ignored or denied. Adams endeavored to sober with the draught of sarcasm Condorcet's intoxicated faith in progress: "Amid all their exultations, Americans and Frenchmen should remember that the perfectibility of man is only human and terrestrial perfectibility. Cold will still freeze, and fire will never cease to burn; disease and vice will continue to disorder, and death to terrify mankind. Emulation next to self-preservation will forever be the great spring of human actions, and the balance of a well-ordered government will alone be able to prevent that emulation from degenerating into dangerous ambition, irregular rivalries, destructive factions, wasting seditions, and bloody civil wars."[18]

Late in life, Adams informed Jefferson that he was, indeed, a believer "in the probable improvability and improvement, the ameliorability and amelioration in human affairs"; but he never could understand the doctrine of perfectibility of the human mind, which appeared to him fantastic as Hindu fakirs' trust in ceremonial repetition as a means of attaining omniscience.[19] Progress, on the contrary, is the slow and painful ascent of the blind led by the one-eyed, dependent upon conservative institutions and the will of God. Real progress would be obliterated, for an indefinite period, by wild snatches at perfection of the sort Condorcet, Mably, Morelly, and Rousseau project. For these theories

postulate either a general sagacity of mind or a general benevolence of impulse which Adams, practiced in the management of
political concerns, knew to be unattainable.

The intelligence and morality which French innovators expect
to find in their new society might be encouraged, it is true, by
education; yet Adams doubted whether mankind ever would be
willing to afford the expense of genuine education for the mass
of men. "Human appetites, passions, prejudices, and self-love will
never be conquered by benevolence and knowledge alone, introduced by human means," he told Samuel Adams.[20] The world
is growing more enlightened, popular opinion asserts; and there
is some truth in the belief that newspapers, magazines, and circulating libraries have made mankind wiser; but with the pride
that accompanies a little new learning comes the peril of popular
vanity, the hazard that all old opinions may be discarded. "If all
decorum, discipline, and subordination are to be destroyed, and
universal Pyrrhonism, anarchy, and insecurity of property are to
be introduced, nations will soon wish their books in ashes, seek
for darkness and ignorance, superstition and fanaticism, as blessings, and follow the standard of the first mad despot, who, with
the enthusiasm of another Mahomet, will endeavor to obtain
them."[21] Himself a man of books and once a schoolmaster, Adams
sneers at Diderot and Rousseau for their praise of idyllic savagery,
their pretended discovery "that knowledge is corruption; that arts,
sciences, and taste have deformed the beauty and destroyed the
felicity of human nature, which appears only in perfection in the
savage state—the children of nature."[22] Yet we cannot expect formal education radically to alter the common impulses of the heart;
only the much more difficult inculcation of morality, which comes
from the snail-slow influence of historical example and just constitutions rather than from deliberate legislation, can effect that
moral improvement which is the real progress of humanity. "There
is no necessary connection between knowledge and virtue. Simple
intelligence has no association with morality. What connection is
there between the mechanism of a clock or watch and the feeling
of moral good and evil, right or wrong? A faculty or quality of

distinguishing between normal good and evil, as well as physical happiness and misery, that is, pleasure and pain, or in other words a *conscience*—an old word almost out of fashion—is essential to morality."[23]

The profound lessons of life are not to be got in schools, nor can they be evaded by experimenting with earthly elysiums. We are as God made us; the nature of our species changes only slowly, if at all; and philosophers who promise to save us from all the pains which the common course of life entails will lead us, instead, into deeper torments. Here Adams is markedly reminiscent of Dr. Johnson. In a passage shot through with a strong beauty, he describes the universal and inescapable emotion of grief, at once chastening and salutary:

The desolated lover, and disappointed connections, are compelled by their grief to reflect on the vanity of human wishes and expectations; to learn the essential lesson of resignation, to review their own conduct toward the deceased, to correct any errors or faults in their future con- duct toward their remaining friends, and toward all men; to recollect the virtues of their lost friend, and resolve to imitate them; his follies and vices, if he had any, and resolve to avoid them. Grief drives men into habits of serious reflection, sharpens the understanding, and softens the heart; it compels them to rouse their reason, to assert its empire over their passions, propensities and prejudices, to elevate them to a superiority over all human events, to give them the *felicis animi immotam tranquiltatem*; in short, to make them stoics and Christians.[24]

The pains and sorrows of our life are essential to the balance of our character; with them lacking, we would not be human; and thus the man who expects to "perfect" the human race would dis- tort and destroy humanity by endeavoring to separate from our nature qualities upon which all our other attributes depend.

5

In wisdom and in impulse, then, says Adams, men are not what French speculators (whether disciples of Voltaire or of Rousseau)

take them to be. Men are foolish, men are corrupted by the passion of emulation and by other appetites; to suppose that men are
sagacious and benevolent is to betray them into anarchy. And in
another respect these French theorists make a moral and psychological blunder quite as grave: they think that, men naturally being
equal, society will be perfect when this state of equality enters into
legislation. But this, Adams knows, is consummate folly: all nature round us cries out that men are unequal from the very constitution of things. The perfectionist who expects to reform society
upon the tableland of equality is ignorant of the real character of
progress.

"That all men are born to equal rights is clear," John Adams
wrote to John Taylor. "Every being has a right to his own, as
moral, as sacred, as any other has. This is as indubitable as a moral
government in the universe." (This view is identical with Burke's,
and the very words are so close to the phrases of the *Reflections*
that one is inclined to think that having read Burke has made the
American's opinion more terse and energetic.) "But to teach that
all men are born with equal powers and faculties, to equal influence
in society, to equal property and advantages through life, is as
gross a fraud, as glaring an imposition on the credulity of the people, as ever was practiced by monks, by Druids, by Brahmins,
by priests of the immortal Lama, or by the self-styled philosophers
of the French Revolution. For honor's sake, Mr. Taylor, for truth
and virtue's sake, let American philosophers and politicians despise
it."[25]

Men do possess moral equality, which is from God; and they
have juridical equality, each a right to his own, the essence of
justice; but that they are so many equipollent physical beings, so
many atoms, is nonsense. This is very like Burke; but one should
not suppose that Adams' belief in natural inequality is derived
from Burke's ideas, however much Burke may have reinforced
it. In the *Defence*, Adams had previously expressed himself with
his invariable candor, refuting Turgot's contention that republics are "founded on the equality of all the citizens" and that
"orders" and "equilibriums" are unnecessary—indeed, harmful.

"But what," wrote Adams of Turgot, "are we to understand here by equality? Are the citizens to be all of the same age, sex, size, strength, stature, activity, courage, hardiness, industry, patience, ingenuity, wealth, knowledge, fame, wit, temperance, constancy, and wisdom?"[26] All his life he continued in the same vein. "The equality of nature is moral and political only, and means that all men are independent," he declared to Abigail Adams. "But a physical inequality, an intellectual inequality, of the most serious kind, is established unchangeably by the Author of nature; and society has a right to establish any other inequalities it may judge necessary for its good. The precept, however, *do as you would be done by*, implies an equality which is the real equality of nature and Christianity...."[27] From this perception of ineradicable differences among individuals, Adams developed his celebrated theory of aristocracy.

Nothing in all the opinions of that blunt but misunderstood man has been more thoroughly misinterpreted and distorted and mistakenly denounced than his concept of aristocracy. The American public did not understand him; nor did Jefferson; nor Taylor—until, that is, he enlightened these two friendly enemies when all three statesmen were old. This confusion is of an origin so early and of a nature so persistent, indeed, that it may best be dissipated by a kind of descriptive catalog.

(1) An aristocrat, in Adams' definition, is any person who can command two votes—his own, and another man's. This is the rudiment of government by those who are best qualified to govern, the literal meaning of "aristocracy." "By aristocracy, I understand all those men who can command, influence, or procure more than an average of votes; by an aristocrat every man who can and will influence one man to vote besides himself. Few men will deny that there is a natural aristocracy of virtues and talents in every nation and in every party, in every city and village."[28]

(2) Aristocracy is not simply a creation of society; it is in part natural, and in part artificial; but in no state can it be eradicated. Its existence may be denied by hypocrites; but it will survive, all the same, for in any society imaginable, some men will exercise political influence over their fellows—some will be followers, others

leaders, and the leaders of political society are aristocrats, call them what we will. "Pick up the first hundred men you meet, and make a republic. Every man will have an equal vote; but when deliberations and discussions are opened, it will be found that twenty-five, by their talents, virtues being equal, will be able to carry fifty votes. Every one of these twenty-five is an aristocrat in my sense of the word; whether he obtains one vote in addition to his own, by his birth, fortune, figure, science, learning, craft, cunning, or even his character for good fellowship, and a *bon vivant*."[29]

(3) The most common form of aristocracy is produced by differences in nature which positive legislation cannot alter substantially. For an aristocrat is a citizen who commands two votes or more "whether by his virtues, his talents, his learning, his loquacity, his taciturnity, his frankness, his reserve, his face, figure, eloquence, grace, air, attitude, movements, wealth, birth, art, address, intrigue, good fellowship, drunkenness, debauchery, fraud, perjury, violence, treachery, pyrrhonism, deism, or atheism; for by every one of these instruments have votes been obtained and will be obtained. You seem to think aristocracy consists altogether in artificial titles, tinsel decorations of stars, garters, ribbons, golden eagles and golden fleeces, crosses and roses and lilies, exclusive privileges, hereditary descents, established by kings or by positive laws of society. No such thing!"[30]

(4) Even an hereditary aristocracy is not dependent upon positive law for its existence. In democratic America, aristocracy of descent continues unchecked. Aaron Burr obtained a hundred thousand votes on the strength of his descent from Jonathan Edwards; in Boston, the Crafts, Gores, Dawes, and Austins constitute a nobility; John Randolph of Roanoke is as much an hereditary aristocrat, by virtue of his great name, as any Montmorenci or Howard.

(5) Aristocracy is not destroyed by alienation of land or confiscation of wealth. "If John Randolph should manumit one of his negroes and alienate to him his plantation, that negro would become as great an aristocrat as John Randolph." Since power follows property, aristocracy may be transferred, but it is not abolished.

(6) Even the effort of the laws to establish equality results in reinforcing of aristocracy. "The more you educate, without a balance in the government, the more aristocratical will the people and the government be." For thus the state creates an elite who command the votes of their less informed fellows.

(7) No people have abolished aristocracy. The Jacobins have not done so, because they have not made all men and women equally wise, elegant, and beautiful. At best, they substitute new individuals for old; an aristocracy remains, perhaps without titles, but still possessing the same political power.

(8) Adams holds no brief for aristocracy: he simply points out that it is a phenomenon of nature, not to be rationally denied. Like most things in nature, aristocracy has its virtues and its vices. Aristocracies have been arrogant and extortionate; but on the other hand, if at times in history aristocracies had not made stands, against monarchs or mobs, "one hideous despotism, as horrid as that of Turkey, would have been the lot of every nation in Europe."

By dint of repetition and expatiation, Adams at length compelled Taylor and Jefferson virtually to concede that aristocracy, in Adams' sense, is an incontrovertible fact. Yet a vague popular impression has persisted that Adams was advocating some sort of oligarchical administration for the United States. In simple fact, Adams was only stating with force and wit a principle that all serious students of politics perceive today. As J. C. Gray puts it, in *The Nature and Sources of the Law*, "The real rulers of a political society are undiscoverable. They are the persons who dominate over the wills of their fellows." Albert Jay Nock remarked that every nation has its aristocracy, and the United States have theirs—an unfortunate sort of aristocracy; he was referring to the ascendancy of plutocrats and politicians, exercising the influence of an aristocracy of the Old Régime without the compulsions of *noblesse oblige*.

This problem of recognizing the aristocracy among a people, checking its vices and utilizing its energies for the benefit of the state, was never far distant from Adams' mind. "There is a voice within us, which seems to intimate, that real merit should govern the world; and that men ought to be respected only in proportion to their talents, virtues, and services. But the question always has been, how shall this arrangement be accomplished?"[31] He found the answer, so far as it ever can be obtained, in a government of checks and balances, and in social arrangements which attach honor, lands, and constitutional powers to men worthy of them, at the same time exercising vigilance over the swelling ambition of aristocrats, natural or artificial. Their honors and preferments must be devised to make them defenders of the people against the encroachments of despotism.

Nature, which has established in the universe a chain of being and universal order, descending from archangels to microscopic animalcules, has ordained that no two objects shall be perfectly alike, and no two creatures perfectly equal. Although, among men, all are subject by nature to *equal laws* of morality, and in society have a right to *equal laws* for their government, yet no two men are perfectly equal in person, property, understanding, activity, and virtue, or ever can be made so by any power less than that which created them; and whenever it becomes disputable between two individuals or families, which is the superior, a fermentation commences, which disturbs the order of all things until it is settled, and each knows his place in the opinion of the public.[32]

What manner of government diminishes this ferment and reconciles men to the social station for which their nature ordains them? This question Adams endeavors to answer when he refutes Turgot.

6

The happiness of society, Adams wrote, is the end of government. So said Bentham; yet for that matter, so did Burke. "From this principle it will follow," Adams continues, writing in the flaming year of 1776, "that the form of government which communicates ease, comfort, security, or, in one word, happiness, to the greatest number of persons, and in the greatest degree, is the best."

These observations sound remarkably utilitarian, and one notes that "liberty," even in 1776, has been omitted from the list of benefits. Adams at once adds, however, "All sober inquirers after truth, ancient and modern, pagan and Christian, have declared that the happiness of man, as well as his dignity, consists in virtue."[33]

Private and public virtues are the primary concern of Adams, who is as much a moralist as Rousseau, though after a different fashion. Adams used the word "liberty" less frequently than did most public men of his age, for at the back of his mind was the conviction that human weakness confounds liberty and license. As nineteenth-century French conservatives (following the lead of Joubert) spoke with emphasis of "justice" as the aim of society, rather than liberty, so Adams preferred the concept of virtue to the concept of freedom. But he did not think the first excluded the second; on the contrary, enduring liberty is the child of virtue. Liberty is not to be got by simple proclamation; it is the creation of civilization and of heroic exertions by a few brave souls. Samuel Adams had told his kinsman that the love of liberty is interwoven in the soul of man. "So it is, according to La Fontaine, in that of a wolf," replied Adams, tartly; "and I doubt whether it be much more rational, generous, or social, in one than in the other, until in man it is enlightened by experience, reflection, education, and civil and political institutions, which are at first produced, and constantly supported and improved by a few....The numbers of men in all ages have preferred ease, slumber, and good cheer to liberty, when they have been in competition. We must not then depend alone upon the love of liberty in the soul of man for its preservation."[34]

Like Burke, Adams knew that true liberty is appreciated only by a few; the mass of men are indifferent to it, except when an appeal to "liberty" will serve their immediate material interests. He feared for freedom in New England itself, since "commerce, luxury, and avarice have destroyed every republican government;"[35] and New England was guilty of the sin of covetousness. "Even the farmers and tradesmen are addicted to commerce," he wrote to Mercy Warren, "and it is too true that property is generally the standard of respect there as much as anywhere."[36] (Students of American history often have forgotten that Adams distrusted the unchecked influence of property as much as he distrusted the unchecked influence of numbers.) Liberty, in short, cannot be discussed in the abstract as if it were totally independent of public virtue and the framework of institutions. Adams' knowledge that freedom is a delicate plant, that even watering it with the blood of martyrs is dubious nutriment, impels him to outline a practical system for liberty under law. Liberty must be under law; there is no satisfactory alternative; liberty without law endures so long as a lamb among wolves. Even the compass of the civil laws does not sufficiently hedge liberty about: under cover of the best laws imaginable, freedom may still be infringed if virtue is lacking. "I would define liberty as a power to do as we would be done by."[37] What sort of government, then, will stimulate this indispensable private and public virtue comprehended in the golden rule? Generally speaking, a republic—which, "although it will infallibly beggar me and my children, will produce strength, hardiness, activity, and sublime qualities in human nature, in abundance. A monarchy would probably, somehow or other, make me rich..."; yet under a monarchy the people "cannot be but vicious and foolish."[38]

A republic of what sort? An aristocracy is a republic, and so is a democracy; either, in its pure form, is inimical to liberty. And here it is that Adams seizes upon Turgot to shake him as if he were a rat in a terrier's jaws. In a letter written on March 22, 1778, to Burke's adversary Dr. Price, the French financier had disparaged the constitutions of the new American states upon the lofty and supercilious principles of the French school. The Americans, Turgot declared, erred in agreeing with Montesquieu that "liberty consists in being subject to the law"; freedom, thought Turgot, should be altogether superior to hampering laws. And why had not the Americans established the "general will" that Rousseau enunciated, rather than aping England in arranging a system of checks and balances, bicameral legislatures, and similar impediments to the immediate will of majorities? Why were they so zealous for local independence, when progress demanded consolidation and centralization? (Here Turgot simply was urging adoption of the administrative principles of the French monarchy, rather than a progressive democratic idea, as Tocqueville makes clear in *The Old Régime*; but Turgot was oblivious to the source of his inspiration.) The states should form a general union, wholly coalesce, become homogeneous. Diversity of laws, manners, and opinions should be eradicated, and uniformity enforced for the sake of progress. In Turgot the mind of a pure economic planner is evident, not the mind of a statesman. Who, he continues, should rule this homogeneous mass of undifferentiated democrats? Why, the people themselves: they should collect "all authority into one centre, the nation."

As Intendant of Limousin, Turgot had been a governor of men; yet he had never really been one of the people; his authority had been ready to hand, conferred upon him by the monarchy, and that there should be difficulty in substituting for the crown a sovereign called "the people" hardly occurred to his mind. But Adams had been one of the people: this abstract reference to a great body of individuals and interests as if they had a single personality exasperated his practical nature. Eight years after Turgot had expressed these views, Adams demolished them in an enormous book hurriedly got up in London to influence the impending Constitutional Convention at Philadelphia, which was presently followed by two more fat volumes under the same title. *A Defence of the Constitutions* fills more than one thousand, two hundred pages in Adams' works—the most thorough treatise on political institutions ever produced in the United States, a task formidable enough to awe the most industrious Dryasdust. Adams tossed off the work in the midst of twenty other labors.

As Burke was to say four years later, the one principle to which the French Revolution, through all its transmigrations, consistently adhered was the idea of simplicity in political structure. The revolutionary thinkers, Burke wrote in the *Reflections*, detested that complexity in a state which really is men's chief safeguard against arbitrary action and oppression. The opposed and conflicting in-

terests within a nation "interpose a salutary check to all precipitate resolutions. They render deliberation a matter, not of choice,
but of necessity; they make all change a subject of compromise,
which necessarily begets moderation; they produce temperaments,
preventing the sore evil of harsh, crude, unqualified reformations,
and rendering all the headlong exertions of arbitrary power, in
the few or in the many, for ever impracticable." To this, *philosophes*
like Turgot were insensible. Absolute liberty and absolute power
in a central government seemed quite compatible to them: all ideas
which interfered with the democratic ideology must be crushed,
all corporate bodies and local prerogatives which impeded the operation of centralization must be abolished. Thus the history of the
Revolution, from the ascendancy of the Girondists to the last days
of the Directory, exhibits one constancy: devotion to fanatic simplicity unalloyed. At first it was the idea of absolute individual
liberty, breaking all the ancient restraints upon action and impulse; at the end, it was the idea of absolute power in the hands
of the centralized administration. Burke and Adams shuddered
at either manifestation of this infatuation with simplicity—France
of 1789, or France of 1797. The progress from the Gironde to the
Directory was natural and inevitable; for, in the words again of
Burke, "When I hear the simplicity of contrivance aimed at, and
boasted of, in any new political constitution, I am at no loss to
decide that the artificers are grossly ignorant of their trade, and
totally ignorant of their duty." Man being complex, his government cannot be simple. The humanitarian theorists who contrive
projects of ingenious simplicity must arrive, before long, at the
crowning simplicity of despotism. They begin with a licentious
individualism, every man deprived of ancient sanctions and thrown
upon his own moral resources; and when this state of things turns
out to be intolerable, as it must, then they are driven to a ponderous and intolerant collectivism; central direction endeavors to compensate for the follies of reckless moral and economic atomism.
Revolutionary idealists of this stamp are faithful to simplicity,
though to nothing else in heaven or earth. They cannot abide any
medium between absolute freedom and absolute consolidation.

Thus, at the inception of modern liberalism, Burke and Adams saw the canker of liberal decay in the flower of liberal vigor. The postulates of the new liberalism, in France, England, and America, depended upon old verities which the liberals themselves already were repudiating: upon the Christian assumption that men are equal in the sight of God, and upon the idea of an enduring moral order divinely sanctioned. The Deists had discarded most of Christian teaching, and Burke and Adams knew that the Deists' intellectual heirs would reject religious dogma and impulse, root and branch. The new liberalism would tolerate no authority. "Liberalism, as the political expression of individualism, therefore espoused freedom for the individual from all personal, arbitrary authority," J. H. Hallowell cogently says. "Starting from the premise of the absolute value and dignity of human personality, liberals necessarily demanded freedom for each individual, from the state, from every arbitrary will. Only when liberalism coupled the contract theory with the belief in objective truth and value, transcending all individuals and binding upon each without promise, could it reconcile freedom from arbitrary authority with the idea of an ordered commonwealth."[39] But the contract theory of society rested upon religious assumptions; and as religious faith decayed among the liberals, their confidence in their own predicates was diseased. More than this, their sentimental individualism soon became shocked at its own practical consequences: the economic competition and the spiritual isolation which resulted from the triumph of their ideas provoked among them a reaction in favor of powerful benevolent governments exercising compulsions. This intellectual and political process, of which France from 1789 to 1797 was the microcosm, now appears to have been the course of liberalism from the eighteenth century to the twentieth. The progress of British liberal politics from Fox to Asquith, of American liberal ideas from Jefferson to Franklin Roosevelt, suggest the rule.

Edmund Burke and John Adams were liberals in the sense that they believed in prescriptive liberties, though not in an abstract liberty. They were individualists in the sense that they believed in individuality—diversity of human character, variety of human action—although they abhorred the apotheosis of Individualism as the supreme moral principle. When the doctrinaire liberals repudiated the idea of Providence, they retained only a moral concept shorn of religious sanctions and left to wither into mere selfishness. Similarly, when the doctrinaire liberals severed political freedom from that political complexity which shelters liberty, they unwittingly hacked the roots of "inalienable rights." Burke touched upon all this in 1790; but Adams, in the *Defence*, had anticipated him.

Turgot, Adams wrote, was blind to the truth that Liberty, practically speaking, is made of particular local and personal liberties; Turgot was ignorant of the great prerequisite for just government, which is recognition of local rights and interests and diversities, and their safeguarding in the state. Turgot was for "collecting all authority into one centre, the nation" (Turgot's own words). "It is easily understood," Adams commented, "how all authority may be collected into 'one centre' in a despot or monarch; but how it may be done when the centre is to be the nation, is more difficult to comprehend....If, after the pains of 'collecting all authority into one centre,' that centre is to be the nation, we shall remain exactly where we began, and no collection of authority at all will be made. The nation will be the authority, and the authority the nation. The centre will be the circle, and the circle the centre. When a number of men, women, and children, are simply congregated together, there is no political authority among them; nor any natural authority, but that of parents over their children."[40]

Either this centralization is an illusion, and authority reposes nowhere; or it is a fact, and therefore a tyranny by those men who in actuality constitute the centre. This dilemma, the conundrum of "plebiscitary democracies" in our age, Adams proceeds to examine in the light of history; for, with Burke, he looked upon history as the source of all enlightened expediency.

As Gilbert Chinard remarks, the *Defence* is a lawyer's brief, rather than a philosophic treatise. But what a brief! Adams is intent upon proving that only a balance of powers—executive, senate, house of representatives, use what equivalent terms you will—makes a free government possible. First he examines modern democratic republics—San Marino, Biscay, seven separate cantons of Switzerland, and the United Provinces of the Low Countries; then he turns to aristocratic republics—nine Swiss examples, and Lucca, Genoa, Venice, and again the United Provinces. Next come three examples of regal republics, England, Poland, and Neuchatel; after that the "Opinions of Philosophers," Swift, Franklin, and Price; presently "Writers on Government," Machiavelli, Sidney, Montesquieu, and Harrington; which lead to "Opinions of Historians," Polybius (Adams' favorite among the ancients), Dionysius of Halicarnassus, Plato, Locke, Milton, and Hume. The seventh chapter is an analysis of twelve ancient democratic republics; the eighth, of three ancient aristocratic republics; and the ninth, of three ancient monarchical republics. It is not necessary to tabulate the contents of the second and third volumes of the *Defence* to be convinced of Adams' erudition. Here is a thirst for information not unworthy of comparison with Aristotle's and Bacon's. And he summarizes all this mass of evidence in a paragraph:

By the authorities and examples already recited, you will be convinced that three branches of power have an unalterable foundation in nature; that they exist in every society natural and artificial; and that if all of them are not acknowledged in any constitution of government, it would be found to be imperfect, unstable, and soon enslaved; that the legislative and executive authorities are naturally distinct; and that liberty and the laws depend entirely on a separation of them in the frame of government; that the legislative power is naturally and necessarily sovereign and supreme over the executive; and, therefore, that the latter must be made an essential branch of the former, even with a negative, or it will not be able to defend itself, but will be soon invaded, undermined, attacked, or in some way or other totally ruined and annihilated by the former.[41]

Without balance in government, there can be no true law; and without law, no liberty. Adams' opinions on sovereignty (the darling of political theorists) are refreshingly direct. Sovereignty is, indeed, properly indivisible, but its exercise may be assigned to counterbalancing bodies or divisions without destroying its efficacy. A simple sovereignty, all power embraced by a single group, lacks balance, by its nature is unjust to the other interests in the commonwealth, and therefore promulgates no true laws—only arbitrary decrees. A divided sovereignty which does not achieve a balance—that is, a sovereignty in which power is allocated to different interests and classes but is allocated unequally—must always be at war, unsuccessfully seeking equilibrium, and consequently possesses no true law. "Longitude, and the philosopher's stone, have not been sought with more earnestness by philosophers than a guardian of the laws has been studied by legislators from Plato to Montesquieu; but every project has been found to be no better than committing the lamb to the custody of the wolf, except that one which is called a *balance of power*."[42] In any state, the sovereignty reposes wherever property resides. America is conspicuous for equality of land-holding. "The sovereignty then in fact, as well as morally, must reside in the whole body of the people."

In the practical art of achieving political balance, Adams had experience; he had dominated the convention that framed the first free constitution for Massachusetts, and his early writings had influenced constitution-makers in other states. He stood for a strong executive, with a veto upon the other two branches of the legislature (for the chief magistrate, although incorporated in the *sovereignty* of the legislature, exercises a separate *authority*); a senate, or upper chamber, substantially representative of wealth and position; a house of representatives, or lower chamber, substantially based upon population. And this division is not made primarily for the protection of the rich, well-born, and able against the mass of the people, but rather to protect the multitude against the ambition of aristocracy, natural or artificial. In Massachusetts, the senatorial seats were allotted to districts in proportion to the direct taxes paid into the state treasury from each area; other methods, too, might serve to distinguish the constituencies electing the members of the upper house from those electing the lower. "The rich, the well-born, and the able, acquire an influence among the people that will soon be too much for simple honesty and plain sense, in a house of representatives. The most illustrious of them must, therefore, be separated from the mass, and placed by themselves in a senate; this is, to all honest and useful intents, an ostracism.... The senate becomes the great object of ambition; and the richest and most sagacious wish to merit an advancement to it by services to the public in the house."[43]

The executive officer should be representative of the people in general, a man of august and independent character, viewing impartially the claims of the other two branches of the government. Parrington objects that Adams provides no means for selecting an executive who would truly represent the mass of people, and not the aristocratic element which tends to dominate all societies. And yet has not the American national presidency developed into very nearly the institution Adams describes, so far as things terrestrial can approach their idea?

Thus power is distributed justly among the chief interests in society; the ineradicable natural aristocracy, to the analysis of which Adams devoted so large a part of his political writings, is recognized and to some extent moulded into a separate body by the institution of a senate; the passion of the moment and the tyranny of the omnipotent legislative organ are checked by constitutional devices. Years before, Adams had inveighed against the defects of a single assembly—it was liable to all the frailties of an individual, it was avaricious, it was ambitious of perpetual power, it was unfit to exercise executive authority, it was too little skilled in law to exercise judicial power, and it tended to adjudge all disputes in its own favor.[44] These evils Turgot's proposal would release upon an unlucky nation; balance alone can keep the lid upon them.

Democracy is feared by Adams no more than he dreads any other unmixed form of government: "I cannot say that democracy has been more pernicious, on the whole, than any of the others. Its atrocities have been more transient; those of the others have been more permanent....Democracy must be an essential, an integral part of the sovereignty, and have a control over the whole government, or moral liberty cannot exist, or any other liberty. I have been always grieved at the gross abuse of this respectable word."[45] But neither can moral liberties endure if democracy be unchecked by other social interests; for that matter, pure democracy destroys itself, for want of wisdom and moderation, and ends in despotism. "Where the people have a voice, and there is no balance, there will be everlasting fluctuations, revolutions, and horrors, until a standing army, with a general at its head, commands the peace, or the necessity of an equilibrium is made appear to all, and is adopted by all."[46] This far-sighted admonition was written three years before Burke stirred himself to warn France and civilization (as Laski very justly comments) of "the military dictatorship he so marvellously foresaw."

As for universal suffrage, Adams offered it no opposition on principle; but he doubted its efficacy, for the aristocracy which must prevail in every society, whether recognized or ignored, will be the real masters under universal suffrage; and they might well be a plundering aristocracy, unfitted by education and experience to be entrusted with the economic power that is inescapably riveted to political authority. "It is hard to say that every man has not an equal right; but admit this equal right and equal power, and an immediate revolution would ensue. In all the nations of Europe, the number of persons who have not a penny is double those who have a groat; admit all these to an equality of power, and you would soon see how the groats would be divided."[47] In America, he was inclined to favor a broad suffrage; but the wisdom of this arrangement was dependent, he knew, upon a continued wide distribution of property, for no man recognized better than Adams the eternal marriage of property and power. He predicted, without the dread of Ames but also without the eagerness of Hamilton, that in a few generations the United States would be populated by more than a hundred million persons. "In future ages, if the present states become great nations, rich, powerful, and luxurious, as well as numerous, their own feelings and good sense will dictate to them what to do; they may make transitions to a nearer resemblance of the British constitution, by a fresh convention, without the smallest interruption to liberty. But this will never become necessary, until great quantities of property shall get into few hands."[48] In this passage Adams displays greater confidence in the wisdom of futurity than he was accustomed to repose in his own generation. A constriction of the franchise, as Tocqueville pointed out, is extremely difficult to enforce—rather like diverting water uphill.

All these treatises and pamphlets, all these letters and masses of evidence, John Adams produced to buttress his simple conservative premise: "My opinion is, and always has been, that absolute power intoxicates alike despots, monarchs, aristocrats, and democrats, and jacobins, and *sans culottes*." His arguments for a proper division of powers have become so familiar to Americans that they may appear wearisome truisms. But it is Adams who made them truisms: his learning and his candor, almost unaided, obstructed in the United States a flooding intellectual sympathy with French theories of idyllic benevolence, omnicompetent single assemblies, and unitary states. He sacrificed his popularity in order to oppose these revolutionary opinions, but in the long run he and his friends prevailed; and modern American government, however disfigured in his eyes by haphazard introduction of the instruments of "direct democracy," nevertheless probably would seem to him sufficient vindication for his political struggle. He was the truest Federalist of them all; for where Hamilton accepted the federal system merely as a tolerable substitute for central government, and where Pickering and Dwight and the other Hartford Convention men adhered to the federal idea only when it suited New England's interest, Adams believed in the federal principle as the best possible government for America. More than any other nation in the world, the United States cling affectionately to the idea of political balance; and in large measure, this is the harvest of Adams' practical conservatism.

A conservative he was always. In 1811, he wrote to Josiah Quincy, "Should I let loose my imagination into futurity, I could imagine that I foresee changes and revolutions such as eye hath not seen nor ear heard...I cannot see any better principle at present than to make as little innovation as possible; keep things going as well as we can in the present train.''[49] Change in America, however enormous, nevertheless has been in a regular train—a legacy from Adams and his coadjutors.

7

In this chapter on Federalists, their great monument has barely been mentioned: the Constitution of the United States of America. It has been the most successful conservative device in the history of the world. Adams' share in the work, however considerable as influence, still was wholly indirect, for Adams was in London when the Convention met. Jefferson was abroad, too, so that the two chief American political thinkers of that age did not participate in the transcendent political accomplishment of their own age—a reflection chastening to any writer who tries to delineate the influence of ideas upon events. But the application and enforcement of the Constitution converted that document, initially a species of compromise between two powerful factions in the States, into the sword of Federalism. Here is an idea which not only outlived the school which gave it being, but flourished with greater vigor after the Federalist party was extinct than ever it had manifested when Federalists presided over the nation.

John Marshall, Chief Justice of the Supreme Court of the United States, was a big, slovenly, shrewd, old-fashioned, lovable man, fond of good living, good company, and good order. He was no philosopher; his entertaining biographer observes that Marshall had only one idea, but that principle was national union. A consistent Federalist, he had been Adams' Secretary of State, and it was Adams who appointed Marshall to the bench which he dignified; but Marshall's Federalism smacked of Hamilton rather than of Adams. In a practical and immediate sense, Marshall accomplished more than either of these two statesmen: he made the Court the arbiter of the Constitution, and he made the Constitution the incarnation of Federalistic conservatism. His opinion in the case of Marbury *vs.* Madison (1803) established the power of the Supreme Court to determine the constitutionality of acts of Congress; in Fletcher *vs.* Peck (1810), federal authority to prevent the states from repudiating their contracts; in Sturges *vs.* Crowninshield (1819), similar jurisdiction over state interference with contracts between private persons; in the Dartmouth College case (1819), the immortality of corporations; in M'Culloch *vs.* Maryland (1819), the "liberal" construction of the Constitution; in Cohens *vs.* Virginia (1820), the supremacy of the Constitution as the transcendent law of the land; in Gibbons *vs.* Ogden (1824), federal power over interstate commerce. These, and his other celebrated opinions, ensured that the United States would fulfill the Federalists' vision of an expanding, united, commercial nation, in which the rights of property and the division of authority were secure. These were conservative tendencies, in part; yet in another sense, they opened the way for illimitable changes of industrialization and consolidation, and they desperately wounded another sort of conservatism, that of the South and the agricultural interest.

Now the astonishing fact about John Marshall's decisions— many of them without precedent of any sort (so far as precedent in a new nation was possible) and undeniably designed to weave into the American social fabric the ideas of their author—is that with only one exception his rulings passed at once into law and were promptly and habitually enforced. Marshall was the last genuine Federalist remaining in public life; throughout almost the whole of his tenure of the office of Chief Justice, he was detested by the presidents in power; and his political philosophy was inconsonant with the professions of faith which dominated the Senate, the House, and the public. If government, as some men think, is a veil for potential force (and if this is true anywhere, it must be true in new states, where as yet prescription and habitual obedience operate imperfectly), how was it that a single bold individual, unsupported by any military power, no matter how exalted his office, could divert the flow of American economic and political energy into what channel he chose?

Resolution accomplishes wonders; but it does not accomplish all this unaided. For one thing, the tendency of the times was with Marshall, for it was becoming increasingly evident that material developments facilitated by Marshall's decisions would operate to the advantage of a considerable portion of the nation—perhaps the majority. And moreover, Marshall was sustained by a steadily augmented body of opinion won over to the Federalistic arguments. John Taylor of Caroline, that energetic old democrat, with great alarm remarked this reaction against egalitarianism and states' powers; many wise and good men, he said, "alarmed by the illusions of Rousseau and Godwin, and the atrocities of the French revolution, honestly believe that these principles have teeth and claws, which it is expedient to draw and pare, however constitutional they may be; without considering that such an operation will subject the generous lion to the wily fox."[50] Adams and the dead Hamilton, despite the collapse of their party, were gaining proselytes from among their formerly embittered opponents; and while these accessions were not to bring a recrudescence of the Federalist party, still this tendency permeated the dominant Republican party until that faction was transformed.

This alembic of conservatism penetrated to the captains of republicanism, indeed, for they were in power; and men in power find it difficult to reject proffered additional authority, from whatever source it comes. With all the indignation of a zealot abandoned by his associates, Randolph of Roanoke cried out that Jefferson, Madison, and Monroe had welcomed powers and preferred measures which in their lean days they denounced as perilous. He was right. Federalistic conservatism crept into the minds of the administration and the public by stealth, and soon mastered the national consciousness—a Federalism diluted and nominally still scorned, but none the less pervasive. After this fashion the American people came to acquiesce in Marshall's decisions, sometimes to applaud them.

And by a prolongation of that influence, the conservative essence of Federalism has endured down to modern America. If it has been a buttress of that national convetousness which Adams detested, still it has been the means of preserving Adams' principle of political balance, liberty under law. Federalism has had a great share in keeping the United States the most conservative power remaining in the world, and thus in the middle of the twentieth century the conservatism of Adams exerts an influence quite as strong as the radical social principles disseminated by his French adversaries. So much John Adams, with his outward vanity and his inward humility, never would have expected.

IV

Romantics and Utilitarians

It is this accursed practice of forever considering *only* what seems *expedient* for the occasion, disjoined from all principle or enlarged systems of action, of never listening to the true and unerring impulses of our better nature, which has led the colder-hearted men to the study of political economy, which has turned our Parliament into a real committee of public safety. In it is all power vested; and in a few years we shall either be governed by an aristocracy, or what is still more likely, by a contemptible democratical oligarcy of glib economists, compared to which the worst form of aristocracy would be a blessing.

—Coleridge's *Table Talk*

CROSSING THE MOUND in Edinburgh after a debate of the Faculty of Advocates on Scottish juridical reform, in 1806, Walter Scott was bantered by the arch-Whig, Jeffrey of the *Edinburgh Review,* and another of his reforming friends. "But his feelings had been moved to an extent far beyond their apprehension: he exclaimed, 'No, no—'Tis no laughing matter; little by little, whatever your wishes may be, you will destroy and undermine, until nothing of what makes Scotland Scotland shall remain.'" And he turned his face to the wall of the Mound to hide his tears.[1] Like Coleridge, Southey, and Wordsworth, Scott per-

ceived in the Utilitarian ideas the enemy of variety in life, the exe-
cutioner of the past; the great Romantics soon declared that the
arid materialism of Bentham was as hostile to beauty and veneration as was Jacobin fury. Burke had known Rousseau for his natural adversary; the Romantics (Burke's disciples politically, yet
tinged somewhat with Rousseauism) struggled against Bentham
as the prophet of the intolerant new industrial secularism.

"Through Bentham, those revolutionary principles against
which Burke fought so hard entered into English politics," Crane
Brinton writes.[2] Despite his own avowed contempt for Rousseau's
sentimentality, Bentham did more to establish egalitarianism in
England than Paine, Priestley, Price, and Godwin accomplished
altogether; he detested Rousseau for his emotionalism, not with
the high religious indignation of Burke. Bentham's ideas subjected modern thought to an overpowering series of radical changes,
which at once reflected and encouraged the advance of industrial
production and the rise of the masses to political power. In part,
these alterations resulted from Utilitarianism proper; in still greater
part, from Marxism, which is Utilitarianism flavored with Hegel
and converted to the uses of the revolutionary proletariat. "The
father of English innovation," writes J. S. Mill, "both in doctrine and in institutions, is Bentham; he is the great subversive."[3]
His analytical method, "breaking into pieces every question before attempting to solve it," was the culmination of Bacon's,
Hobbes', and Locke's methodology, contemptuous of delicate essences, certain that a whole is no more than the sum of its parts;
it is the foundation for every true modern radical's philosophy.

Bentham's test of merit, *utility* (determined in each case by a
judicious weighing of pains and pleasures) appealed powerfully
to the aggressive industrialists of the new age, who disliked phrases
like "right reason," "natural justice," and "good taste" as much
as did Bentham himself. Totally deficient in the higher imagination, unable to grasp the nature of either love or hate, Bentham
ignored spiritual aspiration in man; and, as if to balance the scale,
he never spoke of sin. National character, the immense variety
of human motives, the power of passion in human affairs—these

he omitted from his system; he radiated an absolute confidence in Rationality. Taking his own personality for the incarnation of humanity, he presumed that men have only to be shown how to solve pleasure-and-pain equations, and they will be good; their interests will lead them to co-operation and diligence and peace. He was the narrowest of moralists; and he was the most complacent of political theorists. Politics, like human nature, had no mysteries for him: the solution of all political difficulties lay simply in letting the majority decide every question. This absolute democracy was Rousseau's General Will stripped of its cloudy spirituality.

The object of society is the greatest good of the greatest number: Burke had said as much, yet Burke had meant something very different. The founder of conservatism had understood the complexity of human interests and the subtlety of Good. The greatest good of most men is not likely to reside in their political equality, Burke declared, or in their liberation from prejudice and prescription, or in obsession with economic objects. Their greatest good, said Burke, emanates from their conformity to the providential order of the universe: in piety, in duty, in enduring love. But Bentham swept Burke's world of spirit and imagination contemptuously aside. Bentham never spoke of an Author of our being; religion, to him, was simply a framework for morals. In politics, the greatest good of the greatest number was to be achieved by an egalitarian reconstruction of society upon strictly reasonable lines, a social checkerboard. Universal manhood suffrage, parliamentary reform, a powerful executive, popular education— these, and his projected revolution in the theory and procedure of law, were specifics (soon to become the dogmas of Liberalism) which would guarantee universal liberty and progress. He admitted no need for separation of powers, saw no point in established constitutions; nothing must impede the power of majorities to decide their interests unhampered by the dead hand of the past or the petty objections of reactionaries. Enthroning the majority as sovereign, "he exhausted all the resources of ingenuity in devising means for riveting the yoke of public opinion closer and closer round the necks of all public functionaries," says J. S. Mill, "and excluding every possibility of the exercise of the slightest or most temporary influence either by a minority or by the functionary's own notions of right." Our time knows to its frightful cost the tyranny of virulent mediocrity over minorities; but Bentham, sure that Rationality cannot be overthrown when once established by statute, was resolved to wipe out the very idea of minorities.

After nearly a century and a half of the swelling ascendancy of Benthamite moral notions, as expressed in the creed of nineteenth-century liberalism, John Maynard Keynes, in *Two Memoirs*, expressed what may be the verdict of history upon Utilitarianism. Benthamism, he says, "I do now regard as the worm which has been gnawing at the insides of modern civilization and is responsible for its present moral decay. We used to regard the Christians as the enemy, because they appeared as the representatives of tradition, convention, and hocus-pocus. In truth it was the Benthamite calculus, based on over-valuation of the economic criterion, which was destroying the quality of the popular Ideal." The final *reductio ad absurdum* of Benthamism, Keynes continues, is known as Marxism; drained of spirit and imagination by the gross objectives of the Utilitarians, we have ended defenseless before this brutal descendant of Bentham's philanthropy.[4]

But though it is safe enough today to criticize the poverty of Bentham's moral and political system, his legal reforms still are widely praised. The younger Mill declared that by expelling mysticism from legal philosophy, clearing up the confusion attached to the idea of law in general, demonstrating the necessity for codification, applying the test of utility to material interests, and purging judicial procedure, Bentham conferred an enormous benefit upon society. Men should make and unmake their laws, Bentham thought, upon the principle of utility; law ought to be treated like mathematics or physics, made a tool of convenience; the old illusions that law had a supernatural sanction, an origin superior to man, the Ciceronian and Scholastic notion that it was a human groping after divine enactment, should be dismissed in the interest of efficiency in an industrial age. Twentieth-century political and juridical "realism" and pragmatism, triumphant now in the Supreme Court of the United States and throughout nearly all the world, are derived from Bentham. Possibly, however, the legal philosophy of Bentham (as distinguished from the immediate administrative reform of legal procedure that was accomplished in consequence of his writings) may come to be considered as pregnant with social decay as some thinkers now believe his moral ideas were. Natural-law doctrines, at least in the historical and expedient sense understood by Burke, appear to be undergoing revival. Now it was upon this question of legal reform that Walter Scott took immediate issue with the pupils of Bentham, and in that he showed his sensitive comprehension of Burke's conservative thought. There are two foundations of law, Burke had said: equity and utility. Equity is derived from original justice; utility, properly understood, is a high view of general and permanent interests, and should not be invoked to justify a suppression of private or minority rights. The majority of the people "have no right to make a law prejudicial to the whole community, even though the delinquents in making such an act should themselves be the chief sufferers by it; because it would be made against the principle of a superior law, which it is not in the power of any community, or of the whole race of men, to alter—I mean the will of Him who gave us our nature, and in giving impressed an invariable law upon it. It would be hard to point out any error more truly subversive of all the order and beauty, of all the peace and happiness, of human society, than the position that any body of men have a right to make what laws they please; or that laws can derive any authority from their institution merely and independent of the quality of the subject-matter."[5] This looks forward to the era of the "people's courts" and lawful extirpation of minorities; and Scott, believing with Burke that a ponderous consolidation of government and law on utilitarian principles would be murderous to all old liberties and customs, employed his astonishing talents as novelist and poet to impede this movement.

In the crisis of 1792, wrote Scott, "Burke appeared, and all the gibberish about the superior legislation of the French dissolved like an enchanted castle when the destined knight blows his horn before it.''[6] As Leslie Stephen remarks (and D. C. Somervell echoes him) Sir Walter succeeded in popularizing the proud and subtle doctrines of Burke. The *Reflections* sold by tens of thousands of copies, during the 1790s, but the Waverley novels carried Burke's ideas to a multitude which never could have been reached by pamphlets. ''What Scott did afterwards was precisely to show by concrete instances, most vividly depicted, the value and interest of a natural body of traditions. Like many other of his ablest contemporaries, he saw with alarm the great movement, of which the French Revolution was the obvious embodiment, sweeping away all manner of local traditions and threatening to engulf the little society which still retained its specific character in Scotland....The Radicals denounced them as mere sentimentalists; the solid Whigs, who fancied that the revolution was never to get beyond the Reform Bill of 1832, laughed at them as mere obstructives; by us, who, whatever our opinions, speak with the advantage of later experience, it must be admitted that such Conservatism had its justification, and that good and far-seeing men might well look with alarm at changes whose far-reaching consequences cannot yet be estimated.''[7]

In the Waverley novels, Scott makes the conservatism of Burke a living and a tender thing—in Edie Ochiltree, showing how the benefits and dignity of hierarchical society extend even to the beggar; in Balfour of Burley, illustrating the destructive spirit of reforming fanaticism; in Montrose among the clans, ''the unbought grace of life''; in Monkbarns or the Baron of Bradwardine, the hamely goodness of the old-fashioned laird. The foundations of a civilized moral order are reverence for our forefathers and compliance with our prescriptive duties, Scott seems to say in all his romances; history is the source of all worldly wisdom; contentment lies in piety. Delighting in variety like all the Romantics, repelled by the coarsening pleasure-and-pain principle of conduct, Scott clearly saw in Utilitarianism a system which would efface nationality, individuality, and all the beauty of the past. Utilitarianism was the surly apology for a hideous and rapacious industrialism. Unlike the other Romantic poets, he never felt any impulse toward revolutionary belief; he knew that the welfare of castle and cottage were inseparable, that if we are faithful to tradition, "we are all safe together." Therefore the principles upon which the Utilitarians proposed to reform the law and the courts were detestable to Scott. In his "Essay on Judicial Reform," he makes as cogent a case for juridical prescription as one can find anywhere:

An established system is not to be tried by those tests which may with perfect correctness be applied to a new theory. A civilized nation, long in possession of a code of law, under which, with all its inconveniences, they have found means to flourish, is not to be regarded as an infant colony, on which experiments in legislation may, without much danger of presumption, be hazarded. A philosopher is not entitled to investigate such a system by those ideas which he has fixed in his own mind as the standard of possible excellence. The only unerring test of every old establishment is the *effect* it has actually produced; for that must be held to be good, from whence good is derived. The people have, by degrees, moulded their habits to the law they are compelled to obey; for some of its imperfections, remedies have been found, to others they have reconciled themselves; till, at last, they have, from various causes, attained the object which the most sanguine visionary could promise to himself from his own perfect *unembodied* system.[8]

In style and sentiment, the inspiration of this is Burke. Such is the judgment of men of the world (and scholars in the law) like Burke and Scott, upon the abstractions of a recluse like Bentham, who thinks of life as a mathematical problem. (Curiously enough, several conservative writers have reproached Burke with being "impractical"—Paul Elmer More, who ought to have known better, among them—when the impulse behind modern revolutionary philosophies was produced by two men infinitely less practical than the Whig leader: Rousseau and Bentham.) Law is not manufactured—it grows; society cures its own maladies, or effects its own adjustments, by a process at once natural and providential; the impertinent doctrinaire reformer almost certainly will obstruct this process without providing any passable arbitrary substitute. To Scott, there is something majestic and lovely about this gigantic self-healing action in society; there is something horrid about the chopping and hacking of laws to satisfy a temporary and specious utility. Even the nominally conservative government of 1826, he saw, was infected with this passion for uniformity and utility, ''gradually destroying what remains of nationality, and making the country *tabula rasa* for doctrines of bold innovation. Their loosening and grinding down all those peculiarities which distinguished us as Scotsmen, will throw the country into a state in which it will be universally turned to democracy, and instead of canny Saunders, they will have a very dangerous North-British neighbourhood.''[9] Assimilate the laws of Scotland to the laws of England, and you destroy the character of a people, for law is the expression of their social being; you sow dragon's teeth. This policy is the utility of a simpleton, or of a closet-philosopher. Scott knew his countrymen, and anyone familiar with modern Glasgow or the mining districts of the Lothians and Ayrshire and Fife understands what Scott prophesied when he wrote of ''a very dangerous North-British neighbourhood.''

In the view of men like Burke and Scott, the slowness and clumsiness of old-fashioned law must be tolerated (at least until gradual adjustment may be arranged) for the sake of the safeguards to liberty and property that wither away in any legal system which accords pride of place to speed and neatness. Laws and courts do indeed require constant careful scrutiny and cautious renovation or improvement; but though they may sometimes even require wholesale reformation, still, when that reformation comes, it ought to be conducted after the fashion of Burke's Economical Reform— with tenderness toward ancient prerogatives, with every precaution to make sure that no person or class suffers a particular injustice in the name of some seeming general benefit. Bentham and his school were fiercely impatient of this solicitude for old ways and private rights. Utilitarian disregard for security against state and majority is sufficiently illustrated by Bentham's desire to establish administrative law and administrative tribunals, unchecked by customary rules of justice. Even the eulogist of Bentham's legal reformation must hesitate at this: for the most alarming problem of modern English and American law is the mushroom growth of administrative law, before which the citizen stands almost without recourse; and a phrase that occurs with dreadful monotony in Soviet penal legislation runs "upon the sentence of a court of law or *an administrative body*." Perhaps in ignoring the menace latent in administrative tribunals, Bentham winked at a potential evil more significant than all the juridical anachronisms he succeeded in extirpating.

In the preceding observations, only one facet of Bentham's system has been touched upon, and only one aspect of the Romantic writers' abhorrence. Yet Bentham's juristic utilitarianism and Scott's consequent indignation are representative of the whole struggle between philosophic radicalism and romantic conservatism. What the Romantics dreaded in a world subjected to Utilitarian domination was an indiscriminate destruction of variety, loveliness, and ancient rights in the name of a devouring industrialism and a Philistine materialism. They hated Bentham and James Mill and their associates because Utilitarianism stood for the age of the machine, the hell-hole city, and the barrenness of liberal morality. The Benthamites applauded the transformation of the modern world into a densely-populated industrial community, its obsessing aspiration the indulgence of the senses, its standard a gross mediocrity. "The state of society now leads to such accumulations of humanity, that we cannot wonder if it ferment and reek like a compost dunghill," Scott wrote in his diary, in 1828. "Nature intended that the population should be diffused over the soil in proportion to its extent. We have accumulated in huge cities and smothering manufactories the numbers which should be spread over the face of a country; and what wonder that they should be corrupted?"[10] The false egalitarianism of these new reformers, he believed, was in fact surrender to the most vicious inequality—spiritual inequality. To Maria Edgeworth, he declared with intense feeling: "The state of high civilization to which we have arrived, is perhaps scarcely a national blessing, since, while the *few* are improved to the highest point, the *many* are in proportion tantalized and degraded, and the same nation displays at the same time the very highest and the very lowest state in which the human race can exist in point of intellect....As our numbers grew, our wants multiplied—and here we are, contending with increasing difficulties by the force of repeated inventions. Whether we shall at last eat each other, as of yore, or whether the earth will get a flap with a comet's tail first, who but the reverend Mr. Irving will venture to pronounce?"[11]

Near the end of his life, a Radical mob of artisans, in the county of which he was sheriff, tried to overturn his carriage and do him harm. This shocked Scott more terribly than anything that had occurred in all his career before: the levelling savagery of the future, skulking behind the fantasies of humanitarians like Bentham, had started up Lucifer-like. "And these unwashed artificers are from henceforth to select our legislators," he had written a little earlier. "What can be expected from them except such a thick-headed plebeian as will be 'a hare-brained Hotspur, guided by a whim?"[12] Scott was a man who loved the people; and he contended against a school of reformers who, he cried, were intent upon abolishing the people and substituting efficient human material for the coming utilitarian social mechanism. With his passionate sensibilities, Scott hardly could have borne the fatal impulses of his time, had he not been endowed with a wry Scottish stoicism. "Patience, cousin," he would say, "and shuffle the cards."

The Utilitarians and New Whigs, despite all their professions of worldly wisdom, have no notion of the troubles they have excited nor of how to govern the industrial masses of emancipated individuals whom they praise, Scott had said more than once. In November, 1825, Jeffrey wrote an address to the mechanics warning them against the injurious economic effects of combinations in restraint of trade. That is all very well said, Scott observed; but it will do small good. "It takes only the hand of a Lilliputian to light a fire, but would require the diuretic powers of Gulliver to extinguish it. The Whigs will live and die in the heresy that the world is ruled by little pamphlets and speeches, and that if you can sufficiently demonstrate that a line of conduct is most consistent with men's interest, you have therefore and thereby demonstrated that they will at length, after a few speeches on the subject, adopt it at once. In this case we should have no need of laws or churches."[13]

Scott's influence as novelist and poet, and to a lesser extent as pamphleteer, was incalculably heartening to the Tory party and the conservative impulse through the English-speaking world. The practical political expression of his conservative sentiments, however, is better studied in the character and achievement of Canning; while the real philosopher of conservatism among the Romantic generation is Coleridge. Scott answered Utilitarianism from the heart, Coleridge from the mind, Canning with the weapons of wit and political ingenuity. All three of them fought against the Philosophical Radicals because their romantic imagination told them that Benthamism was a kind of diabolical possession of the modern mind, a lust for reshaping society upon lines which would be as inhuman as they might be precise. The Utilitarians wished to tamper with the living essence of society so that it would accord with their notions of mathematical nicety and administrative convenience. Benthamites never admitted to themselves that the product of distortion, even distortion scientifically engineered, is monstrosity. Like the *philosophes*, the Benthamites despised gothic irregularity and variety; they yearned after the utilitarian squares and boulevards of social planning. The Utilitarians projected long and costly vistas; but at the end of every avenue, the Romantics spied the gallows.

2

Lord Brougham called George Canning a liberal Tory. Others have doubted whether Canning was a Tory at all; and, strictly speaking, he was not; he erected the Conservative party, and made the word "conservative" part of the English political vocabulary. It was his rival and successor Peel, of course, who abandoned the old name "Tory" for "Conservative"; but Canning (who knew better than Peel what conservatism really is) made that transformation possible. Canning's brief ministry, terminated by his unexpected death, marked the end of the old Toryism. He had forced out Wellington and Eldon and the Tory magnates; and though they returned to office after he died, they were crushed in short order by the Reform agitation. By burying the old Toryism, he made possible the survival of conservative opinions.

To link Canning's name with the Romantics is, perhaps, a straining of association. Is this practical, intriguing, intensely ambitious man, witty rather than fanciful, a Romantic? Yet the Romantic poets themselves acknowledged his kinship: the ally of Scott and Coleridge, he also won the admiration of Byron; and Godwin even tried to persuade Canning to lead the Gallophilic radicals, as Paine had invited Burke to marshal English Jacobinism. Disraeli's romantic perception discerned that Canning represented the true line of Tory continuity. George Canning was romantic in the sense that Burke had been romantic: he apprehended the complexity, the variety, the mystery of creation and human nature. He knew that the past governs the present, that motives and wants cannot be reduced to rigid formulas, that "all simple forms of government are bad," that much in human character is beyond mundane laws. His romantic talents enabled him to tower above Liverpool, Addington, Eldon, Wellington, and the whole set of Old Tories, who went for sober fact and security—and therefore were sucked into the maelstrom of 1832. As a young man, editing the *Anti-Jacobin*, Canning exposed the Jacobin folly of applying abstract notions regardless of particular circumstances; as the most successful of all foreign ministers, he rebuffed the Legitimist folly of attempting to apply doctrines of political uniformity among nations by repressive measures; as an English statesman, he endeavored to avert the utilitarian reformers' folly of treating politics as if humanity were governed by rules of geometry and calculus. "It is idle, it is mere pedantry," he exclaimed, "to overlook the affections of nature."[14] Pitt (although he did not enjoy, among his splendid talents, the highest type of imagination) knew the young Canning for the most imaginative and energetic leader of the rising generation, and did all he could to advance him to high place in the Tory party. From Burke and Pitt, Canning derived his political wisdom. Croker and Eldon and the other thinking men among the Old Tories drew their inspiration from the same sources; but while Canning understood how to apply the principles of conservatism to his epoch of change, the Old Tories did not. Canning, who had begun as a Whig, owed nothing to Bolingbroke or the Cavalier tradition; his politics began with the French Revolution; and, unencumbered by the ancient grudges and loyalties of the Tory magnates, he was proportionately better armed for matching conservative intelligence against the threat of pure democracy and the appetite of the new industrialism.

His very flashing sagacity made him suspect to many influential Tories, who had been close to panic ever since 1785; they wanted "none of those confounded men of genius"—thinking sometimes, no doubt, of Calonne, Necker, and Turgot. Even the indomitable Pitt, once so studious of sober reform, so comprehensive in his social views, had shivered at every speculation since 1793, had made Burke's *Reflections* his Bible, and (in the words of Coleridge) proceeded "in an endless repetition of the same *general phrases*....Press him to specify an *individual* fact of advantage to be derived from a war, and he answers, Security! Call upon him to particularize crime, and he exclaims—Jacobinism!" Canning had to win the confidence of a party which had been ridden by fear for a generation. It was a complicated task, and he never quite achieved it. The great Tory proprietors, thinking of his shabby boyhood and his arrogant aspirations, wondered if they dared entrust their defenses to an adventurer, almost a *condottiere*; and the manufacturing and trading interest, for whom Canning and his friend Huskisson accomplished so much, dreaded his boldness. As Coleridge expresses it in *Table Talk*, "The stock-jobbing and moneyed interest is so strong in this country, that it has more than once prevailed in our foreign councils over national honour and national justice. Canning felt this very keenly, and said he was unable to contend against the city train-bands.''

In spite of this hostility, Canning performed miracles in the realm of foreign affairs; but so far as the domestic policies of Britain were concerned, in an immediate sense he accomplished almost nothing. He was prime minister for a mere four months, and then only by Whig tolerance; his only piece of positive legislation during that brief hour of triumph, the Corn Bill, was defeated in the Lords through the influence of Wellington. Not what he did as a conservative, but the example he set for later generations of conservative statesmen, is the reason why his name is prominent in any history of the Conservative Party. The stubborn Tory borough-proprietors deserted Canning the moment he began to form his administration, and the physical exhaustion precipitated by his bold attempt to drag his party after him appears to have been the cause of his early death.

Perhaps no other politician has been so badly misunderstood by his own generation. The Old Tories failed him at the moment when he might have rescued them from their immobility, because they entertained vague fears that he would slide over to liberalism, compromise with the radicals, grant concession after concession until Toryism was pared away altogether. They did not know him. No statesman was less inclined to accept the compromises of uneasy mediocrity or to yield the concessions of timid vacillation. He proposed to retain all the old framework of the British constitution, but to win over, by a vigorous administration, every powerful interest, demonstrating how they could find satisfaction within the English tradition. He was against parliamentary reform; he saw no need for extension of the suffrage; he would have retained the Test and Establishment Acts; he was contemptuous of all doctrines of abstract right and all utilitarian calculations based upon notions of atomic individualism. By efficient government, by admitting the rights of classes and interests when those influences had become clearly entitled to especial consideration, by patching and improving the fabric of the state, he intended to preserve the Britain that Burke had loved.[15]

Why did the Old Tories suspect Canning's loyalty? For two reasons, chiefly: his advocacy of Catholic Emancipation in Ireland, and his popularity in liberal circles because of his struggle against Metternich and Castlereagh. In the first matter, he had done no more than follow the policy recommended by Burke and Pitt, but which George III had frustrated; Catholic Emancipation would have been in its long-run effect a measure healthily conservative, and had it been adoped in 1827, the subsequent history of Ireland and England might have been very different. As for calling the new world into being to redress the balance of the old—why, in this, too, Canning acted in conformity to the conservative system of Burke. Canning had no wish to sponsor the revolutionary spirit in South America or Greece or Portugal; but he understood that a true national spirit of independence, once it has revealed itself and successfully asserted its power, must be accepted as reality; attempts at repression will fail, injuring the conservative cause more than amicable arrangements opportunely concluded. This was no more than the conservative principle Burke had applied to the American Revolution. Indeed, Canning's treatment both of Catholic Emancipation and of the Quadruple Alliance was proof of the profundity of Canning's conservatism. But upon these grounds, the old Tories forsook him; and once he was gone, they huddled behind Peel, who surrendered to the Liberals more than Canning ever dreamed of conceding.

Thus opportunity for salvation under the leadership of genius was lost to the Tories in 1827. Greville, knowing it, wrote three years later: "If Canning was now alive we might hope to steer through these difficulties, but if he had lived we should probably never have been in them. He was the only statesman who had the sagacity to enter into and comprehend the spirit of the times, and to put himself at the head of that movement which was no longer to be arrested. The march of Liberalism (as it is called) would not be stopped, and this he knew, and he resolved to govern and lead instead of opposing it. The idiots who so rejoiced at the removal of this master mind (which alone could have saved them from the effects of their own folly) thought to stem the torrent in its course, and it has overwhelmed them."[16] One of the handicaps

of conservatives in politics is that a great proportion of their supporters, acting as they do upon prejudice and prescription, tend
to shy away from bold ideas and vigorous talents; Canning fell
before this pathetic timidity. Canning had declared that the nation was on the brink of an enormous struggle between property
and population. Only mild and liberal legislation could avert it,
he knew; and then he died. After that, the Reform Bill and the
triumph of utilitarian ideas were inescapable.

But suppose Canning had lived, and had taken the Peels and
Wellingtons and Newcastles and Northumberlands captive, in
time, by the power of his oratory and ingenuity: would the march
of events have been different? Would not a Reform Bill have been
passed, in any event—not in 1832, possibly, but in 1839 or 1842?
Would not the agricultural interest have been overwhelmed, do
what Canning might, by the swelling industrial interest? Would
not progress in English society toward pure democracy ("tyranny and anarchy combined," in Canning's description) have shouldered the Tories aside, no matter who led them, and tramped on
toward the Benthamite ideal of equality? Throughout the nineteenth century, conservatism was endeavoring to impede the
advance of two forces stronger than the armies of the world:
industrialism and democracy. Once eighteenth-century improvement of trade, together with medical and sanitary progress, had
caused a rapid increase of the European population, was not efficient industrialism a necessary consequence, so that the new masses
of humanity might be fed? And once literacy, private judgment,
and the privileges of free contract became general, was not democracy sure to supplant a society of veneration and status? And if
these premises are granted, does not conservatism appear to have
been a mere futile clawing at the skirts of destiny?

But these questions are not simply rhetorical. Certainly the
doubling of the English population between 1740 and 1820 meant
that new sources of productivity must be employed, chiefly those
of the machine; certainly popularization of ideas and extension
of the contractual elements in economic life would require admit-
tance of new interests to a share in the exercise of authority. Yet

it does not follow that the particular *forms* of change which over-whelmed British society were inevitable; and the conservatives ful-filled a high duty in keeping change within the pattern of traditional life, so far as was in their power. Without sturdy conservative op-position, the modern industrialized and egalitarian state might have become a terror to behold. Burke, and the better men among his disciples, knew that change in society is natural, inevitable, and beneficial; the statesman should not struggle vainly to dam the whole stream of alteration, because then he would be opposing Providence; instead, his duty is to reconcile innovation and prescriptive truth, to lead the waters of novelty into the canals of custom. This accomplished, even though he may seem to himself to have failed, the conservative has executed his destined work in the great mysterious incorporation of the human race; and if he has not preserved intact the old ways he loved, still he has modi-fied greatly the ugly aspect of the new ways.

Canning would have acted in this fashion to modify the force and direction of the industrial and democratic energies which loomed before him; and Disraeli learned from his example how this faculty of prudence should be employed. The immediate problem of democracy which confronted Canning was parliamen-tary reform; the immediate problem of industrialism, the corn laws. In either case, his projected course was after the method of Burke.

The British constitution, Canning said, was "the best practi-cal government that the world has ever seen," and he was resolved to do all he could to prevent its subversion by abstract notions of absolute equality and absolute right. Wealth, ability, knowledge, and station qualify men for office; the nation which they administer is a great community united for mutual aid and mutual protec-tion, "respecting and maintaining various orders and ranks, and not only allowing the fair and just gradations of society, but abso-lutely built upon them." The genius of English polity is a spirit of corporation, based upon the idea of neighborhood: cities, par-ishes, townships, guilds, professions, and trades are the corporate bodies which constitute the state. The franchise should be accorded to persons and classes insofar as they possess the qualifications for right judgment and are worthy members of their particular corporations; if voting becomes a universal and arbitrary right, citizens become mere political atoms, rather than members of venerable corporations; and in time this anonymous mass of voters will degenerate into a pure democracy "inlaid with a peerage and topped with a crown," but in reality the enthronement of demagoguery and mediocrity.

What men really are seeking, or ought to seek, is not the right to govern themselves, but the right to be governed well. By efficient and just administration, solicitous to detect and remedy practical economic and political grievances, the quasi-aristocratic constitution of England might be maintained indefinitely; and Canning could have added that had the whole of the government been managed as Huskisson and he ran the Board of Trade and the Board of Control, the Radical demand for extension of the franchise would have had much less support. Social change will indeed make it advisable, from time to time, that new bodies of persons be admitted to share in political power; but they should be considered on the particular merits of their corporate claim, and not as mere individuals seeking to assert a "right" which does not exist in nature.

So long as Canning maintained an ascendancy in Tory councils, the Radicals could stir up little enthusiasm for Reform. In time, Canning or no Canning, some measure of parliamentary reform had to come; but had he or his school had the management of Parliament in the 1830s, probably the Reform Bill would have been a measure intricately wise, patching and pruning the constitution, but not suddenly admitting whole vast masses of population to the franchise upon arbitrary economic considerations, nor abolishing ancient boroughs and rights without regard for either historical association or true utility. As it was, the fine old town for which Canning himself had sat, and Burke and Hampden before him —Wendover, in Buckinghamshire—vanished in the utilitarian Reform of 1832; and with it was whisked away something larger, the whole idea of representation of corporate interests, as contrasted with the view of individuals as so many specks of humanity. Disraeli tried to revive the concept of parliamentary representation as a device for expressing the wants and spirit of towns, callings, and economic occupations; but he could accomplish nothing, for the individualistic dogmas of Liberalism had penetrated too deeply, by 1867, into the political consciousness of England.

As for the coming struggle between agriculture and mechanized industry, Canning's abortive Corn Bill of 1827 promised the beginning of a tolerant and far-seeing balance between the land and the mills. Given Canning's and Huskisson's broad and patient view of political economy, the Tories might have convinced a large portion of their opponents that a prosperous agriculture and a hearty landed gentry and a large rural population were quite as important to the future as the chimneys of Manchester, Leeds, Birmingham, and Sheffield; the wisdom of moderate protective duties might have been conceded, and British rural life might have suffered only minor dislocations throughout the century.* Instead, the barren victory of Wellington and the great proprietors in 1828, maintaining their near-monopoly for a few fleeting years; then Peel, who was not a man of ideas, succumbed through a kind of mental osmosis to the free-trading theories of the Liberals; Cobden and Bright swept everything before them; and Britain became the most thoroughly industrialized country of the world, perilously overpopulated, saddeningly decayed in taste and beauty; more and more, the national tone was set by the Black Country and the swollen seaports, rather than by the rural parishes and tight little towns that had nourished English political stability, English literature, and English charm. The bulk of the population, from the 1840s onward, slipped toward the condition of a proletariat. Disraeli and his Fat Cattle opposition could not reverse the current; but in Canning's time, something might still have been done. Britain could have retained the comparatively balanced economy of France or Germany or America.

*C. R. Fay imagines Huskisson (supposing he had not been killed by the *Rocket* in 1830) rising in the Commons in 1845 to propose a fixed corn duty of five shillings per quarter, the revenues to be applied to Empire settlement—thus providing that the very means of saving British agriculture would be used to alleviate the overpopulation which manufacturing at once sustained and augmented. (Fay, *Huskisson and His Age*, I, 31.)

That would have been a magnificent accomplishment for conservatives, but the hour slipped by; and how the industrial masses of Britain will subsist in the last decade of the twentieth century, their old natural advantages dwindling and the competition of their rivals fiercer than ever before, no man knows.

So much for spilt milk. Canning indicated the most enlightened and astute line of resistance for conservatives, if he did no more. He instilled in conservatism that suppleness of mind and breadth of purpose which have enabled the English conservatives to run a tenacious and reasonably consistent course for a century and three quarters, longer than any other political party in history.

3

"From a popular philosophy and a philosophic populace, Good Sense deliver us!" said Coleridge in his *Lay Sermons*. The inward man does not thrive on the regimen of the circulating library and the periodical press; for Ideas deliberately popularized become the ideologies which set Europe aflame in 1789. When ten thousand men speak with one voice, truly it is the voice of a spirit; but whether the word of God, or the scream of diabolical possession, remains a question the priest and the philosopher must settle. Knowing this, Samuel Taylor Coleridge never aspired to be a leader of the people. Certainly there is no danger that his philosophy—expressed spasmodically, desultorily, and in terms of an eloquence more redolent of seventeenth-century divines than of nineteenth-century reformers—ever will become popular. Although a transcendent master of the English language, Coleridge (to speak of his philosophical and political works) never has been read so much as the treatises of Bentham, who, the more he wrote, sank with dismaying velocity toward pedantic incoherence. For Coleridge speaks in terms of imponderables, Ideas; and Bentham in terms of matter, Statistics. The age of the industrialist and the entrepreneur understood only the latter mode of argument.

Yet the dreamer of Highgate may prove, in the end, more than a match for the eccentric founder of London University. J. S. Mill declared that in Coleridge and Bentham he recognized the two great seminal minds of the nineteenth century, and, despite his own succession to the Utilitarian sceptre of Bentham and James Mill, the younger Mill's sympathies, for the most part, were won by Coleridge. As the current of Philosophical Radicalism rapidly drains, today, into the Serbonian bog of collectivism, the idealistic premises and poetic intuition of the Romantic metaphysician may be left in triumphant possession of the debatable ground over which the two schools fought throughout the nineteenth century. Bentham founded his system upon the dry mechanical rationalism of Locke and Hartley, and upon the sneering skepticism of the *philosophes*. Coleridge adhered to the Church Fathers and Plato, declaring that full though the eighteenth century had been of enlighteners, it had been terribly empty of enlightenment. The former system was shaped round a negation, the latter round a hope; and, however great the immediate popularity of a destructive philosophy may become, in the long run a philosophy of affirmation will conquer it, unless the fabric of civilization itself first disintegrates.

Coleridge as a philosopher stands in the august line of English Christian thought: he continues the tradition to which Hooker, Milton, the Cambridge Platonists, Butler, and Burke, in their several ways, adhered. The writings of Kant and Schlegel were inferior influences upon him; John Stuart Mill blundered in supposing that Coleridge's metaphysical system was imported from Germany. This is no place for an adequate discussion of his metaphysics, however: the lucid Basil Willey has written the best short account of Coleridge's thought.[17] To employ John Stuart Mill's phrases, whenever Bentham considered a received opinion, he asked, "Is it true?" while Coleridge, confronted with the same opinion, asked, "What does it mean?" This is the legacy of Burke—never condemning prejudices because they *are* prejudices, but examining them as the collective verdict of the human species, and endeavoring to make clear the latent meaning in them. Bentham believed that certitude may be secured by scientific analysis and statistical methods. But Coleridge insisted that we never can settle the question of whether an opinion is "true" upon abstract grounds, as if it could be divorced from its context of humanity; all ancient opinions have truth in them; we should try, rather, to apprehend and explain them. For the Understanding, lacking Faith and Intuition, never will suffice to make men wise. Coleridge distinguishes between ''Understanding''—which is ''the mere reflective faculty,'' dependent on the fallible senses, physical perception—and Reason, which is a higher faculty, employing our powers of intuition, the organ of the supersensuous. Understanding is concerned with means, Reason with ends. The Philosophical Radicals, leaving out of their calculations the whole Hyperborean realm of knowledge which is beyond the flesh, would condemn humanity to a philosophy of atheism and death, blotting out that life of spirit which makes life of the body tolerable. This obliteration of the higher instincts of mankind was commenced by Descartes and Locke, and the Benthamites tried to carry it to its ultimate conclusion of a godless and purposeless determinism.

Plato knew more than all the earnest statisticians who would reduce science to an uninspired recording of observable phenomena. Man does not move himself; he does not struggle toward moral existence by Hartley's ludicrous instrument of Association. No, man is drawn forward by a power outside himself, which works through Ideas. An Idea is an immutable spiritual truth communicated to man through the faculty of intuition: the dogmas of religious faith, the principles of morals, the rules of mathematics, and the laws of pure science are apprehended through the intuition (varying in its strength from one man to another), and by no other means can this knowledge be obtained. Ideas are beyond the grasp of the mere Understanding. And Ideas, well or badly apprehended, rule the world. The Benthamite mind, the political-economists' mind, reaches no higher than the useful but limited Understanding, and therefore never attains to general truth— only to particular means and methods. Without Faith to restrain Understanding (and Faith is the product of true Reason), mankind succumbs first to the death of the spirit and then to the death of the body. Coleridge, in the introduction to his second Lay Sermon, caricatures the Utilitarian as a dim-eyed old philosopher who "talked much and vehemently concerning an infinite series of causes and effects," which turns out to be a string of blind men, one following another by clinging to his predecessor's coat-tails, all striding confidently forward. "Who is at the head to guide them?" asks Coleridge; and the contemptuous sage informs him, "No one; the string of blind men goes on for ever without any beginning: for although one blind man cannot move without stumbling, yet infinite blindness supplies the want of sight."[18]

This theory is only the other face of Janus-headed Superstition, Coleridge exclaims. All forms of life are animated by a power which does not originate within them; they progress by eduction. "In the very lowest link in the vast and mysterious chain of Being, there is an effort, although scarcely apparent, at individuation; but it is almost lost in the mere nature. A little higher up, the individual is apparent and separate, but subordinate to anything in man. At length, the animal rises to be on a par with the lowest power of the human nature. There are some of our natural desires which only remain in our most perfect state on earth as means of the higher powers' acting."[19] A Purpose, a Will, emanates from God; this Will has created our humanity, and guides us now in ways beyond our understanding, towards ends which even our reason cannot make out clearly. Providence acts through the instincts and intuitions of our feeble flesh. This being so, the man who takes the materialist, the mechanist, and the Utilitarian for his preceptors in the ends of life is a forlorn fool.

The luminous faith and penetrating intelligence of Coleridge, suggested inadequately in the preceding abstract of his metaphysical doctrines, became a chief force in the reinvigoration of British religious conviction, so gaunt and weary (except for the anti-intellectual tempest of Wesleyism) after its drubbing at the hands of eighteenth-century rationalism. Coleridge foreshadowed the careers of Keble and Newman; he rescued piety and veneration and transcendent metaphysics from Hume; he led the clergy from the indefensible ground of Bibliolatry to the redoubt of Idealism. And he went farther: better even than Burke, he demonstrated that religion and politics are inseparable, that the decay of one must produce the decay of the other. Conservation of our moral order must be paralleled by conservation of our political order. The Church (of which Christianity, "a fortunate accident," is one form, but is not identical with the Idea of a Church itself) lives not merely in partnership with the State, but with it constitutes a unity. Upon considerations of expediency and convenience, we may separate the actual operation of government and of churchly authority; but at bottom, Church and State are forever united. Society cannot subsist unless both of its constituent elements thrive.

This brings us to Coleridge's social conservatism. He was no mere "political Christian"; he attacked the atomic individualism and statistical materialism of the Benthamites because he knew that if the Utilitarians should succeed in discrediting the religious consecration of the state, they would efface the idea of order; and if they should succeed in convincing men that we are only bundles of associated sensations, they would blind humanity to its supernatural and eternal hopes and ends. The pure democrat is the practical atheist: ignoring the divine nature of law and the divine establishment of spiritual hierarchy, he is the unconscious instrument of diabolic powers for the undoing of mankind. Reduce the solemn mystery and infinite variety of human life to the pseudo-mathematical principle of the greatest happiness for the greatest number, and you establish a tyranny of prigs in this world, a hell of loneliness in the world of spirit. "*Your* mode of happiness would make *me* miserable. To go about doing as much *good* as possible to as many men as possible, is, indeed, an excellent object for a man to propose to himself; but then, in order that you may not sacrifice the real good and happiness of others to your particular views, which may be quite different from your neighbour's, you must do *that* good to others which the reason, common to all, pronounces to be good for all. In this sense, your fine maxim is so very true as to be a mere truism."[20] When the Philosophical Radicals deny the existence of the intuitive Reason, they lose any standard for determining what is good and what is bad, and therefore cannot possibly know how to do good to people, or how to seek their own good. Men's politics, especially the politics of the busy-body reformer, are contingent upon their religion.

The transition from Coleridge's most important contribution to theology and metaphysics, *Aids to Reflection* (1825) to his chief religio-political work, *The Constitution of Church and State* (1830) is natural and easy. Religion and society never had been separate entities in Coleridge's mind, not even during his youthful days of enthusiasm for French Liberty; and by 1817 and 1818, indeed, when he published his *Lay Sermons*, he was already aware that the state can be preserved only by the invocation of religious feeling, and that the church can be maintained only by the survival of a state which is conscious of its moral essence. "He threw the weight of his opinion," says H. N. Coleridge, "into the Tory or Conservative scale, for these two reasons:—First, generally, because he had a deep conviction that the cause of freedom and of truth is now seriously menaced by a democratical spirit, growing more and more rabid every day, and giving no doubtful promise of the tyranny to come; and secondly, in particular, because the national Church was to him the ark of the convenant of his beloved country, and he saw the Whigs about to coalesce with those whose avowed principles lead them to lay the hand of spoliation upon it."[21]

Shrewdly, Crane Brinton distinguishes three kinds of conservatives: the conservative of the dictionary, who accepts things as they are; the conservative of the flesh, who, contemptuous of his changing times, idealizes the past; and the philosophical conservative, "the man who works out a consistent and timeless generalization applying to the behavior of men in politics."[22] Coleridge, as the disciple of Burke, is a noble representative of this last type; and his systematic exposition of a conservatism founded upon Ideas commences with the *Lay Sermons*.

Written in the depths of the economic depression that followed the end of the Napoleonic Wars, the Sermons exhort the higher and middle classes to rise superior to Benthamite radicalism. No order can endure if it does not possess itself of Ideas; and during the present discontents, men who lead society must reinforce expediency with principle. Without Ideas, "Experience itself is but a cyclops walking backward, under the fascination of the Past: and we are indebted to a lucky coincidence of outward circumstances and contingencies, least of all things to be calculated on in times like the present, if this one-eyed Experience does not seduce its worshipper into practical anachronisms."[23] Coleridge goes farther than Burke, perhaps, in his search for principle; he doubts the sufficiency of history as a guide; one cannot rely wholly upon knowledge of the past, but must seek the aim of politics, the end for which Providence destines the state; and this may be ascertained only in the Idea of society, which our intuitions let us glimpse dimly. A false conception of the political Idea was the great cause of the French Revolution; only a true conception can save Britain from levelling fallacies: "To the immense majority of men, even in civilized countries, speculative philosophy has ever been, and must ever remain, a terra incognita. Yet it is not the less true, that all the *epoch-forming* Revolutions of the Christian world, the revolutions of religion and with them the civil, social, and domestic habits of the nations concerned, have coincided with the rise and fall of metaphysical systems. So few are the minds that really govern the machine of society, and so incomparably more numerous and more important are the indirect consequences of things than their foreseen and direct effects." In our endeavor to apprehend Ideas, however, we must exercise profound prudence, for the confounding of practical concerns with abstractions was the cardinal error of the Jacobins, "abstract reason misapplied to objects that belong entirely to experience and the understanding."

A prudent examination of the present discontents, Coleridge continues, reveals that the source of national difficulty is "the overbalance of the commercial spirit in consequence of the absence or weakness of the counter-weights." Commerce itself, properly conducted, is indispensable to the nation; but the utilitarian spirit has been degenerating into ungoverned avarice, the moral check upon commerce injured by "the general neglect of all the austerer studies; the long and ominous eclipse of philosophy; the usurpa-

tion of that venerable name by physical and psychological empiricism; and the non-existence of a learned and philosophic public,
which is perhaps the only innoxious form of an *imperium in im-
perio*." The decay of old aristocratic prejudices against greedy
speculation, the undermining of orthodox Christian faith (which
forbids avarice) by the radical dissenting sects, the Highland clear-
ances, the debauching of agriculture to a gross money-getting concern: these particular aspects of a vast and voracious concentration
upon profits are so many illustrations of our sinning confusion
of values. A political economist had told Coleridge "that more
food was produced in consequence of this revolution, that the mut-
ton must be eaten somewhere, and what difference where? If three
were fed at Manchester instead of two at Glencoe or the Trosachs,
the balance of human enjoyment was in favour of the former."
Having watched the "operatives" going to and from the factories, Coleridge disagreed with this learned man. "Men, I still
think, ought to be weighed, not counted. Their worth ought to
be the final estimate of their value."

The conduct of agriculture, like the conduct of the state, requires knowledge of causes and ends. Agriculture's principles are
not identical with those of trade, and the rights of the proprietor
are balanced by his duties. The final causes of agriculture are identical with the final causes of the state. Two negative ends of the
state exist: its own safety, and the protection of person and
property. Three positive ends stand beside these: to make the means of subsistence more easy to each individual; to secure to each
of its members the hope of bettering his condition or that of his
children; and the development of those faculties which are essential to his humanity, that is, to the rational and moral being. Knowing these ends, we must reform our courses, recast our measures,
and make ourselves a better people. "Let us palliate where we
cannot cure, comfort where we cannot relieve; and for the rest
rely upon the promise of the King of Kings by the mouth of his
Prophet, *Blessed are ye that sow beside all waters*."

The seeds of Maurice's and Kingsley's Christian Socialism are
here, although Coleridge himself did not share those aspirations

toward the beneficent welfare-state which Southey expressed. Manufacturing must be regulated, Coleridge said; otherwise, the hope for reform lay in moral improvement of all classes in society, their Christian education and their redemption from materialistic theories. The shape such a moral resuscitation ought to assume was described in *The Constitution of the Church and State, According to the Idea of Each.*

The modifying clause of this title should not be overlooked. Coleridge is not writing of the constitution as it stood in his day, nor as it stood at any particular time in English history; he is writing of the *idea* of church and state, the constitution as it ought to be, "produced by a knowledge or sense of the ultimate aim of each." Ideas exist without men being able to express them definitely or even being consciously aware of their existence. A few men possess Ideas; most men are possessed by them. Providence decreed from the beginning the development of the constitution, and we may hazily perceive the ends of the state in its origins and development; the process gives us a clue. Thus the Idea is in its nature a prophecy. Rousseau, confusing ideas with theories and events, fell into the error of believing the social contract to have been an historical occurrence. No such event ever took place; but the social contract is genuine in the sense which Burke understood—the *idea* of an "ever-originating" contract between God and man and among the several elements of society, a spiritual reality that can be discerned only by spiritual perception.

Now the idea of a State is "a body politic having the principle of unity within itself;" and its unity is the consequence of "the equipoise and interdependence of the great opposite interests...its Permanence and its Progression." Permanence has its sources in the landed interest; Progression, in the commercial, manufacturing, distributing, and professional classes. The major and minor barons—the peers and the knights or franklins—constitute in England the Permanent interest, the burgesses the Progression; both are necessary to the welfare of the state. These classes have been embodied in the two houses of Parliament, with the King to act as beam of the scales. (But the King is much more than this: he is head of the National Church and Clerisy, and the protector and supreme trustee of the Nationalty, and head and majesty of the whole nation.)

In addition to these two estates, a third exists: the Clerisy or Clerks, serving the Church of a nation. Their duty is the maintenance and advance of the moral cultivation of the people. For their endowment, there is set aside a portion of the wealth of the nation, which Coleridge calls the Nationalty, as distinguished from private property, or the Propriety. A part of the duty of the Clerisy is the service of theology; but another part is the function of national education. Some of the members of this estate should be engaged in study and meditation; most, in diffusing knowledge among the people. While the Christian Church has these functions, they do not appertain peculiarly to Christian religion; they are the duties of the clerisy in any nation, under any creed. The Clerisy are the agents of cultivation, and the means of their sustenance, the Nationalty, cannot rightfully be alienated from the Church. A great part of the Nationalty was plundered by the king and the nobility at the Reformation, and this balance ought to be redressed so that the cultivation of national morality and character may be carried forward. (In this denunciation of the Tudor confiscations, Coleridge—with Cobbett as a coadjutor of sorts— is the first of a series of thinkers: after him, Disraeli, and after Disraeli, Belloc.) Such is the Idea of the Constitution. The existing state of things in England is only an approximation of the ideal, with numerous blemishes and disharmonies; the task of the wise reformer is not subversion of the existing order, but its improvement so that it will approach more nearly the Idea of Church and State.

Coleridge hopes for a nation whose affairs will be conducted by gentlemen and scholars, upon high moral principles; it is to be a nation in which the possessors of property recognize the duties that are attached to the land, as well as their concomitant rights. It is to be an aristocratic society, even hierarchical; but justice and wisdom will have a much larger part in it than they occupy now. Classes will be represented carefully in its goverment, and the present preponderance of the landed interest will be modified. The Nationalty will receive back a part of which it has been steadily losing to the Propriety; moral and humane instruction will be restored to the mass of men; and the idea of a national church will be revived in the Church of England, which has been allowed to decline into the position of a mere sect. This program was to become the inspiration of Disraeli and conservative reformers for a century afterward.

Coleridge knew that the tide of modernity was opposed to all this scheme of restoration and conservative improvement. Education, torn from the jurisdiction of the clergy, was being reformed after the Baconian dictum that knowledge is power—transformed upon empirical and utilitarian principles, reduced to the mechanic arts and material sciences, ethics degraded to a digest of the criminal law and lectures on sanitation. The national economy, now dominated by avarice, was being forced into a mould of uniform industrialization, through the instrumentality of the Speenhamland system of poor relief, cotton factories, and "the remainder of the population mechanised into engines for the manufactory of new rich men"; next would come spoliation of the Nationalty, most of what wealth still is reserved for the support of public cultivation to be appropriated by landowners and stockbrokers. The old verities were being displaced by "the mechanico-corpuscular theory raised to the title of the mechanic philosophy" and "a state of nature, or the Oran Outang theology of the origin of the human race, substituted for the first ten chapters of the Book of Genesis." Gin had become the prerogative of the poor, crimes were quadrupled, government was intimidated by clubs of journeymen acting upon abstract theories of inalienable rights divorced from duties. The Liberal and Utilitarian leaders in Parliament failed to grasp the whole grand concept of a "national clerisy or Church, an essential element of a rightly constituted nation, without which it wants the best security alike for its permanence and its progression"; they put their confidence in tract societies, Lancastrian schools, and "lecture bazaars under the absurd name of universities." The State was declining toward subjection to an omnipotent Parliament, defiant of the restraints of the Constitution, contemptuous of the prerogatives of other elements in the nation, substituting the impulse of a numerical majority for the idea of justice. You profess an eagerness for the diffusion of learning, Coleridge admonished the Benthamites, and yet you do not grasp the Idea of knowledge:

But you wish for general illumination; you would spur-arm the toes of society; you would enlighten the higher ranks *per ascensum ab imis*. You begin, therefore, with the attempt to popularise science: but you will only effect its plebification. It is folly to think of making all, or the many, philosophers, or even men of science and systematic knowledge. But it is duty and wisdom to aim at making as many as possible soberly and steadily religious; inasmuch as the morality which the State requires in its citizens for its own well-being and ideal immortality, and without reference to their spiritual interest as individuals, can only exist for the people in the form of religion. But the existence of a true philosophy, or the power and habit of contemplating particulars in the unity and fontal mirror of the idea,—this in the rulers and teachers of a nation is indispensable to a sound state of religion in all classes. In fine, religion, true or false, is and ever has been the centre of gravity in a realm, to which all other things must and will accommodate themselves.[24]

Such was the spirit of the age. Yet true Ideas, having been communicated to those few who can clearly apprehend them, in time trickle down to the mass of men, among whom they become sound prejudices; if the ideas of constitution, church, and state are re-established in the reason of the leaders of society, they may succeed in undoing the Utilitarian corruption of public action and private spirit. Our hope is not in this generation, but in the next, or the generation after that.

The Constitution of Church and State had no significant influence upon the immediate course of affairs. Two years after its publication, Parliament yielded to the Reform rioters and the insistence of Earl Grey and Lord John Russell, displaying in the Reform Bill of 1832 a thorough ignorance of the Idea of the English Constitution. The Reformers forgot that the idea of a state, properly understood, is an aristocracy, said Coleridge; democracy is like the healthful blood which circulates through the veins of a system, but which ought never to appear externally. A pressing need did indeed exist for the reform of representation in Parliament; but the Reform of 1832 could only create new evils: "Now, when the evil and the want are known, we are to abandon the accommodations which the necessity of the case had worked out for itself, and begin again with a rigidly territorial plan of representation!" This would ignore the real need for Parliamentary reform, which was the recognition of the imperial interests of the new Britain which had developed within the past century. "The miserable tendency of all is to destroy our nationality, which consists, in a principle degree, in our representative government, and to convert it into a degrading delegation of the populace. There is no unity for a people but in a representation of national interests; a delegation from the passions or wishes of the individuals themselves is a rope of sand." The Reform of 1832, disfranchising the gentry and the real patriotism of the nation, threw the balance of political power into the hands of the shopkeepers, the least patriotic and conservative of any class. By the methods employed to intimidate the House of Lords, the Reformers subverted the independence of a great order and the harmony of the Constitution. "The mere extension of the franchise is not the evil: I should be glad to see it greatly extended;—there is no harm in that *per se*; the mischief is that the franchise is nominally extended, but to such classes, and in such a manner, that a practical disfranchisement of all above, and a discontenting of all below, a favoured class are the unavoidable results." A brutalizing democracy, unguided by religious consecration, would be the consequence, after some years; and then, "the direct and personal despotism will come on by and by, after the multitude shall have been gratified with the ruin and the spoil of the old institutions of the land."

The ancient ideals of England were surrendered to the stock-jobber and the modern political economist, groaned Coleridge—to the class of persons intent on denationalizing society, men who would dig up the charcoal foundations of the temple of Ephesus

to burn as fuel for a steam-engine. (The National Coal Board,
a hundred and twenty years later, was conducting that sort of operation at Hamilton Palace and Wentworth Woodhouse and other
monuments of the aristocratic national past.) Having subverted
the state, they would turn next upon the church, "the last relict
of our nationalty"; the clerisy, whether priests or teachers, will
be paupers in the Utilitarian society. But the Liberals and Utilitarians would get more than they bargained for:

Necker, you remember, asked the people to come and help him against
the aristocracy. The people came fast enough at his bidding; but, somehow or other, they would not go away when they had done their work.
I hope Lord Grey will not see himself or his friends in the woeful case
of the conjuror, who, with infinite zeal and pains, called up the devils
to do something for him. They came at the word, thronging about him,
grinning, and howling, and dancing, and whisking their long tails in
diabolic glee; but when they asked him what he wanted of them, the
poor wretch, frightened out of his wits, could only stammer forth,—"I
pray you, my friends, be gone down again!" At which the devils, with
one voice, replied,—
      "Yes! yes! We'll go down! We'll go down!
      But we'll take *you* with us to swim or to drown!"[25]

The cheerless atomic individualism of Bentham and the Reformers, predicated upon a sour reasonableness among men, upon the
assumption that enlightened self-interest could replace every antique piety, came to just this end; and the reaction it provoked
was a bitter collectivism, as devoid of ideals as the Utilitarian system. The radical liberalism of Bentham and the Manchester school
is a dead letter now; but the conservative system of thought has
outlived it, in part because Coleridge perceived the reality of ideas,
the role of imagination, and the sanctity of constitutions.

4

If the theories of Bentham and James Mill were the proximate
inspiration of the Reform of 1832, the example of revolutionary

success in France and the muddled ferocity of the working-class mobs who burned Nottingham Castle and the bishop of Bristol's palace were the immediate causes of its passage. "I have heard but two arguments of any weight adduced in favour of passing this Reform Bill," said Coleridge in March, "and they are in substance these:—1. We will blow your brains out if you don't pass it. 2. We will drag you through a horsepond if you don't pass it; and there is a good deal of force in both." Bentham and Scott died in the year of Reform, Coleridge two years later. For nearly half a century, Burke's passionate pleading on behalf of tradition had preserved the constitution of Britain unchanged; now the dyke was breached, and egalitarianism began to inundate English society.

"An Act to provide for the Representation of the People": this abstraction "the people" thus for the first time finds its way into the British Constitution. Previously the people had not been thought of as a homogeneous mass, who might be represented upon a mathematical basis, in equal districts. This was a utilitarian and industrial concept, confusedly recognizing the existence of a new proletariat. Previously men had been represented in their corporate capacities, as freeholders of a town, or tenants of a proprietor, or graduates of a university, or members of a trade or profession. Previously Parliament had reflected the several interests of the realm; hereafter it was to represent a "people" whose will was said to be sovereign, but which had no real common mind or purpose discernible to the candid statesman. The abstractions of Rousseau and Bentham and Hegel had become part of the law of England. Formerly government had been considered as an arrangement among the great interests of the kingdom, for mutual benefit, supported by voluntary contributions called taxes; hereafter government would tend more and more to be an abstract establishment, vested with abstract Austinian "sovereignty," directing society as if the nation were one enormous reformed Panopticon.

Historians have dealt severely with the Reform Bill. The Act of 1832, Hearnshaw wrote a century later (speaking for an influential school of thought) did not reform the old constitution, but created a new one. Certain provisions were beneficial: readjustments of representation to suit the growth of new towns and the decay of old ones, diminution of borough-mongering, enfranchisement of classes which deserved adequate representation. Its premises and its methods, however, were grossly unworthy of a nation with a grand body of political experience.[26]

Far better than Grey or Russell, the imaginative Coleridge understood the proper nature of Parliamentary reform—so J. S. Mill wrote, a few years later. Coleridge had seen that the Reform possessed no principle, and he knew that measures without principle are unprincipled measures. He realized that Reform amounted almost to revolution, but that it contained no remedy for the causes which provoked it. All parties now seem agreed that Coleridge's view was accurate, Mill continues: "The Reform Bill was not calculated materially to improve the general composition of the legislature. The good it has done, which is considerable, consists chiefly in this, that being so great a change, it has weakened the superstitious feeling against great changes."[27]

In the perspective of the twentieth century, this seems a curious apology for 1832. Mill instances the Poor Law Amendment and the Penny Postage Acts for proof of the benefit resulting from popular eagerness for great social changes. Liberalism, with its confidence in illimitable human progress, assumed that great changes, after 1832, would be confined to the promotion of humanitarian legislation. It would have amused Coleridge to find himself admired by a philosopher who thought a Penny Postage Act nearly sufficient compensation for the destruction of the idea of the Constitution. In all Western nations, utilitarianism would eclipse ideas, democracy would swallow the old constitutions; and then having poured out libations to Progress, the states of Europe would rend one another in a frenzy unparalleled since the wars of religion. "It has fallen easily, the old Constitution," Scott wrote in his journal; "no bullying Mirabeau to assail, no eloquent Maury to defend. It has been thrown away like a child's broken toy. Well, *transeat*, the good sense of the people is much trusted to; we shall see what it will do for us. The curse of Cromwell on those whose conceit brought us to this pass. *Sed transeat*. It is vain to mourn what cannot be mended."[28]

V

Southern Conservatism: Randolph and Calhoun

> They who love change, who delight in confusion, who wish to feed the cauldron and make it bubble, may vote if they please for future changes. But by what spell, by what formula are you going to bind all the people to all future time? *Quis custodiet custodes?*

J OHN RANDOLPH of Roanoke, the most singular great man in American history, spoke thus before the Virginia Constitutional Convention in 1829. Madame de Châtenay's description of Joubert would have been apposite to Randolph also: "Like a spirit which has found a body by accident, and manages with it as best it may." At the Convention, his tall, cadaverous figure; his flaming eyes like a devil's or an angel's; his bony accusing finger that had punctuated the prosecution of Justice Chase nearly three decades gone; his tormented face, half a boy's, half a corpse's, framed by his straight black hair that was a memento of his ancestress Pocahontas; his flood of extemporaneous eloquence like a prophet's inspired—for a generation, Congress and America had beheld this Ishmael of politics, this aristocratic spokesman of the Tertium Quids, this slave-holding *ami des noirs*, this old-school planter, this fantastic duellist, this fanatic enemy of corruption, this implacable St. Michael who had denounced Adams and Jefferson and Madison and Monroe and Clay and Webster and Calhoun with impartial detestation. All his career, Randolph dosed himself with brandy to dull the pain of that sickness which, nevertheless, let him live until he was sixty; and now he was turning to opium. He was a man who sometimes saw devils on the stairs; he was a man who told a visitor to his lonely Roanoke cabin, "In the next room a being is sitting at a table, writing a dead man's will with a dead man's hand." And he was also a genius, the prophet of Southern nationalism and the architect of Southern conservatism.

Conservative political policy in the Southern states, which can be traced all the way from George Mason at the Constitutional Convention to the present generation of Southern congressmen, has been rooted in four impulses: a half-indolent distaste for alteration; a determination to preserve an agricultural society; a love of local rights; and a sensitivity about the negro question—the "peculiar institution" before the Civil War, the color-line thereafter. During the early years of the Republic, the former three concerns much overshadowed the last; but by 1806, the dilemma of negro slavery began to creep into the foreground of national politics, and by 1824, John Randolph demonstrated that the problem of slavery was linked inescapably with loose or strict construction of the Constitution, state powers, and internal improvements. From the latter year onward, therefore, the slavery controversy confuses and blurs any analysis of political principle in the South: the historian can hardly discern where, for instance, real love for state sovereignty leaves off and interested pleading for slave-property commences. Both Randolph and Calhoun deliberately entangled the debate on tariffs (at bottom a question of whether the industrial or the agricultural interest should predominate in America), and the debate on local liberties, with the debate on slavery; for thus they were able to rally to their camp a great body of slave-holders who otherwise might have been indifferent to the issues at stake. Years after Appomattox, at a convention of Confederate veterans, that magnificent, simple cavalryman General Nathan Bedford Forrest listened to a series of highflying speeches from his old comrades in arms, by way of apologia for the lost cause; but slavery was scarcely mentioned. Then Forrest rose up, disgruntled, and announced that if he hadn't thought he was fighting to keep his niggers, and other folks' niggers, he never would have gone to war in the first place. Human slavery is bad ground for conservatives to make a stand upon; yet it needs to be remembered that the wild demands and expectations of the abolitionists were quite as slippery a foundation for political decency. The whole grim slavery-problem, to which no satisfactory answer was possible, warped and discolored the American political mind, on either side of the debate, for the earlier two-thirds of the nineteenth century. So far as it is possible, we shall try to keep clear here of that partisan controversy over slavery and to penetrate instead, beneath the froth of abolitionist harangues and Southern fire-eating, to those conservative ideas which Randolph and Calhoun enunciated.

Both the Virginian and the South Carolinian began as democrats and (after a fashion) radicals. When less than thirty years old, Representative John Randolph was the dominant spirit in the Congress of the United States, rejoicing with Jefferson at the collapse of the Federalist party in the election of 1800, determined to break the conservative power of the federal judiciary. At a similar age, a decade later, Representative John C. Calhoun was a War Hawk, a nationalist, an exponent of national improvements at federal expense, and a general innovator. But Randolph grew into the American disciple of Burke, and Calhoun was converted by his early adversary into the Cast-Iron Man, unalterably opposed to "progress," centralization, and abstract humanitarianism. They became conservatives because they perceived that the strong drift of the world was not toward the tranquil, agricultural, old-fangled life they loved, but toward a consolidated and industrialized new order. They rallied round themselves the planter-society of the South, and from 1860 to 1865 the South rendered to the ideas of Randolph and Calhoun the last full measure of devotion.

Between the conservatism of Federalism (especially as advocated by Hamilton) and the conservatism which rose south of Mason's and Dixon's line, a gulf was fixed. The Federalists believed that certain ancient values of society—security of property, stable government, respect for religious conviction, recognition of beneficial distinctions between man and man—could be protected best by a strong common government, vested with extensive powers and capable, indeed, of indefinite expansion. Southerners were convinced that consolidation, political or economic, would breach the wall of tradition and establish in America a unitary state, arbitrary, omnicompetent, manipulated for the benefit of a dominant majority, told by the head—and within that popular majority, for the benefit of the masters of the new industry. (Federalism in the South, which had been led by men like Marshall and Pinckney, dissolved after 1800, or shrank into a vague Whiggism.) In modern America—so far as conservatism can be said to retain a philosophical existence in the minds of politicians—both these conservative impulses, however perverted, still contend against each other and against their common enemies.

Except for Randolph and Calhoun and certain Southern writers in very recent years, the mind of the South has had few competent apologists. Rural societies almost always labor under this disadvantage; cities breed the casuist and the energumen. Yet beneath the violence of the Southern orator and the languor of the Southern private citizen, one can make out a set of assumptions or characteristics, only dimly expressed but none the less real, which give the Southern conservative tradition its curious tenacity. These have been hinted at already; but perhaps they require closer examination.

(1) A preference for the slow processes of natural change, distinguished from artificial innovation—the spirit of "easy does it"; this impulse, so often encountered in warm lands and among rural peoples, was reinforced by a suspicion of the pushing Yankee which commenced in the seventeenth century and is not yet extinct.

(2) A deep affection for agricultural life and a contempt for trade and manufactures. This view, of orgins interesting and complex,

combined with a lack of mineral resources in the Old South to produce general Southern determination neither to be industrialized by Northern enthusiasts nor to submit to taxation, through the tariffs that would subsidize Northern industry.

(3) An assertive individualism, social and political, in some ways even stronger than that of New England. The proud independence of the Southern white made him resent government from any point more remote than his county court-house; and at the same time, the absence from the South of anything like the New England town meeting deprived Southern citizens of that regular voluntary assent to the acts of government which may sometimes modify obdurate individualism. This inclination made the Southerners the most consistent advocates of local liberties and state powers.

(4) An uneasy awareness—sometimes bursting into defiance, sometimes rocked into somnolence—of the immense problem which must exist whenever two races occupy the same territory. The South had to live with the negro; the numbers of the blacks must increase, not diminish; and the menace of a debased, ignorant, and abysmally poor folk, outside the protection of the laws (except as chattels) and substantially outside the pale of the churches—this must always be at the back of the mind of every white Southerner. Upon the ramifications of the economic problem which slavery presented, one cannot enter with any adequacy here. But the riddle of a slave-class, potentially discontented with the whole fabric of established society, must tend to produce in the minds of the dominant people an anxiety to preserve every detail of the present structure, and an ultra-vigilant suspicion of innovation.

In such soil grew Southern political conservatism. This political voice spoke up with clarity only twice, but then it spoke with force and eloquence. Both spokesmen sacrificed high prospects in order to stand by the South: Randolph forfeited the leadership of the House, Calhoun the hope of the presidency. Right or wrong, they were men of bold principle; and either of them expounded a particular conservative doctrine with a lucidity hardly equalled

since. Randolph passionately denounced the democratic proclivity to enlarge the sphere of positive law; Calhoun defended the
rights of minorities.

2

I have said, on a former occasion, and if I were Philip, I would employ
a man to say it every day, that the people of this country, if ever they
lose their liberties, will do it by sacrificing some great principle of government to temporary passion. There are certain great principles, which
if they be not held inviolate, at all seasons, our liberty is gone. If we
give them up, it is perfectly immaterial what is the character of our sovereign; whether he be King or President, elective or hereditary—it is perfectly immaterial what is his character—we shall be slaves—it is not an
elective government which will preserve us.[1]

In 1813, when he expressed these opinions, John Randolph had
made himself one of the most unpopular men in America, unpopular even in the South, for he had cried out against the war
with Britain as it approached and he had denounced the conduct
of the war after it commenced. In later years, a considerable measure of the earlier popularity which had made him the booted and
spurred master of Congress returned to him; and except for one
brief interval, the fascination he exerted over his immediate constituents never failed. As his half-brother Beverley Tucker
remarked, in the eyes of the planters who flocked about Randolph
at Charlotte Court House, his very eccentricities seemed to make
him a kind of dervish invested with wisdom more than human.
Then, too, Virginia was not yet democratic; only freeholders voted.
Democracy generally exhibits an antipathy for eccentricity or any
other manifestation of defiant singularity, as Tocqueville observes,
and it is hardly likely that a candidate of Randolph's poetic fancy
and wild temper could obtain election today. He lived like a knight-
errant, and confessed to an intimate, near the end of his life, that
he had been a Quixote. He was at once the terror and the delight
of Virginia. There at Charlotte Court House, in the heart of the
Southside, in the first fury of his youth he had overwhelmed the

aged Patrick Henry; and at Charlotte Court House, in 1832, the dying Randolph literally bullied the crowd into denouncing Andrew Jackson. "I was not born to endure a master," he once wrote; and, again, "I am like a man without a skin."

Despite all temptations to turn aside into the depths of Randolph's nature, our present purpose is the examination of his ideas; and like Burke's, Randolph's mind was fertile and complex. His political career was no less intricate, although consistent. Because he loved freedom, he could not abide the centralizing intent of Federalism; and because he detested cant and the degradation of the democratic dogma, he could not abide Jeffersonianism. He shivered his lance against both prodigious windmills. His fervent effort to squelch the ominous Federalism of the Supreme Court— that is, the impeachment and trial of Justice Chase—ended in failure, and Randolph's friendly foe John Marshall, one of the few leaders of the age whom Randolph respected and loved, went placidly about his work of consolidation. When presently Randolph's discontent with Jefferson's administration was brought to boiling-point by the Yazoo scandals, the bulk of the Republican party stuck with the president, who had prizes to bestow and protection to extend, and Randolph was left in a hopeless minority with his obdurate Old Republicans, men vowed to political purity, strict construction, extreme economy in government, hard money and no debt, peace with all the world, and the agricultural life. Yet Randolph was one of those men unbearable in triumph (indeed, it is doubtful if Randolph himself liked the possession of power), heroic in adversity: for three decades his hand was against every man's, but near the end of his life he could see the South swinging round to his position.

"Beaten down, horse, foot, and dragoons" was Randolph's own account of the state into which the Old Republicans, the Tertium Quids, were fallen after the passage of Jefferson's Embargo. This was a time of frightful damage to the Southern economy through the non-intercourse acts, the Embargo, the War of 1812, and protective tariffs; this was the era of internal improvements at federal expense, westward expansion, the Bank of the United States, loose construction of the Constitution, and increasing federal ascendancy. A single eloquent voice kept the spirit of state powers and old ways in the public consciousness—until, after the Missouri debate, the Southern states began to revert to their earlier principles, and Vice-President Calhoun, pondering austerely, from his chair above the Senate, the interminable coruscations of Senator Randolph's speeches, was transmuted from an expansionist into a conservative. "Highly talented, eloquent, severe, and eccentric" —this is Calhoun's description of the man of Roanoke—"'not unfrequently wandering from the question, but often uttering wisdom worthy of a Bacon, and wit that would not discredit a Sheridan, every Speaker has freely indulged him in his peculiar manner, and that without responsibility or censure."[2]

The source of a great part of the wisdom of Randolph was Burke—and of Randolph's fierce wit, too: "The little dogs and all, Blanche, Tray, and Sweetheart, see, they bark at me!" John Randolph retorted contemptuously upon Congressmen. This comes from Lear, of course; but Burke had quoted it under identical circumstances. Randolph made no secret of his debt to Burke, and that Randolph's contemporaries did not often recognize the quarter from which came his inspiration—why, Randolph himself observed that one dared quote only Shakespeare and Milton to Congressmen. "We very much doubt," Beverley Tucker wrote of his half-brother, "if he ever became a convert to the views of Burke, until the events of the last four years of Mr. Jefferson's administration led him to suspect that there may be something in the enjoyment of liberty, which soon disqualified a people for that self-government, which is but another name for freedom."[3] From 1805 onward, however, Randolph applied to American questions those first principles of politics laid down by the philosopher of conservatism.

Randolph's speeches and letters never having been collected, one must grope through the dusty volumes of the *Annals of Congress* and fumble with tattered Richmond newspapers to catch the echo of his arrogantly beautiful rhetoric, which once astounded the nation. How orotund and superficial the addresses of Webster and Clay now seem by the side of this darting passion! The reader who wishes to discover the source of the Southern political creed ought to examine Randolph's speeches on Gregg's Resolution (1806), in which he praises free trade and denounces "liberal" constitutional construction; his attack, in the same year, upon proposed federal control of the passage of slaves from one state to another; his speech on foreign relations (December, 1811), in which he opposes the doctrines of racial equality; his fierce remarks concerning legislative representation during the debate on Congressional apportionment (1822); his contempt for levelling, paper guarantees, and consolidation expressed in the controversy over the tariff of 1824; his exposure of the "natural rights" fallacies and political abstractions in the Panama Mission speeches of 1826; and, above all, his part in the Virginia Convention of 1829–1830, when he declared, "Change is not reform." But all these cannot be examined here; instead, our present purpose is to consider Randolph's belief that a democratic passion for legislating is a menace to liberty.

"We see about November—about the time the fogs set in—men enough assembled in the various Legislatures, General and State, to make a regiment," said Randolph, in 1816, to the House of Representatives; "then the legislative maggot begins to bite; then exists the rage to make new and repeal old laws. I do not think we would find ourselves at all worse off if no law of a general nature had been passed by either General or State Governments for the ten or twelve years last past. Like Mr. Jefferson, I am averse to too much regulation—averse to making the extreme medicine of the Constitution our daily food."[4] To this theme, Randolph returned at intervals throughout his life. For him, prescriptive right, common law, and custom afford the real guarantees of justice and liberty. Once men commence tinkering with the body of government, lopping and adding and stimulating and new-modelling, they imperil those old prerogatives and immunities which are the fruit of many generations of growth. Law will change, indeed, with the times; but arbitrary intervention in the process, rude revision upon abstract concepts à la French taste, is a short and nasty way to social caducity. When a people begin to think that they can improve society infinitely by incessant alteration of positive law, nothing remains settled: every right, every bit of property, every one of those dear attachments to the permanence of family, home, and countryside is endangered. Such a people soon presume themselves to be omnicompetent, and the farther their affairs fall into confusion, the more enthusiastic they become for some legislative panacea which promises to cut all knots in Gordian fashion. "For my part, I wish we could have done nothing but talk, unless, indeed, we had gone off to sleep for many years past; and, coinciding in the sentiment which had fallen from the gentleman from New York, give me fifty speeches, I care not how dull or stupid, rather than see one law on the statute book."[5]

"We are a fussical and fudgical people," he said once. The United States in particular are cursed with this modern urge to alter, mutilate, and paralyze by legislative fiat, and the cause of this American delusion is a wild and impractical interpretation of the doctrines of natural equality. Randolph agreed with Smith, Say, and Ricardo that economic man is most prosperous when left to his own devices, and therefore he abhorred legislative regulation of commerce; adhering to the old English view that a parliamentary body really is an assembly of critics, he declared that the regular function of Congress and the state legislatures is not the *creation* of law, but rather the supervision of its just enforcement. Popular vanity does not rest content with this limitation of practical sovereignty, however, and endeavors to interfere in an immense variety of private concerns. Public vanity is turned to personal and class advantage by demagogues and clever speculators, so that government becomes a means for extracting money and rights from one portion of the population to suit the interests of men who manipulate the system. Good political constitutions alone do not suffice to resist this legislative maggot: first the delusion that the state is competent to regulate all things must be exploded, and then power must be counterpoised against power, since mere parchment is no insurance against oppression.

"I must be permitted to say, that there exists, in the nature of man, *ab ovo, ab origine*, of degraded and fallen man—for the first-born was a murderer—a disposition to escape from our own proper duties, to undertake the duties of somebody or anybody else."[6] A people who indulge this disposition in themselves soon are like sea-lawyers in the forecastle, their miserable actual state contrasting with the grandiloquence of their pretensions. On the road from Washington to Roanoke, said Randolph, this high-flying beggary exhibits itself at every inn, squalid as a Spanish *venta:* "We hug our lousy cloaks around us, take another *chaw of tabbacker*, float the room with nastiness, or ruin the grate and fire-irons, where they happen not to be rusty, and try conclusions upon constitutional points."[7] The Academy of Lagado is a fit model for a state committed to perpetual meddling with the laws. In its essence, although in a sense not properly understood by most people, law is indeed natural, the product of Omniscience; but clumsy endeavors to reshape it upon an ill-conceived design of natural equality is the most artificial of all man's endeavors, as destructive of liberty as it is impotent to attain real equality of condition.

Through his disillusion with the practices of democratic republics, Randolph was led to examine the foundations upon which American levelling ideas were built. He found those bases perilously insecure. John Randolph of Roanoke wholly repudiated the common interpretation of the Declaration of Independence, denounced Jefferson as a Pied Piper, and turned his back upon political abstractions to seek security in prescription and in an unbroken vigilance over personal and local rights. As Burke had chosen Rousseau and Price for his antagonists, as Adams had scourged Turgot and Condorcet, Randolph selected Thomas Jefferson, whose "jewels were Bristol stones," as his natural adversary. "As the Turks follow their sacred standard, which is a pair of Mahomet's green breeches, we are governed by the old red breeches of that Prince of Projectors, St. Thomas of Can*ting*bury; and surely Becket himself never had more pilgrims at his shrine than the saint of Monticello."[8]

Men are not born free and equal, said Randolph. Their physical, moral, and intellectual differences are manifest, to say nothing of their difference of birth and wealth. To presume that a mystic ''equality'' entitles the mass of mankind to tinker at pleasure with society, to play with it as a toy, to exercise their petty ingenuity upon it, is to reduce mankind to the only state of life in which anything resembling equality of condition actually prevails: savagery. Jeffersonian levelling doctrines, if taken literally, mean anarchy, ''the chrysalis state of despotism.''

Sir, my only objection is, that these principles, pushed to their extreme consequences—that all men are born free and equal—I can never assent to, for the best of all reasons, because it is not true; and as I cannot agree to the intrinsic meaning of the word Congress, though sanctioned by the Constitution of the United States, so neither can I agree to a falsehood, and a most pernicious falsehood, even though I find it in the Declaration of Independence, which has been set up, on the Missouri and other questions, as paramount to the Constitution. I say pernicious falsehood— it must be, if true, self-evident; for it is incapable of demonstration; and there are thousands and thousands of them that mislead the great vulgar as well as the small....All these great positions, that men are born equally free, and faith without works, are in a certain sense, in which they are hardly ever received by the multitude, true; but in another sense, in which they are almost invariably received by nineteen out of twenty, they are false and pernicious....In regard to this principle, that all men are born free and equal, if there is an animal on earth to which it does not apply—that is not born free, it is man—he is born in a state of the most abject want, and in a state of perfect helplessness and ignorance, which is the foundation of the connubial tie....Who should say that all the soil in the world is equally rich, the first rate land in Kentucky and the Highlands of Scotland, because the superficial content of the acre is the same, would be just as right as he who should maintain the absolute equality of man in virtue of his birth. The ricketty and scrofulous little wretch who first sees the light in a work-house, or in a brothel, and who feels the effects of alcohol before the effects of vital air, is not equal in any respect to the ruddy offspring of the honest yeoman; nay, I will go further, and say that a prince, provided he is no better born than royal blood will make him, is not equal to the healthy son of a peasant.[9]

In this, Randolph's view is identical with that of the man whose overthrow had been Randolph's first political endeavor—John Adams. Randolph proceeds to describe the fallibility of man, his credulity, his egotism, his indolence, his violence; Randolph speaks as a devout Christian, a member of "The Church of England, sir," no mere American Episcopalian. Man is corrupt; and therefore his best chance to attain justice and freedom lies in keeping the hands of ambitious men from that power which invites corruption. "None but the people can forge their own chains; and to flatter the people and delude them by promises never meant to be performed is the stale but successful practice of the demagogue, as of the seducer in private life."[10] Being weak, man may possibly be trusted with his own freedom, but he cannot be trusted to respect other men's liberty, unless the great forces of prescription and veneration demarcate his sphere of governance. Positive law, recently decreed by some transitory congress or other popular body, lacks this buttressing and circumscribing influence of tradition and prejudice; therefore the public should enact new positive law only under the stress of urgent necessity. Rulers will take liberties with new laws where they never would dare infringe upon the old. Even the Constitution of the United States is not sufficiently venerable to restrain the appetites of ambitious men and classes; and the potentialities for increase of power which lie hid in some of its clauses are ominous for the future liberties of America. In the last resort, once men have got into the vice of legislating indiscriminately for immediate purposes and special interests, only force can withstand the masked arbitrary force of "laws" that are no better than exactions.

With all the fanatical and preposterous theories about the rights of man (the *theories*, and not the rights themselves, I speak of), there is nothing but power that can restrain power....You may entrench yourself in parchment to the teeth, says Lord Chatham, the sword will find its way to the vitals of the constitution. I have no faith in parchment, sir, I have no faith in the abracadabra of the constitution; I have no faith in it....There never was a constitution under the sun, in which, by an unwise exercise of powers of government, the people may not be driven to the extremity of resistance by force....If, under a power to regulate trade, you draw the last drop of blood from our veins; if, *secundum artem*, you draw the last shilling from our pockets, what are the checks of the constitution to us? A fig for the constitution! When the scorpion's sting is probing us to the quick, shall we pause to chop logic? Shall we get some learned and cunning clerk to say whether the power to do this is to be found in the constitution, and then, if he, from whatever motive, shall maintain the affirmative, like the animal whose fleece forms so material a part of this bill, quietly lie down and be sheared?[11]

This dolorous plain where naked force battles against naked force is the Ultima Thule to which all people must come who ignore altogether the existence of force in politics, as they ignore most other political realities; it is the Tophet of societies that attempt to treat men as if they were divinely reasonable, competent to legislate upon abstract grounds. The facile assumption that men may safely be entrusted with much power over one another had led to the tariff, internal improvements, and fanciful schemes of foreign policy, all conspiring to begger one part of the nation to the profit of another part. Abstract sentimentality ends in real brutality. Condorcet, Brissot, and Mirabeau were men of good intentions, learning, even genius; but they were metaphysically mad; they trusted in parchment and political gimcracks, regardless of the frailty of human reason, the corruption of human character, and the great dominant interest of civilized life. They insisted upon absolute liberty, or nothing; and they got the latter. "What was the consequence of not stopping to parley with the imprescriptible rights of man, in the abstract? It is that they now have full leisure to meditate on the imprescriptible rights of kings in the concrete...I have seen men who could not write a book, or even make a speech—who could not even spell this famous word Congress (they spelled it with a K) who had more practical sense and were more trustworthy, as statesmen, or generals, than any mathematician, any naturalist, or any literati, under the sun."[12]

If the Constitution cannot be relied upon as a barrier against appetite and force, if the most capacious human intellects cannot apprehend the way to manage society, where may security against power be found? Why, said Randolph, in habitually restricting the scope of government to narrow limits, and in basing all government, and participation therein, upon practical considerations, rather than upon the fancies of the *philosophes* and of Jefferson. Let the objects of government be few and clearly defined; let all important powers, in America, be reserved to the states (as the framers of the Constitution intended), outside the scope of federal authority. Astute lovers of freedom will assert state powers constantly, so that personal and local liberties may endure; the smaller the unit of government, the less possibility of usurpation, and the more immediate and powerful the operation of prescriptive influences. "I, for one, cling to them," said Randolph of the several states, in his reply to Calhoun (January 31, 1816), "because in clinging to them, I cling to my country; because I love my country as I do my immediate connexions; for the love of country is nothing more than the love of every man for his wife, child, or friend. I am not for a policy which must end in the destruction, and speedy destruction, too, of the whole of the State Governments."[13] Calhoun never forgot that debate; and some few years later, he commenced to sacrifice his consuming ambition to the defense of those rights his aristocratic adversary had enunciated.

"The doctrine of states' rights was in itself a sound and true doctrine," writes Henry Adams, inheritor of the Federalist tradition and of an excusable family antipathy toward Randolph; "as a starting point of American history and constitutional law, there is no other which will bear a moment's examination."[14] And the preservation to our present age, despite the great consolidatory tendency of the times, of some degree of states' powers in America—in part, this is the result of Randolph's exhortations. His was the conservatism of particularism, of localism. Without the spirit of particularism, the idea of local associations and local rights, perhaps no sort of conservatism is practicable.

Randolph's second security for justice and liberty lay in common-sense government. "Mr. Chairman, I go for solid security." Most men may be trusted to choose their own representatives, but few can be trusted farther, in politics: illusions of direct democracy lead to direct tyranny. The franchise should be the privilege of citizens whose stake in the commonwealth, and whose moral character, to some extent lift them above the temptations of power to which corrupt human nature is terribly susceptible. Freeholders only should have the vote; property must have its special representation and protection, since property travels with power—"You can only cause them to change hands"; and if power be transferred to the propertyless, soon they will make themselves affluent. Government is not a matter of simple nose-counting: "No, sir, a negro boy with a knife and a tallystick, is a statesman complete in this school." King Numbers, the principle of determining profound questions (really matters to be settled by application of high moral principles and enlightened expediency) by a tally of heads, is the iron despot of modern times. The application of "democratic methods" arbitrarily to every controversy, heedless of particular circumstances and intricacies, is consummate stupidity. "It is not an incantation. It is no talisman. It is not witchcraft. It is not a torpedo to benumb us."[15] Randolph declared he would flee from old Virginia, if the time came when this notion should be applied in all its rigor. Taxation without representation certainly is tyranny, yet precisely this is introduced by democrats who give power to the unpropertied classes: men of property, the rampart of a state, are abandoned to be plundered at discretion by the ochlocracy.

"Among the strange notions which have been broached since I have been in the political theatre, there is one which has lately seized the minds of men, that all things must be done for them by the Government, and that they are to do nothing for themselves: the Government is not only to attend to the great concerns which are its province, but it must step in and ease individuals of their natural and moral obligations. A more pernicious notion cannot prevail. Look at that ragged fellow staggering from the whiskey shop, and see that slattern who has gone there to reclaim him; where are their children? Runnning about, ragged, idle, ignorant, fit candidates for the penitentiary. Why is all this so? Ask

the man and he will tell you, 'Oh, the Government has undertaken to educate our children for us.' ''[16] When unlimited powers
of legislating are surrendered to the mass of men, in obedience
to the dictates of an abstract egalitarianism, such a transfer of private duties to the public burdens surely will follow.

But Jeffersonian political doctrines would not down; they would
efface his beloved "country," Old Virginia, Randolph knew; and
by the time of the Virginia Convention of 1829-1830, their complete triumph was at hand in the Old Dominion. Marshall was
at the Convention, and Madison, and Monroe, old men all of
them, and all perturbed by this wave of constitutional revision
that was sweeping through the seaboard states. Then Randolph's
shrill voice rose above the bumble of talk, and the Convention
listened in an uneasy silence to his supreme warning against the
democratic propensity for incessant alteration. "Change is not reform," he repeated; he eulogized the old constitution of Virginia
as Burke had defended old English ways; he spoke up for the
preponderance of the wealthier eastern counties, for the aristocratic
county courts, for the freehold suffrage, for the vestiges of English institutions. All these were swept away, in 1830, but Randolph's words outlive the society that evoked them. In the history
of American political thought, there have been few speeches or
essays so abundant in striking truths and flashes of insight as his
opening address at the Convention.

Mr. Chairman, the wisest thing this body could do, would be to return
to the people from whom they came, *re infecta*. I am very willing to lend
my aid to any very small and moderate reforms, which I can be made
to believe that this our ancient Government requires. But, far better
would it be that they were never made, and that our Constitution remained unchangeable like that of Lycurgus, than that we should break
in upon the main pillars of the edifice....

It has been better said, than I am capable of saying it, that the lust
of innovation—for it is a lust—that is the proper term for an unlawful
desire—this lust of innovation—this *rerum novarum lubido*—has been the
death of all Republics....Recollect that change is not always amendment.
Remember that you have to reconcile to new institutions the whole mass

of those who are contented with what they have, and seek no change—and besides these, all the disappointed of the other class....[17]

On December 30, 1829, he opposed the insertion of any amending-clause in the new constitution, any invitation to the "maggot of innovation," any suggestion that might arouse the tinkering passions of the next decade or the next generation. Change comes soon enough without paving the way for it. "Sir, the great opprobrium of popular Government is its *instability*. It was this which made the people of our Anglo-Saxon stock cling with such pertinacity to an independent judiciary, as the only means they could find to resist this vice of popular Governments....A people may have the best form of Government that the wit of man ever devised; and yet, from its uncertainty alone, may, in effect, live under the worst Government in the world."[18]

In almost his last remarks at the Convention, Randolph spoke of "a principle which he had learned before he came into public life; and by which he had been governed during the whole course of his life, that it was always unwise—yes—highly unwise, to disturb a thing that was at rest."[19] Here shone the essence of this fierce and gallant man's political wisdom. He had begun as a "Jacobin enragé," and he had learned that society cannot be mended on Procrustes' bed. He saw his Old Virginia dissolving round him; he heard the slavery-question "fire bell in the night" tolling ever louder; in his last year of existence, the Tariff of Abominations and the Force Act threatened to reduce the South to the condition of a subject province. Randolph had hoped that he might end "like a gamecock in the pit"; and while Nullification dismayed America, John Randolph of Roanoke expired as he had lived, with a fantastic nobility.

He left a successor whose ambitions he had always suspected and who at that moment seemed close to ruin: John Caldwell Calhoun. First Randolph had converted Calhoun to strict state-sovereignty views, and presently to a conviction that the foundation of political abstraction which underlay popular American sentiment was treacherous. A few years more, and Calhoun, the son of a heavy-handed frontier democrat, would write that Jeffersonian theories of equality were pernicious:

We now begin to experience the danger of admitting so great an error to have a place in the declaration of our independence. For a long time it lay dormant; but in the process of time it began to germinate, and produce its poisonous fruits....Instead, then, of all men having the same right to liberty and equality, as is claimed by those who hold that they are all born free and equal, liberty is the noble and highest reward bestowed on mental and moral development, combined with favorable circumstance.[20]

The Southern planter-society, which for a time wore an egalitarian mask, had come to perceive its own innate conservatism.

3

That zeal which flared like Greek fire in Randolph burned in Calhoun, too; but it was contained in the Cast-Iron Man as in a furnace, and Calhoun's passion glowed out only through his eyes. No man was more stately, more reserved, more regularly governed by an inflexible will. Calvinism moulded John C. Calhoun's character as it shaped his speeches and books; for though the dogma proper was dying in him as it had decayed in the Adamses—so that Calhoun, like John Adams, squinted toward Unitarianism— still there remained that relentless acceptance of logic, that rigid morality, that servitude to duty; and these things made the man constant in purpose, prodigious in energy.

Unlike Randolph—who possessed, along with his ancient lineage, the richest library in Virginia—all his life Calhoun was a man of few books, relying upon independent meditation. Although many degrees removed from Lincoln's "short and simple annals of the poor," the Calhouns were tough upcountry Carolinians, tried and purged in the Indian terrors of the border, belligerent champions of frontier democracy. Where the boy Randolph read the English novelists and dramatists and Quixote and Gil Blas, the young Calhoun memorized passages from *The Rights of Man*. It was experience of the world, running contrary to his early discipline, that made of him a conservative. At Yale, when a student, he dared to confute the mighty Federalist professor Timothy Dwight; and he entered politics as a Jeffersonian, a nationalist and expansionist, an advocate of internal improvements, and a War Hawk. From the beginning he set his sights high; presently the presidency of the United States became his target. But one moving conviction, which in Calhoun overruled all his other ideas and even mastered his burning ambition, intervened to convert him into the most resolute enemy of national consolidation and of omnicompetent democratic majorities: his devotion to freedom. This principle ruined him as a politician. As a man of thought and a force in history, he was transfigured by it.

"If there be a political proposition universally true," Calhoun said, "one which springs directly from the nature of man, and is independent of circumstances,—it is, that irresponsible power is inconsistent with liberty, and must corrupt those who exercise it. On this great principle our political system rests."[21] Calhoun loved the Constitution of the United States; in him was nothing of Randolph's suspicion of the federal organization from its very inception, "the butterfly with poison under its wings." Because he loved it, he brought it close to destruction in 1832. Because he loved it, he proposed that it be altered—or strengthened—to protect the rights of sectional minorities. Otherwise, said Calhoun, civil war would shake the nation to its foundations; and whatever the outcome of that war, the United States could never again be the same people under the same laws. He was a prophet wholly accurate.

To enter that labyrinth of dead politics and disappointed hopes within which Calhoun's first dozen years as a national politician were encompassed is not to our present purpose. Those were the years when Calhoun listened to Randolph's sarcastic passion, first with stiff antagonism, presently with dawning conviction; then the tariff of 1824 opened like a great crack in the earth before Calhoun, and he knew that in his early years he had sadly misunderstood the nature of politics and the tendency of the nation. He had believed the Republic to be guided by a benevolent popular reason; and now it was manifest that if reason operated in the enactment of the new tariff, it was a malignant reason, calculated to plunder the people of one section in order to benefit a class of persons in another section of the country. Calhoun was no narrow particularist; he had shared the nationalistic ambitions of 1812; but here he discovered a shameless imposition, a contempt for the rights of the South so long as legislation benefited the constituents of a congressional majority. Calhoun had believed the Constitution a secure safeguard against oppression by section or class; and now it seemed that, given selfish interest sufficiently powerful, majorities would warp the Constitution to suit their ends. Calhoun had thought that an appeal to the popular sense of right could redress occasional legislative injustice; and now it could hardly be denied that Congressmen who voted for the tariff of 1824 merely were gratifying the avarice of the people they represented.

A mind like Calhoun's works solemnly and ponderously. He did not at once go over to Randolph and defiance; but with the passage of the years, Calhoun moved unflinchingly toward a repudiation of optimism, egalitarianism, meliorism, and Jeffersonian democracy. Presently he had gone beyond Randolph. Calhoun passionately desired popularity and office, but he did not value these things above his conscience: therefore he surrendered his national reputation in order to protect his state, his section, his order, and the traditions of American rural society. "Democracy, as I understand and accept it, requires me to sacrifice myself *for* the masses, not *to* them. Who knows not that if you would save the people, you must often oppose them?"[22] And Calhoun thought he might be able to save something else besides: the Union. That he failed in every one of these hopes is undeniable. But he did succeed in endowing a dumb and bewildered Southern conservatism with political philosophy; and he described unequivocally the forbidding problem of the rights of individuals and groups menaced by the will of overbearing majorities.

"Stripped of all its covering," Calhoun declared in his terse and inexorable way, "the naked question is, whether ours is a federal or a consolidated government; a constitutional or absolute one; a government resting ultimately on the solid basis of the sovereignty of the States or on the unrestrained will of a majority; a form of government, as in all other unlimited ones, in which injustice, and violence, and force must finally prevail."[23] He was not speaking of South Carolina alone, nor even merely of the Southern states, Calhoun said: once the absolute power of majorities to do as they like with minorities is accepted, the liberties of no section or class are safe. Having reduced South Carolina to submission, the interests which passed the Tariff of Abominations and the Force Act would proceed to other conquests. He predicted a similar exploitation of industrial workers in the Northern cities: "After we are exhausted, the contest will be between the capitalists and the operatives; for into these two classes it must, ultimately, divide society. The issue of the struggle here must be the same as it has been in Europe. Under the operation of the system, wages must sink more rapidly than the prices of the necessaries of life, till the portion of the products of their labor left to them, will be barely sufficient to preserve existence. For the present, the pressure is on our section."[24] These words were written in 1828, two decades before the promulgation of the Communist Manifesto; and they were written by the conservative planter of Fort Hill, who warned the old agricultural interest and the new industrial interest and the yet inchoate masses of industrial labor that when law is employed to oppress any class or section, the end of constitutions and the substitution of ruthless power is at hand. In this fashion the industrial conservatism of Alexander Hamilton, the great Northern manufacturing interest, was invited by the agricultural conservatism of John C. Calhoun to peer into the future.

Groping for a practical remedy, Calhoun turned to Nullification, derived from Jefferson's old Virginia and Kentucky Resolutions: a State might set at defiance any act of Congress clearly unconstitutional, refuse to allow that measure to operate within her boundaries, and appeal to the other states for aid and comfort, so that the unscrupulous majority which had enacted oppressive legislation might behold the power of laws and be compelled to withdraw their claims. Nullification, obviously, was a doctrine full of perils to national existence, and John Randolph told his constituents, "Nullification is nonsense"—a State could not at once be out of the Union and in the Union. President Jackson's intrepid temper had brought matters nearly to a test of force, in which South Carolina would have been crushed, when Henry Clay's compromise (reluctantly endorsed by Calhoun) ignored the principles at stake and for some years glossed over the tremendous problem by reducing the tariff.

Calhoun knew he had failed; and for the eighteen years of life that remained to him, he sought painfully for some means of reconciling majority claims with minority rights, under the rule of law. Nullification had succeeded just this far, that it proved power can be opposed successfully only by power. Yet the essence of civilized government is reliance not upon power, but upon consent. Can the rights of minorities be adjusted to this grand principle of consent? If not, government is an imposition. For, said Calhoun, governments at heart are designed chiefly to protect minorities—numerical minorities, or economic or sectional or religious or political. Preponderant majorities need no protection, and in a rude way can exist without proper government: they have naked force to maintain themselves. The authors of the Constitution had recognized that government is the shelter of minorities, and had done their best to afford protection by strict limitation of federal powers and the added guarantee of a bill of rights. These had not sufficed:

We have acted, with some exceptions, as if the General Government had the right to interpret its own powers, without limitation or check; and though many circumstances have favored us, and greatly impeded the natural progress of events, under such an operation of the system, yet we already see, in whatever direction we turn our eyes, the growing symptoms of disorder and decay—the growth of faction, cupidity, and corruption; and the decay of patriotism, integrity, and disinterestedness. In the midst of youth, we see the flushed cheek, and the short and feverish breath, that mark the approach of the fatal hour; and come it will, unless there be a speedy and radical change—a return to the great conservative principles which brought the Republican party into authority, but which, with the possession of power and prosperity, it has long ceased to remember.[25]

"Conservative principles"—here Calhoun, so early as 1832, has begun to discern a necessity greater than "liberalism" and "progress" and "equality." These conservative principles, if efficacious, must be radical—they must go to the root of things; but their aim is to conserve freedom and order and the quiet old ways men love. Calhoun is talking of American "conservatism" in the year of the English Reform Bill, despite the customary dependence of America upon Britain for philosophical discoveries. One catches here a glimpse of the prescience of a solitary, powerful, melancholy mind which has pierced through the cloud of transitory political haggling to a future of social turbulence and moral desolation.

For eighteen years, then, Calhoun probed in his sober Scotch-Irish mind these conundrums; and in the year after his death there were published two treatises which condensed his meditations into a form as forceful and as logical as Calvin's *Institutes*. The germ of his argument he had expressed cogently in a letter to William Smith, July 3, 1843: "The truth is,—the Government of the uncontrolled numerical majority, is but the *absolute and despotic form of popular governments*;—just as that of the uncontrolled will of one man, or a few, is of monarchy or aristocracy; and it has, to say the least, it has as strong a tendency to oppression, and the abuse of its powers, as either of the others."[26] How is democratic government to be made consonant with justice? *A Disquisition on Government* endeavors to provide a general answer to this question; *A Discourse on the Constitution and Government of the United States* is an application of these general principles to the exigencies of mid-nineteenth-century America.

"Whatever road one travels one comes at last upon the austere figure of Calhoun, commanding every highway of the southern mind," observes Parrington, with that picturesqueness he sometimes attains. "He subjected the philosophy of the fathers to critical analysis; pointed out wherein he conceived it to be faulty; cast aside some of its most sacred doctrines; provided another foundation for the democratic faith which he professed. And when he had finished the great work of reconstruction, the old Jeffersonianism that had satisfied the mind of Virginia was reduced to a thing of shreds and patches, acknowledged by his followers to have been a mistaken philosophy, blinded by romantic idealism and led astray by French humanitarianism."[27] Calhoun, therefore, completes the work of Randolph in demolishing Jefferson's abstract equality and liberty, which rights Jefferson had assumed to be complementary; and Calhoun, accepting Randolph's warning against the tyrannical tendencies inherent in the manipulation of positive law by callous majorities, struggles to devise an effective check upon numerical preponderance.

The old Senator from South Carolina, writing in haste because conscious of his approaching end, makes no endeavor to follow John Adams' historical method for studying effective checks upon arbitrary power. "What I propose is far more limited,—to explain on what principles government must be formed, in order to resist, by its own interior structure,—or, to use a single term, *organism*,—the tendency to abuse power. This structure, or organism, is what is meant by constitution, in its strict and more usual sense."[28] He has commenced, then, by employing a term which since has become of major significance in any discussion of the state, "organism"; and he proceeds in a tenor equally modern. He repudiates root and branch the compact theory of government, as had Burke (except for his metaphorical adaptation of the phrase) and John Adams; government is no more a matter of our choice than is our breathing, being instead the product of necessity. No "state of nature" in which man lived independent of his fellows ever did exist, nor ever can. "His natural state is, the social and political—the one for which his Creator made him, and the only one in which he can preserve and perfect his race." But *constitution*, far from being the product of necessity, must be the work of refined art; and without this tender construction, the end of government must in great measure be baffled. "Constitution is the contrivance of man, while government is of Divine ordination. Man is left to perfect what the wisdom of the Infinite ordained."

Now true constitutions are always based upon the conservative principle: they are the product of a nation's struggles; they must spring from the bosom of the community; human sagacity is not adequate to construct them in the abstract. They are a natural growth; in a sense they are the voice of God expressed through the people; but nature and God work through historical experience, and all sound constitutions are effective embodiments of *compromise*. They reconcile the different interests or portions of the community with one another, in order to avert anarchy. "All constitutional governments, of whatever class they may be, take the sense of the community by its parts,—each through its appropriate organ; and regard the sense of all its parts as the sense of the whole....And, hence, the great and broad distinction between governments is,—not that of the one, the few, or the many,—but that of the constitutional and the absolute."[29]

We should not judge of whether a state is governed justly and freely by the abstract equality of its citizens, therefore. The real question is whether individuals and groups are protected in their separate interests, against monarch or majority, by a constitution founded upon compromise. If (for instance) government, by unequal fiscal action, divides the community into two principal classes of those who pay the taxes, and those who receive the benefits, this is tyranny, however egalitarian in theory. And so Calhoun comes to the doctrine of concurrent majorities, his most important single contribution to political thought. A true majority (to express the concept in its simplest terms) is not a simple head-count: instead, it is a balancing and compromising of interests, in which all important elements of the population concur, feeling that their rights have been respected:

There are two different modes in which the sense of the community may be taken; one, simply by the right of suffrage, unaided; the other, by the right through a proper organism. Each collects the sense of the major-

ity. But one regards numbers only, and considers the whole community as a unit, having but one common interest throughout; and collects the sense of the greater number of the whole, as that of the
community. The other, on the contrary, regards interests as well as numbers,—considering the community as made up of different and conflicting
interests, as far as the action of the government is concerned; and takes
the sense of each, through its majority or appropriate organ, and the
united sense of all, as the sense of the entire community. The former
of these I shall call the numerical, or absolute majority; and the latter,
the concurrent, or constitutional majority.[30]

Calhoun has rejected with scorn the demagogue's abstraction
called "the people." No "people" exists as a body with identical, homogeneous interests: this is a fantasy of metaphysicians;
in reality, there are only individuals and groups. Polling the numerical majority is an attempt to determine the sense of the people, but it is unlikely to ascertain the sense of the true majority:
for the rights of important groups may be altogether neglected under such arrangements. In his *Discourse on the Constitution*, Calhoun
cites as an instance of this injustice the tendency of simple numerical majorities to throw all power into the grasp of an urban
population, in effect disfranchising rural regions. "The relative
weight of population depends as much on circumstances, as on
number. The concentrated population of cities, for example, would
ever have, under such a distribution, far more weight in the
government, than the same number in the scattered and sparse
population of the country. One hundred thousand individuals concentrated into a city two miles square, would have much more
influence than the same number scattered over two hundred miles
square....To distribute power, then, in proportion to population,
would be, in fact, to give the control of government, in the end,
to the cities; and to subject the rural and agricultural population
to that description of population which usually congregate in
them,—and, ultimately, to the dregs of the population."[31]

In general, Calhoun's is a view similar to Disraeli's opinion that
votes should be weighed, as well as counted; yet Calhoun pro-

poses to weigh not merely the individual votes of particular persons, but the several wills of large groups in the nation. He proposes to take into account the differing economic elements, the geographical sections, perhaps yet other distinct interests; and they are to be protected from the encroachments of one another by a mutual negative, or rather a commonly available negative. "It is this negative power,—the power of preventing or arresting the action of the government,—be it called by what term it may,— veto, interposition, nullification, check, or balance of power,— which, in fact, forms the constitution. They are all but different names for the negative power."[32] Perhaps such an arrangement invites the stalemate of the Polish *liberum veto*; but Calhoun believes that common convenience will dissuade these chief interests or groups from petty interference with the conduct of affairs. Promptness of action, indeed, is diminished, but a compensating gain in moral power occurs, for harmony and unanimity and the confidence of security from oppression make such a nation great. In neither of his treatises does Calhoun attempt to outline a precise reorganization of the American government upon these principles, although he suggests that a plural executive might be one means of accomplishing the design: either member of the executive to represent a particular section and to conduct a particular portion of the executive business, such as foreign affairs or domestic matters, but the approval of both officers to be required for the ratification of acts of Congress. Calhoun states that true responsibility for accomplishing beneficial reorganization lies with the North, where the oppressive tariff and the anti-slavery agitation commenced; the North having set this train of events in motion, the North should be prepared to draw up a solution.

Democratic institutions will be safer in a state which has adopted the principle of concurrent majorities, Calhoun proceeds to demonstrate, and under such conditions the suffrage may be extended more widely than prudence would allow otherwise, "but it cannot be so far extended in those of the numerical majority, without placing them ultimately under the control of the more ignorant and dependent portions of the community." Where the theory of the *concurrent* majority prevails, the rich and the poor will not huddle in opposing camps, but will rank together under the respective banners of their sections and interests; the class struggle will be diminished by establishing a community of advantage.

At this point, Calhoun enters upon a kind of digression concerning absolute liberty *vs.* real liberty. Application of the concurrent-majority principle, he says, will allow each section or region to shape its institutions according to its particular needs; a numerical majority tends to impose standardized and arbitrary patterns upon the whole nation, which is an outrage against social liberty. Two ends of government exist: to protect, and to perfect society. Historical origin, character of population, physical configuration, and a variety of other circumstances naturally distinguish one region from another. The means of protecting and perfecting these separate societies must vary accordingly. This is the doctrine of diversity, opposed to the doctrine of uniformity; Calhoun echoes Montesquieu and Burke.

Liberty and security are essential to the improvement of man, and the particular degree and regulation of liberty and security in any society should be locally determined; each people know their own needs best. "Liberty, indeed, though among the greatest of blessings, is not so great as that of protection; inasmuch, as the end of the former is the progress and improvement of the race,— while that of the latter is its preservation and perpetuation. And hence, when the two come into conflict, liberty must, and ever ought, to yield to protection; as the existence of the race is of greater moment than its improvement."[33] Calhoun is referring obliquely to the menace of slavery in the South, here, but with propriety he expresses himself in general terms. Some communities require a greater amount of power than others for self-protection; these local necessities would be recognized by the idea of the concurrent majority, or mutual right of veto.

Liberty *per se* presently becomes Calhoun's topic; and he severs himself completely from Jeffersonian theory. Liberty forced on a people unfit for it is a curse, bringing anarchy. Not all people are equally entitled to liberty, which is "the noblest and highest reward for the development of our faculties, moral and intellectual.'' Liberty and complete equality, far from being inseparable, are incompatible, if by pure equality is meant equality of *condition*. For progress, moral and material, is derived from inequality of condition; and without progress, liberty decays:

Now, as individuals differ greatly from each other, in intelligence, sagacity, energy, perseverance, skill, habits of industry and economy, physical power, position and opportunity,—the necessary effect of leaving all free to exert themselves to better their condition, must be a corresponding inequality between those who may possess these qualities and advantages in a high degree, and those who may be deficient in them. The only means by which this result can be prevented are, either to impose such restrictions on the exertions of those who may possess them in a high degree, as will place them on a level with those who do not; or to deprive them of the fruits of their exertions. But to impose such restrictions on them would be destructive of liberty,—while, to deprive them of the fruits of their exertions, would be to destroy the desire of bettering their condition. It is, indeed, this inequality of condition between the front and rear ranks, in the march of progress, which gives so strong an impulse to the former to maintain their position, and to the latter to press forward into their files. This gives to progress its greatest impulse. To force the front rank back to the rear, or attempt to push forward the rear into line with the front, by the interposition of the government, would put an end to the impulse, and effectually arrest the march of progress.[34]

This is tellingly put, as neat an indictment of the social ennui latent in egalitarian collectivism as the literature of politics affords. Calhoun immediately adds, ''These great and dangerous errors have their origin in the prevalent opinion that all men are born free and equal;—than which nothing can be more unfounded and false.'' He means his observations to be applied particularly to negro slavery, but one may lift them out of their transitory significance and fit them to the tenets of conservatism in our day.

Liberty and security, then, should be measured and applied upon practical and local considerations, rather than upon abstract claims of universal right. Real liberty is best secured by the con-current majority, and thus the impetus toward progress which ac-companies and nourishes liberty is healthiest under the harmony of concurrence. Yet is any arrangement of this sort possible in government? Are not great interests too diverse for concurrence, and is not agreement obtained too tardily for efficient action by the state? Calhoun believes he can answer these objections. Neces-sity will provide sufficient incentive. Cannot the twelve individu-als who compose a jury manage to concur? Will not the necessity of mutual conciliation promote a common good feeling? Supreme among historical examples, was not this veto power an essential characteristic of the Roman Republic? Calhoun will confess the existence of no obstacle which practice and forbearance cannot surmount.

Some persons may object, says Calhoun, that a free press might accomplish all the good he expects from the principle of concur-rent majority. So exalted an opinion of the function of newspapers may seem amusing in the twentieth century, the press not having followed that line of progress which nineteenth-century optimists charted for it; but Calhoun answers the suggestion soberly. His argument is a passable summary of his whole doctrine of con-currence.

What is called public opinion, instead of being the united opinion of the whole community, is, usually, nothing more than the opinion or voice of the strongest interest, or combination of interests; and, not in-frequently, of a small, but energetic and active portion of the whole. Public opinion, in relation to government and its policy, is as much divi-ded and diversified, as are the interests of the community; and the press, instead of being the organ of the whole, is usually but the organ of these various and diversified interests respectively; or, rather, of the parties growing out of them. It is used by them as the means of controlling public opinion, and of so moulding it, as to promote their peculiar interests, and to aid in carrying on the warfare of party. But as the organ and instrument of parties, in government of the numerical majority, it is as incompetent as suffrage itself, to counteract the tendency to oppression and abuse of power;—and can, no more than that, supersede the necessity of the concurrent majority.[35]

Bold and fertile opinions, these. Calhoun's *Disquisition* is open to many of the objections that commonly apply to detailed projects for political reform. He slides quickly over formidable objections, he evades any very precise description of how the principle may be applied, and he really has small hope of any immediate practical consequence from these ideas. Yet these flaws yawn more conspicuously in the great popular reform-schemes of our era—Marxism, Fabian Socialism, distributism, syndicalism, production-planning. Calhoun is not playing Lycurgus; he is describing a philosophical principle, and it is one of the most sagacious and vigorous suggestions ever advanced by American conservatism. The concurrent majority itself; representation of citizens by section and interest, rather than by pure numbers; the insight that liberty is a product of civilization and a reward of virtue, not an abstract right; the acute distinction between moral equality and equality of condition; the linking of liberty and progress; the strong protest against domination by class or region, under the guise of numerical majority—these concepts, provocative of thought and capable of modern application, give Calhoun a place beside John Adams as one of the two most eminent American political writers. Calhoun demonstrated that conservatism can project as well as complain.

4

Randolph's sombre devotion descends into the violence of Beverley Tucker's *Partisan Leader*; Calhoun's exacting logic is followed by a decade of fire-eating, and then explosion. So far as preservation of the Old South was concerned, their conservatism was impotent—indeed, it hurried the Southern states along the road to the Civil War, which in five years did more to extirpate Southern society than a generation of civil domination by the North could have effected. The repressive nervousness of the South after Nul-

lification was no atmosphere encouraging to serious thought, and
the poverty of spirit and body which, like an Old Man of the Sea,
clung upon Reconstruction discouraged any respectable intellectual conservatism. Only vague cautionary impulses guided the
South after 1865, combining with popular distrust of the negro,
and lack of material resources, to slacken the rate of social alteration. The modern South cannot be said to obey any consciously
conservative ideas—only conservative instincts, exposed to all the
corruption that instinct unlit by principle encounters in a literate
age. The affection for state sovereignty, the duties of a gentleman,
and the traditions of society which Randolph and Calhoun ex-
tolled found their finest embodiment in General Lee; and, with
Lee, these ideas yielded to superior force at Appomattox. The political representative of those principles was a man of parts less
exemplary than Lee's, but still a man of high courage and dignity, Jefferson Davis. Eighty years later, progressive vulgarization
of those Southern instincts put into the Mississippi senatorship
that had been Davis' such a man as Theodore Bilbo.

Randolph and Calhoun left no disciples really worthy of their
preceptors, nor did they save the planter-society. Those Southern
fears and prejudices which Randolph's erratic brillance sublimated
into aristocratic libertarianism, and which Calhoun's precise wisdom compressed into a legal brief, broke free from the slender
tether by which these two lonely minds had controlled their fierce
energy. The force of Southern popular enthusiasm was smashed
by the younger violence of Northern industrialism and nationalism; long thereafter, the Southern people groped dazed through
the dark wood of the modern world, unhappily envious of a
mechanized age which was not meant for such as they.

The great majority of Southern people, indeed, never apprehended much more of the doctrines of Randolph and Calhoun
than their apology for slavery and its defense through state powers. The more subtle and enduring details of the conservatism for
which these statesmen spoke were lost upon the common Southern
mind—their distrust of popular fancies, their anxiety for continuity
of institutions, their devotion to an ennobling liberty. Within the

South itself, the levelling and innovating urge that everywhere dominated American life was at work remorselessly all the while Southern orators paid lip-service to the Virginian orator and the Carolinian prophet. A series of state constitutional conventions— Virginia's in 1829–1830 only the first—swept away those protections for property, those delicate balances of power, and those advantages of compromise which Randolph and Calhoun praised; the new constitutions expressed the triumph of doctrinaire alteration. North Carolina in 1835, Maryland in 1836, Georgia in 1839; a second wave in the 'fifties, with change coming to Maryland in 1850–1851, for a second time to Virginia in 1850, and, in the form of constitutional amendments, a large alteration of the Georgia constitution still farther during those years—these popular victories brought greater equality of abstract political right, but hardly greater freedom. Popular demands for equality and simplicity met with no effective opposition in the new Southern states—Alabama, Mississippi, Louisiana, Tennessee, Kentucky, Florida. Thus the way was cleared for the radical constitutions of Reconstruction days, the subsequent disgrace and reaction, and the permanently blighted character of Southern political life.

Democratization and simplification of government were not peculiar to the South, of course, being only the local manifestation of a national tendency; Chancellor Kent, in New York, spoke against it as bitterly as did Randolph in Virginia. The Southern planter-aristocracy could no more withstand this tide of feeling than could, in the North, the Federalists and their heirs the Whigs. Better than anyone else, Tocqueville analyzes this American enthusiasm for constitutional alteration and social levelling. It was the expansive impulse of a people whose links with traditional society were nearly severed and among whom the wide distribution of new land diminished reverence for magistrates and establishments; Rousseau and Paine and even Jefferson did no more than furnish the tinsel with which this buoyant social impulse was trimmed. In America most of all, during the universal flux of the nineteenth century, *things* were in the saddle. Randolph and Calhoun could forge the South into a section, could rally Southerners to a defense of their own economic interests, could impress upon the popular imagination the menace of centralization to the Peculiar Institution; but their talents were insufficient to reinvigorate deeper conservative ideas even in a region so much inclined toward old ways as were the Southern states. They did not much impede the advance of those impulses toward consolidation, secularization, industrialism, and levelling which were everywhere the characteristics of nineteenth-century social innovation.

Randolph and Calhoun both discerned with a good deal of acuity the nature of the threat to tradition, but they could oppose to these revolutionary energies hardly more than their vaticinations and their ability to rouse a rough and confused spirit of particularism among the mass of Southerners. This was not enough. Despite its faults of head and heart, the South—alone among the civilized communities of the nineteenth century—had hardihood sufficient for an appeal to arms against the iron new order which, a vague instinct whispered to Southerners, was inimical to the sort of humanity they knew. Grant and Sherman ground their valor into powder, Emancipation and Reconstruction demolished the loose structure of their old society, economic subjugation crushed them into the productive machine of modern times. No political philosophy has had a briefer span of triumph than that accorded Randolph's and Calhoun's.

Yet they deserve to be remembered, these devoted Southern leaders—Randolph for the quality of his imagination, Calhoun for the sternness of his logic. They illustrate the truth that conservatism is something deeper than mere defense of shares and dividends, something nobler than mere dread of what is new; their arguments, and even their failure, reveal how intricately linked are economic change, state policy, and the fragile tissue of social tranquillity. Perhaps Randolph and Calhoun and other Southern statesmen did not employ to the full that transcendent conservative virtue of prudence which Burke so often commends. But their provocation was severe; and the echo of the fight which a doomed Southern conservatism waged in the name of prescriptive rights has not yet died in the enormous smoky cavern of modern American life.

VI

Liberal Conservatives: Macaulay, Cooper, Tocqueville

You defend the conservative principles on which our ancient system of society in Europe is founded, and the liberty and the individual responsibility attendant upon it; you defend especially the institution of property. You are quite right; you can hardly conceive life without these primary laws, no more can I.

Yet this I own, that this old world, beyond which we neither of us can see, appears to me to be almost worn out; the vast and venerable machine seems more out of gear every day; and though I cannot look forward, my faith in the continuance of the present is shaken....But it is no less the duty of honest people to stand up for the only system which they understand, and even to die for it if a better be not shown to them.
—Tocqueville to Mrs. Grote, July 24, 1850.

TURN WE NOW to the gentiles. British and American liberalism began to flirt with collectivism near the end of the nineteenth century, and since then (as a movement) has surrendered almost without reservation to the intellectual seductions of what Herbert Spencer called "the new Toryism." We are in danger of forgetting how strongly attached the old liberals were to *liberty*. Political liberalism before the middle of the nineteenth century (whatever may be said of economic liberalism) was conservatism of a sort: it intended to conserve liberty. The greater liberals were men imbued with the spirit of Burke. They foresaw in the levelling spirit of their age, in the tendency toward omnicompetent governments, grave peril to personal freedom—a menace even to true human nature. Macaulay furnishes perhaps the most interesting study of the liberal-conservative mind in England; Fenimore Cooper combines these elements in the United States; and Alexis de Tocqueville, a good deal more important than his associates in this chapter, perhaps the only social thinker of the first rank since the end of the eighteenth century, endeavors to reconcile with the inevitable tendency of society those surviving ancient mores and norms which Burke had attested ringingly.

All three of these liberal conservatives were influenced by Burke; Macaulay is one of Burke's more energetic eulogists, and Tocqueville's works are shot through with Burke's ideas. For a long while, Edmund Burke exerted as strong an influence upon the nineteenth-century liberal mind as upon the conservative mind; personal and local freedoms, limitation of the scope of government, and intelligent reform, which meant so much to liberals, all are concepts Burke erected into principles. Gladstone read Burke as earnestly as did Disraeli, and for years it was uncertain which of these two might be the coming Tory leader; Macaulay decided that young Gladstone was the rising light of Toryism, and therefore drubbed him in the *Edinburgh Review*; nor did Gladstone ever disavow Burke's influence. (Burke, Gladstone said, was right in four of the five great questions with which he dealt—the exception, however, being the French Revolution.)[1] This is the liberal affection for the great Whig which occurs repeatedly in the pages of Bagehot, Morley, Birrell, and Woodrow Wilson, which Acton cannot suppress in himself, and which smoulders in collectivists like Laski. Burke taught liberals that liberty is not a novelty to be created, but a legacy to be conserved. "I am at once a Liberal and a Conservative politician," Macaulay told the House of Commons in his last important speech.

And Burke taught them much else. He reinforced in their minds a tenderness for private property and a suspicion of any political power not grounded upon a propertied interest. He reminded them that a "people" is not simply an aggregation of persons told by the head. Burke's misgiving as to Government was nearly so marked as his veneration for the State, and the liberals inherited his ideal of a government which governs so little as it prudently can, which rarely invokes its reserved powers. Such political wisdom they endeavored to apply to the problems of the nineteenth century, to the gigantic forces of democracy and industrialism, to a time when the parson and the squire were succumbing to the sophister and the calculator.

Sometimes Macaulay and Cooper were so ready to appear in the role of conservator as Tocqueville and Mrs. Grote are in the passage which opens this chapter. For in general the liberals feared the future. Nassau Senior, the Grotes, and John Stuart Mill, all Tocqueville's friends, wondered whether democracy could be reconciled with liberty. In the next generation—one can see the tendency in Matthew Arnold—the liberals began to prefer equality over liberty. This consummation of social speculation was dreaded by the three great liberals discussed in this chapter, and its menace induced Tocqueville to write the most astute study of democratic institutions, very likely, that ever will be written. Macaulay has been chosen to represent here the conservative element in British liberalism both because of his resplendent talents and because his deficiencies illustrate those perplexities which now virtually have eradicated the Liberal Party. Cooper is the most forthright thinker, among Americans, who stood for a democracy of elevation against a democracy of degradation. Tocqueville, the only man considered at length in this book who was neither British nor American, is included because he knew the Anglo-American tradition so well, because of his considerable influence upon both nations, and because after Burke he has no peer as a critic of society. Contrary to the general fate of social dialectic, their ideas acquired in the twentieth century a significance even greater than they possessed originally.

2

I have long been convinced that institutions purely democratic must, sooner or later, destroy liberty or civilization, or both. In Europe, where the population is dense, the effect of such institutions would be almost instantaneous....Either the poor would plunder the rich, and civilization would perish; or order and prosperity would be saved by a strong military government, and liberty would perish.
—Macaulay to H. S. Randall, May 23, 1857.

President Franklin Roosevelt, sometimes unfortunate in his choice of ghost-writers, once denounced the preceding passage as an aspersion upon the fair name of American democracy, deriding the false vaticinations of "that English Tory, Lord Macaulay." Thomas Babington Macaulay (although humor was not his strong point) might have chuckled at this unconscious vindication of his fears for the future of civilization in democracies: that a president of the United States should mistake the Whig of Whigs for a Tory, that the president should be oblivious to the internal decay of democratic establishments throughout the world, and that the president should place a demagogic emphasis on "*Lord* Macaulay," a baron conspicuously unbaronial, a commoner for fifty-seven of his fifty-nine years of life. Macaulay made mistakes, but not the particular mistake President Roosevelt thought he was exposing.

Everyone compares Macaulay with Burke, and of course their talents and careers are interestingly similar. Among other coincidences, both had a great deal to do with India, and both as reformers: but reformers of a different stamp. Burke's reforms were intended to purge the English in India from the diseases of arbitrary power and avarice, to secure to the Indians their native laws and usages and religions. For him, prescription was as valid in Madras as in Beaconsfield. This catholic tolerance was not Macaulay's; and with a precipitancy frequently encountered among liberals, Macaulay presumed that institutions and ideas suitable for one people readily may be engrafted—or riveted—upon another people, who are conspicuously different. In 1835, Macaulay was appointed president of the Committee of Public Instruction of the British administration in India, which committee previously had been divided, five to five, over the question of whether the government should continue to encourage Indic learning, or should adopt instead "the promotion of European literature and science among the natives." Macaulay's minute on this subject is a monument at once to the volubility and the shallowness of much nineteenth-century liberalism.[2] All the attention to veneration, to careful investigation, to respect for public rights which Burke would have manifested in similar circumstances, Macaulay sneered away. Upon his recommendation, Lord William Bentinck decreed that Westernization should eradicate the traditional culture of India. To trace the spiritual and intellectual confusion from which Indians have suffered ever since would be tedious and dismaying. E. M. Forster has depicted for us the end-product. Macaulay seemed to discern no difficulty in the way of converting Hindus into Englishmen, preferably Whig Englishmen. Macaulay's error was simply the general error of nineteenth-century colonizers and conquerors, from which few colonial administrations have been exempt; but it remains the act of a man whose conservative instincts were ill-guided and erratic, appalled at the world he himself was helping to introduce. It is a world away from Burke.

Macaulay's understanding of the relations between social cause and social consequence in his own Bleak-Age England was hardly less myopic. Throughout life, he exhibited an increasing uneasiness at the swelling of industrial populations, a terror of their potential political influence and their moral condition; and yet no one more warmly praised industrialization, urban progress, mechanization, and consolidation of every description. This paradox was thoroughly Liberal, Manchester proposing no remedies except a vague confidence in general public education and more of the hair of the dog that bit them—that is, more efficient industrial production. In the *Edinburgh Review*, Macaulay overwhelmed the paternalism of Southey's *Colloquies on Society* with a roar of scorn; but sarcasm would not cure the cancer of the proletariat. Two more generations, and Southey's Tory proposals would become Socialist proposals. A proletariat does not cease to be proletarian because it has been compelled to drowse through state schools or because the price of corn has decreased five shillings a quarter. "If we were to prophesy that in the year 1930 a population of fifty millions, better fed, clad, and lodged than the English of our time, will cover these islands; that Sussex and Huntingdonshire will be wealthier than the wealthiest parts of the West Riding of Yorkshire now are; that cultivation, rich as that of a flower-garden, will be carried up to the very tops of Ben Nevis and Helvellyn; that machines constructed on principles yet undiscovered will be in every house; that there will be no highways but railroads, no travelling but by steam; that our debt, vast as it seems to us, will appear to our grandchildren a trifling encumbrance which might easily be paid off in a year or two—many people would think us insane."[3] Macaulay's prophecy was reasonably close so far as population and debt are concerned; but for most of the rest, it was well he did not see the un-Whiggish England of 1930.

Southey's method, said Macaulay, was "to stand on a hill, to look at a cottage and a factory, and see which is the prettier"—thus to judge societies.[4] Perhaps this is no very practical method; but it may be preferable to the Benthamite calculus, toward which latter view (despite his quarrels with the Utilitarians) Macaulay steadily tended. Francis Bacon was Macaulay's model for a philosopher: "Two words form the key of the Baconian doctrine, Utility and Progress."[5] Materialism rarely has received compliments more lavish than those Macaulay tenders in this essay. He was confident of the illimitable, irresistible progress of applied science and manufactures, perfectly contemptuous of Seneca's moralizing, which he contrasted with the practicality of Bacon. "Shoes have kept millions from being wet; and we doubt whether Seneca ever kept anybody from being angry."[6] Here is a progenitor of dialectical materialism. Macaulay's contentment with industrialism extended even to enthusiasm for the "gay villas" which were commencing to uglify the English landscape.[7]

Despite the nobility of his *Lays* and the brilliance of his *History*, at such moments Macaulay is guilty of the heavy crassness with which Ruskin charged Victorian England. This is middle-class crassness. Now suppose the lower classes have become correspondingly crass, and correspondingly intent upon material development in their own interest; what exhortation from Seneca, or from St. Paul, or even from Thomas Babington Macaulay, will persuade them to docility? Macaulay thought about this problem often; and his only remedy was to keep the poor strictly away from political power. If the masses ever leap to the saddle, all this tranquil, progressive, efficient prosperity will end, Macaulay was sure. He had no intention of conserving Southey's England, but every intention of preserving Manchesterian England. Much of twentieth-century British conservatism's ammunition comes from just such imperilled Liberal depots.

Macaulay became conscious of this danger early in his political career. When speaking on the Reform Bill, in 1831, he declared that universal suffrage would produce a destructive revolution, for "unhappily, the laboring classes in England, and in all old countries, are occasionally in a case of great distress."[8] Given the suffrage, they would violate law and order in a vain endeavor to improve their material lot. When the Chartists were most active, he exclaimed: "My firm conviction is that, in our country, universal suffrage is incompatible, not with this or that form of government, but with all forms of government, and with everything for the sake of which forms of government exist; that it is incompatible with property, and that it is consequently incompatible with civilization."[9] This is the legacy of Locke. Really no cure exists for the inequality of material condition which always will make it impracticable to entrust unpropertied masses with political power: since the richer a country becomes, the more populous it grows, and inequality of incomes increases rather than diminishes. "The increase of population is accelerated by good and cheap government. Therefore, the better the government, the greater is the inequality of conditions; and the greater the inequality of conditions, the stronger are the motives which impel the populace to spoliation. As for America, we appeal to the twentieth century." So Macaulay wrote (March, 1829) in answer to James Mill.[10]

Industrial society, it appears, is permanently saddled with an immense mass of persons who must remain without property, and therefore must be excluded from political influence. This conclusion, among others, induced "Finality Jack" Russell's Whigs to speak of the Reform of 1832 as if it were immutable as the laws of the Medes and the Persians, and inspired the impassioned resistance that Robert Lowe and his Adullamites offered to both Disraeli and Gladstone when the new Reform Bill impended in 1866. Macaulay and his allies contemplated a great and permanent exclusion from the franchise—the exclusion of a genuine and conscious interest; and Burke, though certainly no proponent of sweeping parliamentary reform, had argued more than half a century earlier that the British constitution was not designed to endure such exclusions. Either the exclusion must cease, or the constitution would cease. Disraeli made the former choice in 1866–1867, and made it before the demand had become insufferably strong, so that reform would seem a gift to the newly-enfranchised, not a concession extorted from the masters of society; in this, as in much else, he followed the specific counsel of Burke. The exclusion which Macaulay and Lowe thought indispensable could not possibly endure in modern times, under parliamentary government, unless society should be transformed from a condition of contract to a condition of status. Even if the proletariat ought to be denied political privilege in modern free society, they cannot well be excluded without revolutionary alteration in the structure of the state. But though his position was untenable, Macaulay rendered honorable service to conservatism in defending it to the best of his ability. For his dread of the propertyless multitude led him to harry Utilitarian political theory. In his *Edinburgh Review* articles on "Mill on Government," "The Westminister Reviewer's Defence of Mill," and "The Utilitarian Theory of Government," he bombards the Utilitarians with an accuracy that has more than a touch of Burke's genius, and in a spirit which Burke would have commended.* From this cannonade directed by a man

---

*Repenting, however, of his youthful arrogance toward Mill, Macaulay omitted these articles from the collected editions of his *Critical and Historical Essays.*

really not much separated from them in several respects, the Utilitarians sustained heavy loss. Powerful though the authority of Bentham and James Mill remained, they had been worsted at their own particular tactics of periodical-propagandizing. Macaulay revealed that they "whom some regard as the lights of the world and others as incarnate demons, are in general ordinary men, with narrow understandings and little information."[11] Their *a priori* methods he reduces to their native absurdity, their lack of practical knowledge he unveils mercilessly, their rigid abstractions he impales on his lance. "Mr. Mill is not legislating for England or the United States, but for mankind. Is, then, the interest of a Turk the same with that of the girls who compose his harem? Is the interest of a Chinese the same with that of the woman whom he harnesses to his plough? Is the interest of an Italian the same with that of the daughter whom he devotes to God? The interest of a respectable Englishman may be said, without any impropriety, to be identical with that of his wife. But why is it so? Because human nature is *not* what Mr. Mill conceives it to be; because civilized men, pursuing their own happiness in a social state, are not Yahoos fighting for carrion; because there is a pleasure in being loved and esteemed, as well as in being feared and servilely obeyed?"[12]

Macaulay proceeds to demolish the democratic tenets of the Utilitarians. Mill had contended that men infallibly would pursue their own interest; his argument, then, must apply to the mass of the poor in his Utopian democratic scheme, with a universal franchise; and it would be the interest of the poor to plunder the industrious. True, it might not be to their long-run interest; but if monarchs seldom think in terms of long-run benefit, how can we expect a mass of humble folk to postpone their own gratifications for the sake of posterity?

How is it possible for any person who holds the doctrines of Mr. Mill to doubt that the rich, in a democracy such as that which he recommends, would be pillaged as unmercifully as under a Turkish Pacha? It is no doubt for the interest of the next generation, and it may be for the remote interest of the present generation, that property should be held sacred. And so no doubt it will be for the interest of the next Pacha, and even for the interest of the present Pacha, if he should hold office long, that the inhabitants of his Pachalic should be encouraged to accumulate wealth....But despots we see, do plunder their subjects, though history and experience tell them that, by prematurely exacting the means of profusion, they are in fact devouring the seed-corn from which the future harvest of revenue is to spring. Why, then, should we suppose that the people will be deterred from procuring immediate relief and enjoyment by the fear of distant calamities—of calamities which perhaps may not be fully felt till the times of their grandchildren?[13]

Without venturing into the great salt desert of Utilitarian controversy, still it is worth remarking here that while he dislodged the pillar of universal suffrage supporting the Utilitarian temple, Macaulay brought down a part of the roof, some of it on his own head. He brought into question every point of their logic and their view of human nature; he did them much harm; and because of that, he deserves the thanks of conservatives political and spiritual. For Utilitarianism was the ancestor of "scientific" socialism; at heart, Bentham's principles were illiberal. Bentham looks forward to a society of "planning," and with something of a poetic instinct, rather than from any logical motive, the materialistic Macaulay assaulted him. In so far as Macaulay was the knight-errant of liberalism, he chose the right ogre. The other grandfather of modern socialism was Hegel, from whose doctrines comes the totalitarian aspect of the system; and Tocqueville detected this bend-sinister origin of the Continental Left.[14] Marx's denunciations of his own intellectual progenitors notwithstanding, the two opposing households of Idealism and Utilitarianism produced a formidable bastard. By its side, the English sentimental guild socialism which culminated in William Morris was a puny child. Macaulay had the bravado to assail this powerful school very early, and at the time his criticisms were more damaging, perhaps, than the protests of the Romantic Tories.

This is Macaulay's chief service to the conservative cause. But a different piece of his, written late in life, after he had become a peer in Kensington, is better known. H. S. Randall, the biographer of Jefferson, had expressed surprise that Macaulay did not admire his hero; and the redoubtable Whig replied that he admired very little in American democracy. "The Jefferson politics may continue to exist without causing any fatal calamity" so long as free land is available; but once New England is as thick with people as old England, once wages are low and fluctuating, once vast industrial cities dominate the nation, the democratic government will prove incompetent to restrain the poor from despoiling the wealthy. "The day will come when in the State of New York a multitude of people, none of whom has more than half a breakfast, or expects to have more than half a dinner, will choose a Legislature. Is it possible to doubt what sort of a Legislature will be chosen?...There is nothing to stop you. Your Constitution is all sail and no anchor. As I said before, when a society has entered on this downward progress, either civilization or liberty must perish....Your Huns and Vandals will have been engendered within your own country by your own institutions."[15]

Forcefully expressed, this; and though America has not yet experienced fully the poverty that, Macaulay predicted, would abolish either civilization or freedom, the twentieth century to which he appealed is not yet run out. Gruffly and steadily, Macaulay warned modern society against the illiberal tendency of democracy. But what did he do to arrest the menace? Education was a palliative, he thought: the poor man might be persuaded to "find pleasure in the exercise of his intellect, taught to revere his Maker, taught to respect legitimate authority, and taught at the same time to seek the redress of real wrongs by peaceful and constitutional means."[16] This is asking a great deal from schooling, if we expect it to compensate for desperate social ills. One of Macaulay's chief reasons for deploring the consequences of ignorant violence is pathetic, amusing, and revelatory: that recently there had been "beautiful and costly machinery broken to pieces in Yorkshire." And this man distinguished in pure letters, too! One is tempted to parody Keats. Macaulay did his part to establish that curious modern cult of the God of the Machine. It is not surprising, however, that he over-estimated the power of state education: so did Jefferson and Lowe and Gladstone and Disraeli. John Adams was skeptical, but few other men in the first half of the nineteenth century foresaw the limitations of formal schooling. Aristophanes, who so much doubted whether virtue can be taught, knew more of man. In the country where compulsory education was most thorough, where children were drilled to exalt reason and to respect authority and to seek peaceful redress—in Germany—the social explosion of the twentieth century would be most ferocious.

Macaulay's other preventive was the power of rigid political constitutions, excluding the proletariat from the franchise. That principle proved inadequate to stop the passage of the Reform Bill of 1867, the Parliament Act of 1911, the progressive income-tax and death-duties, the rise of Labour, and parallel developments throughout Western society. The British constitution, contrary to Macaulay's expectation, has resisted these innovations less successfully than the American. So long as a modern state remains liberal in theory, and so long as a great part of its people are substantially proletarians, economic levelling remains a constant pressure. If one is to judge from the course of Western politics since Macaulay's day, this pressure is relieved only by the triumph of illiberal political systems or by some restoration of property, purpose, and dignity to the masses of a nation. Macaulay devised no provision for either course; he was neither a radical nor a true conservative; and so the Whigs from whom he descended are extinct, and the Liberals who succeeded him are moribund.

This brief essay has not been really fair to Macaulay. His incomparable *History* scarcely has been mentioned, or his *Lays* that commemorate the high old Roman virtue. Any schoolboy should know them. Any schoolboy *should*, but he does not: for the Baconian philosophy which Macaulay eulogized, and the system of standardized "practical education" he encouraged, have injured the study of readable history and pure literature. "We must educate our masters," said Lowe, in 1867. Every age gets the schooling it demands, and this age has insisted upon materialistic and egalitarian schooling, so that Macaulay is half forgotten; and presently, no doubt, he would be wholly forgotten, were it not that certain countervailing forces may be already in reaction against the chaos of modern schools. A conservative educational movement may revive Macaulay. Such conservatism as he possessed

was of a kind foredoomed to failure; but he served the conservative cause in a fit of absence of mind, and for that, in addition
to his great gifts, Macaulay deserves remembrance.

3

In Democracies there is a besetting disposition to make publick
opinion stronger than the law. This is the particular form in which
tyranny exhibits itself in a popular government; for wherever there
is power, there will be found a disposition to abuse it. Whoever
opposes the interests, or wishes of the publick, however right in
principle, or justifiable by circumstances, finds little sympathy; for,
in a democracy, resisting the wishes of the many, is resisting the
sovereign, in his caprices. Every good citizen is bound to separate
this influence of his private feelings from his publick duties, and
to take heed that, while pretending to be struggling for liberty, because contending for the advantage of the greatest number, he is
not helping despotism. The most insinuating and dangerous form
in which oppression can overshadow a community is that of popular sway.
                            —Cooper, *The American Democrat*

Anyone who endeavors to trace the parallel development of ideas
in Europe and in America must feel sometimes that he is treating
of superficial resemblances; that the American mind was hardly
more than the mirror of unique social circumstances; and that the
pale ghost of European civilization was as powerless to alter the
course of thought in America as the chorus was impotent to arrest the action in a Sophoclean drama. But Ortega y Gasset, that
urbane and acute defender of European culture, would remark
(in *The Revolt of the Masses*) that even today civilization could not
endure in America, were civilization dead in Europe. In the first
half of the nineteenth century, when America was rawer, the importance of European ideas was correspondingly greater. They
filtered into the United States, often against the protest of an arrogant American public; and the Americans who tempered democratic
overconfidence with old-world prudence ought to receive in our

generation the thanks denied in their own time. The boldest thinker of this description was Fenimore Cooper, belligerently American, unsparingly critical of Americanism.

Cooper was a democrat; but he was the son of a great landed proprietor of conservative opinions, and himself the champion of the Hudson River patroons. This indefatigable controversialist and novelist did his utmost to steer a course between capitalistic consolidation and Southern separatism. He tried quite as hard to reconcile the spirit of a gentleman with political equality. Stubborn as Cato of Utica, and as honest, he never yielded an inch to public delusion nor endured the least infringement of his private rights; and so presently he made himself bitterly detested by popular opinion, in the very democratic society he both defended and chastised with imprudent forthrightness. Unbending rectitude of this sort, however vexatious in its hour, becomes lovable in retrospect. Cooper believed in progress, freedom, property, and gentility. He provides a link between the liberalism of Macaulay and the liberalism of Tocqueville.

Cooper knew American democracy must be purged of its ignorance and roughness if it was to endure. The lawlessness of American agrarian avarice he depicts in old Thousandacres and his brood, in *The Chainbearer*; the brutal individualism of the pioneering spirit, in Ishmael Bush of *The Prairie*; the vulgarity of the American self-made man, in Aristabulus Bragg of *Home as Found*; the ubiquitous professional democrat, in Steadfast Dodge of *Homeward Bound*. And through many of his books runs a pervading distrust of America's anarchic temper, her appetite which respects no prescription, her intolerance that scowls from behind a bombastic affirmation of absolute liberty. Cooper was conservative in every fibre, quite as concerned for tradition, constitutions, and property as were his great legal contemporaries Chancellor Kent and Justice Story. But he saw that no kind of conservatism is possible in America unless political democracy first is made secure and just. America had no political alternative: she could choose only between democracy defecated of popular delusion and democracy corrupted by passion. The regular aim of his literary endeavors was to

demonstrate how any society, if it would be civilized, must submit to moral discipline, permanent institutions, and the beneficent claims of property. This general subjection of appetite to
reason is possible only if a society consents to be led by gentlemen.
Very English, this idea; but of greater importance in the United
States, perhaps, than our age tends to think.

When abroad, Cooper was as aggressively proud of his country as he was critical of America when at home. He was abroad
a good many years, and during that time he wrote three historical
novels of a political turn, intended as warnings to Americans of
how venerable establishments may be corrupted: *The Bravo, The
Heidenmauer,* and *The Headsman.* He feared privilege, consolidation,
and constitutional tinkering quite as much as did Randolph and
the Old Republicans. In *The Heidenmauer,* so wearisomely didactic
as a romance, so interesting as a political exercise, is this vigorous
passage:

However pure may be a social system, or a religion, in the commencement of its power, the possession of an undisputed ascendency lures all
alike into excesses fatal to consistency, to justice, and to truth. This is
a consequence of the independent exercise of human volition, that seems
nearly inseparable from human frailty. We gradually come to substitute inclination and interest for right, until the moral foundations of the
mind are sapped by indulgence, and what was once regarded with the
aversion that wrong excites in the innocent, gets to be not only familiar,
but justifiable by expediency and use. There is no more certain symptom
of the decay of the principles requisite to maintain even our imperfect
standard of virtue, than when the plea of necessity is urged in vindication of any departure from its mandate, since it is calling in the aid of
ingenuity to assist the passions, a coalition that rarely fails to lay prostrate the feeble defenses of a tottering morality.[17]

America was not exempt from this general truth. Her size, indeed, was some protection against corruption; for, Montesquieu
and Aristotle notwithstanding, republics are better on a large than
on a small scale, ''since the danger of all popular governments
is from popular mistakes; and a people of diversified interests and

extended territorial possessions are much less likely to be the subjects of sinister passion than the inhabitants of a single town or
country.''[18] Because centralization would reduce the United States
to the condition of a unitary republic, exposed to the appetites
of mobs and the manipulations of privilege, Cooper remained a
consistent state-powers advocate.[19]

Late in 1833, Cooper and his family returned to America from
an extended Grand Tour; and less than four years later, he found
himself deeply involved in the first of two distressing controversies
which blasted his popularity and injured his prosperity. Both were
the result of popular egalitarian assumptions that Cooper could
not accept. The first affair, trifling in its inception, was an alter-
cation with the people of his community, Cooperstown, who
without permission had used as a public park—and badly scarred—
a bit of land Cooper owned. He expelled the public; for this he
was fantastically reviled by local newspaper editors of the sort Mark
Twain later damned to immortal fame; he sued these persons for
libel, and eventually won, but at the cost of a soured temper and
much litigation. While these suits were in progress, Cooper published *The American Democrat*, a book full of perspicuity and courage,
cogent and dignified. Perhaps it is well this little treatise was written
before the prolongation of his struggle against the editors, and later
the Anti-Rent War, had exacerbated Cooper.

The American Democrat is an endeavor to strengthen democracy
by marking out its natural bounds. In much, the book anticipates
Tocqueville's analysis of American society. Democracies tend to
press against their proper limits, to convert political equality into
economic levelling, to insist that equal opportunity become mediocrity, to invade every personal right and privacy; they set themselves above the law; they substitute mass opinion for justice. But
there are compensations for these vices—or tendencies toward vice.
Democracy elevates the character of the people; it reduces military establishments; it advances the national prosperity; it encourages a realization of natural justice; it tends to serve the whole
community, rather than a minority; it is the cheapest form of
government; it is little subject to popular tumults, the vote replac-

ing the musket; unless excited, it pays more respect to abstract justice than do aristocracy and monarchy.[20] We cherish democracy, therefore; but we do not cherish democracy unlimited and lawless.

"It ought to be impressed on every man's mind, in letters of brass, *'That, in a democracy, the publick has no power that is not expressly conceded by the institutions, and that this power, moreover, is only to be used under the forms prescribed by the constitution. All beyond this, is oppression, when it takes the character of acts, and not unfrequently when it is confined to opinion.'* "[21] How can the public be persuaded of the necessity for these limitations? By exposure of the popular delusions concerning equality and government, and by the influence of gentlemen upon democratic society. "In America, it is indispensable that every well wisher of true liberty should understand that acts of tyranny can only proceed from the publick. The publick, then, is to be watched....Although the political liberty of this country is greater than that of nearly every other civilized nation, its personal liberty is said to be less."[22]

Cooper undertakes to analyze those popular misconceptions which endanger private liberty. Equality is not absolute; the Declaration of Independence is not to be understood literally, not even in a moral sense; the very existence of government infers inequality. And "liberty, like equality, is a word more used than understood. Perfect and absolute liberty is as incompatible with the existence of society, as equality of condition." We adopt the popular polity not because it is perfect, but because it is less liable to disturb society than is any other. Liberty properly is subordinate to natural justice, and must be restrained within limits. False theories of representation, reducing representatives to mere delegates, are a peril to American liberty; so is consolidation, in a system intended, as ours is, for diffusion. A venal and virulent press threatens decent life: "If newspapers are useful in overthrowing tyrants, it is only to establish a tyranny of their own." The inclination of democratic peoples to invade the securities of private life is a shocking perversion of liberal democracy, for "individuality is the aim of political liberty": happiness and depth of character are dependent upon it. With these and similar arguments, often em-

ployed by conservatives but expressed here with a force and precision rarely attained, Cooper attempted to awaken the American public to consciousness of its own vices. He trod on many
toes, and made himself detested, and never got his book read as
it deserves to be.

Together with the need for awakening the people to the necessity
for restraint in exercising their powers, Cooper believed the hope
for democracy lay in the survival of gentlemen, leaders of their
communities, superior to vulgar impulses, able to withstand most
forms of legislative or extra-legal intimidation. "Social station is
that which one possesses in the ordinary associations, and is dependent on birth, education, personal qualities, property, tastes,
habits, and, in some instances, on caprice, or fashion."[23] Social
station is a consequence of property, and so cannot be eliminated
in a civilized society; so long as civilization exists, property is its
support. Our endeavor should be so to arrange matters that the
possessors of superior social station are endowed with a sense of
duty. One man is *not* as good as another, even in the grand moral
system of Providence. "This social inequality of America is an
unavoidable result of the institutions, though nowhere proclaimed
in them, the different constitutions maintaining a profound silence
on the subject, they who framed them probably knowing that it
is as much a consequence of civilized society, as breathing is a
vital function of animal life."[24] Station has its duties, private and
public. We ought to see that those duties are fulfilled by gentlemen.

"All that democracy means, is as equal a participation in rights
as is practicable; and to pretend that social equality is a condition
of popular institutions, is to assume that the latter are destructive
of civilization, for, as nothing is more self-evident than the
impossibility of raising all men to the highest standard of tastes
and refinement, the alternative would be to reduce the entire community to the lowest."[25] The existence of gentlemen is not inconsistent with democracy, for "aristocracy" does not mean the same
thing as "gentlemen." "The word 'gentleman' has a positive and
limited signification. It means one elevated above the mass of society by his birth, manners, attainments, character, and social con-

dition. As no civilized society can exist without these social differences, nothing is gained by denying the use of the term.''[26] Liberal attainments distinguish the gentleman from other people; simple gentlemanlike instincts are not enough. Money, however, is no criterion of gentility. If the gentleman and the lady vanish from a society, they take with them polite learning, the civilizing force of manners, the example of elevated conduct, and that high sense of station which lifts private and public duty above mere salary-earning. If they go, eventually civilization will follow them.

In the book which someone ought to write on the idea of a gentleman, Cooper's remarks deserve an honorable place. Yet they exerted no wide influence. Gentlemen are not altogether extirpated in America, but the social and economic conditions requisite for their survival have always been unfavorable, and are becoming precarious. Only two years after *The American Democrat* was published, the Anti-Rent War in New York, which excited Cooper nearly to frenzy, disclosed how difficult was the position of gentlemen in the United States. For the existence of the gentleman has been founded upon the inherited possession of land; and the radicals of the anti-rent movement were determined that the landed proprietors of central New York should give way to farmers and squatters; no prescription, no title in law, should operate against the demand of the majority for ownership of their fields. In the long run, the farmers and squatters won, through intimidation of the landowners and timidity of the courts before popular enthusiasm. The great proprietors of the Hudson vanished from history. This violation of the rights of property, and the means by which it was accomplished, dismayed Cooper immeasurably. If democratic society were bent upon eradicating the class of gentlemen, how would it provide for its own leadership, how would it retain a high tone? That question never has been answered satisfactorily in the United States; and a marked hostility toward large property in land seems embedded in American character. ''Land reform'' was one of the first American enactments in conquered Japan, dispossessing a conservative and moderate element in Japanese society; and the United States urged upon Italy and El

Salvador "agrarian reform," and for a long while smiled upon those "agrarian reformers" the Chinese Communists. With the same sort of hostility the Manchesterians felt toward the English landed proprietors, American industrial society has resented the survival of landed estates.

"The instability and impermanence of American life," writes Cooper's best critic, "which Cooper in the last half of his career sees as endangering the gentleman's right to his property, and finally, in his last novel, the literal right to life itself, had been one of his themes in the years of his untroubled beginnings....He never found a wholly adequate symbol in which to concentrate his tragic vision, perhaps because in the depths of his nature his heart was cheerful, and the bitterness was on the surface, for all the world to see, in his mind."[27] A staunch optimism never altogether deserted Fenimore Cooper, from whom so many of the best American qualities bristled defiantly. But he lost his fight for a democracy studded with men of good birth and high principle. Most reflective Americans must fall now and then into sober considerations upon the extent of this deficiency. Perhaps the lack of the gentleman in America is most conspicuous in rural regions and small towns and the great empty states of the West, but even in the older cities, society often seems declining into an ennui formerly characteristic only of senescent peoples, for lack of leadership and tone. Perhaps without gentlemen, society bores itself to death. In such a people is no leaven of diversity. "The effect of boredom on a large scale in history is underestimated," writes Dean Inge.[28] Today it seems a force that must be reckoned with. And by this transition, we come to Alexis de Tocqueville.

4

It is believed by some that modern society will be always changing its aspect; for myself, I fear that it will ultimately be too invariably fixed in the same institutions, the same prejudices, the same manners, so that mankind will be stopped and circumscribed; that the mind will swing backwards and forwards forever without begetting fresh ideas; that man will waste his strength in bootless and solitary trifling, and, though in continual motion, that humanity will cease to advance.

—Tocqueville, *Democracy in America*

That facility of the French for generalization, which turned the world upside down, reached its apex in Alexis de Tocqueville. He employed the methods and the style of the *philosophes* and the Encyclopedists to alleviate, more than a half-century later, the consequences of their books. In some respects, the pupil, Tocqueville, excels his philosophical master, Burke: certainly his *Democracy* contains an impartial examination of the new order which Burke never had time or patience to undertake. Tocqueville is a writer who should be read not in abridgement, but wholly; for every sentence has significance, every observation sagacity. The two big volumes of *Democracy* are a mine of aphorisms, his *Old Régime* is the germ of a hundred books, his *Souvenir* is packed with a terse brilliance of narrative that few memoirs possess. Some people besides professors still read Tocqueville. They ought to, because he was the best friend democracy ever has had, and democracy's most candid and judicious critic.

Although he was judge and legislator and foreign minister, and enjoyed a great literary success, Tocqueville felt himself to be nearly a failure. In Macaulay's essay on Machiavelli is a passage which struck the fancy of that omnivorous reader John Randolph, though he did not know the author's name when he came upon the article in the *Edinburgh Review*; Randolph applied this description to his own situation; and certainly Tocqueville's sentiments were similar. "It is difficult to conceive any situation more painful than that of a great man condemned to watch the lingering agony of an exhaused country, to tend it during the alternate fits of stupefaction and raving which precede its dissolution, and to see the symptoms of vitality disappear one by one, till nothing is left but coldness, darkness, and corruption." The spirit of a gentleman and the high talents of remarkable individuals, Tocqueville thought, were sliding into an engulfing mediocrity, and society was confronted with the prospect of a life-in-death. The futility of crying against the monstrous deaf and blind tendency of the times made Tocqueville painfully conscious of his impotence and insignificance. But he was no mere railer against circumstance; he never lost hope of ameliorating those problems which resulted from the levelling inclination of society; and his influence upon posterity has been more considerable than he hoped.

Democratic despotism: in this phrase, which the hesitating Tocqueville adopted only for lack of a better, he described the conundrum of modern society. The analysis of democratic despotism is his supreme achievement as a political theorist, a sociologist, a liberal, and a conservative. "I am not opposed to democracies," he wrote to M. Freslon, in 1857. "They may be great, they may be in accordance with the will of God, if they be free. What saddens me is, not that our society is democratic, but that the vices which we have inherited and acquired make it so difficult for us to obtain or to keep well-regulated liberty. And I know nothing so miserable as a democracy without liberty."[29] Harold Laski remarks that Tocqueville, essentially an aristocrat, was "unable to accept without pain the collectivist discipline" toward which centralized democratic polities remorselessly tend. Legislative power, once it is wholly in the hands of the mass of men, is applied to purposes of economic and cultural levelling.[30] Quite so; the collectivist discipline was more repugnant to Tocqueville—and to any liberal or conservative, of whatever origins—than the worst stupidities of the old régime. Like Aristotle (and some reputable writers have declared that Tocqueville was the greatest political thinker since Aristotle, although Tocqueville himself found little in Aristotle's *Politics* which he thought applicable to modern problems), Tocqueville was always searching for ends. A political system which forgets ends and worships averages, a "collectivist discipline," for Tocqueville was bondage worse than slavery of the old sort. Society ought to be designed to encourage the highest moral and intellectual qualities in man; the worst threat of the new democratic system is that mediocrity will not only be encouraged, but may be enforced. Tocqueville dreads the reduc-

tion of human society to an insect-like arrangement, the real gravi-
tation toward which condition has been described by Wyndham
Lewis in his stories of *Rotting Hill* and by C. E. M. Joad in *Decadence*.[31] Variety, individuality, progress: these Tocqueville struggles to conserve.

Whenever social conditions are equal, public opinion presses with enormous weight upon the mind of each individual; it surrounds, directs,
and oppresses him; and this arises from the very constitution of society
much more than from its political laws. As men grow more alike, each
man feels himself weaker in regard to all the rest; as he discerns nothing
by which he is considerably raised above them or distinguished from
them, he mistrusts himself as soon as they assail him. Not only does
he mistrust his strength, but he even doubts of his right, and he is very
near acknowledging that he is in the wrong, when the great number
of his countrymen assert that he is so. The majority do not need to force
him; they convince him. In whatever way the powers of a democratic
community may be organized and balanced, then, it will always be extremely difficult to believe what the bulk of the people reject or to profess
what they condemn.[32]

Such generalizations, though bold as those of the *philosophes*,
were far better founded upon particular knowledge than had been
the speculations on *a priori* assumptions which characterized the
eighteenth-century social ideas. By his extensive investigations into
American life, by his acquaintance with England, by his political
career, and by his unassuming erudition, Tocqueville was prepared
to pronounce with authority upon human and social nature. He
wrote with care, eager to be just. "Of all writers, he is the most
widely acceptable, and the hardest to find fault with. He is always
wise, always right and as just as Aristides."[33] This is the opinion
of Lord Acton. Tocqueville was determined to escape self-delusion,
at whatever cost to peace of mind. Believing with Burke that Providence paves the way for enormous changes in the world, and that
to oppose such changes when their direction is manifest amounts
to impiety, he was willing to surrender much to the new
democracy—even, to a considerable extent, elevation of mind. "In

the democratic society of which you are so proud,'' said that courageous genius Royer-Collard to Tocqueville, ''there will not be
ten persons who will thoroughly enter into the spirit of your
book.''[34] But Tocqueville was not willing to let democracy become
a cannibal; he would resist, so far as he could, the sacrifice of
democracy's virtues upon the altar of democracy's lusts.

The insidious vice of democracy, Tocqueville discerned, is that
democracy preys upon itself, and presently exists only corrupt and
hideous—still, perhaps, preserving its essential characteristic of
equality, but devoid of all those aspirations toward liberty and
progress which inspired its early triumph. Most critics of democracy had declared that political egalitarianism must end in
anarchy—or, barring that, tyranny. Alexis de Tocqueville was not
in bondage to the past, although he had a strong respect for historical knowledge: the future need not always be like what went before, he wrote, and neither of these hoary alternatives is the
probable consummation of modern egalitarianism. What menaces
democratic society in this age is not a simple collapse of order,
nor yet usurpation by a single powerful individual, but a tyranny
of mediocrity, a standardization of mind and spirit and condition
enforced by the central government, precisely what Laski calls ''the
collectivist discipline.'' He foresaw the coming of the ''social welfare state,'' which agrees to provide all for its subjects, and in turn
exacts rigid conformity. The name democracy remains; but
government is exerted from the top downward, as in the Old
Régime, not from the masses. This is a planners' society, dominated by a bureaucratic elite; but the governors do not form an
aristocracy, for all the old liberties and privileges and individuality
which aristocracy cherishes have been eradicated to make way for
a monotonous equality that the managers of society share.

I think, then, that the species of oppression by which democratic nations
are menaced is unlike anything that ever before existed in the world;
our contemporaries will find no prototype of it in their memories. I seek

in vain for an expression that will accurately convey the whole of the idea I have formed of it; the old words *despotism* and *tyranny* are inappropriate; the thing itself is new, and since I cannot name, I must attempt to define it.

I seek to trace the novel features under which despotism may appear in the world. The first thing that strikes the observation is an innumerable multitude of men, all equal and all alike incessantly endeavoring to procure the petty and paltry pleasures with which they glut their lives. Each of them, living apart, is as a stranger to the fate of all the rest; his children and his private friends constitute to him the whole of mankind. As for the rest of his fellow citizens, he is close to them, but he does not see them; he touches them, but he does not feel them; he exists only in himself and for himself alone; and if his kindred still remain to him, he may be said at any rate to have lost his country.

Above this race of men stands an immense and tutelary power, which takes upon itself alone to secure their gratifications and to watch over their fate. That power is absolute, minute, regular, provident, and mild. It would be like the authority of a parent if, like that authority, its object was to prepare men for manhood; but it seeks, on the contrary, to keep them in perpetual childhood; it is well content that the people should rejoice, provided that they think of nothing but rejoicing. For their happiness such a government willingly labors, but it chooses to be the sole agent and the only arbiter of their necessities, facilitates their pleasures, manages their principal concerns, directs their industry, regulates the descent of property, and subdivides their inheritances; what remains, but to spare them all the care of thinking and all the trouble of living?

Thus it every day renders the exercise of the free agency of man less useful and less frequent; it circumscribes the will within a narrower range and gradually robs a man of all the uses of himself. The principle of equality has prepared men for these things; it has predisposed them to endure them and often to look on them as benefits.[35]

Here a kind of humanitarian Egyptian or Peruvian society is described—just the sort of state British and American collectivistic reformers project today. Most advocates of planned economy, indeed, hardly are able to understand Tocqueville's loathing for an existence like this. The omnicompetent, paternalistic state, guiding all the affairs of mankind, satisfying all individuals' wants, is the ideal of twentieth-century social planners. This arrangement is intended to gratify the material demands of humanity, and twentieth-century social aspiration, so saturated with the ideas of Bentham and of Marx, scarcely conceives of wants that are not material. That men are kept in perpetual childhood—that, in spirit, they never become full human beings—seems no great loss to a generation of thinkers accustomed to compulsory schooling, compulsory insurance, compulsory military service, and even compulsory voting. A world of uniform compulsion is death to variety and the life of the mind; knowing this, Tocqueville felt that the materialism which democracy encourages may so far obsess the public consciousness as to stifle, in all but a few independent souls, the ideas of freedom and variety.

"A native of the United States clings to this world's goods as if he were certain never to die; and he is so hasty in grasping at all within his reach that one would suppose he was constantly afraid of not living long enough to enjoy them. He clutches everything, he holds nothing fast, but soon loosens his grasp to pursue fresh gratifications."[36] This passion of avarice is not a vice peculiar to America, Tocqueville explains; it is a product of democratic times generally. An aristocrat, and the society to which he furnishes the tone, may hold riches in contempt—valor, honor, and pride of family being stronger impulses; but where commercialism fascinates even the most influential class among a people, presently that interest excludes almost all others. The middle classes, by their example, convince the mass of people that aggrandizement is the object of existence. And once the masses embrace this conviction, they do not rest until the state is reorganized to furnish them with material gratifications. Already, in America, this materialism tends toward standardization of character: "This gives to all their passions a sort of family likeness and soon renders the survey of them monotonous."[37] As older nations surrender to the democratic impulse, they succumb to materialism proportionately.

As a governing force in society, materialism is open to two overpowering objections: first, it enervates the higher faculties of man;

second, it undoes itself. Materialism may be a negative vice, rather than a positive: "The reproach I address to the principle of equality is not that it leads men away in the pursuit of forbidden enjoyments, but that it absorbs men wholly in quest of those which are allowed. By these means a kind of virtuous materialism may ultimately be established in the world, which would not corrupt, but enervate, the soul and noiselessly unbend its springs of action."[38] (How much more profound is this than Macaulay's naive delight in "beautiful and costly machinery"!) Presently such absorption in the finite quite eclipses any realization of the infinite; and man, oblivious to the existence of spiritual powers or of God Himself, ceases to be truly human. "Democracy encourages a taste for physical gratification; this taste, if it become excessive, soon disposes men to believe that all is matter only; and materialism, in its turn, hurries them on with mad impatience to these same delights; such is the fatal circle within which democratic nations are driven round. It were well that they should see the danger and hold back."[39]

After some passage of time, this preoccupation with getting and spending undermines the social structure which makes material accumulation possible. "If men were ever to content themselves with material objects, it is probable that they would lose by degrees the art of producing them; and they would enjoy them in the end, like the brutes, without discernment and without improvement."[40] For whatever enlarges the soul, renders the soul more fit for practical abilities in the process. Moral decay first hampers and then strangles honest government, regular commerce, and even the ability to take genuine pleasure in the goods of this world. Compulsion is applied from above as self-discipline relaxes below, and the last liberties expire under the weight of a unitary state. Once a society has slipped so far, almost no barrier remains to withstand absolutism. "Since religion has lost its empire over the souls of men, the most prominent boundary that divided good from evil is overthrown; kings and nations are guided by chance and none can say where are the natural limits of despotism and the bounds of license."[41] The state assumes the right to invade every detail of private life; this usurpation is endorsed by the dislike which undiscriminating democracies manifest toward individual differences; and at length the commerical and industrial impulse which commenced this chain of causation is broken by the importunate interference and insufferable burden of the super-state.

Is this triumph of democratic despotism inevitable? The extension of democratic institutions throughout the whole world is certainly inevitable, Tocqueville answers, and seems so much a work of Providence that we ought to accept it as a process divinely ordained. But the perversion of democratic society into a sea of anonymous beings, social droplets, deprived of true family, true freedom, and true purpose, although terribly possible, is not yet inevitable. Against this, intelligent men should struggle like fanatics; for the Benthamite dream of social organization, in which the lonely, friendless, selfish, and hopeless individual confronts the leviathan state, in which all ancient affections and groupings have been eradicted and materialism has been substituted for traditional duties—this may be averted by the force of ideas, or so we should hope. Eternal vigilance and incessant criticism will be required, however, if the tendency of democratic peoples toward a life-in-death monotony, a Byzantine dreariness, is to be arrested in any degree. The forces which impel mankind toward democratic despotism are of tremendous power. Tocqueville analyzes them at length, notably in the fourth book of the second volume of *Democracy*. Chief among these causes, in addition to the materialism already remarked, are the democratic proclivities to simplicity of concept and structure, to centralization, and to standardization.

First, democratic peoples have a deep-founded dislike for hierarchy, intermediate orders, privileges, and special associations of every description. Complexity and diversity are annoyingly difficult for common minds to appreciate, and this vexation is erected into detestation on principle. Even supernatural beings, intermediate between God and man, tend to fade from the religion of democratic societies; the average man prefers the simple relationship of individual confronting Divinity directly. If democracies will not tolerate angels or devils, they are still less likely to endure vestiges of aristocracy, limited franchises, privileged persons, and those other institutions which interpose barriers between the government and the private concerns of citizens. Thus the trend of democratic simplification is to efface gradually those very safeguards which make libertarian democracy possible. Tocqueville repeatedly describes the function of an aristocracy in protecting freedom. "Nothing in the world is so conservative in its views as an aristocracy. The mass of the people may be led astray by ignorance or passion; the mind of a king may be biased and made to vacillate in his designs; and, besides, a king is not immortal. But an aristocratic body is too numerous to be led astray by intrigue, and yet not numerous enough to yield readily to the intoxication of unreflecting passion. An aristocracy is a firm and enlightened body that never dies."[42] But this instrument for checking arbitrary power and insuring the continuity of civilization invariably is eradicated by a triumphant democracy.

Second, the readiness of democratic states to concentrate in the central government all real power soon poisons at the root true democracy, which is a product of local institutions and self-reliance. More perspicuous than the Federalists and many of the Tories, Tocqueville perceived, as did Randolph and Calhoun, that liberty is intimately connected with particularism. Consolidation is the instrument of innovation and despotism. The Old Régime in France erred in considering consolidation a conservative device: on the contrary, consolidation made possible the overthrow of a multitude of ancient interests by one single wave of revolutionary violence. The consolidated machine of government the Bourbons had established was promptly converted to Jacobinical purposes.

Not only is a democratic people led by its own taste to centralize its government, but the passions of all the men by whom it is governed constantly urge it in the same direction. It may easily be foreseen that almost all the able and ambitious members of a democratic community will labor unceasingly to extend the powers of government, because they all hope at some time or other to wield those powers themselves. It would be a waste of time to attempt to prove to them that extreme centralization may be injurious to the state, since they are centralizing it for their own benefit. Among the public men of democracies, there are hardly any but men of great disinterestedness or extreme mediocrity who seek to oppose the centralization of government; the former are scarce, the latter powerless.[43]

The spectacle of the states of the American union today— resentful yet mendicant-like, fearful of consolidation but cursed with an insatiable appetite for federal grants-in-aid—is sufficient illustration of Tocqueville's observation. Only one thing is safe from revolution, said Tocqueville: centralization. Only one thing could not be set up in France—a free government; and only one thing could not be destroyed—the centralizing principle. Even with men aware of its dangerous nature, "The pleasure it procures them of interfering with everyone and holding everything in their hands atones to them for its dangers."[44] Centralization promises special favors to all sorts of interests, and its possibilities tempt simple democrats almost irresistibly. Yet centralization is wholly inimical to democracy, transferring power to the operator of the machine of government. "I am of the opinion that, in the democractic ages which are opening upon us, individual independence and local liberties will ever be the products of art; that centralization will be the natural government."[45]

Third, democratic nations are enamored of uniformity, standardization; they hate the eccentric, the grand, the private, the mysterious. They demand that legislation be comprehensive and inflexible. "As every man sees that he differs but little from those about him, he cannot understand why a rule that is applicable to one man should not be equally applicable to all others. Hence the slightest privileges are repugnant to his reason; the faintest dissimilarities in the political institutions of the same people offend him, and uniformity of legislation appears to him to be the first condition of good government."[46]

When class and caste vanish, presently even the taste to be different, to be a distinct individual, wanes; men grow ashamed of personality. While in the ages of aristocracy men sought to create imaginary differences even where no actual distinctions existed, in democratic times everything slides toward the blur of mediocrity. "Men are much alike, and they are annoyed, as it were, by any deviation from that likeness; far from seeking to preserve their own distinguishing singularities, they endeavor to shake them off in order to identify themselves with the general mass of the people, which is the sole representative of right and of might in their eyes."[47] Leadership dwindles in consequence, the enlivening energy of contrast evaporates from a people, and men become almost featureless, mere ciphers, identical and interchangeable in the social system. Intelligence shrinks proportionately. As candidates for any sort of advancement appear more and more alike, democracies tend to select men for preferment not by recognition of their peculiar talents, but by wearisome regulations and routines. "From hatred of privilege and from the embarrassment of choosing, all men are at last forced, whatever may be their standard, to pass the same ordeal; all are indiscriminately subjected to a multitude of petty preliminary exercises, in which their youth is wasted and their imagination quenched, so that they despair of ever fully attaining what is held out to them; and when at length they are in a condition to perform any extraordinary acts, the taste for such things has forsaken them."[48] Anyone familiar with American educational tendencies, or with the methods of the civil service, knows well what Tocqueville means. When ambition is deliberately stifled after this fashion, the tone of collective life must suffer.

Altogether, this analysis of democratic follies is a dismaying picture of society's stumbling progress toward a condition of servitude called democracy but in actuality a new absolutism. Its outlines have become clearer in our time. Tocqueville's most succinct description of this yawning peril occurs near the beginnning of his *Democracy*:

I perceive that we have destroyed those individual powers which were able, single-handed, to cope with tyranny; but it is the government alone that has inherited all the privileges of which families, guilds, and individuals have been deprived; to the power of a small number of persons, which if it was sometimes oppressive was often conservative, has succeeded the weakness of the whole community.

The division of property has lessened the distance which separated the rich from the poor; but it would seem that, the nearer they draw to each other, the greater is their mutual hatred and the more vehement the envy and the dread with which they resist each other's claims to power; the idea of right does not exist for either party, and force affords to both the only security for the present and the only guarantee for the future.[49]

What should be done? Marx, in these very years, was full of visions of a world purged utterly of the old order, problems solved in a proletarian upheaval, society reconstituted from base to pinnacle—or rather, all society above the base lopped away. The calm, intricate, and analytical mind of Tocqueville, aware that no knot is really untied after the method Alexander used with Gordius's, turned instead to the weary and unromantic necessity of reconciling old values with new faiths—the conservative function, so much derided, so difficult to execute, quite indispensable to the survival of civilization.

5

"I have always thought that in revolutions, especially democratic revolutions, madmen, not those so called by courtesy, but genuine madmen, have played a very considerable political part. One thing at least is certain, and that is that a condition of semi-madness is not unbecoming at such times, and often even leads to success."[50] This is Tocqueville writing of the frightful days of 1848—when, like ghosts of '93, such raving figures as Blanqui and Barbès invaded the Tribune of the Chamber of Deputies and cried out for a new Terror. Tocqueville was present at the wild street-fighting of the first strong socialist snatch at power; he saw the balloon of Marxism pricked, for the time being; and soon he was foreign minister under Louis Napoleon. The *coup d'état* of 1851 ended the public career of the critic of democracy, who would no more bow to a plebiscitary dictator than to the Parisian mob. That Tocqueville could witness these swings of the revolutionary pendulum and still hope for the future of society is testimony to his conspicuous strength of mind.

Tocqueville believed that men and societies possess free will. He held Hegel and all his school in deep contempt, scoffed at deterministic theories of history, with their chain of fatality, and remarked the factors of chance and unknown causation in historical movements—"chance, or rather that tangle of secondary causes which we call chance." His faith in Providence, genuine and pervasive as Burke's, was wholly opposed to these pretentious theories of fixed fate and national destinies. "If this doctrine of necessity, which is so attractive to those who read history in democratic ages, passes from authors to their readers till it infects the whole mass of the community and gets possession of the public mind, it will soon paralyze the activity of modern society and reduce Christians to the level of the Turks."[51] Great and mysterious movements certainly were at work in the world of the nineteenth century; but opinion and political institutions could modify and mold the action of these tendencies. Even the Old Régime could have been preserved and reformed without indiscriminate destruction, granted a little patience and good conduct: "The revolution broke out not when evils were at their worst, but when reform was beginning. Half-way down the staircase we threw ourselves out of the window, in order to get sooner to the bottom. Such, in fact, is the common course of events."[52] The common course, yes; but not the inevitable course; and a determined stand still could avert the coming of democratic despotism.

True, the difficulties presented by the raw new democracy were extremely formidable. Impatience and ignorance are characteristic of democratic ages; coarsely ambitious men generally are at the helm of state; dignity is wanting in the conduct of affairs, although arrogance is not lacking; the decay of the family, especially in America, to the status of a mere household, removes one of the ancient supports of social tranquillity; human opinions scatter like dust, unable to cohere, and it is hard to rally public opinion to any intelligent concerted action; literary tastes are superficial, reading is hasty; placidity is preferred to nobility; intellectual isolation plagues a community of mind; and, perhaps most dangerous of all, freedom of thought and discussion are badly hampered.

In America the majority raises formidable barriers around the liberty of opinion; within these barriers an author may write what he pleases, but woe to him if he goes beyond them. Not that he is in danger of an auto-da-fé, but he is exposed to continued obloquy and persecution. His political career is closed forever, since he has offended the only authority that is able to open it. Every sort of compensation, even that of celebrity, is refused to him. Before making public his opinions he thought he had sympathizers; now it seems to him that he has none any more since he revealed himself to everyone; then those who blame him criticize loudly and those who think as he does keep quiet and move away without courage. He yields at length, overcome by the daily effort which he has to make, and subsides into silence, as if he felt remorse for having spoken the truth.[53]

All the same, by the force of ideas democracy may be arrested in its descent toward despotism. Only through the influence of mind, and never by violence, may the old ways of society be conserved. Gallantry among the English aristocracy would not save that body, if it could not be supported by a system of ideas. "Military services are not enough to preserve an aristocracy," Tocqueville wrote to Mrs. Grote. "If they were, ours would not now be fallen into dust. For who could lavish life more unreservedly than the nobles of France, in every age, and from the greatest down to the least?...The last gun which defended the old manor-house of Tourlaville, half-sunken in the ground, serves only as a stake to fasten cattle to, and the house itself has been turned into a farm...the fate of an aristocracy which knows how to die, but not how to govern."[54]

Among the props of order in democratic societies, the chief is religion; and Tocqueville found in his American observations some reassurance on this score. Democratic peoples simplify religion, certainly; but it may remain with them as an abiding force, helping to counteract that materialism which leads to democratic despotism. The anti-clericalism which accompanied French democratic struggles is no necessary concomitant of egalitarianism. Separation of church and state, the Roman Catholic priests in America told Tocqueville, establishes a peaceful dominion for religion. "As long as a religion rests only upon those sentiments which are the consolation of all affliction, it may attract the affections of all mankind." Love of self, a vice especially menacing in democracies, is perceptibly checked in the United States by that devotion to unworldly aims which religion inculcates. The American propensity for innovation, which otherwise would be resistless, is compelled to respect the dictates of religious faith, a most important limitation, for it will not abide the theory of omnipotence in the state. American radicals, Tocqueville says, "are obliged to profess an ostensible respect for Christian morality and equity, which does not permit them to violate wantonly the laws that oppose their designs; nor would they find it easy to surmount the scruples of their partisans if they were able to get over their own. Hitherto no one in the United States has dared advance the maxim that everything is permissible for the interests of society, an impious adage which seems to have been invented in an age of freedom to shelter tyrants. Thus, while the law permits the Americans to do what they please, religion prevents them from conceiving, and forbids them to commit, what is rash or unjust."[55] Tocqueville, whose piety was intelligent and enduring, knew that a democratic people with religious faith will respect private rights and the portion of posterity far more reverently than a democratic people who have material success for their goal.

Laws and customs, too, if they are established in the popular affections, may keep a democracy from corrupting itself. Whatever prevents the concentration of power is preservative of freedom and traditional life. In the United States, the federal framework, township government, and the autonomous judicial power all are means for ensuring this separation; and in general, decentralization keeps from the hands of the majority, which would like to be a despot, the chief instruments of tyranny. So long as power can be denied to pure numbers, so long as great fields of human activity are exempt from the influence of government, so long as constitutions limit the scope of legislation—so long as these things endure, democratic despotism is kept at bay. If the democracy can be persuaded to accept as a habit such limitations upon its sovereignty, to approve them from reason and from prejudice, freedom may continue to exist in the same world with equality. The surest support—indeed, the only enduring support—of these checks lies in the customs, the collective habits, of a people; but constitutions may serve to tide nations over times of passion or folly. "The great utility of popular institutions is, to sustain liberty during those intervals wherein the human mind is otherwise occupied—to give it a kind of vegetative life, which may keep it in existence during those periods of inattention. The forms of a free government allow men to become temporarily weary of their liberty without losing it."[56] But he would not attempt to make constitutions immutable, for then they provoke resentment; the reins should be held lightly. "I had long been of opinion that, instead of aiming to make our governments eternal, we should tend to make it possible to change them in an easy and regular manner. Taken all round, I thought this less dangerous than the opposite course; and I thought it best to treat the French people like those madmen whom one should be careful not to bind lest they become infuriated by the restraint."[57] Now that the masses exert direct influence upon the conduct of public affairs, the chief security against abuse of their power resides in attaching them to justice and freedom by that fine mesh of affections and prescriptions which count for so much more than does the weight of positive law.

Vestiges of aristocracy, where they still are encountered, can be employed to temper the impulse of majorities told by the head to exert a tyranny over the whole of society. In America, the class of lawyers, made conservative by their training and their interests, forms a species of artificial aristocracy of talents and influence. Tocqueville knew well that public opinion always detests an aristocracy, however great its merits: "Nothing can be imagined more contrary to nature and to the secret instincts of the human

heart than a subjection of this kind; and men who are left to follow their own bent will always prefer the arbitrary power of a king
to the regular administration of an aristocracy. Aristocratic institutions cannot exist without laying down the inequality of men
as a fundamental principle, legalizing it beforehand and introducing it into the family as well as into society.''[58] In the long run,
then, probably aristocracy everywhere must become extinct. As
its members lose their immediate touch with their dependents and
inferiors, they lose their function as protectors and magistrates;
when the rent-roll increases, ordinarily power diminishes; and as
power slips from the aristocratic fist, then the rents presently are
snatched away. This tendency, sometimes violent, sometimes
almost imperceptible, can hardly be countered. Yet the society
from which aristocracy has vanished, never to rise again, is a civilization open to despotism; and tyranny, once established there,
maintains itself by pandering to the society's vices. The jealousy
for personal liberty which aristocracies possess having been extirpated, omnipotent sovereign and defenseless subject stand face
to face. ''While you preserve your aristocracy, you will preserve
your freedom,'' said Tocqueville to Nassau Senior, on the occasion of the Reform Bill of 1854. ''If that goes, you are in danger
of falling into the worst of tyrannies—that of a despot appointed
and controlled, if controlled at all, by a mob.''[59] France just then
was mastered by the first of these modern ''plebiscitary democracies''; the twentieth-century world knows their every feature.
Cling, then, while you may, to whatever is left of aristocratic pride
and tone, is Tocqueville's advice; even a faint echo of the aristocratic trumpet wakens some resistance to political absolutism.

Still another means of ameliorating democratic faults is public
education. In America, general education kept the people informed
of their immediate rights and duties; and though too often American education is superficial, care and penetration sacrificed to hasty
instruction of the many, still the quantity of instruction has kept
Americans from the ignorant impracticality which produced the
events of 1789 in France. ''It was not want, but ideas, that brought
about the great revolution; chimerical ideas on the relations

between labor and capital, extravagant theories as to the degree in which the government might interfere between the working-man and the employer, doctrines of ultra-centralization which had at last persuaded large numbers that it depended on the state not only to save them from want, but to place them in easy, comfortable circumstances."[60] But Tocqueville did not share that over-weening confidence in the efficacy of schooling which so many statesmen of his century embraced. Literacy and book-learning are of little use unless they are united to "the moral education which amends the heart."

Above all, the well-wisher of modern society should endeavor strenuously to encourage and shelter individual differences, variety of character. Uniformity is the death of high human striving. "In a democratic age the great danger is, you may rest assured, that the component parts of society may be destroyed or greatly enfeebled for the sake of the whole." To this trap the school of Hegel was hurrying. "All that in our day exalts the individual is useful. All that tends to magnify genera, and to ascribe a separate existence to species, is dangerous. This is the natural inclination of the public mind at present. The realistic doctrine carried into politics leads to all the excesses of democracy; it facilitates despotism, centralization, contempt for individual rights, the doctrine of necessity; in short, every institution and every doctrine which permits society to trample men under foot, and considers the nation as everything and the people as nothing."[61] The modern world is madly anxious to realize the dream of the eighteenth-century economists, who believed that the state should do more than govern the nation: it should shape the nation. "It must transform as well as reform its subjects; perhaps even create new subjects, if it thinks fit."[62] Tocqueville dedicated his labors to the defense of men as *men*, to traditional humanity with its lovable ancient strengths and failings; he was horrified at the notion of a "planned" human race. Socialism, of which Morelly and his colleagues were the enthusiastic prophets, is the vehicle of this standardization and dehumanization of man, using the centralized, egalitarian state as its pathway. "So true is it that centralization and socialism are natives of the same soil: one is the wild herb, the other the garden plant.''[63]

Publicly Tocqueville urged incessant attention to these correctives of democracy; but privately, sometimes, he despaired of attempts at reformation, doubting the efficacy of literature in an age of flux and appetite. ''I do not believe that in such times as these the slightest influence can be obtained by such writings as mine, or even by any writings, except by the bad novels, which try to make us still more immoral and ill-conditioned than we are.''[64] An interminable vista of gray uniformity, regimented and hedged remorselessly, individuals totally absorbed in the body politic, stretched in its alkaline nakedness before his mind's eye. ''It is probable that society in general will be melancholy enough for people of our way of thinking—an additional reason for living a great deal with each other,'' he wrote to M. de Corcelle, in 1854. ''I rejoice to find, as time goes on, that I am not one of those who naturally bow before success. The more a cause seems to be abandoned, the more passionately I become attached to it.''[65]

Tocqueville's liberal conservatism is no forlorn cause even yet. To inevitable democracy he rendered the service of strict criticism and projected reform. A. J. P. Taylor thinks Tocqueville failed in his course of action and his analysis of events during 1848: ''The greatest invention of 1848,'' Taylor says, ''which Tocqueville disowned, was Social Democracy; this was the only way in which civilization could be saved....Above all, he who loves liberty must have faith in the people.''[66] This is as if Morelly or Mably were disinterred to criticize Alexis de Tocqueville. For Tocqueville knew all too well the nature of ''Social Democracy,'' a term coined to describe the centralized egalitarian state, which does not so much choke freedom as it simply ignores freedom. And, being Burke's pupil, Tocqueville never could submit to the delusion that ''the people'' exist as an abstraction to be trusted or feared or hated or revered in place of Jehovah. None apprehended better than Burke and Tocqueville the idea of nationality and the eternal union of all generations of mankind; but the people, or masses, do not live a mystical, beneficent existence somehow independent of parties, passions, and the ordinary failings of humanity. The people do not think or act uninfluenced by ideas and leaders. Without ideas and leaders, for that matter, a people cannot truly be said to exist: in the absence of such a leaven, the people subsist only as an amorphous mass of loosely cohering atoms, a tapioca-pudding state, which social planners contemplate with equanimity. The people, under the influence of high principle, sometimes may be elevated to sublimity; they may also shout for Hitler or Stalin or any man who wants to burn a witch. Without the power of those virtuous customs and laws that Tocqueville outlined, the people become Hamilton's "great beast"; and to trust them in the abstract is an act of reckless faith far more credulous than medieval relic-veneration. Just this blind stumbling in the wake of the multitude is the error *Democracy in America* was written to reproach.

VII

Transitional Conservatism:
New England Sketches

From the moment when the great mass of the nations in Europe were taught to inquire why is this or that man possessed of such or such an enjoyment at our expense, and of which we are deprived, the signal was given of a civil war in the social arrangements of Europe, which cannot finish but with the total ruin of their feudal constitutions. It must eventually lead to the destruction of the relics which yet remain of the feudal aristocracy. Whether the arts, the sciences and the civilization of Europe will not all perish with it must yet remain a problem....The *arts* and *sciences* themselves,...genius, talents, and learning, are in the most enlightened periods of human history liable to become objects of proscription to political fanaticism.
—John Quincy Adams to John Adams (July 27, 1795)

THIS REVOLT of the masses against the social establishments, property, and intellectual traditions of the West, commencing in 1789, has continued with only uneasy intermittent truces down to the middle of the twentieth century. John Quincy Adams, judging from his prospect of France, said it might mean the return of barbarism; for popular detestation of the past, once awakened, does not limit itself to annihilation of governments and economies: if the arts and sciences seem prerogatives of a minority, or if they appear to impede gratification of popular appetites, they are involved in the general catastrophe. No possibility could have been better calculated to rouse the mind of New England in opposition to radical innovation. Severe, industrious, practical, and Calvinistic, New England character also displayed a reverence for learning; nowhere, not even in Scotland, were schooling and reading more general; and an informed public opinion began to stir against Gallic notions as soon as the French Revolution commenced. "Resistance to something was the law of New England nature," Henry Adams writes in his *Education*; yet despite their reforming-itch, the New Englanders were in their hearts deeply attached to their ancestral institutions and alarmed at impersonal forces which were sweeping their little civilization into the rapids of nineteenth-century innovation. Even the radical fanaticism of Garrison and his colleagues was only one facet of their nature: Garrison was fully as hostile toward the new industrial masses, as fearful of their potential influence, as he was tender toward negro slaves. In the thought of three New Englanders—whose careers, taken together, extend from the Terror to the Wilderness—one can trace New England's groping for conservative principle. John Quincy Adams, the tireless practical statesman; Orestes Brownson, restless as the son of Agamemnon; Nathaniel Hawthorne, the searcher into mysteries of soul—in all three of them, the conservative instinct struggled for successful expression.

With the coming of democracy and industrialism, the physical and intellectual props of conservative order were knocked away. If civilization was to survive, either these props must be rooted again or some wholly new social architecture devised. New England, which had begun in dissent, was ill qualified for either task: out of sympathy with squire and parson, contemptuous of Jacobin and sophister. But it must be said in apology for New England that the task was Herculean.

Modern industrialism, in Britain and America and most of western Europe, had smashed the economic defenses of conservative society. With accelerating speed, the control of wealth was passing from rural proprietors to industrialists and financiers, from commercial interests of the old sort to great new manufacturing enterprises. In population, predominance was slipping from country to city. And the new possessors of wealth and numbers despised tradition, or else were nearly ignorant of it. The rising entrepreneur, conscious of his recent humble origins, was tempted to contemn the established social structure: his immediate advantage lay in alteration, aggrandizement, consolidation—all forces that are inimical to tradition. The new proletarian of the Bleak Age, rootless and ignorant, sporadically hungry, knew almost nothing of the old values; also he was bored, and change is a show; and his appetites were material. Thus industrial populations, at either extreme, were recruited to liberalism or radicalism—almost never, in the early decades of the nineteenth century, to conservative allegiance. Conservative elements, always tardy in apprehending a great social alteration, for a long time were befuddled by their reverses. The "fat cattle" opposition which Disraeli and Bentinck herded; the planters who huddled behind Randolph of Roanoke; the Yankee merchants and farmers who cheered John Adams—in such groups affection for a prescriptive society still resided, but money and votes were trickling from their grip. The industrial world was a place without veneration.

Toryism, said Newman, is loyalty to persons; but the industrial world was impersonal. Previously, even in America, the structure of society had consisted of a hierarchy of personal and local allegiances—man to master, apprentice to preceptor, householder to parish or town, constituent to representative, son to father, communicant to church. Most men of means had been the magistrates and legislators and exemplars of their neighborhood. What the gentry had been in England, in some degree the Lees and Byrds and Randolphs had been in Virginia, the Van Rensselaers and Schuylers and Coopers in New York, even the old New England families in their seaports and stony townships. Taxation had been genuinely a voluntary contribution for common purposes; government, in its simplicity, was of direct and immediate concern to most elements in the commonwealth; and since social conscience operates most rigorously when social proximity is the rule, this was, by and large, a just society: corruption and negligence would have been too conspicuous to pervade for any length of time the agglomeration of small communities which furnished the strength of this older, decentralized society. Man had to look man in the eye, conscience spoke to conscience. It was a condition of existence comparatively harmonious because few great abuses could be hid. Everyone knows the faults of this seventeenth- and eighteenth-century life; but man being the imperfect creature he is, this society was as well suited to human nature as any in history—best suited, at least, to the Aristotelian view of human nature, which defines the truly natural state as the cultivation of what is highest in man.

This network of personal relationships and local decencies was brushed aside by steam, coal, the spinning jenny, the cotton gin, speedy transportation, and the other items in that catalogue of progress which school-children memorize. The Industrial Revolution seems to have been a response of mankind to the challenge of a swelling population: "Capitalism gave the world what it needed," Ludwig von Mises writes sturdily in his *Human Action*, "a higher standard of living for a steadily increasing number of people." But it turned the world inside out. Personal loyalties gave way to financial relationships. The wealthy man ceased to be magistrate and patron; he ceased to be neighbor to the poor man; he became a mass-man, very often, with no purpose in life but aggrandizement. He ceased to be conservative because he did not understand conservative norms, which cannot be instilled by mere logic—a man must be steeped in them. The poor man ceased to feel that he had a decent place in the community; he became a social atom, starved for most emotions except envy and ennui, severed from true family-life and reduced to mere household-life, his old landmarks buried, his old faiths dissipated. Industrialism was a harder knock to conservatism than the books of the French egalitarians. To complete the rout of traditionalists, in America

an impression began to arise that the new industrial and acquisitive interests are the conservative interest, that conservatism is
simply a political argument in defense of large accumulations of
private property, that expansion, centralization, and accumulation are the tenets of conservatives. From this confusion, from the
popular belief that Hamilton was the founder of American conservatism, the forces of tradition in the United States never have
fully escaped.

That the sudden triumph of democracy should coincide with
the rise of industrialism was in part the product of intertwined
causes; but, however inescapable, it was a conjunction generally
catastrophic. Jeffersonian democracy, designed for a simple agrarian people, was thrust upon an acquisitive, impatient, and often
urbanized mass of men. The nineteenth-century world was a stony field in which to sow equality; weeds came up thick. Yet
however rank the crop of democracy, conservatives could discern
no means for plucking the tares from among the corn. To diminish the franchise, once it had been extended, proved impossible;
to withhold it from new classes, perilous. Paine and Rousseau,
a cheap press, general confidence that legislation could establish
universal happiness, the insurrectionary power which urban mobs
possessed conspicuously throughout most of the nineteenth century, loss of social ascendancy by the old superior orders, substitution of individualism for communal feeling—all these influences
left conservatives nearly impotent. Afraid to make concessions,
afraid to refuse them, they were reduced to the function of trim-
mers. In America, the rapid revision of state constitutions, the
successive extensions of the franchise, the removal of state capitals from eastern cities to western sites—these manifestations of
popular sovereignty were symptoms of general infatuation with
Dinos. Conservative interests were bemused; the Federalist party
smashed, they found no better instrument than the Whig party,
which, though it boasted the talents of Webster and Clay, lacked
truly coherent principle. "A bottomless Whig," Johnson had called
Burke; but it was the American Whigs who more nearly deserved
the epithet. (Perhaps it is time, however, that some of us should

extend to them a more sympathetic consideration than they have had since 1861.)

While industrialism and democracy bombarded conservative ramparts, rationalism and utilitarianism sapped the intellectual foundations of the old system. Leslie Stephen says that Whigs were invincibly suspicious of parsons. This eighteenth-century distrust of sacerdotalism becomes outright denial of faith, in the nineteenth century. Skepticism of Hume's and Voltaire's inspiration had deluged Britain and America; Jeffersonian deism had become almost an official creed among American egalitarians; even conservatives like John Adams and Calhoun abandoned their Calvinistic inheritance for something close to Unitarianism; during his later years, John Quincy Adams suffered agonizing doubts concerning the existence of the Deity. That God willed the state, the conviction of Hooker and Burke, always had been a tremendously energizing principle of conservatism: now, influenced against their instinct by what Glanville calls the "climate of opinion," conservatives were losing their certitude; and with it went their immunity against French and Benthamite rationalism. Conservatism had become uncertain how to reply to sophisters and calculators; the poetic vehemence of the Romantics had deserted them, and they had not yet acquired the methods of the legal and historical conservatives who appeared in Victorian times.

If, then, the conservatism of nineteenth-century New England did not check effectively the flood of innovation, still New England had men of strength and genius. In a more conservative country, old England, this was the time in which Sir Robert Peel gathered up the scraps of conservatism after the debacle of 1832 and compressed them into a party once more. Peel held opinions reasonably like those of our New England conservatives—attached to old ways by instinct, but through reason half convinced of his adversaries' theories; thus he drifted into concession after concession, quite conscientiously—until at length, confident he had the Tories at his back, he was shocked to discover he had turned his back on the Tories. As the prospect of civil war grew formidable, American conservatives had hardly a party either to lead or to repudiate.

2

During recent years, several liberal or radical writers kindly recommended the formation of a true conservative party in the United States. Harold Laski, for instance, declared it would raise the tone of American politics; and Arthur Schlesinger, Jr., had a similar opinion. No doubt they were right. But these gentlemen did not wish conservatism to succeed: they approved it merely to furnish loyal opposition against innovation—an opposition ineffectual except for offering genteel criticism. Mr. Schlesinger approved John Quincy Adams as a model for twentieth-century conservatives. The left-wing advocates of conservative reorganization wish to see a conservative party which, like the English Liberal Party in the twentieth century, would be a medium for transforming existing society into a new collectivist state, an interim party. They approve a conservatism which distrusts its own postulates. John Quincy Adams was the talented representative of such conservative opinion.

Perhaps no man in American political history has been more honest than J. Q. Adams, more diligent, or more firm of immediate purpose. But as a conservative thinker, the second great member of what John Randolph called ''the American house of Stuart'' was vacillating. He had seen Federalism die; he had come to believe, as did Tocqueville, that the growth of democracy was providential; he felt the pressing necessity for conservative principle in the conduct of American affairs, but he never quite discovered how to fix upon it. Brooks Adams, his grandson (half the history of American conservatism, or nearly that, must be an account of the Adamses) declares, ''John Quincy Adams appears to be the most interesting and suggestive personage of the early nineteenth century;'' and in several respects, so the sixth president certainly is. His immense Diary is the best window upon the thought of his age in America, his scientific diligence advanced American learning, and his aspirations for developing national character were eloquently noble. But as a conservative thinker, he was insufficient; as a conservative leader, unfortunate. His suspicion of men's motives exceeded Randolph's; his tone toward his associates was no less haughty; and his personal austerity made impossible the retention of any effective popular following. Lord Lyttleton, who had known Adams the diplomat in Russia and London, once wrote that the second Adams, "of all the men whom it was ever my lot to accost, and to waste civilities upon, was the most doggedly and systematically repulsive. With a vinegar aspect, cotton in his leathern ears, and hatred to England in his heart, he sat in the frivolous assemblies of Petersburg like a bull-dog among spaniels; and very many were the times that I drew monosyllables and grim venom."[1]

John Randolph exclaimed indignantly to Madison, on the occasion of certain shady negotiations for acquiring Florida, "I see, sir, I am not calculated for a politician." J. Q. Adams was not better equipped for that devious vocation, and even when he became president he was ignorant of the intrigues which had secured his election. Crushing defeat at the hands of Jackson in 1828 shocked him immeasurably, further soured his nature, and unsettled his opinions concerning God and man.

Adams first entered political controversy with the publication of his "Letters of Publicola," demolishing Thomas Paine. His long career ended in the midst of his denunciations of slavery and the Southern interest. This half-century of public life had led him from the defense of tradition and property to an humanitarian assault upon the Peculiar Institution which hastened the approach of that conflict destined to consume both true conservatism and true reform in a blaze of passion. He died painfully conscious of his failure to accomplish any of those high hopes for American national character upon which he had expended his life. It is hard to reproach this austerely inspiring man with the collapse of his ideals; but the fact remains that he expected more from men than any true conservative should expect, and he got from them less than many a leader immeasurably Adams' moral inferior can obtain.

Though contemptuous of the doctrines of the French Revolution and hostile toward all political schemes not founded upon a stern morality, Adams himself adhered to certain innovating beliefs which confused and weakened his conservative prejudices. He shared Burke's faith in the principles of social continuity and prescription, but he mingled with these convictions several distinct and even contradictory inclinations. He believed in the idea of progress, for instance—which is not the same thing as believing in Providence; he believed in the possibility of human perfectibility. He believed in consolidation as an instrument for national betterment; he believed in government deliberately guiding the life of its citizens. As for democracy, he never was sure what to believe: again like Tocqueville, he feared for liberty and property under the reign of the majority, yet very often he would praise the democratic spirit with only hinted qualification. "*Democracy*, pure democracy, has at least its foundation in a generous theory of human rights. It is founded on the natural equality of mankind. It is the corner-stone of the Christian religion. It is the first *element* of *all* lawful government upon earth. Democracy is self-government of the community by the conjoint will of the majority of members."[2] From first to last, he leaned dangerously toward identifying virtue with his personal judgment and divine justice with his political fortune.

But he was not conceited. Like most of the Adamses, he seemed vain and pompous in manner; like them all, he experienced at heart a pervasive humility, an incessant Puritanical probing of conscience, a contemptuous self-condemnation of his own faults. He was forever tormented by the thought of what he *should* have been, so that he wrote, near the end of everything, "If my intellectual powers had been such as have been sometimes committed by the Creator of men to single individuals of the species, my diary would have been, next to the Holy Scriptures, the most precious and valuable book ever written by human hands, and I should have been one of the greatest benefactors of my country and of mankind. I would, by the irresistible power of genius and the irrepressible energy of will and the favor of Almighty God, have banished war and slavery from the face of the earth forever. But the conceptive power of mind was not conferred upon me by my Maker, and I have not improved the scanty portion of His gifts as I might and ought to have done.''[3] He sensed that his duty was the conservation of America's moral worth; he knew his age for a time of transition; but how to contend with this grim sphinx, he never properly discovered.

All the same, he made a painful and self-denying effort to guide America by setting his foot in the path Washington had opened. Nationalism, a consolidating federalism ennobled by purposes nearly incomprehensible to the mass of his countrymen, was his political anchor—a nationalism that scorned the materialistic Federalism which Hamilton and Pickering represented, that denounced Southern particularism. He withdrew from the Federalists during the Embargo controversy of 1808, and presently he was surprised to find himself a Republican. Under the Virginia Dynasty, the Republican party so altered its complexion that the son of old John Adams seemed the most eligible successor to James Monroe; thus the younger Adams became president in 1825, and he thought that God had confided to his hands the regeneration of America. A man throughout life at once remarkably shrewd and touchingly naïve, Adams confided in the strength of the Lord at his back; thus when, four years later, democracy overwhelmed him as it had crushed his brave father, the astounded John Quincy Adams wondered whether there existed any God at all.

In consolidation, he thought, lay the means of making America the noblest nation in history. "My system of politics more and more inclines to strengthen the union and its government," he had written in 1816. "It is directly the reverse of that professed by Mr. John Randolph, of relying principally upon the state governments. The efforts of every one of the state governments would be to sway the whole union for its own local advantage. The doctrine is therefore politic enough for a citizen of the most powerful state in the union, but it is good for nothing for the weaker states, and pernicious for the whole.''[4] A mutual detestation separated Adams and Randolph, the most honest men of their generation; and the two divisions of conservative opinion which they represented are not yet reconciled. Tocqueville's warnings against centralized power were lost upon Adams. By proper employment of the revenues and moral leadership possessed by the general government, he thought, human nature might be raised to perfection in America; and that ecstatic vision, almost a medieval mysticism in a Puritanical little nineteenth-century gentleman, induced him to brush aside the problem of local liberties and immediate difficulties. In 1843, at Cincinnati, he re-expressed the persevering dream of a lifetime:

Now the position to which I would invite your earnest and anxious consideration is this: That the form of government, founded upon the principle of the natural equality of mankind, and of which the unalienable rights of individual men are the cornerstone, is the form of government best adapted to the pursuit of happiness, as well as of every individual as of the community. It is the only actual or imaginable human government, in which self-love and social are the same; and I think I am fully warranted in adding that in proportion as the existing governments of the earth approximate to, or recede from, that standard, in the same proportion is the pursuit of happiness, of the community and of every individual belonging to it, promoted or impeded, accomplished or demolished. It is the true republic of Montesquieu—the government of which *virtue* is the seminal principle, and that virtue consisting of the love implanted in every bosom of the community of which it is a member.[5]

In some respects, this out-Jeffersons Jefferson. It is an idealistic moralist's view of society. A firm supporter of the idea of social compact, which he took to be an historical fact; a lover of universal justice; an advocate of incessant improvement—here we see Adams' innovating side. But conservative inclinations and experience kept this optimism in bounds. Bentham, with whom he conversed, horrified Adams by his inhumanly precise social calculus, his materialism, his complacency at the possibility of provoking civil war in England. The judicious reformer operates through means hallowed by Time and sanctified by Providence. For just such reform, American experience had created the federal government, the product of divine will and human compromise. Now was the hour to make this political system the instrument of moral and physical progress. A democracy of elevation should be formed out of the turbulent and disparate elements that inhabited the several states; social disharmonies should be reconciled, local hostilities dissipated.

Internal improvements at federal expense, encouragement of manufactures, conservation of that vast national treasure the public lands of the West, promotion of science, sympathy for the spirit of liberty throughout the world: these constituted Adams' specific program. John Randolph saw in these proposals no more than the scheme of one section to grow rich at the expense of another, no more than a tremendous jobbery, no more than the projects of the Academy of Lagado. And so far as concerns the motives which prompted many supporters of these proposals, Randolph was right. But John Quincy Adams, right or wrong, projected these designs as the fulfillment of Washington's idea of union. Roads and canals and harbors would make the nation truly one, through general benefit; protective tariffs, in the long run, would work to the advantage of all; the public lands, instead of being sacrificed to speculators and squatters, would furnish for generations to come the means of paying for great national enterprises; a new system of weights and measures, a national astronomical observatory, scientific forestry, and similar projects would improve the national understanding and prosper the economy; the United States would receive as members of a larger community those new states, Greece or the South American nations, that had attained in republicanism a higher state of social progress. It would be a conservatism of prosperity and hope, a free and benevolent republic led by gentlemen. It was predicated upon an idea loftier than mere paternalism: upon justice, "a constant and perpetual will of securing to every man his right." It was quite impossible.

For President Adams, in whom the old New England austerity was transmuted into a grand beneficence, reckoned without the inveterate American hostility toward direction from above. More than the denunciations of the "corrupt bargain" between Adams and Henry Clay, more than any merely political difficulty of the administration, what roused the nation to the support of General Jackson and gave Jackson an electoral vote double Adams', the American democracy declined to be directed by central authority. Andrew Jackson, a natural aristocrat—indeed, an autocrat— succeeded the scientist and man of letters, for General Jackson did not propose to bridle the democracy, but to give the nation its head. The public lands, under Jackson, were thrown open to immediate settlement, and the frantic exploitation of everything beyond the Mississippi commenced, from the effects of which America has not recuperated even yet. Internal improvements were discarded with contempt, protective tariffs reduced by compromise, scientific experiments abandoned, foreign policy contracted. Adams felt that he had covenanted with his God. The New England mind never had lost wholly the idea that relationship with Omnipotence is a matter of contract; New England's apologetics abound in references to pious "goodly transactions" between God and His elect. Had God failed John Quincy Adams? Was this the reward of tireless service? Was this the irresistible human progress of which the second Adams had been so confident? Adams, weaker in his faith than Job, was not staunch enough to endure this tribulation. Certainly he never forgave the South for his defeat in 1828, and he hardly forgave his God.

Even the spirit of science, Adams felt, had deserted him and suffered perversion to low uses. Not the high old families like the house of Adams were destined to wield this New England force: instead, the Yankee whittlers and wooden-nutmeg men, the practical inventors and business promoters, kidnaped science and chained it to the service of private avarice. Rather than ennobling the public mind and cementing the social fabric, applied science speedily became the chief weapon of a gross individualism which was anathema to the frugal and righteous Adams, the source of enormous fortunes divorced from duty, the instrument of unscrupulous ambition and rapacious materialism. Presently it commenced to scar the very face of the country which Adams loved, a disfiguring process uninterrupted since his day. Applied science was a revolutionary force, though Adams had mistaken it for a conservative tool. Could there be progress in the world, if this corruption were permitted by Providence? Could there be God? In humiliation of soul, John Quincy Adams left Washington, bitter and nearly hopeless. Despite his outward coldness of demeanor, he never really had obeyed Marcus Aurelius' desolate injunction to those who guide society, "Live as if on a mountain." Nor did an Adams often resign old grudges without reluctance. When his friends returned the ex-president to the House of Representatives, John Quincy Adams began to take his revenge by defying that "Sable Genius of the South" the slave power.

Now John Quincy Adams' detestation of slavery was manifest long before his defeat in 1828, and no hint is intended here that he fulminated against the Peculiar Institution simply because of an old grudge. In 1816, he had disputed with Calhoun on the slavery question: "It is among the evils of slavery that it taints the very sources of moral principle. It establishes false estimates of virtue for vice: for what can be more false and heartless than this doctrine which makes the first and holiest rights of humanity to depend upon the color of the skin. It perverts human reason, and reduces man endowed with logical powers to maintain that slavery is sanctioned by the Christian religion, that slaves are happy and contented in their condition, that between master and slave there are ties of mutual attachment and affection, that the virtues of the master are refined and exalted by the degradation of the slave; while at the same time they vent execrations upon the slave-trade, curse Britain for having given them the slaves, burn at the stake negroes convicted of crimes for the terror of their example, and writhe in agonies of fear at the very mention of human rights as applicable to men of color."[6] But one can hardly doubt that bitterness toward the South, Jackson's South, was an immediate stimulant to Adams' fearless conduct in presenting to Congress, year after year, the abolitionists' petitions.

In defying the furious Southern congressmen by sponsoring the petitions, Adams took pains to remark that he did not endorse the specific views of the petitioners; he defended only their right to petition. John Quincy Adams knew that slavery, like all other

great evils, could not be extirpated satisfactorily by simple legislative decree. Of course he was right in detesting slavery—so did
the great Virginian proprietors; of course he was right in endeavoring to prevent the extension of its blight to the new territories.
But in clothing himself with the bravery of the reformer, Adams
forgot the prudence of the conservative. Reversing the ordinary
process of nature, the youthful opponent of change had become
the aged lieutenant of radical alteration. Already the fanatic voice
of Garrison was crying at his back; and after Adams died, the
leadership of New England descended to the narrow and intolerant humanitarianism of men like Sumner and Phillips, men ready
to dare any number of new plagues if they might eradicate an old
evil.

The Civil War and the suppression of the South so terribly injured intelligent conservatism in America that conservative ideas
have made little truly effective recovery until recent years—and
even now, no satisfactory recovery in the popular mind. Hawthorne, with his attachment to all that was venerable, felt the
menace of abolitionism. "There is no instance, in all history, of
the human will and intellect having perfected any great moral reform by methods which it adapted to that end," he wrote in his
Life of Franklin Pierce; slavery was not to be remedied by legislative contrivance. But John Quincy Adams, having all his life
cherished the conviction that a pious and energetic statesman may
move mountains, was not half so sensitive to the gargoyle faces
that peeked out from behind the abolitionists' petitions. He knew
that abolition could not suffice to solve the problems of the South
and the nation; he loved the Union dearly; no man was less of
a demagogue. But the climate of opinion warmed this cold and
incorruptible New Englander into an uneasy flirtation with the
emotional and radical movement. After Adams, the deluge. That
flood swept away the high and God-fearing dignity of the Republic which his imagination had projected into a future of majestic
tranquillity.

3

"Democracy, simple democracy, never had a patron among men of letters," wrote John Adams, in *A Defence of the Constitutions*. "The people have almost always expected to be served gratis, and to be paid for the honor of serving them; and their applause and adorations are bestowed too often on artifice and tricks, on hypocrisy and superstition, on flattery, bribes, and largesses." Well, somehow every age finds the writers its taste requires, and even before the middle of the nineteenth century, American democracy had begun to generate its eulogists among literary men; presently Whitman was to sing of democracy with a sincerity seldom manifested before and probably impossible to revive in later generations of disillusion. Not only democracy, but those concomitant doctrines still more hostile to the traditional order—the ideas of infinite material progress, perfectibility, and alteration for novelty's sake—obtained their literary devotees among the talents of New England. Emerson's is the greatest name among these literary optimists.

Despite all the conservative threads in the Yankee tapestry, New England's intellectual pattern was perplexed by an enduring streak of tinkering. Rather as Cotton Mather could not resist whittling behind the church door, so New England was incessantly tempted to improve and purify—particularly to improve and purify other people. A Puritanical legacy, this; and prodigiously diluted though the heritage of Puritanism had become in Transcendentalism and Unitarianism, that optimistic meddling-urge remained in full strength. The impulse was responsible in appreciable measure for the outbreak of the Civil War and for the fiasco of Reconstruction. So enduring has been the effect of Yankee censoriousness that the Stowe-version of Southern life, for instance, has continued ever since indelibly marked upon the popular mind of the North; and one perceives its bigoted humanitarianism still at work north of Mason's and Dixon's Line, ensuring that almost any play which celebrates the depravity of Southerners will reward its angel, that almost any romance which exposes the blackness of Southern whites never will be relegated to the category of publishers' remainders. This external or expansive New England conscience, this moral and literary equivalent of the Free Soil movement, found its expression on the one hand in the implacable anti-slavery and anti-Southern energies of Garrison and Parker and Lowell and Charles Francis Adams and Sumner. On the other hand, it was expressed in the misty optimism, social experimenting, and metaphysical creations of Emerson, Ripley, Alcott, Margaret Fuller, and other Transcendentalists and Concord illuminati.

When, as in some of the Transcendentalists and their Unitarian progenitors, the transplanted Germanic idealism which inspired their system seemed to sustain a kind of conservatism, this was by accident, not from the logic of things. Hegel himself was a conservative only from chance and expediency. The whole melioristic, abstract, individualistic tendency of their philosophy was destructive of conservative values. Reliance upon private judgment and personal emotion, contempt for prescription and the experience of the species, a social morality alternately and bewilderingly egocentric or all-embracing (the contradiction so frequently encountered in Rousseau)—these qualities of Emerson's thought gratified a popular American craving which ever since has fed upon Emersonian "Self-Reliance" and "Experience" and "Nature" and his other individualistic manifestoes. Were it not for this affinity with the American intellectual appetite, Emerson might not be remembered, since his essays are not easy reading—piercing sentences or paragraphs sparking amid incoherence of structure, the expression of a mind unsystematic as his friend Carlyle's. But Emerson's speculations were so congenial to the American temper that their influence upon American thought has been incalculably great: one even finds passages from Emerson a favorite exercise in typewriting-manuals, and Emerson has stolen into the soul of such conservatives as Irving Babbitt, sometimes exerting there a disharmonious influence.

Emerson appeals to a variety of egalitarian and innovating impulses common among Americans, all of them earlier remarked by Tocqueville: the passion for simplicity, the dislike of hierarchy,

the impatience with discipline and restriction, the fondness for summary remedies. When he reduces God to the Oversoul, appeals
to individual judgment, extols growth, change, and becoming, and
praises a freedom unfettered by compromise or parchment, then
he reaches an audience vastly larger than the circle of dreamy Transcendentalists. He becomes a prophet of the revolt against authority. Though he is so uncompromisingly individualistic, now and
then his attacks on materialism and ''the present tenures'' of
property foreshadow socialism. This is no paradox. True conservatism, conservatism uninfected by Benthamite or Spencerian
ideas, rises at the antipodes from individualism. Individualism is
social atomism; conservatism is community of spirit. Men cannot exist without proper community, as Aristotle knew; and when
they have been denied community of spirit, they turn unreason-
ingly to community of goods. Despite Emerson's talk of ''the eternal One'' and the Oversoul, despite his outward rejection of
atomism, beneath this veneer lay a philosophical isolation of man
from man. Perhaps a kind of instinctive revulsion against his own
spiritual individualism drove Emerson toward social
collectivism—toward that dour substitute for free harmony, that
solacing uniformity, which Tocqueville calls democratic despotism.

Emerson's specific political notions are almost shocking—
frightening in the first instance for their perilous naïveté, in the
second instance for their easy indifference to uncomfortable facts.
Shrugging aside constitutional safeguards, checks and balances,
devices to secure freedom, prescriptive authorities, he declares that
all we require in government is good will. We must found our
political systems upon ''absolute right,'' and then we will have
nothing to fear. This from a professed admirer of Montesquieu
and Burke! The most optimistic of the *philosophes* was not more
puerile in statecraft. Emerson's political ideal is as impractical as
Thoreau's, without Thoreau's toughness of fibre to furnish an excuse for proof. Rousseau and Hegel are reduced to absurdity by
their confident New England disciple. And when the question arises
of how ''absolute right'' may be established, Emerson falls into
that adulation of the violent hero, the ''wise man,'' which is still

more conspicuous in Carlyle and has been one of the more disastrous delusions of the twentieth century. After years of Transcendental humanitarian preaching, Emerson informs the world that Osawatomie Brown is the destined instrument of absolute right: John Brown, that blood-stained old fanatic, the butcher of innocent men in Kansas and at Harper's Ferry, the archetype of the terrorists who have been at work these past hundred years reducing the science of politics to murder. Brown "made the gallows glorious like the cross." In this tribute to a being at his best moments a monomaniac, at his worst a homicidal horror, one perceives how perilous is the foggy Debatable Land between transcendentalism and nihilism.

"Experience has ever shown, that education, as well as religion, aristocracy, as well as democracy and monarchy, are, singly, totally inadequate to the business of restraining the passions of men, of preserving a steady government, and protecting the lives, liberties, and properties of the people." This admonition by John Adams meant nothing to Emerson. Only the balancing of passion, interest, and power against opposing passion, interest, and power can make a state just and tranquil, said Adams. John Adams believed the existence of sin to be an incontrovertible fact; while Emerson, discarding with the forms of Calvinism the very essence of its creed, never admitted the idea of sin into his system. "But such inveterate and persistent optimism," Charles Eliot Norton remarks of his friend Emerson, "though it may show only its pleasant side in such a character as Emerson's, is dangerous doctrine for a people. It degenerates into fatalistic indifference to moral considerations, and to personal responsibilities; it is at the root of much of the irrational sentimentalism of our American politics."

Recognition of the abiding power of sin is a cardinal tenet in conservatism. Quintin Hogg, in his vigorous little book *The Case for Conservatism*, re-emphasizes the necessity for this conviction. For conservative thinkers believe that man is corrupt, that his appetites need restraint, and that the forces of custom, authority, law, and government, as well as moral discipline, are required to keep sin in check. One may trace this conviction back through Adams to the Calvinists and Augustine, or through Burke to Hooker and the Schoolmen and presently, in turn, to St. Augustine—and, perhaps (as Henry Adams does) beyond Augustine to Marcus Aurelius and his Stoic preceptors, as well as to St. Paul and the Hebrews. Emerson, impatient of tradition, dismisses such disturbing theories. On his fifty-eighth birthday, Emerson remarked, "I never could give much reality to evil and pain." Now evil and pain are the tremendous problems of Christian thought, and a man who cannot "give much reality" to those terrible and inexorable facts is no trustworthy guide for the modern mind. The whole social tendency of Emersonianism has been either to advocate some radical and summary measure, a Solomon's judgment without its saving cunning, or (if this will not suffice) to pretend that the problem does not exist. Few peoples have been so complacent about evil in their midst as have the Americans since the Civil War, and no people have been so ready to deny the very existence of evil. Twentieth-century America presents the spectacle of a nation tormented by crime, urban vice, political corruption, family decay, and increasing proletarianization; and amid this scene the commanding voice is not a Savonarola's, but the chorus of sociologists and psychologists and neo-positivists in pulpits, proclaiming that sin does not exist and "adjustment" will heal every social cancer. Now Emerson did not invent this ostrich-tendency of the American public, but he was its most powerful apologist. If an evil is geographically remote, or peculiar to a section or class (like slavery), solve it by surgery without anaesthetic; if it is close to home, in one's very heart—why, we must be mistaken.

If a foolish consistency is the hobgoblin of little minds, a fatuous optimism frequently is the damnation of expansive minds. As a social optimist ignoring the fact of sin, Emerson was a radical thinker, perhaps the most influential of all American radicals. Believing, with Rousseau, in the supremacy of benevolent instincts, he was ready to discard old ways of society so that ground might be cleared for the new edifices of emotion. Among the warning voices that answered him, those of Hawthorne and Orestes Brownson were the most eloquent.

4

Until Emerson and his circle established the Concord hegemony in American letters, for the most part the literary men of the United States had justified John Adams' dictum by marked conservatism of mind, suspicion of democracy, and love of old ways. Irving and Cooper and Poe participated in this character; and some eminent contemporaries of Emerson, repudiating the works of Transcendentalism, subjected innovation to a criticism which left its mark upon American thought.

The restless mind of Orestes Brownson, a Vermonter, sampled nearly every dissent of Transcendental times, and at length embraced orthodoxy with the fervor of a man who has found sanctuary. Congregationalism, Presbyterianism, Universalism, socialism, atheism, Unitarianism, and revolutionary plotting led by tortuous ways to revulsion against private judgment and, in 1844, to Roman Catholicism. Brownson had known Brook Farm and New Harmony, and now he became one of a community older than the nations. In recent years, more attention has been paid to Orestes Brownson than he had received for the preceding century. (Parrington does not mention him: something like a conspiracy of silence has kept his name out of histories of American thought, perhaps because Brownson's attack on Protestantism in its churchly and social forms does not fit conveniently into the neat categories of conventional intellectual surveys.)[7] Yet he is the most interesting example of the progress of Catholicism as a conservative spirit in America; and if the Catholic portion of the American people has not yet fulfilled Brownson's hopes, still their growing influence has restrained in some degree a popular secularism. The elaborate and subtle history of Catholicism in North America, never satisfactorily written yet, ought to deal thoroughly with Brownson and his *Quarterly Review*.

Burke remarked, more than once, the beneficial influence of Catholicism as a system innately conservative; Tocqueville described its conservative tendency in American life and predicted its growth; in this century, Irving Babbitt wrote that perhaps the Roman Catholic Church (which he did not love) may become the only effective instrument for preserving civilization. Brownson, formerly saturated with every radical speculation and now purged of them all, took up this duty of conservation upon the foundation of religious principle.

"We have heard enough of liberty and the rights of man; it is high time to hear something of the duties of men and the rights of authority."[8] Obedience, submission to God, is the secret of justice in society and tranquillity in life, quite as much as it is indispensable to eternal salvation. To redeem Americans from sectarianism is the task of the intelligent social reformer as well as the duty of the priest; for free political institutions can be secure only when the people are imbued with religious veneration. Democracy, more than any other form of government, rests upon the postulate of a moral law, ordained by an authority superior to human wisdom. But where in the Protestant system or in Transcendentalism is the moral law adequately defined, or its interpretation facilitated? Is not the "moral law" of Concord a mere idealizing of emotion and personal impulse? Blasphemously, the Transcendentalists confound divine love and human love, and religion sinks into a maudlin sentimentality.

Protestantism descends through three states: first, the subjection of religion to the charge of civil government; second, the rejection of the authority of temporal government, and submission of religion to the control of the faithful; third, individualism, which "leaves religion entirely to the control of the individual, who selects his own creed, or makes a creed to suit himself, devises his own worship and discipline, and submits to no restraints but such as are self-imposed."[9] When this last stage is reached, disintegration of the religious spirit is imminent; for man is not sufficient unto himself, reason unaided cannot sustain faith, and Authority is required to preserve Christianity from degenerating into a congeries of fanatic sects and egotistical professions. Under Protestantism, the sect governs religion, rather than submitting to governance; the congregation bully their ministers and insist upon palatable sermons, flattering to their vanity; Protestantism cannot sustain popular liberty because "it is itself subject to popular control, and must follow in all things the popular will, passion, interest, prejudice, or caprice."[10] The modern spirit, of which Protestantism is one expression, detests the idea of loyalty, upon which the whole hierarchy of this world and the next is founded: "What it hates is not this or that form of government, but *legitimacy*, and it would rebel against democracy as quick as against absolute monarchy, if democracy were asserted on the ground of legitimacy. The modern spirit is in every thing the direct denial of the practical reason....It asserts the universal and absolute supremacy of man, and his unrestricted right to subject religion, morals, and politics to his own will, passion, or caprice."[11] This is fatal to democracy, for it stimulates insubordination and disorder, setting everything afloat, and that moral solidarity which makes possible so delicate a government as democracy is broken. Popular religious feeling, which conceivably may be absent in a monarchy or an aristocracy without ruining the social structure, is indispensable to democracy.

Good will is not enough to safeguard freedom and justice: this delusion leads to the triumph of every demagogue and tyrant, and no amount of transplanted Idealism can compensate for the loss of religious sanctions. Men's passions are held in check only by the punishments of divine wrath and the tender affections of piety. The sovereignty of God, far from repressing liberty, establishes and guarantees freedom; authority is not the antagonist of liberty, but its vindicator; Catholics, above all others, should be conservatives, although many Americans of the Catholic faith have fallen into the error that the established order is their enemy, they having come from countries where the government was intolerant of their religion. "Majorities may protect themselves; minorities have no protection but in the sacredness and supremacy of law. The law is right as it is; we must study to keep it so; and if we do, we shall always throw our influence on the conservative side, never on the radical side."[12] Brownson proceeds to anticipate the arguments which extreme Protestants and anti-clerical writers are using in the twentieth century against Romanism, and to refute them. The Church has no desire to meddle in the affairs of government; it endeavors simply to expound the moral laws which just governments obey.

Constitutions cannot be made, says Brownson, agreeing with de Maistre: they are the product of slow growth, the expression of a nation's historical experience, or they are mere paper. "The generative principle of all political constitutions...is Divine Providence, never the deliberate wisdom or will of men." Constitutions must vary as the experience of the people who live under them has varied; and whatever form of government has been long established in a nation, that must be the best permanent framework for the national corporate life. In Europe, monarchy and aristocracy ought to be perpetuated, because the whole tenor of existence there is bound up with these institutions. But in the United States, royalty and nobility never existed, as a native development, nor did king and nobles migrate here. The commons alone migrated to America, and therefore our constitution is framed to suit a nation in which the commons are the only order in the state. Thus republicanism is the best government for America, and the true American conservative will struggle to maintain the Republic in its purity, strictly obeying its laws, cleaving fast to its written Constitution. No human institution is immutable; constitutions must be mended and healed now and then; but the social reformer does not create: he develops, he restores to health, but he knows that he cannot hack a new constitution out of raw humanity.

"Our great danger lies in the radical tendency which has become so wide, deep, and active in the American people." Ceasing to regard anything as sacred or venerable, spurning what is old, injuring what is fixed, setting adrift all religious, domestic, and social institutions, we borrow nothing from the past and ignore the data of experience. We even try to deny that language has exact meaning. The majority of the American people may not approve this radical tendency, but they are silent before ambitious enthusiasts and competing politicians. We shall not escape from this deluge of change and perilous experiment until we recognize the principle of authority: God's authority. This cannot be apprehended without the Church. As Protestantism and its fumbling offshoots decay before our eyes, upon the mound of dissent must rise the fortress of orthodox belief, without which human sin and foible know no limits, without which order and justice perish.

"Men are little moved by mere reasoning, however clear and convincing it may be," Brownson writes in *The American Republic*—which, though one of the more penetrating treatises on American political theory, is a book known to almost no one. "Routine is more powerful with them than logic. A few are greedy of novelties, and are always for trying experiments; but the great body of the people of all nations have an invincible repugnance to abandon what they know for what they know not....No reform, no change in the constitution of government or of society, whatever the advantages it may promise, can be successful, if introduced, unless it has its root or germ in the past. Man is never a creator; he can only develop and continue, because he is himself a creature, and only a second cause."[13] This conservatism of the flesh is itself a providential device, keeping rein upon the lust of ambitious men after innovation. Providence, in essence, is continuing creation; and an irreligious people, denying the reality of Providence, condemn themselves to stagnation.

The process of Roman Catholic proselytizing has been slower, perhaps, than Brownson hoped, but it has been persistent. What a triumphant Catholicism in America may be like—whether, as Tocqueville hints and Evelyn Waugh conjectures, it will be a Catholicism much altered and diluted by American materialism and democracy—the next few generations may begin to learn. They will be fortunate if they can resurrect the active intelligence of Orestes Brownson to reconcile orthodoxy with Americanism.

Caleb Weatherbee, the Catholic crippled eccentric of Salem, in Santayana's *The Last Puritan*, says movingly: "I live in the future too, thinking of those who will come after us in this teeming America, not—fortunately for them—the heirs of my body, but in some measure, I am sure, the vindicators of my mind. We were always a circumcized people, consecrated to great expectations. Expectations of what? Nobody knows: yet I believe God has revealed to me something of the direction of his providence. I thank Him for my deformity, because without it I should probably have been carried headlong—what strength have I of my own?—by the running tide of our prosperity and triviality, and never should have conceived that we in America are not addressed to vanity, to some gorgeous universal domination of our name or manners, but that without knowing it we are addressed to repentance, to a new life of humility and charity.'' It is not beyond the realm of possibility that the stern New England current of dissenting piety may reunite with the stream of orthodoxy, as it did in the person of Brownson, and wash American character in the waters of repentance. The shock of Hiroshima and Nagasaki may have ushered in, unknown to almost everyone, that new life of humility and charity; and fresh national trials, whatever they may inflict upon the structure of society, are likely to assist this transformation of the New England conscience.

5

The most influential conservative thinker of this transitional New England period, however, was Nathaniel Hawthorne, the "boned pirate," the master of allegory, that humorous, melancholy man obsessed with the problems of conscience. Sensitive equally to the terrible and the comic, he was at once an active politician and a dreamer. And Hawthorne restored to the American mind that doctrine of sin which Emerson and his school so studiously ignored.

Some recent writers, anxious in this age of unrest to buttress popular sovereignty by every means at the disposal of the scholar, have been rather ludicrously eager to demonstrate that because Hawthorne was a Democrat, he must have been a democrat. He was; but so was Fenimore Cooper. Hawthorne disliked snobbery and pretence and the commercial affections of the Whigs; he wished to be proud of America; and his very fascination with the dead past occasionally tempted him into an uneasy expression of hope for the present and the future. Yet very few other Americans have been so congenitally conservative as Hawthorne, so steeped in tradition and suspicious of alteration. His democracy was the democracy of his friend President Franklin Pierce, an intelligent, moderate, and honest gentleman of considerable talents with whom political partisans and historians have dealt brutally. Like Pierce, Hawthorne knew that the curse of Southern slavery could not be dissipated by punitive legislation or Northern intimidation. He detested slavery, but he knew that its existence being contrary to the trend of economic forces and moral convictions throughout the world, with the passage of time servitude would fade away without need for interference from the federal government. Governmental meddling and private fanaticism could imperil the Union, but they could not resolve great social questions like this. No man ever was more justly hanged than John Brown, he declared in contempt of Emerson and Thoreau and Lowell. If Hawthorne's moderation had been more widely emulated, North and South, America might have kept to the path of tradition which, Hawthorne knew, was the secret of English political tranquillity. Yet all this is of small importance to us now: Hawthorne's particular political opinions are no great matter today, but his underlying social and moral principles possess enduring significance. He influenced American thought by his perpetuation of the past and by his expression of the idea of sin.

Conservatism cannot exist anywhere without reverence for dead generations. The incessant movement and alteration of life in America, the absence of true family continuity, even the perishable fabric of American building, unite in tempting the United States to ignore the past. All Scott's genius was required to remind nineteenth-century Britain that any generation is only a link in an eternal chain; and the problem of persuading Americans to look backward to their ancestors was still greater. Irving, Cooper, and Hawthorne (with historians like Parkman) succeeded in waking the American imagination; they created, out of rude and fragmentary materials, a vision of the American heritage which still helps direct the amorphous mass of the American people into a national ideal originated among a few English-speaking folk along the Atlantic shore. The work of all three writers exerted a conservative energy, and Hawthorne's possessed the most enduring intellectual strength. In the solitude of his haunted chamber in Salem, he learned how hard was the task of a romancer in a land without the mystery and awe of antiquity; he taught himself to conjure up the ghost of old New England, and his necromancy gave to American thought and letters a bent still discernible. Yvor Winters somewhat enigmatically describes this influence as Maule's curse, or American obscurantism. Winters does not seem to mean political obscurantism in any sense commonly understood; but it is true that Hawthorne, more than anyone else in American letters, punctured the bubble of "enlightenment" which Emerson's school was endeavoring to puff up still further. Hawthorne was no idolizer of the past; he knew the past to have been black and cruel, often; but for that very reason, apprehension of the past ought to be fundamental to the projecting of any social reform. Only through scrutiny of the past can society descry the limitations of human nature.

And Americans, of all peoples who ever existed, cared least about their past. It is curious, Hawthorne remarks in *The Marble Faun*, that Americans pay for portrait busts: "The brief duration of our families, as a hereditary household, renders it next to a certainty that the great-grandchildren will not know their father's grandfather, and that half a century hence, at farthest, the hammer of the auctioneer will thump its knock-down blow against his blockhead, sold at so much for the pound of stone!" In the England of Burke, veneration of one's forefathers still was a natural social impulse, and contempt for old ways an artificial novelty. But in the America of Hawthorne, expectation of change was greater than expectation of continuity, the lure of the future more powerful than the loyalty of the past; although some measure of veneration still was as essential to society as it had ever been, nevertheless veneration had become the creation of artifice. It was necessary to hew out an artificial reverence, that men might look backward to their ancestry and by corollary look forward to their posterity. Hawthorne was the best of those writers who leavened the American temper with a respect for old things.

And that part of the American past which was Hawthorne's especial province, Puritan New England, exerted an influence in the long run substantially conservative. Though born of a stern dissent, Puritanism in America soon manifested a character more demandingly orthodox, according to its own canons, than the comparative leniency of Anglicanism. In *The Scarlet Letter*, retrospectively in *The House of the Seven Gables*, in many of the *Twice Told Tales* and *Mosses from an Old Manse*, that Puritan spirit is disclosed with inimitable perspicacity and candor: fiercely censorious, bold, resolute, industrious, allied with free political institutions, introspective, repressive of emotion, seeking after godliness with a zeal that does not spare self-love, self-pity, or even worldly ambition. Much to fear here, something to hate, a great deal to hold in awe. The Puritan character, for all its enduring influence upon the American mind through the agency of its gentler New England descendants, stands poles apart from the common aspirations and impulses of modern American life. Cautious of action, suspicious of alteration and expansion, repressive of self, armored in a steely theology, Puritanism detests the materialistic, hedonistic appetites that predominate in modern America, and Puritanism is abhorred by the modern spirit. Puritanism is moral conservatism in its extreme form; and of all the varieties of mutiny that the modern world suffers, moral revolution is the most violent. But because of Hawthorne, America never has been able to forget the Puritans, either their vices or their virtues. Upon American society today, the memory of Puritanism still exerts some degree of restraint, if only by holding out the other extreme of remorseless discipline; and this conservative vestige of old New England belief will linger, embalmed by Hawthorne, so long as anyone reads American literature.

Yet this achievement, magnificent though it would be in a lesser man, is merely incidental to Hawthorne's chief accomplishment: impressing the idea of sin upon a nation which would like to forget it. Hawthorne never was an historical romancer principally; his burning interest was morality; and, writing moral allegories such as no man had written since Bunyan, he chastened American optimism by declaring with all the powers of his imagination that sin, in quality and quantity, is virtually constant; that projects of reform must begin and end with the human heart; that the real enemy of mankind is not social institution, but the devil within us; that the fanatic improver of mankind through artificial alteration is, very commonly, in truth a destroyer of souls.

Now belief in the dogma of original sin has been prominent in the system of every great conservative thinker—in the lofty Christian resignation of Burke, in the hard-headed pessimism of Adams, in the melancholy of Randolph, in the "Calvinistic Catholicism" of Newman. But Hawthorne dwells almost wholly upon sin, its reality, nature, and consequences; the contemplation of sin is his obsession, his vocation, almost his life. Here he becomes a major preceptor of conservatives. "True civilization," Baudelaire wrote in his journal, "does not lie in progress or steam or table turning. It lies in the diminution of the marks of original sin." Though so radically different in mind and heart, Hawthorne and Baudelaire were close together in this view. By heroic efforts, Hawthorne suggests, man may diminish the influence of original sin in the world; but this struggle requires nearly his undivided attention. Whenever man tries to ignore sin, some avenging angel intervenes, progress material and spiritual collapses, and the reality of evil is reimpressed upon men's minds by terror and suffering. Only one species of reform really is worth attempting: reform of conscience.

Not that Hawthorne is a true Puritan, or perhaps even a strict Christian. His novels are not tracts. He dissects the anatomy of sin with a curiosity insatiable and even cruel. In *The Scarlet Letter*, and again in *The Marble Faun*, he suggests that sin, for all its consequences, nevertheless may be an enlightening influence upon certain natures—indeed, ennobling: although it burns, it wakens. We still do not know all the secrets of the riddle of sin; perhaps our regeneration is impossible without its agency. "Is Sin, then— which we deem such a dreadful blackness in the universe—" he makes Kenyon speculate fearfully, near the end of *The Marble Faun*—"is it, like Sorrow, merely an element of human education, through which we struggle to a higher and purer state than we could otherwise have attained? Did Adam fall, that we might ultimately rise to a far loftier paradise than his?'' But whatever sin effects, we must reckon with sin as the greatest force that agitates society. Those impulses toward cruelty, destruction, and ruthless self-gratification that forever are fighting to master our inner nature—the man whose psychology ignores these, corrupts society and himself. Hawthorne flatly contradicts Emerson; and in *The Blithedale Romance*, as in a half-dozen short stories, he describes the catastrophe of humanitarianism between moral blinkers. Nathaniel Hawthorne did not convince America of the necessity for taking sin into every social calculation: to men of the twentieth century, sin remains a most uncomfortable theory, and an age that has beheld human beings consumed in the furnaces of Buchenwald, or worked to death like old horses in the Siberian arctic, still pretends that sin is no more than a theological sham. Even a critic like R. C. Churchill, often astute, an inheritor of the old English Liberal tradition, writes doggedly of ''the barbarous, pre-civilized notion of Original Sin.''[14] No, Hawthorne did not make the doctrine of sin popular; but he left a good many people uneasily or resentfully aware that possibly it is true. This is his powerful conservative achievement. A lurking consciousness of sin has haunted American letters ever since.

''A revolution, or anything that interrupts social order, may afford opportunities for the individual display of eminent virtues,'' wrote Hawthorne in his sketch ''The Old Tory''; ''but its effects are pernicious to general morality. Most people are so constituted that they can be virtuous only in a certain routine.'' This is Burke's mind, through and through. Hawthorne returns to this theme of moral conservatism throughout his works, but his most deliberate analysis of the destroying power of sinful impulses, once revolutionary moral precepts are practised, is *The Blithedale Romance*; his most terse analysis is contained in three short stories of *Mosses from an Old Manse*: ''The Hall of Fantasy,'' ''The Celestial Railroad,'' and ''Earth's Holocaust.''

It was impossible, situated as we were, not to imbibe the idea that everything in nature and human experience was fluid, or fast becoming so; that the crust of the earth in many places was broken, and its whole surface portentously upheaving; that it was a day of crisis, and that we ourselves were in the critical vortex. Our great globe floated in the atmosphere of infinite space like an unsubstantial bubble. No sagacious man will long retain his sagacity, if he live exclusively among reformers and progressive people, without periodically returning into the settled system of things, to correct himself by a new observation from that old standpoint.

It was time for me now, therefore, to go and hold a little talk with the conservatives, the writers of the North American Review, the merchants, the politicians, the Cambridge men, and all those respectable old blockheads who still, in this intangibility and mistiness of affairs, kept a deathgrip on one or two ideas which had not come into vogue since yesterday morning.

With this good-natured contempt, Hawthorne turned his back upon the idealists and radicals of Brook Farm, upon Emerson and Alcott and Ripley and Margaret Fuller and all that ''knot of dreamers.'' For they had forgotten the sinfulness of man, and with it, the proper functions and limits of moral and social action. *The Blithedale Romance* is the history of a fanatic reformer, Hollingsworth, who is determined to redeem criminals by appealing to their higher instincts; and when all is done, he is grimly resigned to attempting the reformation of one criminal only, himself. ''The besetting sin of a philanthropist, it appears to me,'' says Hawthorne through the mouth of Coverdale, ''is apt to be a moral obliquity. His sense of honour ceases to be the sense of other honourable men. At some point of his course—I know not exactly when or where—he is tempted to potter with the right, and can scarcely forbear persuading himself that the importance of his public ends renders it allowable to throw aside his private conscience.'' Hollingsworth, for the sake of his dream, helps destroy the socialistic community he had joined (although it was doomed to dissolution in any case, from the impracticality of its Fourieristic projects); he causes the suicide of the emancipated woman who loved him; temporarily he abandons an innocent girl in peril, for the prospect of funds to found his refuge for criminals; and in projecting a general elevation of "higher instincts," he loses his own. Such a man, like the abolitionist, like the collectivist, forgets that most people can be virtuous only in a certain routine. That moral discipline broken, society relapses into its original state of chaotic sin. Morality is an artifice most fragile.

In "The Hall of Fantasy," an allegory of the innovating passion which plagued Hawthorne's America, he describes with a certain sighing sympathy the "self-styled reformers that peopled this place of refuge. They were the representatives of an unquiet period, when mankind is seeking to cast off the whole tissue of ancient custom like a tattered garment....Here were men whose faith had embodied itself in the form of a potato, and others whose long beards had a deep spiritual significance. Here was the abolitionist, brandishing his one idea like an iron flail." These were the seekers after earthly perfection; but another dweller in the Hall of Fantasy, Father Miller, with his prophecies of imminent destruction for all mankind, "scatters all their dreams like so many withered leaves upon the blast." Only in another world than this, Hawthorne intimates, will perfection be found.

In "The Celestial Railroad," Hawthorne imitates *The Pilgrim's Progress* (so strong an influence upon both Irving and Hawthorne) and—like C. S. Lewis in *The Great Divorce*—describes a journey from the City of Destruction to the Celestial City. Mr. Smooth-it-away, a director of the new railway between those points, escorts the travellers and explains how modern progress and material improvement have banished the consequences of sin and quelled the pangs of conscience. The Slough of Despond has been bridged with tracts, Evangelist's scroll is replaced by a convenient pasteboard ticket, pious colloquy along the way has yielded to polite gossip, the burdens of guilt now are deposited in the baggage car, the dispute between Beelzebub and the keeper of the wicket gate has been compromised, Mr. Greatheart has been superseded by Apollyon as chief engineer, the Valley of Humiliation has been filled up with materials from the Hill Difficulty, Tophet has been explained away as the crater of a half-extinct volcano, Giant Transcendentalist has inherited the cavern of Pope and Pagan, Vanity Fair is full of eloquent clergymen, Despair's castle has been converted into a house of entertainment. But the Lord of the Celestial City, it turns out, has refused an act of incorporation for this remarkably convenient railroad; and the travellers, leaving the train for the ferry which they expect to carry them over to the City, are confounded to find that they are Charon's passengers, bound for a destination quite different. So much for modern blindness to moral absolutes.

"Earth's Holocaust" is the destruction of the past by innovating modern mankind, carting off to a bonfire on the Western prairie everything that dead ages venerated. Pedigrees, noble crests, badges of knighthood, and all the trappings of aristocracy are tossed in; a despairing gentleman cries, "This fire is consuming all that marked your advance from barbarism, or that could have prevented your relapse thither." But purple robes and royal sceptres follow; and strong drink, and tobacco, and the weapons of war, and the gallows—and presently marriage certificates, and money, and a shout rises that deeds to property must burn, and all written constitutions. The bonfire is augmented, very soon, by millions of books, the literature of the ages: "The truth was, that the human race had now reached a stage of progress so far beyond what the wisest and wittiest men of former ages had ever dreamed of that it would have been manifest absurdity to allow the earth to be any longer cumbered with their poor achievements in the literary line." To replenish the pyre, the people soon drag up surplices, mitres, crosiers, crosses, fonts, chalices, communion tables, pulpits—and the Bible. "Truths which the hearers trembled at were nothing but a fable of the world's infancy"—so into the holocaust with Holy Writ.

Now it seems that every vestige of the human past has been destroyed in this magnificent reform, and mankind may luxuriate in primitive innocence. But "a dark-complexioned personage" reassures the despairing reactionaries. "There's one thing that these wiseacres have forgotten to throw into the fire, and without which all the rest of the conflagration is just nothing at all"—the human heart. "And, unless they hit upon some method of purifying that foul cavern, forth from it will reissue all the shapes of wrong and misery—the same old shapes or worse ones—which they have taken such a vast deal of trouble to consume to ashes. I have stood by this livelong night and laughed in my sleeve at the whole business. Oh, take my word for it, it will be the old world yet!"

This was the substance of Hawthorne's resolute conviction: that moral reformation is the only real reformation; that sin always will corrupt the projects of enthusiasts who leave sin out of account; that progress is a delusion, except for the infinitely slow progress of conscience. But Hawthorne, like Pierce, was broken in the whirlwind of fanaticism, Northern and Southern, which wailed onward to Sumter, and then raved triumphant from Manassas to Appomattox. "The Present, the Immediate, the Actual, has proved too potent for me," Nathaniel Hawthorne wrote in the last year of his life, the year of Gettysburg. "It takes away not only my scanty faculty, but even my desire for imaginative composition, and leaves me sadly content to scatter a thousand peaceful fantasies upon the hurricane that is sweeping us all along with it, possibly into a Limbo where our nation and its polity may be as literally the fragments of a shattered dream as my unwritten Romance."[15]

From the hurricane-fanned conflagration of reforming enthusiasm and sinful appetite which became Civil War and Reconstruction, American moral and political conservatism has not yet recovered, and perhaps never can. "Believe me, the fire will not be allowed to settle down without the addition of fuel that will startle many people who have lent a willing hand thus far," growls the observer in "Earth's Holocaust." Thus the New England idealists, when the war was burned out, discovered aghast that from its ashes writhed the corruption, brutality, and baneful ignorance which were supposed to have been roasted in their integument dogma of sin.

VIII

Conservatism with Imagination: Disraeli and Newman

> We are not indebted to the Reason of man for any of the great achievements which are the landmarks of human action and human progress. It was not Reason that besieged Troy; it was not Reason that sent forth the Saracen from the Desert to conquer the world; that inspired the Crusades; that instituted the Monastic orders; it was not Reason that produced the Jesuits; above all, it was not Reason that created the French Revolution. Man is only truly great when he acts from passions; never irresistible but when he appeals to the imagination. Even Mormon counts more votaries than Bentham.
>
> —Benjamin Disraeli, *Coningsby*

TWO JEWS INTRODUCED the new conservatism and the new radicalism: Disraeli and Marx. For three decades, though poles apart in society, they inhabited the same London. The showy proprietor of Hughenden, chaffing, beguiling, or astounding the House of Commons; the sour toiler at the British Museum, where (as Cunninghame Graham says) learned men of all nations wear out their eyes for a pittance that a dock-walloper would scorn—these two children of Israel, either the son of a Jewish father who had divorced himself from the old orthodoxy, perceived that the liberal society of the nineteenth century was doomed to suicide. Marx proposed to efface the whole extant social order and substitute a collectivistic life shaped upon a thorough materialism; Disraeli was determined to resuscitate the virtues of an older order.

If Ricardo is acknowledged as the greatest of the liberal economists, a case may be made that the three principal movements in English social thought, from the accession of Victoria to the present day, have been dominated by leaders imbued with the Hebrew tradition, none of whom wholly succeeded in breaking free from his Jewishness. Disraeli, at least, never sought to sever this bond; for, though a professed Anglican, he gloried in his ancestry and the "great Asian mystery" that had conquered Europe. Christianity, he said, was the culmination of Hebraism; conservative society was the temporal expression of Hebraic moral principle.

Yet it is exaggeration to speak of Disraeli as if conservative ideas in Victorian times were sustained entirely by his fervid and baroque imagination. He did, indeed, resurrect Toryism as a political movement, saving it from amalgamation with a utilitarian Liberalism. He attracted to conservatism a popular following that, a hundred and fifty years after his Reform Act, still can win a majority in the House of Commons. His novels and speeches set in the English mind a myth of the Tory heritage (myths are true in essence, however fanciful in detail), and so diverted into conservative quarters much of that romantic enthusiasm which in France and Germany flared as a revolutionary force. But Disraeli, though immensely clever as a novelist, splendidly resourceful as a party leader, wonderfully shrewd as a diplomat, was not precisely a philosopher. His genius was the manifestation of a lavish imagination, sometimes erratic. Metaphysical first principles, to which Burke turned with reluctant majesty, to which Coleridge applied his convoluted talents with dreamy relish, hardly entered Disraeli's books and speeches except as flashing epigrams or vasty Oriental secrets, veiled from vulgar sight like dwellers in a seraglio. The master of philosophical conservatism in the Victorian age was Newman, who shares this chapter with the author of *Sybil* and *Con-*

tarini Fleming. However incongruous in character, these two were
the chief conservators of traditional English ideas and forms, in
their time. Yet Disraeli was a kind of intruder upon Toryism, long
distrusted by the men whose cause he was resolved to redeem;
and Newman seemed to most of his contemporaries an apostate
from English traditions, forgetting Canterbury for Rome. Often
it requires a man who is not quite one of them to wake conservatives from their congenital lethargy. Sir Robert Peel, whom the
Tories trusted far more than ever they had trusted Canning, led
them unwittingly to the brink of destruction.

In 1848, when Marx and Engels issued the Communist Manifesto, Disraeli was assuming leadership of the Tory party; and
Newman, at the Oratory in Birmingham, was on the eve of his
struggle to establish a Catholic University in Dublin. In 1867, when
the first volume of *Capital* appeared, Disraeli effected his Reform;
and Newman was halfway between the *Apologia pro Vita Sua* and
A Grammar of Assent. All three careers, however inconsonant, were
protests against Liberalism. Marx, Disraeli, and Newman believed
that Liberalism, though so confident of its own immortality, was
not long for this world, being no more than a transitional doctrine, an evanescent blossom. Though Liberalism imagined itself
to be a glorious new flower, in fact, these critics perceived, it was
a parasite upon the decayed trunk of the old order: the morals
and politics of Liberalism took their sustenance from the traditional soil which Liberalism repudiated, and if that order perished,
they must wither. The skepticism of Benthamites and Manchesterians could flourish only in a society still controlled substantially
by orthodox belief; Liberal parliamentarianism was sustained by
the aristocratic loyalties of the old England. Let orthodoxy and
traditional political establishments die, and Liberalism must sink
into the grave after them. Marx looked forward with a ferocious
joy to this consummation and demise of middle-class ascendancy;
Disraeli and Newman endeavored to save piety, order, and freedom by restoring the balance which Utilitarianism had overthrown.

Whether in scholars like Bentham and Mill and Grote, or in men of affairs like Cobden and Bright and Chadwick, the quality most conspicuously lacking in Liberals was higher imagination. They went for facts, adoring the particular, however isolated, almost in defiance of the Decalogue. This passionate attachment to facts, the legacy of Bacon and Locke, has had a depressing effect upon the British and the American mind ever since. "It is difficult not to feel that for some English historians," Duncan Forbes comments, "a thought of Coleridge's, say, still seems somehow less 'real,' less of a hard 'fact,' than a migration of herring or an Act of Parliament. The history of ideas has never been as eagerly pursued in England as it has been elsewhere."[1] Transcending English empiricism, neither Disraeli nor Newman was afraid of ideas; they understood the power of imagination, and its role in history; and so, in an inferior sense, did Marx. Despite Marx's formal adherence to Utilitarian concepts of argument and proof, despite his belligerent determination to be scientific, his influence has been that of a man of imagination—an imagination begrimed and fettered, true, but still participating in the world of ideas, superior to the tyranny of particular facts. "To consider whether Marx was 'right' or 'wrong'; to dredge Volumes I and III of *Capital* for inconsistencies or logical flaws, to 'refute' the Marxian system is, in the last resort, sheer waste of time," says Professor Alexander Gray; "for when we consort with Marx we are no longer in the world of reason or logic. He saw visions—clear visions of the passing of all things, much more nebulous visions of how all things may be made new. And his visions, or some of them, awoke a responsive chord in the hearts of many men."[2] Though assertedly a materialist, in truth Marx was an idealist, indoctrinated by Hegel; and this aspect of his character, which he endeavored to strip from himself as if it were Nessus' shirt, accounts nevertheless for his victory over the Utilitarians whose method he imitated. He dealt, however mistakenly, with ends; the Liberals, with means and particulars; and the mass of men being governed by imagination more than reason, in such a struggle the odds favor the visionary.

For Marx, the end of human endeavor was absolute equality of condition. He was under no illusion as to equality in a hypothetical state of nature: equality never before had existed in society, he knew; he sneered at all concepts of natural right. Equality would be no restoration, but a creation. Men are not equal by nature; the socialist must level them by legislation and economic device. "In order to establish equality, we must first establish inequality"—is this not the most significant sentence in *Capital?* The clever, the strong, the industrious, the virtuous, must be compelled to serve the weak and stupid and slack and vicious; nature must submit to the socialist art, so that an Idea may be vindicated. "Marx's faith in his untutored intuitions of ethical knowledge, illustrated in his unquestioning adherence to the goal of communism, his philosophy of history, and his assertion of the unique efficacy of the method of revolution in social development, are examples of an apriorism which is the essence of idealism," J. L. Gray writes.[3] Arbitrary though this ethical end Equality is, in it resides more imagination than in the endless reiteration of "the greatest happiness of the greatest number." Thus the radical impulse which the Liberals once employed has deserted Benthamism for Marxism. The principle of Envy, shrouded in verbiage, vanquishes naked Self-Interest.

The imagination, and the ends, of Disraeli and Newman were of another nature. They abhorred the idea of equality. Their end was Order; order in the realm of spirit, order in the realm of society. In religious faith, a belief which recognizes the divine character of the church, an immortal corporation independent of the state; in politics, a system which admits social diversity, hierarchy of rights and duties. Disraeli, who baptized Tory democracy, moulded his concept of English society round the core of aristocratic principle; Newman, who did much to save the church from being a mere tool of political authority, looked upon the life of the spirit as ascent to truth and upon education as the ladder to this transcendent wisdom. Both of them knew that the phrase "law and order" is not tautological: law, sacred or mundane, depends upon order, hierarchy of spirit and idea, gradation of society.

The careers of these imaginative conservatives, and their grim adversary's of whose existence they were scarcely aware, stretch across the half-century between the Liberal triumph of the 'thirties and the Conservative revival of the 'eighties. This was the age of Liberalism, from the adoption of the Reform Act of 1832 until the Reform of 1867 made its consequences felt. Politically, it was the half-century of the lower middle classes, "government by grocers," enfranchised in 1832; economically, the epoch of triumphant Manchesterianism, free trade, free enterprise, and competitive individualism; intellectually, the era of popularized Utilitarianism; religiously, the age of ecclesiastical commissions and Evangelicalism, the Pharisaical Clapham Sect and Trollope's Reverend Mr. Slope. In the life of the masses, it was the day of hell-holes, the plight of the urban industrial populations described by Saint-Simon and by Engels, the Britain that groans and reeks in the pages of *Hard Times* and *Bleak House* and persists into Mayhew's *London Labour and the London Poor* and Gissing's *Workers in the Dawn*. Chartism was its manifestation during the years when Disraeli contended against Peel, and Newman went over to Rome; but Chartism was only one symptom of a dread which dogged all ranks of society.[4] It was the England of *Sybil, or The Two Nations*.

The "Hungry 'Forties" were not in truth peculiarly hungry: the population was better fed than it had been in the 'thirties, or the 'twenties, and the 'fifties were better fed still, as a general prosperity penetrated to the lower strata of society—at the same time staving off the agricultural depression which the Old Tories had been sure would follow on the heels of Corn Law repeal. The disorders pictured in *Sybil*, like the spirit of Chartism itself, were allayed by cheap bread and higher wages. Marx, though prescient in many things, never was farther from the mark than when he predicted increasingly desperate poverty for the working classes; for from 1848 onward, the material condition of industrial populations has improved throughout Western nations, except for comparatively brief intervals of war and economic dislocation. But Disraeli and Newman, lamentable though they knew the material condition of the new proletariat to be, saw that physical poverty was not the cardinal problem of Victorian society. The evil extended deeper far: it was the curse of a populace cut off from the continuity of humanity, deprived of religious consolation, political tradition, decency of existence, true family, education, and possibility of moral improvement. The vast majority of men always had been poor; but perhaps never, since the triumph of Christianity, had they been so bored and hopeless, condemned to monotonous labor in the grimiest and grittiest of hideous towns, in a milieu philosophically dedicated to material success and moral individualism.

Having seen the fruits of Liberalism, Disraeli and Newman, in their separate ways, became Tory reformers. Marx, detesting bourgeois ascendancy, nevertheless would have substituted a society with all the spiritual or anti-spiritual characteristics of that system, but dominated by manual laborers. Disraeli as a statesman, Newman as a philosopher, recognized in radicalism of this sort simply the further corruption of human existence upon Utilitarian principles. Faith, loyalty, and tradition were the bases of their social thought; they would restore to humankind what a voracious industrialism and a corroding Benthamite philosophy had defaced. Their instrument was the power of imagination.

2

What place was there for Tory principles, asks Keith Feiling, in the charnel-house of the shattered Tory party after passage of the Reform Bill of 1832? And he answers:

Much; if they realized that since the Revolution they had exhausted themselves in defence of eighteenth-century Whig monopolies, wherein a landed aristocracy should have all political power, and this power should be buttressed by an exclusive Church. If they cut away this incrustation, if they examined their original native forces in the light of the new world round them, they might yet find things to do and survivals of imperishable value. There was a Church, with a spiritual integrity and a spiritual sanction for a historical society. There was a Crown, tarnished, hated, and partisan now, but still with a role to play. And there was a people. For the present it was neglected, faction-ridden, almost revolutionary. But it was capable, as it might prove desirous, of living its new life and finding new happiness within ancient bounds and old affections. It might respond, not to bitter revolutionary formula or sentimental ideal, but to that balanced measure of life, that liberty in order, which had been set forth by Hooker, Burke, and Coleridge, and lately exemplified, with whatever shortcomings, by Pitt, Liverpool, Huskisson, and Canning.[5]

Appropriately, this passage has the ring of Disraeli. For Benjamin Disraeli transmuted fallen reaction into rising conservative courage.

The Jews, says Sidonia in *Coningsby*, are essentially Tories. "Toryism indeed is but copied from the mighty prototype which has fashioned Europe. And every generation they must become more powerful and more dangerous to the society which is hostile to them." For, denied the privileges of full citizenship, Jews are driven into radical movements and secret societies. Their instincts as a people remain conservative, nevertheless; as Disraeli writes in *Lord George Bentinck*, "They are the trustees of tradition, and the conservators of the religious element. They are a living and the most striking evidence of the falsity of that pernicious doctrine of modern times, the natural equality of man....They have also another characteristic, the faculty of acquisition....Thus it will be seen that all the tendencies of the Jewish race are conservative. Their bias is to religion, property, and natural aristocracy; and it should be the interest of statesmen that this bias of a great race should be encouraged and their energies and creative powers enlisted in the cause of existing society."[6]

The Jewish radical is an anomaly: the traditions of race and religion, the Jewish devotion to family, old usage, and spiritual continuity, all incline the Jew toward conservatism.* It is exclusion from society which provokes the Jewish social revolutionary.

---

*For a recognition of these tender yet enduring characteristics, described by a writer politically radical, see Arthur Miller's short story "Monte Saint Angelo" in *The Cornhill Magazine*, summer, 1951.

Karl Marx, never able to free himself from this complex resentment, became a hater of Jewry as well as of capitalism; but Disraeli, ignoring the hoots of "Jewboy" which greeted him at the hustings, declared that Sinai and the Hebrew prophets would save Western society from being reduced to powder by Benthamite notions. Friedrich Gentz, the friend of Metternich and translator of Burke, represented the true tendency of Jewish social thought, said Disraeli; and more eminently still, Disraeli himself showed how modern Jewish character may attach itself with a virile affection to the institutions of what once was called Christendom.

A stripe luxuriant, Eastern, perhaps Semitic, runs through Disraeli's sparkling imagination, even more characteristic of the man than were his flamboyant clothes. But though his may have been a fancy sometimes marred by extravagance and conceit, still it shone a faculty creative and incisive, consuming the dry bones of Utilitarianism in a blaze of color and high exhortation. This it was, quite as much as the Reform of 1867 and successful imperialism, which defeated the stiff rationalism of the Liberals. "The false English nobles, and their Jew" did more than terminate the ascendancy of the lower middle classes: they exploded the Liberal assumption that politics would be governed increasingly by the soberly rational citizen, weighing and balancing material interests.

Early in his career, Disraeli's imagination conceived a theory of the English constitution which dominated his course until his death in 1881—although modified in his later years by political expediency and wearying responsibility. The seeds of this growth were sown by Coleridge; Disraeli the Tory radical cultivated them as a program for Young England, and even today they nurture the mind of the Tory party, although that party has received tremendous accessions from Liberalism. It is interesting to contrast this vision of Disraeli with the inflamed vision of Karl Marx. Either propounded a theory of classes. Marx insisted that warfare among classes is inevitable, in time must be catastrophic, and will end with the absorption of all classes into the proletariat, establishing a classless society. Disraeli declared that the real interests of classes are not inimical; that they are bound together in the nation's welfare; and his aim in politics was the reconciliation of classes, reunion of the two nations of the nineteenth century, rich and poor, into one state—but this reunion a vindication and restoration of class, not its abolition. Class is order; without order, law crumbles. The intelligent Tory, invoking the old sense of order and obligation, must struggle to infuse into modern industrial life the aristocratic spirit, reviving that loyalty to persons and places which is the rudiment of every high conservative impulse. British democracy depends upon the continued existence of a true sense of class.

Assuming form during the reign of the Plantagenets, said Disraeli, the English constitution comprehends a system of recognized orders and classes in the state, each with its peculiar privileges, so acknowledged and balanced as to afford every great interest in the commonwealth its voice in the affairs of the realm. In Tudor times, the violence of the Reformation hurt this balance, reducing the Church as a separate order in the kingdom, abolishing endowments for educating the poor, and throwing into the hands of great nobles a mass of landed property which ever since has enabled certain of these magnates, banded into a party which became the Whigs, to exercise an unjust preponderance, bullying Crown and Commons. The attempt of the Crown to resist this ascendancy precipitated the Civil Wars, and the extreme measures of the Parliamentarians rallied round the King a party truly Tory. The Revolution escaped from the grasp of the great magnates, who found themselves saddled with the Commonwealth. Dissatisfied with the Restoration, the Whigs brought in William III, hoping to make him a Doge on the pattern of the Venetian oligarchy; but he baffled them. Their discomfiture was transitory, however—for, compelling Anne to acknowledge Hanoverian succession, they obtained foreign kings who indeed must submit to being treated as doges. George III stood up against them; they had nearly trounced him, nevertheless, when the French Revolution burst upon the world, and Burke led over to Pitt a large part of the Whig strength. Since then, the Whigs had remained a party inordinately ambitious, seeking to establish their monopoly of power at whatever cost to the ordering of the commonwealth. In such a peer as the Duke of Bedford lay the gravest menace to English liberties and traditions.

The Tories, devoted to Crown, Church, and the privileges of the nation, have the duty of resisting this Venetian Constitution which Whigs and Liberals advocate. The Reform Bill of 1832 (Disraeli continues) was a further ruthless step toward the destruction of national tradition and character: among its other vices, the act abolished ancient popular franchises in towns like Preston, which had spoken for the lower orders of the realm; so the reformers silenced bitter and genuine grievances. Restriction of political power to a particular class was Whig policy; recognition of the right of all classes to be heard, Tory principle. These ideas are set out in *A Vindication of the English Constitution* (1835), *The Letters of Runnymede* (1836), *Coningsby* (1844), *Sybil* (1845), and in Disraeli's earlier speeches.

Tory recovery after 1832, under Peel, had been no more than a sham: Sir Robert had obtained office by sacrificing principle. A great statesman except when he had to deal with the future, Peel suffered from a lack of imagination more revolutionary in its consequences than a library of Jacobin pamphlets. His Tamworth Manifesto conceded to the Whigs, in substance, their chief demands, and when Peel yielded on the Corn Law question, the economic bulwark of the old Tory interest fell, and with it, all too probably, the security of the country gentlemen, as a class a most useful element in English society. Disraeli, Bentinck, and the squires in the House of Commons (what Bagehot called "the Army of Fogies"), outraged, repudiated Peel and reconstituted the Tory party during their years in the political wilderness.* In time, this resuscitated party, led by Derby and Disraeli, was sufficiently strong to win office precariously; and after 1873, the Conserva-

---

*Some two hundred and fifty Tory country gentlemen followed Bentinck and Disraeli into the lobbies on the Corn Law division. In 1951, only fifteen members of the House of Commons, in all parties, described themselves as "landowners."

tives obtained a preponderance which (with one short interval) enabled them to govern Britain for three decades.

Now what was it, in the ideas of Disraeli, that provided the Conservatives with spirit enough to recover from Peelism and to dominate a nation more heavily industrialized than any other in the world? What enabled the party of the country gentlemen to hold office well into the twentieth century, when they had thought themselves irretrievably ruined in 1845? How did Disraeli's theory of English history take shape as a political philosophy? The fascination of Disraeli's personality, and the details of his long struggle against Gladstone, often obscure estimates of his accomplishment. When admirers of Lord Beaconsfield endeavor to sum up his achievements, sometimes one is confronted with a miscellaneous list of innovations—the Reform of 1867, the Factory Acts, aid to schools, commencement of a program of public housing—as if these were of themselves conservative measures. In truth, Disraeli's positive legislation sometimes was inconsistent with his theory, and in any case inferior to it. His really important achievement, as a political leader, was implanting in the public imagination an ideal of Toryism which has been immeasurably valuable in keeping Britain faithful to her constitutional traditions. The Primrose League mattered more than Suez. A foreigner who travels today through West Riding, say, from Leeds to Sheffield, or through any other densely-settled British industrial region, must be astonished that Conservative governments can exist in Britain. Yet many of the workingmen who live in these grim brick rows or in the monotony of the new council-houses vote for Conservative candidates; in the country at large, the Tories claim millions of supporters among the regular trade-union members, and many more among the laboring classes in general. Britain, which Saint-Simon thought ripe for proletarian revolution during Liverpool's ministry, was still Tory enough in 1951 to make Churchill prime minister and in 1986 to sustain a Tory lady in that office. Nowhere else in the modern world has a unified conservative party enjoyed such continuity of purpose and such enduring popular support. In great part, this is the triumph of Disraeli.

"The people of this country have ceased to be a nation," says Tancred. "They are a crowd, and only kept in some rude provisional discipline by the remains of that old system which they are daily destroying." Here is the kernel of Disraeli's social theories: the idea of the nation. Repudiating the social atomism of the Benthamites, despising the class-hostility of the rising socialists, he reminded Englishmen that they are not simply an aggregation of economic units, not simply soldiers in a class struggle: they constitute a nation, and of that nation the Crown, the aristocracy, and the Church are the guardians. The fabric of nationality has been terribly rent, and must be repaired. British liberty has consisted in a balance of orders; but this has been corrupted by Whigs and Utilitarians, who do not understand, or who actually detest, the principle of nationality, in which no class is forgotten. The House of Commons has become almost absolute, controlled substantially by an exclusive economic class, rigidly defined by the ten-pound franchise; the House of Lords has been degraded by the mauling it suffered in 1832, so that it is scarcely more than a court of registration; the Crown has come to be looked upon as a mere symbol, rather than the shield of the realm; the Church is being treated as a simple agency of moral discipline, to be managed and despoiled by Parliament. And the mass of Englishmen, the peasantry and the forgotten town laborers, are hideously neglected, abandoned to ignorance, vice, monotony, and poverty. They have less voice in affairs than they had in the Middle Ages. The nation is rotting. It is not an age of political corruption, but something worse, "an age of social disorganization, far more dangerous in its consequences, because far more extensive."[7] What wonder that the Utilitarian system, though it is now dying away, awoke some response in an age of social torpor? "Anointed Kings turned into chief magistrates, and therefore much overpaid; Estates of the Realm changed into parliaments of virtual representation, and therefore requiring real reform; Holy Church transformed into national establishment and therefore grumbled at by all the nation for whom it was not supported. What an inevitable harvest of Sedition, Radicalism, Infidelity!"[8]

The old Whigs, with their predilection for a Venetian oligarchy; the Liberals, who speak for a smug Philistine class; the Radicals, steeped in the dreary doctrines of political uniformity and Manchesterian economics—these parties hold out no hope to the nation of England. If reform is to come, it must be the work of a reinvigorated Toryism. The Tories must save the true Commons of the land. Disraeli was contemptuous of the abstract term "people," so much in vogue with radicals, which bewildering noun really is "a term of natural philosophy and not of political science."[9] In *Runnymede*, again, he declares, "The phrase 'the people' is sheer nonsense. It is not a political term. It is a phrase of natural history. A people is not a species; a civilized community is a nation."[10] A sentimentalized and undefined "people" is not the object of Disraeli's solicitude: he would rescue from their misery simply the lower classes of Britain, disfranchised and disinherited.

What these classes had become, Disraeli describes in *Sybil*; and the blue books bear him out. The peasant had sunk to an "agricultural labourer" synonymous with pauper, subsidized by the parish to keep wages low; the industrial workers are denizens of Wodgate, or Hell-House Yard, at the mercy of the tommy-shopkeeper, huddled in swarming thousands, "lodged in the most miserable tenements in the most hideous burgh in the ugliest country in the world." They are brutally ignorant of religion, or at best believe in "our Lord and Saviour Pontius Pilate who was crucified to save our sins; and in Moses, Goliath, and the rest of the Apostles." And this mob is increasing. "I speak of the annual arrival of more than three hundred thousand strangers in this island," says Gerard, the socialist. "How will you feed them? How will you clothe them? How will you house them? They have given up butcher's meat; must they give up bread? And as for raiment and shelter, the rags of the kingdom are exhausted and your sinks and cellars already swarm like rabbit warrens." The bastard children are dosed with laudanum, and, if they survive, thrust out into the street to shift for themselves; the population works four days out of seven, and is drunken the other three. What is there to conserve in this society?

A vast deal remains to be conserved, or restored. After this terrible indictment, Disraeli remains a Tory. "Loyalty is not a phrase, Faith is not a delusion, and Popular Liberty something more diffusive and substantial than the profane exercise of the sacred rights of sovereignty by political classes." Men cannot improve a society by setting fire to it: they must seek out its old virtues, and bring them back into the light. England is great still, capable of regeneration; but if committed to the hands of the doctrinaire innovator, she must fall. As Disraeli said twenty years after the publication of *Sybil,*

You have an ancient, powerful, richly-endowed Church, and perfect religious liberty. You have unbroken order and complete freedom. You have landed estates as large as the Romans', combined with commercial enterprise such as Carthage and Venice united never equalled. And you must remember that this peculiar country, with these strong contrasts, is not governed by force; it is not governed by standing armies; it is governed by a most singular series of traditionary influences, which generation after generation cherishes because it knows that they embalm custom and represent law....And these mighty creations are out of all proportion to the essential and indigenous elements and resources of the country. If you destroy that state of society, remember this— England cannot begin again.[11]

The remedies? They lay, first of all, in the revival of a feeling of nationality, community, repudiating Utilitarian selfishness and individualism. Those sufferers in the hell of Wodgate were as much Englishmen as the bankers of the City. With this must come the restoration of true religious feeling; for Disraeli, though no theologian, was deeply pious, and the Angel of Sinai spoke to him as commandingly as to Tancred—if less dramatically. There must follow a series of political and economic amendments: the renewal of reverence for the Crown; the reinvigoration of the Church; the preservation of local government; the establishment of commercial codes that take cognizance of the agricultural interest; fairness to Ireland; physical improvement of the condition of the laboring people, "by establishing that labour required regulation as much as property." And this must be restoration, not revolution. Young England aspired to a great deal, and accomplished some of this—accomplished more, perhaps, than one realizes on first reflection. The Conservatives succeeded, under the guidance of Disraeli, in preserving venerable institutions which Bentham confidently had expected to be extirpated by the middle of the nineteenth century. A hundred years after Disraeli became the leader of the Tories, the Crown was held in greater affection than ever before, whatever the diminution of its political function; the Lords survived, for all the Parliament Act of 1911, and fifteen peers were ministers in the Labour government; the Church of England, though still only in name the church of most Englishmen, nevertheless remained established and endowed; the *arrondissement* had not replaced the parish, nor the *gendarmerie* the constable; the condition of the laboring classes, confounding the predictions of Marx, was better than ever before. And alone among the great powers of the earth, Britain had experienced no revolution or civil war throughout the nineteenth and twentieth centuries. This is a magnificent conservative achievement, the work of Disraeli, who taught a confused and almost-ruined party the principles of Bolingbroke and Burke and Coleridge.

The Toryism of Disraeli convinced Englishmen that the lower classes were not forgotten, that the English nation did indeed still live, that the masters of society had a common interest with the masses of society. The humanitarian legislation of Shaftesbury and his colleagues had something to do with all this; but mere positive law does not keep a nation contented; the problem of social tranquillity is not the problem of want. "No orator ever made an impression by appealing to men as to their plainest physical wants," Walter Bagehot writes, "except when he could allege that those wants were caused by some one's tyranny."[12] Disraeli proved that Conservatism was not tyranny; it was more popular than Liberalism.

Yet the final proof of Toryism's popular sympathies which Derby and Disraeli found it necessary to supply may turn out to have been, in the long run, the death-warrant of conservatism.

That, of course, was the Reform Bill of 1867, admitting to the franchise the urban laboring classes. "It was not merely a question of political tactics," Nigel Birch writes; "Disraeli had a profound belief that democracy is Tory, and events have not proved him wrong."[13] This is sanguine; nor, indeed, is it accurate to say that Disraeli felt any firm confidence in democracy. The Reform Bill which passed was not the bill he had drawn up, and he was in a mood of dejection throughout the turbulent days of debate; events were moving faster even than the supple Disraeli could behold without dismay. Thirty years earlier, it is true, he had written that the English constitution was "an aristocratic constitution founded on an equality of civil rights," by virtue of its peculiar government, "in fact a noble democracy."[14] In his *Vindication*, he had remarked, "If we examine not only the political constitution, but the political condition of the country, we shall in truth discover that the state of our society is that of a complete democracy, headed by an hereditary chief, the executive and legislative functions performed by the two privileged classes of the community, but the whole body of the nation entitled, if duly qualified, to participate in the exercise of those functions, and constantly participating in them."[15] Yet this was limited and traditional democracy; absolute and doctrinaire democracy he dreaded nearly so much as Lord Salisbury did. In 1865, he hoped that the House would "sanction no step that has a tendency to democracy, but that it will maintain the ordered state of free England in which we live." Privileges should indeed be granted to the laboring classes, but not as absolute rights, he said during the debate in 1867: "Popular privileges are consistent with a state of society in which there is great inequality of conditions. Democratic rights, on the contrary, demand that there should be equality of conditions as the fundamental basis of the society which they regulate."[16] Democracy once triumphant, he knew, would enforce equality of condition; and the Britain of one hundred years later confirmed his foreboding.

He wished to give preponderance to no single class in the nation: a broad extension of the franchise would accord that dangerous preponderance to the artisans. Yet he recognized the necessity for settling the parliamentary reform question on some basis, quieting the dangerous agitation for organic change. He hoped the Act of 1867 would be final; of course it was not: a third Reform, 1884–1885, enfranchised agricultural laborers and miners and other householders in the counties, swept away the seats held by the small agricultural boroughs, and dealt the *coup de grace* to the ancient aristocratic and territorial interest. Preponderance in the House of Commons passed finally to the industrial towns. Women, and everyone else still excluded, received the franchise in succeeding enactments (1918 and 1928), until the Socialists completed the Benthamite and Chartist program of "one man, one vote" by abolishing the university seats eight decades after Disraeli's Reform. The Tories were indeed shooting Niagara. But what else could have been done? Walter Bagehot, the most sagacious of Liberals, knew that 1867 was simply the sequel to 1832, much though he abhorred the dishing of the Whigs: "The reformers of 1832 destroyed intellectual constituencies in great numbers without creating any new ones, and without saying, indeed without thinking, that it was desirable to create any. They thus by conspicuous action, which is the most influential mode of political instruction, taught mankind that an increase in the power of numbers was the change most to be desired in England. And of course the mass of mankind are only too ready to think so."[17] The Act of 1832 had reduced enfranchisement to mere financial qualification; after that, popular opinion was sure to demand reduction of qualifications until universal suffrage was attained.

"Few pages in our modern political history are more discreditable than the story of the 'Conservative' Reform Bill of 1867," said Lecky, a generation later. This is harsh; still, passage of the Act might have been better handled. The "fancy franchises"—plural votes for the educated, the thrifty, the propertied, the leaders of men, to ensure that votes might be weighed as well as counted— were lost in the confusion of debate, with Liberals and Tories and Radicals endeavoring to outdo one another in generosity toward the electors they were about to enfranchise. The Tories, lacking an absolute majority in the House of Commons, ended by passing a bill that resembled only vaguely their original proposal, which had been hedged about with safeguards and reservations. Gladstone had announced in 1864, "I venture to say that every man who is not presumably incapacitated by some consideration of personal unfitness or of political danger is morally entitled to come within the pale of the Constitution." Thus it came to pass; and voting ceased to be considered a privilege, and became a "moral right." How far private property, individuality, and decency in government may survive under absolute democracy is not yet certain. But the wisdom and vigor of the party Disraeli reconstituted certainly provided a leadership for the new democracy which kept it sober and honest during its first years of emancipation.

The working man is not congenitally a radical, Disraeli said at the Guildhall in 1874; he refused to share the fear that laboring men will never return a conservative government. "We have been told that a working man cannot be conservative, because he has nothing to conserve—he has neither land nor capital; as if there were not other things in the world as precious as land and capital!" The working man has liberty, justice, security of person and home, equal administration of law, unfettered industry. "Surely these are privileges worthy of being preserved!...And if that be the case, is it wonderful that the working classes are Conservative?"[18] Fifteen decades later, some of them are conservative yet, though they may have forgotten long ago what party passed the Act of 1867; the worst fears of Lowe's Adullamites have not been realized. Disraeli's ideal of a government truly national, not a government of preponderant class, however injured by the rise of doctrinaire Socialism as a parliamentary party, is not dead.

Five years after its passage, Disraeli said that the Act of 1867 was founded on a confidence that the great body of the English people are conservative. The objects of Toryism, he explained, are maintenance of the old institutions of the country, preservation of the Empire, and elevation of the condition of the people.[19] Disraeli's party had no reason to be ashamed of its performance in these matters. They had come a long way since, in 1833, the party was thought to be nearly defunct, "except by a few old battered crones of office, crouched round the embers of faction which they were fanning, and muttering 'reaction' in mystic whispers." They had come a long way since, in 1845, Peel turned his back upon the country gentlemen. And they survive as a powerful and intelligent party near the end of the twentieth century chiefly, perhaps, because of the imaginative gifts of the "old Jew gentleman sitting on the top of chaos." Here and there Disraeli failed; but in large part, he succeeded in diverting the torrent of progress into the canal of tradition.

3

People say to me, that it is but a dream to suppose that Christianity should regain the organic power in human society which once it possessed. I cannot help that; I never said it could. I am not a politician; I am proposing no measures, but exposing a fallacy, and resisting a pretence. Let Benthamism reign, if men have no aspirations; but do not tell them to be romantic, and then solace them with glory; do not attempt by philosophy what once was done by religion. The Ascendancy of Faith may be impracticable, but the reign of Knowledge is incomprehensible. The problem for statesmen of this age is how to educate the masses, and literature and science cannot give the solution.
    —John Henry Newman, "The Tamworth Reading
       Room" (1841)

Newman, indeed, was no politician. His only important essay directly touching upon politics is "Who's to Blame?" (1855), provoked by English disasters in the Crimea; otherwise, politics in his writings is only a faint shadow of theology and the theory of knowledge. But real conservatism, too, transcends politics. Newman was a consistent Tory, attached to the principle of aristocracy and the concept of loyalty to persons; yet this is not his important contribution to conservative thought. Suffused with that sense of the vanity of worldly things which is highly characteristic of great conservatives, he dealt with the problems of society only because the Benthamites and other radicals seemed determined to force him and his allies into political controversy. ''Starting then with the being of a God, (which, as I have said, is as certain to me as the certainty of my own existence, though when I try to put the grounds of that certainty into logical shape I find a difficulty in doing so in mood and figure to my satisfaction,) I look out of myself into the world of men, and there I see a sight which fills me with unspeakable distress. The world seems simply to give the lie to that great truth, of which my whole being is so full....The sight of the world is nothing else than the prophet's scroll, full of 'lamentations, and mourning, and woe.' ''[20] This sensitive and subtle man lived in an age, however, in which Caesar claimed the things that are God's; and so Newman spent his life in arguments and struggles abhorrent to his contemplative nature.

Keble, Pusey, Newman, Hurrell Froude, and the whole body of the Tractarians commenced in 1833 their struggle against the encroachments of Utilitarian measures upon the Church. The Reform Act was followed by a wave of Liberal legislation designed to reshape the Church of England; and that policy was formed chiefly by the body of opinion which elected the first Reform Parliament—the Nonconformist middle classes. So long as Parliament had been an assembly of Anglicans, so long as the Test and Corporation Acts prohibited the seating of Dissenters, Romanists, and Jews, the Church of England rested content with its subordination to the Lords and Commons; but now this was swept away. Hereafter, it seemed, the House of Commons was to be dominated, or at best heavily influenced, by Nonconformists and secular rationalists, hostile toward the Establishment, often bent upon expressing in statute the enmity and contempt for the Church which Bentham and James Mill avowed. The assault upon the Church began promptly; and, though presently it was abated both by the strength of the Oxford Movement and by the alarm raised among Evangelicals and even Nonconformists, the Church of England has been afraid of the state ever since. Establishment of the Ecclesiastical Commission, arrogating to the laity control over church revenues; bullying of great prelates, notably the Bishop of Durham, out of their ancient prerogatives; commutation of tithes, in 1836; assumption of cathedral endowments (to anticipate) by the Ecclesiastical Commissioners between 1852 and 1868; just before Keble's Assize Sermon, the suppression of ten Irish bishoprics by the government—these, the Tractarians knew, were only the beginning of a secularizing process which, if not impeded, would end in the humanitarian psuedo-religion advocated by the Utilitarians. Things never went so far as Bentham and Mill hoped. The Tractarians, aided by an inchoate public attachment to the Church, averted disestablishment, disendowment, and that plundering of Church property which swept across Europe after 1830, extending even to the citadels of orthodoxy in Italy, Spain, and Portugal.

This was a considerable conservative accomplishment, but there is no need to dwell upon it here. When Mr. Harding, in *The Warden*, loses the emoluments of Hiram's Hospital to the Ecclesiastical Commissioners (stirred up by Tom Towers of the *Jupiter*), one sees the nature of the struggle between the high-and-dry church and the triumphant Liberals as well as it is expressed anywhere; and Trollope pictures in the debate of the feeble bedesmen about the justice of this, and in their conquest by the professional agitator, a victory of Utilitarian concepts—assisted by those selfish impulses which the Utilitarians founded their system upon—over prescriptive arrangements. But the race was not, in the end, to the Reverend Mr. Slope and Mrs. Proudie, or even to Tom Towers of the *Jupiter*. By 1850, as G. M. Young writes, Coleridge (and the Oxford Movement that was his grandchild) had defeated Bentham. The Church was more than a moral police-force, and society more than an aggregation of individuals. The Tractarians insured that "the corporate and sacramental aspect of the Church should re-emerge, and that religion would have to find a place for feelings of beauty, antiquity, and mystery, which the ruling theology had dismissed or ignored as worldly or unprofitable or profane."[21] Flirtations of some later Anglo-Catholics with radical collectivism notwithstanding, the Oxford Movement was an English conservative phenomenon of enduring importance. By his leadership among the Tractarians, Newman helped to resuscitate the traditional elements in Anglican faith; and when he went over to Roman Catholicism, he exercised there, too, a conservative influence upon a body of persons long hostile toward the English state, and raised permanently the intellectual standards of that growing communion, so that the chief thinkers among British Catholics, more than a century later, were conservatives in the line of Cardinal Newman.

For the student of conservative general ideas, however, these particulars (important though they were in the development of modern English thought) are not so interesting as the philosophical principles which Newman enunciated after he left Oxford for the Oratory of St. Philip Neri at Birmingham. His theory of knowledge and his idea of education: these are conservative concepts that, susceptible of universal application, flash out from the social controversies of modern Britain and modern America. Politics, any observant scholar soon finds, stretches upward into the problems of ethics, and ethics, in turn, is surmounted by the problems of religious faith. Newman continues the philosophical chain of Hooker and Burke, who knew that society subsists upon faith. This conviction is clear in Newman's early sermons and essays, but it attains fruition in *An Essay on the Development of Christian Doctrine* (1845), *The Idea of a University* (1853), *A Grammar of Assent* (1858), and *Apologia pro Vita Sua* (1864). Most cogently, perhaps, it is expounded in "The Tamworth Reading Room," which was published in the *Times* in February, 1841, and reprinted in *Discussions and Arguments* (1872). As a framework for the exposition of Newman's conservative beliefs, "The Tamworth Reading Room" serves very well.

Sir Robert Peel, who fought with all his energies to save the Conservative party from extinction after 1832, brought upon himself obloquy from the two greatest conservatives in Victorian times. "Peel was an example of the mistake of supposing that even the highest practical abilities are sufficient, without philosophical insight, to save a politician from grave errors," Lord Hugh Cecil writes. "The weakness of the practical mind is that while it clearly sees the actual existing circumstances of the case, it has small power of foresight."[22] The strong practical manufacturer of Tamworth compounded away, in the Tamworth Manifesto (1834), all the real principles of political Toryism, said Disraeli; and in his address at the opening of the Tamworth Reading Room (1841), Peel surrendered the intellectual premises of old England into the hands of the Utilitarians, said Newman. Cobden was shrewd when he "did not wholly despair of Peel": for quite as Sir Robert gradually was persuaded of the free-traders' case, so this defender of religious establishments let his own mind be captured by the metaphysical and educational principles of Utilitarianism, the concepts of Bentham and Brougham. Conservatism, political and spiritual, had to be rescued from a guardian thus seduced; and while Disraeli freed Toryism from the Peelites and re-established the line of demarcation between parties, Newman reaffirmed the venerable religious opposition to the Baconian idea of "knowledge as power" and to the Utilitarian ambition that education might become an instrument for material aggrandizement.

At the opening of the Tamworth Library, Peel had declared (in the homiletic vein he often exercised) that men must be educated, or they will be vicious, and Useful Knowledge is the instrument of their redemption; that "physical and moral science rouses, transports, exalts, enlarges, tranquillizes, and satisfies the mind"; that science is a neutral ground on which men may meet regardless of politics and religion. This is the view Brougham expounded at the inauguration of London University. Physical science will be even a source of consolation and pleasure at the hour of death. Disciples of Bentham (though embellishing their preceptor's arid prose with an imagery at once amatory and evangelical), Brougham and Peel spoke of knowledge as a means of obtaining power over nature, and improving men morally; of education, as practical training for success in this endeavor. But they wholly omitted religion, and its science of theology, from their scheme. Religion is controversial; therefore it has no place in the public instruction, they believed—even Sir Robert, the champion of the Church of England. Their concept of knowledge and education is shot through with fallacies.

For secular knowledge is not the principle of moral improvement, says Newman; nor is it the direct means of moral improvement; nor the antecedent of moral improvement. Secular knowledge is not a principle of social utility, nor a principle of action. Without personal religion, secular knowledge commonly is a tool of unbelief. Conviction is not produced by the logic of words, nor by the accumulation of facts. Physical science cannot bring certitude, for the most plausible scientific theories are no more than probable suppositions founded upon such scanty facts as we are able to grub together in our fumbling human way. Men are not going to be good because they have been taught assorted facts, or because they have been instructed in the art of doubting. True knowledge is not the product of orderly reason, of Benthamite logic, of data carefully weighed; no man bases his actions upon these abstract grounds. Bentham and Mill themselves, though they profess a system of principles rigidly scientific, in reality built their logic of words upon presuppositions and experiences of which, likely enough, they were not themselves conscious. No, knowledge is not the result of an instruction in physical and moral science. Like virtue, knowledge really is the product of a subtle process which men apprehend imperfectly at best: this is what Newman later called the Illative Sense.

In morals, as in physics, the stream cannot rise higher than its source. Christianity raises men from earth, for it comes from heaven; but human morality creeps, struts, or frets upon the earth's level, without wings to rise. The Knowledge School does not contemplate raising man above himself; it merely aims at disposing of his existing powers and tastes, as is most convenient, or is practicable under circumstances. It finds him, like the victims of the French Tyrant, doubled up in a cage in which he can neither lie, stand, sit, nor kneel, and its highest desire is to find an attitude in which his unrest may be least.[23]

Thus practical knowledge leaves man in torment. The heart is not reached through the reason. Dread of the unseen is the only known principle of subduing moral evil, but this is left quite out of consideration by Utilitarian educators. Scientific facts do not relieve modern man's boredom, nor offer him a hope above the vanity of human wishes. "If in education we begin with nature before grace, with evidences before faith, with science before conscience, with poetry before practice, we shall be doing much the same as if we were to indulge the appetites and passions, and turn a deaf ear to the reason."[24] Without a foundation of first principles, science itself is worthless—a meaningless accumulation of unrelated facts. Our first principles are not obtained by heaping together data, after Bacon's method, and drawing inferences. "Life is for action. If we insist on proofs for everything, we shall never come to action: to act you must assume, and that assumption is faith." Reason does not impel our impressions and our actions; it *follows* them.

If, then, we do not form our lives, or even our sciences, upon a logic of words or a museum of specimens, what actually is the source of our first principles, of our governing motives? What precisely is this Illative Sense of Newman? In *The Grammar of Assent*, he defines it briefly thus: "It is the mind that reasons, and that controls its own reasonings, not any technical apparatus of words and propositions. This power of judging and concluding, when in its perfection, I call the Illative Sense." Here we have a use of "sense" parallel to "good sense," "common sense," "a sense of beauty;" it is a uniform faculty which, however, may be employed in different measures, may be attached to particular subject-matters, which employs a method of reasoning above logic (resembling modern mathematical calculus in its principle), and is the ultimate test of truth and error in our inferences. It varies in its force and purity from one individual to another, and true intellectual improvement consists in the strengthening and perfecting of the Illative Sense.[25] As the phrase implies, the Illative Sense is constituted by impressions that are borne in upon us, from a source deeper than our conscious and formal reason. It is the combined product of intuition, instinct, imagination, and long and intricate experience. Yet the Illative Sense is not infallible in any man: assumptions which are an act of the Illative Sense may be founded upon mistaken elements of thought, and thus lead to error. We must correct our own particular Illative Sense by reference to Authority; for Authority, which is a sort of filtered collective Illative Sense, provides the purgation of individual error. As Newman wrote in his essay on John Keble (1846), "Conscience is an authority; the Bible is an authority; such is the Church; such is Antiquity; such are the words of the wise, such are hereditary lessons; such are ethical truths; such are historical memories, such are legal saws and state maxims; such are proverbs; such are sentiments, presages, and prepossessions."

In the physical sciences, it is true, the common test of probability is physical fact, submitted to the physical senses and tested by them. But history, ethics, and similar studies must be undertaken and tested by the Illative Sense and by Authority. "In such sciences, we cannot rest upon mere facts, because we have not got them. We must do our best with what is given us, and look about for aid from any quarter; and in such circumstances the opinions of others, the traditions of ages, the prescriptions of authority, antecedent auguries, analogies, parallel cases, these and the like, not indeed taken at random, but, like the evidence from the senses, sifted and scrutinized, obviously become of great importance."[26]

If, then, the Illative Sense is the ultimate sanction of belief and action, what shall we say of the Utilitarian concept of knowledge? Blind to the very existence of the Illative Sense, Bentham's disciples omit from their calculations the cardinal means to wisdom; and with it they omit religious faith. Vaguely cognizant that religious truth cannot be apprehended by any of their methods—and defiantly certain that, upon their tests, theology cannot be a science—Utilitarians studiously ignore Faith. But religion, even considered merely on utilitarian grounds, is the strong prop of society, the consolation of lonely man, the sanction of justice, the deterrent of evil. In any of these concerns, nothing will serve but religion. Thus the Utilitarians—and Sir Robert Peel, insofar as he is their convert—undermine the footing of their utilitarian order. "How sad that he who might have had the affections of many, should have thought, in a day like this, that a Statesman's praise lay in preserving the mean, not in aiming at the high; that to be safe was his first merit, and to kindle enthusiasm his most disgraceful blunder! How pitiable that such a man should not have understood that a body without a soul has no life, and a political party without an idea, no unity!"[27]

Utilitarianism is a philosophy of death: its morbidity is the consequence of Benthamite emphasis upon Doubt. With Descartes, the Utilitarians doubt all things in heaven and earth; and this is consummate folly. For Doubt is a surly, envious, egotistic emotion, a bitter denial of everything but the sullen self; and one learns nothing by doubting. Doubt never can be wholly assuaged in many things, but we must manage to live despite our doubts (which are a condition of our imperfect temporal nature). "We must make up our minds to be ignorant of much, if we would know anything. And we must make our choice between risking Science, and risking Religion."[28] The man who cultivates practical training at the expense of neglecting his Illative Sense makes a sorry bargain. Deny the Illative Sense, and doubt is inescapable; admit it, and one may climb from doubt to certitude in some matters. "Doubt itself is a positive state, and implies a definite habit of mind, and thereby necessarily involves a system of principles and doctrines all its own. Again, if nothing is to be assumed, what is our very method of reasoning but an assumption? and what our nature itself?...Of the two, I would rather have to maintain that we ought to begin with believing everything that is offered to our acceptance, than that it is our duty to doubt of everything. The former, indeed, seems to be the true way of learning."[29] Belief follows action: Coleridge had said much the same thing. But Newman does not imply that, in most cases, the intellect can perceive truth intuitively. The Illative Sense, which resolves doubt, is more than intuition. "We know, not by a direct and simple vision, not at a glance, but, as it were, by piecemeal and accumulation, by a mental process, by going round an object, by the comparison, the combination, the mutual correction, the continual adaptation, of many partial notions, by the employment, concentration, and joint action of many faculties and exercises of mind.''[30] This union and concert is a matter of training; and thus Newman, having shown that Utilitarian principles of education are *not* a way to genuine knowledge, is led to describe the true educative process.

It is no paradox that the adversary of Liberalism was the noblest exponent of liberal education. If ''Liberalism'' was an odious word to Sir Robert Peel, to Newman it was anathema. He first heard that word, he said, in connection with the opinions of Byron and his admirers. ''Afterwards, Liberalism was the badge of a theological school, of a dry and repulsive character, not very dangerous in itself, though dangerous as opening the door to evils which it did not itself either anticipate or comprehend. At present it is nothing else than that deep, plausible skepticism,...the development of human reason, as practically exercised by the natural man.''[31] In religion and in politics, the essence of Liberalism is private judgment; and to Newman, who venerated authority, judgment of grave questions according to the impudent and fallible dictates of one's own petty personal understanding was an act of flagrant impiety, approaching diabolic possession, the sin of spiritual pride. Liberals postulate the supremacy of human reason (that is, of the dry logical reason which Bentham exemplified), and hold Christian humility in contempt; they believe fatuously in the natural goodness and infinite improvability of man.

But liberal education is another matter: this is a use of ''liberal'' far more ancient and more pure, a true understanding of liberty, which is freedom to live within the compass of God's ordinances, not freedom to doubt and demolish. Liberal education is the intellectual training of free men. No Victorian was better suited to define liberal education than was Newman, the exemplar of traditional liberal learning at its highest, the light of Oxford. Possessed of a mind marvellously capacious and inquiring, though operating (to its advantage) within the confines of a majestic intellectual tradition, Newman ''is perhaps the only Englishman [G. H. Bantock remarks] to question the whole basis of contemporary 'civilization,' and raise the deepest problems of the relationship of the individual ego to the external world."[32]

Brinton, discussing Newman's searching criticism of scientific methods and assumptions, goes so far as to call him a pragmatist in the twentieth-century sense.[33] But Brinton confuses William James' belief that only particular facts are knowable, with Newman's belief that scientific theories, *per se*, cannot bring certitude. If in any sense Newman was a pragmatist, it is in the old meaning of that word— which, properly understood, expresses the "genius of Anglicanism," according to Paul Elmer More: "Rightly understood it may be said that among philosophers Plato was the supreme pragmatist, in so far as he sought to defend his belief in Ideas as facts more real than the objects of nature by showing that there is a spiritual intuition larger, deeper, more positive and trustworthy, more truly scientific, than the clamorous rout of physical sensations."[34] The really speculative, catholic, and liberal mind of Newman, aware that "the problem for statesmen of this age is how to educate the masses," turned to consideration of the discipline which makes men at once servants of God and masters of themselves.

"If virtue be a mastery over the mind, if its end be action, if its perfection be inward order, harmony, and peace, we must seek it in graver and holier places than Libraries and Reading-rooms."[35] Education, at heart, is a *discipline*, not a pleasure nor a consolation nor an alternative to idleness. Education itself cannot teach virtue, but the discipline which accompanies true education is like the discipline which virtue, too, requires. And the root of education is the study of theology; of virtue, religious faith. The first four discourses of *The Idea of a University* are devoted to proving that theology is indeed a science, indispensable to any sound system of knowledge; then Newman considers the general question of what higher education ought to be. His immediate endeavors here—the attempt to establish a Catholic University in Dublin— came to nothing; their ultimate influence, to more than most educationists realize.[36]

The problem of the age was indeed the education of the masses; but with that precise problem, Newman does not deal directly.

When he writes of education, it is the training of the leading elements in society. As a Tory, he knew that leadership must precede any mass-movement; the leaders provided, the problem is two-thirds solved. Both leaders and masses, however, require an education founded upon religious principle, an intellectual discipline which recognizes what the Utilitarian pedant does not, that "The various busy world, spread out before our eyes, is physical, but it is more than physical; and, in making its actual system identical with his scientific analysis, such a Professor as I have imagined was betraying a want of philosophical depth, and an ignorance of what a University Teaching ought to be. He was no longer a teacher of liberal knowledge, but a narrow-minded bigot."[37] The Edinburgh Reviewers, who would remodel universities upon a narrow plan of utilitarian efficiency, are in reality the most illiberal of men. They are unaware that "Religious Truth is not only a portion, but a condition of general knowledge. To blot it out is nothing short, if I may so speak, of unravelling the web of University Teaching."

To describe a University is easier than to define adequately a liberal education.* By a liberal discipline, says Newman in Discourse V, "A habit of mind is formed which lasts through life, of which the attributes are, freedom, equitableness, calmness, moderation, and wisdom; or what in a former discourse I have ventured to call the philosophical habit." Liberal studies are especially characteristic of a university and of a gentleman—as opposed to *servile*, the employments in which the mind has little part. We do wrong if we claim too much for this discipline: "Its direct business is not to steel the soul against temptation or to console it in affliction, any more than to set the loom in motion, or to direct the steam carriage; be it ever so much the means or the condition of both material and moral advancement, still, taken by and large, it as little mends our hearts as it improves our temporal circumstances." It cannot directly instill virtue: "Quarry the granite rock

---

*Newman's most moving description, probably, is that which concludes "What Is a University?" in *The Office and Work of Universities.*

with razors, or moor the vessel with a thread of silk; then you may hope with such keen and delicate instruments as human knowledge and human reason to contend against those giants, the passion and the pride of man.'' At its best, it remains a method, a discipline, for teaching the mind right reason and modesty of intellectual aspiration. ''A young man of sharp and active intellect, who has had no other training, has little to show for it besides a litter of ideas heaped up into his mind any how.''[38] Liberal education brings *order* into an active intellect; the university hardly can hope to do more.

This process of training, by which the intellect, instead of being formed or sacrificed to some particular or accidental purpose, some specific trade or profession, or study or science, is disciplined for its own sake, for the perception of its own proper object, and for its own highest culture, is called Liberal Education; and though there is no one in whom it is carried as far as is conceivable, or whose intellect would be a pattern of what intellects should be made, yet there is scarcely any one but may gain an idea of what real training is, and at least look towards it, and make its true scope and result, not something else, his standard of excellence.[39]

Not Learning or Acquirement, but Thought or Reason exercised upon Knowledge, is the end of intellectual training; and as for Knowledge proper, that is its own end. The real aim of education is ''the clear, calm, accurate vision and comprehension of all things, as far as the finite mind can embrace them, each in its place, and with its own characteristics upon it.''

This idea of a university, and of educational ends, seems infinitely remote, perhaps, from the shape that training of the intellect has assumed in the English-speaking world. Newman's own Catholic University expired; Oxford and Cambridge and the Scottish universities gradually accepted many of the Utilitarian innovations; and the new provincial universities of England, situated in the swollen industrial towns, generally endeavored to imitate the pattern of the University of London, commended in 1827 and 1828 by Brougham and Lushington. As for the developing system of state-supported public education (the first subsidy had been appropriated in 1842), it tended steadily to adopt a character secular and utilitarian. The Benthamites were determined that the state must become the universal educator; substantially, they succeeded. Quarrels between the Anglican establishment and the Nonconformists threw supervision of education more and more into the hands of government, and in the state schools—except for "simple Bible teaching"—the severance of schooling from the church was complete. Robert Lowe, as head of the Education Department in 1862, commenced levelling bad schools up—and good schools down; for, being perhaps the most true-blue Liberal among all Liberals of his generation, he had little in common with Newman. When, in 1867, Lowe spoke of the pressing necessity for "educating our masters," he was closer far in spirit to Brougham than to Newman or Disraeli; and the consequent Education Act of 1870 was pushed through Parliament by Forster on the plea that "Upon the speedy provision of elementary education depends our industrial prosperity." "Technical education" was the scheme of Liberal Britain. Practical instruction to equip Britain for meeting German competition, said an influential Nottingham manufacturer, was the great need, and it must be compulsory: "If we continue to fight with our present voluntary system, we shall be defeated."[40] The Benthamite ideal—secular, uniform, universal education prescribed by the state, free and compulsory (a coupling of words suggestive of the democratic despotism that the Philosophical Radicals did not heed)—began to be realized in 1870. In this direction the schools moved steadily, until the Education Act of 1902 accelerated the process enormously, extending it to secondary education and still further centralizing and standardizing the system. The Act of 1902, sponsored by Arthur Balfour, was in substance a socialist policy, strenuously urged by Sidney Webb in *Fabian Tract No. 106*. Here, as in so many other respects, the new consolidating socialism insinuated itself into the party which that great aristocrat Lord Salisbury had dominated only a few years earlier.

"By their system of state education all would be thrown into the same mint, and all would come out with the same impress and superscription," Disraeli had said in 1839. "They might make money, they might make railroads; but when the age of passion came, when those interests were in motion, and those feelings stirring, which would shake society to its centre, then...they would see whether the people had received the same sort of education which had been advocated and supported by William of Wykeham."[41] The notions of Gradgrind, mingled with a Rousseauistic sentimentality, have come to dominate state-supported education in both Britain and America; and now that the age of passion is here, a part of the thinking public seems to be waking in alarm to the menace of quasi-education divorced from religious principle.*

Conservative thinkers, however, ought to be judged not simply by what they failed to avert, but more by what they preserved. Newman has kept in the minds of innumerable professors and teachers and educated men an ideal of education which continues to struggle (sometimes with unaccustomed success, at present) against the degradation of learning into technical training, against the intolerant secularization of universities and schools, on behalf of truly humane learning. Into an age that staggers under the urban proletariat, its Old Man of the Sea, so that sometimes schools are scarcely more than jails to contain children until the law allows them to work, Newman's books have preserved the concept of an

---

*How thoroughly the educational convictions of Newman have been forgotten or quashed among twentieth-century educationists may be suggested by the following desultory observations:

1) A hundred years after Newman went to Dublin, the Director of the Department of Education at Oxford was M. L. Jacks, an ardent disciple of Rousseau and John Dewey, eager for "integrated" schooling to dominate the whole child, based upon the pleasure-principle. Incidentally, Jacks was among the last of those Liberals whom Newman detested.

2) In the monthly journal *Tomorrow*, a reviewer objected to Canon Bernard Iddings Bell's vigorous book in the tradition of Newman, *Crisis in Education*, on the ground that Dr. Bell seemed to think education ought to form Christian gentlemen—as if (in the reviewer's eyes) the ideas of Newman and Dr. Arnold had no validity in America, where Christians and gentlemen are anachronistic.

education designed for liberal gentlemen, without whom any society stifles. In America, at least, the parochial schools, and the universities endowed by religious bodies, still retain some influence; and most such foundations, whether they know it or not, find in Newman the best expression of their educational theories.

One of the fiercest conflicts of first principles in the nineteenth century, Newman wrote in 1858, was over whether government and legislation ought to be of a religious character, or not; "whether the state has a conscience; whether Christianity is the law of the land; whether the magistrate, in punishing offenders, exercises a retributive office or a corrective; or whether the whole structure of society is raised upon the basis of secular expediency. The relation of philosophy and the sciences to theology comes into the question. The old time-honoured theology, during the last forty years, has been vigorously contending with the new; and the new is in the ascendant."[42] A century and a quarter later, the new is in the ascendant still. But that grim utilitarian expediency continues to be opposed by the ancient religious view of society—this is Newman's bequest, in greater part than some historians of ideas acknowledge, to the England whose spiritual and literary tradition he loved and enriched.

4

No Reform Bill can be final, Bulwer Lytton exclaimed in 1859. "Democracy is like the grave—it perpetually cries, 'give, give,' and, like the grave, it never returns what it has once taken. But you live under a constitutional monarchy, which has all the vigour of health, all the energy of movement. Do not surrender to democracy that which is not yet ripe for the grave." The period of Benthamism, says Dicey in his *Law and Opinion in England*, commencing about 1825, came to an end between 1865 and 1870; it was followed by the period of collectivism. If Derby and Disraeli ushered in the age of collectivism, it was because they perceived, sooner than the Liberals, that Benthamism was a sterile thing, a dry and withered branch, as Newman had declared; and already the yellow leaves were fluttering down from it. The near-socialism of John Stuart Mill in his later years, the conversion of old John Bright to advocacy of lavish public expenditure for the general welfare—these are tokens of the change in the climate of opinion. Utilitarianism, in motive, was an apology for the industrial expansion of England; and that process accomplished, as a conscious social force Utilitarianism shrivelled, though it left its premises to Marxism and Fabianism and social planning and the age of industrial corporations.

In 1875, shortly after the Conservatives had conciliated the working classes by amending the laws concerning friendly societies and conspiracy, Walter Bagehot wrote: "Putting reactionary policy, then, aside, there remains for Conservatives only the choice between the ignorant Democratic Conservatism of the masses, and that of steadily supporting the moderate policy recommended by the educated caution of the soberest men of both parties."[43] Generally speaking, Conservatism since then has inclined toward the latter course. The Tory Radicalism of Lord Randolph Churchill, with its ambiguous slogan "We must trust the people," never captured the bulk of the party; instead, the Conservatives have steadily augmented their ranks by accessions of strength from the splintering Liberals, Joseph Chamberlain's adherence the most important of these gains. But whether the candor and clarity of Conservative ideas have been strengthened proportionately is doubtful. Bagehot's advocacy of a conservatism of capitalists has been fulfilled; and that fulfillment has worked rather as if the ghost of Peel rose up to undo the achievement of Disraeli.

It was that genial and humane Liberal Bagehot, too—the best critic of his own time, and, incidentally, an admirer of Newman, though hardly of Disraeli—who understood that the old order of things was being effaced not so much through the agency of democracy, in itself, as by a tremendous social force that converts modern nations into states close-knit and sensitive to novelty, like Athens and Florence: the nineteenth-century triumph of government by discussion. Discussion it was that broke the cake of custom in Christendom, that engulfed Burke's prejudice and prescription, that subverted men's ancient reluctance to abandon the ways of their ancestors. The era of Disraeli and Gladstone, a time of speeches and sermons and parliamentary excitement, constituted a revolutionary phenomenon—the swift alteration of society by the immediate influence of public opinion and debate. Democracy was the fruit of public discussion, not its seed. "Since Luther's time there has been a conviction more or less rooted, that a man may by an intellectual process think out a religion for himself, and that, as the highest of all duties, he ought to do so. The influence of the political discussion, and the influence of the religious discussion, have so long and so firmly combined, and have so effectually enforced one another, that the old notions of loyalty, and fealty, and authority, as they existed in the Middle Ages, have now over the best minds almost no effect."[44] This is the Private Judgment against which Newman inveighed. Referring to Bulwer Lytton's comparison of democracy to the grave, Bagehot remarks that this analogy is equally apt for discussion. "Once effectually submit a subject to that ordeal, and you can never withdraw it again; you can never again clothe it with mystery, or fence it by consecration; it remains for ever open to free choice, and exposed to profane deliberation."[45]

Private judgment and free discussion, the indispensable postulates and chief supports of Liberalism, were made possible in the nineteenth century by a cheap press (soon to be cheap and nasty), speedy communication, and urban concentration of population; thus the chief European nations obtained the advantages of the ancient city-states, and were exposed to the dangers of public opinion as it had fermented there. Disraeli and Newman, in their defense of tradition, authority, and old loyalties, swam against this roaring current; and their success in rousing popular sympathy for prescriptive verities (this force taken into account) was heroic. In a time when the fountains of the great deep seemed to be broken up—an age much like that of Greece in the fifth century—Disraeli had the subtlety to weld the fragments of conservative political instinct into a robust party, and Newman had the wisdom to arm the Christian mind against the conquering host of utilitarians and materialists. Britain shot Niagara in 1867; that cataract, however, really ought to be called Discussion, not Democracy; and conservatism, refreshed by these two men of creative imagination, was hardy enough to survive the shock.

Discussion and private judgment, rather than the physical suffering which Marx predicted, have provided the stimulus to incessant experiment and alteration throughout the past century and a half. Marxism has been embraced by many not because they suffer, but because it is a new field for protest and private judgment. Is the voracity of discussion indeed so insatiable as the appetite of the grave? If it is, then are permanence and continuity impossible for modern society? Three checks upon the empire of unbridled discussion seem possible: the deliberate revival of the concept of traditional wisdom, the growth of public boredom with talk and with change itself, and the coming of catastrophes which teach men to distrust their own opinions. The latter two contingencies appear to be impending in our generation; but either of them is a merciless disciplinarian; and the conservative who hopes to spare society an age of misery needs must endeavor to resuscitate that political faith which is not mere personal interest, that wisdom beyond physical facts which supplants doubt by assent— the system of Disraeli and the system of Newman.

IX

Legal and Historical Conservatism:
a Time of Foreboding

If I am asked, What do you propose to substitute for universal suffrage? Practically, what have you to recommend? I answer at once, Nothing. The whole current of thought and feeling, the whole stream of human affairs, is setting with irresistible force in that direction. The old ways of living, many of which were just as bad in their time as any of our devices can be in ours, are breaking down all over Europe, and are floating this way and that like haycocks in a flood. Nor do I see why any wise man should expend much thought or trouble on trying to save their wrecks. The waters are out and no human force can turn them back, but I do not see why as we go with the stream we need sing Hallelujah to the river god.

-Sir James Fitzjames Stephen,
Liberty, Equality, Fraternity

AFTER 1867, conservative elements in British society found themselves steadily reinforced by recruits from the old Liberal and Whig and Utilitarian bands. Alarmed at the trend of Gladstonian Liberalism, at the increasing powers of the state, at the aggressiveness of the labor movement, and at the flattery paid to the vast new electorate, the middle classes (so long the driving force behind Liberalism) began to transfer their allegiance to the Tories. As early as the 'fifties, Bagehot perceived, and unmistakably by the middle 'seventies, true Conservative and Liberal interests were approaching identity; and small difference remained between a "conservative Liberal" and a "liberal Conservative." Both had the duty of setting bounds to the expansion of a voracious democracy and a ponderous state. The Tories, who since the beginning of the century had been sturdy opponents of the Utilitarians' social atomism and defenders of the state as a moral agency, now found that the balance had swung the other way: the constitution of English society was threatened by a secular collectivism, as a political movement the instrument of the poor who were now enfranchised. Herbert Spencer, his Radicalism outraged by this new and more formidable peril to individualism, published *Man versus the State* in 1884, becoming a kind of ally of the Conservatives, now less repugnant to political individualists than were the rising collectivistic humanitarians. "It was the Tory party that had changed, or at any rate seemed to change, from the champion of paternalism against all manner of dissenters to the champion of individualism against all manner of socialists," Sir Ernest Barker observes.[1] Not in *Man versus the State,* however, does one find the genuinely conservative ideas of late Victorian times. Three great scholars in law and history sustained the true conservative impulse: J.F. Stephen, with *Liberty, Equality, Fraternity* (1873); Henry Maine, with *Popular Government* (1885); and W.E.H. Lecky, with *Democracy and Liberty* (1896).

The strength of Conservatism, says Bagehot, has not emanated chiefly from intellectual conviction. Two enduring sentiments, instead, have nourished the attachment of most conservatives: the old cavalier feeling of loyalty; and (what animates the "party of order" in the Continent) the feeling of fear—"dread that their shop, their house, this life—not so much their physical life as their whole mode and sources of existence—will be destroyed and cast away." Modern British conservatives (Bagehot wrote in 1856) manifest an earnestness which lifts them above the mere Toryism of enjoyment and the despicable conservatism of shrinking terror. But a conservatism of reflection is not yet general in England: "In the face of questioning classes, every unthinking Conservative endangers what he defends—he is a vexation to the Liberal, and a misfortune to his country."[2] The measured and sober apologetics which English conservative thought required still more urgently after 1867 were produced by a convert from Utilitarianism "with rather an aggressive development of conscience"; by a scientific historian of institutions, recruited from among the liberals; and by an Anglo-Irish scholar, steeped in the ideas of Burke.

The emergence of socialism as a distinct political movement in the 'seventies, a threat to the whole extant society of Britain, alarmed old-school Manchesterians as much as it disquieted Tories. But the Labour Party not yet having come into being (though the Labour Representation League elected two of its thirteen candidates in the general election of 1873), socialists could influence the course of Parliament only through the process of converting men of the dominant parties to socialistic views. As the Radicals, before 1832, had penetrated the ranks of the Whigs, so Socialists now began to filter among the Liberals—even among the ranks of the Conservatives. This insemination is evident in the later thought of John Stuart Mill, whom the conservative writers accurately perceived to be the chief storm-cloud of this changing climate of opinion; the hereditary high-priest of Utilitarianism, the leader of that restless stirring of secularism and experiment which the Philosophic Radicals had managed to utilize for their ends fifty years earlier, was moving from the extreme of individualism toward collectivism without being conscious of inconsistency. "The Saint of Rationalism" (Gladstone's description of J.S. Mill) was himself as much divorced from the life of old England as were the now-enfranchised working classes whom, though dreaded and despised by him, he yet helped to provide with social doctrines. "The Bible, the Church of England, the ancient Universities and grammar-schools, the parsonage, the country-house—all these things which have played so large a part in making and embodying the national tradition [R.J. White comments] were for many years outside his ken."[3] Mill and the other leading Utilitarians had not even the Bible, which meant nearly everything to the Noncomformist critics of conservative society. As much as man may be, John Stuart Mill was pure and humorless intellect, disgusted with the flesh, dubious of the spirit. Though totally unlike Mill in temperament and taste, the urban proletariat of Victorian England shared this with him, that they lived a life which lacked the Bible, the Church, the University, the grammar-school, the parson, the squire.

Mill felt his misgivings about political radicalism. In the *Essay on Liberty,* he echoes Tocqueville's dread of democratic despotism; in *Representative Government,* he recommends a system of elaborate artificial checks upon general suffrage similar to Disraeli's fancy franchises. It was Mill's extreme secularism, rather than his particular political ideas, which made him the enemy of all discerning conservatives. For he was eager to sweep the veneration out of social life, replacing it by the ''religion of humanity,'' in which man would adore himself, found his moral system upon utilitarian reason, and consider every prescriptive custom of mankind simply as an ''experiment in living.'' Man would mould his universe closer to his heart's desire. Poverty, disease, vicissitudes of fortune, every other ill from which men suffer—these may be eradicated by the rational planner of the new society. ''All the grand sources, in short, of human suffering are in a great degree, many of them almost entirely, conquerable by human care and effort,'' Mill writes in *Utilitarianism.* These superior human beings, as they progress toward material perfection, will cease to require the childish comforts of religious consolation; present sufferings abolished, they will shrug their shoulders at the prospect of eternal life. Mill is the harbinger of the twentieth-century socialists' lavish hopes for material comfort—for instance, John Strachey's prediction that life itself may be prolonged indefinitely by the welfare state. And his meliorism (and Comte's) was the immediate inspiration of a crowd of anti-religious and anti-traditional popularizing writers.*

---

*Winwood Reade, for instance, whose *The Martyrdom of Man* (1872) concludes, ''Famine, pestilence, and war are no longer essential for the advancement of the human

Though Stephen, Maine, and Lecky were none of them perfectly orthodox in belief, they recognized in this virulent secularism, this overweening confidence in human benevolence and human sagacity, a menace to everything old, settled, and lofty in society. If Mill's collectivistic version of Utilitarianism, and its ally Positivism, should capture the popular fancy, these conservatives foresaw, the debasing of civilization would follow—the coming of life without principle, in which the ordinary motives to integrity that had governed the operation of Western society since Charlemagne would be dissolved in the acid of general selfishness. Every state must have its masters; and out of the chaos of popular politics unlighted by moral principle would come the new tyrants, themselves emancipated from hoary convention and consequently the more ruthless. In the chilly egalitarian society at which John Stuart Mill hinted, in the godless social ritualism of Comte with its scientist-dictator-priests, the conservatives of later Victorian years made out the features of a life not worth living. They set about refuting the corrosive rationalism of Mill by a conservative rationalism; but they knew the tide was against them.

The substantially native English materialism of Mill was reinforced by the strong influence which Comte's ideas began to exert in Great Britain, particularly upon historians and scientists, in the 'seventies and 'eighties. Disseminated by George Eliot, Frederic Harrison, John Morley, Huxley, and a crowd of interpreters, Positivism was applauded in England chiefly because it purported to brush away old theological and metaphysical concepts of life, re-establishing thought upon a basis severely scientific.* Liberals like Morley could embrace this new morality

---

race. But a season of mental anguish is at hand, and through this we must pass in order that our posterity may rise. The soul must be sacrificed; the hope in immortality must die. A sweet and charming illusion must be taken from the human race, as youth and beauty vanish never to return."

*Just how truly scientific, in any enduring sense, Comte's system was, may be suggested by his uncritical acceptance of Gall's phrenological theories—which, Comte declared, disproved the theological doctrine of human depravity by detecting an "organ of benevolence" in every brain.

without much noticing the cult of Sociolatry and the absolute state which Comte erected upon this premise. But the Narcissene self-worship of humanity was an inseparable part of Comte's philosophy: man must adore something, and, having denied God, he will find his deity somewhere much lower than the angels. And the planned state, dominated by the industrialist and the scientist, administered by a committee of bankers, supported by a vast uniform proletariat, leaving nothing to individual aspiration, repudiating democracy root and branch, liberty surrendered to the concept of control—this follows naturally from Auguste Comte's postulates. For men, having been instructed deliberately that there are no supernatural sanctions for moral conduct, must be made to conform and to labor either by naked force or by elaborate social machinery. The emancipated English admirers of Comte could not see that Positivism, as a social system, meant the very opposite of emancipation, the antithesis of liberalism. Men should be at liberty to demolish theology; but they should have liberty in nothing else—Comte himself was sufficiently frank in this declaration; and the Victorian conservatives understood him better than did his own disciples.

Mill's humanitarian rationalism and Comte's collectivistic Positivism, despising and dismissing the Past, promised mankind a future abounding in earthly delights—chaste ones—upon the Utilitarian happiness-principle. But the historical and juridical school of English thinkers knew, with Burke, that the past refuses to be dismissed, for it is the voice of all human wisdom. Derided, the Past exacts its vengeance. The study of laws, social institutions, and the history of morals informed Stephen, Maine, and Lecky that people abruptly deprived of piety and common usage cannot discern the Future at all; they apprehend only the Present; and, drifting down the shallow uncharted estuary of sensual impulse and confused desire, they ground upon the shivering sands of social apathy.

2

"It is a thousand pities that J.F. Stephen is a judge," the Earl of Beaconsfield, in the last year of his life, wrote to Lytton; "he might have done anything and everything as leader of the future Conservative party." This was 1881, eight years after Stephen published *Liberty, Equality, Fraternity*. Promptly upon its publication, Fitzjames Stephen had stood as a Liberal in Dundee, had been eclipsed by one of the new-style collectivistic Liberals, and had come to realize that he was a conservative through and through. But as a practical politician, Stephen met his end in 1873. He had been reared as a strict Utilitarian and Claphamite; he had become the "Benthamee Lycurgus" of India, and in India had learned that force, not discussion, binds society together; baffled in politics, he turned to his judicial career, and wrote his monumental history of the criminal law. Perhaps too stern, blunt, and Puritanical to be a successful party leader (despite Disraeli's suggestion) in the nineteenth century, this resolute and manly Victorian was the author of what Sir Ernest Barker calls "the finest exposition of conservative thought in the latter half of the nineteenth century."[4]

Hobbes, Locke, Bentham, and John Austin disciplined Stephen's mind, and he never repudiated these teachers; but in effect he rejected their innovating and skeptical side. For one tremendous error of the secular reformers made J.F. Stephen into a conservative: they ignored the depravity of man. As with John Adams, the Puritanical view of human nature aroused Stephen against sentimental humanitarians, against the rootless liberty of Mill and the "benevolent organ" of Comte. And his inherent distrust of weak and erring humanity convinced him, as it convinced his friend Carlyle, that political institutions are no more than a veil for force. Fitzjames Stephen's skeptical brother Leslie told the younger Oliver Wendell Holmes, in 1873, that Fitzjames had been "a good deal corrupted by old Carlyle";[5] he had become a preacher of religious dogmas. But the dogmas were not always orthodox. J.F. Stephen could defend Pilate; he could say, "If Christianity really is what much of the language which we often hear used implies, it is false and mischievous," and that if the Sermon on the Mount really means to forbid defense of the nation's honor, then the Sermon on the Mount ought to be disregarded.[6] His was the God of the Prophets and the Puritans, infinitely powerful, "one who, whatever he may be in his own nature, has so arranged the world or worlds in which I live as to let me know that virtue is the law which he has prescribed to me and to others."[7]

Love is not the word to use toward such a Being; what men must feel for Him is awe, the rational and virile way to think of God. Mill, and Comte's pupils, were resolved to eradicate awe from the world; but with awe gone, the whole sanction for virtue and the whole motive of struggle would be snatched from mankind, so that life would become first meaningless, then intolerable. The Religion of Humanity which French and English positivists professed was, in substance, just this:

"The human race is an enormous agglomeration of bubbles which are continually bursting and ceasing to be. No one made it or knows anything worth knowing about it. Love it dearly, oh ye bubbles." This is a sort of religion, no doubt, but it seems to me a very silly one.[8]

John Stuart Mill, the target of Stephen's heavy guns, protested that Stephen's book was "more likely to repel than to attract."[9] Of course Mill was quite right, in his time. *Liberty, Equality, Fraternity* exerted no wide immediate influence; it ran counter to both the current of Victorian self-confidence and the popular collectivistic promises which had defeated Stephen at Dundee. But his unflinching and sombre essay, the production of a practical jurist steeped in the Old Testament and Milton, transcends the brief optimism of Victorian prosperity. Liberty is a word of negation, says Stephen; equality is something less, a mere word of relation; and fraternity, as a general social impulse, never existed and never can exist. The motto of the Republic had become the creed of a religion, and that a religion of destructive heresies. Stephen intended his book as a refutation, upon Utilitarian principles, of this innovating creed, a species of appeal from the New Utilitarians to the Old; but in truth, Stephen himself was something more than a Utilitarian, quite as Burke had been something more than a Whig. The economic and the legal concepts (with some modification) of Bentham, Ricardo, and James Mill were shared by Fitzjames Stephen: he demonstrated easily that J.S. Mill was an apostate from this school of belief.

As the old Utilitarianism breaks up after 1870, indeed, one may distinguish at least three offshoots from the blasted trunk of Benthamism. There is Stephen's endorsement of the economic and legal principles of the early Utilitarians; but Stephen realizes that the metaphysical and moral basis of Benthamism is inadequate. There is John Stuart Mill's prolongation of Utilitarian skepticism and humanitarianism; but Mill abandons the economic and political individualism of his preceptors. Third, there is the Idealism of Green, Bradley, Bosanquet, and their associates, mingling Hegel with Bentham, retaining the democratic and reforming proclivities of the Utilitarians, but exchanging the Benthamite happiness-principle in society for an idealization of the state derived from German philosophy. J.F. Stephen's concept of the state and its origins—unlike Green's—closely resembles the idea of Burke: this, with his concurrence (again like Burke) in the economic principles which Adam Smith had defined, and his severe opinion of human nature, led Stephen to conservatism. He added to conservative political thought an analysis of the relationship between discussion and force which until then never had been clearly expressed.

In one respect, certainly, the younger Mill remained the genuine Utilitarian, and J.F. Stephen was the anti-Benthamite: like Sir James his father, Stephen insisted that everything in society is derived from religious truth. Disagreeing with Newman and Ward, still more hostile toward the "liberal" theologians, Stephen declared that positivists and liberals provide no satisfactory sanctions for morality in their creeds; "but he was equally opposed to sham sanctions and sham claims to authority," says his brother. However the Victorian battle between theologians and Darwinians might end, the need for religious sanctions to preserve society would remain unaltered. Devotees of abstract liberty, equality, and fraternity, devoid of awe and reverence, trudge insensately toward servility, bondage, and barbarity. Stephen's grim piety resembles Hesiod's:

> Zeus rules the world, and with resistless sway,
> Takes back tomorrow what he grants today.

The state cannot leave religion out of its cognizance; for the state is a religious establishment, and law is the instrument of social vengeance, created to enforce morality.

"Man has a fearful disease," says Stephen, describing the tenets of Calvin, "but his original constitution is excellent. Redemption consists not in killing but in curing his nature." The perversity and corruption of our nature, demonstrated by our vices, make men subject to miserable bondage—from which God rescues the elect. "Speak or fail to speak of God as you think right, but the fact that men are deeply moved by ideas about power, wisdom, and goodness, on a superhuman scale which they rather apprehend than comprehend, is certain. Speak of original sin or not as you please, but the fact that all men are in some respects and at some times both weak and wicked, that they do the ill they would not do, and shun the good they would pursue, is no less certain. To describe this state of things as a 'miserable bondage' is, to say the least, an intelligible way of speaking. Calvin's theory was that in order to escape from this bondage men must be true to the better part of their nature, keep in proper subjection its baser elements, and look up to God as the source of the only valuable kind of freedom—freedom to be good and wise."[10] This is the foundation of Stephen's politics; and one may remark a strong similarity to the New England Puritanical tradition, from John Adams to Irving Babbitt. Mill, Stephen wrote, believed that if men are emancipated from restraint and endowed with equality, they will live as brothers; but "I believe that many men are bad, a vast majority of men indifferent, and many good, and that the great mass

of indifferent people sway this way or that according to circumstances, one of the most important of which circumstances is the
predominance for the time being of the bad or good."[11] Universal suffrage, and the whole idea of equality, defy this necessity
for leadership by the virtuous; the egalitarians try to omit morals
from their politics—an impossibility. "I think that wise and good
men ought to rule those who are foolish and bad."

The realm of politics and the realm of morals do not exist in
separate spheres, Comte notwithstanding; the state exists to enforce a moral system, to redeem men from the impulses of the
flesh and their ignorance. And morality, in turn, must be supported by the sanction of religious faith, or it cannot stand. "The
whole management and direction of human life depends upon the
question whether or not there is a God and a future state of human
existence. If there is a God, but no future state, God is nothing
to us. If there is a future state, but no God, we can form no rational guess about the future state."[12] Lacking God and a future
state, men must act either according to impulse or in obedience
to "common utilitarianism," the "ordinary current morality which
prevails among men of the world"; but even this latter rough system of behavior eventually will collapse, without the sustaining
force of a nobler belief held by a minority of mankind. If, however, God and a future state do exist, reasonable men will base
their conduct upon "a wider kind of utilitarianism." Believing
in Providence, they will surmise that they "transcend the material world in which they are placed, and that the law imposed on
them is this—Virtue, that is to say, the habit of acting upon principles fitted to promote the happiness of men in general, and especially those forms of happiness which have reference to the
permanent element in men, is connected with, and will, in the
long run, contribute to the individual happiness of those who practice it, and especially to that part of their happiness which is connected with the permanent elements of their nature. The converse
is true of vice."[13] This conviction of Stephen's may be Utilitarianism, but it surely is a long way from Bentham's Greatest Happiness Principle, and equally remote from Leslie Stephen's attempt
to establish a science of morality upon rational and material proofs.

Whatever system of principles men adhere to, however, the religion of "Liberty, Equality, Fraternity" is pernicious; "for, whichever rule is applied, there are vast numbers of matters in respect of which men ought not to be free; they are fundamentally unequal, and they are not brothers at all, or only under qualifications which make the assertion of their fraternity unimportant."[14] So far as liberty, equality, and fraternity have any existence or meaning in modern society, they are rooted in Christian morality; and if positivists and rationalists succeed in their endeavor to explode the religious convictions of society, they will bury in the ruins those very liberal social principles which the school of Mill professes to live by. The sanction of faith obliterated, the pseudo-religion of 1789 cannot long survive. Men who cannot hope for salvation or dread damnation will make a Roman candle of their world.

Thus the philosophical assumption upon which Mill's *Liberty* rests is itself rotten to the core; but even if we confine our criticism of Mill's system to the narrow bounds of his rationalistic method, says Stephen, still Mill's position is untenable, being actually shaped in conformity to vague sentiments the origin of which Mill himself hardly admits, and not truly manufactured according to the Utilitarian standards that Mill thinks he speaks for. The fundamental internal error of J.S. Mill's politics is just this: he thinks that society can be ruled by discussion. But the tremendous impelling power in all societies is force.

In Stephen's definition, force is not simply physical compulsion: the fear of Hell is a kind of force, too: and deference to public opinion is in essence force; and even discussion itself is a decent drapery over force, a convention by which men expend in talk some of their ferocious energies, and end, perhaps, by counting heads instead of breaking them—but societies tolerate this veil only when opposing interests are more or less evenly balanced, and when the issues to be settled are not desperately important to the contending parties. Stephen does not refer to Bagehot's remarks on discussion in *Physics and Politics,* for that book had been published only the year before, as Stephen, sailing home from India, wrote the essays which were united to make *Liberty, Equality, Fraternity*. But Bagehot's opinion that Victorian England was a society dominated by Discussion was not wholly inconsonant with Stephen's own view. Opinions, true or false, do indeed help to direct the action of society. Opinions can result in action only through force or the threat of force, however; and if the *Essay on Liberty*, for instance, changes public opinion through discussion and eventually alters society itself in some respects, this comes about because a body of determined men make it clear that, in the last resort, they are ready to employ their force in support of their opinions. It was not Bentham's *Fragment on Government* which compelled the Reform of 1832; governors of the state, and great established interests, do not yield to pure dialectic; what demanded the surrender of 1832 was the mob at Nottingham and at Bristol. *A Fragment on Government*, or rather the ideas which that work represented, certainly had filtered down to the mob; but the ultimate sanction for change was the employment of unadorned force.

Mill had written that compulsion is justifiable in society only until the "time when mankind have become capable of being improved by free and equal discussion." Was there ever a time, asks Stephen, at which no man could be improved by discussion? Are not even savages improved by discussion, and do they not employ it? But every previous society has found it necessary to reinforce discussion by the buttress of force, and our age cannot afford to dispense with this prop to order. "No such period has as yet been reached anywhere, and there is no prospect of its being reached anywhere within any assignable time." Let us be candid: force (or the potentiality of it) is, if anything, more influential in our own time than in previous ages. Lincoln employed a force which would have crushed Charlemagne and his peers like so many eggshells. "To say that the law of force is abandoned because force is regular, unopposed, and beneficially exercised, is to say that night and day are now such well-established institutions that the sun and moon are mere superfluities."[15] Through their armies, their police, and their means of rapid communication, modern states are supported by a potential force more promptly and effectively employed, in case of need, than ever before. The comparative orderliness of our society is the product not of logic-chopping and diffident persuasion, but of this reservoir of force.

To ignore the role of force, as Mill does, is to expose society to the contagion of a ravaging sickness. For the mass of men require restraint; they cannot adequately curb their own passions or their own sloth, and so must be compelled to acknowledge the suzerainty of law, which is sanctioned by force. "Estimate the proportion of men and women who are selfish, sensual, frivolous, idle, absolutely commonplace and wrapped up in the smallest of petty routines, and consider how far the freest of free discussion is likely to improve them. The only way by which it is practically possible to act upon them at all is by compulsion or restraint...It would be as wise to say to the water of a stagnant marsh, 'Why in the world do you not run into the sea? You are perfectly free.'"[16] This is not all. Nature, abhorring a vacuum, always supplies force to fill any conspicuous cavity in society, and if the state abandons its sacred function of directing social force into the service of law, then new groups and agencies will seize the opportunity to use force for their own ends, subverting law and the state—indeed, perhaps creating a new state governed by themselves upon the ashes of the preceding state which forgot its own function. Labor unions or dissenting sects will thrust their particular wills upon the rest of humanity, if government eschews force and supinely accepts the notion that it can employ only discussion in its own defense.

Nor is force, generally considered, an evil: rather, it arms the sanction which lies behind whatever good men do. It must be employed to keep men from building anew their Tower of Babel. It is the corrector of our vices. There are times when toleration becomes a vice, because it exceeds its proper sphere of mitigating struggle and, growing excessive, aims at the complete suppression of those contests which provide the stimulus to life. Then force may be employed justly to curb a licentious toleration. There are times when liberty, too—at best a negative expression—threatens all decent folk, and must be put down by force; to this, modern doctrines of liberty are tending: "The cry for liberty, in short, is a general condemnation of the past and an act of homage to the present in so far as it differs from the past, and to the future in so far as its character can be inferred from the character of the present."[17] When excessive liberty thus becomes destructive of our civilized inheritance, it must be quashed; and from time immemorial, only force has been able to deal with the arrogance of groups whose appetite for novelty is boundless. Already modern "liberty" has shattered most of the old forms in which discipline was a recognized and admitted good, and has produced few new forms to replace them. "Liberty," continually glorifying the present, has become incompatible with "a proper sense of the importance of the virtue of obedience, discipline in its widest sense"—incompatible, that is to say, with real civilization. Force, whether physical or moral, is ordained by Providence to save us from this anarchic impulse.

We are *not* living in an age of discussion, then; manifestly this is a time of force; indeed, the survival of compulsion is the chief protection to our order and culture. But even if Mill and Comte were able to dispense with the sanctions of physical force and moral awe, even if they could manage (*per impossibile*) to substitute a Religion of Humanity for a supernatural faith of veneration and fear—why, what sort of life would Comte's "ritualistic Social Science Association," or Mill's milksop paradise for rationalists, inflict upon abused humanity? They appear to want a world "like a Stilton cheese run away with by its own mites," measured quantitatively by abundance of population, and perhaps by quantitative education. "Enthusiasts for progress are to me strange enough. 'Glory, glory: the time is coming when there will be six hundred million Chinese, five hundred million Hindoos, four hundred million Europeans, and Heaven only knows how many hundred million blacks of various shades, and when there will be two British Museums, each with a library. "Ye unborn ages, crowd not on my soul." ' "[18] What is this progress that positivists applaud? It seems to be an increasing effeminacy, a softness of life, men "less earnestly desirous to get what they want, and more afraid of pain, both for themselves and others, than they used to be. If this be so, it appears to me that all other gains, whether in wealth, knowledge, or humanity, afford no equivalent. Strength, in all its forms, is life and manhood. To be less strong is to be less of a man, whatever else you may be."[19] The passengers on some ocean liner of the future may be immunized against the roll of the waves by an ingenious device, but they will not know the exultation of the old seafarer. So far as the positivists can define their "progress," or anyone else can define that evanescent vision, progress seems to be a weakening of fibre; and the rational man who hastens its coming must have degenerated from his sires.

What, for that matter, is happiness? Mill thinks he can test it, and plan the happy society. What conceit! "Where are we to find people who are qualified by experience to say which is the happier, a man like Lord Eldon or a man like Shelley; a man like Dr. Arnold or a man like the late Marquis of Hertford; a very stupid prosperous farmer who dies of old age after a life of perfect health, or an accomplished delicate woman of passionate sensibility and brilliant genius, who dies worn out before her youth is passed, after an alternation of rapturous happiness with agonies of distress?"[20]

These questions never can be answered; they are "like asking the distance from one o'clock to London Bridge." The legislator and the moralist never really try to obtain the happiness of each individual: they simply endeavor to persuade or compel men to accept their particular view of life. The positivists' aspiration to complete a design for making men happy, and—still more presumptuous—to arrange that each man's happiness shall count for as much as another's, is their crowning absurdity. Here Stephen makes mincemeat of his adversaries; and in demolishing them, he annihilates the cardinal principle of his own nominal preceptor, Bentham. The grand scheme of God is inscrutable; the object of life is virtue, not pleasure; and obedience, not liberty, is the means of its attainment.

But even setting aside the vanity of Progress and Happiness—
the Positivist goals—the system of Comte and Mill is internally
discordant. True equality excludes liberty (here Stephen reiterates the arguments of Burke, Tocqueville, and others); real equality
is not attainable, and is contemplated only by men capable of thinking they can make playing-cards equal in value by shuffling the
pack; equality is a big name for a small thing. Look at America,
and ask yourself whether equality is the end of man—whether the
rapid production of an ''immense multitude of commonplace, self-
satisfied, and essentially slight people is an exploit which the whole
world need fall down and worship.''

As for fraternity—who really believes in it? ''It is not love that
one wants from the great mass of mankind, but respect and
justice.'' Are we really brothers? ''Are we even fiftieth cousins?''
And though we should be, is not this relationship too abstract for
any practical action in our vale of tears, with so many more pressing problems about us? To proclaim every man your brother is
to deny that any particular man has claims of kinship upon you.
''Humanity is only I writ large, and love for Humanity generally
means zeal for MY notions as to what men should be and how
they should live.''[21] Persons like Mill or Rousseau, despising their
own age and most actual men, seem curious advocates for indiscriminate love of Humanity. Purported affection for the amorphous mass of mankind is in fact usually the inordinate expansion
of ego, the sham of a man who is determined to melt everything
established in society and to imprint his own seal upon the drip-
ping red wax of a new world. And, supposing such men should
succeed in effecting their purpose, whom would they satisfy? Not
themselves, certainly. In their atomized society, every man dragging out his days in a lonely condition of complete equality and
liberty, men would exist as the damned, reduced to a dead level,
''offering no attractions to the imagination or the affections.''

Words are tools which break in one's hand, Stephen remarks
in an aside: put a powerful strain upon them, and an advantage
is given in argument to the inferior thinker over the superior. ''The
things which cannot be adequately represented by words are more

important than those which can." Is this a Utilitarian speaking? Or is Stephen, in instinct, system, and mature experience, not rather a conservative in whom the Anglican and Puritan traditions commingle, superficially clothed in Utilitarian method? "It seems to me that we are spirits in prison," he continues, "able only to make signals to each other, but with a world of things to think and to say which our signals cannot describe at all."[22] Here speak out the awe and humility with which Burke regarded the great mysterious incorporation of the human race, and here the complacent materialism of Bentham shrinks to insignificance.

Powerful though he was in argument, somehow his book did fail Stephen as a tool, and the sentimental egalitarianism of Mill's later days, which Stephen decried as the degeneracy of human vigor, has won ten or twenty times as many readers as *Liberty, Equality, Fraternity*. *An Essay on Liberty* flattered the popular assumption of self-sufficiency; Stephen flailed against the crowd like Samson among the Philistines. But whose book the twentieth century has vindicated in the debate over force versus discussion, there hardly can be much doubt; and whose analysis of the sanctions that rule human action was the keener, the mounting calamities of all the world attest.

3

Conversing with Sir Henry Maine early in 1882, Lord Acton objected to Maine's defense of primogeniture in a recent lecture; this, said Acton, was Legitimacy, giving a Tory tinge to the entire paper. "You seem to use Tory as a term of reproach," replied Maine. Acton was taken aback. A friend of his, nominally a Liberal, tolerant of Toryism? "I was much struck by this answer—much struck to find a philosopher, entirely outside party politics, who does not think Toryism a reproach."[23] Three years later, Maine would write a book intensely conservative: *Popular Government*. He had begun his adult life by despising Disraeli; he ended it in a deep pessimism, aghast at the blind tendency of society, which was stumbling along a path of retrogression. Like Spencer (whose *Man versus the State* Maine endorsed), like Stephen, like a dozen other leading Victorians whose allegiance originally had been Liberal or Radical, Sir Henry Maine changed his political affiliation but not his views. It was Liberalism, and the times, that changed: abandoning its old devotion to personal freedom, Liberalism took up the cause of the material welfare of the masses. Men of sober learning, in reaction, began to go over to the cause which Disraeli's kaleidoscopic imagination had kept alive; and before long, surprise at finding a philosopher who respected Toryism was impossible even for Acton.

Acton himself, after the Reform of 1885, could not ignore the collectivistic inclinations of Liberalism; but he excused them—at least the "academic socialism" of Continental thinkers, of which, he conceded, Gladstone was becoming the English representative—as somehow the intellectual drift of the time. "I quite agree with Chamberlain, that there is latent Socialism in the Gladstonian philosophy. What makes me uncomfortable is his inattention to the change which is going on in these things...But it is not the popular movement, but the travelling of the minds of men who sit in the seat of Adam Smith that is really serious and worthy of all attention."[24] Though this is loyalty to Gladstone, is it loyalty to Acton's own principle of liberty? Or to the principle of progress? Maine, even more keenly aware of the earnest flirtation which scientists and political economists were conducting with collectivism, saw in this affair infidelity to both freedom and progress; for progress is measured in terms of freedom. If the movement of society from status to contract is the index of progress, then socialism is disastrous reaction.

Progress, said Maine, is rare in the procession of history; but it is real. Therefore—although never active in British practical politics—he commenced as a moderate Liberal in the tradition of Burke, endeavoring to promote cautious reform, reconciling old interests with new energies, preparing society for necessary change, preserving what is best in the ancient order. His Indian career displays this influence of Burke, this respect for native custom and culture, this calm devotion to a society that is a spirit or a living thing, not a mere mechanical contrivance. Writers on politics who imply that Burke and his school opposed change *per se* err seriously. Beneficial change is the Providential instrument of social preservation, said Burke, a conservative force; but we must not fall into the confusion of thinking that all change is reform. The world experiences both improvement and decay; the latter tendency is the easier path, though ruinous at last; and statesmen must train themselves and the people to distinguish healthy change from processes of dissolution. When Maine became convinced that the drift of change in Western society was retrogressive, he became a conservative.

The intensive study of social history made Maine into a pessimist, writes Sir Ernest Barker: "History has with Maine, what it tends to have with many of us, a way of numbing generous emotions. All things have happened already; nothing much came of them before; and nothing much can be expected of them now."[25] This is a neat judgment. But is it just to Maine? As the founder of modern comparative social studies, as a prodigious historical scholar, as perhaps the most penetrating observer of Indian society, Maine knew that human progress, or even the wish for it, is a fragile creation; but he did not despair of it. On the contrary, progress—by which Maine means, chiefly, the promotion of a high state of intellectual attainment, and of liberty under law—has been active in the West for some centuries. The index of its success is the trend from status to contract among peoples, and its principal instruments are private property and freedom of contract. The life of the mind, and the liberty of persons, flourish in a society diversified, economically individualistic, and characterized by several property (as distinguished from the various forms of communal ownership). A society in which men freely contract for economic ends tends to be progressive; modern collectivism, then, is stifling.

The general thesis of Maine's studies in the history of institutions is not dismal: granted prudence and sagacity, mankind may progress—granted these, and the heritage of the Greeks, that is. For progress is a Greek creation; when Greek ideas expire, society is static:

To one small people, covering in its original seat no more than a hands-breadth of territory, it was given to create the principle of Progress, of movement onwards and not backwards or downwards, of destruction tending to construction. That people was the Greek. Except the blind forces of Nature, nothing moves in this world which is not Greek in its origin. A ferment spreading from that source has vitalized all the great progressive races of mankind, penetrating from one to another, and producing results accordant with its hidden and latent genius, and results of course often far greater than any exhibited in Greece itself. It is this principle of progress which we Englishmen are communicating to India...There is no reason why, if it has time to work, it should not develop in India effects as wonderful as in any other of the societies of mankind.[26]

Yet the mass of mankind tend always to stagnate: they prefer custom and habit to innovation; the hand of the Past lies heavy on them. There was nothing of the reactionary in Maine, who knew that the source of social wisdom is knowledge of dead ages, but that dreary imitation of what once lived will stifle the most gifted peoples. The very science of jurisprudence, which writers on the law often assume to be immutable (even Bentham and Austin inclining toward this opinion), however stable, must change with the passage of the generations.[27] Indian natives, including the young intellectuals with a veneer of Western ideas, are oppressively attached to the past; and even with Europeans, "It may be that too much of the sloughed skin of the past hangs about us, and impedes and disorders our movements...Although there is much in common between the Present and the Past, there is never so much in common as to make life tolerable to the men of the Present, if they could step back into the Past. There is no one in this room to whom the life of a hundred years since would not be acute suffering, if it could be lived over again."[28] A people who love their past intelligently will think of their national future; and if we are solicitous for posterity, we must investigate the historical causes of progress and vitality. Maine was the pupil of Savigny—who, in turn, was the pupil of Burke even more than he was the pupil of Hegel. "History is the only true way to attain a knowledge of our own condition," Savigny wrote in 1815. Savigny employed historical jurisprudence to oppose the radical notions derived from the fancied Rights of Man; Maine found in the history of institutions a corrective of sweeping schemes for social improvement.

Such investigation will be fruitful only if undertaken upon methods truly scientific, Maine believed. The five brilliant volumes of his social studies constitute a foundation for this scientific history; modern legal thought and sociology and political speculation, as well as historical method, are deeply indebted to Maine. In this or that he has been corrected or amended; Maine himself expected nothing else; but the bulk of his writing looms still majestic in accuracy and outlook. History must teach, he declared, "that which every other science teaches, continuous sequence, inflexible order, and eternal law." Historical truth must be like the truths of the astronomer and the physiologist. This is setting the sights very high; but Maine made a beginning. The purpose of his *Ancient Law,* as indeed of all his works, was to re-establish historical judgments on this solid base. History is *not* Philosophy teaching by example: the *a priori* suppositions that ruled the French school in the eighteenth century, and which plague Utilitarian thinkers despite their professions of scientific realism, must yield to laborious and conscientious historical investigation.

The need for attaining this method of historical study is urgent; otherwise, Benthamism (despite the unpopularity of the founder's name) will carry everything before it in the sphere of legislation. Benthamism suffers from woeful imperfections in its theory of human nature; application of the comparative method to the study of customs, motives, and ideas may alleviate this narrowness of Utilitarianism. Political economists, like Benthamites in general, "greatly underrate the value, power, and interest of that great body of custom and inherited idea which, according to the metaphor which they have borrowed from the mechanicians, they throw aside as friction. The best corrective which could be given to this disposition would be a demonstration that this 'friction' is capable of scientific analysis and scientific measurement."[29] Checks upon the rigid

Benthamite calculus lacking, historians and jurists are betrayed into errors endowed with a potency for social injury that hardly can be exaggerated. The Utilitarian tenets led Buckle, for instance, to inform the public that since the natives of India subsist upon rice, since "the exclusive food of the natives is of an oxygenous rather than a carbonaceous character, it follows by an inevitable law that caste prevails, that oppression is rife, that rents are high, and that custom and law are stereotyped." The only trouble with all this is that, in point of fact, the common Indian food is *not* rice.[30] Similarly, the Austinian doctrine of sovereignty (so fraught with latent menace to free institutions) is constructed upon abstractions and *a priori* reasonings of this character; the Analytical Jurists ignore or reject particular historical antecedents, national differences, and "the whole enormous aggregate of opinions, sentiments, beliefs, superstitions, and prejudices, of ideas of all kinds, hereditary and acquired, some produced by institutions and some by the constitution of human nature."[31] From this blindness the conscientious historian must redeem modern thought. If he fails, and the Benthamites have their way with legislation, society will be treated as a mechanical contrivance. Freedom and progress, which are things of the spirit, do not long survive such a régime. "Just as it is possible to forget the existence of friction in nature and the reality of other motives in society except the desire to grow rich, so the pupil of Austin may be tempted to forget that there is more in actual sovereignty than force, and more in laws which are the commands of sovereigns than can be got out of them by merely considering them as regulated force." Maine's words have had their weight in England; but the American pragmatic school of juridical thought, Maine's contemporary Holmes eminent among them, disregarded his injunctions.

We cannot enter here upon the breadth and depth of Maine's own contribution toward this conservative history on a scientific plan. His great reputation endures. "What pure reason and boundless knowledge can do," said Acton, "without sympathy or throb, Maine can do better than any man in England."[32] This dispassionate historian of laws and customs established a vastly influential school of research and speculation. And his own immediate conclusions from the imposing mass of his investigations were socially conservative without reservation.

In their early and barbarous states of society, men exist in a condition of status: individual personality manifested only in rudimentary form, property the possession of the group, subsistence, gratification of hopes, marriage, life itself wholly dependent upon the community. Progress consists of a release from this bondage; and civilized people exist in a condition of contract, possessing several property, and able to develop fully their individual talents.

The movement of the progressive societies has been uniform in one respect. Through all its course it has been distinguished by the gradual dissolution of family dependency, and the growth of individual obligation in its place. The Individual is steadily substituted for the Family, as the unit of which civil laws take account...Nor is it difficult to see what is the tie between man and man which replaces by degrees those forms of reciprocity in rights and duties which have their origin in the Family. It is Contract. Starting, as from one terminus of history, from a condition of society in which all the relations of Persons are summed up in the relations of Family, we seem to have steadily moved towards a phase of social order in which all these relations arise from the free agreement of individuals.[33]

Private property and contract make possible the variety of personality, the wealth, the leisure, and the fertility of invention that sustain civilization. The prudent statesman, feeling that there is a half-mysterious link between contract and noble culture (Maine said at Calcutta in 1862), ''will shrink from tampering with so powerful an instrument of civilization.'' Immediate advantages in seeming expediency or popular approbation must not be allowed to outweigh this enduring necessity for respecting the system of contract. Indeed, contract is one of the more efficient means of moral education, teaching through the necessity of exact performance how much depends upon fidelity.[34] Here Maine's praise of contract and individual economic responsibility, though similar in some respects to that of the Liberal economists, really transcends Utilitarian thought (he being hostile toward the Manchesterians, in fact, thinking they would cause the loss of India) and rises to the plane of Burke and Smith.

Civilized societies are competitive societies. Their competition is economic and civil; another kind of competition is found even among the most savage peoples living in a condition of status, but it is a terrible competition. The study of primitive societies refutes the notion that all men are brothers, and that all men are equal. "The scene before us is rather that which the animal world presents to the mental eye of those who have the courage to bring home to themselves the facts answering to the memorable theory of Natural Selection. Each fierce little community is perpetually at war with its neighbour, tribe with tribe, village with village."[35] The idyllic fantasies of Rousseau are exploded by the sober historian. If a civilized people abandon civilized competition, after a steady course of retrogression they will find themselves forced back upon the murderous competition of natural selection. It is quite true that joint ownership, by community or family, is older than private ownership of land; but this only demonstrates that private proprietorship is a part of progress. Ferocious though competition is between groups in a primitive condition of life, in their domestic transactions competition is feeble. Economic competition—in exchange and in the acquisition of property—is relatively modern in origin; and what is more, in its complete form it is distinctively Western. It is a mighty benefit, essential to the higher forms of progress.

The socialist endeavors to deduce from these facts that the primitive economic arrangements of men ought to be humanity's present economic condition; that several property ought to be abolished in favor of renewed communal ownership. But modernity in institutions is no proof of injustice; rather, it is presumptive of high development. One conclusion the scientific historian, impartial though he should be in most matters, may draw from his study of property as an institution:

Nobody is at liberty to attack several property and to say at the same time that he values civilization. The history of the two cannot be disentangled. Civilization is nothing more than a name for the old order of the Aryan world, dissolved but perpetually reconstituting itself under a vast variety of solvent influences, of which infinitely the most powerful have been those which have, slowly, and in some parts of the world much less perfectly than others, substituted several property for collective ownership.[36]

Henry Maine entertained these opinions long before the bitter dispute over the Reform Bills of 1884 and 1885, when the survival of the House of Lords seemed threatened again, when the Radicalism of Chamberlain mastered Gladstone's reluctance to enlarge the suffrage, when the tendency of Liberalism toward a new collectivism became increasingly palpable. Maine's "Tory" book *Popular Government* marked no new stage, then, in his intellectual development; he was applying the historical judgments of his tremendous scholarship to the drift of governments throughout Western society. It is a work melancholy in tone, but not so gloomy as his friend Stephen's; and not so powerful, either. Sometimes the admirer of Maine is disappointed in *Popular Government.* Though lucid and courageous, the book does not always penetrate to first principles; unhappy, perhaps, when compelled by a feeling of duty to turn from scientific history to contemporary politics, Maine sometimes seems concerned more with the particularities of Democracy than with the roots of society. But *Popular Government* remains worth reading today.

Modern popular government was born with a lie in its mouth: the assumption of a State of Nature, taught by Rousseau. "Democracy is commonly described as having an inherent superiority over every other form of government. It is supposed to advance with an irresistible and pre-ordained movement. It is thought to be full of the promise of blessings to mankind: yet if it fails to bring with it these blessings, or even proves to be prolific of the heaviest calamities, it is not held to deserve condemnation. These are the familiar marks of a theory which claims to be independent of experience and observation on the plea that it bears the credentials of a golden age, non-historical and unverifiable."[37] But how the performance of democracy contrasts with its pretensions! The sober student of history will note the fact "that since the century during which the Roman Emperors were at the mercy of the Praetorian soldiery, there has been no such insecurity of government as the world has seen since rulers became delegates of the community.'' Maine cites the failure of democracy in Germany, Italy, Spain, Latin America; its awful turbulence in France; its stimulation of the fell spirit of Nationalism. What else was to be expected? In practice, universal suffrage tends to be the natural basis of a tyranny; at best, government by wire-pullers.*

But it is not a charge against democracies that they incline toward intellectual innovation; on the contrary, they are more commonly guilty of a deadening ultra-conservatism of thought. They detest the Darwinian theory, and the hard truths of Malthus; they oppose true progress: ''It seems to me quite certain that, if for four centuries there had been a very widely extended franchise and a very large electoral body in this country, there would have been no reformation of religion, no change of dynasty, no toleration of Dissent, not even an accurate Calendar.''[38] They insist, instead, upon being flattered by vague generalities about their own virtue and infallibility. Unable to exercise a genuine common volition—such a thing as the general will does not exist in nature—they allow government to fall into the hands of professional manipulators and plundering cabals. Most men are as bored with practical politics as they are with progress and enlightenment, and can be persuaded to cast their votes or volunteer their languid support to a party by one influence only: corruption. There are two kinds of public bribery—the first the spoils of office, the second ''the directer process of legislating away the property of one class and transferring it to another. It is this last which is likely to be the corruption of these latter days.''[39]

May anything be done to save this democracy from itself—this popular government which is in deadly peril of setting its own laws at defiance and mercilessly oppressing individuals or minorities? Maine holds out some hopes. The first measure of salvation is the more accurate defining of the word ''democracy.'' Men must be brought to see that democracy means a form of government, and

---

*Ralph Adams Cram, in *The End of Democracy* (1937), reiterates this catalogue of disaster, with more recent instances.

nothing more: it is not an end in itself, but a proposed means to justice, freedom, and progress; we must be purged of the delusion that Democracy is Vox Dei. Certainly we ought to know by now that to consult the hoarse voice of Democracy is as hazardous as consulting the Greek oracles. "All agreed that the voice of an oracle was the voice of a god; but everybody allowed that when he spoke he was not as intelligible as might be desired, and nobody was quite sure whether it was safer to go to Delphi or to Dodona." Democracies must first be taught modesty about their own functions; beyond this, the principal safeguard for popular government will be found in exact and august constitutions, like that of the United States.

Where Stephen seeks to emphasize the moral majesty of law in general, Maine aspires to attach a sanctity to constitutional documents. Only in America has democracy manifested a considerable success; and a great part of that accomplishment results from the wise conservatism of the Federal Constitution. Avoiding the peril of a single assembly (toward which Britain is drifting), recognizing the rights of the several states and the necessity for limiting the power of positive legislation, capping the system (though almost unintentionally) with the dignified check of a Supreme Court, the fathers of the American Republic devised an instrument of government unparalleled as a conservative power for ordered liberty. In its inspiration, the American Constitution is British; but Britain now needs to learn from her children. With Guizot, Maine praises *The Federalist* as the greatest application in history of the elementary principles of government to practical administration. "It would seem that, by a wise Constitution, Democracy may be made nearly as calm as water in a great artificial reservoir; but if there is a weak point anywhere in the structure, the mighty force which it controls will burst through it and spread destruction far and near."[40]

Some men hope for different remedies. They foresee, for instance—Renan among them—the formation of an intellectual aristocracy, an elite. "Society is to become the Church of a sort of political Calvinism, in which the Elect are to be the men with

exceptional brains.'' But would such an aristocracy—not that it
is likely to obtain ascendancy—really be beneficent? From ''an
ascetic aristocracy of men of science, with intellects perfected by
unremitting exercise, absolutely confident in themselves and absolutely sure of their conclusions,'' what sort of treatment would
the heart and spirit of society get?[41] Maine, with the instinct of
the true conservative, dreads this projected new privileged order;
but in any case, if ever a conflict between Democracy and Science
comes, ''Democracy, which is already taking precautions against
the enemy, will certainly win.'' For Democracy abhors cultural
progress, or any manifestation of superiority.

The world, as Machiavelli put it, is made up of the vulgar. Into
their hands, the Benthamite politics put unrestricted political
power; and they are proceeding promptly enough to undo all the
rest of Bentham's work. ''The 'Anarchical Sophisms' which he
exposed have migrated from France to England, and may be read
in the literature of Advanced Liberalism side by side with the
Parliamentary Fallacies which he laughed at in the debates of a
Tory House of Commons.''[42] The progress from status to contract was the work of aristocratic minds; the retrogression from
contract to status will be the achievement of a democratic complacency.

What Engels, in 1877, called ''the negation of the negation''
was slouching forward behind the curtain of Democracy: private
property, the achievement of Contract, was menaced with sociali-
zation, or a return to primitive Status. If this reaction should be
consummated, civilization must sink proportionately to the barbarism that is described by Status. Degeneration is not inevitable; it is merely probable. ''No doubt, if adequate causes are at
work, the effect will always follow; but, in politics, the most powerful of all causes are the timidity, the listlessness, and the super-
ficiality, of the generality of minds. If a large number of
Englishmen, belonging to classes which are powerful if they exert
themselves, continue saying to themselves and others that
Democracy is irresistible and must come, beyond all doubt it will
come.''[43] So Maine wrote. But the Reforms of 1884 and 1885 had

broken in influence the most energetic of those classes that Maine spoke of, the landed proprietors; and Britain was now committed to party competition for the franchises of men who little apprehended the significance of several property, and rarely tasted of it.

4

One finds *Democracy and Liberty*, in two fat volumes, on the shelves of any decent second-hand bookshop. Lecky's *History of England in the Eighteenth Century* still is in demand, and perhaps always will be; the *History of European Morals* is read, too; but his political treatise never has attracted the attention it deserves. Although markedly digressive, and in part concerned with what are now dead controversies, *Democracy and Liberty* is the most thorough manual of conservative politics produced during the nineteenth century.

"Protestantism in one aspect," says Leslie Stephen, "is simply rationalism still running about with the shell on its head."[44] Applied to Lecky, this witticism contains much truth. At once an earnest Protestant and the historian of rationalism, he retained his faith in the being of a benevolent Deity while he scoffed at superstition and sacerdotalism. Roman Catholicism, he was convinced, lingered only as a dying cult—one of his less fortunate predictions, though it had seeming justification in the 'seventies; Christianity, to survive in a world of science and industry, must be purged of the relics of fable and simple credulity. The Hell of orthodoxy, which to Fitzjames Stephen was the most real and indispensable element in Christianity, seemed to Lecky the horrid invention of revolting imaginations, the grotesque survival of brutal times, impossible for a rational man to admit into his moral system. But Lecky did not embrace the Religion of Humanity. As a defense of intuitive moral ideas against the inductive or utilitarian school of moralists, the first chapter of *A History of European Morals* probably has no peer in modern scholarship, and reflects Lecky's abiding and touching confidence in a loving God: "I suspect that many moralists confuse the self-gratulation which they suppose a virtuous man to feel, with the delight a religious man experiences from the sense of the protection and favour of the Deity.''[45]

The reader of *The Rise and Influence of Rationalism* or of *The Map of Life* will find the idea of Providence, however, so important to Burke's philosophy, conspicuous by its absence. It is not denied; but it is scarcely affirmed. The rational religion of Lecky has pruned away nearly all of traditional Christianity except an intuitive morality, the imitation of Christ, and the Golden Rule. Yet the essence of Christianity lives still, Lecky thinks:

If it be true Christianity to dive with a passionate charity into the darkest recesses of misery and of vice, to irrigate every quarter of the earth with the fertilizing stream of an almost boundless benevolence, and to include all the sections of humanity in the circle of an intense and efficacious sympathy; if it be true Christianity to destroy and weaken the barriers which had separated class from class and nation from nation, to free war from its harshest elements, and to make a consciousness of essential equality and of a genuine fraternity dominate over all accidental differences; if it be, above all, true Christianity to cultivate a love of truth for its own sake, a spirit of candour and of tolerance towards those with whom we differ—if these be the marks of a true and healthy Christianity, then never since the days of the Apostles has it been so vigorous as at present, and the decline of dogmatic systems and of clerical influence has been a measure if not a cause of its advance.[46]

Are these indeed the marks of a true and healthy Christianity? Or are they possibly the marks of that sentimental humanitarianism which Lecky detested? At any rate, Lecky (thorough Old Whig that he was) remained invincibly suspicious of parsons, confident that the priest must give way to the rational moralist; and the affirmation that ''orthodoxy is my doxy,'' the rock upon which Johnson, Burke, Coleridge, Newman, and lesser men had built their conservatism, yields in Lecky to tolerant endorsement of the Sermon on the Mount, which Fitzjames Stephen had declared to be boggy ground for any practical social system. *Securus judicat orbis terrarum:* this spirit, missing in Lecky, is a premise without which most men's conservatism tends to falter, when confronted with a sea of troubles.

Religious veneration, then, cuts a poor figure in Lecky's manual of conservatism, though Lecky defends church establishments upon the ground of utility. And despite his immense knowledge of moral philosophy, even moral considerations receive little attention in *Democracy and Liberty*. In that work (published in 1896, the year in which, after a long literary career, Lecky took his seat in the House of Commons) we perceive the nineteenth century merging into the twentieth: the controversy over faith and morals, which exercised nineteenth-century thinkers more than anything else, gives way to questions of economics and of political techniques. Benthamism, although forsaken as a consistent system, has subtly conquered nearly everyone: the political economists' blue-books supplant the sermon and the oration. This renunciation of religious and moral arguments apart, Lecky is Burke speaking at the end of the nineteenth century. In 1855, when Lecky entered Trinity College, Dublin, he acquired the *Reflections on the Revolution in France;* and his annotated old copy was in his pocket for forty years, on his solitary walks in Ireland and Switzerland.[47] Abhorrence of radical change, Burke's cardinal political principle, is the theme of *Democracy and Liberty.*

Throughout the decade that intervened between the publication of Maine's *Popular Government* and the appearance of *Democracy and Liberty,* organic change seemed to be sapping the continuity of British society. The old Jew gentleman no longer sat on the top of chaos; even men who had cordially detested him, among them Lecky, reluctantly wished Disraeli alive again, to restrain with his exotic arts the djinn of popular impulse which (in their opinion) he had released. Gladstonian Liberalism, furious at having been dished in 1867, was endeavoring to gratify the new electorate at the expense of Tory interests, and Salisbury's Conservatives entered perforce into this competition. In its immediate consequences, the Third Reform of 1884-1885 seemed more revolutionary than the measures of 1832 and 1867. Essentially, as Lecky wrote, the belief of the new radicals was that "in the hands of a democracy taxation should be made the means of redressing the inequalities of fortune, ability, or industry; the preponderant class voting and spending money which another class are obliged to pay.''[48] Prescriptive right of every sort was shaken; and, as Burke had predicted, ''No species of property is secure when it once becomes large enough to tempt the cupidity of indigent power.'' Indigent power sat in the House of Commons after 1885.

The Fabian Society was founded in 1884: Sidney Webb, Bernard Shaw, and their friends began to undermine the intellectual defenses of Victorian England, almost at the very time when a Radical government struck down the Parliamentary bulwarks of the territorial proprietors. No old dominant class ever really relinquishes power until its nerve has failed—until, losing confidence in its own virtue and its own justness, that powerful order allows the sceptre or the sword to slip from its grasp, mesmerized rather than vanquished. This process had begun in England many years before; now the intellectual socialists brought it nearer to culmination. Marxism, in its original virulence or in its milder variants, now had to be considered as a most serious influence in the world of ideas, not the eccentric fabrication of an embittered exile. Socialism, said Lecky, was become something greater than a simple political scheme: ''Its teaching has evidently permeated great masses of men with something of the force, and has assumed something of the character, of a new religion, rushing in to fill the vacuum where old beliefs and old traditions have decayed.''[49]

Fabian literary socialism was calculated to appeal particularly to the new crowd of half-educated young people, trained in the state schools set up in compliance with the Education Act of 1870, augmented by the compulsory feature added in the Act of 1876, and crowned by the adoption of free schooling in 1891. Industrialists had demanded the establishment of state schools to supply technical training; they soon were to find that the stream of clerks and ambitious artisans whom the schools produced could think of other things than efficient production. As Denis W. Brogan remarks of the Western-educated clerical class in India, ''The man who can keep accounts can also read John Stuart Mill, Macaulay, and Marx.''[50] By 1892, more than seven million pounds sterling was being spent annually by school boards in England and Wales. This alone would have made necessary a radical revision of the taxation-system and a radically large increase in the amount of taxation. Lecky perceived that the political value of education was overrated: "The more dangerous forms of animosity and dissention are usually undiminished, and are often stimulated, by its influence. An immense proportion of those who have learnt to read, never read anything but a party newspaper—very probably a newspaper specially intended to inflame or mislead them—and the half-educated mind is peculiarly open to political Utopias and fanaticisms."[51] Some of these people (Gissing describes them in *The Nether World*) read atheist pamphlets; others read Fabian Tracts.

As education became thoroughly secularized and modernized, so local government, the fortress of Tory political spirit, became democratized. Disraeli had said that the parochial constitution was more important than the national constitution; now all that was amended. The squire and the parson lost their ancient grip upon administration of justice in the counties when the Local Government Act of 1888 (passed by a Conservative government) established the county councils; and the Liberals, in 1894, set up the parish councils and the urban and rural district councils. The old idea of ordination and subordination in rural localities was thus repudiated by the state; the principle of popular election supplanted it. The Act of 1894 did something more: it abolished property qualifications for vestrymen and poor-law guardians; it swept away the rating qualification for voting. Thus the class that paid the expenses of local government was lost in the mass of those who might benefit from such expenditures. Taxation without representation has more forms than one. "The country gentlemen who chiefly managed her county government," said Lecky of the old system, "at least discharged their task with great integrity, and with a very extensive and minute knowledge of the districts they ruled. They had their faults, but they were more negative than positive."[52] A man familiar with county and local councils today may make his comparisons.

With all this went a voluminous body of social legislation— housing for the working-classes, sanitary improvements, factory laws, workmen's compensation laws, a civil service vastly enlarged; and all had to be paid for; and the army and navy estimates increased steadily. Between 1870 and 1895, the national public expenditure increased from seventy million pounds to a hundred million. In 1874, the income tax was only twopence in the pound; by 1885, it rose the highest point hitherto, eightpence; and after 1894, it began to climb farther upward. Many of the Liberals themselves feared the graduated income-tax; Gladstone had been eager to abolish income-tax entirely, and opposed death duties on landed estates; but the death duties which Sir William Harcourt introduced in his budget of 1894 triumphed, for Manchesterian dislike of landed property afforded the death duties a sanction. When the Conservatives regained office next year, they dared not repeal the duties: already the middle-class element in the Conservative Party outweighed the landed interest, and the need for revenue was pressing. "There could hardly be a greater departure from what used to be called orthodox political economy," Lecky wrote, "than the duties of Sir William Harcourt. The first principle of taxation according to the older economists, is that it ought to fall upon income and not upon capital. In England one of the two largest direct taxes annually raised is now a highly graduated tax falling directly upon capital. ...Its most oppressive features are that there is no time limit, so that in the not improbable event of two, three, or even four owners of a great property dying in rapid succession, the tax has the effect of absolute confiscation, and that no distinction is drawn between property which produces income and is easily realisable and the kinds of property which produce little or no income and which is difficult or impossible to realise."[53] Thus the derelict country house casts its shadow before: higher death duties, two great wars to slaughter the sons of county families, more income taxes, the addition of taxes upon "unearned" income—so the end of the whole pattern of rural Britain begins to take shape in 1894.

Unearned income from land, said Lecky, is of all forms of wealth generally that most beneficial to society. "Society is a compact chiefly for securing to each man a peaceful possession of his property, and, as long as a man fulfills his part in the social compact, his right to what he has received from his father is as valid as his right to what he has himself earned." People who live upon inherited property have done more for England, by far, than the great bulk of self-made rich men. William Wilberforce, John Howard, and Lord Shaftesbury were of this class—and Lecky might well have added his own name, so eminent among the great scholars who have obtained from ample private means the leisure and the learning by which they add to the sum of civilization. Nor are these famous names all. "Great inherited properties usually carry with them large and useful administrative duties, and no class of men in England have, on the whole, lived better lives, and contributed more to the real well-being of the community, than the less wealthy country gentlemen who, contenting themselves with the moderate incomes they inherited, lived upon their estates, administering county business, and improving in countless ways the condition of the tenants and their neighbours."[54] A whole century after the time of which Lecky wrote, a large proportion of the remaining landed families of Britain still performed those duties, under dismaying handicaps, with a conscientiousness unequalled in any other nation.

The Independent Labour Party was founded in 1893. Three years later, Lecky still could write that the New Unionism and the Socialists had been crushed at the general election of 1895, that conservative tendencies were dominant in the working-class centers, and that the avowed Socialist party, so powerful in the Continent, scarcely existed in the English Parliament. But how long might this endure? Like Irving Babbitt in twentieth-century America, Lecky dreads the plutocracy as much as the program of Hyndman and Morris:

It is not the existence of inherited wealth, even on a very large scale, that is likely to shake seriously the respect for property: it is the many examples which the conditions of modern society present of vast wealth acquired by shameful means, employed for shameful purposes, and exercising an altogether undue influence in society and in the State. When triumphant robbery is found among the rich, subversive doctrine will grow among the poor. When democracy turns, as it often does, into a corrupt plutocracy, both national decadence and social revolution are being prepared. No one who peruses modern Socialist literature, no one who observes the current of feeling among the masses in the great towns, can fail to perceive their deep, growing, and not unreasonable sense of the profound injustices of life.[55]

This is like Coleridge in the *Lay Sermons,* or Disraeli in *Sybil*; but it is seventy to fifty years nearer the culmination of an epoch when wealth is divorced from social duty.

In these matters, as in so much, Lecky is the best spokesman of the landed element and the upper-middle classes in late-Victorian days. He is the bold opponent of a democracy that destroys the balance of interests in the community, upon which depends the Constitution; he warns against a democracy that loves regulation and restriction, foreseeing a day not distant when (as Elie Halévy writes) employer and worker in Britain, losing their energies, will form "an unconscious alliance against that appetite for work, that zeal for production by which British industry had conquered the markets of the world."[56] A tendency to democracy, says Lecky, "does not mean a tendency to parliamentary government, or even a tendency toward greater liberty." Quite the contrary: the democracy taking form in Britain seems to be the rudiment of socialism; and Lecky agreed with Herbert Spencer that "socialism is slavery, and the slavery will not be mild."

The rush and tumult of modern life, the constant succession of new impressions and ideas, the destruction of continuity, the appetites of jaded political palates, the decay of family feeling— these unite to reinforce "what may be called the unintelligent conservatism of English Radicalism." Class bribery is the latest instrument of those destructive forces which have been trying since 1789, or earlier, to undermine the fabric of English life. This

radicalism has preserved a constant character, despite its own detestation of continuity, and moves in a few old, well-worn grooves.

The withdrawal of the control of affairs from the hands of the minority
who, in the competitions of life, have risen to a higher plane of fortune
and instruction; the continual degradation of the suffrage to lower and
lower strata of intelligence; attacks upon institution after institution; a
systematic hostility to the owners of landed property, and a disposition
to grant much of the same representative institutions to all portions of
the Empire, quite irrespectively of their circumstances and characters,
are the directions in which the ordinary Radical naturally moves...To
destroy some institution, or to injure some class, is very commonly his
first and last idea in constitutional policy.[57]

The socialists are proceeding to take command of this long-
established radical tendency in Britain; but to it they are adding
elements of compulsion and permanent regulation which make
it still more ominous than before. Universal military training, the
most crushing burden that the state can impose upon its people,
the most terrible curse to the better types of humanity—highly
strung, sensitive, and nervous—is found in conjunction with levelling democracy, not merely by coincidence. The armed horde is
a concomitant of egalitarian socialism and state planning; and it
is a natural reaction of any society which has abandoned all the
old habitual and internal disciplines, so that it must rely (as Burke
predicted) upon arbitrary external disciplines. Individuality, like
imagination, must vanish from a people among whom socialism
triumphs.

But can socialism actually succeed in dominating Britain? It is
essentially opposed to free trade and international commerce, the
sustenance of English life. In the future, industrial conditions
doubtless will be greatly modified. Different taxation, new laws
of inheritance, co-operative endeavors, governmental direction of
industry, legislation for social welfare—these changes probably will
come. ''But the proposed changes which conflict with the fundamental laws and elements of human nature can never, in the long

run, succeed. The sense of right and wrong, which is the basis of the respect for property and for the obligation of contract; the feeling of family affections, on which the continuity of society depends, and out of which the system of heredity grows; the essential difference of men in aptitudes, capacities, and character, are things that never can be changed, and all schemes and policies that ignore them are doomed to ultimate failure."[58] In 1896, Lecky was criticized for his pessimism; nine decades later, the observer of life in Marxist states would envy Lecky's optimism.

Menaced thus by the new collectivism of the closing third of the nineteenth century, the inheritors of Burke's liberal ideas were reconciled to the conservatives. Stephen, Maine, and Lecky defended contract against status. Sentimental collectivism would harden into crushing servitude, they knew. Marx and Engels looked forward to the "negation of the negation," the return of status, with an apocalyptic eagerness. So, indeed, writers less radical have viewed this drift of things. The fashionable paternal statism of the 1920s and 1930s abounded in endorsements of a return to status. Even Dean Roscoe Pound explained in 1926 that the course of law throughout the twentieth century, it seems, refutes Maine's thesis: society now is moving triumphantly from contract to "relation" (a kind of modernized and modified status) and therefore relation-status must represent a higher stage in progress—unless we have been progressing backward.[59]

Just so—unless we have been progressing backward. The modern recrudescence of status in society may be progress, with its pillars the contact-man, the ration-queue, the giant corporation, the giant union, the labor camp, the *levée en masse,* and the police agent. If this is progress, however—this life of the amorphous housing-estate and the mass-hypnotism of television—why, one can but say, with President Lincoln, "For those who like that sort of thing, that is the sort of thing they like."

X

Conservatism Frustrated: America, 1865—1918

Whatever the result of the convulsion whose first shocks were beginning to be felt, there would still be enough square miles of earth for elbow-room; but that ineffable sentiment made up of memory and hope, of instinct and tradition, which swells every man's heart and shapes his thought, though perhaps never present to his consciousness, would be gone from it, leaving it common earth and nothing more. Men might gather rich crops from it, but that ideal harvest of priceless associations would be reaped no longer; that fine virtue which sent up messages of courage and security from every sod of it would have evaporated beyond recall. We should be irrevocably cut off from our past, and be forced to splice the ragged ends of our lives upon whatever new conditions chance might leave dangling for us.

—James Russell Lowell, "Abraham Lincoln"

SPLICING THE RAGGED ENDS: to this melancholy occupation, men of a conservative bent were condemned after Appomattox. The ruined South hardly could afford the luxury of any species of thought—there, every nerve was strained, for decades, to deal hastily with exigencies, somehow to make a dismembered economy stir again, in some fashion to reconcile negro emancipation with social stability. So, for a long time after 1865, the South has no philosophers; and her disenfranchised leaders are employed, half dazed, in writing apologia—Stephens and Davis, notably—or in mending resignedly the fabric of civilization, with Lee.

The obligations of conservative restoration therefore lay with the mind of the triumphant North; but the Northern intellect, which practically was the New England intellect, faltered before this enormous task, being ill equipped for it. The crabbed conservative strain which wound through New England character and reached its most humane expression in Hawthorne was, in essence, a conservatism of negation; now, burdened with the necessity for affirmation and reconstruction, the New England mind shied and groaned and cursed at these perplexities. For years, too, the masters of New England—not the State Street men, but leaders like Charles Francis Adams and Sumner and Everett and Parker and Emerson, the men of thought and statecraft—had been engaged in a dangerous, self-righteous flirtation with radicalism, political abstractions, and that kind of fanatic egalitarianism which Garrison represented. Their conservative instincts were bewildered by the passion of this moral crusade and by the influence of Transcendentalism; they scarcely remembered, any longer, where to look for the foundations of a conservative order; and so when we speak of the "conservative" thought which existed in the Gilded Age, really we mean a set of principles very like English Liberalism, which honest and confused men are trying to apply to conservative ends. This conservative longing may be traced with reasonable distinctness in the ideas of James Russell Lowell, E.L. Godkin, Henry Adams, and Brooks Adams—a half-century of frustration, from the beginning of Reconstruction to the brink of the First World War.

The New England reformers thought they had struck down evil incarnate when they crushed the Sable Genius of the South; and their horror at the corruption and chaos of the Gilded Age was intensified proportionately as they discovered the extent of their own previous naïveté. They had dreaded an era of Jefferson Davis; but now they were in an era of Thaddeus Stevens, and of worse than Stevens. The merciless and vulgar old ironmaster, indeed, looked conspicuously admirable by the side of the Conklings and Mortons, the Butlers and Randalls, the Chandlers, Blaines, and Boutwells who scrabbled in the dust of a country blighted even worse spiritually than physically. Presently the reformers grasped that their great general, Grant, was a groping dupe. They had been intent on abstract virtue, and now they awoke to find their fellow-Republicans, the oligarchs of their party, intent upon concrete plunder. The Mountain had yielded to the Directory. At this spectacle of national corruption, they stared helpless for a while, and then did what they could to restore a measure of decency. But before they could effect any substantial amelioration, the South had been reduced to a poverty of economy and spirit from which it has not yet recovered, and the nation exposed to a régime of self-seeking which left its stamp upon the character of the United States. The South was condemned to a permanent political hypocrisy, in fact disfranchising the black population which the amended Constitution elevated to a nominal equality; the North poisoned itself with avarice. It was cruel work, splicing the ragged ends; and if the splicing was clumsily done, still only men of high gifts could splice at all.

Even after the reddest wounds of the War and Reconstruction had begun to heal, the state of the nation was dismaying. This was the age of the exploiting financiers, the invincible city bosses with Tweed their *primus inter pares,* and the whole rout of grasping opportunists who are the reverse side of the coin of American individualism. Bryce's calm chapters in *The American Commonwealth* tell the story. This was the age, too, of a relentless economic centralization, a dull standardization, and an insatiable devastation of natural resources. Presently an abused public begins to stir in heavy resentment, and then in active protest; and that public resolves to cure the ills of democracy by introducing a greater degree of democracy. If government is corrupt—why, make it wholly popular: and so the last third of the nineteenth century experiences the successful advocacy of direct democratic devices. The election of judges and of executive officials, the abolition of the last exceptions to universal manhood suffrage, the revision of constitutions, the direct primary, the popular election of United States senators, presently the popular initiative and referendum and recall—these instruments of extreme democracy are proposed, praised, and gradually enacted. They are designed to purify; more commonly, they stultify proper government. True party responsibility is almost destroyed, so that the pressure-group bullies legislatures and the representative sinks closer and closer to the status of delegate. Such democracy, however direct in name, is a sham: real power is captured (except for sporadic reform-movements) by special interests and clever organizers and the lobbies. A long way removed, this, from New England visions of the American future.

As the public grows irate at deception and exploitation, the demagogue and the fantastic, and a variety of economic and social visionaries, frighten what remains of true conservative opinion. The rise of wild politicians like Tillman in the Southern states, the menace of the Populists, Bryan and Free Silver, the tremendous strikes which rage during the administration of the only strong and intelligent president of the time, Cleveland: these symptoms demonstrate both that abuse is countered by abuse, and (in Lowell's words) "the fatal change (to me a sad one) from an agricultural to a proletary population." Jefferson's America is as much eclipsed as John Adams'; if freedom, decency, and order are to be conserved, thinking men must contend against the whole eyeless, brutal tendency of a mechanized society.

Add to this the gradual popularization of Darwin's theories, the increasing influence of Positivism and a pragmatic spirit older than Pragmatism, the triumph of cheap and unscrupulous newspapers: the problem of a moral conservation of American standards—or any standards—becomes acute. American character, individualistic, covetous, contemptuous of restraint, always had been stubborn clay for the keepers of tradition to mould into civilization. Now it threatens to become nearly anarchic, to slip into a ditch of spiritual atomism. What can be done? Lowell speculates uneasily; Godkin scourges the age in the *Nation*; the four sons of Charles Francis Adams try to fight their way into the thick of practical affairs, but are repulsed, and Henry and Brooks Adams pry bitterly into the probabilities of social destiny.

2

Belittling James Russell Lowell has become fashionable. Parrington does it; and in Laski's *The American Democracy* is a more recent specimen of this cavalier treatment.[1] Lowell did not possess original genius. But how civilized a man, and how versatile! Whoever reads Lowell's letters is not likely to dismiss him summarily, and the shrewd and erudite Leslie Stephen held Lowell in profound respect. Lowell founded the major American school of literary criticism; he was a poet of high, if limited, talent; and he represented the best in Brahmin culture. As a student of society, he was guilty of grave inconsistencies and vacillations. But his life extended through a baffling age, from the Virginia Dynasty to the Mauve Decade. If he furnishes no enduring political maxims, still he best exemplifies the frustration of conservatism in his age, in doubt about democracy, in doubt about industrialism, in doubt about the future of the American people.

At the beginning of his career, Lowell, like Disraeli—but more seriously than Disraeli—flirted with radicalism; his early poetry was deliberately radical: "I believe that no poet in this age can write much that is good unless he gives himself up to this tendency. For radicalism has now for the first time taken a distinctive and acknowledged shape of its own. So much of its spirit as poets in former ages have attained (and from their purer organization they could not fail of some) was by instinct rather than by reason. It has never till now been seen to be one of the two great wings that upbear the universe."[2] This is amusingly suggestive of Marxist "proletarian poetry" in the 1930's. But some of this radicalism stuck: he became an unswerving abolitionist, and although he never joined the most radical faction of that body, his bitterness toward everything Southern was implacable. Like almost all sensitive New Englanders, he was shocked by the Mexican War and the Southern appetites that provoked it; this inspired the *Bigelow Papers,* the beginning of his reputation; and he denounced slavery, Southern political principles, and Jefferson Davis with a virulence that makes them unpleasant reading now, leaguing himself with Garrison although he knew that fanatic for "a blackguard," like "every leader of reform." Northern men of conscience had reason to be shocked at much that occurred south of Mason's and Dixon's Line; but Southerners had as good cause to resent the supercilious intolerance of New England; and Lowell's blind detestation, which endured well into Reconstruction, did not sit well on the pupil of Burke.

For Lowell was always a discerning admirer of Burke, and he confessed his own essential conservatism. "I was always a natural Tory," he wrote, with playful candor, to Thomas Hughes in 1875, "and in England should be a staunch one. I would not give up a thing that had roots to it, though it might suck up its food from graveyards."[3] Born in an old mansion on Tory Row, Cambridge, and reared in the orthodoxies of Brahmin New England, he remained all his days substantially a defender of tradition, moral and social, despite inconsistencies like his Abolitionism. "Conservative" is regularly a term of commendation with Lowell. In a passage like the following, one perceives how much in love he was with the philosophy and style of Burke:

None of our great poets can be called popular in any exact sense of the word, for the highest poetry deals with thoughts and emotions which inhabit, like rarest sea-mosses, the doubtful limits of that shore between our abiding divine and our fluctuating human nature, rooted in the one, but living in the other, seldom laid bare, and otherwise visible only at exceptional moments of entire calm and clearness.[4]

His encomium of Lincoln (which did much to establish an enduring popular veneration for the President) is praise of the conservative democrat, a statesman after Burke's heart, who combined a disposition to preserve with an ability to reform. It is some proof of Lowell's catholic grasp of human nature, incidentally, transcending the narrow Brahminism sometimes pinned to his name, that he could love—almost worship—this Illinois politician so foreign to Cambridge. Anyone who reads of Charles Francis Adams' first interview with President Lincoln realizes the gulf of manners and education between Massachusetts Bay and Springfield, Illinois. ''Among the lessons taught by the French Revolution there is none sadder or more striking than this, that you may make everything else out of the passions of men except a political system that will work, and that there is nothing so pitilessly and unconsciously cruel as sincerity formulated into dogma. It is always demoralizing to extend the domain of sentiment over questions where it has no legitimate jurisdiction; and perhaps the severest strain upon Mr. Lincoln was in resisting a tendency of his own supporters which chimed with his own private desires, while wholly opposed to his convictions of what would be wide policy.''[5] Macaulay could not have put this better.

Although never himself a Radical Republican, Lowell was allied with the vengeful and virulent elements of Republicanism until the impeachment of President Johnson showed him the depths of spite and arbitrary vanity to which the Republican Party was descending. Then, rather shamefacedly (for he had detested Johnson and Seward), Lowell turned to the reform element among the Republicans, and, like Godkin, spent many years in the assault on city bosses and the spoils-system, often displaying remarkable courage. President Hayes made Professor Lowell minister to Spain and then to England, for which he was eminently qualified, and some of Lowell's more interesting reflections grew out of these years abroad. But one cannot look to Lowell for any consistent exposition of conservative ideas. Much in his age frightened him: the decay of manners, the corruption of morals, the discontent of a proletarian population, the mass-mind that is the consequence of intellectual vulgarization and speedy communication, the disturbance of American life by a deluge of immigrants. His solutions are faltering and vague, but his criticisms often glow with conservative acuity and prudence.

"I have always been of the mind that in a democracy manners are the only effective weapons against the bowie-knife," he wrote to a friend, "the only thing that will save us from barbarism."[6] After the Civil War, Lowell's chief contribution to politics was his endeavor to preserve the remnants of a gentlemanly tradition in defiance of the Gilded Age. Perhaps the best expression of his social conservatism is a letter to Joel Benton, in 1876, when Lowell had been the target of violent journalistic and popular abuse for daring to condemn Jim Fisk, Boss Tweed, and their creatures on the occasion of the Centenary of the United States. The Lowell of the *Bigelow Papers* had seemed to think that if only Senator Webster, General Cushing, and other conservatives were squelched, and the South brought to heel to the New England conscience, infinite moral progress awaited the United States. These prerequisites had been attained; and Lowell was horrified at the result:

What fills me with doubt and dismay is the degradation of the moral tone. Is it or is it not a result of Democracy? Is ours a "government of the people by the people for the people," or a Kakistocracy rather, for the benefit of knaves at the cost of fools? Democracy is, after all, nothing more than an experiment like another, and I know only one way of judging it—by its results. Democracy in itself is no more sacred than monarchy. It is man who is sacred; it is his duties and opportunities, not his rights, that nowadays need reinforcement. It is honour, justice, culture, that make liberty invaluable, else worse than worthless if it mean only freedom to be base and brutal....And as long as I live I will be no writer of birthday odes to King Demos any more than I would be to King Log, nor shall I think *our* cant any more sacred than any other. Let us all work together (and the task will need us all) to make Democracy possible. It certainly is no invention to go of itself any more than the perpetual motion.[7]

But work together how? In part, Lowell meant the administrative and purgative devices that Godkin and Higginson and the rest were intent upon—an able civil service, improved education, an aroused public conscience. But sometimes he went deeper. To

Thomas Hughes, he wrote of his trip to Cincinnati, where the sight of the peaceful fields along the railway heartened him: "Here was a great gain to the sum of human happiness, at least, however it may be with the higher and nobler things that make a country truly inhabitable. Will they come in time, or is Democracy doomed by its very nature to a dead level of commonplace? At any rate, our experiment of innoculation with freedom is to run its course through all Christendom, with what result the wisest cannot predict. Will it only insure safety from the more dangerous disease of originality?"[8]

"Originality," the infatuation with novelty and intellectual experiment, became steadily more repugnant to Lowell; he dreaded the influence of Darwinian ideas; he scowled upon the pretensions of physical and biological studies to omniscience. Like Burke, he trusted to the intellectual bank and capital of the ages. "I think the evolutionists will have to make a fetish of their protoplasm before long. Such a mush seems to me a poor substitute for the Rock of Ages—by which I understand a certain set of higher instincts which mankind have found solid under their feet in all weathers. At any rate, I find a useful moral in the story of Bluebeard. We have the key put into our hands, but there is always one door it is wisest not to unlock."[9] Just so; yet the majority of mankind, in defiance of Lowell, appeared bent upon violating that fatal chamber; the locks were broken, and every shrouded mystery was being tumbled into the daylight. To all elements in society, the great globe itself began to seem insubstantial. If even the natural order was in question, could men be expected to leave the social order governed by mere prescription? Lowell knew how important to civilization is a general assent to social continuity:

One of the strongest cements of society is the conviction that the state of things into which they are born is a part of the order of the universe, as natural, let us say, as that the sun should go round the earth. It is a conviction that they will not surrender except on compulsion, and a wise society should look to it that this compulsion is not put upon them. For the individual man there is no radical cure, outside of human nature itself, for the evils to which human nature is heir.[10]

So Lowell declared in his celebrated English address on "Democracy." Lowell's recent biographer exposes the inconsistencies and hesitancies that mar this speech;[11] yet it is studded with reflections worth remembering, among them his observations on education. The modern world being plagued with an indiscriminate curiosity, would education itself accomplish anything toward the conservation of civilized order? Lord Sherbrooke had told Englishmen to educate their future rulers. But will this suffice? "To educate the intelligence is to enlarge the horizon of its desires and wants. And it is well that this should be so. But the enterprise must go deeper and prepare the way for satisfying those desires and wants in so far as they are legitimate."[12]

Thus we return to the uncomfortable query, "How?" And again Lowell is rather evasive. With a touch of Disraeli, he does indeed say that "Democracy in its best sense is merely the letting in of air and light"; and he had once remarked, in a similar vein, "Habitual comfort is the main fortress of conservatism and respectability, two old-fashioned qualities for which all the finest sentiments in the world are but a windy substitute."[13] He would give the proletariat he pitied and dreaded a stake in society. "What is really ominous of danger to the existing order of things is not democracy (which, properly understood, is a conservative force), but the Socialism, which may find a fulcrum in it. If we cannot equalize conditions and fortunes any more than we can equalize the brains of men—and a very sagacious person has said that 'where two men ride of a horse one must ride behind'—we can yet, perhaps, do something to correct those methods and influences that lead to enormous inequalities, and to prevent their growing more enormous."

Still he was silent as to the means. He detested the labor unions; he denounced the eight-hour-day legislation; he knew that "State Socialism would cut off the very roots in personal character." Generally, Lowell had small ability as a practical statesman; and this same inability to grasp political actualities (natural enough in an old Brahmin gentleman who was severed from the society of his birth by "the change from New England to New Ireland") is the defect of his last important social utterance, "The Place of the Independent in Politics" (1888). Here he returns to his consistent dislike of party, declaring, "It has been proved, I think, that the old parties are not to be reformed from within." But this is falling back upon Washington's simple hope for a government without factions, and ignores what Burke should have taught every statesman, that if true party be lacking, any government is captured by the clique or the demagogue. If parties cannot be reformed from within, democracy probably cannot be reformed at all. Lowell's ground is much firmer under his feet when he enunciates literary and general truths, which he does here in his remarks on Burke as a political philosopher:

Many great and many acute minds had speculated upon politics from Aristotle's time downwards, but Burke was the first to illuminate the subject of his observation and thought with the electric light of imagination. He turned its penetrating ray upon what seemed the confused and wavering cloud-chaos of man's nature and man's experience, and found there the indication, at least, if not the scheme, of a divine order. The result is that his works are as full of prophecy, some of it already fulfilled, some of it in the course of fulfillment, as they are of wisdom. And this is because for him human nature was always the text and history the comment.[14]

Although in much smaller measure, some of these endowments were Lowell's own; and accordingly he still has meaning for the student of conservative ideas. Nothing so thoroughly unfits a man for pleasing the voters as the possession of a college education, said E.L. Godkin; and Godkin used his friend Lowell as an illustration. Lowell was "as patriotic an American as ever lived," a thorough democrat; but he was out of tune with the multitude. The West never took to him; the New York *Tribune* even denied he was a "good American," and the Republican Party wrote "Ichabod" on him. "The cause of all this really was that his political standards differed from theirs. He lived in an earlier republic of the mind, in which the legislation was done by first-class men, whom the people elected and followed. In a republic in which the multitude told the legislators what to do, he never really was at home."[15] The influence of the Virginian mind upon American politics expired in the Civil War; and the influence of the New England mind, which Lowell so eminently represented, withered in the Gilded Age.

3

> The rise of the newspaper press—furnishing to every man the materials for an opinion of some sort about public affairs, and the opportunity to say something about them, whether well or ill judged—had naturally a paralyzing effect on aristocratic pol-icy, and would have led to the downfall of aristocratic states even if the French Revolution had never occurred....When every man in the state knew, or thought he knew, what ought to be done, the period of government by small trained minori-ties had passed away.
>
> —E.L. Godkin, *Unforeseen Tendencies*
> *of Democracy*

Edwin Lawrence Godkin, a brilliant editor, spent his life strug-gling with "that greatest difficulty of large democracies, the difficulty of communicating to the mass common ideas and im-pulses." In his youth a rising light among the English Liberals, Godkin transferred to the United States his high and severe tal-ents, making the *Nation* a power in the land, influencing Lowell, leaguing his energies with the sons of Charles Francis Adams and with Higginson and Norton and the conservative reformers who did their best to shame the corruptors of the democratic ideal. A thinker in the Whig line of Macaulay, shrewder as a critic than as a prophet, the contemptuous adversary of protective tariffs, so-cialism, and all other affronts to Manchesterian political economy, he hoped to assist in the redemption of his adopted country and of his ideal of enlightened democracy; his instrument was a "grave,

decorous, and mature'' press like England's, to counterbalance
the puerility and frivolity of popular American newspapers. Certainly the newspaper press of the Gilded Age was bad enough;
but worse was possible, and as H.S. Commager remarks of Godkin, ''He lived to see the advent of that 'yellow journalism, which
he thought the nearest approach to Hell in any Christian state,'
and of 'a blackguard boy with several millions of dollars at his
disposal' who presumed to dictate the policies of the nation; but
he was too proud to follow where the Pulitzers and Hearsts led.
He retired at the turn of the century, somehow serene though
defeated, seeing journalism vulgarized, the 'chromo' civilization
which he had once derided triumphant, and his adopted country
embarked upon paths of conquest which he thought disastrous.
His like was not seen again.''[16]

Hope of turning the popular press to ends conservative of old
decencies and ideals died hard. Henry Adams' chief aspiration
was the editorship of a New York daily; and this unachieved,
Adams withdrew into a conviction of his own total failure, apparently unaware that the ultimate influence of his actual mission to
the classes would be greater than any possible effect of his frustrated ephemeral mission to the masses. The wholesome—if sometimes erratic—social conservatism of men like Godkin, Adams,
Curtis, and Theodore Roosevelt gave way, either side of the ocean,
to the calculated hysteria of Pulitzer and Hearst, the nominal political conservatism and actual social demoralization of Northcliffe
and Rothermere. But that some decent newspapers survive in an
age of mass-emotion, that the press still can be, on occasion, the
preceptor as well as the seducer of public opinion, is in part the
legacy of Godkin's criticism and Godkin's standards. His *Nation,*
after an interesting succession of editors, still endures, although
presently as the rasping voice of a sentimental collectivism which
is nearly everything that Godkin detested. Government by college graduates, Godkin's half-wistful hope for the future of
democracy; the old-style ''educated man in a democracy'' of whom
Godkin often wrote—these are hardly more than shadows now,
partially because of the educational reforms accomplished by

Godkin's ally President Eliot of Harvard, and men of his utilitarian mind. Yet somehow the United States blunders along; the spectacle of public corruption, though dismaying, really is not perceptibly worse than in Godkin's day, and the decisions of public assemblies are not much more dangerous than they were during the last third of the nineteenth century. No one can say how much Godkin and his colleagues had to do with the rousing of a public conscience that has kept crime and folly in some degree under surveillance, but it is certain they had their part in it.

Probably Godkin's essay "The Growth and Expression of Public Opinion," reprinted in *Unforeseen Tendencies of Democracy*, is his most penetrating contribution to the analysis of modern society. Accepting democracy as natural and inescapable—expressing a confidence in its permanence, indeed, which the experience of this century has proved ill-founded—the reforming editor now and then replied with acuity to some of the strictures upon popular government advanced by Tocqueville and Maine and Lecky. He was so incautious as to predict that "probably the world will not see another dictator chosen for centuries, if ever";[17] he feared not the dissolution of democracy, but rather degradation, the consequence of general mediocrity in mind and character straying bewildered through the labyrinth of civil society. "The really alarming feature connected with the growth of democracy is, that it does not seem to make provision for the government of this new world."

Quite as the modern reading public suffers from an increasing incapacity for continuous attention, so the people, suffering from chronic boredom with politics, are only occasionally roused to action—and then, commonly, ignorant action. To supply a government which the people will not furnish, there come forward the boss and the machine, allied with criminals and titanic spongers on the public; and though the people may be vaguely disgusted and discontented with this misgovernment, their resentment seldom amounts to more than "swinging the pendulum"—allowing one party hardly more than a single term in office, but replacing them with men of similar stamp. Democracies tend to disregard or to envy special fitness, and thus to exclude their natural leaders from office; and America in particular lacks any large class to furnish leadership: "The absence of anything we can call society, that is, the union of wealth and culture in the same persons, in all the large American cities, except possibly Boston, is one of the most marked and remarkable features of our time."[18] This paralysis of reason and decency in government is nearly completed by the modern state being shorn, in popular opinion, of those elements of consecration and veneration which Burke thought indispensable to order. "The state has lost completely, in the eyes of the multitude, the moral and intellectual authority it once possessed. It does not any longer represent God on earth. In democratic countries it represents the party which secured most votes at the last election, and is, in many cases, administered by men whom no one would make guardians of his children or trustees of his property. When I read the accounts given by the young lions of the historical school of the glorious future which awaits us as soon as we get the proper amount of state interference with our private concerns for the benefit of the masses, and remember that in New York, 'the state' consists of the Albany Legislature under the guidance of Governor Hill, and in New York City of the little Tammany junta known as 'the Big Four,' I confess I am lost in amazement."[19]

Even a state thus plundered and mauled, stripped of moral armor, might be tolerable if only the activity of government were confined to its ancient bounds. But modern populations, upon whom a popular press bestows presumption without knowledge, are resolved to extend the functions of government immeasurably beyond its old duties of defense and maintenance of internal order; for the public is now fascinated with the possibility of obtaining necessities and comforts through action of the state, even to the exclusion of those liberties which once were so resounding a rallying-cry. Economic appetites, now the masters of all classes, incline the public to demand a paternalistic regime; they encourage a variety of cheap Utopian fancies, as popular as they are gross; they lead almost invariably to manipulation of the value of money by the state, with its consequent inflation and insecurity; they are an excuse for profuse public expenditure; they make the labor question doubly dangerous; and the delusion, already dismayingly general, that prosperity depends upon the action of government, must lead to socialism, if wholly triumphant—to a common poverty of body and mind which masquerades as common gratification. "The rule of the many must always be the rule of the comparatively poor, and, in this age of the world, the poor have ceased to be content with their poverty. They seek wealth, and, in times when wealth is accumulating rapidly, they seek it eagerly. We cannot change this state of affairs. We must face the problem as it is presented to us. That problem is, I do not hesitate to say, the great problem of government in every civilized country—how to keep wealth in subjection to law; how to prevent its carrying elections, putting its creatures on the judicial bench, or putting fleets and armies in motion in order to push usurious bonds up to par."[20] Corrupt and stupid governments may be tolerated when their activities are confined by prescription to a small and certain sphere; in this age of aggrandizement, however, corrupt and stupid governments deliver us up precipitately to class warfare and international anarchy.

What can be done to restrain these appetites and to purge society of its ailments? Godkin's medicine, like his diagnosis, suffers from his preoccupation with economic and political questions, in their narrower sense: like nearly all his philosophical school, like Macaulay and J.S. Mill, he can escape the narrow legacy of the rationalist tradition only at rare moments; often he seems to think of society as a machine, efficient or inefficient, which may be injured or repaired by certain technical operations. Yet he does not ignore the complexity of these questions; he does not entertain the pleasing illusion, so common in America, that every problem has a simple solution if only men can manage to hit upon it, or that every problem has a solution at all. For instance, " 'The labor problem' is really the problem of making the manual laborers of the world content with their lot. In my judgment this is an insoluble problem. No discoveries nor inventions will ever solve it as long as population continues to press close on the available products of human industry. The causes of the dissatisfaction of the masses with their condition may change from age to age, but the dissatisfaction will continue, and the blame will be always laid on those who have a larger share of the world's goods than others.''[21] Godkin advocates certain practical remedies, now appearing almost ludicrous in their inadequacy; but, every once in a while, he shows himself conscious that all these depend for their efficacy upon a moral condition to which most modern desires run counter, and which can be checked, if checked at all, only by a sense of duty approaching religious consecration in the publicist, the professor, the leader of party.

Godkin's immediate remedies or palliatives were civil-service reform, the referendum, the initiative, the frequent constitutional convention, and the likelihood that failure by governments in their management of the economy would provoke a restoration of *laissez-faire:*

I do not look for the improvement of democratic legislatures in quality within any moderate period. What I believe democratic societies will do, in order to improve their government and make better provision for the protection of property and the preservation of order, is to restrict the power of these assemblies and shorten their sittings, and to use the referendum more freely for the production of really important laws. I have very little doubt that, before many years are elapsed, the American people will get their government more largely from constitutional conventions, and will confine the legislatures within very narrow limits and make them meet at rare intervals....After a very few years' experience of the transfer of the currency question, which has now begun, to the management of popular suffrage, the legal tender quality of money, which is now behind the whole trouble, will be abolished, and the duty of the government will be confined simply to weighing and stamping.[22]

Well, this is drawing out Leviathan with a hook, and Godkin, for all his reading of Burke and Tocqueville, never had a prophet's eye. Yet this seemed to be the tendency of his times: the initiative, the referendum, the recall, and all that series of devices to remedy democracy by more democracy, spread across America—

and since have been conspicuous chiefly in their abuse or their
moribund neglect. They have served the unscrupulous boss or political manipulator better than they have served the reformer, it
being still easier to persuade men to sign petitions than to dominate
a party caucus; and even pragmatic America has frowned upon
the idea of managing ordinary political affairs by the extreme medicine of constitutional conventions. Awarding positions in the civil
service upon the basis of examinations does not touch the chief
powers and plums of government; and far from withdrawing
authority from the state into their own hands, the people have permitted, with only occasional grumbling, concentration of new powers in the executive branch. Managed currencies have succeeded
in obliterating any fixed standard of value; instead of submitting
to gold, they have taken gold captive. To examine further the
failure of Godkin's proposals would be tedious and captious. He
lost faith in them himself, privately, and confessed to Charles Eliot
Norton, in 1895, "You see I am not sanguine about the future
of democracy. I think we shall have a long period of decline like
that which followed the fall of the Roman Empire, and then a
recrudescence under some other form of society. Our present tendencies in that direction are concealed by great national
progress."[23]

Godkin's limitations were the limitations of the whole school
of "classical" nineteenth-century liberals whenever they endeavored to turn conservative and check the flood of innovation which
only a little while earlier had swept them to their perch of intellectual eminence. Like Lord John Russell, all of them yearned after
finality; but industrialism and democracy and the complex current of popular desires burst through their artifices of electoral
qualifications and ingenious political gimcracks. Liberalism was
the child of an honest, if sometimes myopic, "reasonableness,"
the assumption that society could be induced to follow courses
strictly logical and practical; and when the masses insisted on remaining unreasonable, the liberals drowned in the fierce waters
they had mistaken for a millpond. That Godkin, by intellectual
descent hardly a conservative at all, should have been the most

respectable opponent of innovation in the Gilded Age, is evidence sufficient of the dismal fatigue that American conservatism suffered during those hard years.

Yet it would be wrong to imply that Godkin was a failure. He perceived the real nature of modern public opinion, that vast fumbling creature hungry for something to satisfy the craving engendered by his nominal literacy. Godkin tried, with courage and perseverance, to make the press an instrument of political purgation and a disseminator of good taste, to establish moral principle in the empire of journalism. But four months before his death, he wrote to Norton, "The grand place we promised to occupy in the world seems to be completely out of sight....The worst of it is that the cheap press has become a great aid and support in all these things. It has by no means turned out, as it was expected to, a teacher of better manners and purer laws."[24] If journalism in general has become what Arthur Machen once called it, "that damnable vile business," still there are journals which remember Godkin and men like him. And what should we do without them?

For a keener examination of modern society, however—for recognition that politics is only the skin of social being—one needs to turn from "the New Jerusalem of the *Nation*" to two sombre and disappointed brothers, Henry and Brooks Adams. Their friend Godkin hoped to the last that by opening some sluice, resorting to some pump, the flood of their age might be compelled to subside into a democratic reservoir of opinion. The fourth generation of the house of Adams, deciding after some brief experience of life that reason and benevolence do not govern humanity, proceeded to inquire into those laws of force which were hurrying all civilization toward catastrophe. "The men become every year more and more creatures of force, massed about central power-houses," wrote Henry Adams, old and solitary in Washington, that city which Joseph de Maistre declared (with more truth than his detractors perceive) never would become an actual community. Upon this dim-eyed and perhaps imbecile world, Godkin had tried to bestow clear vision. The few thousand readers of Godkin's *Nation*, the few hundred readers of Lowell's and Adams' *North*

American Review, had ceased to constitute public opinion, or possibly even to shape public opinion in any direct sense. "Society laughed a vacant and meaningless derision over its own failure," said Adams, looking back to Black Friday. In Henry and Brooks Adams, the conservative instinct abandoned aspiration to control society; it sought only to understand.

4

> Today finishes, I apprehend, the silver period of our society, and gives it the *coup-de-grace.* We must now brace ourselves to the struggle for gold. Unless you and I are wholly in error, this struggle has got to break much old crockery and *bric-à-brac,* and to make a clear field for some new variety of social, political, and economic man. I have of late tended to see in it the compulsion which is to suppress still more the individual and to make society still more centralized and automatic, but the fun is in the process, and not in the result. The process bids fair to be long enough to furnish us with more than a life-long amusement.
>
> —Henry Adams to Brooks Adams, October 23, 1897

To dislike Henry Adams is easy. Full of the censoriousness which was so prominent a characteristic in his great ancestors, mercilessly candid in his estimate of everyone, often mocking even toward what he loved best, perfectly certain that his great-grandfather and grandfather and father had been consistently right and their adversaries sunk in delusion or hypocrisy, but swearing by no other certitudes—this gloomy yet humorous man, whom Albert Jay Nock calls the most accomplished of all the Adams family, is the most irritating person in American letters; and the most provocative writer, and the best historian, and one of the more penetrating critics of ideas. The best cure for vexation with Henry Adams is to read his detractors; for against his Olympian amusement at a dying world and his real inner modesty, their snarls and quibbles furnish a relief which displays Adams' learning and wit as no amount of adulation could.

A case might be made that Henry Adams represents the zenith of American civilization. Unmistakably and almost belligerently American, the end-product of four generations of exceptional rectitude and remarkable intelligence, very likely (despite his autobiography) the best-educated man American society has produced, Adams knew the history of medieval Europe as well as he knew the administration of Jefferson, understood Japan and the South Seas as he understood New England character, and perceived as no other American of his generation did the catastrophic influence that modern science would exert upon the twentieth-century mind and society. But the product of these grand gifts was a pessimism deep and unsparing as Schopenhauer's, intensified by Adams' long examination and complete rejection of popular American aspirations. Henry Adams' conservatism is the view of a man who sees before him a steep and terrible declivity, from which there can be no returning: one may have leisure to recollect past nobility; now and then one may perform the duty of delaying mankind for a moment in this descent; but the end is not to be escaped.

In any account of American conservatism, the house of Adams and Harvard College must occupy a space conspicuously disproportionate, on the face of things. But one may say, without much exaggeration, that this family and that college *were* the conservative mind, at least in the North. Henry and Brooks Adams carry right into the triumphant imperial America of 1918 the courageous and prescient conservative tradition that John Adams founded in the days of the Boston Massacre. Harvard, at the end of the nineteenth century and the begining of the twentieth, manifests in Henry Adams, Charles Eliot Norton, Barrett Wendell, George Santayana, and Irving Babbitt the legacy of conservative republicanism which was one face of New England's genius. As professor of history at Harvard, for a few years, and editor of the *North American Review*, Adams exercised upon the American mind an influence still discernible, commencing in pupils and disciples like Henry Osborn Taylor and Henry Cabot Lodge and Ralph Adams Cram, and extending now in some degree to every respectable university and college in America, but this sort of influence Adams cared little for; first he hoped to become a leader of political society through the law, and later through the press; defeated in both aspirations, he turned to Chartres and the thirteenth century for consolation. "There are two things that seem to be at the bottom of our constitutions," he wrote in 1858, from Berlin, to Charles Francis Adams, Jr.; "one is a continual tendency toward politics; the other is family pride; and it is strange how these two feelings run through all of us." Fifty-three years later, it was clear to Adams how both political attainment and gratification of family pride had been frustrated for the fourth generation of his house. "I have always considered that Grant wrecked my own life, and the last hope or chance of lifting society back to a reasonably high plane. Grant's administration is to me the dividing line between what we hoped, and what we have got."[25] In the Gilded Age and its aftermath, an Adams could not lead with success or serve with honor.

What are the sources of the monstrous corruption of modern life, the sickness Adams detected in England and on the Continent and in the comparative innocence of American civilization? He spent half his life asking that question. When a very young man at the American legation in London, Adams read John Stuart Mill, and Tocqueville, and the other liberals, and presently Comte, and Marx; but though all these authors left some trace upon Adams, he dismissed the liberals with a wry smile, retained from Comte only the idea of phase, and observed of Marx, "I think I never struck a book which taught me so much, and with which I disagreed so radically in conclusion."[26] His convictions were inherited ideas, substantially, the convictions of John Adams and John Quincy Adams. His *History of the United States during the Administrations of Jefferson and Madison*, in style and method the finest historical work by an American, judges those fateful years with the impartial dislike his grandfather and great-grandfather felt for both Jeffersonians and Hamiltonian Federalists; his novel *Democracy* expresses the high contempt of the Adams breed for a nation led by Blaines and Conklings, living a complex lie. What is wrong with this society, whose gifts befoul, warping the character of Roosevelt and of Taft, cheapening even his intimate friend Hay? Adams rejected the popular answers to this question, as he rejected the popular specifics; and turning, like his ancestors, to science and history for enlightenment, he saw at work in modern times the culminating stages of a tremendous and impersonal process of degradation which had commenced centuries before, was signalized in his age by the triumph of gold over silver as a standard of value, and would rumble on resistlessly to further consolidation and centralization until socialism should be ascendant everywhere; then socialism, and civilization, would rot out.

"Modern politics is, at bottom, a struggle not of men but of forces," he wrote in his *Education*. "The conflict is no longer between the men, but between the motors that drive the men, and the men tend to succumb to their own motive forces."[27] For centuries, society has frenziedly sought centralization and cheapness and incalculable physical power; now all these things are near to attainment; and they mean the end of civilized life. Once man turned from the ideal of spiritual power, the Virgin, to the ideal of physical power, the Dynamo, his doom was sure. The faith and beauty of the thirteenth century, this descendant of the Puritans declared, made that age the noblest epoch of mankind; he could imagine only one state of society worse than the rule of the capitalists in the nineteenth century—the coming rule of the trade unions in the twentieth century.

Adams' devotion to the mind and heart of the thirteenth century has exposed him to a hail of criticism, some shrewd, some shallow. The naïve idea, promulgated by certain historians of the American mind, that Adams either ignored or was ignorant of the disorder and physical dread of that age, would have been beneath Adams' contempt: there has been no man since who could teach medieval history to Henry Adams. He knew perfectly the danger and discomfort of the Middle Ages; and he knew quite as well that happiness is more dependent upon tranquil mind and conscience than upon material circumstance. "He transformed the Middle Ages by a process of subtle falsification, into a symbol of his own latter-day New England longing," Yvor Winters writes;[28] but if this charge is better founded than its predecessor, still it remains vague; and Paul Elmer More inflicts a more serious blow when he observes of *Mont-Saint-Michel and Chartres,* "There is a fateful analogy between the irresponsibility of unreasoning Force and unreasoning Love; and the Gods of Nietzsche and of Tolstoy are but two faces of one God. To change the metaphor, if it may be done without disrespect, the image in the cathedral of Chartres looks perilously like the ancient idol of Dinos decked out in petticoats."[29] Did Adams, after all, nowhere perceive anything but Whirl, even in thirteenth-century Chartres? "I am a dilution of a mixture of Lord Kelvin and St. Thomas Aquinas," he told Brooks. His grandfather's tormenting doubt of the existence of Providence and Purpose seems to have condemned succeeding generations of the Adams family to an hereditary reluctant skepticism, a Maule's Curse more malign than the spell upon the House of Seven Gables. (It is curious that General Hamilton was the initial instrument of their discomfiture, General Jackson the agent of their disillusion, and General Grant the gross confirmer of their skepticism.) Yet if faith had been no more than a charming illusion even in the age of Aquinas, still it had been a beneficent delusion, Henry Adams implied. To it had succeeded a more delusory worship of Force, by 1900 incarnate in the dynamos at the Paris Exposition. "My belief is that science is to wreck us, and we are like monkeys monkeying with a loaded shell," he wrote to Brooks in 1902.[30]

Decay of religious conviction and the Christendom it sustained had led down to "a society of Jews and brokers"; the Trust was an instrument for converting the remnants of the old free community, for which the Adamses had struggled, into the complete consolidation of a monolithic state; and the despot, the anarchist, and the gold-standard lobbyist all were partners of the Trust. The next stage of society would be "economic Russianization"; thought already was regarded with distrust, and with the final triumph of centralization, individuality would be suppressed utterly. State socialism was nearly inevitable and wholly odious; it would triumph over capitalism because it is cheaper, and modern life always rewards cheapness. Confiscation by the state, of which the beginning could be discerned in death duties, was only a few generations off. Labor, rapidly gaining mastery over the capitalists, would blackmail society until the older order was quite effaced. "I maintain that...we are already in principles at the bottom,—that is, at the great ocean equi-potential,—and can get no further. I prove it by the fact that I live here in Paris, or there in Washington, at the mercy of any damned Socialist or Congressman or Tax-assessor, and that I can't enter the Port of New York without being made to roll on the dock, to be kicked and cuffed and spit upon by a dirty employee of a dirtier Jew cad who calls himself collector, and before whom the whole mass of American citizens voluntarily kneel." The ruling impulse of modern humanity, indeed the very laws of natural phenomena, made this end certain. As the "conservative Christian anarchist" he whimsically called himself, Adams contended against this tide, most hotly in 1893, upon the silver question. "He thought it probably his last chance of standing up for his eighteenth-century principles, strict construction, limited powers, George Washington, John Adams, and the rest."[31]

Gold crushed silver, as the Trust and the Socialist (really the same people under different names) were crushing out individual personality. "The attraction of mechanical power had already wrenched the American mind into a crab-like process....The mechanical theory, mostly accepted by science, seemed to require that the law of mass should rule."[32] The capitalists, expiring in their hour of triumph, must yield in their turn to greater force. "It is the socialist—not the capitalist—who is going to swallow us next, and of the two I prefer the Jew."[33] Society, in short, obeys Gresham's Law (as Albert Jay Nock later put it): the cheap drives out the dear; and in the long run, civilization itself will be too dear for survival.

The process of degradation was now too far advanced for any exertion of will to hamper its course. Some 2,500 years of this evolution had brought us near the finish of things, he wrote to Brooks Adams in 1899: "I give it two more generations before it goes to pieces, or begins to go to pieces. That is to say, two generations should saturate the world with population, and should exhaust all the mines. When that moment comes, economical decay, or the decay of an economical civilization, should set in."[34] The resources of nature, like those of spirit, are running out, and all that a conscientious man can aspire to be is a literal conservative, hoarding what remains of culture and of natural wealth against the fierce appetites of modern life. The whole idea of progress, whether that theory entertained by John Adams' old enemy Condorcet or the biological version of the Darwinians, had been nonsense. "That, two thousand years after Alexander the Great and Julius Caesar, a man like Grant should be called—and should actually and truly be—the highest product of the most advanced evolution, made evolution ludicrous. One must be as commonplace as Grant's own commonplaces to maintain such an absurdity. The progress of evolution, from President Washington to President Grant, was alone enough to upset Darwin."[35]

And man's very acquisition of scientific knowledge was to become the instrument of his moral and physical destruction. The discovery of the nature of radium, in 1900, meant the beginning of a revolution which must end in disintegration. "Power leaped from every atom, and enough of it to supply the stellar universe showed itself running to waste at every pore of matter. Man could no longer hold it off. Force grasped his wrists and flung him about as though he had hold of a live wire or a runaway automobile....If Karl Pearson's notions of the universe were sound, men like Galileo, Descartes, Leibnitz, and Newton should have stopped the progress of science before 1700, supposing them to have been honest in the religious convictions they expressed. In 1900 they were plainly forced back on faith in a unity unproved and an order they had themselves disproved. They had reduced their universe to a series of relations to themselves. They had reduced themselves to motion in a universe of motions, with an acceleration, in their own case, of vertiginous violence."[36] The Virgin had ceased to inspire faith; the Dynamo, or science, had lost all significance; Whirl remained.

In three essays, reprinted in *The Degradation of the Democratic Dogma*, Adams condensed these reflections with melancholy lucidity into "a historical study of the scientific grounds of Socialism, Collectivism, and Humanitarianism and Democracy and all the rest": "The Tendency of History" (1894), "The Rule of Phase Applied to History" (1909), and "A Letter to American Teachers of History" (1910). Shorn of Adams' supporting evidence, the general argument he advances may be put briefly enough. It is just this: as the exhaustion of energy is an inevitable condition of all nature, so social energies must be exhausted, and are now running out; and many of the types of "progress" upon which we congratulate ourselves are no more than symptoms and afflictions of this decay. The Laws of Thermodynamics are our doom. By the Law of Dissipation, nothing can be added to the sum of energy, but intensity must always be lost. Work can be done only by degrading energy, as water can work only by running downhill. Society does its work at the same price; and as scientists accept this sombre fact, they are becoming oppressed by a stifling pessimism. All vital processes suffer degradation, inevitably incident to their operation; the growth of the brain enfeebles the human body, for instance. A supernatural will or directive power seems to account for the existence of energy, but this power does not provide for the replenishing of energy. Even the rise of human consciousness was a phase in the decline of vital force. Human activity reached its point of greatest intensity in the Middle Ages, with the Crusades and the cathedrals; since then, true vitality has been waning rapidly. The year 1830, which marked the beginning of a gigantic harnessing of natural physical energies in the service of man, at the same time enfeebled humanity, for power gains at the expense of vitality. Industrialized, we are that much nearer to social ruin and total extirpation. "The dead alone give us energy," says Le Bon, and we moderns, having severed our ties with the past, are not long for this world.

Future historians must be guided by a knowledge of physics; and if the dilemma of degradation of energy is to be explained away, another Newton will be required. As perhaps the ape, a hundred thousand years ago, groped dimly for further development of his kind, and failed, so mankind now is trapped by the failure of its energies and by the depletion of those natural resources that men have plundered wantonly. Human evolution has passed perihelion, after the fashion of the Comet of 1843, and now, with terrible speed, we are rushing away from the day of our nobility. Adams applies the law of squares to the problem of modern decay, and suggests that the Mechanical Phase of modern history, beginning in 1600, reached its highest authority about 1870, and then turned sharply into the Electric Phase, which may be considered under way by 1900; and the Electric Phase will endure only until 1917, when it will pass into the Ethereal Phase—and more prophecies beyond this. Adams' celebrated predictions of the outbreak and duration of the First World War, of a possible subjugation by Thought of "the molecule, the atom, and the electron to that costless servitude to which it has reduced the old elements of earth and air, fire and water…" are by-products of this rule of phase. But prolongation of such resources cannot prevent the final total degradation of energy.

In this catastrophe, the social degradation represented by triumphant consolidation and its heir socialism are developments quite as natural and fatal as the general extinction of energy. Socialism must be succeeded by social rot, a disguised blessing, since socialism's continuance would be unendurable; indeed, it is in itself corruption. Politics, too, will end as water does, at sea-level, or like heat, at 1^0 Centigrade. Like the Comet, humanity hurtles into the oblivion of eternal night and endless space.

Christian orthodoxy believes in an eternity which, as it is superhuman, is supra-terrestrial; and the real world being a world of spirit, man's fate is not dependent upon the vicissitudes of this planet, but may be translated by divine purpose into a realm apart from our present world of space and time. In this certitude, Christians escape from the problem of degradation of energy; but Adams, however much he might revere the Virgin of Chartres as incarnation of the idea and as a symbol of eternal beauty, could not put credence in the idea of Providence. He was determined that history must be "scientific"; although so independent of mind, he complied willingly with the well-known tendency of metaphysics and theology to follow the lead of scientific theory; he found it impossible to disbelieve Thomson and Pearson and Kelvin. If science "should prove that society must at a given time revert to the church and recover its old foundation of religion, it commits suicide."[37] The phase of religion was far nobler, to Adams' mind, than the phase of electricity; but he felt himself borne irresistibly along by the wave of progress. One might revere the Virgin, in the Electric Phase; but one could not really worship. The blunt nonconformist piety of John Adams gave way to the doubts of John Quincy Adams, the humanitarianism of Charles Francis Adams, the despair of Henry Adams. Belief in Providence, so enduringly rooted in Burke's conservatism, was lost in the vicissitudes of New England's conservative thought.

Just one moral support in trial was nearly sufficient, Adams once wrote to Henry Osborn Taylor, and that the Stoic—but only "in theory." Marcus Aurelius was Adams' type of highest human attainment, and with the Antonine ended the story of moral adjustment. Irving Babbitt refers to "the desolate and pathetic Marcus Aurelius," and indeed the spectacle of the Emperor's devouring loneliness takes on renewed and frightening significance when contemplated with his disciple Henry Adams in the foreground. "The kinetic theory of gas is an assertion of ultimate chaos," said Adams. "In plain words, Chaos was the law of nature; Order was the dream of man....The Church alone had constantly protested that anarchy was not order, that Satan was not God, that pantheism was worse than atheism, and that Unity could not be proved as a contradiction."[38] Karl Pearson seemed to agree with the Church; and so, in passionate desire, did Adams himself; but his overmastering Adams rationality could not submit to his heart. Paul Elmer More, a conservative of the next generation, writes thus of Henry Adams' frustrated conservative loyalties:

This breed of New England, of whom he was so consciously a titled representative, had once come out from the world for the sake of a religious and political affirmation—the two were originally one—to confirm which they were ready to deny all the other values of life. For the liberty to follow this affirmation they would discard tradition and authority and form and symbol and all that ordinarily binds men together in the bonds of habit. But the liberty of denying may itself become a habit. The intellectual history of New England is in fact the record of the encroachment of this liberty upon the very affirmation for which it was at first the bulwark. By a gradual elimination of its positive content the faith of the people had passed from Calvinism to Unitarianism, and from this to free thinking, until in the days of our Adams there was little left to the intellect but a great denial.[39]

Here an heir of Hooker and Laud sits in judgment on an inheritor of Mather and Cotton. Deprived of the sanctions of religion, does conservative instinct verge toward extinction? The ideas of the house of Adams, carried by Henry Adams to their twentieth-century philosophical culmination, obtained their political summary in the writings of Brooks Adams—like his brother, fascinated by that determinism the consequences of which he hated.

5

Just how far the acceleration of the human movement may go it is impossible to determine; but it seems certain that, sooner or later, consolidation, having reached its limit, will necessarily stop. There is nothing stationary in the universe. Not to advance is to go backward, and when a highly centralized society disintegrates under the pressure of economic competition, it is because the energy of the race has been exhausted.
                    —Brooks Adams, preface to the French
                    edition of *The Law of Civilization
                    and Decay*

Brooks Adams confessed himself to be an eccentric; and so he was; but he belonged to the grand tradition of eccentricity, and published his novel and gloomy doctrines with the old Adams fearlessness. Whether he ought to be called a conservative is more debatable. He was disgusted with American society in his day; his books were calculated to win the attention of the free-silver men and the socialists; he thought inertia was social death, and that the only chance for survival lay in acceptance of progress and adjustment to change; he denounced the capitalists and bankers nearly so vehemently as Marx had done—and in several particulars, notably his economic determinism, Brooks Adams' ideas ran parallel with Marx's. All the same, he detested the very process of change which he urged society to accept, longed hopelessly for the republic of Washington and John Adams, condemned democracy as symptom and cause of social decay, and toward the end of his days professed his faith in the church of his ancestors. His detestation of capitalism resulted from his abhorrence of turbulent competition; he seems to have been desperately hungry for stability and order; but by the logic of his own economic and historical theories, permanence never is found in this universe.

In this crisis of my fate [the panic of 1893] I learned, as a lawyer and a student of history and of economics, to look on man, as a pure automaton, who is moved along the paths of least resistance by forces over which he has no control. In short, I reverted to the pure Calvinistic philosophy. As I perceived that the strongest of human passions are fear and greed, I inferred that so much and no more might be expected from a pure democracy as might be expected from any automaton so actuated. As a forecast I suggested that the first great social movement we might expect, should be the advent of something resembling an usurer's paradise, to be presently followed by some such convulsion as has always formed a part of such conditions since the beginning of time.[40]

This is the general theme of his four books, *The Law of Civilization and Decay, America's Economic Supremacy, The New Empire,* and *The Theory of Social Revolutions;* they expound his cyclical theory of history and his conviction that man is the prisoner of economic force. Civilization is the product of centralization, and grows up about the centers of exchange; as the agents of central political and economic organization subdue the men of simpler rural economies—the Romans conquering their provinces, the middle classes accomplishing the Reformation, the proprietors evicting the yeomen, Spain crushing the Indians—civilization grows richer and richer. The highest product of this civilization, ironically enough, is the usurer; he extirpates the military classes which once predominated; but the usurer and his gross culture seem to infect the race with morbid afflictions, quite as they stifle the spirit of art. Social vitality dwindles, the great centralized economy no longer can operate efficiently, decay and collapse follow, and de-centralized, barbarous life is triumphant once more—to be suc-ceeded, in the course of centuries, by a repetition of the same bloody and purposeless history.

The economic center of the civilized world—which determines the social equilibrium—has shifted westward throughout history: Babylon to Rome, Rome to Constantinople, Constantinople to Venice, Venice to Antwerp. It flourished in Holland so late as 1760, but by 1815 it was in London; the tide has been running since toward America, and that transfer of economic and political power now is nearly complete—so Brooks Adams wrote in 1900. The Spanish-American War was a token of American economic supremacy. England is faced with a long and dreadful decay, and America must take precautions to avoid participating in the ulti-mate collapse of Britain. A tremendous contest begins to loom be-tween the power of Asia, possibly dominated by Russia, and the American power; the question will be decided in China and Korea, and in years to come, the mineral resources of China will produce a new economic phase. To win in this competition will require intense centralization: "If expansion and concentration are neces-sary, because the administration of the largest mass is the least costly, then America must expand and concentrate until the limit of the possible is attained; for Governments are simply huge cor-porations in competition, in which the most economical, in propor-tion to its energy, survives, and in which the wasteful and slow are undersold and eliminated."[41]

Cheapness of production and distribution is the source of suc-cess in economic life, and therefore in civilization. Centralization probably is proportionate to velocity, and the most vertiginous nation triumphs over its neighbors. These contentions are sustained by an examination of Syrian, Persian, Hellenic, Roman, Central Asian, Flemish, Spanish, and Russian civilizations.

Although the immediate consequence of competition and centralization is success, its ultimate effect is degradation. The usurer, whose whole view is economic, is at once the most complete product of civilization and the most limited and ignoble type of man. "To this money-making attribute all else has been sacrificed, and the modern capitalist thinks in terms of money more exclusively than the French aristocrat or lawyer before the French Revolution ever thought in terms of caste."[42] Too stupid even to glimpse the necessity for revering and obeying the law that shelters him from social revolution, the capitalist lacks capacity sufficient for the administration of the society he has made his own. Woman and the producer and the man of thought already have been debased by the rule of capitalism or state socialism—two sides of a coin—so that no vitality remains in society to prevent a sickening decay. Democracy, simultaneously the ally and the dupe of this soulless material civilization, fails to fulfill the duties of sacrifice and leadership; so the structure of social organization collapses, and the dreary cycle of endeavor commences afresh.

Yet despite his contempt for capitalistic society, despite his hereditary antipathy toward centralization, despite his abhorrence of socialism, despite his wholehearted rejection of cheapness as the real standard of achievement, still Brooks Adams accepted the triumph of consolidation as inevitable. He urged cooperation in the process as a counterpoise to the insatiable capitalist, as homage to the instinct for self-preservation. Conservatism, social inertia, obedience to tradition—these attitudes are doomed to destruction by the impersonal processes of economic destiny. Conservatism, he writes, "resists change instinctively and not intelligently, and it is this conservatism which largely causes those violent explosions of pent-up energy which we term revolutions....With conservative populations slaughter is nature's remedy."[43] Our educational institutions should adjust themselves to this tremendous process of change, that they may make its progress less violent. We should dismiss the emotional instinct to keep things as they are, and regard government dispassionately, as we would any other business, accepting moral change, too, like all other alteration; for nothing can be done to prevent its ultimate overwhelming victory. "In American industry friction will infallibly exist between capital and labor; but that necessary friction may be indefinitely increased by conservatism. History teems with examples of civilizations which have been destroyed through an unreasoning inertia like that of Brutus, or the French privileged classes, or Patrick Henry."[44] We must hold every judgment in suspense, subject to new evidence. "There is but one great boon which the passing generation can confer upon its successors: it can aid them to ameliorate that servitude to tradition which has so often retarded submission to the inevitable until too late."[45]

The trouble with this injunction is that Brooks Adams neither obeyed nor believed it. No man was less calculated to submit in silence to a future régime of centralization and stifling grossness; no man was less inclined to abandon the moral rigor of the Adams family for a suspension of certitude. The conclusions of Brooks Adams rub his every prejudice the wrong way. If he had really believed in resigned cooperation with the coming order, of course he would not have written his books. The Adams family—Henry most of all—had a way of expressing themselves in sardonic paradox or grim exaggeration which has led, frequently, to misinterpretation; yet one hardly can maintain that Brooks Adams' whole philosophy was an exercise in irony. It appears rather to be a half-perverse growl of protest: Adams had been taken captive by the determinists, and was endeavoring to wear his chains with dignity. In fact, the hideous uniformity which he foresaw, and compliance with which he counselled, made up the vision of terror that John Adams and all his seed had fought against for nearly a century and a half. Expansion, consolidation, and dispassionate reception of change, which he pretended to recommend, he really knew to be the poison of everything he honored, and this half-suppressed groan of torment persisted in escaping from him, giving the lie to his theories.

For the process of competition and consolidation had caused the war of 1914-1918, he wrote; and the degradation of leadership which that process entailed had made the establishment of a wise peace impossible. Even more horrifying was the unsexing of women by the industrial capitalistic movement. The sexual instinct had been suppressed in our thought, ignored in our education, and converted in woman to a shameful and shamefaced imitation of man. "The woman, as the cement of society, the head of the family, and the centre of cohesion, has, for all intents and purposes, ceased to exist. She has become a wandering isolated unit, rather a dispersive than a collective force."[46] The family principle decays so that the whole structure of life is in peril. Our system of law, too, is corrupted by the poison. Taxation is making social diversity and inheritance of property negligible. The democratic proclivity for levelling downward, which we see in the trade union, conflicts with nature's system of competition, and a gigantic explosion must be the consequence. "Social war, or massacre, would seem to be the natural ending of the democratic philosophy." If this is the probable future after we submit to resistless change, it seems curious to recommend abandonment of tradition for the sake of tranquil adjustment. Brooks Adams never attained consistency in his argument with himself; his erudite and picturesque books are full of brilliant generalizations and curious deductions, but empty of orderly affirmation.

He was certain only of dissolution. "Hardly had Washington gone to his grave when the levelling work of the system of averages, on which democracy rests, began....Democracy is an infinite mass of conflicting minds and of conflicting interests which, by the persistent action of such a solvent as the modern or competitive industrial system, becomes resolved into what it is, in substance, a vapor, which loses in collective intellectual energy in proportion to the perfection of its expansion."[47] The new American empire, the coming American economic supremacy, must therefore be accompanied by a loss in intelligence and freedom which would efface the American system of Washington or Adams or Jefferson. We must face this expansive prospect of material triumph and spiritual extirpation; indeed, we must embrace it: "Americans in former generations led a simple agricultural life. Possibly such a life was happier than ours. Very probably keen competition is not a blessing. We cannot alter our environment. Nature has cast the United States into the vortex of the fiercest struggle which the world has ever known. She has become the heart of the economic system of the age, and she must maintain her supremacy by wit and by force, or share the fate of the discarded."[48]

There is a ring of Huxley and Spencer in this, the echo of "competitive evolution" and aggressive positivism; the chains of Brooks Adams' captivity to the scientific determinists clank. After all, might not "sharing the fate of the discarded" be preferable to sharing the fate of the victors, in a contest of this description, where the sacrifices seem to exceed the prizes? This is imperialism without the assurance of Roosevelt or Chamberlain, without the hope and consecration of Kipling. From the viewpoint of orthodox Christianity, it would be better far to join the discarded, rather than enter voluntarily upon the next phase of degradation; but Brooks Adams' religious convictions, like his brother's, were hardly more than vestigial. Marxism's ravages upon traditional society have not been inflicted chiefly by revolutionary proselytizing: the corrosive influences of Marxist deterministic theories, instead, have sapped the resolution of men who despise the Marxist creed as a whole. The prophecies of Marxism are of the order which accomplish their own fulfillment, if they are given initial credence. Comte, Marx, and the exponents of scientific positivism destroyed in Henry and Brooks Adams the belief that had made the Adams family great: the idea of Providence and Purpose.

Such were the fortunes of American conservative belief in a swaggering half-century. Limitless expansion was the passion of that age, and the forces of aggrandizement pressed their assault upon the broken walls of prescription and convention. The ruin of the South deprived the nation of that region's conservative influence. It opened the way for protective tariffs undreamed of before, for exploitation of the empty West, for the triumph of urban interests over the rural population, for a system of life in which culture was wholly subordinated to economic appetite. The immigration this age demanded to satisfy its booming industries changed the character of the American population, so that Lowell's "New Ireland" soon was engulfed by the deluge of Italians, Poles, Portuguese, and Central Europeans whose bewilderment secured the urban bosses in their mastery of public life. The cake of custom was worse than broken: it was ground underfoot. The American educational system, relied upon to discipline this rough age and assimilate these alien masses, was itself confused and lowered in tone by the inundation of change. And, appetite whetting yet newer appetite, the nation blundered with McKinley into an unblushing rapacity, with Theodore Roosevelt into a rubicund belligerence—so the Adams brothers declared. Genuine conservatives found no chance to catch their breath.

Even had conservatives been able to command any substantial body of public opinion, they scarcely would have known what way to lead the nation. Unsettled in their first principles by the claims of nineteenth-century science, doubting their old metaphysical postulates, they shrank before the Positivists, the Darwinians, and the astronomers. Lowell endeavored to ignore the new science; Brooks Adams was reduced to nihilism by his deductions from it. By the time the First World War ended, true conservatism was nearly extinct in the United States—existing only in little circles of stubborn men who refused to be caught up in the expansive lust of their epoch, or in the vague resistance to change still prevalent among the rural population, or, in a muddled and half-hearted fashion, within certain churches and colleges. Everywhere else, change was preferred to continuity.

The automobile, practical since 1906, was proceeding to disintegrate and stamp anew the pattern of communication, manners, and city-life in the United States, by 1918; before long, men would begin to see that the automobile, and the mass-production techniques which made it possible, could alter national character and morality more thoroughly than could the most absolute of tyrants. As a mechanical Jacobin, it rivalled the dynamo. The productive process which made these vehicles cheap was still more subversive of old ways than was the gasoline engine itself. Henry Ford, the Midas of velocity, swept out of memory the simplicities of his boyhood; and, growing old, he sought a refuge within the brick walls of his gigantic open-air museum of antiquities, a man of physical forms astonished by the influence of gadgets on ideas. The mass-production methods of which he was the most eminent exploiter were accomplishing more to alter human nature than even the steam-engine had done, dissolving pride of station and family. "It destroys the social prestige of traditional occupations and skills and with it the satisfaction of the individual in his traditional work," Peter Drucker says of the assembly-line and the new-style industrialism. "It uproots—quite literally—the individual from the social soil in which he has grown. It devaluates his traditional values, and paralyzes his traditional behavior."[49]

Government was doing its best to equal the velocity of the industrial world. The federal income-tax amendment to the Constitution, passed in 1913, was accepted as a painful expedient in emergency, as it had been in England after Corn Law repeal; and, as in England, neither political party could contrive to abolish income tax when the emergency was past. As an instrument for deliberate social alteration, the income tax soon would supplement that unconscious force, the second industrial revolution. Buffeted by these innovations and others nearly so formidable, their very principles confounded with apologies for "free enterprise" and the self-made man, it is no wonder that the conservatives were routed; it is a matter for surprise that they did not surrender incontinently. "The various horizons which you and I have passed through since the '40's are now as remote as though we had existed in the time of Marcus Aurelius," Henry Adams wrote, in the last month of his life, to his friend Gaskell; "and, in fact, I rather think that we should have been more at home among the Stoics, than we could ever hope to be in the legislative bodies of the future."[50] It was 1918, and America was the greatest power of the world, and if the old verities were to be conserved at all, America must take up the cause.

XI

English Conservatism Adrift:
the Twentieth Century

"You have given these people," it is said, "a say in the management of the kingdom, and yet you won't allow them a share in that of the businesses in which they work." Now if this is to be interpreted, as logically it may be, "You have given Dick Turpin your pistols, and you object to his using them so as to make you give him your purse," there *is* something in it. As an argument against the folly of giving the pistols, it is admirably conclusive, though sadly belated. Otherwise it is belated only.
   —George Saintsbury, *A Second Scrap Book*

AFTER 1895, the Conservative party had the support of interests so powerful and so various that in any other period of English history its position would have been invulnerable. Led by Lord Hartington, the old Whig landed families had come over to the Tories in 1886; and these Liberal Unionists were leagued with Joseph Chamberlain's imperialistic Radicals. The upper classes and the upper-middle classes—indeed, the preponderant part of the great middle classes—now were Conservative: for the first time in history, the Tory party had the general support of the rich.

The Tories had something still more valuable: popular endorsement of the new imperialism told for them. Disraeli, foreseeing this wave of expansion and imperial feeling, had identified Conservative policy with it; but he had acted from more motives than simple expediency. Accepting the decay of British agriculture as irreparable in a nation dominated by its urban populations, anticipating the fierce industrial competition of Germany and America and other powers, he had known that conservative policy would be given short shrift in a nation impoverished, overpopulated, and oppressed by a shrinking horizon. Imperial resources and imperial markets were the best insurance against such a future. Thus Disraeli's imperialism was consistent enough with his conservatism, even though generally imperial expansion is full of risks for any conservative society. Be this as it might, the Tories now were the political beneficiaries of British imperial ambitions, and Lord Salisbury's talents at the foreign office had established the Conservatives' reputation as trustees of English honor and English interests abroad.

In his bluff and dexterous way, Salisbury still dominated the Conservatives and Unionists with conspicuous success. Abhorring organic change, he had managed to patch and prune British institutions so effectively that, on the face of things, the old order still seemed virtually unaltered: 1867 and 1884 had not destroyed the British constitution or the British character. In the House of Commons, his nephew, Arthur Balfour, was the Conservative leader—a philosopher, a man of letters, charming, eloquent, immensely clever. The aged and baffled Gladstone had resigned in March, 1894; the Liberals went out of office fifteen months later; and in the general election of July, 1895, the Unionists obtained a majority of 152 over Liberals and Nationalists combined. Chamberlain's radical energies were poured into the colonial office. Conservatism had not seemed so well entrenched since the times of Pitt.

Their old enemies the Liberals were weaker in spirit and support than they had been since the days of Fox; and they were doomed to further splintering; their only legislative success in 1894, Harcourt's death duties, marked their immersion in the collectivistic current. "We are all Socialists now."* From this time forward, Liberals did not know quite what they believed, and the public detected their vacillation. They were to win again in 1906, but never after. Their philosophical postulates—the political economy of Manchester, the ethics and sociology of the Mills—were dissolving before their eyes. Liberalism, by demolishing the old habitual arrangement of life in England and surrendering power to the mass of the people, had rendered itself obsolete; it did not know how to meet the twentieth century. Power somehow had slipped from the hands of statesmen, said Lord Salisbury, but "I should be very much puzzled to know into whose hands it has passed." If that grand aristocrat no longer managed to hold the reins of society, Liberals certainly could not hope to dominate the new era. The formulas of nineteenth-century Liberalism, G. M. Young writes, had grown impossibly antiquated:

Those canons were grounded on the premiss that at any time there would be a number—and an always increasing number—of men and women interested in the ordering of public affairs, and able to make their interest felt: felt, not spasmodically at election time, but continuously; by reading, by discussion, by thinking things out for themselves and talking them over with their neighbours. But this premiss rested in turn on the assumption that the operations of government would always be within the comprehension of the sober citizen using diligence in his affairs, and that he would be interested because, if only as a contributor to public opinion, he felt that he could do something about them. What that Liberalism did not anticipate—could not anticipate—was that the increasing complexity, the mere range, of government would carry it beyond his comprehension: and that the volume of knowledge possessed by government puts its actions beyond the control of public opinion as that Liberalism conceived it: knowledge is power, and, as I have suggested, both the physical and psychological power of a modern government, wielded perhaps by a compact, resolute minority conscious of its purpose, might go far beyond the power of any despotism yet conceived.[1]

*Sir William Harcourt, however, could not recollect having uttered this phrase that clings to his name.

Here the Liberals were routed by the reappearance of a quality
in human nature which Tories always had known to be more or
less constant: the ineffectuality of reason as a guide for most men.
"Reason has small effect upon numbers," Bolingbroke had written
three hundred years before. "A turn of imagination, often as violent and as sudden as a gust of wind, determines their conduct."
The confusion of public opinion in the twentieth century vindicated this old Tory assumption. Yet the triumphant Conservative party, facing only a shattered and bewildered opposition, fell
at the end of a decade; and it never has recovered properly from
that fall. What happened to conservatism in Britain at the turn
of the century? The proximate political causes for the Tory defeat in 1906 are easily listed—the failure of Chamberlain's tariff-
reform campaign; Nonconformists' resentment at the Education
Act of 1902; importation of Chinese coolies into South Africa; the
Taff Vale decision which had held trade unions responsible for
the acts of their members. But such miscellaneous grievances,
strong though these were, do not ruin a great party. The really
impelling causes of the Conservatives' disaster lay deeper: the decay of Victorian confidence, and the swelling influence of the socialists.

The year of Queen Victoria's death, 1901, also marked the end
of Victorian economic progress. Real wages, rising fairly steadily
since 1880 (increasing by a third, altogether, during twenty years)
reached a tableland shortly after the turn of the century, and then
refused to budge. The competition of Britain's industrial rivals,
assisted by the protective tariffs of their governments, had combined with the restrictive practices of the powerful British trade
unions and with a curious slackness of British businessmen
(remarked by Alfred Marshall, and later by Halévy) to imperil
the foreign markets upon which the survival of Britain depends.
The depressions of 1873 and 1883 hinted at the future. This menace was gigantic; but for the time being, it amounted to no more
than a cessation of economic progress; if real wages did not rise
much, neither did they fall perceptibly during the first decade of
the twentieth century. But to a people infatuated with the idea

of progress, taught by Benthamism and Liberalism and many conservatives that they had every right to expect a steady increase of
material wealth and general happiness, mere stability is indistin-
guishable from decline. Ever since the 1840's, the material condition
of the masses had been improving in Britain; now more than sixty
years of advance was halted by forces which, for the most part,
were beyond the control of any political party; but modern populations (encouraged by the cheap press) tend to expect governments
to provide sustenance, and to blame governments for calamities
that are world-wide—indeed, for acts of God. Behind the Conservatives' debacle of 1906 lay a vague popular impression that somehow the affairs of Britain were being mismanaged: progress, which
the masses had been told was inevitable, somehow was being impeded. Earlier, this disquietude had furnished popular support for
imperialism, the public sensing that (as George Orwell wrote half
a century later) if the English people were confined to their insular
resources, "We would all be very poor and have to work very
hard." Britain had lost most of her comparative advantage in
manufacturing; to some extent, she was suffering from an absolute
decline of natural advantages; and no party, or political philosophy,
could remedy that.* But nations in which the average man has the
franchise are not so sweetly reasonable as Bentham had expected.

When Balfour's government struggled to retain office in 1905,
then, they labored under this handicap, immense though impon-
derable. Balfour was not the best of political tacticians, but it is
improbable that Disraeli could have won an election under such
circumstances. This difficulty was the consequence of material conditions working upon an uneasy electorate; equally disastrous to
the Unionist government was the influence of the reorganized and
aggressive socialist movement, which now had freed itself from

---

*The real incomes of the laboring classes did, indeed, increase sporadically during
the twentieth century, particularly after the Second World War, so that some optimistic statisticians calculate that real wages were augmented by fifty per cent between 1900
and 1950; but nearly the whole of this gain was achieved by deliberate economic levelling under the compulsion of positive law, not by a general increase of social wealth.
See J. H. Huizinga's articles "The Bloodless Revolution," *The Fortnightly*, April and
May, 1952.

its early utopianism and exoticism, so that it loomed in muscular hardihood just behind the Liberals. Since the successful London Dock Strike of 1889, both industrial unionism (as distinguished from the older trades-unionism) and the political activity in labor unions had increased apace; and the Fabians, turning from "the inevitability of gradualism," sought alliance with these practical collectivists.

Led by Asquith and Lloyd George, Liberals saw their best chance for survival, accordingly, in advocacy of radical social reform. The rising generation of Liberal politicians hastened to embrace a program of economic levelling, as Joseph Chamberlain had risen earlier upon the wave of radical alteration, and as Sir William Harcourt had employed this impulse to establish the new death-duties. But Socialism was not to be contented with the Liberal *via media:* Balfour, defeated, perceived that the fifty-three Labourites elected to the House of Commons in 1906 were more significant than the 377 Liberals. For the first time a formidable Labour group sat in Parliament; henceforth the real struggle in English politics would occur between conservatives and socialists.

2

For apprehending distinctly the nature of the ground-swell that was disturbing English society in the times of Salisbury and Balfour, one hardly can do better than to read the books of George Gissing. That connoisseur of misery, born in a room above a chemist's shop in grimy Wakefield and destined to spend most of his life in dismal lodgings in Islington or Clerkenwell or Tottenham Court Road, began as a political and moral radical, a positivist and a socialist. "We have a destructive task to perform; we must destroy the State-Church, and do our utmost to weaken its hold upon the popular mind," he wrote to his brother in 1879. "By hacking away here, and ploughing there, surely the field will at length be got into something like a state fit for the sower."[2] Gissing came to know the modern proletariat, and the rough side of human nature, as well as did any sensitive man in England;

and that knowledge made him a conservative. Progress? He had caught a glimpse of what way Progress led. In 1892, he wrote to his sister Ellen, ''I fear we shall live through great troubles yet, owing to the social revolution that is in progress.... We cannot resist it, but I throw in what weight I may have on the side of those who believe in an aristocracy of *brains,* as against the brute domination of the quarter-educated mob.''[3] *The Private Papers of Henry Ryecroft* (published in 1903, the year Gissing died) is the book of a natural Tory: ''And to think that at one time I called myself a socialist, communist, anything you like of the revolutionary kind! Not for long, to be sure, and I suspect that there was always something in me that scoffed when my lips uttered such things. Why, no man living has a more profound sense of property than I; no man ever lived, who was, in every fibre, more vehemently an individualist.''[4] This modern age—as Mad Jack shrieks in *The Nether World*—literally is Hell; but the socialist state will be its innermost circle.

Gissing's early patrons, Frederic Harrison and John Morley, converted him for a while to Positivism; Gissing's lonely nature, nevertheless, soon showed him the terrible solitude of human existence deprived of ends; and his analysis of modern life, whether in the slums out of which he spun his grim reputation or among the fashionable people he came to know later in his brief career, revealed the inevitable tendency of a society which has lost its sanction for moral conduct. He never could restore his own faith; but his portraits of clergymen of the old school—Mr. Wyvern in *Demos,* or the rector in *Born in Exile*—disclose his longing after vanished certitudes. He repudiated the intolerant agnosticism of his youth, when he had written that he could not condescend to be converted by men who were convinced merely through their sentiments. ''Establish your dogmas on a scientific basis, in clear relation with the hierarchy of human knowledge, and we ungrudgingly grant them a place in our system''—so he had told his sister in 1880.[5] Two decades later, he confessed his folly; science, whether speculative or applied, is a chief instrument for increasing the misery of our time: ''I hate and fear 'science' because of my conviction that, for long to come if not for ever, it will be the remorseless enemy of mankind. I see it destroying all simplicity and gentleness of life, all the beauty of the world; I see it restoring barbarism under a mask of civilization; I see it darkening men's minds and hardening their hearts; I see it bringing a time of vast conflicts, which will pale into insignificance 'the thousand wars of old,' and, as likely as not, will whelm all the laborious advances of mankind in blood-drenched chaos.''[6]

The boy who wrote *Workers in the Dawn* (1880), brimming with Ruskinian socialism, aspired to be "the mouthpiece of the advanced Radical party." But social reform went the way of positivism, as Gissing came to maturity and saw the denizens of mean streets for what they were: four years later, Waymark in *The Unclassed* dissects Gissing's own youthful socialism, compounded of sentimentality and egotism. "I often amuse myself with taking to pieces my former self. I was not a conscious hypocrite in those days of violent radicalism, workingman's-club lecturing, and the like; the fault was that I understood myself as yet so imperfectly. That zeal on behalf of the suffering masses was nothing more nor less than disguised zeal on behalf of my own starved passions. I was poor and desperate, life had no pleasures, the future seemed hopeless, yet I was overflowing with vehement desires, every nerve in me was a hunger which cried out to be appeased. I identified myself with the poor and ignorant; I did not make their cause my own, but my own cause theirs. I raved for freedom because I was myself in the bondage of unsatisfiable longing."[7] Thereafter Gissing renounced socialism of every variety, declaring his intention to devote himself to literary art; but his artistry, for years after, was the revelation of social misery.

Like Waymark, he was not born to be a radical. He could not love the poor and ignorant: taken as a body, they were detestable to him, loathsome as the industrial ugliness and urban depravity that hemmed them in. The suffering masses cannot rule their own passions: they are not fit to rule society. This is the theme of *Demos* (1886), in which the working-class socialist hero, Richard Mutimer, turns out to be a working-class socialist scoundrel, corrupted by ambition and prosperity, as the novel develops; and the ruined young squire who undoes Mutimer's philanthropic projects is a better and a wiser man. Gilbert Grail, in *Thyrza* (1887) is a different manner of working-man, humble and generous; but the slums crush him. Gissing's best story of the London proletariat is *The Nether World* (1889), the most terribly convincing of his earlier novels—"certainly in some respects his strongest work, *la letra con sangre*," says Thomas Seccombe, "in which the ruddy drops of anguish remembered in a state of comparative tranquillity are most powerfully expressed."[8] Gissing had done with socialism; it was *duty* he spoke of now, not rights; the only reform possible was reform of one's own character.

Clerkenwell, where the Hospitallers' Arch rises begrimed from the wrack of a submerged epoch, is the heart of *The Nether World*. "Go where you may in Clerkenwell, on every hand are multiform evidences of toil, intolerable as a nightmare." The struggle of decent character against the corruption of poverty is the thread that joins the straining people of this merciless book; when it ends, no happiness remains for anyone; but then, happiness was hardly to be thought of. Happiness aside, two people have beaten Poverty in some sense, for they have clung to their duties with a dogged resignation; they have been true to the best that was in them. *The Nether World* begins in one graveyard and ends in another. Sidney Kirkwood and Jane Snowdon, hope lost and love denied, meet on a cloudy spring morning three years after life beat them, join hands over a tombstone, say farewell, and go their separate ways back to the monotony of duty. From the degradation of modern city-life—frightful at its worst in Shooter's Gardens, insufferably drab even in the decent dullness of Crouch End—Gissing perceives no sanctuary but that of stoic acceptance and self-amendment. At Kirkwood's dreams of social justice, at John Hewett's zeal for universal suffrage, he smiles pityingly. In this hard Gissing-world, the whole duty of man is to stand siege within the fortress of his character.

Gissing's later novels, for the most part, are a prolonged protest against the frustrations and loneliness of modern life throughout all social classes. This is the world of over-education, of *The New Grub Street,* where Harold Biffen takes poison in the park. It is the world of woman free and miserable, delineated in *The Emancipated, The Odd Women, In the Year of Jubilee,* and *The Whirlpool.* This is the world of pretense and ruinous egotism, of *Denzil Quarrier* and *Born in Exile* and *Our Friend the Charlatan.* And Gissing's whole endeavor is a work of moral conservatism. Modern reformers' fanatic determination to make the laboring classes dissatisfied is a curse to us all. "It is one of the huge fallacies of the time," says Wyvern in *Demos.* "No, these reforms address themselves to the wrong people; they begin at the wrong end. Let us raise our voices, if we feel impelled to do so at all, for the old simple Christian rules, and do our best to get the educated by the ears."[9] Such a preacher is Gissing in his later books. But he has small hope of social regeneration.

For the arrogant secularism of modern thought is destroying everything beautiful in our literature and philosophy; the sound old parson is giving way to whited sepulchres like the Reverend Bruno Chilvers of *Born in Exile,* who declares in private, "The results of science are the divine message to our age; to neglect them, to fear them, is to remain under the old law whilst the new is demanding our adherence, to repeat the Jewish error of bygone time. Less of St. Paul and more of Darwin! less of Luther and more of Herbert Spencer!"[10] And the new collectivism, whether called socialism or by some name more palatable to the Philistines who are masters in this time, designs to efface the variety and individuality which make even the mere life of the flesh tolerable. "May we not live long enough," Gissing wrote in 1887, "to see democracy get all the power it expects!"[11] In 1879, he had expected the year 1900 to be fertile in great things; but when the turn of the century came round, he looked into the jaws of a monstrous social caducity. "The barbarisation of the world goes merrily on. No doubt there will be continuous warfare for many a long year to come. It sickens me to read the newspapers; I turn as much as possible to the old poets.... Who knows what fantastic horrors lie in wait for the world? It is at least a century and a half since civilization was in so bad a state.''[12] Harvey Rolfe, in the last pages of *The Whirlpool* (1897), growls a half-ironic endorsement of the new imperialism: it is release from our damning moral confusion.

That graceful and grave little book *The Private Papers of Henry Ryecroft,* expressing an ennobled Epicureanism, was published in 1903, while Gissing, at St. Jean de Luz, was dying of consumption when scarcely past forty. It is the testament of a man who loved everything venerable in England, from open fires to church bells; and as a conservative influence, possibly it has done more to remind thoughtful men of the truth and beauty residing in old ways than have all the Tory speeches in Hansard this century. Gissing abjures every innovating heresy; and to what remains of a better world, he says, we must cling with the tenacity of men suspended above an abyss. He is no friend of the people. "Every instinct of my being is anti-democratic, and I dread to think of what our England may become when Demos rules irresistibly." Men taken in the mass become blatant creatures, ready for any evil. "Democracy is full of menace to all the finer hopes of civilisation, and the revival, in not unnatural companionship with it, of monarchic power based on militarism, makes the prospect dubious enough. There has but to arise some Lord of Slaughter, and the nations will be tearing at each other's throats."[13] Against these terrors of the mass-mind and the anarchic impulse, the chief protection is the English political tradition: Englishmen rise superior to abstruse political theory.

Their strength, politically speaking, lies in a recognition of expediency, complemented by respect for the established fact. One of the facts particularly clear to them is the suitability to their minds, their tempers, their habits, of a system of polity which has been established by the slow effect of generations within this sea-girt realm. They have nothing to do with ideals: they never trouble themselves to think about the Rights of Man. If you talk to them (long enough) about the rights of the shopman, or the ploughman, or the cat's-meat-man, they will lend ear, and, when the facts of any such case have been examined, they will find a way of dealing with them. This characteristic of theirs they call Common

Sense. To them, all things considered, it has been of vast service; one
may even say that the rest of the world has profited by it not a little.
That Uncommon Sense might now and then have stood them in better
stead is nothing to the point. The Englishman deals with things as they
are, and first and foremost accepts his own being.[14]

Democracy is alien to English tradition and rooted sentiment; the
future of England depends upon reconciling the aristocratic idea
(and the spirit of deference which Bagehot, regretfully, had seen
vanishing forty years before) with the problems of the grey-coated
multitude. "The democratic Englishman is, by the laws of his own
nature, in parlous case; he has lost the ideal by which he guided
his rude, prodigal, domineering instincts; in place of the Right
Honourable, born to noble things, he has set up the mere Plebs,
born, more likely than not, to all manner of baseness. And, amid
all his show of loud self-confidence, the man is haunted with misgiving."[15]

Thus the convictions of Burke are echoed at the inception of
the twentieth century by an "unclassed" novelist from the mill-
country of West Riding, in an era when the most popular leader
of the Conservative party is a Radical manufacturer from Birmingham, successful in capturing the gold and diamonds of South Africa
for the forty-two million people of a Britain from which Victorian
heartiness is ebbing away. Toward the future of England as Joseph
Chamberlain saw it, or as Sidney Webb saw it, George Gissing
felt an overwhelming detestation. In this factory-shadowed and
depersonalized nation, as likely as not, "the word Home will have
only a special significance, indicating the common abode of retired labourers who are drawing old-age pensions." Even comfort, once the especial characteristic of England, seems to be
perishing, killed by new social and political conditions: "One who
looks at villages of the new type, at the working-class quarters of
towns, at the rising of 'flats' among the dwellings of the wealthy,
has little choice but to think so. There may soon come a day when,
though the word 'comfort' continues to be used in many languages,
the thing it signifies will be discoverable no where at all."[16]

This will be the spiritual famine of the Nether World spread to the whole of society; and Gissing stares upon the prospect of this tidy socialistic Inferno as if, like Farinata, he had great scorn of Hell. This will be the culmination of our social revolutions. Such of us as still are men, then, will hold fast by shaken constitutions and fading beauties so long as there is breath in us.

3

Arthur Balfour, one of the most interesting and least successful party leaders of the past hundred years, doubtless would have endorsed Gissing's remark that practical politics is the diversion of the quarter-educated. He was a philosopher, but not an original political thinker: like his uncle Lord Salisbury, he combined distrust of political generalization with indifference to popularity. This is not to depreciate his talents as a politician: one of those fortunate gentlemen who can walk over fresh snow without leaving tracks, he was a master of ambiguity and compromise, when he chose, and for a time he could please nearly everyone. The amiability of his nature, indeed, led him—despite his penetration of men's motives and his political dexterity—into his principal inconsistencies and failures: the Education Act of 1902, Zionism and the Balfour Declaration, and his polite evasion of any real policy concerning tariff reform. As a conservative, his principle of action, like Lord Salisbury's before him, was astute delay and amelioration. More than the socialism of Webb and Shaw, the conservatism of Salisbury and Balfour had the right to call itself Fabian.

This was the sort of conservatism which George Saintsbury praises; and after 1867, certainly, it was a prudent reaction from Disraeli's betrothal of Conservatism to Tory Democracy. Upon a well-founded impulse of alarm, the Conservatives repudiated the emotional levelling Toryism of Lord Randolph Churchill, and Balfour dissociated himself from the "Fourth Party" of Churchill, Gorst, and Drummond-Wolff. "That there are certain nets which, though displayed in the sight of the bird, with other birds already caught in them—nay, with the whole process of spreading and results of capture liberally revealed again and again—retain their fatality, is common enough knowledge,'' Saintsbury writes. ''Almost the most modern is what is called Tory Democracy.''[17]

Balfour saved Conservatism from the net of Tory Democracy, on the one hand, and perhaps from unconditional surrender to the Birmingham brand of new conservatism, on the other. Sir John Gorst, a few months after the Tory defeat in 1906, still thought that in unquestioning faith in the people lay the chief hope for Toryism, ''that Church and King, Lords and Commons, and all other public institutions are to be maintained so far, and so far only, as they promote the welfare and happiness of the common people.'' The sentimental devotion of Churchill and Gorst to an abstract ''people,'' somehow aloof from classes, economic interests, and individual fallibility, was a perversion of Disraeli's idea of nationality, and nothing more; Disraeli himself had repudiated the idea of the ''people'' long before. Under Balfour's leadership, after 1891, the Conservatives sheered away from this confidence in *vox populi,* which Lord Rosebery had defined as the wolf of radicalism in the sheepskin of Toryism. Professor W.L. Burn observes, ''Did Gorst mean that any change, however revolutionary, was laudable so long as it was carried by a Tory or Conservative government? Might the sword of Damocles drop at any moment so long as the thread was cut by a Tory knife?''[18] This affection for party above principle was what Salisbury (while still Viscount Cranborne) had found disquieting in Disraeli. In an age full of tremendous social and economic changes, simple faith in the people never would do; the people themselves, so far as they can be said to exist as a homogeneous body, do not know what they want or where they stand, once change has swept away their familiar landmarks; and Salisbury and Balfour endeavored to provide old-style aristocratic leadership and precaution in a time of mass-action.

Thus Conservatism's twentieth-century Scylla was evaded, for the time being; but there remained Charybdis, which was the metamorphosed Radicalism of Joseph Chamberlain and the industrial interest he represented, also democratic, but hardly sentimental—imperialistic, instead, and nonconformist or secular, contemptuous of the landed interest, and bent upon material change, perhaps through paternalistic legislation. The charm and tact of Balfour had something to do with taming these Gothic auxiliaries to the Tory legion, reconciling their objectives with conservative principles, so that Chamberlain served under Balfour willingly when Salisbury withdrew from political life. "We can't always help things going to the Devil," Saintsbury wrote in 1924, "but we can make them go slowly, and sometimes turn them out of the Diabolic way." This was the policy of Salisbury and Balfour both with their Unionist recruits and with the affairs of Britain. The grand principle of sound conservatism militant, Saintsbury added, is this: "Fight for it as long as you possibly can consistently with saving as much of it as you possibly can; but stave off the fighting by gradual and insignificant concessions where possible."[19] Balfour acted upon similar assumptions. But such maneuvers did not avert the Liberal victory of 1906 or the Labor victory of 1924.

To put the blame upon Arthur Balfour—as most Conservatives did in 1911, when they virtually compelled his resignation as leader—is a confused reaction against the impotence which the Tory party felt once the familiar contests of Victorian times all began to slip away, a new kind of economic class struggle supplanting the political and moral controversies that had been the themes of parliamentary discussion ever since 1832. Balfour was a man of the nineteenth century, the Conservatives felt, a magnificent virtuoso contemptuous of politics and economics—a dilettante, or something very like one, in the iron age. They wanted safe, practical minds—and when they got them, in Bonar Law or Stanley Baldwin or Neville Chamberlain, they discovered they needed a different sort of leadership, after all, and turned to Winston Churchill. Arthur Balfour, then, was struggling not simply against the altered spirit of the age, but against the altered constitution of his own party. Conservatism was the faith of the country gentlemen still, but they had ceased to dominate its councils. The Reforms of 1884 and 1885, much though they had diminished the influence of the landed classes, still had only reflected an earlier economic eclipse of the country interest. When Peel abandoned the Corn Laws, the dyke of agricultural prosperity was breached; but a general prosperity in England concealed for a generation the extent of the damage. The agricultural depression of 1877 inflicted upon all of rural Britain a poverty very slowly alleviated; and Disraeli, convinced ever since the fall of Peel that a party committed to protective duties for agriculture could not hope to govern England, made no attempt to shelter the landowners and the rural population behind a sea-wall of new tariffs—although the Continental powers already were adopting just such measures to check rural depopulation and excessive urbanization. Germany and France and the other states of Europe needed peasants to fill the ranks of their conscript armies; Britain did not. She still could recruit police-constables enough from the villages, and with that the dominant classes of the cities felt satisfied. By the middle of the twentieth century, England would have difficulty finding even police-recruits in a society that allotted scarcely more than five per cent of its labor-force to agriculture.

Arthur Balfour, therefore, as an eminent member of the old landed aristocracy of Britain, the class possessing leisure and wealth and rural antecedents which had dominated England since time out of mind, was not truly representative of twentieth-century Conservatives. Wealth, as well as population, had passed to manufacturing occupations and regions; and political power refuses to be parted long from money and force. The nineteen years of Unionist supremacy that ended in 1906, R. C. K. Ensor remarks, "may be looked on as a successful rally of the governing families to maintain their position, propped and modified by their alliance with the ablest leader of the upstarts—Chamberlain."[20] Even had Balfour been an abler practical politician, the old governing classes of England could not have prolonged for many years their capitulation to an urban democracy that had forgotten the idea of deference. Balfour did not fail, except so far as his whole order failed; and they did not abandon their duties, but had their duties snatched from their reluctant hands. The British aristocracy, as a body the most intelligent and conscientious upper class the Western world has known, never became decadent; they simply were inundated, so that after 1906 they were compelled to stand powerless while their property followed their political influence into the custody of the cities and the industrial masses. Of that aristocracy, Balfour was worthy to be the leader in their last years of ascendancy—though less as a statesman, perhaps, than as a great gentleman of many talents.

"I am more or less happy when being praised; not very uncomfortable when being abused; but I have moments of uneasiness when being explained," Balfour said of himself. His subtle nature will not be explained here; and, for that matter, no one has attempted it, for there is no satisfactory biography of Lord Balfour. In the sphere of conservative social thought, nothing that Balfour said or did matters so much as what he was, or rather what culture and class he epitomized. In the light of later days, Balfour's very indolence and aloofness seem virtues, now that political authority is in the grasp of the energumen and the statistician. D. C. Somervell compares him with Lord Melbourne: "It is a measure of his personal distinction that such a man should have risen to the premiership, seeing that he took or appeared to take so little interest in most of the problems of the people he governed....Balfour, too, was an autumn rose, a bloom of the finest perfume blossoming dangerously late in its season when the frosts were already setting in."[21] He cared for music and philosophy a great deal more than for politics; and though he wrote little on politics that is worth reading now, his speculative studies in theology have an enduring value, conservative in the sense that the accomplishment of Newman was conservative.

The substance of Balfour's four philosophical volumes—*A Defense of Philosophic Doubt* (1879), *The Foundations of Belief* (1895), *Theism and Humanism* (1915), and *Theism and Thought* (1923)—is nearly akin to Pascal's maxim that the Heart has reason which the Reason knows not. Balfour is skeptical as Newman is skeptical: acutely conscious that the postulates of modern science do not rest upon absolute knowledge, but are derived from sources similar to those of religious conviction. If only the data of physical researches and sensory evidence be allowed by thinking men, then we must labor forever in the agonies of doubt. Balfour agrees with Francis Bacon in this, if in nothing else, that he who begins in doubt may end in certainty. A higher skepticism is preparation for wisdom—not the narrow destructive skepticism of the egoist, deliberately seeking unbelief, but instead an intellectual recognition of the want of evidence. Skepticism need not destroy belief; it may serve, on the contrary, to expose the unjustifiable complacency of unbelievers. Balfour hopes by an enlightened skepticism, which extends to skeptical consideration of the claims of "exact" science, to restore some measure of confidence among men "who surrender slowly and unwillingly, to what they conceive to be unanswerable argument, convictions with which yet they can scarcely bear to part; who, for the sake of Truth, are prepared to give up what they had been wont to think of as their guide in this life, their hope in another, and to take refuge in some of the strange substitutes for Religion provided by the ingenuity of these latter times."[22] The truly reasonable skeptic will discover the presumption of these strange substitutes, Positivism among them; and thus skepticism is the instrument of piety. It led Balfour to Theism, belief in a Being who is not simply a misty Unity or Identity, but "a God whom men can love, a God to whom men can pray, who takes sides, who has purposes and preferences, whose attributes, howsoever conceived, leave unimpaired the possibility of a personal relation between Himself and those whom He has created."[23]

The truth of what Coleridge called the Reason, and Newman called the Illative Sense, is what Balfour sets against both naturalistic materialism and anti-Christian idealism. Men who demand material and mensurable evidence of the transcendent ask what is not in nature; they endeavor to solve mysteries simply by denying that mysteries exist. "They search for proofs of God, as men search for evidence about ghosts or witches. Show us, they say, the marks of His presence. Tell us what problems His existence would solve. And when these tasks have been happily accomplished, then will we willingly place Him among the hypothetical causes by which science endeavours to explain the only world we directly know, the familiar world of daily experience.'' But this is treating God as if He were an entity, a separable part of reality, when ''He is Himself the condition of scientific knowledge.''[24] Knowledge, love, and beauty cannot endure in a world that acknowledges only Nature; they have both their roots and their consummation in God, and people who deny God must lose both the definition and the appreciation of knowledge, love, and beauty.[25] Balfour, like Joubert, implies that it is not hard to know God, provided one does not try to define him. Religion and science are neither inimical nor exclusive, properly understood; both must rely upon intuitions and intimations beyond the simple evidence of the senses; and men who endeavor to reduce religion to matter-of-fact morality, or elevate science to the estate of a dogmatic creed, have shut their eyes to the sources of wisdom that distinguish civilized men from primitive beings.

A similar trust in authority, prescription, and moral intuition constituted the politics of Arthur Balfour. These were the principles of Burke; and, like Burke, Balfour knew how to apply them in practical administration, as his performance when he was Secretary for Ireland attested. But for a man so learned and on occasion so practical, he was curiously short-sighted in his larger political prophecies and hopes. The Education Act of 1902 is an instance of this defect: ''I did not realize that the Act would mean more expense and more bureaucracy,'' he confessed later. Another is his conduct of Conservative resistance to the Liberal government in 1906, employing the vast Tory majority in the House of Lords to quash the innovating legislation of the jubilant Liberals and Labourites—which led to the Parliament Act of 1911 and the reduction of the Lords to near-impotence. Errors of judgment may be repaired easily enough when they involve no more than matters of governmental policy; but when they are involved with organic change, their effect is liable to be permanent. It was Balfour's misfortune to be the leader of Conservatism at a time when the taste for organic change had become itself almost institutional.

In his very slowness to perceive such probabilities, as in his distaste for economics and finance, Balfour was representative of the old-fashioned Conservative interest, the legacy of the Cecils and the other great houses. Balfour was the witty and cultivated voice of traditional Britain, still gallant amid the jostling twentieth century. "The difference between Joe and me," Balfour said of Chamberlain, "is the difference between youth and age: I am age."[26] It was quite true. Chamberlain's state socialism and industrial imperialism were the wave of the future, while the ascendancy of the old governing classes of England ended with Balfour. Henry Adams, who saw in himself and his brothers the representatives of the dying old America, recognized in Balfour his English counterpart. Upon Balfour's resignation of the Conservative leadership, Adams wrote to his brother Charles Francis that strong and interesting personalities were vanishing from the world:

The *Lives* of our contemporaries now fill our bookshelves, and not one of them offers a thought. Since the Civil War, I think we have produced not one figure that will be remembered a life-time…. What is more curious, I think the figures have not existed. The men have not been born.

If they had existed I should have attached myself to them, for I needed them bad. As life has turned out, I am dying alone, without a twig to fall from. I might as well be a solitary woodchuck on our old Quincy hills as winter comes on. We leave no followers, no school, no tradition…. I am rather interested to see that Arthur Balfour has succumbed to the same conditions here. He can't force the coming generation. He expresses it rather well too.[27]

Certainly Balfour left no political inheritor. Bonar Law, who succeeded him, stood for the transformed Conservative party, the party of industry and commerce. From the general election of 1906 until the Conservative resurgence in 1922, a flood of radical legislation broke up the old society from which Balfour came. Political power had indeed slipped from the hands of statesmen of the old sort, who formed and directed public opinion; but, as Stephen had said, power that the state relinquishes will be seized by other organizations and individuals. The Benthamite theory that sovereignty should be relinquished to the custody of the innumerable individuals who make up society, each acting for himself and exerting an equal weight in the decision of public matters, attained its culmination in the Plural Voting Act of 1913 and the Representation of the People Act of 1918; thereafter—with exceptions of no great significance—the principle of one person, one vote would operate unchecked. The electorate now consisted of eighteen million men and women, each presumed to vote intelligently after individual consideration of the issues in question. But political power, defying Act of Parliament, refused to be atomized. The influence of which old classes and bodies had been deprived was assumed by new—by the labor unions, especially, and by reorganized political parties, strictly disciplined, which proceeded to squeeze out the independent member of Parliament. The economic and political individualism which the Benthamite school had expected to result from universal suffrage never existed for a moment; instead, political leaders hastened to flatter and to satisfy popular desire for positive legislation facilitating the new collectivism. The Trade Disputes Act of 1906, the Finance Act of 1909-10, the Parliament Act of 1911, the Trade Unions Act of 1913, and lavish state expenditure were the immediate results of the conservatives' rout. Labour was enormously strong now; old-age pensions had commenced; and the rest of the welfare state was taking form. Lloyd George had initiated his program of making the rich pay ransom. Political equality was complete; to equality of condition the reforming mind was irresistibly attracted.

Two years after the catastrophe of 1906, Balfour spoke at Newnham College on Decadence. "National character is subtle and elusive," he said; "not to be expressed in statistics nor measured by the rough methods which suffice the practical moralist or statesman. And when through an ancient and still powerful state there spreads a mood of deep discouragement, when the reaction against recurring ills grows feebler, and the ship rises less buoyantly to each succeeding wave, when learning languishes, enterprise slackens, and vigour ebbs away, then, I think, there is present some process of social degeneration which we must perforce recognize, and which, pending a satisfactory analysis, may conveniently be distinguished by the name of 'decadence.' " No sociology exists which can determine precisely whether a state of decadence has been attained in a nation. It appears that decadence is quite as normal in communities as is progress. Concerning our society, however, "whatever be the perils in front of us, there are, so far, no symptoms either of pause or retrogression in the onward movement which for more than a thousand years has been characteristic of Western civilisation."[28] Professor C. E. M. Joad, in 1948, attempted to express a more concise definition of decadence: the loss of an object in life. Conservative leaders, despite the influence of Disraeli and Stephen, did not often think directly in terms of social ends, even after 1906.

In the spring of 1914, Balfour delivered his Gifford Lectures on Theism and Humanism at the University of Glasgow; and with his fee, he purchased a pair of wrought-iron garden gates for his estate of Whittinghame. In the scroll-work were set the letters "1914." In that year the onward movement of Western civilization shuddered to a halt; and morbid symptoms of social ennui had spread across the face of Balfour's society nearly a decade earlier.

4

How is one to sum up the work of W. H. Mallock, which fills twenty-seven volumes, exclusive of ephemerae? Mallock is remembered chiefly for one book, *The New Republic,* and that his first, composed while he still was at Oxford—"the most brilliant novel ever written by an undergraduate," says Professor Tillotson, justly.[29] (It is also the most brilliant accomplishment in its *genre,* after Thomas Love Peacock; and perhaps it is equal to Peacock at his best.) But other books of Mallock's are worth looking into still— his theological and philosophical studies, his didactic novels, his zealous volumes of political expostulation and social statistics, even his books of verse.

"He had astonishing acuteness, great argumentative power, wide and accurate knowledge, excellent style," Saintsbury says of Mallock. "He might have seemed—he did seem, I believe, to some—to have in him the making of an Aristophanes or a Swift of not so much lessened degree.... And yet after the chiefly scandalous success of *The New Republic* he never 'came off.' To attribute this to the principles he advocated is to nail on those who dislike those principles their own favourite gibe of 'the stupid party.' *We* know brains when we see them, even if they belong to the enemy. Exactly what was the flaw, the rot, the 'dram of eale,' I do not know—it lay in faults of taste and temper, perhaps."[30] In the past two or three decades, interest in Mallock has revived somewhat, probably stimulated by that conservative resurgence for which Mallock hoped, and the lines of which he predicted. *Is Life Worth Living?*, *Social Equality*, and *The Limits of Pure Democracy*, together with Mallock's charming autobiography, are especially deserving of attention from anyone interested in the conservative mind. Mallock died in 1923, half forgotten even then; but he has had no equal among English conservative thinkers since. He spent his life in a struggle against moral and political radicalism: for bulk and thoroughness, quite aside from Mallock's gifts of wit and style, his work is unexcelled among the body of conservative writings in any country.

By inheritance a country gentleman of ancient family, by inclination a poet, Mallock turned himself into a pamphleteer and a statistician on the Benthamite pattern, all for the sake of the old English life that he describes lovingly in his *Memoirs of Life and Literature*—the splendid houses, the good talk, the wines and dinners, the tranquillity of immemorial ways. This may be the conservatism of enjoyment, but Mallock defended it by the conservatism of the intellect. For its sake he spent his life among blue-books and reports of the income-tax commissioners; he accomplished unassisted what the research staff of the Conservative Political Centre now carries on as a body. "Throughout almost all his books is to be noticed the aspiration after a Truth which will give the soul something more than 'a dusty answer'; it is everywhere evident," says Sir John Squire.[31] In the search for this truth, he assailed some of the most formidable personages of his day— Huxley, Spencer, Jowett, Kidd, Webb, Shaw. And none of these writers, not even Bernard Shaw, came off well from a bout with Mallock.

In boyhood, Mallock "unconsciously assumed in effect, if not in so many words, that any revolt or protest against the established order was indeed an impertinence, but was otherwise of no great importance."[32] His first aspiration as a conservative was the restoration of classical taste in poetry. But as he grew, he came to realize "that the whole order of things—literary, religious, and social—which the classical poetry assumed, and which I had previously taken as impregnable, was being assailed by forces which it was impossible any longer to ignore." He turned to the defense of orthodox religion against the positivists and other worshippers of skeptical science. Although all his life inclining toward Roman Catholicism ("If Christianity means anything definite—anything more than a mood of precarious sentiment—the only logical form of it is that represented by the Ecumenical Church of Rome"), and observing complacently that his *Doctrine and Doctrinal Disruption* had impelled certain serious Anglicans to join the Roman communion, still he entered the Church of Rome only on his deathbed.

It was the Tory radical Ruskin who encouraged feelings of awe and piety in the ultra-conservative Mallock; and Ruskin (as "Mr. Herbert"), preaching from his improvised pulpit in that unforgettable villa of *The New Republic,* expresses the aim of Mallock's general endeavor when he says that we moderns cannot pipe back the gods of the Greeks:

The Atheism of the modern world is not the Atheism of the ancient: the long black night of the winter is not the swift clear night of the vanished summer. The Greek philosopher could not darken his life, for he knew not from what mysterious source the light fell upon it. The modern philosopher does know, and he knows that it is called God, and thus knowing the source of light he can at once quench it. What will be left you then if this light be quenched? Will art, will painting, will poetry be any comfort to you? You have said that these were magic mirrors which reflected back your life for you. Well—will they be any better than the glass mirrors in your drawing-rooms, if they have nothing but the same listless orgy to reflect? For that is all that will be at last in store for you; nay, that is the best thing that possibly can be in store for you; the only alternative being not a listless orgy for the few, but an undreamed-of anarchy for all. I do not fear that, however. Some will be always strong, and some will be always weak; and though, if there is no God, no divine and fatherly source of order, there will be, trust me, no aristocracies, there will still be tyrannies. There will still be rich and poor; and that will then mean happy and miserable; and the poor will be—as I sometimes think they are already—but a mass of groaning machinery, without even the semblance of rationality; and the rich, with only the semblance of it, but a set of gaudy, dancing marionettes, which it is the machinery's one work to keep in motion.[33]

Mallock, like Ruskin, was an artist and a moralist; to him, the notion of material Progress was ludicrous and hideous. "Mr. Saunders" (Professor Clifford), in *The New Republic,* defines progress as "such improvement as can be verified by statistics, just as education is such knowledge as can be tested by examinations." Mallock saw how statistical fallacies were destroying the civilization reflected in the marvellous conversations of *The New Republic.* Sixty years later, in all England there was scarcely a country house left where such a company might meet in comfort—nor, indeed, did much remain of the society that could talk thus; he glimpsed this prospect; and so Mallock, "something of a man of the world, something of a poet, a scholar, a logician, a stylist, a critic, fastidious but not heartless, a realist with a touch of the mystic" (as Squire describes him) cudgelled socialists and positivists for half a century. *The New Republic,* which had made Jowett and Huxley and Tyndall and Clifford wince terribly, was followed by a satire upon the positivists, *The New Paul and Virginia,* or *Positivism on an Island,* in which Mallock marooned the unfortunate Professor W. K. Clifford (under the name of Professor Paul Darnley) together with Virginia St. John, a young woman of lively antecedents, who "found herself, at the age of thirty, mistress of nothing except a large fortune." Next, in 1880, he published *Is Life Worth Living?*, probably the most serious and searching attack to which the spirit of positivism has been subjected. He exposed atheism and agnosticism to an analysis calculated to demonstrate their results in the realm of morals, appealing "to the intellect, a sense of humor, and what is called a knowledge of the world" rather than to pure religious emotion.

The message of *Is Life Worth Living?* is a more thorough expounding of the author's declaration of faith: that morality and happiness cannot subsist without the foundation of supernatural religion. The "band-work" which positivists cry up as a substitute for piety never can build a Civitas Dei. "Social conditions, it is true, we may expect will go on improving; we may hope that the social machinery will come gradually to run more smoothly. But unless we know something positive to the contrary, the outcome of all this progress may be nothing but a more undisturbed ennui or a more soulless sensuality. The rose-leaves may be laid on more smoothly, and yet the man that lies on them may be wearier or more degraded."

When man loses sight of moral ends, his degradation commences. Self-reproach comes, without possibility of absolution; and self-weariness; and indifference.[34] The positivistic thinkers, whose early training has been religious, and who know little enough of the world, imagine that their own tame and narrow emotions are all that humanity has to discipline. If they succeed in revolutionizing the moral convictions and character of most men, they will learn how close the beast lies beneath the skin of humanity. Even those among whom habitual desire to do right still operates are corrupted by the moral indifference which follows on the heels of irreligion. "The whole prospect that environs them has become morally colourless; and they discern in their attitude towards the world without, what it must one day come to be towards the world within. A state of mind like this is no dream. It is a malady of the modern world—a malady of our own generation, which can escape no eyes that will look upon it. It is betraying itself every moment around us, in conversation, in literature, and in legislation."

Against the logic of scientific negation, there is no recourse but to face the grim question bravely: to ask ourselves whether orthodox religion is true or false. Can lost faith be recovered? Are we to accept the positivists' contention that external proofs must determine the validity of religion, or may the tradition and discipline of the Church convince us that atheism is itself unscientific? The man who venerates his ancestors and thinks of his posterity will stand up resolutely against these Vandals of the intellect, who are reducing modern civilization to ashes:

Upon this Empire, as upon that of Rome, calamity has at last fallen. A host of intellectual barbarians has burst in upon it, and has occupied by force the length and breadth of it. The result has been astounding. Had the invaders been barbarians only, they might have been repelled easily; but they were barbarians armed with the most powerful weapons of civilisation. They were a phenomenon new to history: they showed us real knowledge in the hands of real ignorance; and the work of the combination thus far has been ruin, not reorganization. Few great movements at the beginning have been conscious of their own true tendency; but no great movement has mistaken it like modern Positivism. Seeing just too well to have the true instinct of blindness, and too ill to have the proper guidance from sight, it has tightened its clutch upon the world of thought, only to impart to it its own confusion. What lies before men now is to reduce this confusion to order, by a patient and calm employment of the intellect.

After the publication of this moving book, Mallock turned for some years from philosophy and morals to political economy and sociology. The rise of the Social Democratic Federation, the popularity of Henry George's ideas, and even the economic notions of his old mentor Ruskin alarmed him powerfully: *Social Equality,* the first of his seven books on politics and economics, was the result, appearing in 1882. Mallock's ideas underwent some refinement, and his tables of statistics some amendment, during the years that elapsed before the publication of his last sociological volume, *The Limits of Pure Democracy* (1919); but his principles and his method did not alter. Mallock's aim was to establish a conservative system of thought on scientific grounds. The radicals, claiming science for their own, were inventing or warping statistics to suit their purposes; the old Tory contempt for political economy tended to keep Conservatives from answering false statistics with true; and Mallock, with little encouragement from most Conservative leaders, set himself to redress the balance.

Almost from its beginnings, the Conservative party had been pitifully weak in its grasp of political economy. Burke has possessed an admirable mastery of the subject, and Pitt had understood finance; but (except for Huskisson and Herries, neither of whom was a proper leader of men) from their times to the later years of Salisbury's government, economists had been Liberals, and the Liberals had trounced the Conservatives repeatedly in this field. "The difficulties in the way of formulating a true scientific conservatism, which the masses shall be able to comprehend, I am the last person to ignore," Mallock wrote in 1920. "There is the difficulty of formulating true general principles. There is the difficulty of collecting and verifying the statistical and historical facts, to which general principles must be accommodated. There is the difficulty of bringing moral and social sentiments into harmony with objective conditions which no sentiments can permanently alter. There is the difficulty of transforming many analyses of fact into a synthesis moral and rational, by the light of which human beings can live; and feeling my way slowly, I now attempted to indicate what the nature of such a synthesis would be. In so doing I felt that political problems of life reunited themselves with those which are commonly called religious, and with which, during my earlier years, my mind had been alone engaged."[35] Now that the old Liberals were succumbing to theories of socialism, the need for a conservative economics was desperate.

The old conservative arguments are obsolete, Mallock wrote. For the prescriptive rights, the traditionary influences, the ancient respect for property and order, all have been shattered by successive waves of political and economic thought ever since Rousseau. No longer can conservatives rely upon these ancient verities: our traditions have to be sheltered now, rather than utilized as defenses.

Ideology and "scientific" system and statistical method have been employed exclusively by the innovators. "All that bears any semblance of organized thought or system has belonged to the attacking party; and, force excepted, it has been met by nothing but an obsolete dogmatism that cannot even explain itself."[36] It is of no avail to protest that the Radical doctrines are merely an appeal to envy; that is begging the question; for if the doctrine of equality be true, "we must consider envy to be as sound a guide in politics as reverence by religious men is considered to be in religion." The supreme issue to be determined, then, is simply this: is the doctrine of social equality true, or is it false? Are the Radicals right when they say that the perfection of society requires equality? Would civilization, and would the poor, gain from the establishment of equality? What is the relationship between progress and equality? To some extent, Mallock advances answers to all these questions in *Social Equality;* but his arguments are strengthened in *Labour and the Popular Welfare* (1894).

When it is scientifically considered—so runs Mallock's argument in all his political works—the doctrine of equality will be exposed as a fallacy; for equality is the death of progress. Throughout history, progress of every sort, cultural and economic, has been produced by the desire of men for *inequality.* Without the possibility of inequality, a people continue on the dreary level of bare subsistence, like Irish peasants; granted inequality, the small minority of men of ability turn barbarism into civilization. Equality benefits no one. It frustrates men of talent; and it reduces the poor to a poverty still more abject. In a densely-populated civilized state, it means near-starvation for the poor. For inequality produces the wealth of civilized communities: it provides the motive which induces men of superior abilities to exert themselves for the general benefit. About one-sixteenth of the British population, in this age, is responsible for producing two-thirds of the national income.[37]

How is it that socialists fail to recognize the immense value of superior abilities, which would be suppressed under a system of social equality? Their fundamental error is the labor theory of wealth, as expounded by Marx, who got its rudiment from

404 THE CONSERVATIVE MIND

Ricardo. Labor (Marx notwithstanding) is *not* the cause of most of our wealth: unaided, labor produces merely a bare subsistence. Man is not a laboring animal naturally: without especial incentive, he works as little as will enable him to sustain life. "Labor in itself is no more the cause of wealth than Shakespeare's pen was the cause of his writing 'Hamlet.' The cause is in the motives, of which labor is the outward index." The principal motive is inequality; and the principal producer of wealth is not Labor, but *Ability*. Mallock defends the importance of great men against Macaulay and Spencer. Individual genius is a tremendous social force; and the talents of great men save the poor from sinking into barbarism. Reduce great men, or merely men of energy and talent, to the boredom of equality, and you reduce the mass of men proportionately.

Ability, the chief productive faculty, is a natural monopoly: it cannot be redistributed by legislation, though it may be crushed. "Ability is a kind of exertion on the part of the individual which is capable of affecting simultaneously the labour of an indefinite number of individuals, and thus hastening or perfecting the accomplishment of an indefinite number of tasks." It is the faculty which directs labor, in short; which produces inventions, devises methods, supplies imagination, organizes production and distribution and protection, maintains order. In a civilized state, Ability and Labor cannot exist separately, and therefore one cannot estimate with perfect exactness the proportion of wealth produced by either; but of the national income (in 1894) of thirteen hundred million pounds, Labor produced not more than five hundred million pounds, whilst eight hundred million pounds at least was demonstrably the product of Ability. Labor without Ability is simply the primitive effort of natural man to obtain subsistence. Recognizing that mankind cannot prosper by mere labor, society hitherto has endeavored to encourage Ability by protecting its incentives.

Capital, so bitterly assailed by socialists, is simply the production-fund of all society; it is the control of Intellect over Labor. Inheritance of property, detested by the party of progress, is one of the most important incentives to Ability, satisfying the instinct of bequest and simultaneously providing for saving and the accumulation of capital. By admitting the claims of Ability, society has obtained tremendous gains for the laboring classes, which Labor unaided never could have attained. During the first sixty years of the nineteenth century, the income of the laboring classes, per capita, rose so greatly that by 1860 it equalled the total income of *all* classes in 1800—as if, in 1800, the entire wealth of Britain has been divided among the laboring people. And the process has continued. In 1880, the income of the laboring class alone was equal to the income that *all* classes had received in 1850. "This represents a progress, which the wildest Socialist would never have dreamed of promising." Indeed, not only has the wealth of the laboring classes increased absolutely, but it has grown proportionately; the rich and the middle classes now have a smaller share of the total income than formerly; and this is because Labor, ceasing to be simple unskilled manual effort, is acquiring special talents and therefore sharing in the rewards of Ability.[38]

If this process continues (Mallock wrote in 1894) for thirty years longer, at the end of that time the laborers will have their incomes doubled. Yet the uninformed cupidity of the poorer classes threatens progress. It is natural to seek greater prosperity, even through the agency of government; but if this fancied prosperity is attained by despoiling the other elements in society, it will stifle Ability and will lead, in short order, to general poverty and eventual barbarism. The demand for an absolute social equality, on the premise of a fancied natural justice, is as ruinous as the pretended economy to be obtained by abolishing the Monarchy, thus saving a million pounds a year—which, however, comes to less than sixpence halfpenny per head of population. "It costs each individual less to maintain the Queen that it would cost him to drink her health in a couple of pots of porter."[39] The socialist, ready to abolish the established government of Britain in order to relieve a laboring man of paying sixpence, would commit a folly no less grave in abolishing incentives to Ability.

These ideas are applied to the management of affairs in *Aristocracy and Evolution* (1898). Sociologists generally have ignored the fact of congenital inequality, Mallock begins. More than ever before, in our society the direction of the economy is in the hands of a comparative few. Our wage-capital, and our whole system of production, require direction by a small number of men, who represent Ability. This is both just and expedient. The "party of progress" has foolishly depreciated the role of strong and intelligent men in civilization. Really they are the mind of society; public opinion as the spontaneous creation of the masses never has existed; what we call public opinion forms round exceptional men. Upon the encouragement and recognition of these men depends civilization. The average man should be taught to embellish his lot, not to endeavor to escape from it. Democracy exhibits a perilous tendency to repudiate leadership—to insist that the men who manage great affairs shall be "exceptional only for such qualities as practical activity and a quick apprehension of the wishes of other people, which would enable them to do what their many-headed master bade them; but they would have to be wanting in any strength of mind or originality which might tempt them to act out of harmony with their master's temper at the moment, or what is the same thing, to any acts beyond their master's comprehension, even though such acts might be for his future benefit."[40] Abolish this true leadership of Ability restrained by a traditional moral and political system, and the laboring classes, after an interval of terror in which they would be helpless as so many sheep, must submit to new masters whose rule would be harder, more arbitrary, and less humane than the old.

Though our society, like all civilized communities, requires aristocratic principles for its successful administration, nevertheless it remains a society of free association and voluntary endeavor; the necessity for direction by a comparative few does not bring about the subjection of the many. This is because the services of Ability are secured by adequate rewards: compulsion is not required where men are persuaded by incentives. The Fabians declare their readiness to efface this voluntary cooperation; they speak, instead, of a "law of civic duty," which implies punishment of those who shirk. But though socialism may be able to enforce Labor by the task-master's whip, no state can compel Ability to perform its natural function. Under compulsion, Ability sinks to the level of mere Labor; no man will exert unusual talents if he is to get no reward; and Sidney Webb's escape into economic slavery (by which the Fabians think they evade the fear of want) really would result in permanent want for everyone. Mallock's *A Critical Examination of Socialism* (1908), in which these concepts are explained, remains perhaps the most lucid dissection of collectivistic errors.

In *The Limits of Pure Democracy* (1919), Mallock's social ideas are summarized in the light of the Russian Revolution. The primary producer of our modern wealth, vastly augmented since the beginning of the nineteenth century, is Directive Mind; yet Directive Mind, or Ability, receives as its reward no more than one-fifth of this increment. Mankind ought not to complain at the rewards of Directive Mind, but to be surprised that they are so modest. In politics and in productive endeavor, the authority of the few is derived not from any merely legal sanction, or from any theory of divine right, but from nature: the aristocracy or oligarchy of modern times is a phenomenon of general benefit. "In any great and civilized State *Democracy only knows itself through the co-operation of oligarchy*,...the many can prosper only through the participation in benefits which, in the way alike of material comfort, opportunity, culture, and social freedom, would be possible for no one unless the many submitted themselves to the influence or authority of the super-capable few."[41] Socialism first repudiates this legitimate leadership and then, in reaction from its own failure, demands a dictator. Out of the application of pure democracy in Russia will come a host of squalid new oligarchs, dominated by a tyrant who, secretly repudiating the ideas upon which he rose, still will continue to exhort the masses to "revolution" and "democracy" while he proceeds to stamp out resistance to a new absolutism, necessary because revolution has made the life of everyone intolerable.

From the twin menace of atheism and social retrogression, we can be delivered if we have the courage to face our tasks. On the one hand, we must revive in our own hearts those religious convictions which are not truly inconsonant with modern knowledge, but transcend it; on the other, we must counteract the socialists' appeal to envy by convincing the mass of men that society is conducted for their benefit. Mallock unites the issues of religious faith and social conservatism in his later novels, little read nowadays. Agnosticism prepares the way for social chaos. Mistaking the lessons of modern science, the positivists and their allies throw men upon their private moral resources:

Science having, as they supposed, expelled God from nature, they practically looked upon the change that was thus effected as comparable to man's loss of a sort of celestial schoolmaster, who had indeed managed his business for him, but in many ways was very objectionable; and the schoolmaster being dead they conceived of the human race as left in a free, even if in rather a forlorn condition, to construct for itself, in defiance of nature, a little private universe of its own, like a sort of Dotheboys Hall which has got rid of its Squeers, and whose orphans propose henceforward to educate and to board themselves. But such Agnostics practically failed to realize what was in theory even for themselves a truism, that the precise train of reasoning which freed them from an intelligent God, reduced them to mere puppets of that nature which it was their enlightened programme to oppose.[42]

So Mallock wrote in *The Reconstruction of Belief* (1905). The new democracy of Dotheboys Hall refuses to be conducted on principles of pure reason; fierce personal passion and contempt for civilization are its moral characteristics. And the social arrangements of the "party of progress," compelling everyone to trade on his private stock of reason, denying the natural inequality between man and man, repudiating leadership and mistaking confiscation for augmentation of wealth, are the mundane equivalent of the spiritual anarchy that positivism invites. Mallock endeavored, over fifty years, to countervail this intellectual revolution by a campaign of candid and lucid propaganda, trusting that "the mischief, religious, social and political, which 'advanced' thought has done, may in time, by a rational development of conservative thought,

be undone, and the true faiths be revived, on which the sancti-
ties, the stabilities, and the civilisation of the social order depend."[43] He did not underestimate the difficulty of this
conservative labor, but he never lost hope, even though he lived
amid what seemed to many the dissolution of English culture.

The plausible democratic optimism and evolutionary progres-
sivism of Benjamin Kidd (who was the especial object of Mallock's
criticism in *Aristocracy and Evolution*), popularized in Kidd's *Social
Evolution* (1894), had an immediate influence upon public opinion much stronger than Mallock's books, or even Herbert
Spencer's—and Mallock knew it. Kidd and his school, forsaking
being in their quest for *becoming*, abandoned the past for a complacent faith in the future of evolving mankind. W. H. Mallock knew
that the battle was not to such as Kidd. But after the turn of the
century, Mallock must have felt himself to be the tiring champion of the proscribed minority: social Darwinians dominated the
English and American mind until Sir Edward Grey saw the lights
going out all over Europe.

"From the evolutionist's viewpoint neither man or society was
of a determinate nature and therefore could not be studied as
such," Ross Hoffman observes. "Hence conservative philosophy
of the kind that examines the nature of institutions and seeks to
apprehend the principles by which they live, to make judgments
upon them by reference to the permanent norms of human nature, and to discover the means of conserving and prospering the
good values, came to seem irrelevant to the subject of discussion.
That is the prime reason why there was so little conservative political and social philosophy worthy of the name in the early years
of this century."[44]

To some extent, Mallock's trust rested upon the expectation
of steady material improvement in the condition of the whole population, as had been so conspicuously the course of the economy
between 1850 and 1890; but the lagging of British industry after
1900, and the terrible blow of the war, further inclined the poorer classes toward the idea of a radical redistribution of income,
rather than a cooperative increase of it. Even so, Mallock did not

despair; for he knew that ideas, in the long run, have immense power. If the conservative mind does indeed contrive to arrest the decay of Western civilization, Mallock will deserve great credit for being the author of a reasoned conservative apologetic. After the first flush of enthusiasm, he did not expect to move mountains:

Arguments are like the seed, or like the soul, as Paul conceived of it, which he compared to seed. They are not quickened unless they die. As long as they remain for us in the form of arguments they do no work. Their work begins only, after a time and in secret, when they have sunk down into the memory, and have been left to lie there; when the hostility and distrust they were regarded with dies away; when, unperceived, they melt into the mental system, and, becoming part of oneself, effect a turning round of the soul.[45]

Mallock's books have helped in this subtle transformation; and their influence may continue to filter through society, the temper of the time being what it is.

5

Except for those whose struggle for life was so hard as to leave them no time or desire for self-deception, the world became a matter of acting and make-believe, giving such falsity to every value, such crooked perspective to every event, that when the greatest tragedy in human history came, every nation was equally surprised and unprepared, though each had, in reality, done nothing else except prepare for it, consciously or unconsciously, during the previous half-century. The war, certainly, was the final triumph of the system. Every man, the world over, was forced to fight to make the world safe for Democracy, whether he believed in it or not—though the war itself was undoubtedly due to the very form of government for which he was now urged to fight, and one, in any case, peculiarly unsuited for the prosecution of a successful war....The people of every country allowed only the most brutalized and hypocritical of their countrymen to come to the top and rule them, thereby proving how much they had gained by education and the other blessings which they owed to the system.

—Sir Osbert Sitwell, *Triple Fugue*

Of British conservatism between the two World Wars, it is difficult to write anything worth reading. Stanley Baldwin, a courageous man, rescued his party from its ruinous entanglement with Lloyd George; but one cannot look to Baldwin for general ideas. As for the rank and file of Conservatives in the House of Commons, Baldwin described them to Keynes as "a lot of hard-faced men who look as if they had done very well out of the war." The Prime Minister was still more contemptuous, with reason, of the barons of the penny press who aspired to dominate the Conservative party. Conservatism between the wars felt itself fortunate if it succeeded in holding fast to what it had, as when the General Strike of 1926 was broken; positive action, in that time of increasing economic distress, hardly was thought of. Neville Chamberlain's social reforms, after the pattern his father had cut, were simply ameliorations of life in the mass-age, differing in degree rather than in kind from the Socialists' program; Winston Churchill's work at the Treasury was undone by the depression years. The Conservative politicans of the 'thirties, observes Professor Burn, did almost nothing to stave off the coming of the new Leviathan:

Having abandoned the old aristocratic concept of government they did nothing to create a new aristocracy: they relied confidently on their skill in riding the wild horses of democracy; they were gamblers who would pocket their winnings and pay their losses cheerfully without seeking to alter the rules of the game. What did they do to maintain the family as the basic unit of society? There may be answers to this question, but they are not, in recollection, very obvious....A certain tolerance and a certain efficiency, of which Baldwin and Chamberlain were the respective representatives; and, in addition, the opportunity to pad oneself against the more unpleasant impacts of society. The process of proletarisation was allowed to continue, but a man who was sufficiently wealthy could withdraw himself from contact with it. The chief difference today is that the process of proletarisation has been accelerated while most of the exemptions have been cancelled.[46]

And conservative thought, apart from political activity, suffered from the same blight. Chesterton and Belloc, although outside the true line of descent in conservative ideas, though sentimentally democratic and economically fanciful, did more to nourish the old conservative impulse during those dark times than did the men who should have carried on the tradition of Burke. Distributism, however involved with individualistic fallacies, offered more of an answer to the ills of modern life than did the pensions and doles of the Conservative and Liberal and Labour parties; *Orthodoxy* in some sort echoed the ideas of Coleridge and Newman; *The Servile State* reflected the postulates of Bolingbroke and Disraeli. But Belloc and Chesterton were only auxiliaries of conservatism. Where were the marshals?

Some, like George Wyndham, had been overborne by the ugliness of twentieth-century political life and had died before their hour; others, like F. E. Smith, never fulfilled their early promise. And many young men whom interest and inheritance should have secured to the conservative cause were seduced from it by the general bewilderment of the British mind in this era, by fond hopes of Russian inspiration, and by sedulous attention from collectivistic thinkers. Dean Inge compresses it all into his best essay, "Our Present Discontents," in the first volume of *Outspoken Essays*. These were the days of Fabian intellectual hegemony, when social radicalism at last began to force its way into Oxford and Cambridge; these were the fruits of idealistic speculation of the sort Lord Keynes describes among the young men gathered round Professor G. E. Moore: "We repudiated all versions of the doctrine of original sin, of there being insane and irrational springs of wickedness in most men. We were not aware that civilisation was a thin and precarious crust erected by the personality and the will of a very few, and only maintained by rules and conventions skillfully put across and guilefully preserved. We had no respect for traditional wisdom or the restraints of custom....As cause and consequence of our general state of mind we completely misunderstood human nature, including our own."[47]

A few of the younger generation had seen through this pose of negation: T. E. Hulme, for instance, who died in the War. The democratic ideology, said Hulme, is really a body of middle-class thought originating in the eighteenth century, and has no true connection with the working-class movement. The revolutionary impulse of our times, inflamed by this union of eighteenth-century aspiration with the new proletarian discontent, cannot bring forth social life, being itself senile. "Liberal Socialism is still living on the remains of middle-class thought of the last century. When vulgar thought of today is pacifist, rationalist, and hedonist, and in being so believes itself to be expressing the inevitable convictions of the instructed and emancipated man, it has all the pathos of marionettes in a play, dead things gesticulating as though they were alive. Our younger novelists, like those Roman fountains in which water pours from the mouth of a human mask, gush as though spontaneously from the depths of their own being, a muddy romanticism that has in reality come through a very long pipe."[48] But the Fabian creed continued to be propagated, penetrating steadily to new strata of society; and presently it found expression through the Left Book Club, and through the neglected or embittered schoolteacher, too often himself representative of that intellectual proletariat which is the peculiar product of modern economies and modern humanitarianism.*

Lord Birkenhead (F. E. Smith), in the year he died, published a half-whimsical prophecy entitled *The World in 2030 A.D.* Whether taken seriously or not, it is an odd book to be written by a Tory; for the world of 2030 A.D., as Birkenhead imagined it, would have eliminated disease, war, poverty—and, substantially, human nature. It would be a world ruled by the psychologist and the statistician, practicing ectogenesis, living on synthetic nutriment, emancipated from every vestige of mystery and the old web of individuality. It would be the dream of Bentham—or, to some, the chasm of the covetous, in Dante's Fourth Circle, where of all the lost infernal creatures, these are most terribly stripped of personality, forever nameless:

---

*Colm Brogan's schoolmaster of this description, in *The Democrat at the Supper Table*, is worthy of Peacock or Holmes or Mallock.

That ignoble life,
Which made them vile before, now makes them dark,
And to all knowledge indiscernible.

George Saintsbury, passing two unknown men on a bridge, was startled to hear one of them tell his companion, "There goes the biggest Tory in England." His nameless critic was accurate: Saintsbury was the most forthright inheritor of Toryism among all the thinking men of the 'twenties. And Professor Saintsbury, writing of the Benthamite and socialistic utopias like the society Lord Birkenhead suggested, found them hideous and dismaying:

Put away all thought of the crime and agony which would have to be gone through in order to bring about the Socialist Utopia; get it some-how brought about by fairy agency; could there, even then, be anything more loathsome than one wide waste of proletariat-Cocqcigrue comfort; everybody as good as the President; everybody as "well educated" as everybody else; everybody stationed, rationed, regulated by some kind of abstract "State"—as equal, and really as free, as pigs in a sty, and not much better deserving the name of man, or the manly chances of position, possession, genius, ancestry, and all that differentiates us from the brutes?[49]

Here beckons the alternative to a conservative society. Except for the possibility of providential retribution upon human presumption, taking the shape of frightful war, the conservative cast of mind remains the only effective barrier to the triumph of this new existence.

XII

Critical Conservatism:
Babbitt, More, Santayana

If this catastrophe of our publick liberty should be miraculously delayed or prevented, still we shall change. With the augmentation of wealth, there will be an increase of the numbers who may choose a literary leisure. Literary curiosity will become one of the new appetites of the nation; and as luxury advances, no appetite will be denied. After some ages we shall have many poor and a few rich, many grossly ignorant, a considerable number learned, and a few eminently learned. Nature, never prodigal of her gifts, will produce some men of genius, who will be admired and imitated.
                —Fisher Ames, "American Literature"

B Y THE BEGINNING of the First World War, the United States in some degree fulfilled Ames' prophecy. An expansive and complacent democracy, luxurious and often bored, exhibiting great poverty and great wealth but too little of that modest private security its founders had designed, in which nearly everyone was schooled and almost no one educated, had become the most powerful state of the century—indeed, of the ages, perhaps. As a nation, the Americans were rich; but true leisure remained a scarce commodity, little commended, sometimes despised; and therefore it is surprising that this era was dignified by a body of philosophical and literary criticism more substantial than any in previous American history—commensurate, indeed, with the best in English thought and letters. A mature nation, however scornful of intellectual attainments, could not evade the obligation to tolerate a few men of ideas.

Three of these men, pre-eminently, were conservative thinkers, rowing against the vertiginous social currents of the Harding and Coolidge and Hoover years. Two, Irving Babbitt and Paul Elmer More, were inheritors of the Puritan mind of New England, even though they transcended that severe tradition; and the third, George Santayana, really a cosmopolitan, reared in the Catholic faith and proud of his Spanish blood, still was influenced powerfully by the New England genius. Massachusetts and her neighbors were almost insignificant on the map of the United States, now, and their congressional representation was scarcely greater; but still they leavened a nation which often treated civilization as no more than a material fabric.

These years of vulgarity and presumption produced, or provoked, other conservative thinkers, as well. It would be interesting to write of Ralph Adams Cram, a great architect and an heir to the Romantics, who spoke up for Henry Adams' medievalism; or of Albert Jay Nock, who venerated four oddly-assorted thinkers —Burke, Jefferson, Herbert Spencer, and Henry George—and wrote that serenely contemptuous autobiography, *Memoirs of a Superfluous Man*, which is likely to be an enduring conservative influence in American thought; or the Southern Agrarians, among them Donald Davidson and Allen Tate, who endeavored to remind America of the virtues of the Old South. Even H.L. Mencken had his conservative side, displayed with eccentric virulence in *Notes on Democracy*. There was a conservative press, of sorts, superior to the vulgarized conservatism of the daily newspapers and the slick magazines: certain Southern quarterlies, and the short-lived *Bookman*, and the equally evanescent *American Review*. If this book pretended to be a history of American intellectual movements, much ought to be said, also, about the revival of Thomism in the universities. But this book is not such a history—instead, only an essay suggesting the progress of certain conservative ideas; and so Babbitt, More, and Santayana are chosen here, somewhat arbitrarily, as the most significant representatives of the American conservative impulse after 1918.

If one were compelled to select a practical American politician in either great party, during this century, who recognized a consistent system of conservative or radical ideas, where would he turn? Theodore Roosevelt, young or old, stood chiefly for expansion and Teddy, as Henry Adams said; Cleveland really had been a better conservative. William Howard Taft was a passable president and a good chief justice, but no philosopher. Henry Cabot Lodge, the pupil of Adams, was an able writer and a shrewd politician, but nothing higher. Woodrow Wilson, who read Burke, was a maze of contradictions. The elder Senator Robert Taft was bold enough to call himself a "liberal conservative," but most party leaders of recent years have shied at any system of thought; like Franklin Roosevelt, they have fled from principle with the consummate agility of men who are enamored of their popularity. Yet as political philosophy decayed among the politicians, it flourished among the professors: Babbitt, More, and Santayana, none of whom ever entered practical politics, looked upon the turbid confusion of American society and charted its currents. More and Babbitt hoped to assist in a spiritual regeneration of American life; in them, the dismayed aloofness of Henry Adams was succeeded by dogged endeavor to achieve conservative moral reform.

Conceivably it is an ominous sign for any society—Burke might have thought so—when men of letters must take up the burden which a dwindling remnant of old-fashioned philosophical statesmen have resigned. Whether this is true or not, certainly the conservative elements in a nation are menaced when rural population commences to decline; and that significant trend began in 1916, in which year the American farm population (although almost from the commencement of the Republic it had been declining relative to the total population) rose to its peak of nearly thirty-three million persons and began to slide downward in numbers, absolutely and apparently irretrievably. Rural virtues and loyalties, together with the influence and vigor of the small towns, were yielding to the social centralization that the Adams brothers had loathed and predicted, to the industrialism which had risen alongside democracy and which now threatened to master its comrade. The America of Jefferson and John Adams was being effaced; Hamilton's scheme was triumphant, after all, though Hamilton might have been aghast at his creation's smug and grossly intolerant face. It was a society dominated by hazy sentimentality and concrete appetite, waking to knowledge of its own awful strength, ready to patronize or to lord it over the rest of the world, afraid of responsiblity, impatient of admonition. Could it be restrained from destroying its own past, shattering its own constitution, and then turning upon the other nations to enforce its vague aspiration toward a general materialistic civilization, secular and uniform, infatuated with mediocrity, sick with the ruin of leadership? Twentieth-century America was incomparably stronger than Jacobin France, and different both in objective and in structure; yet if conservatives could not succeed in directing or softening these waves of social force, the consequences to civilization might be more overwhelming than those of the French Revolution. This is a problem beyond the resources of politicians; it can be comprehended in nothing less than moral philosophy and religious faith, if comprehended at all. We are struggling with it still, harder than before; and the great contest in American society is the assault of the forces of moral and political aggrandizement upon the forces of moral and political stability.

The belligerent expansive and naturalistic tendencies of the era found their philosophical apologist in John Dewey. No philosopher's style is more turgid; but Dewey's postulates, for all that, are simple and quite comprehensive. He commenced with a thoroughgoing naturalism, like Diderot's and Holbach's, denying the whole realm of spiritual values: nothing exists but physical sensation, and life has no aims but physical satisfaction. He proceeded to a utilitarianism which carried Benthamite ideas to their logical culmination, making material production the goal and standard of human endeavor; the past is trash, the future unknowable, and the present the only concern of the moralist. He propounded a theory of education derived from Rousseau, declaring that the child is born with "a *natural* desire to do, to give out, to serve," and should be encouraged to follow his own bent, teaching being simply the opening of paths. He advocated a sentimental egalitarian collectivism with social dead-level its ideal; and he capped this structure with Marxist economics, looking forward to a future devoted to efficient material production for the satisfaction of the masses, a planners' state. Every radicalism since 1789 found its place in John Dewey's system; and this destructive intellectual compound became prodigiously popular, in short order, among that distraught crowd of the semi-educated and among people of more serious pretensions who found themselves lost in a withered world that Darwin and Faraday had severed from its roots. Intensely flattering to the presumptuousness of the modern mind, thoroughly contemptuous of authority, Dewey's books were a mirror of twentieth-century discontent; and the gray haze of the Utilitarian future toward which Dewey led the rising generation was not immediately repellent to a people who had submitted themselves to the lordship of sensation. Veneration was dead in Dewey's universe; indiscriminate emancipation was cock of the walk. This was the imperialistic craving of America and the twentieth century given a philosophic mask. Babbitt, More, and Santayana, in their several ways, defied this apotheosis of appetite.

2

As if they recognized in him their most formidable adversary, writers of the Left have attacked Irving Babbitt with a vituperation somewhat startling when one remembers that this abuse is directed against a contemplative Harvard professor of comparative literature. Oscar Cargill, in his *Intellectual America*, exclaims furiously, "We know not in what superstitious eighteenth century sectarianism Babbitt was reared, but his lack of salivary control at the mere mention of *science* or *democracy* suggests the rural hymn singer and sermon note-taker, rather than the cosmopolitan.'' Harold Laski, in *The American Democracy,* declares that Babbitt won no pupils. Ernest Hemingway, fuming at Babbitt's faith in human dignity, says he wants to know how genteel Babbitt will be when he dies. As a matter of fact, Babbitt was a big, earnest Ohioan who worked on a Western ranch in his youth, studied at Harvard and at Paris, wandered afoot in Spain, fought against the currents other men rode to success, and died with remarkable fortitude, working to the last to convince America that man cannot remain human unless he restrains his appetites. Although friendly to religion, he remained suspicious of all churches; if he detested the corruption of American principles, still he is one of the most thoroughly native of American writers. Aristotle, Burke, and John Adams were his mentors in social thought. Founding the school of American philosophy which he called humanism, he left behind him an influence which may endure long after Laski has been nearly forgotten at the London School of Economics. In him, American conservatism attains maturity.

The heart and essence of Babbitt's intellectual system, says his ally Paul Elmer More, is contained in a footnote to Babbitt's criticism of Rousseau in *Literature and the American College,* his first book:

The greatest of vices according to Buddha is the lazy yielding to the impulses of temperament (*pamâda*); the greatest virtue (*appamâda*) is the opposite of this, the awakening from the sloth and lethargy of the senses, the constant exercise of the active will. The last words of the dying Buddha to his disciples were an exhortation to practice this virtue unremittingly.

The disciplinary arts of *humanitas*—that exercise of Will which distinguishes man from beast—are dying of neglect in this era; contemptuous of the realm of spirit which Buddha and Plato alike describe, modern man is corrupted by a gross naturalism, reducing all things to a single sensate level. If man forgets the dual nature of existence, he stifles his higher self, which is ruled by the law for man, as contrasted with the law for thing which governs the senses; thus he commits suicide. Having destroyed his higher self, a man dooms his lower self too, for without the directing power of Will, he tumbles into the anarchy of the beasts. In our time the task for the humanist is to remind society of its spiritual reality. Babbitt and his colleagues are merciless toward the humanitarian, as distinguished from the true humanist. Humanitarians in the tradition of Bacon and Rousseau are sentimentalists who think that all human problems may be resolved by the application of physical remedies. The humanitarian's indiscriminate utilitarian method engenders hostility toward that hierarchy of values which erects distinctions between saint and sinner, scholar and barbarian. Intent upon an egalitarian condition for society, the humanitarian tries to extirpate those spiritual essences in man which make possible truly *human* life.

Irving Babbitt's enemies promptly labelled this advocacy of spiritual self-discipline and subordination of the senses "Puritanism," as if that were *per se* its condemnation. And it is Puritanical, the creed of humanism—in the sense that Plato and Augustine were Puritans. Babbitt and More rejected Calvinism with abhorrence as a system corrosively deterministic; their faith rested upon the premise of free will; and yet it remains true enough that something of the old New England austerity lived in both these Middle Westerners and gave them the iron resolution to speak up for dualism and the life of spirit in an era dedicated to the senses and sentimentality. The humanist, wrote Babbitt in his first book, "believes that the man of to-day, if he does not, like the man of the past, take on the yoke of a definite doctrine and discipline, must at least do inner obeisance to something higher than his ordinary self, whether he calls this something God, or, like the man of the Far East, calls it his higher Self, or simply the Law. Without this inner principle of restraint man can only oscillate violently between opposite extremes, like Rousseau, who said that for him there was 'no intermediary term between everything and nothing.' "[1] The saving of civilization is contingent upon the revival of something like the doctrine of original sin.

For a student of social conservatism, the most important book among Babbitt's seven volumes is *Democracy and Leadership*; and since (as More observes) Babbitt was a "rotary" writer, touching upon the essentials of his system in each of his books rather than developing his ideas in sequence, a close examination of this courageous essay provides a tolerable view of the whole of his humanistic system. It was published in 1924, when American millionaires pushed up like mushrooms; and Babbitt was as contemptuous of millionaires as he was of Jacobins. "A few more Harrimans and we are undone," he had written sixteen years earlier. For he knew that the Rockefellers and Harrimans represented the same forces as did John Dewey: they stood for the delusion that men can be improved upon utilitarian principles. If, as Lloyd George said, the future will be taken up even more than is the present with economic problems—why, the future will be superficial. That naturalism which began at least as early as the Renaissance, was made "scientific" by Bacon, and was popularized by Rousseau, now has progressed to a degree which imperils the structure of social life. The old bulwarks of prejudice and prescription have been demolished by the popularization of naturalistic ideas in every segment of society; and the humanist can counter this radicalism only by winning men to an alternative system of ideas. "Progress according to the natural law has been so rapid since the rise of the Baconian movement that it has quite captivated man's imagination and stimulated him to still further concentration and effort along naturalistic lines. The very magic of the word progress seems to blind him to the failure of progress according to the human law," Babbitt had written in 1919.[2] Humanists now must remind the world that there is law for man and law for thing, or resign themselves to catastrophe. Forms and restrictions will not keep society from destroying itself, if ideas are lacking: "The attempt to oppose external and mechanical barriers to the freedom of the spirit will create in the long run an atmosphere of stuffiness and smugness, and nothing is more intolerable than smugness. Men were guillotined in the French Revolution, as Bagehot suggests, simply because either they or their ancestors had been smug.

Inert acceptance of tradition and routine will be met sooner or later by the cry of Faust: *Hinaus ins Freie!*"[3] Perhaps no generation ever was more smug than Babbitt's; and the very radicals among his audience, enveloped in their own interesting unconscious smugness, quite certain of evolutionary proletarian bliss, called Professor Babbitt an obscurant because he predicted the coming of chaos.

Rousseau, first among the theorists of radical democracy, the most eminent contemner of civilization, gave the wrong answers to the right questions. He denied the duality of human experience, and relied upon the régime of the senses as the means to general happiness. Rousseau's (and Whitman's) sentimental dream of democratic fraternity is, like utilitarian theories, a particular aspect of humanitarianism, or the naturalistic movement. Humanitarianism omits the keystone of the arch of humanity, which is Will. "As against expansionists of every kind, I do not hesitate to affirm that what is specifically human in man and ultimately divine is a certain quality of will, a will that is felt in its relation to his ordinary self as a will to refrain."[4] This power, peculiar to man, of invoking a check upon the impulses of sense, even upon the impulses of reason, is what makes him *human*. The surrender of Rousseau to desire, the surrender of the Utilitarians to avarice, end in the dehumanization of our race. If social reform is substituted for self-reform, emotional anarchy presently undoes every project of the humanitarian. In *Literature and the American College,* Babbitt had distinguished between humanist and humanitarian; in *The Masters of Modern French Criticism,* he had analyzed the decay of standards and the rise of relativism; in *The New Laokoon,* he had examined the anarchy in literature and art that is consequent upon decline in standards; in *Rousseau and Romanticism,* he had said that the imagination holds the balance of power between the higher and lower natures of man, and that Rousseau's idyllic imagination corrupted the aspirations of modern man. Now, in *Democracy and Leadership,* he was endeavoring "to show that genuine leadership, good or bad, there will always be, and that democracy becomes a menace to civilization when it seeks to evade the truth...On the appearance of leaders who have recovered in some form the truths of the inner life and repudiated the errors of naturalism may depend the very survival of Western civilization." *Democracy and Leadership* is perhaps the most penetrating work on politics ever written by an American—and this precisely because it is not properly a political treatise, but really a work of moral philosophy. "When studied with any degree of thoroughness," Babbitt wrote in his first paragraph, "the economic problem will be found to run into the political problem, the political problem into the philosophical problem, and the philosophical problem itself to be almost indissolubly bound up at last with the religious problem." Many political scientists have paid small attention to this book. But if science is more than the accumulation and classification of physical data, Babbitt's view of politics is science upon a high plane.

Modern politics, like modern civilization in general, says Babbitt, long has been exposed to the disintegrating influence of the naturalist. "The naturalist no longer looks on man as subject to a law of his own distinct from that of the material order—a law, the acceptance of which leads, on the religious level, to the miracles of other-worldliness that one finds in Christians and Buddhists at their best, and the acceptance of which, in this world, leads to the subduing of the ordinary self and its spontaneous impulses to the law of measure that one finds in Confucianists and Aristotelians." In politics, the father of this modern denial of a higher will—*i.e.*, a moral system to which man can appeal from his own lower nature—is Machiavelli, who, with the aversion all naturalists display for dualism, would not allow men to possess a divided allegiance, fealty to both a mundane state and the City of God. Yet Machiavelli and his followers are not true realists: "The Nemesis, or divine judgment, or whatever one may term it, that sooner or later overtakes those who transgress the moral law, is not something that one has to take on authority, either Greek or Hebraic; it is a matter of keen observation." With Hobbes, this negation of morality enters English political thought, and we continue to suffer from its poison. "If one is to refute

Machiavelli and Hobbes, one must show that there is some universal principle that tends to unite men even across national frontiers, a principle that continues to act even when their egoistic impulses are no longer controlled by the laws of some particular state supported by its organized force.'' The utilitarian temper encouraged by Locke further degraded the venerable concept of public office as a consecrated trust, and ''if the aristocratic principle continues to give way to the equalitarian denial of the need of leadership, parliamentary government may ultimately become impossible.''

Upon the ruins of the medieval idea of government which Machiavelli and his followers undermined, Rousseau erected a kind of quasi-religious political contrivance, supplied with its own myths from his idyllic imagination, inspired by the notion that pity has primacy among human emotions. The sentimental doctrine of the General Will, which Rousseau produced to mortar this system together, from the beginning was full of menace. ''By this device Rousseau gets rid of the problem that has chiefly preoccupied political thinkers in the English tradition—how, namely, to safeguard the freedom of the individual or of minorities against a triumphant and despotic majority.'' Rousseau's fallacious new dualism, that which postulates the citizen in his private capacity and the citizen as a member of the community, may provide the apology for a tyranny more crushing than anything Rousseau himself denounced.

Burke, continues Babbitt, perceived all this; and Burke knew, better than anyone else, that the only kind of conservatism which can survive is an imaginative conservatism. But the strong tendency of the times impaired his appeal to the traditional conservative symbols of the imagination: Baconian love of novelty and change, discovery piled on discovery, the hope that we are moving toward some ''far-off divine event,'' undid the defenses of prejudice and prescription and ''a wisdom above reflection'' upon which Burke relied to save true liberalism. Modern conservatives, or liberals, must find other instruments and methods.

These new instruments of conservation will need to be ingenious; for they must be employed against the tremendous imperialistic instinct of modern democracy. It is an error (as Mirabeau said) to suppose that democracy and imperialism are inimical; they will hunt together in our time, as they did in Periclean Athens and Revolutionary France. Japan, if converted to democracy, will be many times more dangerous than when governed by a conservative aristocracy, content with the present arrangement of things. Eight years later, Babbitt returned to this theme in *On Being Creative*, taking note of André Siegfried's dread of the American's "consciousness, still more dangerous, of his 'duties' toward humanity."[5] Imperialism is one aspect of man's ancient expansive conceit, which the Greeks knew would bring hubris, and then blindness, and finally nemesis. "Man never rushes forward so confidently, it would sometimes seem, as when he is on the very brink of the abyss." Humility, which Burke ranked high among the virtues, is the only effectual restraint upon this congenital vanity; yet our world has nearly forgotten the nature of humility. Submission to the dictates of humility formerly was made palatable to man by the doctrine of grace; that elaborate doctrine has been overwhelmed by modern presumption, the self-reliance which radiates from Rousseau and Emerson; "and it is not as clear as one might wish that European civilization can survive the collapse of this doctrine." Babbitt himself never embraced the idea of grace; but he perceived its transcendent importance, as had Pascal and the Jansenists, and his frequent return to this topic foreshadows the fascination of Christian novelists and apologists with the doctrine of grace during recent decades.

With the decline of the doctrine of grace and with the theological confusion that the Reformation admitted, a doctrine of work began to take its place—but a concept almost wholly divorced from its old theological namesake. Francis Bacon expounded this exaltation of labor above piety and contemplation; Locke carried it to its utilitarian extreme in his Second Treatise; Adam Smith echoed him, Ricardo enlarged upon the idea, Marx reduced "work" to the purely quantitative view. "The attempt to apply the utilitarian-sentimental conception of work and at the same time to eliminate competition has resulted in Russia in a ruthless despotism, on the one hand, and in a degrading servitude, on the other." How are we to escape from this fallacious concept of the nature of work? The humanitarians are guilty of participation in this error: "Even when they do not fall into the cruder quantitative fallacies, they conceive of work in terms of the natural law and of the outer world and not in terms of the inner life."

But "work" really is a thing very different from this; and Babbitt appeals to Buddha and Plato for his definition. True work, the higher work, is labor of the spirit, self-reform; and this brings us to the nature of Justice. "The Platonic definition of justice as doing one's own work or minding one's own business has perhaps never been surpassed." The only true freedom, Babbitt adds, is the freedom to work. "It is in fact the quality of a man's work that should determine his place in the hierarchy that every civilized society requires." They who work with their minds should rank above those who work with their hands; but men engaged in a genuinely ethical working are higher still. Any real civilization must relieve certain individuals of the necessity for working with their hands, so that they may participate in that leisure which is an indispensable preparation for leadership.

These leaders in spirit and mind must be taught to rise superior to material possessions; and this cannot be accomplished without a genuinely ethical or humanistic working. "To proclaim equality on some basis that requires no such working will result ironically. For example, this country committed itself in the Declaration of Independence to the doctrine of natural equality. The type of individualism that was thus encouraged has led to monstrous inequalities and, with the decline of traditional standards, to the rise of a raw plutocracy...The remedy for such a failure of the man at the top does not lie, as the agitator would have us believe, in inflaming the desires of the man at the bottom; nor again in substituting for real justice some phantasmagoria of social justice." Such substitution generally brings fanatical attacks on property itself, and presently upon thrift and industry; it provokes suppression of competition, which is necessary to rouse man from his native indolence. From the confusion of decreeing an absolute equality without any properly understood ethical basis, America never has recovered: "It is not yet clear that it is going to be possible to combine universal suffrage with the degree of safety for the institution of property that genuine justice and genuine civilization both require." Inflation of the currency will be the most common and subtle form of this peril.

Every man must find his happiness in work or not at all. Yet in our time the mass of men are bored with their labor—a consequence, partially, of the humanitarians' misunderstanding of the essence of work. Their inability to define love and liberty has brought us to similar bafflement in these vast matters. In substance, the humanitarians' failure is the product of their ignorance of man's ethical will, of the fact that his only real peace is spiritual peace. In our pupilage to the humanitarians, we have lost sight of standards; upon the restoration of standards depends the preservation of our civilized life and our humanity.

"Commercialism is laying its great greasy paw upon everything (including the irresponsible quest of thrills); so that, whatever democracy may be theoretically, one is sometimes tempted to define it practically as standardized and commercialized melodrama...One is inclined, indeed, to ask, in certain moods, whether the net result of the movement that has been sweeping the Occident for several generations may not be a huge mass of standardized mediocrity; and whether in this country in particular we are not in danger of producing in the name of democracy one of the most trifling brands of the human species that the world has yet seen." What is it that has persuaded America to accept the quantitative test in all things, so that "the American reading his Sunday paper in a state of lazy collapse is perhaps the most perfect symbol of the triumph of quantity over quality that the world has yet seen"? The loss of true leadership is both cause and effect of our deficiency in standards. "One should, therefore, in the interests of democracy itself seek to substitute the doctrine of the right man for the doctrine of the rights of man." Frequently democracy has been no more than an attempt to eliminate the qualitative and selective principles in favor of abstract theories of the general will. In the United States, this struggle between true and false liberalism, qualitative and quantitative democracy, has been substantially the contest between Washington's liberty and Jefferson's liberty. Jefferson wished to emancipate men from external control; but he never understood, as Burke knew, how power without and power within always must remain in ratio; so that every diminution of power on the part of the state, unless it is to result in injury to society, should be accompanied by an increase of self-control in individuals. The Epicurean and speculative Jefferson disliked the whole idea of rigid self-discipline, to which the house of Adams was devoted; and Jefferson's example encouraged the expansive and coarsely individualistic tendencies of Americans. Judicial control, uncongenial to Jefferson in either its political or its ethical form, remains a chief guarantee of our liberty; but it has been terribly injured by our proclivity toward imperialism and quantitative judgment.

The Federal Constitution and the Supreme Court and other checks upon immediate popular impulse are to the nation what the higher will is to the individual. Where our society succeeds, usually it is in consequence of this restraining influence in our thought and political structure; where it fails, often it is in consequence of our sentimental humanitarianism: "We are trying to make, not the Ten Commandments, but humanitarianism work— and it is not working. If our courts are so ineffective in punishing crime, a chief reason is that they do not have the support of public opinion, and this is because the public is so largely composed of people who have set up sympathy for the underdog as a substitute for all the other virtues." The utilitarian energumen, with his emphasis on "outer working," moves further and further toward a dehumanized society: "The type of efficiency that our master commercialists pursue requires that a multitude of men should be deprived of their specifically human attributes, and become mere cogs in some vast machine. At the present rate even the grocer in a remote country town will soon not be left so much initiative as is needed to fix the price of a pound of butter."

Where are we to discover the leaders who may redeem us from all this? Their great merit must be humility; nothing else will serve. Thus the scientist is disqualified, for we know his presumption; and the artist-aristocrat would be quite as disagreeable. To trust in the divinity of the average, dispensing with leadership altogether —a popular notion—is worse folly still; and the fickleness of the public has made even the radical reformer lose faith in this dream. No, in this hour when our need for leadership is desperate, when our power extends across oceans and gropes blindly for lack of direction, it will not save us to "evolve under the guidance of Mr. H.L. Mencken into second-rate Nietzscheans." Leadership can be restored only by the slow and painful process of developing moral gravity and intellectual seriousness, turning back to the strength of traditional doctrines—the honesty with which they face the fact of evil. Our spiritual indolence can be overcome only by a re-examination of first principles. "The basis on which the whole structure of the new ethics has been reared is, as we have seen, the assumption that the significant struggle between good and evil is not in the individual but in society. If we wish once more to build securely, we may have to recover in some form the idea of 'the civil war in the cave.' "

We need to examine our definition of work—which depends upon our definition of nature. What we mean by "liberty," in turn, depends upon our meaning for "work." Our regeneration is contingent, then, upon resort to Socratic methods, involving these definitions and those of "justice" and "peace." This is no mere question of the Schools. "The time may come, if indeed it has not come already, when men will be justified in asserting true freedom, even, it may be, at the cost of their lives, against the monstrous encroachments of the materialistic state." We must purge ourselves of the notion that pure equality is consonant with liberty and humility. The need for restoration of standards in our life means that we shall have to ascertain some ethical centre. The ethical state is possible, human nature being susceptible to right example. But our ethical centre must be more than our current adulation of "service." The real leader is no mere humanitarian; his sanctions come from will and conscience.

When all is said, we are brought back to the question of Will. The "idealist" and "realist" schools of political thought, both rooted in naturalism, will not do for our time. Anyone who transcends naturalism "ceases in about the same measure to be either a humanitarian idealist or a Machiavellian realist. He becomes aware of a quality of will that distinguishes man from physical nature and is yet natural in the sense that it is a matter of immediate perception and not of outer authority." Is there not a power independent of our senses, independent even of our ordinary reason, to which we may appeal against our very selves? In sober fact, do men have souls, or do they not? Upon one's solution of this inquiry rests the basis of politics; for if men do not possess souls, if there is no higher will, then they may as well be treated as parts of a machine—indeed, they cannot be treated otherwise. Babbitt contemplates politics upon a height too giddy for many men to ascend; but his postulates granted, politics cannot be discussed satisfactorily upon any other level.

One plane is higher still, Babbitt remarks at the end of his desultory but noble book: and that is the plane of grace. "Traditionally the Christian has associated his liberty and his faith in a higher will with grace." But Babbitt cannot persuade himself to clamber to that crag; he is not really sure it exists; and he endeavors to express his system in "terms of work," ethical work, the activity of the higher nature of man, as distinguished from communion with God. He stops short of Burke, therefore, and Hooker, and the Schoolmen. Paul Elmer More came to believe that one dare not halt at the level of work, but must press on for security to religious faith.

Justice has not been done here to Babbitt. His great erudition is only suggested; his intricate mind is obscured by the curtness of this summary. He joined the broken links between politics and morals, and that is a work of genius. He knew that the conservation of the old things we love must be founded upon valid ideas of the highest order, if conservatism is to withstand naturalism and its political progeny. "The conservative nowadays," he ob-

serves in one of his numerous moments of sharpshooting prescience, "is interested in conserving property for its own sake, and
not, like Burke, in conserving it because it is an almost indispensable support of personal liberty, a genuinely spiritual thing." Babbitt's teachings already have had some influence in guiding
American conservative thinkers to positions more tenable. His influence may grow, attracting to the austere cause of Work and
Will a succession of the men whom a nation economically mature
must find if that nation is to be something more than a machine.

3

On North Avenue in Cambridge, once, Babbitt suddenly
clenched his hands and exclaimed to Paul Elmer More, "Great
God, man, are you a Jesuit in disguise?" Babbitt endeavored all
his life to teach himself tolerance toward churches; but it was otherwise with More; and that far-ranging critic remarks, with something like a smile, "I have never been able to answer the question
satisfactorily."[6]

Though he was born in Missouri, More stands conspicuous in
the tradition of New England thought—as, indeed, so much that
is called "Middle Western" today is really the New England mind
and character transplanted. With a sense of dedication rare in his
generation, while still a young man he retired to the hamlet of
Shelburne, in New Hampshire, so that he might find the leisure
and the detachment necessary for contending intelligently with our
modern complexity; and then returning into the world, intellectually armored, very like a prophet, he struggled as lecturer and
essayist and editor of the *Nation* against the pragmatism of James,
the naturalism of Dewey, the sentimentality of the socialists, the
presumption of a people who had forgotten the truth of dualism.
He disciplined himself into mastery of English prose style; and
as a critic of ideas, perhaps there has not been his peer in England or America since Coleridge. "All differences of opinion,"
Cardinal Manning once observed, "are at bottom theological."
More's adherence to this principle became his great strength; com-

mencing as a thorough skeptic, he ended as the most eminent Anglican thinker in the history of the United States, possibly the most
learned American theologian of any communion.

The first of the eleven volumes of More's *Shelburne Essays* was
published in 1904. Through this glowing critical series, through
the five volumes of *The Greek Tradition,* through the *New Shelburne
Essays* that were published in the last decade of his life, runs a stern
continuity: the insistence that for our salvation in this world and
the other, we must look to things of the spirit, accept the duality
of human nature, remind ourselves that the present moment is
of small consequence in the mysterious system of being. If, with
William James, we resign ourselves to the stream of time and
change, we invite inner and outer catastrophe:

Sometimes as I consider with myself how this illusion daily more and
more enthralls and impoverishes our mental life by cutting off from it
all the rich experience of the past, it is as though we were at sea in a
vessel, while a fog thickened, closing in upon our vision with ever narrower circle, blotting out the far-flashing lights of the horizon and the
depths of the sky, throwing a pall upon the very waves about us, until
we move forward through a sullen obscurity, unaware of any other
traveller upon that sea, save when through the fog the sound of a threatening alarm beats upon the ear.[7]

Much read in Burke and Newman, More understood that when
generation thus ceases to link spiritually with generation, first civilization and then human existence itself must shrivel. And men will
ignore the past and the future, he came to believe, without a pervasive belief in the reality of the transcendent. Man must lead a
double life, More wrote in concluding the first volume of *Shelburne
Essays,* balancing between law for man and law for thing, never
losing the distinction between his public and his private duty. Our
modern social confusion, intellectually considered, is the consequence of confounding the sphere of private morality with the
sphere of public activity. This is the enormous error of the
humanitarians. When the religious impulse is contracted to mere

"brotherhood of man," fratricide is not far distant. Near the end of the third volume of the *New Shelburne Essays* (1936), More repeated this declaration: "The one effective weapon of the Church in her campaign against the unnecessary evils of society, her one available instrument for bringing into play some measure of true justice as distinct from the ruthless law of competition and from the equally ruthless will to power of the proletariat, is through the restoration in the individual human soul of a sense of responsibility extending beyond the grave."[8] *Pleonexia,* the "perpetual and restless desire of power after power, that ceaseth only in death," can be restrained by no force in this world—solely by an inner human check which is of supernatural origin.

Its religious instincts suppressed or bewildered, our society must find its way back to permanence, or die. Modern romanticism and modern science, though superficially inimical, share a disastrous impressionism; for both have surrendered to the theory of ceaseless flux, with no principle of judgment except the shifting pleasure of the individual. This is Pragmatism, the cancer of our intellect. In such times, the man of conscience must declare boldly that he is a reactionary; otherwise formlessness in philosophy and letters will become formlessness in society, impotent acceptance of change, leading to the individualism of Cobden or the collectivism of Marx—in either case, the stifling of civilization by material forces; or, this bulwark failing in turn, then anarchy. "The saying has gone abroad that strength means joy in change and that he who would question change is reactionary and effeminate." Yet is a reactionary nothing more than a coward before innovation, no more than a slave of the Past? "Reaction may be, and in the true sense is, something utterly different from this futile dreaming; it is essentially to answer action with action, to oppose to the welter of circumstance the force of discrimination and selection, to direct the aimless tide of change by reference to the co-existing law of the immutable fact, to carry the experiences of the past into the diverse impulses of the present, and so to move forward in an orderly progression. If any young man, feeling now within himself the power of accomplishment, hesitates to be called a reactionary, in the better use of this term, because of the charge of effeminacy, let him take courage."[9]

A manual to candid and intelligent reaction against the philosophy of flux is *Aristocracy and Justice,* the ninth volume of the *Shelburne Essays* (1915). How are men to be saved from themselves? How are they to be saved from their drifting lassitude, the product of a facile evolutionary philosophy, which must end (if not arrested) in a catastrophe of which the war that began in 1914 is merely a foreshadowing? In the realm of society, men require an aristocracy to lead them aright. To acknowledge this aristocracy, we must be frankly and nobly reactionary. "We have the naked question to answer: How shall a society, newly shaking itself free from a disguised plutocratic régime, be guided to suffer the persuasion of a natural aristocracy which has none of the insignia of an old prescription to impose its authority?"[10] To persuade victorious democracy that it must resurrect aristocracy: this is the tremendous practical problem in our politics.

The cant phrase that "the cure of democracy is more democracy" lies; the real cure must be not more, but *better* democracy. Improvement never can come from the mass itself; it must be the work of natural aristocracy, which "does not demand the restoration of inherited privilege or a relapse into the crude dominion of money; it is not synonymous with oligarchy or plutocracy. It calls rather for some machinery or some social consciousness which shall ensure both the selection from among the community at large of the 'best' and the bestowal on them of 'power'; it is the true consummation of democracy." Our first step toward the creation or resuscitation of natural aristocracy ought to be a reform of our institutions of higher learning.

Like a great old tree, our society has been dying at the top. The educated classes are in danger of turning traitors to the civilization which sustains them—deluded by humanitarianism, perhaps ignorant of their own proper duties. "At other times the apprehension has been lest the combined forces of order might not be strong enough to withstand the ever-threatening inroads of those who envy barbarously or desire recklessly; whereas today the doubt is whether the natural champions of order themselves shall be found loyal to their trust, for they seem no longer to remember clearly the word of command that should unite them in leadership.''

Idealists like G. Lowes Dickinson count upon a ''slow, half-conscious detachment of all of them [the leaders of modern society] who have intelligence and moral force from the interest and active support of their class.''[11] (The Harrimans whom Babbitt contemned in one generation as the unabashed exemplars of utilitarian avarice become in the next generation zealots for the welfare state.) That decay of the venerable humanistic intellectual discipline in higher education, of which decadence President Eliot's innovations at Harvard are a symptom, is a chief cause of this bewilderment or treason of the clerisy. We have forgotten the Magna Carta of our education —Sir Thomas Elyot's *Boke Named the Governour*. ''The scheme of the humanist might be described in a word as a disciplining of the higher faculty of the imagination to the end that the student may behold, as it were in one sublime vision, the whole scale of being in its range from the lowest to the highest under the divine decree of order and subordination, without losing sight of the immutable veracity at the heart of all development, which 'is only the praise and surname of virtue.' This was no new vision, nor has it ever been quite forgotten. It was the whole meaning of religion to Hooker, from whom it passed into all that is best and least ephemeral in the Anglican Church. It was the basis, more modestly expressed, of Blackstone's conception of the British Constitution and of liberty under law. It was the kernel of Burke's theory of statecraft. It is the inspiration of the sublimer science, which accepts the hypothesis of evolution as taught by Darwin and Spencer, yet bows in reverence before the unnamed and incommensurate force lodged as a mystical purpose within the unfolding universe.''[12] Lacking such an education, men have no hold upon the past; they are at the mercy of every wind of doctrine.

For real liberty—the liberty of true distinction, not the fierce levelling freedom of envy—the leaders of society require a liberal education. With such a discipline, they can serve as a true natural aristocracy, mediating between plutocracy and egalitarian democracy. The soul of this humanistic discipline is study of the classics; they teach man the meaning of Time, and "confirm him in his better judgment against the ephemeral and vulgarizing solic- itations of the hour." When our universities and colleges devote themselves to turning out specialists and technicians and business- men, they deprive society of its intellectual aristocracy and, pres- ently, undermine the very social tranquillity upon which modern specialization and technical achievement are founded.

Yet the precise means of ensuring the life of a natural aristocracy is not so important a question as the principle upon which a true aristocracy will manage the affairs of mankind. That principle is Justice, and the existence of civilization hangs on this. But how may Justice be defined? More offers a series of definitions, with the aim of demolishing the sentimental term "social justice" which has been so useful an instrument to radicalism. Put very simply, justice is "the act of right distribution, the giving to each man his due"; but that, to have real meaning, requires further defini- tion of *right* and *due*. When we examine more closely the impulse called justice, we find that it is "the inner state of the soul when, under the command of the will to righteousness, reason guides and the desires obey"—or, briefly, "Justice is happiness, happi- ness is justice." What, then, is social justice? More condemns im- partially Nietzsche's "will to power" and its opposite, the humanitarian, socialistic ideal of absolute equality. Social justice, instead, is "such a distribution of power and privilege, and of property as the symbol and instrument of these, as at once will satisfy the distinctions of reason among the superior, and will not outrage the feelings of the inferior." No absolute rule exists for striking this balance, no more than there is any absolute code of morals for individual conduct; but the same criterion applies to it that is our means of approaching individual justice: "Social justice and personal justice both are measured by happiness." The legislator must distinguish nicely between superiority and egotism, special merit and public contentment. It is a work of mediation, of compromise, and we must resign ourselves to the fact that along with justice there always must remain some individual deprivation or scarcity, which we are too prone to call "injustice." We are not perfect or perfectible creatures; and if we would be in harmony with Nature, we must not damn the nature of things (like Porson trying to blow out the mirrored image of a candle-flame) and demand that absolute Justice which does not reside in this world.

Property, without which civilization cannot endure, is really "the magnifying of that natural injustice [the initial inequality of men] into that which you may deplore as unnatural injustice, but which is a fatal necessity, nevertheless. This is the truth, hideous if you choose to make it so to yourself, not without its benevolent aspect to those, whether the favorites of fortune or not, who are themselves true—ineluctable at least." Unless we call civilization a mistake, any attempt to ignore natural inequality and propertied inequality is sure to cause general unhappiness. "Security of property is the first and all-essential duty of a civilized community." Life is a primitive thing; we share it with the beasts; but property is the mark of man alone, the means of civilization; therefore, says More in a bold phrase which has infuriated his humanitarian opponents, "To the civilized man the *rights of property are more important than the right to life.*"

He goes farther still. So important is property to truly human existence, that even if men rob under cover of the laws (for no set of laws can be perfect), "It is better that legal robbery should exist along with the maintenance of law, than that legal robbery should be suppressed at the expense of law." For the worst thing which can happen to law is its over-extension, its expansion to fields in which it cannot be competent; then disrespect for law in all its capacities will become general. If you deny a fact, the fact will control you. This is true of property. "You may to a certain extent control it and make it subservient to the ideal nature of man; but the moment you deny its rights, or undertake to legislate in defiance of them, you may for a time unsettle the very foundations of society, you will certainly in the end render property your despot instead of your servant, and so produce a materialized and debased civilization."

When property is insecure, the spirit of materialism flourishes. In such times of want, intellectual leisure is denounced popularly as abnormal and anti-social; the scholar is detested. "There is something at once comical and vicious in the spectacle of those men of property who take advantage of their leisure to dream out vast benevolent schemes which would render their own self-satisfied career impossible." Private ownership, production, and distribution are indispensable to the progress of society; and we need to strengthen ourselves "against the insidious charms of a misapplied idealism." Transfer the ancient prerogatives of property to the labor which produces property, and our venerable institutions, the Church and the University most of all, are in terrible peril. "For if property is secure, it may be the means to an end, whereas if it is insecure it will be the end itself."

In a century when the aristocratic principle, the classical idea of justice, and the institution of property all are menaced, what effective stand can conservatives take? Great advantages are with the radicals—the seductions of flattery, the opportunism which deals with immediate material needs to the exclusion of distant considerations, the force of humanitarian sympathies. "It is not strange, therefore, that the history of England since the Revolution of 1688, with intervals of timid delay, has been the record of a gradual yielding to the steady thrust of opportunism." The conservative can appeal to the imagination of men; but he must be sure his own imagination is sound and true. The conservative must make certain of the rectitude of his own morality. He has now to contend against the New Morality, that vague but virulent social passion which, if it means anything, "means the reconstruction of life at the level of the gutter." Humanitarianism, usurping the place of the Church, endeavors to ignore the existence of Sin and to erect sympathy into a social theory, leaving individual responsibility out of account. Sympathy and justice are confounded.

Confronted with such disheartening odds, the conservative must retire into himself for a space, so that he will remember "that his nature is not simple and single, but dual," a reflection of incalculable ethical value. Within him is a truer self, an inner check, "unchanged amid continual change, of everlasting validity above the shifting values of the moment." Guided by this intuition, "he will know that the obligation to society is not the primal law and is not the source of personal integrity, but is secondary to personal integrity. He will believe that social justice is in itself desirable, but he will hold that it is far more important to preach first the responsibility of each man to himself for his own character." Abjuring cant, he will discover a fortitude which may yet suffice to defend the old morality against a collective and sentimental humanitarianism that, without conservative opposition, would devour its own sustenance incontinently.

And by way of conclusion, More undertakes a final definition of justice: "the Everlasting Morality of distinctions and of voluntary direction opposed to the so-called New Morality of drifting." Aristocratic leadership and a voluntary society are allied naturally; the morality of flux rapidly sweeps through the stage of humanitarianism into the stage of collective compulsion. Politics leads to morals.

Morals, in turn, must lead to religious faith. In the last volume of the *Shelburne Essays*, More suggests that fear is an inevitable factor in human conduct; and, religious fear absent, men soon become subject to fears of a description more immediate and more difficult to alleviate, the fear of class war, or of destitution, or of subjugation to the machine. "As we contemplate the world converted into a huge machine and managed by engineers, we gradually grow aware of its lack of meaning, of its emptiness of human value; the soul is stifled in this glorification of mechanical efficiency. And then we begin to feel the weakness of such a creed when confronted by the real problems of life; we discover its inability to impose any restraint on the passions of men, or to supply any government which can appeal to the loyalty of the spirit. And seeing these things we understand the fear that is gnawing at the vitals of society." Humanitarians, having dissolved the old loyalties and prescriptions, find themselves defenseless before the boss, the union-leader, the political policeman, the very pitiless machine-

society they had welcomed. Fear, like injustice and sin, will not
be eradicated from the world; but the fear of modern civilization
is a terror peculiarly hideous. What is to be done? "It looks as
if, first of all, we needed somehow or other to get the fear of God
back into society."[13]

This said, Paul Elmer More turned to the second great phase
of his contribution to American philosophy and letters, that study
of Platonism and Christianity he called *The Greek Tradition*. In
Platonism and in *The Religion of Plato*, he analyzed Platonic dualism, with its distinct realms of idea and matter, recognizing in
the constitution of man the existence of a power beyond himself.
More traced the revolt of Stoic and Epicurean monistic systems
against this dualism in *Hellenistic Philosophies*. Next, in *The Christ
of the New Testament*, he wrote the greatest American work of Christian apologetics, assailing the modernists with all the weight of
his erudition and all the majesty of his style. Belief in the Incarnation is in conformity to reason: for the supernatural, if it is to
be apprehended clearly by man, must make itself felt in natural
forms; and historical evidences for the powers of Christ carry overwhelming conviction. "At least of Christianity, whatever may be
said of other forms of faith," he wrote later, in *The Catholic Faith*,
"one thing is certain, that it depends upon revelation, that without
revelation the belief of the Christian is a baseless assumption."[14]
With *Christ the Word*, More completed his vindication of orthodoxy;
and though these books cannot be properly discussed here, they
dealt a most serious blow to the theological modernism of the twentieth century, establishing strongly that premise of metaphysical
dualism upon which More's critical and social ideas were built.
An heir to the Puritan mind, More had perceived that Puritanism, with all its dogged power, still remained only a courageous
negation; and he returned to an affirmation as bold in the twentieth century as Puritanical dissent had been in the seventeenth.

"The *Shelburne Essays* and the five volumes of *The Greek Tradition*," Walter Lippmann once wrote, "are more than the
monumental work of a literary critic. They are a record of con-

tinuous religious discovery within a nature that combines in ex-
quisite proportions a delicate sensibility with a hard-headed instinct for reality. It makes no particular difference whether one
agrees with all his particular judgements; to read him is to enter
an austere and elevated realm of ideas and to know a man who,
in the guise of a critic, is authentically concerned with the first
and last things of human experience.''[15] Nothing else in American
letters, for union of constancy with power of execution, equals
More's intricate countermine to radical naturalism in philosophy
and radical humanitarianism in social controversy. More resolved
to counteract the influence of men like John Dewey, ''with a precious panacea for the calamities of history,'' infatuated of ne-
oterism, the itch for change; and certainly the pragmatists seem
unhappily simple by the side of More. For him, sin and redemption, justice and grace, were realities which the naturalists can ignore only at the cost of brutalizing society; and, after eight decades
of controversy, the tide appears to be turning slowly in More's
favor.

He knew that a high conservatism requires imagination; he knew
that it requires something even rarer and nobler, consecration.
''It is true that religion, or religious philosophy, as its friends and
foes have seen from the beginning, is an alleviator of discontent
and a brake upon innovation,'' More said in 1921; ''but the content it offers from the world of immaterial values is a necessary
counterpoise to the mutual envy and materialistic greed of the
natural man, and the conservatism it inculcates is not the ally of
sullen and predatory privilege but of orderly amelioration.''[16]
These are the sentiments of a reactionary philsopher who dignified reaction, who reminded a hurrying generation that the American and the English and the Christian and the Greek pasts are
not dead, and that the stream of being in which the pragmatists
splash may be tumbling down to a Dead Sea. Between the pessimism of Henry Adams and the strong faith of More is a chasm,
and its presence suggests that both the deterministic theories of
the Adams brothers and the naturalistic confidence of Positivism
in ''some far-off divine event'' may retreat before a revived theism.

With Babbitt and More, American conservative ideas experienced a reinvigoration attesting the coquetry of History and the mystery of Providence.

4

"He feared me," George Santayana writes of his friend Andrew Green. "I was a Mephistopheles masquerading as a conservative. I defended the past because once it had been victorious and had brought something beautiful to light; but I had no clear expectation of better things in the future. He saw looming behind me the dreadful spectres of death and of truth."[17] Like Green, the educated public of America often has been charmed and perturbed simultaneously by the dispassionate and versatile Santayana—who, though exerting so strong an influence upon American thought, rarely confessed himself to be an American; forty years of American association were insufficient to wash away the Spanish birth he cherished and the cosmopolitan position—a blend of aesthetic Catholicism with skepticism—from which he viewed American and English ideas with a quizzical urbanity. In that amusing, discursive, and melancholy novel *The Last Puritan*, one perceives how deeply he penetrated into Anglo-American character and institutions, and how he never really was assimilated to them. As a conservative thinker, he has illuminated British and American society with an exotic light; yet his discipline was English and New-English; Burke, for instance, strides through Santayana's books (*Winds of Doctrine* being a title extracted from Burke and St. Paul), and even the Genteel Tradition of New England letters which Santayana dissected was woven into his education. If not part of American society, still he was inside that society in a way Tocqueville never could attain.

After the theistic humanism of Babbitt and More, the materialism of Santayana may seem a weakening of the conservative fibre, a postscript to Henry Adams. Yet Santayana's metaphysics, though at odds with dualism, repudiates the common sort of mechanism, exposes the egoism of the Idealists, and, with a good-natured nudge, consigns James' pragmatism to the nursery. "The intellectual world of my time alienated me intellectually. It was a Babel of false principles and blind cravings, a zoological garden of the mind, and I had no desire to be one of the beasts."[18] Something Hellenistic suffuses the thought of Santayana, who agrees with Plato that only the knowledge of ideas can be literal and exact, while practical knowledge necessarily is mythical in form; but, like the Hellenistic moralists, he cannot accept a thoroughgoing dualism. "To double the world would unspiritualize the spiritual sphere; to double the truth would make both truths halting and false. There is only one world, the natural world, and only one truth about it; but this world has a spiritual life possible in it, which looks not to another world but to the beauty and perfection that this world suggests, approaches, and misses."[19]

Spirit lives only through matter; divine purpose, which we delineate in our myths, is real, but manifested only in natural ways; nothing is immortal, not even the forms of beauty to which Santayana's books are devoted. His naturalism is not irreligious, he says; religion and the poetry of mythology are not mere childish science, but endure as "subtle creations of hope, tenderness, and ignorance," true in a lofty sense which grubby isolated facts never can attain; Christianity, productive of so much virtue and beauty, has no enemy in him. But he cannot subscribe with his reason to these venerable orthodoxies. All things perish, the most ancient opinions among them, and the philosopher will smile tolerantly at progress and decay, content with the immense variety of character and phenomena. If this cosmic urbanity diminishes Santayana's consistency and his will, still only an heroic thinker can resign himself cheerfully to contemplation of the flux, too terrible even for Heraclitus or Empedocles. Often the imperturbable Santayana, in Boston, Berlin, London, Avila, or Rome, is very like Stilbo (described by Seneca), tranquil amid the sack of Megara, indifferent to catastrophe, indifferent to the conquering Demetrius who, enthroned, wonders at the philosopher. What has he lost? Goods, daughters, his house? All these are nothing, only "the adventitious things that follow the beck of fortune"; permanence is nothing; he retains his self, and all the consolations of natural beauties and mysteries.

Such grand placidity colors Santayana's social thought. "For myself, even if I could live to see it, I should not be afraid of the future domination, whatever it may be. One has to live in some age, under some fashion; I have found, in different times and places, the liberal, the Catholic, and the German air quite possible to breathe; nor, I am sure, would communism be without its advantages to a free mind, and its splendid emotions. Fanatics, as Tacitus said of the Jews or Christians, are consumed with hatred of the human race, which offends them; yet they are themselves human; and nature in them takes its revenge, and something reasonable and sweet bubbles up out of the very fountain of their madness."[20] Beneath this generous tolerance, however, Santayana adheres to a firm and haughty standard for judging dominations and powers: a good society is beautiful, a bad society ugly. Upon this ground, he builds his conservatism and his condemnation of the direction modern life has taken.

In the course of a conversation with John D. Rockefeller, Santayana mentioned Spain's population; and the millionaire, after a pause, murmured, "I must tell them at the office that they don't sell enough oil in Spain." Here in one sentence leered the ugliness and barrenness of the modern age. "I saw in my mind's eye," adds Santayana, "the ideal of the monopolist. All nations must consume the same things, in proportion to their population. All mankind will then form a perfect democracy, supplied with rations from a single centre of administration, as is for their benefit; since they will then secure everything assigned to them at the lowest possible price."[21] This utilitarian utopia, prophesied by Henry and Brooks Adams as the triumph of the cheapest, starves the realm of spirit and the realm of art as no other domination can. The culmination of liberalism, the fulfillment of the aspirations of Bentham and Mill, and of the French and American democratic spokesmen, it is also the completion of capitalism. It is communism. Rockefeller and Marx were merely two agents of the same social force—an appetite cruelly inimical to human individuation, by which man has struggled up to reason and art.

Through half a century, from his early *Reason in Society* to his late *Dominations and Powers*, Santayana was consistenly contemptuous of the innovation which despoils the world in the name of efficiency and uniformity, consistently quick to defend the conservation of social harmony and tradition. "A reformer hewing so near to the tree's root never knows how much he may be felling," he wrote in 1905. "Possibly his own ideal would lose its secret support if what it condemns had wholly disappeared." Individualism is the only ideal possible; and if individuals are subordinated to the state, it is only that they may fulfill their devotion to things rational and impersonal, a higher individualism. For a time, democracy and individualism exhibit a parallel growth; but presently democratic legislation presumes to regulate all things, and industrial liberalism, supported by democracy, aspires to replace individuality by efficient standardization; thus the man who loves beauty and variety will endeavor (like Socrates in *Dialogues in Limbo*) to puncture the bubbles of social planners who have forgotten the real aim of society, the life of mind and art.

"It is unfortunate to have been born at a time when the force of human character was ebbing, when the tide of material activity and material knowledge was rising so high as to drown all moral independence," says Peter Alden in *The Last Puritan*. This ebbing of real humanity has been accelerated by the whole "liberal" movement, Santayana wrote in 1926: "That comfortable liberal world was like a great tree with the trunk already sawed quite through, but still standing with all its leaves quietly rustling, and with us dozing under its shade. We were inexpressibly surprised when it fell and half crushed us; some of us are talking of setting it up again safely on its severed roots."[22] But the shell of Christendom has been broken, and a new spirit, that of emancipated, atheistic, international democracy, is dragging us toward an industrial socialistic future. Liberalism, once professing to advocate liberty, now is a movement for control over property, trade, work, amusements, education, and religion; only the marriage bond is relaxed by modern liberals. "The philanthropists are now preparing an absolute subjection of the individual, in soul and body, to the instincts of the majority—the most cruel and unprogressive of masters; and I am not sure that the liberal maxim, 'the greatest happiness of the greatest number,' has not lost whatever was just or generous in its intent and come to mean the greatest idleness of the largest possible population."

This is no perversion of liberalism, but simply its natural progression. Liberalism (fortunately) has been always a secondary state, living like a saprophyte on the tissue of the previous age, inheriting its monuments, feelings, and social hierarchy. "Liberalism does not go very deep; it is an adventitious principle, a mere loosening of an older structure."[23] Manifestly, in our time, it is simply a transition from Christendom, aristocracy, and family-economy to an overwhelming utilitarian collectivism. By the horrors of competition and the trial of war have the liberals been discredited. Santayana's essay "The Irony of Liberalism," included in *Soliloquies in England*, is a funeral sermon over the aspirations of Bentham and Cobden and J. S. Mill. Modern liberalism—though the ancients knew better—wanted to enjoy both liberty and prosperity simultaneously. Prosperity involving subjection to things, however, soon it appears that the real love of the liberals is not for liberty, but for progress; and by "progress" the liberals mean expansion. "If you refuse to move in the prescribed direction, you are not simply different, you are arrested and perverse. The savage must not remain a savage, nor the nun a nun, and China must not keep its wall." Tradition is suspect to the liberal; he insists upon reform, revision, restatement: "A man without traditions, if he could only be materially well equipped, would be purer, more rational, more virtuous than if he had been an heir to anything. *Weh dir, dass du ein Enkel bist!* Blessed are the orphans, for they shall deserve to have children; blessed the American!" But logically, the application of liberal doctrines would lead to a Nietzschean world, if anywhere, and no one who has tasted the actual liberal system seems to like it; for if it represses its Nietzschean squint, it turns out dismally hollow. Even for the rich, a liberal system is an agony of doubt and hesitation. "I find no sense of moral security among them, no happy freedom, no mastery over anything. Yet this is the very cream of liberal life, the brilliant success for the sake of which Christendom was overturned, and the dull peasantry elevated into factory-hands, shopkeepers, and chauffeurs.''

When the aim of life is to imitate the rich, and ''opportunity'' is made generally available, general discouragement is the consequence. No paradox, this: the average man, formerly content in his special craft or his old simplicities, is hopelessly out of the running in the race for wealth, and exhausts himself very early, and lingers on only in boredom. Despite its pretenses, the liberal system has degraded the masses. The mediocre man ''then becomes a denizen of those slimy quarters, under the shadow of railway bridges, breweries, and gasworks, where the blear lights of a public house peer through the rain at every corner, and offer him the one joy remaining in life.'' Nominally literate, this populace is manipulated by the press, dosed with every variety of superstition, bullied by the advertiser and the propagandist. ''Liberalism has merely cleared a field in which every soul and every corporate interest may fight with every other for domination. Whoever is victorious in this struggle will make an end of liberalism; and the new order, which will deem itself saved, will have to defend itself in the following age against a new crop of rebels.'' The present-day liberal, become an advocate of the tyranny of the state in every field, offers as an apology his intention of freeing the people. ''But of freeing the people from what? From the consequences of freedom.''

In the preface to *Dominations and Powers*, Santayana wrote from his Roman convent, ''If one political tendency kindled my wrath, it was precisely the tendency of industrial liberalism to level down all civilizations to a single cheap and dreary pattern.'' Even material well-being, in the long run, is jeopardized by material development of this description; the best we can hope for is a gradual slackening of economic pace. An empty atomic individuality replaces real individual character: ''When all are uniform the individuality of each unit is numerical only.'' Men have then indeed become Burke's flies of a summer. In this ponderous organized blindness, chivalry (which Santayana praises nearly in the tone of Burke) is dead, supplanted by a cringing anxiety to be safe. The banners of liberalism are snatched by the communists, for the liberals have failed in both their aspirations, material comfort and moral liberty. Liberalism "had enabled mankind to grow far more numerous and more exacting in its standard of living; it had multiplied instruments for saving time and labour; but paradoxically had rendered life more hurried than ever before and labour more monotonous and in itself less rewarding. The people had been freed politically and nominally by being given the vote, and enslaved economically in being herded in droves under anonymous employers and self-imposing labour leaders. Meanwhile the liberal rich, who had expected to grow richer and did so when individually enterprising, became poorer and idler as a class, and more obviously withdrawn from the aristocratic leisure, sports, and benevolent social and intellectual leadership which they had supposed themselves fitted for. Nothing was rationalized by the liberal régime except the mechanism of production. Society meantime had been unhinged, and rendered desperate, and governments had been either incapacitated by intellectual impotence or turned into party tyrannies."[24]

Acting under the illusion that graceful yielding would ensure general peace, the liberals relaxed the traditional order. "When we have conceded everything that anybody clamours for," they thought, "everyone will be satisfied; and then if any picturesque remnant of the traditional order is left standing, we shall at last be able to enjoy it safely and with a good conscience." But the liberal's dearest friend and ally, the reformer, had a Will of his own to satisfy, a secret and consuming intolerance of the old order or anything out of harmony with his own ingenious schemes. While any opposition exists to the consummation of his ego, he will allow no peace in society. And can that ego ever rest? The first half of the twentieth century has shown the liberals that their own wealth, taste, and intellectual liberty are intended to vanish in the next reformation. "The concupiscence of the flesh, the concupiscence of the eyes, and the pride of life exhaust and kill the sweets they feed upon; and a lava-wave of primitive blindness and violence must perhaps rise from below to lay the foundations for something differently human and similarly transient.''

The conceit of the present generation of reformers is the "freedom" of uniformity, Russian style or American style, in which man feels himself content because personal opinion is eradicated and he knows no other condition. Whether educated "to be like Stalin" or to "adjust to the group" after the notion of John Dewey, the tendency of these gigantic states is toward a sheep-population, though achieved in Russia by harsh compulsion, in America by contagion and attraction. A militant demand for unanimity leads to a society hyponotized by the statistical psychologist, the strings and wires of the human psyche in his hands, and he commissioned to pull them. His subjects are the proletariat, "an ugly modern word for an ugly thing," a vast crowd of exiles in their own country, who have nothing in common but the mere physical and vital powers of man, whatever traces of civilization linger among them rapidly dying in their nondescript and unsettled society. They have no art, no religion, no friends, no prospects; work for them is an evil, so that their chief effort is to diminish work and increase wages. This endeavor failing in the long run (for they multiply like wild animals), proletarians become equal in one thing, certainly: in their misery. How long can an elite of administrators and statisticians, themselves starved of imagination by an education grossly acquisitive and presumptuous, hold together such a society? Santayana hints at some hope for converting this body of administrators into a timocracy; but, neglecting the means, he slips rapidly into another topic.

The schoolmaster Cyrus P. Whittle, in *The Last Puritan*, is a type of the bitter reforming zealot who is bringing this proletarian planners'-society closer. His joy is to vilify all distinguished men; but he has his secret devotion, his species of religion. "Not only was America the biggest thing on earth, but it was soon going to wipe out everything else; and in the delirious dazzling joy of that consummation, he forgot to ask what would happen afterwards. He gloried in the momentum of sheer process, in the mounting wave of events; but minds and their purposes were only the foam of the breaking crest; and he took an ironical pleasure in showing how all that happened, and was credited to the efforts of great and good men, really happened against their will and expectation." Affection and dread run mingled through Santayana's analysis of America, especially in *Character and Opinion in the United States* (1920). A new type of American, foreign to the sour uprightness of the old Yankee, has made his appearance—"the untrained, pushing, cosmopolitan orphan, cock-sure in manner but not too sure in his morality." Social radicalism is in the American's blood, although because of his individualism and rough comradeship, "it will take some hammering to drive a coddling socialism into America." The American's preoccupation with quantitative standards, his insistence upon conformity, are ominous for the future. "America is all one prairie, swept by a universal tornado. Although it has always thought itself in an eminent sense the land of freedom, even when it was covered with slaves, there is no country in which people live under more overpowering compulsions." Is civilization indeed to be remoulded by this overweeningly confident nation, the Cyrus P. Whittles bringing down everything not incontestably American?

The tradition of English and American liberties (which are a world away from "absolute liberty") now struggles against "an international democracy of the disinherited many, led by the disinherited few," that "would abolish those private interests which are the factors in any cooperation, and would reduce everybody to forced membership and forced service in one universal flock, without property, family, country, or religion."[25] A society led by "Niebelungen who toil underground over a gold they will never use," creatures of the narrow utilitarianism that liberals approved, threatens to make proletarianism universal. Occidental civilization has abused the whole concept of production, complicating life without ennobling the mind; and this is especially true in America. Materialism, confused with tradition, is turned into a sort of religion, and more and more America inclines toward a universal crusade on behalf of this credo of mechanized production and mass consumption. Americans seldom perceive the terror just underfoot: "A barbaric civilization, built on blind impulse and ambition, should fear to awaken a deeper detestation than could ever be aroused by those more beautiful tyrannies, chivalrous or religious, against which past revolutions have been directed."[26]

What hope remains for saving the life of reason and the tradition of liberties? Santayana, who is inclined to believe that material forces are the real agent in historical change, reproves our "attributing events to the conscious ideals and free will of individuals."[27] Yet it is not always futile to defy the times: when Charles I had the choice of dying as a traitor for resisting the apparent will of his people, or of leading them to their moral ruin, his sacrifice did achieve its aim in part, sheltering the deep roots of Church and monarchy, preserving a refinement in English life and feeling.[28] The lover of reason and beauty will contend against a brutal mechanized monotony with all his powers; and conceivably he may so modify any domination that in some measure nobility of mind will endure under the yoke.

Santayana left America in 1912; he abandoned London and Oxford, too, after some years, withdrawing from this vertiginous world, a very old man, to that most conservative of all places, Rome: Rome, where nothing dies but of extreme caducity, where Nero's ghost, metamorphosed to a monstrous crow, roosted on a bough for a millennium, and where the last of the Stuarts languishes in Canova's marble under the dome of St. Peter's. There the agony of a blind society, burning in its own furnaces, pursued him, so that St. Benedict's abbey upon Monte Cassino was smashed to powder while he wrote in his cloister, and Nuremburg, the great medieval center of craftsmanship, was erased by modern techniques. He wrote on, nobly sane in a generation of frenzy; and surely the civilization which possessed a Santayana retains some chance for regeneration.

5

Except under the pressure of some enormous event, general ideas filter only slowly into the mind and conscience in democratic societies. The immediate effect of the writings of Babbitt, More, and Santayana upon the conduct of affairs in America was imperceptible; their influence upon private opinion, restricted to small circles and scattered individuals in the vastness of the United States. Even the First World War did not shake American confidence in the strong tendency of things; in its result, it seemed a vindication, rather, of liberal, humanitarian, and pragmatic impulses; and it reinforced tremendously, out of its frightful energies, three social impulses which the critical conservatives detested: the conversion of political power to the ends of a levelling humanitarianism, the development of a new and complex American imperialism, and the infection of all segments of society by a gross hedonism.

The instrument of the first was the graduated income-tax, which Wilson, like that curiously similar great liberal Gladstone, embraced only as a temporary expedient—but which, again like Gladstone, he could not manage to detach from the social body after the emergency was done. Together with the inheritance tax, this device was irresistibly tempting to social reformers, almost impossible to restrain within the strict necessities of ordinary government; as John Randolph had said, property must follow power; and a people long possessed of universal suffrage, from the beginning committed to social equality, and just now commencing to nibble at the bait of social planners—this people could not long be withheld from experimenting with their pulsating new engine of change. The power to tax certainly is the power to destroy; humanitarians confidently believed it was the power to create, as well. The rights of property, in a nation increasingly industrialized and experiencing the growth of a proletariat of alien origins, inevitably would be contrasted with the rights of men. Paul Elmer More, like Burke, had said these rights were not separable, property being the highest among the social rights of mankind; but this does not make a popular slogan. The only matter for surprise is that the transfer of wealth from propertied persons to propertyless persons, by means of positive legislation, has not proceeded even faster since 1918—considering the intellectual confusion of propertied and conservative people in the United States.

As for imperialism, the national appetite that had consumed Louisiana, the Southwest, the Pacific Coast, Hawaii, Puerto Rico, and the Philippines was now more voracious than ever; and, as before, it was clothed in the motley garments of liberalism and manifest destiny. Trouncing Mexico and Nicaragua was American imperialism of the old sort, further afield, and would be countered by the old sort of opposition; but a more insidious and portentous imperialism, applauded rather than denounced by humanitarians, began to take form: a resolution that all the world should be induced to embrace American principles and modes of life, founded upon the immense presumption that American society is the final superior product of human ingenuity. Colonel House's recommendations to President Wilson for a common exploitation of Africa by the great powers foreshadows this ambition; and soon after the war, it becomes much clearer, and the prophetic afflatus impels Bertrand Russell to predict a coming American military occupation of Europe in the interest of American capitalism, and Georges Duhamel to write *America the Menace*, and C. E. M. Joad to describe *The Babbitt Warren*. The new imperialism, economic rather than military, perhaps yet more cultural than economic, was an impulse of origins far deeper than the claims of American creditors. It was more Wilsonian than Rooseveltian, and its crusading democratic sympathies are suggested by the fact that the Democratic party, previously the voice of protest against aggrandizement, ever since Wilson's day has tended to stand for "active participation" in the affairs of Europe and Asia. Irving Babbitt said that should Japan adopt democracy, she must be watched with trembling; and in America, popular sympathies endorsed the Americanization of the world with an abandon untempered by aristocratic reserve. As an expression of national moral disapproval, the hostility toward Germany and Japan that preceded the Second World War had something of the old New England loftiness of principle; but it was marked just as strongly by the fanatic intolerance of opposition and the overweening priggishness which were characteristic of the New England reformers. Presently the same democratic opinion, impatient for victory, approved revival of the methods that General Sherman had introduced into American warfare. More and more, unguided by any well-understood objectives or any consistent reliance upon that inner check which the humanists defined, American foreign policy came to resemble the aspiration of Cyrus P. Whittle.

In the realm of morals, religion declined steadily toward the credo of "service" which Babbitt and More had analyzed; the educational ideas of John Dewey, disavowing all checks, inner or outer, captured the schools; and Teapot Dome was only one bubble upon the surface of the cauldron of American ethical confusion. A nation intent upon gratification of appetites chose for the presidency the shoddiness of Harding, the mediocrity of Coolidge, and the honest frustration of Hoover. The United States had come a long way from the piety of Adams and the simplicity of Jefferson. The principle of real leadership ignored, the immortal objects of society forgotten, practical conservatism degenerated into mere laudation of "private enterprise," economic policy almost wholly surrendered to special interests—such a nation was inviting the catastrophes which compel society to re-examine first principles.

Franklin Roosevelt, the representative of humanitarian indignation, ascended in immediate consequence. Fortunately for American traditions, Roosevelt was not really a radical—less given to innovation than Joseph Chamberlain or Lloyd George. Unfortunately for American conservatism, Roosevelt, who had no system of ideas, repeatedly accepted the suggestions of doctrinaire social reformers and tinkers. But Roosevelt's success made Americans of conservative tendencies begin to think; and the benefits of that awakening are yet incalculable. Liberal humanitarianism in the United States found itself embarrassed, to put the matter mildly, when the Second World War was won—won at the expense of Hiroshima and Nagasaki and all they meant to the American conscience, won at the expense of consuming centralization at home, the maintenance of permanent armies abroad. American liberalism displayed all the weakness and vacillation Santayana ascribes. But after the New Deal and the Fair Deal, what direction?

America in victory needed a genuine conservatism more than ever before in her history, to redeem her from ungoverned will and appetite. In the humanistic discipline of Babbitt, in the theistic elevation of More, in the urbane humility of Santayana, the spirit of such a conservatism subsists. May these ideas be transmitted to the great uneasy mass of the American people who vote and labor and struggle over the dollar? If not, the infinitely repressive and monotonous future domination sketched by Santayana may impend, whether called ''communism'' or ''the American way of life.'' The new American conservative must accomplish something more difficult than chastening Russia: he must chasten himself.

XIII

Conservatives' Promise

I, who mourn the distant vistas of mankind,
The stooks, like castles built of gold,
Flashing on far horizons,
The voices of the priests and cries of warriors,
United to create a myth, life-giving,
I can tell how far we have descended,
How thickly muffled, numbed, how far condemned—
Without the gambler's hope to a gambler's life,
Where the highest prize is a week in a Butlin camp,
And the forfeit, a star's disruption.
                    —Sir Osbert Sitwell, *Demos the Emperor*

CONSERVATIVES HAVE BEEN ROUTED, although not conquered. But what of their adversaries? The hopes of the
Jacobins were broken by the Directory; they were ground
under Napoleon's heel; and their ghosts were exorcised in 1848
and 1871. Benthamites were checked effectively by the Romantic
writers, by their own pedantry, and by the new collectivism, so
that they dissolved as a coherent force after the 1870's. Positivists
succumbed to their absurdities, and although positivism still stirs
in the popular consciousness, as a movement it resembles a turtle

crawling with its head gone. Sentimental socialists, of the school of Kingsley and Morris, sank into the slough of Marxism or expired in the arid climate of twentieth-century industrialism. Marxism and its offshoots have been made hideous in British and American eyes by the practical demonstrations of applied Marxism in Russia and China.

In both great English-speaking nations, conservative convictions have maintained a political and intellectual continuity for two centuries, while the radical parties that detested tradition have dissolved successively, adhering to no common principle among them except hostility to whatever is established. British Socialism, though several times successful in attaining power, repeatedly has sickened of itself and surrendered political leadership to the Conservatives.

In America, no important public man confesses himself to be a socialist; and when one prominent politician, Henry Wallace, flirted with doctrinaire collectivists, he was repudiated by his former admirers. The American "New Left," posturing fantastically in the 1960's, speedily alienated the public and proceeded to expire in little acts of isolated violence. Liberalism and Populism and Fascism and Syndicalism and nearly every other organized ideology of the "party of progress" have been discredited in America and Britain.

Conservatives have retreated a long way since the French Revolution burst out; now and again they have fled headlong; but they have not despaired when defeated in the field. The radicals have been able to rouse the appetite for novelty and the passion of envy among modern peoples; the conservatives have been able to fortify themselves within the inertia and the tradition of man; and these latter are powerful walls still. Certainly the conservatives have been routed, forced back from ditch to palisade; yet today, when the radicals' ranks are decimated and afflicted by internecine ferocity, conservatives have such an opportunity for regaining ground as they had not seen since the day when modern radicalism issued its challenge to prescriptive society by decorating "this hell-porch of a Hotel de Ville" with human heads on pikes.

How much conservatives have lost since July 14, 1789, has been suggested in the preceding chapters of this prolonged essay. What they have retained, in Britain and America, remains greater than what they have forfeited. The celebrants of the Feast of Reason, could they see the Anglo-American civilization of 1972, would be astonished to find Christian belief still enduring on either side of the Atlantic. If the churches of Britain are not altogether in sound condition, still they are little weaker than they were in 1789. The latitudinarian parsons (many of whom, Burke knew, held revolutionary sympathies at the beginning of the troubles in France) have successors more diligent, if no more conservative. The America that Jefferson described to a Barbary bey as "not a Christian nation" is simultaneously the home of muscular Protestantism and a chief prop of Rome. As Tocqueville predicted, democratic times have altered the practice of religion, but they have not worked the ruin of religious conviction. Thus the basis of any conservative order, religious sanction, remains tolerably secure.

As for political institutions, the outward shape of things has altered little in either Britain or the United States; and even the inward constitution has changed only in an orderly fashion, with few exceptions. The British Constitution still depends upon Crown in Parliament; it still acknowledges the ancient rights of Englishmen. The House of Commons remains a powerful body of critics; the House of Lords, however reduced in authority, provides some check upon the appetites of the hour; the sovereign and the idea of monarchy are respected by every important political faction. In America, the Federal Constitution has endured as the most sagacious conservative document in political history; the balance of interests and powers still operates, however threatened by recent centralization; and almost no one with a popular following advocates the overthrow of American political establishments.

Private property, which both aristocratic and middle-class elements in the conservative interest believe to be indispensable to an orderly society, remains an institution of immense power in America and Britain, and few propose its abolition. "Nationalization" has lost its appeal in Britain; general appetite for durable private possessions never was greater in America than it is today. Income taxes and corporations' growth may have injured the foundation of private ownership, but the edifice stands in no imminent danger of collapse.

Respect for established usage and longing for continuity are not dead, either, among English-speaking peoples. Despite the disruptive forces of mass-communication, rapid transportation, industrial standardization, a cheap press and other mass media, and Gresham's Law working in affairs of the mind, despite the radical effects of vulgarized scientific speculation and weakened private morality, despite the decay of family economy and family bonds, most men and women in the twentieth century still feel veneration for what their ancestors affirmed and built, and they express a pathetic eagerness to find stability in a time of flux. So the uprooting of humanity by proletarianization is not yet irreparable, and conservatives may appeal to an unsatisfied emotion of potency.

Of the six premises of conservative belief that are listed in the introductory chapter of this book, then, four at least continue to move most people in America and Britain. The conservatives' rout has been most injurious where the principle of leadership—the idea of order and class—is concerned, and also in the problem of combining reverence with the spirit of self-reliance, moral and social. Conservatism's most conspicuous difficulty in our time is that conservative leaders confront a people who have come to look upon society, vaguely, as a homogeneous mass of identical individuals whose happiness may be obtained by direction from above, through legislation or some scheme of public instruction. Conservatives endeavor to teach humanity once more that the germ of public affections (in Burke's words) is "to learn to love the little platoon we belong to in society." A task for conservative leaders is to reconcile individualism—which sustained nineteenth-century life even while it starved the soul of the nineteenth century—with the sense of community that ran strong in Burke and Adams. If conservatives cannot redeem the modern masses from the sterile modern mass-mind, then a miserable collectivism impoverishing body and soul impends over Britain and America—the collectivism that has submerged eastern Europe and much of Asia and Africa, the collectivism (as Orwell wrote) of "the stream-lined men who think in slogans and talk in bullets."

The prospect of this collectivism, affrighting even some obdurate radicals of the West, is the immediate impulse behind a revival of popular conservatism in Britain and the United States. True, American or British collectivism would not be identical with the communism of the Soviet Union or of China. In England, A.L. Rowse's description of "progressive" education is applicable to British collectivism generally: "Observe that there is a certain flavour of totalitarianism about it: it is just the form our totalitarianism would take—kindly, humane, fussy, bureaucratic, flat, insipid, like a minor civil servant's dream, without energy or power, hazard or enterprise, the standards set by people who cannot write English, who have no poetry or vision or daring, without the capacity to love or hate. It is very English, very lower-middle-class. How I loathe this whole conception of life—such a contrast to the great ages of our history, the pomp and colour of the Elizabethan, the gusto and creative vitality, the contrasts, the rich and jostling variety, the proliferating fertility of the Victorian; the world of Shakespeare and the world of Dickens!"[1]

In the United States, where obedience to positive law and regulation notoriously is less habitual than in Britain, the new collectivism probably would be a magnified Prohibition torment—a welter of defiance, crime, corruption, evasion, repression, and decaying morality, in which only the violent and the vicious could prosper. Even all the elaborate apparatus of the modern total state could not suffice to govern tolerably a country so populous, so vast, and so rooted in individualism as the American Republic.

Liberals and socialists, on either side of the Atlantic, may be quite as alarmed as were Tweedledum and Tweedledee at their "monstrous crow, as big as a tar-barrel" when they are confronted by the shape of the modern total state. But they are no better equipped than were that pair to contend against the menace.

Subjecting the failure of twentieth-century American liberalism to close analysis would be breaking a butterfly upon the wheel.

It may suffice to quote from one of the wittier and more independent writers of the twentieth century, Malcolm Muggeridge, who calls liberalism a death-wish: "Liberalism will be seen historically as *the* great destructive force of our time; much more so than communism, fascism, nazism, or any of the other lunatic creeds which make such immediate havoc. . . . It is liberalism which makes the Gadarene swine so frisky; as mankind go to their last incinerated extinction, the voice of the liberal will be heard proclaiming the realization at last of life, liberty, and the pursuit of happiness."[2]

One is reminded of Matthew Arnold's description of liberals' confusion in his own time, when, in *Essays in Criticism*, he makes his liberals exclaim, " 'Let us have a social movement, let us organize and combine a party to pursue truth and new thought, let us call it *the Liberal party*, and let us all stick to each other, and back each other up.' . . . In this way the pursuit of truth becomes really a social, practical, pleasurable affair, almost requiring a chairman, a secretary, and advertisements; with the excitement of an occasional scandal . . . but, in general, plenty of bustle and very little thought. To act is so easy, as Goethe says; to think is so hard!"

American liberalism of this sort slides down to dusty death— some of its adherents seduced into political freakishness, fellow-travelling, or the gulf beyond (as in Lionel Trilling's novel *The Middle of the Journey*), others lapsing into apathy, yet others turning conservative: a movement, this last, similar to the course of the rising talents of England after 1793. To the young, to militant "minorities," and to the discontented generally, American liberalism has become a dreary "establishment." "Today the Park, tomorrow the World" ran the legend on a gigantic sign in Grant Park during the New Left demonstrations at the Democratic Convention at Chicago in 1968. It was against the liberals' smugness that those extremists rose up. Although the New Left can no more take the World than they could hold the Park, their wrath may suffice to tumble the liberals' house of cards.

British liberalism's collapse is yet more catastrophic. As a parliamentary party, the Liberals are virtually extinct. Under

Asquith, Liberalism endeavored to stand somewhere just a trifle to the right of Labour; Lewis and Maude sum up Liberalism's last days of hope in *The English Middle Classes:*

Liberalism, in short, was to receive the spoils of office as commission for the job of honest broker in the redistribution of power and wealth between the classes and the masses. Labour was urged to hold its hand for the time being: "if farmers and traders are threatened with a class war they will surely sulk and harden into downright Toryism." Labour's political problem was neatly outlined—how to win middle-class support for a new deal which would be largely to the material disadvantage of the *bourgeoisie*. It was not until 1945 that the problem seemed to be resolved, and when the dust had settled, it was seen that the "honest broker" was dead.[3]

The intellectual dilemma of those liberals who have survived the debacle of their party was suggested by the disquietude of Lord Beveridge, architect of the British welfare state, in his declining years. Dismayed at the immorality and selfishness of a populace all too ready to assume that they now have only to obtain from centralized authority—without much personal exertion—their share of an inexhaustible common fund, Lord Beveridge (reviewing for the *Spectator* Rowntree's and Lavers' *English Life and Leisure*, in 1951) wrote: "Can a country whose destiny (in part at least) is in the hands of a people so irresponsible and so ignorant hope to be well governed?"[4] He suggested that the franchise be made contingent upon the passing of some intelligence-test, thus abandoning pure democratic notions. In a radio broadcast on December 31, 1951, he remarked, "We have somehow to carry on an aristocratic tradition in Britain without the aristocrats." As to the means for resolving this paradox, he was vague. To such lamentations the humanitarianism of latter-day liberals generally is reduced.

As for socialists, they seem impotent beneath the giant shadow of Marxist collectivism, as do the liberals whom they vanquished or absorbed. In America, scarcely any professed pure socialists can be discovered—even Norman Thomas, after he retired from campaigning, having come to concede that private economic enterprise is tolerable, and more than tolerable, in many fields. Lacking support from the labor unions, no American socialist innovator could gain ground; and whatever tinge of socialism once existed among some union leaders has faded almost to invisibility.

The British socialists are riven into factions. Even the New Town and Council-House concept of society is dependent upon public energy and a living belief; and the more nearly socialism seemed to approach substantial enactment in recent years, the less public support or even acquiescence was forthcoming: zeal died. The semi-religous enthusiasm of the old sentimental socialists, the dissenting-chapel spirit diverted to secular concerns, ceased to animate these reformers three decades ago. C.E.M. Joad confessed in the pages of the *New Statesman and Nation*, "Socialism is no longer a creed to conjure with. It is like a hat which has lost its shape because so many wear it; rightly or wrongly, few of us now look to it to revivify our early hopes."

Finding that most men seem to lack motive for performing duties in society, now that ordinary rewards for ordinary integrity have been diminished, the socialists are dismayed; they begin to wonder whether their theory of human nature can be at fault. G.D.H. Cole concluded that "Socialism is an unworkable system without a new social drive such as the Communists have managed to give it," and proposed, somewhat hazily, more "democratization" and decentralization of the Welfare State. P.C. Gordon Walker, sometime Labour secretary of state for commonwealth relations, frankly became hopeful of devising new compulsions: "The new State will also directly augment authority and social pressure by new powers of punishment and compulsion. So far from withering away, as in theory both the individualist and the total State should, the new State, if it is to bring into being and serve the better society, must create new offenses and punish them."[5] And E.H. Carr spoke even more candidly: "The donkey needs to see the stick as well as the carrot. . . . I confess that I am less horror-struck than some people at the prospect, which seems to be unavoidable, of an ultimate power of what is called direction of labour resting in some arm of society, whether in an organ of state or trade unions."[6]

One begins to hear the phrases of Orwell's Ingsoc. Just after Labour's defeat at the polls in 1959, Aneurin Bevan told the House of Commons that when in office, the Socialists never had found ways to reconcile socialist planning with democracy—and so, in a sense, had let power slip from their hands in perplexity. Aldous Huxley, so early as 1927, had detected the quasi-religious character of British socialism, and the doubts that were sure to wear away that creed:

In the early stages of that great movement which has made the whole of the West democratic, there was only discontent and a desire for such relatively small changes in the mode of government as would increase its efficiency and make it serve the interests of the discontented. A philosophy was invented to justify the malcontents in their demands for change; the philosophy was elaborated; conclusions were relentlessly drawn; and it was found that, granted the assumptions on which the philosophy was based, logic demanded that the changes in the existing institutions should be, not small, but vast, sweeping, and comprehensive. . . . Becoming familiar, a dogma automatically becomes right. . . . The transformation of the theory of democracy into theology has created a desire for progress in the direction of more democracy among numbers of people whose material interests are in no way harmed, and are even actively advanced, by the existing form of government which they desire to change. This spread of socialism among the middle classes, the spontaneous granting of humanitarian reforms by power-holders to whose material advantages it would have been to wield their power ruthlessly and give none of it away—these are phenomena which have become so familiar that we have almost ceased to comment on them.[7]

There, in a paragraph or two, is the history of radicalism since 1789. When, at length, the egalitarian society was attained without limit in Russia, and every social democrat outside the Communist party perceived that it was equality in misery, these dogmas were exploded. "Without a new social drive such as the Communists have managed to give it. . . ." This ominous phrase is a death sentence for the Fabian faith in which G.D.H. Cole had his being.

The Benthamite doctrine of rational self-interest and the Rousseauistic doctrine of human benevolence both have gone glimmering; there remain the police agent and the camp for "saboteurs," as in Russia, or else the old motives to morality and duty that conservatives always had believed in: religious sanctions, tradition, habit, and private interest restrained by prescriptive institutions. It remains to be seen whether, within this century, the conservatives can contrive to restore the old motives to integrity. The alternative to such a recovery appears to be not liberalism, nor socialism, but something far grimmer.

2

> Those who put their faith in worldly order
> Not controlled by the order of God,
> In confident ignorance, but arrest disorder
> Make it fast, breed fatal disease,
> Degrade what they exalt.
> —T. S. Eliot, *Murder in the Cathedral*

One century after Macaulay predicted the growth of a proletariat in American cities, what Arnold Toynbee calls the "internal proletariat" began to act there quite as Macaulay had expected. Simultaneously, the "external proletariat," the embittered and impoverished dupes of ideology in Asia and Africa and eastern Europe and much of Latin America, began to threaten the seats of the mighty in Washington and London.

This challenge to the "permanent things," to the great traditions of the civil social order, has become as fierce as it was in Burke's day. Armed doctrines are more frightfully armed. The liberal era of complacency draws to its end; and if ever moral imagination and power of decision were required, the hour is now.

However moribund the ideologies of liberalism and old-style socialism may have become, the lust for change never lacks agents.

Throughout the world, a new levelling theory and system seem to be taking substance: China's "cultural revolution," though abandoned, was only the more extreme form of this phenomenon, which would sweep away the patrimony of civilized man. There exist always two aspects of order: the outer order of the commonwealth and the inner order of the soul. So it is that, in our years, conservatives confront the tremendous dual task of restoring the harmony of the person and the harmony of the republic: neither can endure long if the other has surrendered to Dinos.

The new revolutionary theory and system would bring first anarchy, and then total servitude; the instruments for both are more efficacious than they were in any other time. The new order, erected upon ruins, would be what Tocqueville called "democratic despotism," but harsher far than he expected that tyranny to grow. In some sense, it would be what James Burnham called the "managerial revolution": super-bureaucracy, arrogating to itself functions that cannot properly appertain to bureau or cabinet; the planned economy, encompassing not merely the economy proper, however, but the whole moral and intellectual range of human activities; the grand form of *Planwirtschaft*, state planning for its own sake, state socialism devoid of the generous aims that originally animated some early socialists.

In a confused way, mixed up with the notion of some mysterious deliberate conspiracy against freedom, George Orwell succeeded in awaking the dread of the British and the American public against this new domination by his novel *Nineteen-Eighty-Four*, much as Aldous Huxley had stirred up a vague alarm earlier by his *Brave New World*. (One may add that this new order closely resembles the régime of the Antichrist in Vladimir Solovyov's fable, written ninety years ago: "Ye shall be as gods," the malcontent masses are told by the evangels of the new dispensation; but those who dissent end in furnaces.)

Ideas of the efficacy and beneficence of "planning" for socialistic ends have helped to clear the way for this Behemoth; but its reality would be crueller to the old-style socialist than his worst visions of old-style capitalism. In the new-style collectivism, power is loved for its own disciplinary sake; regulation becomes an end rather than a means; and the state sustains the industrial discipline.

Democracy, in the old sense, must be sacrificed to the New Society; freedom, in the old sense, must be forgotten. How long might the planned society retain the theory and form of socialism? Is it possible that the new order might serve ends so foreign to the old humanitarian socialism as to be no more socialistic than such "people's democracies" as Albania are democratic? ("Freedom?" Lenin exclaimed. "Freedom? What for? What for?")

George Orwell described the classes and occupations from which the managers and planners for the new absolute state are being recruited, "made up for the most part of bureaucrats, scientists, technicians, trade-union organizers, publicity experts, sociologists, teachers, journalists, and professional politicians . . . whose origins lay in the salaried middle class and the upper grades of the working class," and who "had been shaped and brought together by the barren world of monopoly industry and centralized government," schooled beyond their intellectual capacities, lacking property, lacking religious faith, lacking ancestors or expectation of posterity, seeking to gratify by the acquisition of power their loneliness and their nameless anxieties. From precisely these elements in society the personnel of bureaucracy and Party in revolutionary eastern Europe, in China, and in parts of Africa have been recruited. The intellectual servitude of this class is described unforgettably by one who had experienced it—Czeslaw Milosz, in *The Captive Mind;* yet Polish communism has been mild by the side of the Chinese undertaking, and a systematic destruction of the order of the soul still more catastrophic may be conceived. The masters of the New Society are themselves servile. They are not socialists like Morris or Cunninghame Graham or even Hyndman; they do not resemble Norman Thomas or Clement Attlee; they are the new élite, though they constitute no aristocracy of birth or of nature. They are at once jailers and jailed.

Saint-Simon and Comte were the fathers of this totally planned society—of what Andrew Hacker calls "the spectre of predictable man." Some seeds of this misrule may be detected in Utilitarianism, too, despite the individualism of Bentham's disciples. Wilhelm Röpke, that penetrating social thinker in the line of Burckhardt, calls the total planners' ideal "eternal Saint-Simonism, " and he describes their dream as "that attitude of mind which is the outcome of a mixture of the hubris of the natural scientist and engineer mentality of those who, with the cult of the 'Colossal,' combine their egotistical urge to assert themselves; those who would construct and organize economics, the State, and society according to supposedly scientific laws and blueprints, while mentally reserving for themselves the principal *portefeuilles*. And so we observe those collectivist social engineers of the type of a Wells or a Mannheim who quite openly admit the point of view of 'society as a machine' and who would thus seriously like to see realized the nightmare of a veritable Hell of civilization brought about by the complete instrumentation and functionalization of humanity."[8]

This would not be capitalism, nor yet socialism; it is the colossal state created for its own sake. Socialists may help to erect this structure; they will not endure to administer or enjoy it. The New Society, if constructed on this model, at first might seem a convenient arrangement for enforcing equality of condition. But its structure—as if a chthonian instinct had inspired its building—especially facilitates ends quite different, the gratification of a lust for power and the destruction of all ancient institutions in the interest of the new dominant élites. It is C.S. Lewis' *That Hideous Strength*.

The grand Plan requires that the public be kept constantly in an emotional state closely resembling that of a people at war: this lacking, obedience and co-operation wane, for the old motives to duty are lost to sight in the machine-society. "Work, sacrifice, and the achievement of targets must be hammered into the public sleeping and waking, eating and drinking," John Jewkes points out. "The statesman must adopt every trick and device to mould the ideal economic man for the purpose. Cupidity ('the golden age is just around the corner'); narrow patriotism ('our community must stand on its own feet'); fear ('the struggle is one for survival') and hatred ('the laggards must be run to earth'): the use of all these are now well-established methods of the planned economy.''⁹

When faith in a transcendent moral order, duty to family, hope of advancement, and satisfaction with one's task have vanished from the routine of life, Big Brother appears to show the donkey the stick instead of the carrot. A powerful new element in society hopes to play the role of Big Brother, to manage all human concerns. "There are many in all parties who look forward to the time when virtually the whole of the population will be dependent on the State for the whole of the amenities of life," says Douglas Jerrold. "Those who do so are the representatives of the most powerful class of the present day who, like the ruling classes which have preceded them, work in unspoken alliance toward common ends. This class is the new aristocracy of the pen and the desk, the professional organizers and administrators, who not only control the executive government (itself a province of vastly increasing importance), but also the machinery of organized labour and organized capital, and who now wish to assume not only the direction of all our great productive undertakings but, through the control of education and doctoring, the private lives of all the citizens.''¹⁰

Such a New Society will require a New Morality—quite as Rousseau endeavored to supply a New Morality for his fancied era of emancipation. But moral systems are not constructed readily by social engineers. The old religious and ethical imperatives demolished, compulsion must take their place if the great wheel of circulation is to be kept turning. When the inner order of the soul is decayed, the outer order of the state must be maintained by merciless severity, extending even to the most private relationships. Some zealots for the New Order are not reluctant to accept this prospect.

For, sensing their growing opposition, the radical planners display an increasing belligerence. If democracy cannot be persuaded, then democracy must be intimidated. The terrorism of such groups as "Maoists" in lands very different from China is not the only form which this movement assumes. The rhetoric of certain less violent political figures suggests their captivity to the *libido dominandi*. There is A.J.P. Taylor, an English Socialist who wishes the country "to be ruled by people who never had top-hats." He is vexed at farmers who expect good agricultural prices; when social planning is thoroughly entrenched, the rustic will be taught his place. "The peasant no longer respects us; our last chance is to make him fear us. We must get the fetters on him before he starves us out." Marx knew that socialism assumes the economics of plenty; and for this, the towns must keep the upper hand. "He wanted to finish the struggle for good and all by liquidating the peasantry; but, failing this Utopian solution, the towns have to practice the doctrine which is the basis of all civilized life: 'We have the Maxim gun, and they have not.' "[11]

Such is the mentality, and such the prospect, of the New Elite and the New Society. During the remainder of the twentieth century, the principal endeavor of imaginative conservatives is likely to be resistance to the ideas of a total society, through recovery of an order which will make the total state unnecessary and impracticable. But simple expostulation and lamentation cannot resist the growth of *Planwirtschaft*; conservative factions have committed that error too often. If, by the year 2000, justice, liberty, and hope still are general characteristics of Western social thought and community, the credit for the revival of private and public norms may belong to the school of genuinely reforming and critical conservatism that is a growing influence in America and even in Britain.

In those countries, ordinarily a generation must elapse before a body of ideas sufficiently rouses the public to purposeful action: J. M. Keynes' aphorism that today's classroom lectures become tomorrow's slogans of the crowd in the street is something of a hyperbole. In the United States, the intellectual recovery of conservative ideas commenced early in the 1950's; so perhaps Americans are well along their path toward some reinvigoration of the private and the public order.

Their destination will be determined by the quality of their moral imagination. In other books, this writer has touched upon particular present discontents, and possible remedies; it would be unsuitable to suggest a conservative program in the present prolonged essay, which is chiefly an exercise in the history of ideas. Yet it must be said here that today's conservative thinker addresses himself to certain primary difficulties of the modern civil social order. If he fails, much must fall.

In essence, the body of belief that we call "conservatism" is an affirmation of normality in the concerns of society. There exist standards to which we may repair; man is not perfectible, but he may achieve a tolerable degree of order, justice, and freedom; both the "human sciences" and humane studies are means for ascertaining the norms of the civil social order, and for informing the statesman and the reflecting public of the possibilities and the limits of social measures.

The twentieth-century conservative is concerned, first of all, for the regeneration of spirit and character—with the perennial problem of the inner order of the soul, the restoration of the ethical understanding and the religious sanction upon which any life worth living is founded. This is conservatism at its highest; but it cannot be accomplished as a deliberate program of social reform, "political Christianity." As Christopher Dawson observes, "There is a tendency, especially among the English-speaking Protestant peoples, to treat religion as a kind of social tonic in order to extract a further degree of moral effort from the people."[12] If the conservatives' effort comes to no more than this, it will not succeed. Recovery of moral understanding cannot be merely a means to social restoration: it must be its own end, though it will produce social consequences. In the words of T.S. Eliot, "If you will not have God (and he is a jealous God) you should pay your respects to Hitler or Stalin."

The conservative is concerned with the problem of leadership, which has two aspects: the preservation of some measure of reverence, discipline, order, and class; and the purgation of our system of education, so that learning once more may become liberal in the root sense of that word. Only just leadership can redeem society from the mastery of the ignoble elite.

The conservative is concerned with the phenomenon of the proletariat—which word does not signify the poor only. The mass of modern men must find status and hope within society: true family, links with the past, expectations for the future, duty as well as right, resources that matter more than the mass-amusement and mass-vices with which the modern proletarian (who may be affluent) seeks to forget his loss of an object. The degeneration of the family to mere common house-tenancy menaces the essence of recognizable human character; and the plague of social boredom, spreading in ever-widening circles to almost every level of civilized existence, may bring a future more dreary than the round of life in the decaying Roman system. To restore purpose to labor and domestic existence, to give men back old hopes and long views and thought of posterity, will require bold imagination.

The conservative is concerned with resistance to the armed doctrine, the clutch of ideology. He endeavors to restore the right reason of true political philosophy; he insists that although we cannot create the Terrestrial Paradise, we can make our own Terrestrial Hell through infatuation with ideology. And he declares that while this recovery of political normality is in process, we must hold the line—often by hard diplomatic and military decisions—against the adversaries of order and justice and freedom.

The conservative is concerned with the recovery of true community, local energies and co-operation; with what Orestes Brownson called "territorial democracy," voluntary endeavor, a social order distinguished by multiplicity and diversity. Free community is the alternative to compulsive collectivism. It is from the decay of community, particularly at the level of the "little platoon," that crime and violence shoot up. In this realm, misguided "liberal" measures have worked mischief that may not be undone for decades or generations, especially in the United States. Miscalled "urban renewal" (actually the creation, often, of urban deserts and jungles), undertaken out of mixed humanitarian and profiteering motives, has uprooted in most American cities whole classes and local communities, under dubious cover of federal statute; inordinate building of highways has had the same consequence. Urban rioting, the swift increase of major crimes, and the boredom that en-

courages addiction to narcotics are products of such foolish programs. In the phrase of Hannah Arendt, "the rootless are always
violent." So it is that the conservative talks of the need for roots
in community, not of more measures of "mass welfare."

And of course the conservative is concerned with a number of
other primary questions, and with a vaster array of prudential
questions, to which the answers must vary with the circumstances
and the time. With Burckhardt, the twentieth-century conservative separates himself from the "terrible simplifiers." As H. Stuart
Hughes remarks very truly, "Conservatism is the negation of ideology." There exists no simple set of formulas by which all the ills
to which flesh is heir may be swept away. Yet there do exist general
principles of morals and of politics to which thinking men may
turn.

"And the more thoroughly we understand our own political tradition, the more readily its whole resources are available to us,
the less likely we shall be to embrace the illusions which wait for
the ignorant and the unwary." So said a learned disciple of Burke,
Michael Oakeshott, in his inaugural lecture upon assuming the
professorial chair at the London School of Economics and Political Science, which previously had been occupied by radical scholars, Graham Wallas and Harold Laski. These fallacies, he
continued, are "the illusion that in politics we can get on without
a tradition of behavior, the illusion that the abridgement of a tradition is itself a sufficient guide, and the illusion that in politics
there is anywhere a safe harbour, a destination to be reached or
even a detectable strand of progress. The world is the best of all
possible worlds, and everything in it is a necessary evil."[13]

This is a world away from the mentality of the total planner.
"As a negative impulse, conservatism is based on a certain distrust of human nature, believing that the immediate impulses of
the heart and visions of the brain are likely to be misleading
guides." So wrote Paul Elmer More, in 1915. "But with this distrust of human nature is closely connected another and more positive factor of conservatism—its trust in the controlling power of
the imagination." In this same essay on Disraeli, More observed

that "Conservatism is in general the intuition of genius, whereas liberalism is the efficiency of talent."[14] By the 1980's, conservatives were exercising once more those powers of imagination and intuition. The New Elite might find it necessary to reckon with the Resurrected Philosophers.

3

> Both the successes and the failures in the American social experience strengthen the classically conservative belief—the orthodox medieval belief, indeed—that all human concerns are properly linked according to a hierarchy of values. Some aspects of life exist, that is, for the sake of others, and these latter are more important.
>
> —Rowland Berthoff, *An Unsettled People*

As the power of centralized government increases, political leaders—immersed in adminstrative duties of increasing complexity and bound to ceremonial functions—have less time for reflection. The last American president to do his own thinking was Herbert Hoover; the last British prime minister of intellectual distinction was Arthur Balfour.* So it is that when one discusses social thought in recent decades, one rarely turns to those who occupy high political office: the ideas expressed by those men are put into their heads by others, and their very words ordinarily come from the typewriters of anonymous or quasi-anonymous members of their staffs—who, in turn, often echo the phrases of influential publicists or scholars. To the historian, the sociologist, the political scientist, and the poet (of whatever political persuasion), the historian of social thought in the twentieth century must look for seminal ideas. Such writers and scholars of a conservative bent, especially in the United States, have reasserted their belief strongly during the past thirty years.

---

*Winston Churchill, indeed, was a lively journalist and popular historian; but T. S. Eliot's strictures upon Churchill's rhetoric and political intellect probably will be sustained by the judgment of later times.

So late as 1950, Lionel Trilling could deny that conservative thought survived in America. "In the United States at this time," he wrote, "liberalism is not only the dominant but even the sole intellectual tradition. For it is the plain fact that nowadays there are no conservative or reactionary ideas in general circulation. This does not mean, of course, that there is no impulse to conservatism or to reaction. Such impulses are certainly very strong, perhaps even stronger than most of us know. But the conservative impulse and the reactionary impulse do not, with some isolated and some ecclesiastical exceptions, express themselves in ideas but only in action or in irritable mental gestures which seek to resemble ideas."[15]

Liberal concepts had gone dry and hollow, Trilling continued, but he could perceive no alternative body of ideas. At the time he wrote, true enough, the conservative tradition seemed to be atrophied: it remained eloquent only among such latter-day Southern Agrarians as Donald Davidson, Allen Tate, Cleanth Brooks, and Richard Weaver, or such clergymen as Bernard Iddings Bell. Yet scarcely had Trilling written those lines than a powerful revival of "traditional" and "prescriptive" ideas made itself felt—whether by writers who called themselves conservative or by men who preferred freedom from attachment to that or any other political label. Since 1950, perhaps two hundred serious books of a conservative cast of thought have been published in America, and a goodly number in Britain; several periodicals professedly conservative have appeared, and a bibliography of important conservative essays might require as many pages as this present volume contains. In earlier editions of this book, some attempt was made to discuss or to mention a variety of recent conservative thinkers; but their number has grown so considerable that one must rest content with brief representative specimens; even a mere list of names would be cumbersome and incomplete.

About 1950, the domination of the "liberal intellectual" seemed secure. Men conservatively inclined are not eager to be styled "intellectuals"; for that term itself is joined to the secular cult of the rationalistic Enlightenment. What occurred after 1950 was this:

conservative thinkers demonstrated that "intellectuals" enjoy no monopoly of intellectual power, and that intellectualism and right reason are not synonymous terms. The principal poets of the twentieth century, indeed, never had submitted to the hegemony of liberal intellectualism: it may suffice to mention, for the moment, the names of Eliot, Yeats, and Frost. But after 1950, there occurred a revival also of conservative conviction in what we call "social studies" or the "human sciences."

It was not conservatives only who had grown weary of the arrogance of the self-proclaimed "intellectual." About the time when the first edition of this book was published, someone wrote to Bertrand Russell inquiring after his definition of an "intellectual." Russell replied forthrightly:

"I have never called myself an intellectual, and nobody has ever dared to call me one in my presence.

"I think an intellectual may be defined as a person who pretends to have more intellect than he has, and I hope that this definition does not fit me."

Being well acquainted with the signification of words, Russell spoke with some authority on the modern usage of "intellectual." The word has had an interesting history. In the seventeenth century, it was indeed employed as a noun, chiefly to describe a person who holds that all knowledge is derived from pure reason. It had even then, and earlier, a denigratory implication. The more common term for this concept was "intellectualist." Bacon wrote mordantly, in the *Advancement of Learning*, of the intellectualist as an abstract metaphysician: "Upon these intellectualists, which are, notwithstanding, commonly taken for the most sublime and divine philosophers, Heraclitus gave a just censure." Hume demolished the eighteenth-century intellectuals, who took Reason for their guide to the whole nature of man; they were the *a priori* reasoners, on the model of Locke. Coleridge—like Hume, however, not using the word "intellectual"—attacked them as the devotees of the mere Understanding, "the mere reflective faculty," as distinguished from the Reason, or organ of the supersensuous.

As a noun descriptive of persons, "intellectual" scarcely appeared at all in nineteenth-century dictionaries. So far as the term
was employed, it meant the "sophisters and calculators" whom
Burke had scorned, the abstract *philosophes*; it was a category
despised equally, though for different reasons, by Romantics and
Utilitarians. It was closely linked with an unimaginative
secularism: Newman attacked Sir Robert Peel for giving way to
it. All in all, "intellectual" meant what Bacon had suggested, a
person who overrates the understanding. By implication, an intellectual neglected the imagination, the powers of insight and
wonder, and the whole realm of being that is beyond private rational perception.

The twentieth-century employment of "intellectual" appears
to be derived from the jargon of Marxism. It is directly linked
with the notion of a body of schooled and highly rational persons
bitterly opposed to established social institutions—outcasts in a
sense, men who go out to the Cave of Adullam, uprooted, passionate for change. The word implies an opposition between the
life of the mind and the life of society—or, at least, a hostility between "advanced social thinkers" and the possessors of property
and power. In the definition of the twentieth-century dictionaries,
an intellectual is "a person of a class or group professing or supposed to possess enlightened judgment with respect to public or
political questions."

Until the 1920s, London and New York knew few of these intellectuals. "Mr. Trotsky of the Central Cafe," in Vienna, could
walk into the street and make a revolution; but he lacked Anglo-
Saxon colleagues. American and British scholars, generally speaking, were not alienated. And it remains true today, as Russell's
remarks suggest, that many of the better-educated Englishmen
and Americans are hostile to defecated rationality. Only when a
doctrinaire hostility toward traditional religion, "capitalism," and
established political forms began to make itself felt in Britain and
America, what with the growing influence of Marxism and other
European ideologies in the 1920s and the vague discontents of the
Depression, did a number of educated Americans and Englishmen begin to call themselves intellectuals.

From the first, American intellectuals were identified with a political and social movement loosely called "liberalism"—very different in some respects from the English liberalism it thought it emulated, and ranging all the way from a mild secularism to outspoken sympathy with the Soviet Union. Often it was linked, philosophically, with pragmatism and with various experimental undertakings in education and practical morality. It tended rapidly to become an ideology, with its secular dogmas and slogans. Lionel Trilling deliberately uses the terms "liberal" and "intellectual" almost synonymously.

One may add that there existed reasons for this desertion of many educated Americans to ideology. The disquietude of reflective persons in a country apparently given over to getting and spending, the condition of the underpaid professor or teacher in an acquisitive environment, the decay of the old American respect for learning—a decay which seemed actually to grow more alarming in direct proportion to the ease with which high-school diplomas and college degrees were obtained, on the principle that whatever is cheap has little value—all these influences tended to produce alienation of scholar and writer from established American society. "Intellectuals" appeared in America when the works of the mind began to lose ground in public influence.

This term "intellectual" having been identified with "liberal," it scarcely is surprising that Lionel Trilling discovered no conservative intellectuals; one might as well have sought for carnivorous vegetarians. But actually the man of intellectual strength need not be alienated from his cultural patrimony and his society; he may be a member of what Coleridge called the clerisy. There existed an earlier model than Trilling's: the American scholar as described by Orestes Brownson in his address "The Scholar's Mission," at Dartmouth College, in 1843:

I understand by the scholar no mere pedant, dilettante, literary epicure or dandy; but a serious, robust, full-grown man; who feels that life is a serious affair, and that he has a serious part to act in its eventful drama; and must therefore do his best to act well his part, so as to leave behind him, in the good he has done, a grateful remembrance of his having been. He may be a theologian, a politician, a naturalist, a poet, a moralist, or a metaphysician; but whichever or whatever he is, he is it with all his heart and soul, with high, noble—in one word, *religious* aims and aspirations.

By 1950, there was need for such scholars: Trilling had found the liberal imagination virtually bankrupt. The "liberal intelligentsia," a rootless body of people intellectually presumptuous, on a European model, manifestly were incompetent to offer intellectual guidance to a people for whom they felt either contempt or a condescending and unrealistic pity. "The scholar is not one who stands above the people," Brownson had said, "and looks down on the people with contempt. He has no contempt for the people; but a deep and all-enduring love for them, which commands him to live and labor, and, if need be, to suffer and die, for their redemption; but he never forgets that he is their instructor, their guide, their chief, not their echo, their slave, their tool." Scholars of that character, remembering with T.S. Eliot that they participated in a tradition and would be puny if that tradition were lacking, began to challenge the liberal intellectuals almost at the time when Trilling doubted their existence.

If the universities generally submitted to the liberal intellectuals' ascendancy, still the sympathetic public for conservative thinkers was larger than the liberals'. In foreign affairs, about 1950, both America and Britain had set themselves against the "armed doctrine," ideology supported by the arms of the Communist powers. In domestic concerns, the menace of the mass-society, of Tocqueville's "democratic despotism," had entered into the public consciousness. Might there be some alternative to ideology and mindless centralization? In one form or another, that question was being asked by a large part of the literate public. Thus conservatively-minded scholars, if they possessed imagination and could write tolerably well, found the ground made ready for them. In America, public-opinion polls began to show that an increasing proportion of the public called itself "conservative"—whatever the average man might mean by that; this proportion rose steadily, as the revival of conservative ideas made headway; at this writing, according to the polls, people calling themselves "conservative" make up by far the largest single element in the American population—indeed, if one combines with them those who call themselves "moderate" or "middle-of-the-road," three-fourths of the American public classify themselves in opposition to liberalism and radicalism.

In the social disciplines, considerably to the surprise of the long-dominant element in many learned societies, a conservative bent—the work of a minority, but of a lively minority—became discernible. By laboring for social coherence and a measure of stability, the conservative social scientists argued, their disciplines might achieve more for mankind than ever they had in their melioristic phase.

It would be well for scholars in the human sciences, they declared, to address themselves to the concerns of genuine community, local and voluntary, rather than clearing the way for an egalitarian collectivism. The little platoon is oppressed today by the forces of consolidation and centralization; but it may be reanimated. If it expires, society is left to boredom and apathy.

It would be well to direct their energies to the examination of voluntary and private associations, rather than to planning new activities for the unitary state. It would be well to admit some moral imagination to their researches: to look into the deeper meanings within religious belief, rather than to play the old game of exploding "superstitions of the childhood of the race"; to abandon the sterile and sometimes disingenuous notion of a "value-free science," and to reaffirm the existence of a moral order.

It would be well for them to renew the classical definition of justice, "to each his own"; to recognize diversity and variety, rather than standardization of life, as goals of the tolerable society; to admit the virtues of order and class; to encourage the development of talented leadership, rather than to sing the praise of universal mediocrity.

It would be well for scholars in the human sciences to speak

up for permanence, as against change on principle; for man's longing for continuity is among his deepest impulses, and this yearning often is frustrated in the twentieth century. If the need of the
eighteenth century was for emancipation, the need of the twentieth
is for roots. When, through the influence of such studies, politicians and the public have acquired some understanding of community, the springs of volition, social ethics, the attractions of
diversity, and the necessity for roots in culture and in place, then
it may become possible to confront intelligently the disorder of
this age—and to apply intelligent remedies: so the conservative
thinkers in the human sciences reasoned. But if the makers of opinion in the human sciences offer nothing better than the shallow
assumptions of latter-day humanitarianism and the thin palliatives of mass-welfare legislation—why, the age must await the
return of the gods of the copybook headings.

Since 1950, a considerable body of literature in this field of
reformed social science has been published: in history, in sociology,
in political theory, in economics, in psychology, even in pure
philosophy (if that may be classified here as one of the human
sciences). For purposes of fairly close examination, we confine ourselves here to one of the earlier studies of this sort, which remains
in the first rank: *The Quest for Community* (entitled, in a later edition, *Community and Power*), by Robert A. Nisbet, published in 1953.

Dr. Nisbet aspires to restore to true significance such terms as
"community," "liberalism," "individuality," and "democracy."
He seeks to save the concept and the reality of community, and
to rescue sociological speculation from its infatuation with Benthamite dogma and method. He begins candidly and confidently:

One may paraphrase the famous words of Karl Marx and say that a
specter is haunting the modern mind, the specter of insecurity. Surely
the outstanding characteristic of contemporary thought on man and society is the preoccupation with personal alienation and cultural disintegration. The fears of the nineteenth-century conservatives in Western
Europe, expressed against a background of increasing individualism,
secularism, and social dislocation, have become, to an extraordinary

degree, the insights and hypotheses of present-day students of man in society. The widening concern with insecurity and disintegration is accompanied by a profound regard for the values of status, membership, and community.[16]

Tocqueville looms large in *The Quest for Community*—as he does in the books of John A. Lukacs, a philosophical historian whose work in part parallels the sociological studies of Nisbet. Tocqueville's dread of democratic despotism, his concern for local liberties, associations, and individuals, and his warning against the corrupting forces of material aggrandizement and consolidation are the principal topics with which Nisbet is concerned, in his analysis of the nature of true community:

The family, religious association, and local community—these, the conservatives insisted, cannot be regarded as the external products of man's thought and behavior; they are essentially prior to the individual and are the indispensable supports of belief and conduct. Release man from the contexts of community and you get not freedom and rights but intolerable aloneness and subjection to demoniac fears and passions. Society, Burke wrote in a celebrated line, is a partnership of the dead, the living, and the unborn. Mutilate the roots of society and tradition, and the result must inevitably be the isolation of a generation from its heritage, the isolation of individuals from their fellow men, and the creation of the sprawling, faceless masses.

The towering moral problem of our time, Nisbet reasons, is the problem of community lost and community regained. We long desperately for a sense of continuity in our existence, and a sense of direction; these are denied to most of us by the decay of family, the obliteration of the old guild-organization, the retreat of local spirit before the centralized state, and the forlorn condition of religious belief. The most conspicuous result of the revolutionary destruction of traditional society—a result, too, of mass industrialism—has been the creation of the Lonely Crowd: a mass of individuals without real community, aware that they matter to no one, and often convinced that nothing else matters. The assault on institutional religion, on old-fashioned economic methods, on family authority, and on small political communities has set the individual free from nearly everything, truly: but that freedom is a terrifying thing, the freedom of a baby deserted by his parents to do as he pleases. In reaction against these negative liberties, presently the confused and resentful masses incline toward any fanaticism that promises to assuage their loneliness— the Communist or Fascist parties, the lunatic dissidence of dissent, the totalist state with its delusions.

Increasingly, individuals seek escape from the freedom of impersonality, secularism, and individualism. They look for community in marriage, thus putting, often, an intolerable strain upon a tie already grown institutionally fragile. They look for it in easy religion, which leads frequently to a vulgarization of Christianity the like of which the world has not seen before. They look for it in the psychiatrist's office, in the cult, in functionless ritualizations of the past, and in all the other avocations of relief from nervous exhaustion.

Collectivism, the antithesis of true community, "comes to reveal itself to many minds as a fortress of security, against not only institutional conflicts but conflicts of belief and value that are internal to the individual." It is not poverty that induces the masses to support totalitarian parties, but the longing for certitude and membership. "To say that the well-fed worker will never succumb to the lure of communism is as absurd as to say that the well-fed intellectual will never succumb. The presence or absence of three meals a day, or even the simple possession of a job, is not the decisive factor. What is decisive is the frame of reference. If, for one reason or another, the individual's immediate society comes to seem remote, purposeless, and hostile, if a people come to sense that, altogether, they are victims of discrimination and exclusion, not all the food and jobs in the world will prevent them from looking for the kind of surcease that comes with membership in a social and moral order seemingly directed toward their very souls."

Institutions decay when they are deprived of function; thus the family is disintegrating before our eyes not because of "sexual maladjustment'' and ''family tensions'' (those darling phrases of certain sociologists), but because it has been deprived of its old economic and educational advantages. So it is with aristocracy, local government, guild, church, and the other elements which bound man to man for many centuries. It is doubtful whether new voluntary associations have helped in considerable degree to supply the sense of community that these institutions nourished; and thus the social planners, who once expected to arrange matters easily by a Benthamite calculus, ''frequently find themselves dealing not simply with the upper stratum of decisions, which their forebears assumed would be the sole demand of a planned society, but often with baffling problems which reach down into the very recesses of human personality.''

All history, and modern history especially, in some sense is the account of the decline of community and the ruin consequent upon that loss. In this process, the triumph of our modern state has been the most powerful factor. ''The single most decisive influence upon Western social organization has been the rise and development of the centralized territorial state.'' There is every reason to regard the state in history as, to use a phrase that Gierke applied to Rousseau's doctrine of the General Will, ''a process of permanent revolution.'' Hostile toward every institution which acts as a check upon its power, the nation-state has been engaged, ever since the decline of the medieval order, in stripping away one by one the functions and prerogatives of true community—aristocracy, church, guild, family, and local association. What the state seeks is a tableland upon which a multitude of individuals, solitary though herded together, labor anonymously for the state's maintenance. Universal military conscription and the ''mobile labor force'' and the concentration-camp are only the more recent developments of this system. The ''pulverizing and macadamizing tendency of modern history'' that Maitland discerned has been brought to pass by ''the momentous conflicts of jurisdiction between the political state and the social associations lying intermediate to it and the individual.'' The same processes may be traced in the history of Greece and Rome; and what came of this, in the long run, was social ennui and political death. All those gifts of variety, contrast, competition, communal pride, and sympathetic association that characterize man at his manliest are menaced by the ascendancy of the omnicompetent state of modern times, resolved for its own security to level the ramparts of traditional community.

Liberation from the dead hand of the past was the object of the devotees of romantic emancipation and of the ''will of the people.'' But because men who ignore the past are condemned to repeat it, this expected emancipation from prescription has become, in the twentieth century, a tyranny more thorough and inescapable than anything known to the despotisms of antiquity, let alone the Old Régime, throughout half of Europe and a large part of the rest of the world. ''Permanent revolution'' means permanent insecurity and permanent injustice. The grim dream of Marx (whose ''withering away of the state'' was in part simply a terminological trick and in part self-deception) is the logical culmination of the levelling and centralizing doctrines popularized, in different guises, by Rousseau and Bentham. Marx predicted the ultimate merging of all things into an amorphous and characterless whole— even ''the gradual abolition of the distinction between town and country, by a more equal distribution of population over the country.'' And as the old elements of true community have been hacked away, men increasingly have been induced to bring Marx's dream to fulfillment, seeking in the vast impersonal state a substitute for all the old associations that, dimly, they know they have lost.

The nineteenth century, Nisbet says, was many things; but most of all, it was the century when the political masses emerged, created by the new industrialism and the destruction of custom and community. ''Between the state and the masses there developed a bond, an affinity, which however expressed—in nationalism, unitary democracy, or in Marxist socialism—made the political community the most luminous of visions. In it lay salvation from economic misery and oppression. In it lay a new kind of liberty, equality, and fraternity. In it lay right and justice. And in it, above all else, lay community.''

So the total community, the omnipotent state, found in the new restless masses the instrument for its triumph. This total state means to destroy all rivals to its power and to subordinate all human relationships to its might. The slogan of the total state varies from country to country and year to year; it does not really matter, this slogan, for it is no more than a pretext, a mere rallying-cry to unite the masses against minorities and against venerable associations. "It can as well be radical equality as inequality, godly piety as atheism, labor as capital, Christian brotherhood as the toiling masses." In all of its forms, however, modern totalitarianism is *not* constructive, but ruinous. The Nazi and Fascist parties were destructive instruments, made possible by the hysteria and the loneliness of the masses who enthusiastically supported them; though now and again these ideologies might endeavor to disguise themselves by talk of "family" and "tradition," this was no better than sham: their nature and object was revoluntionary. "Far from being, as is sometimes absurdly argued, a lineal product of nineteenth-century Conservatism, totalitarianism is, in fact, the very opposite of it." The totalist order destroys minorities by force and terror, but employs flattery and bribery to retain the support of the masses. The modern total state never is an *unpopular* creation.

Because it flourishes upon rootlessness among the masses, the total state detests and endeavors to obliterate knowledge of the past. "A sense of the past is far more basic to the maintenance of freedom than hope for the future. . . . Hence the relentless effort by totalitarian governments to destroy memory. And hence the ingenious techniques for abolishing the social allegiances within which individual memory is given strength and power of resistance."

The leaders of yesteryear's liberalism assumed that man is sufficient unto himself; and that assumption was fallacious, for man cannot subsist without community. Individualism and popular sovereignty, the two chief objects of the liberals, have been overwhelmed by the masses and the total state. But the conservatives, who never abandoned the idea of community, still retain vitality, and with them lies the hope for arresting the might of political totalism. "Whatever the basic intellectual significance of existentialism, its present popularity, especially in Western Europe, is one more example of the flamelike attraction that moral atomism and solipsism have for the disinherited and the alienated. When even the ideas of humanitarian liberalism are consigned by the intellectual to the same charnel house that holds the bones of capitalism and nationalism, his emancipation is complete. He is now free—in all his solitary misery." Rousseau and his disciples were resolved to force men to be free; in most of the world, they triumphed; men are set free from family, church, town, class, guild; yet they wear, instead, the chains of the state, and they expire of ennui or stifling loneliness:

It is absurd to suppose that the rhetoric of nineteenth-century individualism will offset present tendencies in the direction of the absolute political community. Alienation, frustration, the sense of aloneness—these, as we have seen, are the major states of mind in Western society at the present time. The image of man is decidedly different from what it was in the day of Mill. It is ludicrous to hold up the asserted charms of individual release and emancipation to populations whose most burning problems are those arising, today, from moral and social release. To do so is but to make the way of the Grand Inquisitor the easier. For this is the appeal . . . of the totalitarian prophet—to "rescue" masses of atomized individuals from their intolerable individualism.

Yet true individuality is desperately needed in our age; and so is real democracy—not unitary democracy, like that of Turgot or Rousseau, but the democracy that means genuine participation of the citizen in communal affairs; and so is liberty—though not the dogmatic "liberalism" of the last century. All these are barriers against total power. How may true individuality and democracy and liberal spirit contend successfully against Leviathan? Why, first of all, by acting upon the principle that the will is free. More than anything else, the influence that has aided the growth of the total state has been the assumption that such is the ineluctable course of history. The prophecies of Marx, like the prophecies of Knox, were of the order of those that work their own fulfillment. If conviction of the inevitability of gradualism prevails in the minds of men a few years longer, "the transition from liberal democracy to totalitarianism will not seem too arduous or unpleasant. It will indeed be scarcely noticed save by the 'utopians,' the 'reactionaries,' and similar eccentrics."

Centralization and political collectivism, nevertheless, are not irresistibly ordained, the fashionable current of opinion among the intellectuals notwithstanding. "Among modern intellectuals the cardinal sin is that of failing to remain on the locomotive of history, to use Lenin's expressive phrase." The fashionable intellectual is wrong through and through in this assumption, as he is wrong in nearly everything else. Men are rational beings, not creatures of circumstances purely; they still have it in their power to arrest this totalist evil, which becomes a necessity only to societies hopelessly decadent.

To check centralization and usurping of power, Nisbet continues, we require a new *laissez-faire*. The old *laissez-faire* was founded upon a misapprehension of human nature, an exaltation of individuality (in private character often a virtue) to the condition of a political dogma, which destroyed the spirit of community and reduced men to so many equipollent atoms of humanity, without sense of brotherhood or of purpose. And this old *laissez-faire*, once confronted with the brute force of the masses and the intricate machine of collectivism, necessarily collapsed because it had no communal force behind it; the individual stood defenseless before the commissar. Our new *laissez-faire*, however, "will hold fast to the ends of autonomy and freedom of choice." It will commence not with the abstract Economic Man or Citizen, but with "the personalities of human beings as they are actually given to us in association." The new *laissez-faire* will endeavor to create conditions "within which *autonomous groups* may prosper." It will recognize as the basic social unit the *group:* the family, the local community, the trade union, the church, the college, the profession. It will seek not unity, not centralization, not power over masses of people, but rather diversity of culture, plurality of association, and division of responsibilities. Repudiating the error of the total state, it will restore the sort of State through which, as Burke said, Providence designed that men should seek their perfection as persons. In such a state, the primacy of ethics is recognized, and the true freedom of the person, which subsists in community, will be guarded jealously.

With variations, what Nisbet writes has been expressed by a good many scholars during these past two decades. The variations are to be expected and welcomed: for conservatism is not an ideology, but instead a mode of looking at human nature and society. It is unnecessary, indeed, that a scholar calls himself a "conservative" to share substantially this understanding of means for recovering order in the person and in the community. To name only American writers of recent decades, concerned with the "human sciences," would fill this chapter with too long a roster. These scholars are linked, however loosely, in assertion of the permanent things against the demands of eager ideology. Many of them—historians, economists, political theorists, sociologists—write well, and stand high in the Academy. In the long run, quite conceivably, their influence will be powerful upon the rising generation of serious journalists, publishers, clergymen, teachers, public men, and other molders of popular opinion. No new radical system of belief has appeared to do battle with them: their ideological adversaries are merely latter-day Marxists or anarchists who have learned nothing and forgotten nothing during the past several decades. The conservative scholars are resisted, nevertheless, by the intellectual apathy of the American and British democracies—by populations as yet only vaguely aware that the order they have known must be renewed, or else must perish. What today's conservative thinkers have to fear, then, is not defeat in an intellectual contest, but rather eucatastrophe: that is, the collapse of the whole moral and social structure of modern civilization, before their arguments can move the minds and courses of the crowd. They know that this may be "the last hour before the fall."

These scholars have not been moved by those ideological prophecies which are meant to work their own fulfillment. Among them, cheerfulness will keep breaking in. A conservative historian of social institutions, Rowland Berthoff, speaks for them when he affirms that despite the disorders of American life, despite the neglect of community, much remains to conserve and to renew:

Fortunately the curious cycle through which American society had passed in its first 360 years left a growing sense that the good society could not be built merely by cutting the individual adrift from all institutions and structures. At best, too much of his energy and attention had to be devoted to keeping the society going at all....At worst, the detached individual had become fearful, embittered, and unable to look beyond material success to any higher value of life. For a higher freedom—liberation of his energy and talents for cultural and spiritual self-fulfillment—evidently the support of a stable, well-founded social structure was as necessary as the checks and balances of the new economic system. By the late 1960s Americans were perhaps closer to ensuring the individual a positive and many-sided liberty than at any time in at least a century and a half. If in their perennial aspiration toward a great society they could keep a reasonable balance between change and order, economic mobility and social stability, they might yet bring about the new birth of freedom, the city upon a hill, the beacon to all mankind, of the long-troubled American dream.[17]

To the intellectuals, the scholars had not yielded. And their learning is allied nowadays with the armed vision of the poets.

4

For, dear me, why abandon a belief
Merely because it ceases to be true?
Cling to it long enough, and not a doubt
It will turn true again, for so it goes.
Most of the change we think we see in life
Is due to truths being in and out of favor.
As I sit here, and oftentimes, I wish

> I could be monarch of a desert land
> I could devote and dedicate forever
> To the truths we keep coming back and back to.
> —Robert Frost, "The Black Cottage"

Society's regeneration cannot be an undertaking wholly political. Having lost the spirit of consecration, the modern masses are
without expectation of anything better than a bigger slice of what
they possess already. Dante says that damnation is a terribly simple state: the deprivation of hope—or, as Christ speaks in the York
Mysteries,

> Ye cursed caitiffs, from me flee,
> In hell to dwell without an end.
> There shall ye nought but sorrow see
> And sit by Sathanas the fiend.

How to restore a living faith to the lonely crowd, how to remind men that life has ends—this conundrum the twentieth-
century conservative faces. Along with the consolations of faith,
perhaps three other passionate human interests have provided the
incentive to performance of duty—and the reason for believing
that life is worth living—among ordinary men and women: the
perpetuation of their own spiritual existence through the life and
welfare of their children; the honest gratification of acquisitive
appetite through accumulation and bequest of property; the com-
forting assurance that continuity is more probable than change—in
other words, men's confidence that they participate in a natural
and a moral order in which they count for more than the flies of
a summer. With increasing brutality, the modern temper—first
under capitalism, then under state socialism—has ignored these
longings of humanity. So frustration distorts the face of society
as it mars the features of individuals. The behavior of modern
society now exhibits the symptoms of a consummate hideous frustration.

"I think it would be very wicked indeed to fit a boy for the
modern world," say Evelyn Waugh's luckless classics-master Scott-

King, in *Scott-King's Modern Europe*. To adjust oneself or others to the shape of things which the positivistic planner has in mind, or to the present temper of society, would be conformity with a dread boredom. Triumphant social boredom is at once death and hell for a civilization. So the conservative seeks to look beyond humanitarian sociology.

Not to the statistician, then, but to the poet, do many conservatives turn for insight. If there has been a principal conservative thinker in the twentieth century, it is T. S. Eliot, whose age this is in humane letters. Eliot's whole endeavor was to point a way out of the Waste Land toward order in the soul and in society.

"Conservatism is too often conservation of the wrong things," Eliot wrote in *The Idea of a Christian Society*, "Liberalism a relaxation of discipline; revolution a denial of the permanent things." The conservatism of Eliot is not the attitude of the dragon Fafnir, muttering "Let me rest—I lie in possession."

In the mind of Eliot, English and American conservative experiences are joined, for he listened to Irving Babbitt at Harvard, and lived most of his life in London. One of the kindliest of men, Eliot entered with some reluctance upon political controversy; but once in the struggle, he bore himself with courage.

In *The Idea of a Christian Society* (1939) and *Notes towards the Definition of Culture* (1948), the most influential poet and critic of his age, the unsparing spectator of the Waste Land of modern culture, took up the defense of the beliefs and customs that nourish civilization, bitterly aware that we are "destroying our ancient edifices to make ready the ground upon which the barbarian nomads of the future will encamp in their mechanized caravans." This menace is imminent: for our mechanical civilization already has accustomed masses of the population to the notion of society as a machine. "The tendency of unlimited industrialism is to create bodies of men and women—of all classes—detached from tradition, alienated from religion, and susceptible to mass suggestion: in other words, a mob. And a mob will be no less a mob if it is well fed, well clothed, well housed, and well disciplined."[18]

No friend to pure democracy, Eliot believed in class and order; for that very reason, he distrusted the new elite, recruited from this mob of the spiritually improverished. Trained at uniform state schools in the new orthodoxies of secular collectivism, arrogant with the presumption of those who rule without the restraining influences of tradition and reverence and family honor, such an elite must be no more than an administrative corps; they cannot become the guardians of culture, as were the old aristocracies. "The elites, in consequence, will consist solely of individuals whose only common bond will be their professional interest; with no social cohesion, with no social continuity. They will be united only by a part, and that the most conscious part, of their personalities; they will meet like committees. The greater part of their 'culture' will be only what they share with all the other individuals composing their nation."[19]

No high culture is conceivable in a society dominated by this arid caste of officialdom. Can we save the civilization that remains to us, battered though it has been in this century? "We must proceed to consider how far these conditions of culture are possible, or even, in a particular situation at a particular time, compatible with all the immediate and pressing needs of an emergency. For one thing to avoid is a *universalized* planning; one thing to ascertain is the limits of the plannable."[20]

In such passages, he went to the heart of the matter. Fairly early, Eliot called himself a royalist, rather than a conservative. Here he had in mind a distinction between Toryism and the unimaginative fusion of factions that made up the English Conservative party between the two World Wars. In terms of political principle, despite that, Eliot was conservative enough—or reactionary, as he said of himself. This was made clear in his lecture (1956) to the Conservative Political Centre on "The Literature of Politics." It was no accident that the dominant poet of the twentieth century—who, with reason, saw himself in the line of Vergil and Dante—stood up conspicuously as a defender of norms in culture and in the civil social order.

He combined in himself, Eliot confessed, "a Catholic cast of mind, a Calvinistic heritage, and a Puritanical temperament." Nowadays Dante and Milton hold some common ground against the advocates of what C. S. Lewis called "the abolition of man." Much of Eliot's early popularity may have been founded upon a ludicrous misapprehension of his intentions: a feeling, especially among the rootless and aimless of the new generation, that Eliot spoke for the futility and fatuity of the modern era, all whimper and no bang—a kind of Anglo-American ritualistic nihilism.

Eliot's real function, for all that, was one of conserving and restoring: melancholy topographer of the Waste Land, but guide to recovered personal hope and public integrity. Having exposed the Hollow Men, diseased by life without principle, Eliot—like Vergil in a comparable age—showed the way back to the permanent things. "When I wrote a poem called *The Waste Land*," he said in his "Thoughts after Lambeth" (1931), "some of the more approving critics said that I had expressed 'the disillusionment of a generation,' which is nonsense. I may have expressed for them their own illusion of being disillusioned, but that did not form part of my intention."

The struggle to uphold the permanent things has no surcease. As Eliot wrote in his essay on Francis Herbert Bradley, "If we take the widest and wisest view of a Cause, there is no such thing as a Lost Cause, because there is no such thing as a Gained Cause. We fight for lost causes because we know that our defeat and dismay may be the preface to our successors' victory, though that victory itself will be temporary; we fight rather to keep something alive than in the expectation that it will triumph." In every period, some will endeavor to pull down the permanent things, and others will defend them manfully.

No less than politicians do, great poets move nations, even though the generality of men may not know the poets' names. When the chief poet and critic of the century sets his hand to "redeeming the time: so that the Faith may be preserved alive through the dark ages before us; to renew and rebuild civilization, and save the World from suicide"—why, it is conceivable that he may undo Marx and Freud, not to mention captains and

kings. As much as any man in his time, Eliot foresaw the destruc-
tion of order, and labored to avert total ruin. In the pageant *The Rock* (1934), his chorus intones that warning:

> It is hard for those who live near a Police Station
> To believe in the triumph of violence.
> Do you think that the Faith has conquered the World
> And that lions no longer need keepers?

A few months after *The Rock* first was performed, Adolf Hitler made himself German Führer. Until the end of time, Eliot knew, lions will need keepers, and the Faith will find martyrs. Through the whole of Eliot's writing there runs the idea of a community of souls: a bond of love and duty joining all the living, and also those who have preceded us and those who will follow us in this moment of time. That perception may outlast the ideological dog-mas of this century.

It has been a chief purpose of good poetry to reinterpret and vindicate the norms of human existence. Generally the poet knows that we were not born yesterday. Certainly some poets have been radicals: there is the Promethean defiance of Shelley. And yet neither "romantic" nor "proletarian" poetic dissent has long dominated the republic of letters. Just past the summit of the Romantics' revolutionary enthusiasm, Shelley was answered by Coleridge, Wordsworth, Southey, and Scott; while even Byron thought Shelley's first principles nonsensical. From the beginnings of European literature until this century, the enduring themes of serious poetry have been those of order and permanence. After some decades of protest and negation, twentieth-century poetry returns to an affirmation of continuity and lasting truths.

John Betjeman's *Collected Poems* (1959) have enjoyed a popular-ity rare since the days of *Childe Harold* and *Idylls of the King*. And Betjeman, Tory wit, lover of things ancient, architect and cham-pion of preservation, stood for what has been called "the conser-vatism of enjoyment": for the satisfaction of generation linking with generation. Better than any polemicist, Betjeman—in "The

Planster's Vision"—rouses us to the peril of the possible future spiritless despotism of mediocrity, the totally planned society of the egalitarian visionary:

> *I* have a Vision of The Future, chum,
> The workers' flats in fields of soya beans
> Tower up like silver pencils, score on score:
> And Surging Millions hear the Challenge come
> From microphones in communal canteens
> "No Right! No Wrong! All's perfect, evermore."

Only this one poem of Betjeman's is directly political. The conservative need not be a practical politician; for that matter, the conservative poet may not call himself conservative, nor even know that his first assumptions have something in common with those of Cicero or Burke. There come times when conservatively-inclined poets turn to political verse about the controversies of the hour: Canning, Frere, and other members of the *Anti-Jacobin Review* circle, for instance. Yet ordinarily such is not their more enduring work. The conservative impulse rarely produces so memorable a long political poem as Sir Osbert Sitwell's *Demos the Emperor*, with its gloomily splendid prologue.

Not often in his treatment of prudential and existential concerns, but frequently in his deeper assumptions concerning the soul, justice, and order, a poet reveals the political background of his vision. So it is that there were poetic conservatives long before "conservative" became a noun of politics. No mere defender of the establishments of the hour, the poet is loyal to norms, not to factions; thus, with Ben Jonson, he scourges the follies of the time. Every age is out of joint, in the sense that man and society never are what they ought to be; and the poet senses that he is born to set the time right—not, however, by leading a march to some New Jerusalem, but by rallying in his art to the permanent things. Even good poets commonly considered radical—William Morris, for one—often are not looking for a brave new world, but instead seek to restore what once was, and so may be again.

Homer, "the blind man who sees," looked with high scorn upon the brutal and unjust "Age of Heroes," as Eric Voegelin points out in his *World of the Polis*. Surviving perhaps from an earlier and better culture, Homer appealed to the assembly of gods for judgment upon a debased age. Sophocles, constant to normative truth in a century undone by sophistry, exhorted the Athenians to obey divine injunctions, superior to the edicts of man. Vergil, seeking to restore civilization after a generation of civil war, took for his themes the high old Roman virtue and the life-giving Roman piety. Dante, seeing the medieval order shattered by ignorance, selfishness, and crime, described in his vision the antagonist realms of order and disorder.

In English letters, dominated by normative and ethical convictions more strongly than is any other national body of literature, the conservative cast of opinions scarcely requires mention. The emphasis of Milton upon ordered liberty; the politics of Dryden, anticipating Burke's; the Tory principles of Swift and Pope; the doctrines of ordination and subordination, so strong in Johnson; the conservative Christian humanism of Coleridge; Yeats' passionate attachment to tradition and continuity—these are so many instances of the point. But one cannot undertake here an historical survey of poets' opposition to what Samuel Johnson, in *Irene*, called "the lust of innovation." It may suffice to observe that most influential English and American poets of the twentieth century have been conservators of the permanent things.

Robert Frost may have expressed mild reservations about the word "conservative," but his own political conservatism is undeniable. Some radical critics like to quote Frost's early remark that he never was a radical when young, for fear he might be a conservative when old. However that may be, Frost never flirted with radicalism; and the conservative character of his later years is suggested by "The Figure a Poem Makes," the preface to his *Collected Poems*. "We prate of freedom," he wrote there. "We call our schools free because we are not free to stay away from them until we are sixteen years of age. I have given up my democratic prejudices and now willingly set the lower classes free to be completely taken care of by the upper classes. Political freedom is nothing to me. I bestow it left and right....More than once I should have lost my soul to radicalism if it had been the originality it was mistaken for by its young converts.''

For the neoterist and doctrinaire reformer, Frost had no fellow-feeling. Harrison, in ''A Case for Jefferson,'' is a Freudian and Marxist, though of pure Yankee stock:

> He dotes on Saturday pork and beans.
> But his mind is scarcely out of his teens.
> With him the love of country means
> Blowing it all to smithereens
> And having it all made over new.

One reason for Frost's popular successes, aside from his high talent, is his affinity with the old America, and with views of humanity and art older still. From tradition came his strength.

A Tory poet, Kipling, prophesied that the gods of the copybook headings with fire and slaughter would return; and so have they come among us again, and they smite with increasing fury. A chastened generation looks for the principles of order. The skies grow dark, and sober counsels obtain a hearing; as Chesterton wrote in *The Ballad of the White Horse*—

> The wise men know what wicked things
>   Are written on the sky,
> They trim sad lamps, they touch sad strings,
> Hearing the heavy purple wings,
> Where the forgotten seraph kings
>   Still plot how God shall die.

Yet such champions of orthodoxy as Chesterton go gaily in the dark. Not to the romantic liberal enthusiast, nor to the glowering proletarian poet, nor to the versifying nihilist, can a chastened generation turn. They must look, instead, to the poetic defenders of normality, though for a time such poets lay under a cloud. As

Kipling expressed this, in "The Fabulists," written during the
first great war of this time of troubles—

> When desperate Folly daily laboreth
>   To work confusion upon all we have,
> When diligent Sloth demandeth Freedom's death,
>   And banded Fear commandeth Honour's grave
> Even in that certain hour before the fall
> Unless men please they are not heard at all.

The poets of permanence have begun to please again. It even
is conceivable that Fafnir-conservatives may listen to them. If that
should come to pass, some sting might be drawn from the definition of "conservative" in Ambrose Bierce's *Devil's Dictionary*:
"Conservative, *n*. A statesman who is enamored of existing evils,
as distinguished from the Liberal, who wishes to replace them with
others."

In the present decade, liberalism and socialism lie prostrate,
and for the most part fallen from public favor. A New Order,
nevertheless, struggles to arise: an order of the lords of misrule,
described in *Troilus and Cressida*—

> Strength should be lord of imbecility,
> And the rude son should strike the father dead:
> Force should be right; or rather, right and wrong
> Between whose endless jar justice resides,
> Should lose their names, and so should justice too.
> Then everything includes itself in power,
> Power into will, will into appetite.

Nothing is but thinking makes it so. If men of affairs can rise
to the summons of the poets, the norms of culture and politics
may endure despite the follies of the time. The individual is foolish;
but the species is wise; and so the thinking conservative appeals
to what Chesterton called "the democracy of the dead." Against
the hubris of the ruthless innovator, the conservative of imagination pronounces Cupid's curse:

They that do change old love for new,
Pray gods they change for worse.

NOTES

CHAPTER I

1. Hearnshaw, *The Social and Political Ideas of Some Representative Thinkers of the Revolutionary Era*, p. 8.
2. Simpson, *Memoir, Letters, and Remains of Tocqueville*, II, p. 260.
3. Feiling, *Toryism*, pp. 37–38.

CHAPTER II

1. Quoted in Cobban, *Edmund Burke and the Revolt Against the Eighteenth Century*, p. 85.
2. Buckle, *History of Civilization in England*, I, pp. 424–25.
3. J. G. Baldwin, *Party Leaders*, pp. 144–45.
4. Cecil, *The Young Melbourne*, p. 20.
5. Birrell, *Obiter Dicta*, Second Series, pp. 188–89.
6. Burke, "Thoughts on the Present Discontents," *Works*, I, p. 323.
7. Tocqueville, *The Old Régime*, pp. 33–34.
8. Bissett, *Edmund Burke*, p. 429.
9. Wilson, "Edmund Burke and the French Revolution," *The Century Magazine*, LXII, No. 5, p. 792.
10. Burke to Lord Fitzwilliam, November 29, 1793—Wentworth Woodhouse Papers, Book I, 945 (Sheffield Public Library).
11. P. P. Howe, *The Life of William Hazlitt*, p. 60.
12. MacIver, *The Modern State*, p. 148.
13. "Appeal from the New to the Old Whigs," *Works*, III, p. 79.
14. MacCunn, *The Political Philosophy of Burke*, p. 127.
15. "Reflections on the Revolution in France," *Works*, II, p. 370.
16. *Ibid.*, pp. 363–64.
17. Woolf, *After the Deluge*, p. 177.
18. "Speech on the Petition of the Unitarians," *Works*, VI, p. 115.
19. Cobban, *Edmund Burke*, p. 93.
20. "Tracts on the Popery Laws," *Works*, VI, p. 22.
21. *Ibid.*, pp. 32–33.
22. *Ibid.*, pp. 21–22.
23. Hooker, *Ecclesiastical Polity*, Book V, Chapter 69.
24. Buckle, *op. cit.*, I, pp. 418–19.
25. "Speech on the Petition of the Unitarians," *Works,* VI, pp. 112–13.
26. "Reflections," *Works*, II, p. 359.
27. *The World*, No. 112.
28. "Reflections," *Works*, II, pp. 366–67.
29. "Appeal from the New Whigs," *Works,* III, pp. 111–12.
30. Wallas, *Human Nature in Politics*, pp. 182–83.
31. Babbitt, *Democracy and Leadership*, p. 116.
32. "Letter to Sir Hercules Langrische on the Catholics" (1792), *Works,* III, p. 340.
33. Hoffman and Levack, *Burke's Politics*, pp. xiv–xv.

34. "Speech on Fox's East-India Bill," *Works*, II, p. 278.
35. "Letters on a Regicide Peace," *Works*, II, p. 278.
36. "Reflections," *Works*, II, pp. 334-35.
37. "Tracts on the Popery Laws," *Works*, VI, pp. 29-30.
38. ."Appeal from the New Whigs," *Works*, III, pp. 108-9.
39. "Reflections," *Works*, II, p. 335.
40. *Ibid.*, pp. 322-23.
41. "Regicide Peace," *Works*, II, p. 216.
42. "Petition of the Unitarians," *Works*, VI, p. 124.
43. "Reflections," *Works*, II, pp. 331-32.
44. "Appeal from the New Whigs," *Works*, III, pp. 108-9.
45. "Reform of Representation," *Works*, VI, pp. 145-47.
46. "Reflections," *Works*, II, p. 310.
47. "Appeal from the New Whigs," *Works*, III, p. 83.
48. *Ibid.*, p. 85.
49. "Reflections," *Works*, II, pp. 332-33.
50. *Ibid.*, p. 325.
51. Thomson, *Equality*, p. 68.
52. "Thoughts on the Present Discontents," *Works*, I, p. 323.
53. "Speech on a Bill for Repeal of the Marriage Act" (1781), *Works*, VI, p. 171.
54. "Appeal from the New Whigs," *Works*, III, p. 85.
55. *Ibid.*, p. 86.
56. "Reflections," *Works*, II, p. 307.
57. Burke to Lord Fitzwilliam, November 21, 1791—Wentworth Woodhouse
     Papers, Book I, p. 712 (Sheffield Public Library).
58. Willey, *The Eighteenth-Century Background*, pp. 244-45.
59. Maugham, "After Reading Burke," *The Cornhill Magazine*, winter, 1950-51.

CHAPTER III

1. Fay, *English Economic History, Mainly since 1700*, p. 48.
2. *The Federalist*, No. 17.
3. "The Continentalist," No. V, April 18, 1782, *Works of Hamilton*, I, p. 255.
4. *Ibid.*, p. 263.
5. John Quincy Adams to John Adams, July 27, 1795, *Writings of J. Q. Adams*, I,
     pp. 388-89.
6. "The Stand," *Works of Hamilton*, V, p. 410.
7. Fisher Ames, "Dangers of American Liberty," *Works* (1809), p. 434.
8. J. Q. Adams, "Parties in the United States," *Selected Writings of John and J. Q.
     Adams*, pp. 325-26.
9. Ames, letter of October 26, 1803, *Works*, p. 483.
10. Ames, letter of March 10, 1806, *Works*, p. 512.
11. Ames, letter of November 6, 1807, *Works*, p. 519.
12. Hamilton, *Works*, VI, p. 391.
13. *Selected Works of John and J. Q. Adams*, p. 148.
14. John Adams, *Works*, VI, pp. 402-3.
15. *Ibid.*, VI, p. 516.
16. *Ibid.*, VI, p. 232.
17. *Ibid.*, IV, pp. 444-45.

18. *Ibid.*, VI, p. 279.
19. *Ibid.*, X, p. 101.
20. *Ibid.*, VI, p. 416.
21. *Ibid.*, VI, p. 275.
22. *Ibid.*, VI, p. 518.
23. *Ibid.*, VI, pp. 519-20.
24. *Ibid.*, X, p. 218.
25. *Ibid.*, VI, p. 454.
26. *Ibid.*, IV, p. 389.
27. *Ibid.*, I, p. 462.
28. *Ibid.*, VI, pp. 451-52.
29. *Selected Writings of John and J. Q. Adams,* p. 169.
30. John Adams, *Works,* VI, p. 457.
31. *Ibid.*, VI, p. 249.
32. *Ibid.*, VI, pp. 285-86.
33. *Ibid.*, IV, p. 193.
34. *Ibid.*, VI, p. 418.
35. *Ibid.*, IX, p. 602.
36. *Selected Writings of John and J. Q. Adams,* pp. 57-58.
37. John Adams, *Works,* X, p. 377.
38. *Selected Writings of John and J. Q. Adams*, pp. 208-9.
39. Hallowell, *The Decline of Liberalism as an Ideology,* p. 23.
40. John Adams, *Works,* IV, p. 301.
41. *Ibid.*, IV, p. 579.
42. *Ibid.*, IV, p. 431.
43. *Ibid.*, IV, p. 290.
44. *Ibid.*, IV, p. 290.
45. *Ibid.*, VI, pp. 477-78.
46. *Ibid.*, IV, p. 588.
47. *Ibid.*, X, p. 267.
48. *Ibid.*, IV, p. 359.
49. *Ibid.*, IX, pp. 630-31.
50. Taylor, *Construction Construed and Constitutions Vindicated,* p. 77.

CHAPTER IV

1. Lockhart, *Scott,* II, p. 111.
2. Brinton, *English Political Thought in the Nineteenth Century,* p. 15.
3. Leavis, *Mill on Bentham and Coleridge,* p. 42.
4. Keynes, *Two Memoirs,* pp. 96-97.
5. Burke, "Tracts on the Popery Laws," *Works,* VI, p. 22.
6. Lockhart, *Scott,* X, p. 32.
7. Leslie Stephen, *Hours in a Library,* I, pp. 163-64.
8. Lockhart, *Scott,* III, pp. 305-6.
9. *Ibid.*, VIII, p. 290.
10. *Ibid.*, IX, p. 218.
11. *Ibid.*, IX, p. 298.
12. *Ibid.*, X, p. 50.
13. *Ibid.*, VIII, p. 124.

14. Quoted by Feiling, *Sketches in Nineteenth Century Biography*, p. 39.
15. See Petrie, *Life of Canning*, pp. 136–37.
16. *The Greville Diary*, I, pp. 317–18.
17. Willey, *Nineteenth Century Studies*, pp. 1–44.
18. Coleridge, *Lay Sermons*, pp. 149–50.
19. *Table Talk*, p. 52; see also *Aids to Reflection*, p. 105.
20. *Table Talk*, p. 135.
21. Preface to *Table Talk*, p. 10.
22. Brinton, *op. cit.*, pp. 74–75.
23. *Lay Sermons*, pp. 46–47.
24. *The Constitution of Church and State*, p. 79.
25. *Table Talk*, p. 118.
26. Hearnshaw, *Conservatism in England*, pp. 190–91.
27. Leavis, *op. cit.*, p. 152.
28. *Journal of Sir Walter Scott, 1829–1832*, pp. 154–55.

CHAPTER V

1. *Annals of Congress*, Twelfth Congress, Second Session, pp. 184–85.
2. "Onslow to Patrick Henry," *Works of Calhoun*, VI, p. 347.
3. Tucker, "Garland's Life of Randolph," *Southern Quarterly Review*, July, 1851.
4. *Annals of Congress*, Fourteenth Congress, First Session, p. 1132.
5. *Ibid.*, Seventeenth Congress, First Session, pp. 820–21.
6. *Register of Debates*, Nineteenth Congress, Second Session, II, pp. 125–29.
7. Garland, *Randolph of Roanoke*, II, p. 345.
8. *Ibid.*, II, p. 347.
9. *Register of Debates, op. cit.*
10. Richmond *Enquirer*, April 1, 1815.
11. *Ibid.*, June 4, 1824.
12. *Register of Debates, op. cit.*
13. *Annals of Congress*, Seventeenth Congress, First Session, pp. 844–45.
14. Adams, *John Randolph*, p. 273.
15. *Proceedings and Debates of the Virginia State Convention*, p. 317.
16. *Ibid.*, p. 319.
17. *Ibid.*, p. 492.
18. *Ibid.*, pp. 789–91.
19. *Ibid.*, p. 802.
20. Calhoun, "Discourse on the Constitution," *Works*, I, pp. 511–12.
21. "The South Carolina Exposition and Protest," *Works*, VI, p. 29.
22. Coit, *Calhoun*, p. 335.
23. Calhoun, *Works*, VI, p. 75.
24. *Ibid.*, VI, p. 26.
25. *Ibid.*, VI, p. 192.
26. *Ibid.*, VI, p. 229.
27. Parrington, *Main Currents In American Thought*, II, pp. 71–72.
28. "Disquisition on Government," *Works*, I, p. 7.
29. *Ibid.*, pp. 36–37.
30. *Ibid.*, p. 29.
31. "Discourse on the Constitution," *Works*, I, pp. 397–98.

32. "Disquisition on Government," *Works,* I, p. 35.
33. *Ibid.,* p. 55.
34. *Ibid.,* pp. 56-57.
35. *Ibid.,* p. 75.

CHAPTER VI

1. See Morley, *Life of Gladstone,* II, p. 530.
2. Macaulay's argument is summarized in Trevelyan, *Life and Letters of Lord Macaulay,* I, 353-54. But James Mill was the great architect of this policy in India. See Duncan Forbes, "James Mill and India," *The Cambridge Journal,* October, 1951.
3. "Southey's Colloquies on Society," *Miscellaneous Works of Macaulay,* I, pp. 433-34.
4. *Ibid.,* pp. 405-6.
5. "Lord Bacon," *Miscellaneous Works,* II, p. 410.
6. *Ibid.,* p. 411.
7. See Cotter Morison, *Macaulay,* p. 170.
8. *Miscellaneous Works,* V, p. 19.
9. *Ibid.,* V, p. 258.
10. "Mill's Essay on Government," *Miscellaneous Works,* I, p. 316.
11. *Ibid.,* p. 280.
12. *Ibid.,* pp. 310-11.
13. *Ibid.,* p. 315.
14. For an energetic defense of Hegel's collectivism, however, see C. E. Vaughan, *Studies in the History of Political Philosophy before and after Rousseau,* II, p. 163.
15. The complete text of this letter is printed in H. M. Lydenberg (ed.), *What Did Macaulay Say about America?* (New York, New York Public Library, 1925).
16. *Miscellaneous Works,* V, p. 450.
17. Cooper, *The Heidenmauer,* pp. 65-66.
18. *The Bravo,* pp. iii-iv.
19. See "On the Republick of the United States," in *The American Democrat.*
20. *The American Democrat,* pp. 54-61.
21. *Ibid.,* pp. 139-40.
22. *Ibid.,* p. 141.
23. *Ibid.,* p. 71.
24. *Ibid.,* p. 76.
25. *Ibid.,* p. 89.
26. *Ibid.,* p. 112.
27. Grossman, *James Fenimore Cooper,* pp. 263-64.
28. Inge, *The End of an Age,* p. 216.
29. Simpson, *Memoir, Letters, and Remains of Tocqueville,* II, p. 384.
30. Laski, "Tocqueville," in Hearnshaw, *Social and Political Ideas of some Representative Thinkers of the Victorian Age,* pp. 111-12.
31. Joad, *Decadence,* p. 393.
32. *Democracy in America,* II, p. 261.
33. Acton, *Lectures on the French Revolution,* p. 357.
34. Simpson, *Memoir,* II, p. 64.
35. *Democracy in America,* II, p. 318.

36. *Ibid.*, II, p. 136.
37. *Ibid.*, II, pp. 228–29.
38. *Ibid.*, II, p. 133.
39. *Ibid.*, II, p. 145.
40. *Ibid.*, II, p. 148.
41. *Ibid.*, I, p. 327.
42. *Ibid.*, I, p. 236.
43. *Ibid.*, II, pp. 367–68.
44. Tocqueville, *Recollections,* p. 202.
45. *Democracy in America,* II, p. 296.
46. *Ibid.*, II, p. 289.
47. *Ibid.*, II, p. 282.
48. *Ibid.*, II, pp. 245–46.
49. *Ibid.*, I, p. 10.
50. *Recollections,* p. 143.
51. *Democracy in America,* II, p. 88.
52. Tocqueville to Freslon, September 28, 1853 (Simpson, *Memoir,* II, pp. 234–35).
53. *Democracy in America,* I, p. 264.
54. Tocqueville to Mrs. Grote, February 24, 1855 (Simpson, *Memoir,* II, p. 279).
55. *Democracy in America,* I, p. 305.
56. "France before the Revolution," Simpson, *Memoir,* I, p. 256.
57. *Recollections,* p. 216.
58. *Democracy in America,* I, pp. 420–21.
59. Simpson, *Memoir,* II, p. 251.
60. Tocqueville, *The Old Régime,* p. viii.
61. Simpson, *Memoir,* II, p. 251.
62. Tocqueville to Senior, April 10, 1848 (Simpson, *Memoir,* II, p. 91).
63. Simpson, *Memoir,* II, pp. 59–60.
64. *Ibid.*, II, pp. 410–11.
65. *Ibid.*, II, p. 271.
66. Taylor, *From Napoleon to Stalin,* p. 66.

CHAPTER VII

1. Bagot, *George Canning and His Friends,* II, p. 362.
2. Adams' address to his constituents, September 17, 1842, in Quincy, *Memoir of the Life of John Quincy Adams,* pp. 382–83.
3. *The Degradation of the Democratic Dogma,* pp. 34–35.
4. *Writings of John Quincy Adams,* VI, p. 60.
5. *Selected Writings of John Adams and John Quincy Adams,* pp. 400–401.
6. *Memoirs of John Quincy Adams,* V, pp. 10–11.
7. An exception is R. H. Gabriel's chapter on "Democracy and Catholicism," in *The Course of American Democratic Thought.*
8. Brownson, *Essays and Reviews,* p. 352.
9. *Ibid.*, pp. 374–75.
10. *Ibid.*, p. 379.
11. *Ibid.*, pp. 307–8.
12. *Ibid.*, p. 320.
13. *The American Republic,* p. 54.

14. R. C. Churchill, *Disagreements,* p. 197.
15. Hawthorne, dedicatory preface to *Our Old Home* (1863).

CHAPTER VIII

1. Duncan Forbes, *"Historismus* in England," *The Cambridge Journal,* April, 1951, p. 391.
2. Alexander Gray, *The Socialist Tradition,* p. 331.
3. J. L. Gray, "Karl Marx and Social Philosophy," in Hearnshaw, *Social and Political Ideas...of the Victorian Age,* pp. 130-31.
4. A succinct description of these conditions is to be found in R. H. Mottram's chapter "Town Life and London," in Young, *Early Victorian England,* I, p. 167.
5. Feiling, *The Second Tory Party,* p. 396.
6. Disraeli, *Lord George Bentinck,* pp. 498-99.
7. Disraeli, *Coningsby,* Book IV, Chapter III.
8. *Ibid.,* Book VII, Chapter II.
9. *Ibid.,* Book I, Chapter VII.
10. Disraeli, *Letters of Runnymede,* p. 270.
11. Monypenny and Buckle, *Disraeli,* V, p. 410.
12. Bagehot, "The English Constitution," *Works,* V, p. 164.
13. Birch, *The Conservative Party,* p. 20.
14. Disraeli, "The Spirit of Whiggism," in *Letters of Runnymede,* p. 283.
15. Disraeli, *Vindication of the English Constitution,* pp. 203-4.
16. Kebbel, *Selected Speeches of the Earl of Beaconsfield,* I, p. 546.
17. Bagehot, "Lord Althorp and the Reform Act of 1832," *Works,* VII, p. 62.
18. Monypenny and Buckle, *Disraeli,* X, pp. 351-52.
19. Kebbel, *Selected Speeches,* II, pp. 530-33.
20. *Apologia pro Vita Sua,* Chapter V.
21. Young, *Early Victorian England,* II, p. 472.
22. Lord Hugh Cecil, *Conservatism,* p. 68.
23. Newman, *Discussions and Arguments,* p. 272.
24. *Ibid.,* pp. 274-75.
25. Newman, *A Grammar of Assent,* p. 353.
26. Newman, *The Development of Christian Doctrine,* p. 180.
27. *Discussions and Arguments,* p. 305.
28. *Ibid.,* p. 280.
29. *A Grammar of Assent,* p. 377.
30. *The Idea of a University,* Discourse VII, Part I.
31. *Apologia pro Vita Sua,* Chapter V.
32. G. H. Bantock, "Newman and Education," *The Cambridge Journal,* August, 1951; also see Chapter V of Bantock's *Freedom and Authority in Education.*
33. Brinton, *English Political Thought in the Nineteenth Century,* pp. 163-64.
34. Paul Elmer More, "The Spirit of Anglicanism," in More and Cross, *Anglicanism,* p. xxxii.
35. *Discussions and Arguments,* p. 268.
36. See Fergal McGrath's *Newman's University: Idea and Reality.*
37. *The Idea of a University,* Discourse III, Part 6.
38. *Lectures and Essays on University Subjects,* p. 359.

39. *The Idea of a University,* Discourse VII, Part I.
40. Quoted in Jarman, *Landmarks in the History of Education,* pp. 264-68.
41. Monypenny and Buckle, *Disraeli,* II, pp. 62-63.
42. *A Grammar of Assent,* p. 379.
43. Bagehot, "Lord Salisbury on Moderation," *Works,* IX, p. 174.
44. Bagehot, "Physics and Politics," *Works,* VIII, p. 114.
45. *Ibid.,* p. 104.

CHAPTER IX

1. Sir Ernest Barker, *Political Thought in England from Herbert Spencer to the Present Day,* p. 128.
2. Bagehot, "Intellectual Conservatism," *Works,* IX, pp. 255-58.
3. R. J. White, "John Stuart Mill," *The Cambridge Journal,* November, 1951, p. 93.
4. Barker, *op, cit.,* p. 172.
5. Quoted in Annan, *Leslie Stephen,* p. 205.
6. *Liberty, Equality, Fraternity,* pp. 317-18.
7. *Ibid.,* p. 311.
8. *Ibid.,* p. 291.
9. Quoted in Leslie Stephen, *Life of Sir James Fitzjames Stephen,* p. 339.
10. *Liberty, Equality, Fraternity,* pp. 45-46.
11. *Ibid.,* pp. 263-64.
12. *Ibid.,* p. 319.
13. *Ibid.,* pp. 303-4.
14. *Ibid.,* p. 319.
15. *Ibid.,* p. 231.
16. *Ibid.,* p. 31.
17. *Ibid.,* p. 173.
18. *Ibid.,* p. 178.
19. *Ibid.,* p. 221.
20. *Ibid.,* p. 271.
21. *Ibid.,* p. 283.
22. *Ibid.,* pp. 297-98.
23. *Letters of Lord Acton to Mary Gladstone,* p. 119.
24. *Ibid.,* p. 212.
25. Barker, *op. cit.,* p. 167.
26. Maine, *Village Communities,* pp. 238-39.
27. Maine, *Early Law and Custom,* p. 361.
28. Maine, *Village Communities,* pp. 290-91.
29. *Ibid.,* pp. 232-33.
30. *Ibid.,* pp. 214-15.
31. Maine, *Early Institutions,* pp. 360-61.
32. *Letters of Acton to Mary Gladstone,* p. 31.
33. Maine, *Ancient Law,* Chapter V.
34. Duff, *Memoir and Speeches of Maine,* pp. 90-91.
35. *Village Communities,* pp. 225-26.
36. *Ibid.,* p. 230.
37. Maine, *Popular Government,* pp. vii-viii.
38. *Ibid.,* p. 98.
39. *Ibid.,* p. 106.

40. *Ibid.*, p. 111.
41. *Ibid.*, pp. 189–90.
42. *Ibid.*, p. 85.
43. *Ibid.*, pp. 73–74.
44. Leslie Stephen, *Life of J. F. Stephen*, pp. 309–10.
45. Lecky, *History of European Morals from Augustus to Charlemagne*, I, p. 67, note.
46. Lecky, *The Rise and Influence of Rationalism in Europe*, I, pp. 186–87.
47. See Lecky's address at Dublin University on the centenary of Burke's death, in Elizabeth Lecky's *Memoir of Lecky*, pp. 305–6.
48. Lecky, "Old-Age Pensions," *Historical and Political Essays*, p. 300.
49. Lecky, *Democracy and Liberty*, II, p. 353.
50. D. W. Brogan, *The Price of Revolution*, p. 139.
51. *Democracy and Liberty*, I, pp. 319–20.
52. *Ibid.*, pp. 301–2.
53. *Ibid.*, pp. xviii–xix.
54. *Ibid.*, II, pp. 500–1.
55. *Ibid.*, pp. 501–2.
56. Halévy, *History of the English People in the Nineteenth Century*, V, p. x.
57. *Democracy and Liberty*, I, p. 155.
58. *Ibid.*, II, p. 369.
59. Pound, *Interpretations of Legal History*, pp. 54–55.

CHAPTER X

1. Parrington, *The Romantic Revolution in America*, pp. 466–68; Laski, *The American Democracy*, pp. 419–20.
2. *Letters of James Russell Lowell*, I, pp. 78–79.
3. *Ibid.*, II, p. 153.
4. Lowell, *Among My Books*, II, p. 251.
5. Lowell, "Abraham Lincoln," *Political Essays*, p. 186.
6. Lowell to Miss Norton, March 4, 1873, *Letters*, II, p. 103.
7. *Letters*, II, p. 179.
8. *Letters*, II, pp. 194–95.
9. Lowell to Miss Norton, *Letters*, II, p. 276.
10. Lowell, *Political and Literary Addresses*, p. 36.
11. R. C. Beatty, *James Russell Lowell*, pp. 275–78.
12. *Political and Literary Addresses*, pp. 34–35.
13. Lowell to Godkin, October 10, 1874, *Letters*, II, p. 150.
14. *Political and Literary Addresses*, p. 197.
15. Godkin, *Problems of Modern Democracy*, p. 201.
16. Commager, *The American Mind*, p. 68.
17. Godkin, *Unforeseen Tendencies of Democracy*, p. 138.
18. *Problems of Modern Democracy*, p. 325.
19. *Ibid.*, pp. 173–74.
20. *Ibid.*, pp. 109–10.
21. *Ibid.*, p. 193.
22. *Ibid.*, pp. 297–98.
23. Ogden, *Life and Letters of Godkin*, II, p. 199.
24. *Ibid.*, II, p. 253.

25. *Letters of Henry Adams,* I, 5; II, pp. 575-76.
26. *Letters of Adams,* II, p. 49.
27. *The Education of Henry Adams,* pp. 421-22.
28. Winters, *In Defense of Reason,* p. 173.
29. P. E. More, *Shelburne Essays,* XI, p. 140.
30. *Henry Adams and His Friends,* p. 529.
31. *The Education of Henry Adams,* p. 335.
32. *Ibid.,* p. 501.
33. *Henry Adams and His Friends,* p. 438.
34. *Ibid.,* p. 463.
35. *The Education of Henry Adams,* p. 266.
36. *Ibid.,* pp. 494-95.
37. *The Degradation of the Democratic Dogma,* p. 131.
38. *The Education of Henry Adams,* p. 451.
39. More, *Shelburne Essays,* XI, p. 123.
40. *The Degradation of the Democratic Dogma,* pp. vii-viii.
41. Brooks Adams, *America's Economic Supremacy,* p. 133.
42. Brooks Adams, *The Theory of Social Revolutions,* p. 208.
43. Brooks Adams, *The New Empire,* p. xiii.
44. *Ibid.,* p. xxxiv.
45. *Ibid.,* p. 211.
46. *The Degradation of the Democratic Dogma,* p. 119.
47. *Ibid.,* pp. 108-9.
48. *The New Empire,* p. xxxiv.
49. Drucker, *The New Society,* p. xvii.
50. *Letters of Henry Adams*, II, p. 648.

CHAPTER XI

1. G. M. Young, *Last Essays,* pp. 60-61.
2. *The Letters of George Gissing to his Family*, p. 3.
3. *Ibid.,* pp. 326-27.
4. *The Private Papers of Henry Ryecroft,* p. 113.
5. *Letters of Gissing,* p. 71.
6. *Ryecroft,* pp. 268-69.
7. *The Unclassed,* Chapter XXV.
8. Seccombe, introduction to *The House of Cobwebs,* p. xxvi.
9. *Demos,* Chapter XXIX.
10. *Born in Exile,* Part V, Chapter I.
11. *Letters of Gissing,* p. 199.
12. *Ibid.,* pp. 47, 371.
13. *Ryecroft,* p. 56.
14. *Ibid.,* p. 131.
15. *Ibid.,* pp. 136-37.
16. *Ibid.,* pp. 203, 256.
17. Saintsbury, *A Second Scrapbook,* p. 318.
18. W. L. Burn, "English Conservatism," *The Nineteenth Century,* January, 1949, p. 11.
19. Saintsbury, *A Last Scrapbook,* pp. 155-58.
20. R. C. K. Ensor, *England, 1870-1914,* p. 388.

21. D. C. Somervell, *British Politics since 1900*, p. 49.
22. Balfour, *A Defense of Philosophic Doubt*, pp. 326-27.
23. Balfour, *Theism and Humanism*, p. 21.
24. *Ibid.*, pp. 273-74.
25. Balfour, *Theism and Thought*, pp. 32-33.
26. Julian Amery, *The Life of Joseph Chamberlain*, IV, p. 464.
27. *Letters of Henry Adams*, II, p. 576.
28. Balfour, *Essays Speculative and Political*, pp. 32, 49.
29. Tillotson, *Criticism and the Nineteenth Century*, p. 124.
30. Saintsbury, *A Second Scrapbook*, pp. 178-80.
31. Squire, introduction to *The New Republic*, p. 10.
32. Mallock, *Memoirs of Life and Literature*, pp. 251-52.
33. Mallock, *The New Republic*, p. 281.
34. Mallock, *Is Life Worth Living?*, p. 148.
35. *Memoirs of Life and Literature*, p. 135.
36. Mallock, *Social Equality*, p. 22.
37. Mallock, *Labour and the Popular Welfare*, p. 233.
38. Mallock, *Social Reform* (1914), p. 331.
39. *Labour and the Popular Welfare*, p. 147.
40. Mallock, *Aristocracy and Evolution*, p. 180.
41. Mallock, *The Limits of Pure Democracy*, p. 392.
42. Mallock, *The Reconstruction of Belief*, p. 303.
43. *Memoirs of Life and Literature*, p. 273.
44. Ross Hoffman, *The Spirit of Politics and the Future of Freedom*, p. 45.
45. *Is Life Worth Living?*, p. 241.
46. W. L. Burn, "English Conservatism," *The Nineteenth Century*, February, 1949, p. 72.
47. J. M. Keynes, *Two Memoirs*, pp. 99-100.
48. T. E. Hulme, *Speculations*, p. 254.
49. Saintsbury, *A Scrap Book*, p. 48.

CHAPTER XII

1. Babbitt, *Literature and the American College*, p. 60.
2. Babbitt, *Rousseau and Romanticism*, p. 374.
3. *Ibid.*, p. 25.
4. Babbitt, *Democracy and Leadership*, p. 6.
5. Babbitt, *On Being Creative*, p. 232.
6. More, *On Being Human* (New Shelburne Essays, III), p. 27.
7. More, *Shelburne Essays*, VII, pp. 201-2.
8. *On Being Human*, p. 158.
9. *Ibid.*, pp. 268-69.
10. *Shelburne Essays*, IX, p. 21.
11. *Ibid.*, VII, p. 191.
12. *Ibid.*, IX, p. 56.
13. *Ibid.*, XI, p. 256.
14. More, *The Catholic Faith*, p. 170.
15. Quoted in Robert Shafer's *Paul Elmer More and American Criticism*, p. 271.
16. *On Being Human*, p. 143.

17. Santayana, *The Middle Span,* p. 149.
18. *Ibid.,* pp. 35–36.
19. Santayana, *The Realm of Spirit,* p. 219.
20. Santayana, *Soliloquies in England,* p. 188.
21. *The Middle Span,* p. 134.
22. Santayana, *Winds of Doctrine,* p. vi.
23. *Soliloquies in England,* p. 176.
24. Santayana, *Dominations and Powers,* p. 348.
25. Santayana, *Character and Opinion in the United States,* p. 226.
26. Santayana, *Reason in Society,* p. 69.
27. *The Middle Span,* p. 169.
28. *Dominations and Powers,* p. 384.

CHAPTER XIII

1. A. L. Rowse, "University Education for All?", *The National Review* (London), November, 1949.
2. Malcolm Muggeridge, "Books," *Esquire,* September, 1965.
3. Lewis and Maude, *The English Middle Classes,* p. 64.
4. Lord Beveridge, "English Life and Leisure," *The Spectator,* June 8, 1951.
5. Gordon Walker, *Restatement of Liberty,* p. 319.
6. Carr, *The New Society,* pp. 57–58.
7. Huxley, *Proper Studies,* pp. 24–28.
8. Rôpke, *Civitas Humana,* p. 63.
9. Jewkes, *Ordeal by Planning,* p. 228.
10. Jerrold, *England: Past, Present, and Future,* pp. 307–8.
11. Taylor, "Town versus Country," *The New Statesman and Nation,* October 20, 1951, p. 439.
12. Dawson, *Beyond Politics,* p. 21.
13. Oakeshott, *Political Education,* p. 28.
14. More, *Aristocracy and Justice,* pp. 168, 186. See also A. H. Dakin, *Paul Elmer More,* p. 159.
15. Lionel Trilling, *The Liberal Imagination,* p. ix.
16. Robert A. Nisbet, *The Quest for Community* (title of second edition, *Community and Power*), pp. 3, 25, 31, 37, 187, 245, 278–9.
17. Rowland Berthoff, *An Unsettled People: Social Order and Disorder in American History,* pp. 478–9.
18. Eliot, *The Idea of a Christian Society,* p. 21.
19. Eliot, *Notes towards the Definition of Culture,* p. 47.
20. *Ibid.,* p. 109.

A Select Bibliography

THERE ARE LISTED below books mentioned in the preceding chapters, with some additional useful references. The edition of Burke's works cited in the notes is that of Bohn's Standard Library (London, 1854-57, 9 vols.), which is fairly frequently encountered. Of the new scholarly edition of Burke (Oxford University Press), only two volumes have been published at this writing: *Party, Parliament, and the American Crisis, 1766-1774* (Vol. II, 1981, edited by Paul Langford); and *India: Madras and Bengal, 1774-1785* (Vol. V, 1981, edited by P. J. Marshall).

Acton, John Emerich Edward Dalberg (first Baron Acton). *Lectures on Church and State.* Edited by Douglas Woodruff. London, 1952.

(Acton, Lord). *The Correspondence of Lord Acton and Richard Simpson,* Vol. I. Edited by Josef L. Altholz and Damian McElrath. Cambridge, England, 1971.

Acton, Lord. *Essays in the Liberal Interpretation of History.* Edited by William H. McNeill. Chicago, 1967.

Acton, Lord. *The History of Freedom and Other Essays.* Edited by John Neville Figgis and Reginald Vere Laurence. London, 1907.

Acton, Lord. *Lectures on the French Revolution.* Edited by Figgis and Laurence. London, 1916.

Acton, Lord. *Lectures on Modern History.* Edited by Figgis and Laurence. London, 1950.

(Acton, Lord). *Letters of Lord Acton to Mary Gladstone.* Edited by Herbert Paul. London, 1904.

Adams, Brooks. *America's Economic Supremacy.* Edited by Marquis Childs. New York, 1947.

Adams, Brooks, *The Law of Civilization and Decay.* Introduction by Charles A. Beard. New York, 1943.

Adams, Brooks. *The New Empire.* New York, 1903.

Adams, Brooks. *The Theory of Social Revolutions.* New York, 1913.

Adams, Brooks and Henry. *The Degradation of the Democratic Dogma.* New York, 1920.

Adams, Henry. *The Education of Henry Adams.* Boston, 1918.

(Adams, Henry). *Henry Adams and His Friends: a Collection of His Unpublished Letters.* Edited by H. D. Cater. Boston, 1947.

Adams, Henry. *History of the United States during the Administrations of Jefferson and Madison.* 9 vols. New York, 1890-98.

Adams, Henry. *John Randolph.* Boston, 1895.

(Adams, Henry). *Letters of Henry Adams.* Edited by W. C. Ford. 2 vols. Boston and New York, 1930 and 1938.

Adams, Henry. *The Life of Albert Gallatin.* Philadelphia, 1880.

Adams, Henry. *Mont-Saint-Michel and Chartres.* Boston, 1933.

(Adams, John). *Correspondence of John Adams and Thomas Jefferson.* Edited by Paul Wilstach. Indianapolis, 1925.

(Adams, John). *Diary and Correspondence of John Adams.* Edited by L. H. Butterfield. 4 vols. Cambridge, Mass., 1961.

(Adams, John). *Statesman and Friend: Correspondence of John Adams with Benjamin Waterhouse.* Edited by W. C. Ford. Boston, 1927.

Adams, John. *Works.* Edited by Charles Francis Adams. 10 vols. Boston, 1851.

(Adams, John Quincy). *Memoirs of John Quincy Adams.* Edited by C. F. Adams. 12 vols. Philadelphia, 1874-77.

Adams, John Quincy. *Parties in the United States.* New edition. New York, 1941.

(Adams, John Quincy). *The Writings of John Quincy Adams.* Edited by W. C. Ford. 7 vols.

New York, 1913–17.

Ames, Fisher. *Works*. Boston, 1809. Also there is now available a two-volume new edition of Ames' writings, edited by W. B. Allen (Liberty Classics, Indianapolis, 1983).

Anderson, Theodore. *Brooks Adams, Constructive Conservative*. Ithaca, 1951.

Annan, Noel. *Leslie Stephen: His Thought and Character in Relation to His Time*. London, 1951.

Arendt, Hannah. *The Origins of Totalitarianism*. Second edition, Cleveland, 1958.

Arnold, Matthew. *Essays in Criticism*. Third edition, London, 1875.

Babbitt, Irving. *Democracy and Leadership*. Boston, 1924.

Babbitt, Irving. *Literature and the American College*. Boston, 1908.

Babbitt, Irving. *The Masters of Modern French Criticism*. Boston, 1912.

Babbitt, Irving. *The New Laokoon*. Boston, 1910.

Babbitt, Irving. *On Being Creative*. Boston, 1932.

Babbitt, Irving. *Rousseau and Romanticism*. Boston, 1919.

Babbitt, Irving. *Spanish Character, and Other Essays*. Boston, 1940.

(Bagehot, Walter). *The Works and Life of Walter Bagehot*. Edited by Mrs. Russell Barrington. 10 vols. London, 1915.

Bagot, Josceline (ed.). *George Canning and His Friends*. 2 vols. London, 1909.

Balfour, Arthur James (first Earl of Balfour). *Chapters of Autobiography*. London, 1930.

Balfour, Arthur James. *A Defense of Philosophic Doubt*. Second edition, London, 1920.

Balfour, Arthur James. *Essays Speculative and Political*. London, 1921.

Balfour, Arthur James. *The Foundations of Belief*. Second edition, London, 1895.

Balfour, Arthur James. *Theism and Humanism*. London, 1915.

Balfour, Arthur James. *Theism and Thought: a Study in Familiar Beliefs*. London, 1923.

Bantock, G. H. *Freedom and Authority in Education*. London, 1952.

Bantock, G. H. *T.S. Eliot and Education*. London, 1970.

Barker, Sir Ernest. *Church, State, and Study*. London, 1930.

Barker, Sir Ernest. *Political Thought in England from Spencer to the Present Day*. London, n.d.

Barker, Sir Ernest. *Reflections on Government*. Oxford, 1942.

Becker, Carl L. *The Heavenly City of the Eighteenth-Century Philosophers*. New Haven, 1932.

Bemis, Samuel Flagg. *John Quincy Adams*. 2 vols. New York, 1950 and 1956.

Beringause, Arthur F. *Brooks Adams*. New York, 1955.

Bernhard, Winfred E. A. *Fisher Ames, Federalist and Statesman*. Chapel Hill, 1965.

Berthoff, Rowland. *An Unsettled People: Social Order and Disorder in American History*. New York, 1971.

Beveridge, Albert J. *The Life of John Marshall*. 4 vols. Boston, 1916.

Biggs-Davison, John. *George Wyndham: a Study in Toryism*. London, 1951.

Birch, Nigel. *The Conservative Party*. London, 1949.

Blake, Robert. *Disraeli*. London, 1966.

Boorstin, Daniel. *America and the Image of Europe*. New York, 1960.

Boorstin, Daniel. *The Americans*. 3 vols. New York, 1958, 1965, and 1973.

Boorstin, Daniel. *The Decline of Radicalism: Reflections on America Today*. New York, 1969.

Boorstin, Daniel. *The Genius of American Politics*. Chicago, 1953.

Boorstin, Daniel. *The Image, or What Happened to the American Dream*. New York, 1962.

Boorstin, Daniel. *The Lost World of Thomas Jefferson*. Boston, 1948.

Boulton, James T. *The Language of Politics in the Age of Wilkes and Burke*. London, 1963.

Bredvold, Louis. *The Brave New World of the Enlightenment*. Ann Arbor, 1961.

Bredvold, Louis. *The Intellectual Milieu of John Dryden*. Ann Arbor, 1934.

Brightfield, Myron F. *John Wilson Croker*. Berkeley, 1940.

Brinton, Crane. *English Political Thought in the Nineteenth Century*. Cambridge, Mass., 1949.

Brinton, Crane. *The Political Ideas of the English Romanticists*. New York, 1926.

Brogan, Colm. *The Democrat at the Supper Table.* London, 1946.
Brogan, Denis W. *The Price of Revolution.* London, 1951.
Brownson, Orestes. *Selected Essays.* Edited by Russell Kirk. Chicago, 1955.
Brownson, Orestes. *Works.* 20 vols. Detroit, 1882 to 1887.
Bruce, William Cabell. *John Randolph of Roanoke.* 2 vols. New York, 1922.
Buckle, Henry Thomas. *History of Civilization in England.* 2 vols. London, 1857 and 1861.
(Bulwer Lytton). *Lord Lytton's Pamphlets and Sketches.* London, 1875.
Burke, Edmund. *Correspondence.* Edited by Thomas W. Copeland. 10 vols. Chicago, 1958 to 1970.
Burke, Edmund. *The Speeches of the Right Honourable Edmund Burke.* 4 vols. London, 1816.
Burke, Edmund. *Works.* 9 vols. Bohn edition, London, 1854-57.
Calhoun, John C. *The Papers of John C. Calhoun.* Edited by Clyde N. Wilson, W. Edwin Hemphill, *et. al.* 16 vols. Columbia, S.C., 1949-84.
Calhoun, John C. *Works.* Edited by R. K. Crallé. 6 vols. New York, 1851-56.
Canavan, Francis. *The Political Reason of Edmund Burke.* Durham, N.C., 1960.
Canning, George. *Speeches, with a Memoir.* 6 vols. London, 1830.
Cargill, Oscar. *Intellectual America: Ideas on the March.* New York, 1948.
Carr, Edward Hallett. *The New Society.* London, 1951.
Cecil, Lady Gwendolyn. *The Life of Robert, Marquis of Salisbury.* 2 vols. London, 1921.
Cecil, Lord David. *The Young Melbourne.* London, 1939.
Cecil, Lord Hugh. *Conservatism.* London, 1912.
Chinard, Gilbert. *Honest John Adams.* Boston, 1933.
Churchill, Lord Randolph. *Speeches, 1880-1882.* 2 vols. London, 1889.
Churchill, Winston. *Lord Randolph Churchill.* 2 vols. London, 1906.
Cobban, Alfred. *Edmund Burke and the Revolt against the Eighteenth Century.* London, 1929.
Coit, Margaret L. *John C. Calhoun: American Portrait.* Boston, 1950.
Coleridge, Samuel Taylor. *Aids to Reflection.* Edited by Thomas Fenby. London, 1867.
Coleridge, Samuel Taylor. *The Constitution of Church and State, according to the Idea of Each.* Edited by H. N. Coleridge. London, 1852.
Coleridge, Samuel Taylor. *Lay Sermons.* Edited by Derwent Coleridge. Third edition, London, 1852.
Coleridge, Samuel Taylor. *Philosophical Lectures, 1818-1819.* Edited by Kathleen Coburn. London, 1949.
Coleridge, Samuel Taylor. *Table Talk and Omniana.* Edited by T. Ashe. London, 1884.
Cone, Carl B. *Burke and the Nature of Politics.* 2 vols. Lexington, Ky., 1957 and 1964.
Cooper, James Fenimore. *The American Democrat.* Edited by H.L. Mencken. New York, 1931.
Cooper, James Fenimore. *Works.* Mohawk edition, New York, n.d.
Copeland, Thomas W. *Our Eminent Friend, Edmund Burke.* New Haven, 1949.
Cram, Ralph Adams. *The End of Democracy.* Boston, 1937.
Cram, Ralph Adams. *The Nemesis of Mediocrity.* Boston, 1921.
Dakin, Arthur Hazard. *Paul Elmer More.* Princeton, 1960.
Davidson, Donald. *The Attack on Leviathan: Regionalism and Nationalism in the United States.* Chapel Hill, 1938.
Davidson, Donald. *Still Rebels, Still Yankees.* Baton Rouge, 1957.
Dicey, Albert V. *Lectures on the Relations between Law and Public Opinion in England in the Nineteenth Century.* London, 1905.
Disraeli, Benjamin. *Novels.* Introduction by Philip Guedalla. 12 vols. Bradenham edition, London, 1926-27.
Disraeli, Benjamin. *Lord George Bentinck.* London, 1852.

Disraeli, Benjamin. *The Runnymede Letters.* Introduction by Francis Hitchman. London, 1895.

(Disraeli, Benjamin). *Selected Speeches of the Right Honourable the Earl of Beaconsfield.* Edited by T. E. Kebbel. 2 vols. London, 1882.

Disraeli, Benjamin. *Vindication of the English Constitution in a Letter to a Noble and Learned Lord.* London, 1855.

Drucker, Peter. *The New Society: The Anatomy of the Industrial Order.* New York, 1949.

Duff, Sir M.E. Grant. *Sir Henry Maine: a Brief Memoir of His Life with Some of His Indian Speeches and Minutes.* London, 1892.

Duggan, Francis X. *Paul Elmer More.* New York, 1966.

Eliot, Thomas Stearns. *After Strange Gods.* London, 1934.

Eliot, T.S. *Collected Plays.* London, 1962.

Eliot, T.S. *Collected Poems, 1909-1962.* London, 1963.

Eliot, T.S. *To Criticize the Critic.* London, 1965.

Eliot, T.S. *Essays Ancient and Modern.* London, 1943.

Eliot, T.S. *The Idea of a Christian Society.* London, 1939.

Eliot, T.S. *Notes towards the Definition of Culture.* London, 1948.

Eliot, T.S. *On Poetry and Poets.* London, 1957.

Eliot, T.S. *The Sacred Wood.* London, 1950.

Eliot, T.S. *Selected Essays, 1917-1932.* London, 1932.

Eliot, T.S. *The Use of Poetry and the Use of Criticism.* London, 1933.

Fay, C.R. *English Economic History, mainly since 1700.* London, 1940.

Fay, C.R. *Huskisson and His Age.* London, 1951.

Feiling, Keith. *The Second Tory Party, 1714-1832.* London, 1938.

Feiling, Keith. *Toryism, a Political Dialogue.* London, 1913.

Gabriel, Ralph Henry. *The Course of American Democratic Thought.* New York, 1940.

Garvin, J.L., and Amery, Julian. *The Life of Joseph Chamberlain.* 4 vols. London, 1932-51.

Gissing, Algernon and Ellen (eds.). *Letters of George Gissing to Members of His Family.* London, 1927.

(Gissing, George). *The Letters of George Gissing to Eduard Bertz, 1887-1903.* Edited by Arthur C. Young. New Brunswick, N.J., 1961.

Gissing, George. *Born in Exile.* London, 1892.

Gissing, George. *Critical Studies of the Works of Charles Dickens.* Edited by Temple Scott. New York, 1924.

Gissing, George. *The Crown of Life.* London, 1899.

Gissing, George. *Demos.* London, 1886.

Gissing, George. *The Emancipated.* London, 1890.

Gissing, George. *Eve's Ransom.* London, 1895.

Gissing, George. *The House of Cobwebs.* London, 1906.

Gissing, George. *In the Year of Jubilee.* London, 1894.

Gissing, George. *The Nether World.* London, 1889.

Gissing, George. *New Grub Street.* London, 1891.

Gissing, George. *The Odd Women.* London, 1893.

Gissing, George. *Our Friend the Charlatan.* London, 1901.

Gissing, George. *The Private Papers of Henry Ryecroft.* London, 1903.

Gissing, George. *Thyrza.* London, 1887.

Gissing, George. *The Unclassed.* London, 1884.

Gissing, George. *The Whirlpool.* London, 1897.

Gissing, George. *Will Warburton.* London, 1905.

Gissing, George. *Workers in the Dawn.* London, 1880.

Godkin, Edwin Lawrence. *Problems of Modern Democracy*. New York, 1898.
Godkin, E.L. *Reflections and Comments, 1865-1895*. New York, 1895.
Godkin, E.L. *Unforeseen Tendencies of Democracy*. Boston, 1893.
Gordon Walker, P.C. *Restatement of Liberty*. London, 1951.
Gray, Alexander. *The Socialist Tradition*. London, 1946.
Gray, John Chipman. *The Nature and Sources of the Law*. New York, 1916.
Grossman, James. *James Fenimore Cooper*. Stanford, 1967.
Habsburg, Otto von. *The Social Order of Tomorrow: State and Society in the Atomic Age*. London, 1959.
Halévy, Elie. *The Growth of Philosophic Radicalism*. New edition, London, 1934.
Halévy, Elie. *A History of the English People in the Nineteenth Century*. 6 vols. Revised edition, London, 1952.
Halévy, Elie. *Thomas Hodgskin*. London, 1956.
Hallowell, John H. *The Decline of Liberalism as an Ideology*. Berkeley, 1943.
Hallowell, John H. *The Moral Foundation of Democracy*. Chicago, 1954.
Hamilton, Alexander. *The Papers of Alexander Hamilton*. Edited by Harold C. Syrett. 10 vols. New York, 1961-66.
Hamilton, Alexander. *Works*. Edited by Henry Cabot Lodge. 9 vols. New York, 1886.
Haraszti, Zoltán. *John Adams and the Prophets of Progress*. Cambridge, Mass., 1952.
Harrod, Roy F. *The Life of John Maynard Keynes*. London, 1951.
Hart, Jeffrey. *Viscount Bolingbroke, Tory Humanist*. London, 1965.
Hawthorne, Nathaniel. *Complete Works*. 12 vols. Riverside edition, Boston, 1883.
Hayek, F.A. *The Counter-Revolution of Science*. Glencoe, Ill., 1952.
Hearnshaw, F.J.C. *Conservatism in England*. London, 1933.
Hearnshaw, F.J.C. (ed.). *The Social and Political Ideas of Some Representative Figures of the Age of Reaction and Reconstruction*. London, 1932.
Hearnshaw, F.J.C. (ed.). *The Social and Political Ideas of Some Representative Figures of the Revolutionary Era*. London, 1931.
Hearnshaw, F.J.C. (ed.). *The Social and Political Ideas of Some Representative Figures of the Victorian Age*. London, 1930.
Hicks, Granville. *Figures of Transition: a Study of British Literature at the End of the Nineteenth Century*. New York, 1939.
Himmelfarb, Gertrude. *Lord Acton: a Study in Conscience and Politics*. New York, 1952.
Hoffman, Ross J.S. *Edmund Burke, New York Agent*. Philadelphia, 1956.
Hoffman, Ross J.S. *The Spirit of Politics and the Future of Freedom*. Milwaukee, 1951.
Hoffman, Ross J.S., and Levack, Paul (eds.). *Burke's Politics*. New York, 1949.
Hogg, Quintin. *The Case for Conservatism*. London, 1947.
Hulme, T.E. *Speculations: Essays on Humanism and the Philosophy of Art*. Edited by Herbert Read. London, 1936.
Huxley, Aldous. *Proper Studies*. London, 1927.
Inge, William Ralph. *The End of an Era*. London, 1948.
Inge, W.R. *Our Present Discontents*. New York, 1939.
Inge, W.R. *Outspoken Essays*. First and Second Series, London, 1919 and 1923.
Jerrold, Douglas. *England: Past, Present, and Future*. London, 1950.
Jewkes, John. *Ordeal by Planning*. London, 1949.
Joad, C.E.M. *Decadence: a Philosophical Inquiry*. London, 1948.
Joubert, Joseph. *Pensées and Letters*. Edited by H.P. Collins. London, 1928.
Kenner, Hugh. *The Invisible Poet: T.S. Eliot*. New York, 1959.
Keynes, John Maynard. *Two Memoirs*. London, 1949.
Kirk, Russell. *Edmund Burke: a Genius Reconsidered*. La Salle, Ill., 1986.

Kirk, Russell. *Eliot and His Age: T.S. Eliot's Moral Imagination in the Twentieth Century.* New York, 1972.

Kirk, Russell. *Enemies of the Permanent Things: Observations of Abnormality in Literature and Politics.* La Salle, Ill., 1985.

Kirk, Russell. *John Randolph of Roanoke: a Study in American Politics.* Indianapolis, 1978.

Kirk, Russell, and McClellan, James. *The Political Principles of Robert A. Taft.* New York, 1967.

Kirk, Russell. *A Program for Conservatives.* Chicago, 1962.

Korg, Jacob. *George Gissing: a Critical Biography.* London, 1963.

Kuehnelt-Leddihn, Erik von. *Liberty or Equality: the Challenge of Our Time.* London, 1952.

Kurtz, Stephen G. *The Presidency of John Adams.* Philadelphia, 1957.

Labaree, Leonard W. *Conservatism in Early American History.* New York, 1948.

Laski, Harold. *The American Democracy.* New York, 1948.

Laski, Harold. *Political Thought in England from Locke to Bentham.* London, 1920.

Leavis, F. R. (ed.). *Mill on Bentham and Coleridge.* London, 1950.

Lecky, Elizabeth. *A Memoir of the Right Honourable William Hartpole Lecky.* London, 1909.

Lecky, William Hartpole. *Democracy and Liberty.* 2 vols. London, 1896.

Lecky, W.E.H. *Historical and Political Essays.* London, 1908.

Lecky, W.E.H. *A History of England in the Eighteenth Century.* 8 vols. London, 1878-92.

Lecky, W.E.H. *History of European Morals from Augustus to Charlemagne.* 2 vols. London, 1869.

Lecky, W.E.H. *History of the Rise and Influence of the Spirit of Rationalism in Europe.* 2 vols. London, 1865.

Lecky, W.E.H. *Leaders of Public Opinion in Ireland.* 2 vols. London, 1912.

Lecky, W.E.H. *The Map of Life: Character and Conduct.* London, 1899.

(Lecky, W.E.H.). *A Victorian Statesman: Private Letters of W.E.H. Lecky, 1859-1878.* Edited by H. Montgomery Hyde. London, 1947.

Lewis, Roy, and Maude, Angus. *The English Middle Classes.* London, 1949.

Lindbom, Tage. *The Tares and the Good Grain.* Translated by Alvin Moore, Jr. Macon, Ga., 1983.

Lippincott, Benjamin. *Victorian Critics of Democracy.* Minneapolis, 1938.

Lipsky, George A. *John Quincy Adams: His Theory and Ideas.* New York, 1950.

Lockhart, J.G. *Memoirs of the Life of Sir Walter Scott.* 10 vols. Edinburgh, 1853.

(Lowell, James Russell). *Letters of James Russell Lowell.* Edited by Charles Eliot Norton. 2 vols. London, 1894.

Lowell, James Russell. *Writings.* Riverside edition, 10 vols., Boston, 1890.

Lowi, Theodore J. *The End of Liberalism: Ideology, Policy, and the Crisis of Public Authority.* New York, 1969.

Lukacs, John, *Historical Consciousness, or the Remembered Past.* New York, 1968.

Lukacs, John. *The Passing of the Modern Age.* New York, 1970.

Macaulay, Thomas Babington. *Miscellaneous Works.* Edited by Lady Trevelyan. 5 vols. New York, 1880.

MacCunn, John, *The Political Philosophy of Burke.* London, 1913.

Mackail, J.W., and Wyndham, Guy. *Life and Letters of George Wyndham.* 2 vols. London, n.d.

Mackintosh, Sir James. *Memoirs.* Second edition, 2 vols. London, 1836.

Mahoney, Thomas H.D. *Edmund Burke and Ireland.* Cambridge, Mass., 1960.

Maine, Henry Sumner. *Ancient Law.* London, 1906.

Maine, Henry Sumner. *Dissertations on Early Law and Custom.* London, 1883.

Maine, Henry Sumner. *The Early History of Institutions.* Fourth edition, London, 1890.

Maine, Henry Sumner. *Popular Government.* London, 1886.
Maine, Henry Sumner. *Village-Communities in the East and West.* Third edition, London, 1876.
Mallock, William Hurrell. *Aristocracy and Evolution.* London, 1898.
Mallock, W.H. *Atheism and the Value of Life.* London, 1884.
Mallock, W.H. *Classes and Masses.* London, 1896.
Mallock, W.H. *A Critical Examination of Socialism.* London, 1908.
Mallock, W H. *The Heart of Life.* London, 1901.
Mallock, W.H. *A Human Document.* London, 1892.
Mallock, W.H. *The Individualist.* London, 1899.
Mallock, W.H. *Is Life Worth Living?* London, 1880.
Mallock, W.H. *Labour and the Popular Welfare.* London, 1895.
Mallock, W.H. *The Limits of Pure Democracy.* London, 1919.
Mallock, W.H. *Memoirs of Life and Letters.* Second edition, London, 1920.
Mallock, W.H. *The New Paul and Virginia, or Positivism on an Island.* London, 1879.
Mallock, W.H. *The New Republic.* Introduction by Sir John Squire. Rosemary Library edition, London, n.d.
Mallock, W.H. *The Reconstruction of Belief.* London, 1892.
Mallock, W.H. *Studies of Contemporary Superstition.* London, 1895.
Mallock, W.H. *The Veil of the Temple.* London, 1904.
Manchester, Frederick, and Shepard, Odell (eds.). *Irving Babbitt, Man and Teacher.* New York, 1941.
Mathew, David. *Acton: the Formative Years.* London, 1946.
Mayer, J.P. *Prophet of the Mass Age: a Study of Alexis de Tocqueville.* London, 1939.
McClellan, James. *Joseph Story and the American Constitution.* Norman, Oklahoma, 1971.
McDowell, R.B. *British Conservatism, 1832-1914.* London, 1959.
McGrath, Fergal. *Newman's University: Idea and Reality.* London, 1951.
Menczer, Béla (ed.). *Catholic Political Thought, 1789-1848.* London, 1952.
Minogue, Kenneth R. *The Liberal Mind.* New York, 1963.
Mises, Ludwig von. *Human Action.* London, 1949.
Molnar, Thomas. *The Counter-Revolution.* New York, 1969.
Molnar, Thomas. *The Decline of the Intellectual.* New York, 1961.
Molnar, Thomas. *The Future of Education.* Foreword by Russell Kirk. New York, 1970.
Montgomery, Marion. *T. S. Eliot: an Essay on the American Magus.* Athens, Georgia, 1970.
Monypenny, W. F., and Buckle, G. E. *The Life of Benjamin Disraeli, Earl of Beaconsfield.* 6 vols. London, 1910-20.
More, Paul Elmer. *The Catholic Faith.* Princeton, 1931.
More, Paul Elmer. *Christ the Word.* Princeton, 1927.
More, Paul Elmer. *Hellenistic Philosophies.* Princeton, 1921.
More, Paul Elmer. *New Shelburne Essays.* 3 vols. Princeton, 1928-36.
More, Paul Elmer. *Platonism.* Princeton, 1928.
More, Paul Elmer. *The Religion of Plato.* Princeton, 1921.
More, Paul Elmer. *Shelburne Essays.* 11 vols. Boston, 1904-21.
Morison, J. Cotter. *Macaulay.* London, 1882.
Morley, John. *The Life of William Ewart Gladstone.* 2 vols. London, 1908.
Neill, Thomas P. *The Rise and Decline of Liberalism.* Milwaukee, 1953.
Newman, John Henry. *Apologia pro Vita Sua.* London, 1864.
Newman, John Henry. *Discussions and Arguments on Various Subjects.* London, 1872.
Newman, John Henry. *An Essay in Aid of a Grammar of Assent.* London, 1858.
Newman, John Henry. *An Essay on the Development of Christian Doctrine.* London, 1845.

Newman, John Henry. *Essays Critical and Historical.* 2 vols. London, 1871.

Newman, John Henry. *The Idea of a University Defined and Illustrated.* London, 1853.

Newman, John Henry. *Lectures and Essays on University Subjects.* London, 1859.

Newman, John Henry. *The Office and Work of Universities.* London, 1856.

Niemeyer, Gerhart. *Between Nothingness and Paradise.* Baton Rouge, 1971.

Nisbet, Robert A. *Conservatism: Dream and Reality.* Minneapolis, 1986.

Nisbet, Robert A. *The Quest for Community.* New York, 1953 (also published, 1962, under the title *Community and Power*).

Nisbet, R.A. *Social Change and History.* New York, 1969.

Nisbet, R.A. *The Sociological Tradition.* New York, 1966.

Oakeshott, Michael. *Rationalism in Politics, and Other Essays.* New York, 1962.

Oakeshott, Michael. *The Voice of Poetry in the Conversation of Mankind.* London, 1959.

Ogden, Rollo. *Life and Letters of Edwin Lawrence Godkin.* 2 vols. New York, 1907.

Parkin, Charles. *The Moral Basis of Burke's Political Thought.* Cambridge, England, 1956.

Parrington, Vernon L. *Main Currents in American Thought.* New York, 1930.

Peel, Sir Robert. *Speeches in the House of Commons, 1810–1840.* 4 vols. London, 1853.

Petrie, Sir Charles. *George Canning.* London, 1930.

Pound, Roscoe. *Interpretations of Legal History.* Cambridge, Mass., 1923.

Quincy, Josiah. *Memoir of the Life of John Quincy Adams.* Boston, 1858.

Röpke, Wilhelm. *Civitas Humana.* London, 1948.

Röpke, Wilhelm. *The Social Crisis of Our Time.* Chicago, 1950.

Rossiter, Clinton. *Conservatism in America.* New York, 1955.

Rossiter, Clinton. *Alexander Hamilton and the Constitution.* New York, 1964.

Rowntree, B. Seebohm, and Lavers, G.R. *English Life and Leisure: a Social Study.* London, 1951.

Saintsbury, George. *The Earl of Derby.* London, 1892.

Saintsbury, George. *Scrap Books.* 3 vols. London, 1922–24.

Salomon, Albert. *The Tyranny of Progress: Reflections on the History of French Sociology.* New York, 1955.

Samuels, Ernest. *The Young Henry Adams.* Cambridge, Mass., 1948.

Santayana, George. *Character and Opinion in the United States.* New York, 1920.

Santayana, George. *Dialogues in Limbo.* New York, 1948.

Santayana, George. *Dominations and Powers.* New York, 1951.

Santayana, George. *The Last Puritan.* New York, 1935.

Santayana, George. *The Life of Reason.* 4 vols. New York, 1948.

(Santayana, George). *The Letters of George Santayana.* Edited by Daniel Cory. New York, 1955.

Santayana, George. *Persons and Places.* 3 vols. New York, 1944–53.

Santayana, George. *The Realm of Spirit.* New York, 1940.

Santayana, George. *Soliloquies in England and Later Soliloquies.* New York, 1922.

Santayana, George. *Winds of Doctrine.* New York, 1926.

(Scott, Walter). *The Journal of Sir Walter Scott, 1829–1832.* Edinburgh, 1946.

Scruton, Roger. *The Meaning of Conservatism.* New York, 1980.

Shafer, Robert. *Paul Elmer More and American Criticism.* New Haven, 1935.

Sitwell, Sir Osbert. *Demos the Emperor.* London, 1949.

Sitwell, Osbert. *Triple Fugue.* London, 1924.

Smith, F.E. (first Earl of Birkenhead). *Law, Life, and Letters.* 2 vols. London, 1927.

Smith, F.E. *The World in 2030 A.D.* London, 1930.

Smith, Page. *John Adams.* 2 vols. New York, 1962.

Somervell, D.C. *English Politics since 1900.* London, 1950.

Somervell, D.C. *English Thought in the Nineteenth Century.* London, 1947.

Southey, Robert. *Essays Moral and Political.* 2 vols. London, 1832.

Southey, Robert. *Sir Thomas More; or Colloquies on the Progress and Prospects of Society.* 2 vols. London, 1829.

Stanlis, Peter. *Edmund Burke and the Natural Law.* Ann Arbor, 1958.

Starzinger, Vincent E. *Middlingness:* Juste Milieu *Political Theory in France and England, 1815-48.* Charlottesville, Va., 1965.

Stephen, Sir James Fitzjames. *A History of the Criminal Law of England.* 3 vols. London, 1883.

Stephen, J.F. *Liberty, Equality, Fraternity.* London, 1873.

Stephen, Sir Leslie. *The English Utilitarians.* 3 vols. London, 1900.

Stephen, Leslie. *History of English Thought in the Eighteenth Century.* 3 vols. Third edition, London, 1902.

Stephen, Leslie. *Hours in a Library.* 3 vols. London, 1879.

Stephen, Leslie. *Life of Sir James Fitzjames Stephen.* London, 1895.

Strauss, Leo. *Liberalism, Ancient and Modern.* New York, 1968.

Talmon, J.L. *The Origins of Totalitarian Democracy.* London, 1952.

Talmon, J.L. *Political Messianism: the Romantic Phase.* New York, 1960.

Tate, Allen. *Reactionary Essays on Poetry and Ideas.* New York, 1936.

Taylor, A.J.P. *From Napoleon to Stalin: Comments on European History.* London, 1950.

Taylor, John, of Caroline. *Construction Construed, and Constitutions Vindicated.* Richmond, 1820.

Taylor, John, of Caroline. *An Inquiry into the Principles and Policy of the Government of the United States.* Edited by R.P. Nichols. New York, 1950.

Thomson, David. *Equality.* Cambridge, England, 1949.

Tillotson, Geoffrey. *Criticism and the Nineteenth Century.* London, 1951.

Tinder, Glenn. *The Crisis of Political Imagination.* New York, 1964.

Tocqueville, Alexis de. *Democracy in America.* Edited by Phillips Bradley. 2 vols. New York, 1948.

Tocqueville, Alexis de. *The European Revolution;* and *Correspondence with Gobineau.* Edited by John Lukacs. New York, 1960.

(Tocqueville). *Memoir, Letters, and Remains of Alexis de Tocqueville.* Edited by M.C.M. Simpson. 2 vols. London, 1861.

Tocqueville, Alexis de. *The Old Régime and the French Revolution.* Translated by Stuart Gilbert. New York, 1955.

Tocqueville, Alexis de. *Recollections.* Translated by George Lawrence; edited by J.P. Mayer and A.P. Kerr. New York, 1970.

Trevelyan, G. Otto. *The Life and Letters of Lord Macaulay.* 2 vols. New York, 1875.

Trevor, Meriol. *Newman.* 2 vols. New York, 1962.

Trilling, Lionel. *The Liberal Imagination: Essays on Literature and Society.* New York, 1950.

Utley, T.E. *Essays in Conservatism.* London, 1949.

Vaughan, C.E. *Studies in the History of Political Philosophy before and after Rousseau.* 2 vols. Manchester, 1925.

Vivas, Eliseo. *The Moral Life and the Ethical Life.* Chicago, 1950.

Voegelin, Eric. *The New Science of Politics: an Introductory Essay.* Chicago, 1952.

Voegelin, Eric. *Order and History.* 4 vols. Baton Rouge, 1956-1974.

Voegelin, Eric. *Science, Politics and Gnosticism.* Chicago, 1968.

Weaver, Richard. *Ideas Have Consequences.* Chicago, 1948.

Weaver, Richard. *Life without Prejudice.* Chicago, 1956.

Weaver, Richard. *The Southern Tradition at Bay.* New Rochelle, N.Y., 1968.

Weaver, Richard. *Visions of Order.* Baton Rouge, 1964.

Whitehead, Alfred North. *Adventures of Ideas.* London, 1942.

Willey, Basil. *The Eighteenth Century Background.* London, 1940.

Willey, Basil. *Nineteenth Century Studies: Coleridge to Matthew Arnold.* London, 1949.

Williamson, René de Visme. *Independence and Involvement: a Christian Re-orientation in Political Science.* Baton Rouge, 1964.

Wilson, Francis Graham. *The Case for Conservatism.* Seattle, 1951.

Wiltse, Charles M. *John C. Calhoun.* 3 vols. Indianapolis, 1944–1951.

Winters, Yvor. *In Defense of Reason.* New York, 1947.

Woolf, Leonard. *After the Deluge: a Study of Communal Psychology.* London, 1931.

Wyndham, George. *Essays in Romantic Literature.* London, 1919.

(Wyndham). *George Wyndham Recognita.* Edited by Charles T. Gatty. London, 1917.

Young, G.M. (ed.). *Early Victorian England, 1830–1865.* 2 vols. London, 1934.

Young, G.M. *Last Essays.* London, 1950.

INDEX